Beginning Spanish 101 and 102

Kim Potowski • Silvia Sobral • Laila M. Dawson

Howard Community College

WILEY *Custom*
LEARNING SOLUTIONS

Custom Brief Contents

Y SUS NACIONALIDADES

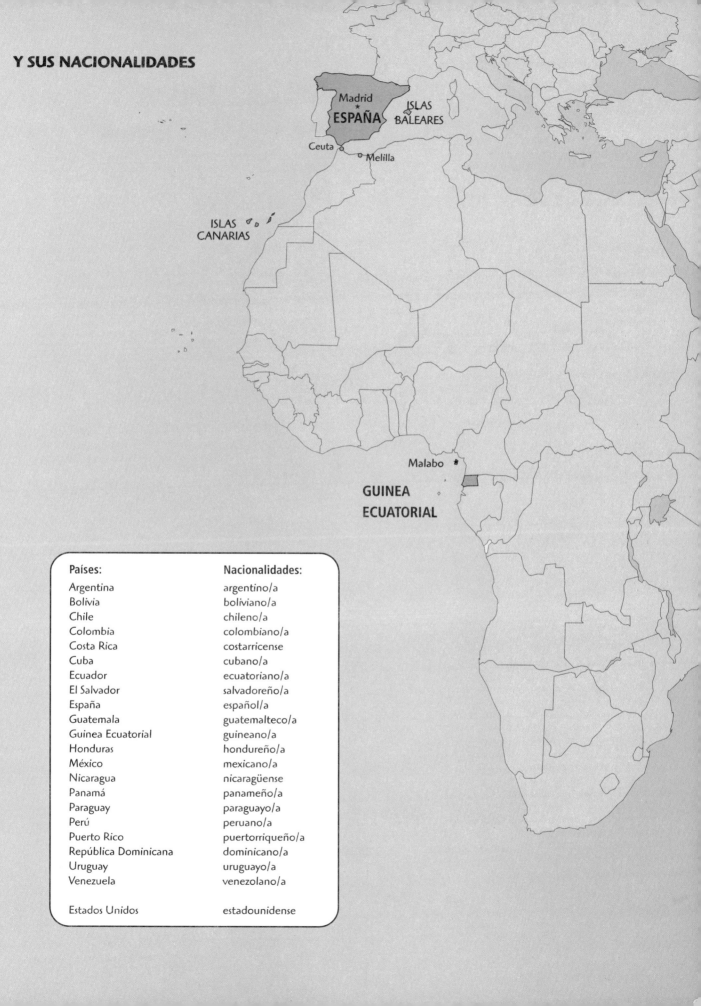

Madrid ★
ESPAÑA ISLAS BALEARES
Ceuta
Melilla
ISLAS CANARIAS

Malabo ★
GUINEA
ECUATORIAL

Países:	Nacionalidades:
Argentina	argentino/a
Bolivia	boliviano/a
Chile	chileno/a
Colombia	colombiano/a
Costa Rica	costarricense
Cuba	cubano/a
Ecuador	ecuatoriano/a
El Salvador	salvadoreño/a
España	español/a
Guatemala	guatemalteco/a
Guinea Ecuatorial	guineano/a
Honduras	hondureño/a
México	mexicano/a
Nicaragua	nicaragüense
Panamá	panameño/a
Paraguay	paraguayo/a
Perú	peruano/a
Puerto Rico	puertorriqueño/a
República Dominicana	dominicano/a
Uruguay	uruguayo/a
Venezuela	venezolano/a
Estados Unidos	estadounidense

Expresiones útiles en clase

¿Qué dicen los profesores?

Abre la puerta/ la ventana.

Abran el libro en la página...

Lee/Lean* las instrucciones del ejercicio...

Lee/Lean en voz alta.

Cierra/Cierren el libro/ el cuaderno.

Escucha/Escuchen.

Repite/Repitan (la palabra...)

Traduce/Traduzcan (la palabra...)

Ve/Vayan a la pizarra, por favor.

Escribe/Escriban la siguiente oración: ...

Contesta/Contesten esta pregunta: ...

Estudia/Estudien los verbos.

Siéntate/Siéntense, por favor.

Trabaja/Trabajen con un/a compañero/a.

Trabaja/Trabajen en grupos de cuatro.

What do professors say?

Open (to one person) the door/window.

Open (to more than one person) your book
    to page . . .

Read the instructions/directions for
    exercise . . .

Read aloud.

Close your book/notebook.

Listen.

Repeat the word . . .

Translate the word . . .

Go to the chalkboard, please.

Write the following sentence: . . .

Answer this question: . . .

Study the verbs.

Please sit down.

Work with a classmate.

Work in groups of four.

¿Qué dicen los estudiantes?

Profesor/a, tengo una pregunta.

¿Cómo se dice... en español/ inglés?

¿Qué significa (la palabra)?

Perdón, repita la palabra/ la oración/
    la pregunta/ la respuesta, por favor.

Perdón, ¿en qué página/ ejercicio/
    lección/ capítulo estamos?

¿Cómo se escribe... ?

Más despacio, por favor.

What do students say?

Professor, I have a question.

How do you say . . . in Spanish/in English?

What does (the word) . . . mean?

Pardon me, please repeat the
    word/sentence/question/answer.

Pardon me, what page/exercise/
    lesson/chapter are we on?

How do you spell . . .?

More slowly, please.

---

*The two verb forms correspond to a command to one single person (tú) and more than one person (ustedes): Lee (tú)/Lean (ustedes.)

ALL THE HELP, RESOURCES, AND PERSONAL SUPPORT YOU AND YOUR STUDENTS NEED!

2-Minute Tutorials and all
of the resources you & your
students need to get started
www.wileyplus.com/firstday

Student support from an
experienced student user
Ask your local representative
for details!

Collaborate with your colleagues,
find a mentor, attend virtual and liv
events, and view resources
www.WhereFacultyConnect.com

Pre-loaded, ready-to-use
assignments and presentations
www.wiley.com/college/quickstart

Technical Support 24/7
FAQs, online chat,
and phone support
www.wileyplus.com/support

Your *WileyPLUS*
Account Manager
Training and implementation suppor
www.wileyplus.com/accountmanag

MAKE IT YOURS

Dicho y hecho

NINTH EDITION

Beginning Spanish

Kim Potowski
University of Illinois at Chicago

Silvia Sobral
Brown University

Laila M. Dawson
Professor Emerita, University of Richmond

WILEY

John Wiley & Sons, Inc.

VICE PRESIDENT AND EXECUTIVE PUBLISHER	Jay O'Callaghan
DIRECTOR, WORLD LANGUAGES	Magali Iglesias
SENIOR DEVELOPMENTAL EDITOR	Elena Herrero
PROJECT EDITOR	Glenn A. Wilson
ASSOCIATE EDITOR	Maruja Malavé
ASSISTANT EDITOR	Lisha Perez
PROJECT ASSISTANT	Alejandra Barciela
ASSOCIATE DIRECTOR OF MARKETING	Jeffrey Rucker
MARKETING MANAGER	Tiziana Aime
SENIOR MARKETING ASSISTANT	Susan Matulewicz
MARKET SPECIALIST	Elena Casillas
SENIOR PRODUCTION EDITOR	William A. Murray
SENIOR MEDIA EDITOR	Lynn Pearlman
MEDIA PROJECT MANAGER	Margarita Valdez
SENIOR PHOTO EDITOR	Elle Wagner
DIRECTOR, CREATIVE SERVICES	Harry Nolan
ILLUSTRATION STUDIO	Escletxa, Barcelona, Spain
COVER DESIGN	Maureen Eide
FRONT COVER IMAGE	Cosmo/Condina/SuperStock
BACK COVER IMAGE	Aflo Relax/Masterfile

This book was set in ITC Highlander Book by Curriculum Concepts International and printed and bound by R.R. Donnelley.

This book is printed on acid-free paper. ∞

Founded in 1807, John Wiley & Sons, Inc. has been a valued source of knowledge and understanding for more than 200 years, helping people around the world meet their needs and fulfill their aspirations. Our company is built on a foundation of principles that include responsibility to the communities we serve and where we live and work. In 2008, we launched a Corporate Citizenship Initiative, a global effort to address the environmental, social, economic, and ethical challenges we face in our business. Among the issues we are addressing are carbon impact, paper specifications and procurement, ethical conduct within our business and among our vendors, and community and charitable support. For more information, please visit our website: www.wiley.com/go/citizenship.

ISBN: 978-0-470-88060-9
BRV ISBN: 978-0-470-91782-4

Printed in the United States of America

10 9 8 7 6 5 4 3 2 1

Kim Potowski

I was raised on Long Island, New York, which is now wonderfully much more Spanish-speaking than before. I completed a Ph.D. in Hispanic linguistics and Second Language Acquisition at the University of Illinois at Urbana-Champaign despite a two-year hiatus teaching English in Mexico City and learning to talk *chilango*. I have been at the University of Illinois at Chicago since 1999 and work with heritage Spanish-speaking populations in K-12 and university contexts.

Much love to Cliff Meece and to Gayle and Tom Meece Sr. for all of your support.

Soon after becoming *Licenciada* in English Philology in Spain, I arrived at the University of Illinois at Urbana-Champaign to pursue a M.A. in Teaching English as a Second Language. A few weeks later, I first faced a classroom believing that my job consisted in explaining grammar rules and their exceptions, giving examples, correcting mistakes. My academic work in Applied Linguistics and experience teaching English and Spanish have proved to me that language learning and teaching are much more complex and exciting processes. *Dicho y hecho* brings together my experience and that of my co-authors for a text that we hope will facilitate teaching and learning while making it a meaningful, enjoyable endeavor.

Dedico este trabajo a mis profesores, estudiantes y colegas, de quienes sigo aprendiendo, y especialmente a mis padres, Eusebio y María de los Ángeles, por enseñarme, inspirarme y apoyarme siempre.

Silvia Sobral

Laila Dawson

Dicho y hecho's first edition had its beginnings during an 11,000-mile road trip through Mexico in the late 1970's. Since that time *Dicho* has been an integral part of my life journey, with inspiration drawn from my passion for teaching and my love for Hispanic countries and their cultures. I was born in Buenos Aires, Argentina, and attended bilingual schools there and in Mexico City. This foundation eventually led me to graduate studies at the University of Wisconsin and a teaching career, first at Virginia Union University, and then at the University of Richmond, where I helped develop and directed the Intensive Spanish Program. I also accompanied students on study-abroad programs in Spain, Venezuela, Ecuador, and Costa Rica, and on service-learning projects in Honduras. In my retirement, I work on community integration projects in the bilingual and bicultural town of Leadville, Colorado, teach ESL to immigrant women, and continue to travel extensively.

It is with great joy that I now pass the *Dicho y hecho* torch on to two extraordinary teachers and authors, Kim and Silvia, and dedicate this book to my beloved newest grandchild, Emmanuelle Soledad.

	Así se dice	**Así se forma**

	Así se dice	Así se forma

	Así se dice	**Así se forma**

Cultura	Dicho y hecho	Así se practica

Preface

Dicho y hecho offers a straight-forward, user-friendly approach to beginning Spanish. Over 30 years of research in second language acquisition indicate that numerous and varied input activities are required *before* asking students to produce output using a new structure or new vocabulary.

Dicho y hecho provides students with abundant input of new forms and structures before moving them smoothly through guided practice to output. This empirically proven language teaching methodology informs activity sequences throughout the entire program. The easy-to-implement, lively approach so characteristic of *Dicho y hecho* makes learning Spanish an attainable goal, and offers students and instructors alike a truly enjoyable experience. Watch language bloom in your classroom as you begin using *Dicho y hecho.*

Dicho y hecho is flexible enough to fit the increasing variety of course formats, contact-hours, and determinations of scope for beginning level courses. For the first time ever, the program is available in its traditional 15-chapter format, and in this briefer 12-chapter format, each of which is thoroughly supported by *WileyPLUS,* an innovative, research-based, online environment for effective teaching and learning that supplements and complements the printed content.

Hallmarks of the *Dicho y hecho* program

A complete program. With nearly 400,000 satisfied users and counting, *Dicho y hecho* offers a complete program designed to support you and your students as you create and carry out your course. Each chapter, integrating vocabulary, grammar, and cultural content into a cohesive unit, has been carefully developed to follow a consistent sequence of linguistic and cultural presentations, practice activities, and skill-building tasks both in print and online.

ACTFL Standards. From its first edition, *Dicho y hecho* has provided a framework for the development of all four language skills (listening, speaking, reading, and writing) in activities that focus on meaningful and achievable communication. In recent editions, including this one, ACTFL's five Cs (communication, culture, connections, comparisons, and communities) have been woven into explanations, activities, culture notes, and cultural essays, strengthening the fabric of the entire program.

Flexible and easy-to-adapt. While it focuses on the essentials that students need to master beginner level language and cultural awareness, *Dicho y hecho* is flexible enough to adapt to any kind of course in the curriculum. Whether used on its own or, supplemented with online or printed materials, it maintains a clear direction for students, and solidly grounds them in the basics of the language.

Diverse and engaging activities. *Dicho y hecho* combines a broad array of class-tested and innovative activities that involve all language skills (listening, speaking, reading, and writing) and range from input processing to guided and structured output and opportunities for spontaneous and open-ended expression. Whole-class activities are interwoven with individual, paired, and small group exercises, all of which are sequenced to provide a varied pace and rhythm to every class meeting.

Grammar as a means for communication. Grammar is presented with precise, simple explanations, clear charts, and abundant example sentences that draw immediate connections between forms and their communicative use. Carefully sequenced activities take students from input comprehension to effective self expression.

High-frequency vocabulary and active use. Thematic units in each chapter present a selection of varied, practical, and high-frequency vocabulary in visual and written contexts. Activities range from identification in the chapter-opening art scenes and input-based exercises to personal expression and situational conversations that use the new vocabulary, resulting in effective acquisition of new words.

Integrated and interesting cultural information throughout. Through an appealing combination of readings, maps, photos, and realia in the *Cultura* section, and *Notas culturales* that appear frequently throughout each chapter, *Dicho y hecho* introduces students to the geography, politics, arts, history, and both traditional and contemporary cultural aspects of the countries and peoples that make up the Spanish-speaking world.

Features of the Brief Edition

Dicho y hecho, **Brief Edition** focuses on authentic, purposeful communication in activities driven by input processing principles that move students comfortably and naturally from input to output, and ultimately to the negotiation of meaning.

- Each activity set in the brief edition ensures that there is additional structured practice of new forms seamlessly woven into the communicative fabric. Activity directions are in Spanish beginning in *Capítulo 6.*

- *Dicho y hecho* sections at the end of the chapter bring a consistent, balanced, and process-based approach to the development of the four basic language skills. Most notably, we have included a wide variety of strategies specific to the development of each skill. *Para leer* includes high-interest, authentic readings with activities that develop students' reading comprehension skills and invite critical response and personal reaction to each selection. *Para conversar* develops conversational skills with the application of strategies and an awareness of context and register. *Para escribir* provides steps for writing as a process for each writing task, and includes strategies for developing good writing skills. And *Para ver y escuchar* is driven by video input, where the visual and aural senses are simultaneously engaged, making for more realistic listening practice.

- *Nota cultural* culture notes throughout each chapter present current and interesting information on a range of topics from customs to day-to-day life to important artists, writers, and other historical figures, many with lively photos. The first *Cultura* section in each chapter explores the geography and cultures of the Spanish-speaking world, highlighting a particular country or group of countries, while the second sharpens focus on an aspect of the chapter theme from a Hispanic perspective. Pre-reading activities (*Antes de leer*) tap into background knowledge and create curiosity, while post-reading (*Después de leer*) activities reinforce comprehension and invite critical, personal, and comparative response.

- Two fully integrated strands of video, one situational, the other cultural. Lively situational dialogs that use chapter vocabulary and structures in the *VideoEscenas* section, and topical documentary segments in the *Dicho y hecho* section are presented with straight-forward strategies and carefully crafted activities to develop solid listening skills through a process-based approach.

- Design enhances the straight-forward, user-friendly nature of the program. Lexical and structural information is well identified, transitions from presentation to practice are obvious, and association of art, photos, realia, side-bar material to particular activities is very clear.

- *Así se pronuncia* and *Escenas* listening section from the previous edition are now integrated into the lab manual portion of the Activites Manual.

Visual Walkthrough

Overview

Chapter openers establish the theme and communicative goals and set the cultural focus, listing all of the chapter's vocabulary, grammar, and culture sections, as well as the topics around which skills will be developed in the *Dicho y hecho* section.

CAPÍTULO **4** PLUS

¡A la mesa!

Así se dice

¡A la mesa!
Las comidas y las bebidas
¿Cuál es tu preferencia?
Tengo hambre

Así se forma

1. The verb *gustar*
2. Stem-changing verbs
3. Counting from 100 and indicating the year
4. Interrogative words (A summary)

Cultura

- México
- Las comidas en el mundo hispano

Dicho y hecho

Para leer:
Pedro y la fábrica de chocolate
Para conversar:
¿Qué comemos?
Para escribir:
Comer en la universidad
Para ver y escuchar:
La comida hispana

By the end of this chapter you will be able to:

- Buy and talk about food in a market, restaurant, etc.
- Express likes and dislikes. Talk about actions, desires, and preferences in the present
- Express large quantities, prices, and dates
- Ask for specific information

ENTRANDO AL TEMA

1. Which factors do you think most strongly influence your eating habits in general: cost, time, flavor, health, family, etc?

2. What Hispanic foods or dishes have you tried? Have you heard of any that you would like to try?

Entrando al tema

Two or three thought-provoking questions spark thinking about the chapter theme and cultural topics.

Así se dice

Active vocabulary is presented in illustrations with labels and speech bubbles, or in highly contextualized comprehensible texts. English translations are provided for items that may be particularly difficult to understand solely through visual or textual context. *WileyPLUS* provides audio for each of the vocabulary words in *Así se dice* section.

Así se forma

Grammar information is presented in functional, clear, and concise language, usually accompanied by an illustration showing use of the particular structure. Explanations feature example sentences using the chapter context and vocabulary. *WileyPLUS* offers *Animated Grammar Tutorial* for each of the grammar points, and *Verb Conjugator* where needed.

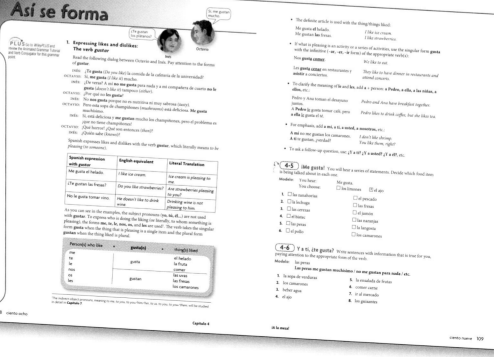

Actividades

Vocabulary and grammar presentations are followed by a series of communicative activities moving from input/comprehension and guided output/production activities in which form-meaning connections are made to activities that invite original and spontaneous use of the vocabulary and structures for personal expression and meaningful communication with classmates. A portion of the in-text activities are also available online in *WileyPLUS*.

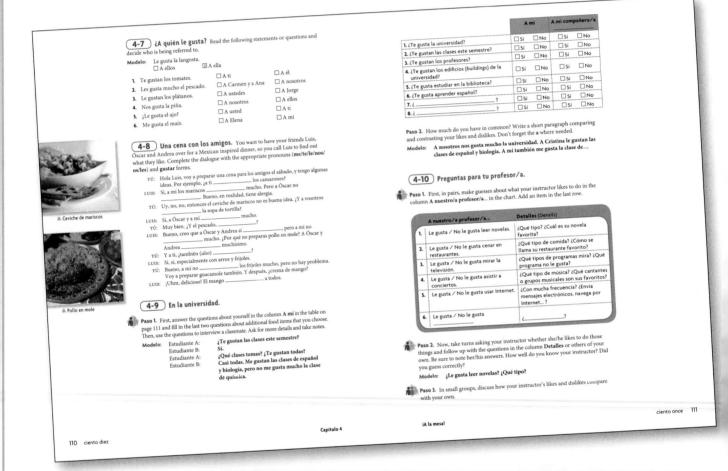

4-7 ¿A quién le gusta? Read the following statements or questions and decide who is being referred to.

Modelo: Le gusta la langosta.
☐ A ellos   ☒ A ella

1. Te gustan los tomates.
2. Les gusta mucho el pescado.
3. Le gustan los plátanos.
4. Nos gusta la piña.
5. ¿Le gusta el ajo?
6. Me gusta el maíz.

☐ A ti   ☐ A él
☐ A Carmen y a Ana   ☐ A nosotros
☐ A ustedes   ☐ A Jorge
☐ A nosotros   ☐ A ellos
☐ A usted   ☐ A ti
☐ A Elena   ☐ A mí

4-8 Una cena con los amigos. You want to have your friends Luis, Óscar and Andrea over for a Mexican inspired dinner, so you call Luis to find out what they like. Complete the dialogue with the appropriate pronouns (**me/te/le/nos/os/les**) and **gustar** forms.

TÚ: Hola Luis, voy a preparar una cena para los amigos el sábado, y tengo algunas ideas. Por ejemplo, ¿a ti _____ los camarones?
LUIS: Sí, a mí los mariscos _____ mucho. Pero a Óscar no _____. Bueno, en realidad, tiene alergia.
TÚ: Uy, no, no, entonces el ceviche de mariscos no es buena idea. ¿Y a vosotros _____ la sopa de tortilla?
LUIS: Sí, a Óscar y a mí _____ mucho.
TÚ: Muy bien. ¿Y el pescado, _____?
LUIS: Bueno, creo que a Óscar y Andrea sí _____ pero a mí no _____ mucho. ¿Por qué no preparas pollo en mole? A Óscar y Andrea _____ muchísimo.
TÚ: Y a ti, ¿también (*also*) _____?
LUIS: Sí, sí, especialmente con arroz y frijoles.
TÚ: Bueno, a mí no _____ los frijoles mucho, pero no hay problema. Voy a preparar guacamole también. Y después, ¿crema de mango?
LUIS: ¡Uhm, delicioso! El mango _____ a todos.

▲ Ceviche de mariscos

▲ Pollo en mole

4-9 En la universidad.

Paso 1. First, answer the questions about yourself in the column **A mí** in the table on page 111 and fill in the last two questions about additional food items that you choose. Then, use the questions to interview a classmate. Ask for more details and take notes.

Modelo: Estudiante A: ¿Te gustan las clases este semestre?
          Estudiante B: Sí.
          Estudiante A: ¿Qué clases tomas? ¿Te gustan todas?
          Estudiante B: Casi todas. Me gustan las clases de español y biología, pero no me gusta mucho la clase de química.

	A mí		A mi compañero/a	
	☐ Sí ☐ No		☐ Sí ☐ No	
1. ¿Te gusta la universidad?	☐ Sí ☐ No		☐ Sí ☐ No	
2. ¿Te gustan las clases este semestre?	☐ Sí ☐ No		☐ Sí ☐ No	
3. ¿Te gustan los profesores?	☐ Sí ☐ No		☐ Sí ☐ No	
4. ¿Te gustan los edificios (*buildings*) de la universidad?	☐ Sí ☐ No		☐ Sí ☐ No	
5. ¿Te gusta estudiar en la biblioteca?	☐ Sí ☐ No		☐ Sí ☐ No	
6. ¿Te gusta aprender español?	☐ Sí ☐ No		☐ Sí ☐ No	
7. ¿_____?	☐ Sí ☐ No		☐ Sí ☐ No	
8. ¿_____?	☐ Sí ☐ No		☐ Sí ☐ No	

Paso 2. How much do you have in common? Write a short paragraph comparing and contrasting your likes and dislikes. Don't forget the *a* where needed.

Modelo: A nosotros nos gusta mucho la universidad. A Cristina le gustan las clases de español y biología. A mí también me gusta la clase de…

4-10 Preguntas para tu profesor/a.

Paso 1. First, in pairs, make guesses about what your instructor likes to do in the column **A nuestro/a profesor/a…** in the chart. Add an item in the last row.

	A nuestro/a profesor/a…	Detalles (*Details*)
1.	Le gusta / No le gusta leer novelas.	¿Qué tipo? ¿Cuál es su novela favorita?
2.	Le gusta / No le gusta cenar en restaurantes.	¿Qué tipo de comida? ¿Cómo se llama su restaurante favorito?
3.	Le gusta / No le gusta mirar la televisión.	¿Qué tipos de programas mira? ¿Qué programa no le gusta?
4.	Le gusta / No le gusta asistir a conciertos.	¿Qué tipo de música? ¿Qué cantantes o grupos musicales son sus favoritos?
5.	Le gusta / No le gusta usar Internet.	¿Con mucha frecuencia? ¿Envia mensajes electrónicos, navega por Internet…?
6.	Le gusta / No le gusta	¿_____?

Paso 2. Now, take turns asking your instructor whether she/he likes to do those things and follow up with the questions in the column **Detalles** or others of your own. Be sure to note her/his answers. How well do you know your instructor? Did you guess correctly?

Modelo: ¿Le gusta leer novelas? ¿Qué tipo?

Paso 3. In small groups, discuss how your instructor's likes and dislikes compare with your own.

Capítulo 4   ¡A la mesa!

110   ciento diez

ciento once   111

Nota de lengua

Short notes throughout each chapter provide additional grammatical and usage information relevant to the vocabulary and major structures presented as well as practiced in the activities.

NOTA DE LENGUA

- **Mucho** and **poco** do not change in gender and number when they modify verbs.
  Comemos **mucho/poco**.   We eat a lot/little.

  When they modify nouns, **mucho** and **poco** do change in gender and number to agree with the noun.

  Comemos **muchas** verduras y **poca** carne.

- Spanish uses the preposition **de** (*of*) to join two nouns for the purpose of description.
  helado **de** vainilla   vanilla ice cream
  jugo **de** naranja   orange juice

  How many combinations can you come up with?

Cultura

The first *Cultura* section in each chapter focuses on a particular country or group of countries and offers an eclectic mix of brief readings, captioned photographs, and realia that bring to life the histories and cultures of Spanish–speakers around the world. The second *Cultura* section explores an aspect of the chapter theme from a Hispanic perspective. Questions in *Antes de leer* pique curiosity and tap into background knowledge, and *Después de leer* follow–up questions check comprehension, then invite critical response through comparison and personal expression. Videos for Cultura sections are hosted in *WileyPLUS*. Also *Map Quizzes* can be found online to help students with their geography skills.

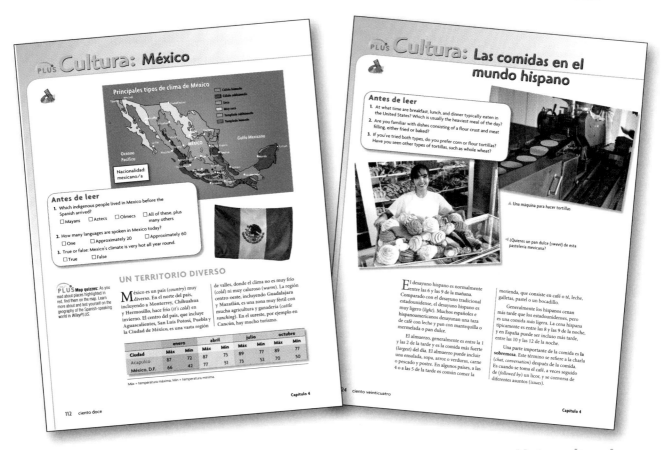

NOTA CULTURAL

La comida mexicana vs. la comida Tex-Mex

Tex-Mex is a term given to food, music, and other cultural products based on the combined cultures of Texas and Mexico. Many ingredients of Tex-Mex cooking are common in Mexican cuisine, although other ingredients are unknown in Mexico. Tex-Mex food encompasses a wide variety of dishes such as burritos, chimichangas, nachos, fajitas, tortilla chips with salsa, and chili con carne, all of which are usually not found in Mexico.

Nota cultural

These notes on the products, practices, and important people of the country or countries featured in the chapter's *Cultura* section, as well as notes about cultural phenomena common to Spanish speakers across national boundaries, appear throughout each chapter, and appeal to a wide array of interests.

VideoEscenas: ¿La nueva cocina?

▲ Paloma y Pedro pasean por la tarde, quieren tomar algo y deciden entrar en un restaurante de "nueva cocina".

Paso 1. Answer these questions before you watch the video.

1. What types of cuisine and specific dishes do you like best when you eat out?
2. What is the strangest thing you have eaten?
3. What do you think "new cuisine" could be like?

Paso 2. Watch the video paying attention to the main ideas and indicate which of the following statements are true (**cierto**) or false (**falso**).

	Cierto	Falso
1. Paloma y Pedro quieren (*want*) cenar.	☐	☐
2. El restaurante sirve cocina tradicional.	☐	☐
3. A Paloma le gusta su postre.	☐	☐
4. Pedro piensa (*thinks*) que su helado va a ser muy bueno.	☐	☐

Paso 3. Look at the questions below and watch the video again. This time focus on the specific information you need to answer the questions. You may take notes as you listen.

1. ¿Qué quieren tomar Paloma y Pedro?
2. ¿Por qué quiere entrar Paloma en este restaurante?
3. ¿De qué manera son inusuales los postres de Paloma y Pedro?
4. ¿Cómo reacciona Pedro a la "nueva cocina" de este restaurante?

Paso 4. In small groups, share your opinions.

¿Quieres probar (*try*) este tipo de "nueva cocina"? ¿Por qué sí o por qué no?

Capítulo 4

116   ciento dieciséis

VideoEscenas

Activities based on a short, situational video segment develop listening practice. Each video segment uses the chapter's vocabulary and grammar in a concise, practical, and natural context. Activities that follow move from pre-viewing questions establishing the general context and triggering recall of vocabulary, comprehension questions checking for understanding, and expansion questions inviting personal or critical response. Video for *Videoescenas* can be found in *WileyPLUS*.

SITUACIONES

In pairs or groups of three, you and your friend(s) are going out for dinner tonight but each one of you wants to go to a different restaurant. Try to persuade your friends to go to your favorite restaurant by telling them what type of food they serve, describing the dish(es) you think they would really like, what they have for dessert, etc. Make a decision and be ready to share it with the class.

Situaciones

These role-play activities present interactive, often humorous problem-solving situations that must be worked out using the language presented and practiced in the chapter.

Investig@ en Internet

These boxes prompt exploration of authentic Spanish-language Internet sources with specific goals for finding, bringing back, and sharing information.

INVESTIG@ EN INTERNET

Busca en Internet el sitio de Chef Merito. ¿Qué producto es nuevo para ti (*for you*)? ¿Qué producto deseas probar (*try*)?

Dichos

Each chapter has one or two *Dichos* boxes with sayings from the Spanish-speaking countries along with a thought-provoking question.

DICHOS

Querer es poder.
¿Puedes explicar este dicho en español?

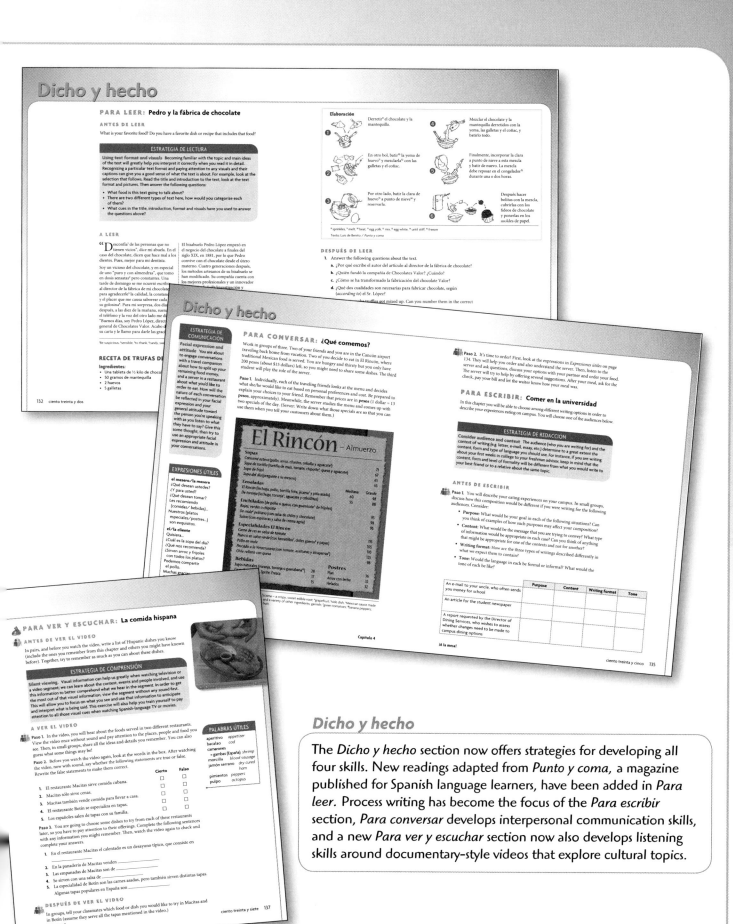

Dicho y hecho

The *Dicho y hecho* section now offers strategies for developing all four skills. New readings adapted from *Punto y coma*, a magazine published for Spanish language learners, have been added in *Para leer*. Process writing has become the focus of the *Para escribir* section, *Para conversar* develops interpersonal communication skills, and a new *Para ver y escuchar* section now also develops listening skills around documentary-style videos that explore cultural topics.

Repaso de vocabulario activo

Vocabulary presented within the chapter's *Así se dice* sections and practiced throughout in activities is collected here, organized into thematic groupings and parts of speech, and provided with English translations. All Spanish words are hyperlinked in *WileyPLUS* to listen to their pronunciation.

Repaso de vocabulario activo

Adjetivos y expresiones adjetivales
al horno *baked*
a la parrilla *grilled*
caliente *hot*
frío/a *cold*
frito/a *fried*
mucho/a/os/as *much, a lot, many*
otro/a/os/as *another/other*
poco/a/os/as *little (quantity), few*

Adverbios
más/menos *more/less*
mucho/poco *a lot/a little*
también *also*
todavía *still*

Conjunciones
cuando *when*
lo que *what (that which)*
porque *because*
que *that, which, who*

Palabras interrogativas
¿Adónde? *(To) where?*
¿Cómo? *How?*
¿Cuál/es? *Which (one/s)?*
¿Cuándo? *When?*
¿Cuánto/a/os/as? *How much?/How many?*
¿De dónde? *From where?*
¿De quién? *Whose?*
¿Dónde? *Where?*
¿Por qué? *Why?*
¿Qué? *What? Which?*
¿Quién/es? *Who?*

el desayuno *breakfast*

Las legumbres y las verduras *Legumes and vegetables*
el brócoli *broccoli*
la cebolla *onion*
los frijoles *beans*
los guisantes *peas*
las judías verdes *green beans*
la lechuga *lettuce*
el maíz *corn*
la papa/la patata *potato*
las papas fritas *French fries*
el tomate *tomato*
la zanahoria *carrot*

Las frutas *Fruits*
la banana/el plátano *banana*
la cereza *cherry*
la fresa *strawberry*
el limón *lemon*
la manzana *apple*
el melocotón/el durazno *peach*
la naranja *orange*
la pera *pear*
la piña *pineapple*
la sandía *watermelon*
la uva *grape*

Las carnes, los pescados y los mariscos *Meat, fish, and seafood*
el bistec *steak*
el camarón/la gamba *shrimp*
la carne de cerdo/puerco *pork*
la carne de res *beef*
la chuleta de cerdo/puerco *pork chop*
la hamburguesa *hamburger*
el jamón *ham*
la langosta *lobster*
el pescado *fish*

el pollo *chicken*
la salchicha/el chorizo *sausage*
la tocineta/el tocino *bacon*

Las bebidas *Beverages*
el agua *water*
el café *coffee*
la cerveza *beer*
el jugo/el zumo *juice*
la leche *milk*
el refresco *soda drink*
el té *tea*
el vino *wine*

Los postres *Desserts*
la galleta *cookie*
el helado *ice cream*
el pastel *pie, pastry*
la torta *cake*

Otras comidas y condimentos *Other foods and condiments*
el aceite *oil*
la aceituna *olive*
el ajo *garlic*
el arroz *rice*
el azúcar *sugar*
el cereal *cereal*
la crema *cream*
la ensalada *salad*
el hielo *ice*
el huevo *egg*
los huevos revueltos/fritos *scrambled/fried eggs*
la mantequilla *butter*
la mermelada *jam*
el pan *bread*
el pan tostado *toast*
la pimienta *pepper*
el queso *cheese*
la sal *salt*
el sándwich/el bocadillo *sandwich*
la sopa *soup*
el vinagre *vinegar*

Verbos y expresiones verbales
almorzar (ue) *to have lunch*
cocinar *to cook*
comprar *to buy*
costar (ue) *to cost*
desear *to want, to wish*
dormir (ue) *to sleep*
entender (ie) *to understand*
gustar *to like*
necesitar *to need*
pedir (i) *to ask for, to order*
pensar (ie) *to think*
poder (ue) *to be able, can*
preferir (ie) *to prefer*
preparar *to prepare*
querer (ie) *to want, to love*
servir (i) *to serve*
tomar *to take, to drink*
vender *to sell*
volver (ue) *to return, to go back*
quisiera *I would like*
tener (irreg.) (mucha) hambre *to be (very) hungry*
tener (mucha) sed *to be (very) thirsty*

Capítulo 4

Autoprueba y repaso

I. The verb *gustar*. Write questions according to the model and then answer them. Use the correct form of **gustar** and the appropriate corresponding pronoun.

Modelo: ¿A tu hermano / las legumbres?
¿A tu hermano le gustan las legumbres?
Sí, le gustan las legumbres. O, No, no le gustan...

1. ¿A tus padres / tomar café?
2. ¿A ustedes / la comida italiana?
3. ¿A ustedes / desayunar temprano?
4. ¿A tu abuela / los postres?
5. ¿A ti / los frijoles negros?

II. Stem-changing verbs. Write questions to your friends using the **ustedes** form of the verb. Then write answers to the questions using the **nosotros** form.

Modelo: entender el ejercicio
¿Entienden el ejercicio?
Sí, entendemos el ejercicio. O, No, no entendemos el ejercicio.

1. poder cocinar
2. querer ir al supermercado
3. almorzar a las doce todos los días
4. preferir cenar en un restaurante o en la cafetería
5. normalmente pedir postres en los restaurantes

III. Counting from 100 and indicating the year.

A. Mr. Trompa, a very wealthy man, is going to buy everything his two daughters need to start college. How much money does he need to buy two of each of the following items? Follow the model and write out the numbers.

Modelo: Un libro de psicología cuesta $90.
Dos cuestan ciento ochenta dólares.

1. Un libro de arte cuesta $125.
2. Una buena calculadora cuesta $170.
3. Una impresora cuesta $450.
4. Una computadora con teclado y monitor cuesta $1,400.
5. Un televisor para el cuarto cuesta $750.
6. Un coche nuevo cuesta $25,000.

B. Write out the following famous years.

1. Colón llega a las Américas: 1492
2. La creación de la Armada Invencible de España: 1588
3. La Declaración de Independencia de EE.UU.: 1776
4. La caída (*fall*) del Muro de Berlín: 1989
5. La caída de las Torres Gemelas: 2001

IV. Interrogative words. Use various interrogative words to obtain more information.

Modelo: Ana no come en la cafetería.
¿Dónde come? O, ¿Por qué no come en la cafetería?

1. Ana no bebe vino.
2. La sandía no es su fruta favorita.
3. No trabaja por la mañana.
4. No es de Buenos Aires.
5. No tiene veinte años.
6. No vive en la residencia estudiantil.
7. No va a la librería ahora.
8. No está enferma hoy.

V. General review. Answer the following questions about yourself and your friends. Use complete sentences.

1. ¿Qué comes en el desayuno?
2. ¿Cuál es tu postre favorito?
3. ¿Qué frutas te gustan más?
4. ¿Dónde quieres cenar esta noche?
5. ¿Cuántas horas duermes (generalmente) por la noche?
6. Tú y tus amigos, ¿pueden estudiar toda la noche sin dormir?

VI. *Cultura.*

1. Name two or three differences between Hispanic cultures and your culture with regards to diet and eating habits.
2. Describe the difference between a **tortilla** made in México and a **tortilla** made in Spain.
3. What are some of the largest contributors to México's economy?

Answers to the *Autoprueba y repaso* are found in **Apéndice 2.**

¡A la mesa!

Autoprueba y repaso

This end-of-chapter review is a handy and effective tool for checking basic mastery of the chapter concepts and preparing for quizzes and exams. An answer key appears in Appendix 2 for easy self-correction.

The Complete Program

The Complete Program

To receive a review or desk copy of any of these program components, please contact your local Wiley sales representative, call our Sales Office at 1.800.237.2665, or contact us online at www.wiley.com/college/potowski.

Student Textbook

978-0-470-90688-0

The textbook includes 12 thematically-based chapters, an access code to download accompanying video and the audio from our Companion Sites at www.wiley.com/college/potowski.

Annotated Instructor's Edition

978-0-470-90701-6

The Annotated Instructor's Edition contains side notes with suggestions for teaching, meaningful structural exercises, suggestions for varying or expanding communicative activities, and transcripts of audio input for listening activities. These annotations are especially helpful for first-time instructors.

Activities Manual

978-0-470-93791-4

The Activities Manual is available in print or online and contains two components:

- A Workbook that links reading and writing, builds vocabulary, practices grammar, and helps students develop personal expression and composition skills. Some activities are self correcting and the answer key appears at the end of the Activities Manual.

- A Lab Manual to be used with the Lab Manual Audio files available digitally on *WileyPLUS* and on the Instructor and Student Companion Sites (access codes are required). The Lab Manual includes a variety of contextualized listening comprehension activities, followed by the *Escenas,* at the end of each chapter, and the *Así se pronuncia* in chapters 1 to 8. The Answer Key to the written responses in the *Lab Manual* and the audio scripts are available as an electronic file on the **Dicho y hecho** Instructor Companion Website at www.wiley.com/college/potowski and in *WileyPLUS* as an Instructor Resource.

Dicho y hecho Video

www.wileyplus.com

The **Dicho y hecho** Video presents situational and topical video segments designed to work with activities in the corresponding chapters of the text. Each video segment features interactions between native speakers of Spanish in the U.S. and abroad, in professional or social settings, and models language usage or explores cultural topics. Video segments are available digitally in *WileyPLUS* and on the Instructor and Student Companion Sites. Please contact your Wiley Representative as the video can also be delivered as a DVD.

 WILEYFLEX

Students have more options than the traditional textbook. Consider an eBook, loose-leaf binder version or a custom publication. Learn more about our flexible pricing, flexible formats and flexible content at www.wiley.com/college/wileyflex.

WILEYPLUS

www.wileyplus.com

WileyPLUS is an innovative, research-based, online teaching and learning environment that integrates relevant resources, including the entire digital textbook, in an easy-to-navigate framework that helps students study more effectively. Online Activities Manual available with our Premium version.

WileyPLUS builds students' confidence because it takes the guesswork out of studying by providing a clear roadmap to academic success. With *WileyPLUS,* instructors and students receive 24/7 access to resources that promote positive learning outcomes. Throughout each study session, students can assess their progress and gain immediate feedback on their strengths and weaknesses so they can be confident they are spending their time effectively.

What do students receive with *WileyPLUS?*

A Research-based Design. *WileyPLUS* provides an online environment that integrates relevant resources, including the entire digital textbook with audio and video hyperlinks, in an easy-to-navigate framework that helps students study more effectively.

- *WileyPLUS* adds structure by organizing textbook into a more manageable content.
- Related supplemental material reinforce the learning objectives.
- Innovative features such as self-evaluation tools improve time management and strengthen areas of weakness.

One-on-one Engagement. With *WileyPLUS* for ***Dicho y hecho,* Ninth Edition,** students receive 24/7 access to resources that promote positive learning outcomes. Students engage with related activities (in various media) and sample practice items, including:

- Wimba Voice Response Questions and Wimba Voiceboards
- Animated Grammar Tutorials
- Videos with Activities
- Listening Activities for vocabulary
- Audio Flashcards
- Verb Conjugator
- Map Quizzes
- Self-tests for Additional Practice
- English Grammar Checkpoints
- *Panoramas culturales:* a website with a wealth of activities and information on the 21 Spanish-speaking countries of the world
- Practice Handbook
- La pronunciación

Measurable Outcomes. Throughout each study session, students can assess their progress and gain immediate feedback. *WileyPLUS* provides precise reporting of strengths and weaknesses, as well as individualized quizzes, so that students are confident they are spending their time on the right things. With *WileyPLUS,* students always know the exact outcome of their efforts.

What do instructors receive with *WileyPLUS* ?

WileyPLUS provides reliable, customizable resources that reinforce course goals inside and outside of the classroom as well as visibility into individual student progress. Pre-created materials and activities help instructors optimize their time:

– Syllabi
– Media enriched PowerPoint Slides
– Image Gallery
– Gradable Reading Assignment Questions (embedded with online text)
– Question Assignments
– Testbank
– Video activities with answer key and video scripts in Spanish and English
– Exams with anser key, audio files, and scripts

Gradebook: *WileyPLUS* provides access to reports on trends in class performance, student use of course materials and progress towards learning objectives, helping inform decisions and drive classroom discussions.

WileyPLUS. **Learn More.**   www.wileyplus.com

Powered by proven technology and built on a foundation of cognitive research, *WileyPLUS* has enriched the education of millions of students, in over 20 countries around the world.

If you are interested in a version that includes the electronic Activities Manual, please contact your sales representative for information about *WileyPLUS Premium*.

Student Companion Site

www.wiley.com/college/potowski/

The Student Companion Site contains electronic Activities Manual, complimentary Self-tests, the *Panoramas culturales* section, audio flashcards, Verb Conjugator accompanying audio for the textbook and the Lab Manual, and videos.

Instructor Companion Site

www.wiley.com/college/potowski/

The Instructor Companion Site includes the student resources above plus exams and digital Test Bank and test audio files. It also includes the image gallery, answer keys for the exams and the Lab Manual, audio and video scripts, and PowerPoint presentations.

Acknowledgments

No project of the scope and complexity of *Dicho y hecho* could have materialized without the collaboration of numerous people. The author team gratefully acknowledges the contributions of the many individuals who were instrumental in the development of this work.

The professionalism, dedication, and expertise of the John Wiley & Sons, Inc. staff who worked with us have been both indispensable and inspirational. To Jay O'Callaghan, Vice President and Executive Publisher, who oversaw the administrative aspects of the entire project, bore the ultimate responsibility for its completion, and never failed to be approachable, we are very grateful. We also thank Magali Iglesias, Director of World Languages, for the vast expertise she brings to the project. We are also very grateful to William A. Murray, Senior Production Editor, for his expertise, flexibility, creativity, inordinate patience, and dedication to the project. We extend our thanks and appreciation to Elle Wagner, Photo Editor, for facilitating the photo selections that enhance the text. Nor can we neglect to thank the Marketing team lead by Jeffrey Rucker, Associate Director of Marketing, with Tiziana Aime, Marketing Manager, and Elena Casillas, Market Specialist, for creating a brilliant advertising program that will position *Dicho y hecho* favorably in the marketplace, and for their enthusiasm, creativity, and dedication in meeting Spanish instructors around the country.

We thank Lynn Pearlman, Senior Media Editor, for her creativity in coordinating the outstanding media ancillaries that supplement the text. We would also like to acknowledge everyone at Curriculum Concepts International. Our Project Editor Glenn Wilson did an absolutely outstanding job reading text, making insightful suggestions, and keeping the project on task and organized.

Most of all, we offer heartfelt appreciation and most profound gratitude to our wonderful Senior Developmental Editor, Elena Herrero, for her unfaltering devotion to *Dicho y hecho,* her tireless hands-on involvement with us, her talent, expertise, and diligence in turning a manuscript into a book, her kind flexibility with our demanding schedules, and—most importantly—her friendship and confidence in us as authors.

We are grateful to the loyal users of *Dicho y hecho,* who over the years have continued to provide valuable insights and suggestions. And finally, for their candid observations, their critically important scrutiny, and their creative ideas, we wish to thank the following reviewers and contributors for this edition from across the nation:

Amy Adrian, *Ivy Tech Community College;* Ana Afzali, *Citrus College;* Sandra Barboza, *Trident Technical College;* J. Raúl Basulto, *Montgomery College;* Anne Becher, *Colorado University-Boulder;* María Beláustegui, *University of Missouri, Kansas City;* Mara-Lee Bierman, *SUNY Rockland Community College;* Virgilio Blanco, *Howard Community College;* Ana Boone, *Baton Rouge Community College;* Maryann Brady, *Rivier College;* Catalina Castillón, *Lamar University;* Daria Cohen, *Rider University;* Rifka Cook, *Northwestern University;* Mayra Cortes-Torres, *Pima Community College;* Debra Davis, *Sauk Valley Community College;* Patricia Davis, *Darton College, Main Campus;* William Deaver, Jr., *Armstrong Atlantic State University;* Aurea Diab, *Dillard University;* Carolyn Dunlap, *Gulf Coast Community College;* Linda Elliott-Nelson, *Arizona Western College;* Luz Escobar, *Southeastern Louisiana University;* Jill Felten, *Northwestern University;*

María Ángeles Fernandez, *University of North Florida;* Leah Fonder-Solano, *University of Southern Mississippi;* Sarah Fritz, *Madison Area Technical College;* Jennifer Garson, *Pasadena City College;* Thomas Gilles, *Montana State University;* Andrew Gordon, *Mesa State College;* Dennis Harrod, *Syracuse University;* Candy Henry, *Westmoreland County Community College;* Lorena Hidalgo, *University of Missouri, Kansas City;* Laurie Huffman, *Los Medanos College;* Martha Hughes, *Georgia Southern University;* Jessica E. Hyde-Cadogan, *University of New Haven;* Nuria Ibáñez, *University of North Florida;* Mary Lou Ippolito, *Trident Technical College;* Shelley Jones, *Montgomery College;* Karl Keller, *University of Alabama in Huntsville;* Mary Jane Kelley, *Ohio University;* Isidoro Kessel, *Old Dominion University;* Sharyn Kuusisto, *City College of San Francisco;* Deborah Lemon, *Ohlone College;* Leticia P. López, *San Diego Mesa College;* José López-Marrón, *CUNY Bronx Community College;* Joanne Lozano, *Dillard University;* Dora Y. Marrón Romero, *Broward College;* Kara McBride, *St. Louis University, Frost Campus;* Nelly A. McRae, *Hampton University;* Elaine Miller, *Christopher Newport University;* Nancy Mínguez, *Old Dominion University;* María Eugenia Moratto, *University of North Carolina, Greenboro;* María Yazmina Moreno-Florido, *Chicago State University;* Asha Nagaraj, *Northwestern University;* Sandy Oakley, *Palm Beach Community College;* María de los Santos Onofre-Madrid, *Angelo State University;* Sue Pechter, *Northwestern University;* Rose Pichón, *Delgado Community College;* Kay Raymond, *Sam Houston State University;* Deborah Rosenberg, *Northwestern University;* Laura Ruiz-Scott, *Scottsdale Community College;* Clinia Saffi, *Presbyterian College;* Phillip Santiago, *Buffalo State College;* Román Santillán, *Medgar Evers College, CUNY;* Karyn Schell, *University of San Francisco;* William Schott, *University of Missouri, Kansas City;* Luis Silva-Villar, *Mesa State College;* E. Esperanza Simien, *Baton Rouge Community College;* Roger Simpson, *Clemson University;* Dawn Slack, *Kutztown University of Pennsylvania;* Víctor Slesinger, *Palm Beach Community College;* Nori Sogomonian, *San Bernardino Valley College;* Benay Stein, *Northwestern University;* Roy Tanner, *Truman State University;* Sara Tucker, *Howard Community College;* Mayela Vallejos-Ramírez, *Mesa State College;* Michael Vermy, *SUNY Buffalo State College;* Kathleen Wheatley, *University of Wisconsin-Milwaukee;* U. Theresa Zmurkewycz, *St. Joseph's University.*

Kim Potowski

Silvia Sobral

Laila Dawson

Nuevos encuentros

Así se dice

Nuevos encuentros
  Las presentaciones
  Saludos y despedidas
  Expresiones de cortesía
Los números del 0 al 99
El alfabeto
Los días de la semana y los
  meses del año
  ¿Qué día es hoy?
  ¿Cuál es la fecha de
    hoy?/¿Qué fecha es hoy?
Decir la hora

Así se forma

1. Identifying and describing
  people: Subject pronouns
  and the verb *ser*
  Los cognados

Cultura

- Greetings
- Hispanic nationalities

By the end of this chapter
you will be able to:

- Meet and greet each other
- State where you are from and learn the origins
  of others
- Describe yourself and others
- Exchange phone numbers, e-mail addresses,
  and birthdays
- Tell time

ENTRANDO AL TEMA

1. What are these people probably saying to each other?
  ¡Hola!   **Gracias.**   **Hasta mañana.**

2. Is there anyone that you kiss on the cheek when you greet
  them? Would you kiss someone on the cheek whom you
  just met?

We will explore these questions in this chapter.

El gusto es mío. ¿De dónde es usted, profesora?

Buenos días, profesora Falcón, le presento a mi amigo Octavio.

Mucho gusto, Octavio.

Soy de Mendoza, Argentina.

Soy de Colombia, ¿y tú?

¿Cómo te llamas?	
¿Cómo se llama?	*What's your name?*
Me llamo...	*My name is . . .*
Buenos días	*Good morning*
Te/Le presento a...	*I want to introduce you to . . .*
Encantado/a	*It's nice to meet you*
Mucho gusto	*I'm pleased to meet you*
¿De dónde eres?	*Where are you from?*
Soy de...	*I'm from . . .*

Inés

Octavio

la profesora Falcón

Nuevos encuentros

Las presentaciones (*Introductions*)

In Spanish, there are two ways of addressing someone and, therefore, there are two equivalents of the English *you*: **tú** and **usted**. In general, use **tú** with classmates, relatives, friends, and others in a first-name basis relationship; use **usted** with professors and other adults in a last-name basis relationship.

Informal (with classmates)
Hola, me llamo...,
¿Cómo te llamas (tú)?

Formal (with instructor)
Buenos días, me llamo...
¿Cómo se llama (usted)?

- To say you are pleased to meet someone, you can say:

Mucho gusto.
Encantado. (*said by males*)/**Encantada.** (*said by females*)

- To ask where someone is from, say:

Informal
¿De dónde eres?

Formal
¿De dónde es usted?

- To say where you are from, say: **Soy de...**

Saludos y despedidas (*Greetings and expressions of farewell*)

Observe and compare the following conversations. The first introduces some formal greetings (**los saludos**) and the second presents their informal equivalents, as well as expressions of farewell (**las despedidas**).

Formal

PROF. RUIZ:	**Buenos días, señorita.**	*Good morning, Miss.*
	(Buenas tardes, señora.)	*(Good afternoon, Ma'am.)*
	(Buenas noches, señor.)	*(Good evening, Sir.)*
SUSANA:	**Buenos días.**	*Good morning. How are you?*
	¿Cómo está usted?	
PROF. RUIZ:	**Muy bien, gracias.**	*Very well, thanks. And you?*
	¿Y usted?	
SUSANA:	**Bien, gracias.**	*Fine, thanks.*

NOTA DE LENGUA

- There is no Spanish equivalent for *Ms*. Use **señora** or **señorita** as appropriate.
- In many Spanish-speaking countries, **tarde** is used while there is still daylight.
- **Buenos días** and **Buenas tardes/noches** are also used in informal settings, especially the first time you see people during a given day, and may also be used as a farewell.

Informal

LUIS:	**¡Hola!**	*Hello!/Hi!*
OLGA:	**¡Hola! ¿Cómo estás?**	*How are you?*
	(¿Qué tal?)	*(How's it going?)*
LUIS:	**Fenomenal. ¿Y tú?**	*Terrific. And you?*
OLGA:	**Regular.**	*OK./So-so.*
LUIS:	**¿Qué pasa?**	*What's happening?*
	(¿Qué hay de nuevo?)	*(What's new?)*
OLGA:	**Pues nada. Voy a clase.**	*Not much. I'm going to class.*
LUIS:	**Bueno (Pues), hasta luego.**	*Well, see you later.*
	(Hasta mañana.)	*(See you tomorrow.)*
	(Hasta pronto.)	*(See you soon.)*
	(Chao.)	*(Bye./So long.)*
OLGA:	**Adiós.**	*Good-bye.*

NOTA DE LENGUA

You may have noticed that Spanish has two verbs expressing *to be*:

ser   **Soy** de México.
estar   ¿Cómo **está** usted?

You will study **estar** and the differences between **ser** and **estar** in later chapters.

NOTA DE LENGUA

Spanish uses an upside-down question mark at the beginning of a question and an upside-down exclamation point at the beginning of an exclamation.

¿? = **signos de interrogación**
¡! = **signos de exclamación**

1-1 **¿Quién... ? (Who . . . ?)** Refer back to pages 4 and 5 to see who . . .

1. are greeting informally?
   a. Carmen y Alfonso   **b.** Inés y la profesora Falcón

2. is introducing one person to another informally?
   a. Javier   **b.** Inés

3. are introducing themselves?
   a. Linda y Manuel   **b.** Alfonso y Carmen

4. is introducing one person to another formally?
   a. Javier   **b.** Inés

5. is asking about someone's origin informally?
   a. Pepita   **b.** Octavio

1-2 **¿Formal o informal?** Listen to the following people as they greet each other and indicate whether they are addressing each other in a formal or informal manner.

	Formal	Informal
1.	☐	☐
2.	☐	☐
3.	☐	☐
4.	☐	☐

1-3 **¿Cómo estás?** Listen and choose the appropriate response to each greeting or question.

1. **a.** Me llamo Juan.   **b.** Hola, ¿qué tal?   **c.** Soy de Estados Unidos.

2. **a.** Muy bien, ¿y tú?   **b.** Pues nada.   **c.** Gracias.

3. **a.** Fenomenal.   **b.** Soy de México, ¿y tú?   **c.** Hasta pronto.

4. **a.** Muy bien, gracias.   **b.** Pues nada.   **c.** Bueno, pues, hasta luego.

5. **a.** ¿Qué pasa?   **b.** Buenas tardes.   **c.** Chao.

 1-4 **Las presentaciones.**

Paso 1. Move around the classroom and talk to at least five of your classmates and your instructor. Take notes in a chart like the one below.

- Greet them (remember to greet your instructor with formal forms!).
- Introduce yourself and learn their names.
- Find out where they are from.
- Say good-bye.

Modelo: Estudiante A: **Hola, me llamo Antonio. Y tú, ¿cómo te llamas?**
            Estudiante B: **Me llamo Raquel. ¿Cómo estás?**
            Estudiante A: **Muy bien, gracias. ¿De dónde eres?**

Nombre	Es de...

Paso 2. Find one of the classmates you met earlier. Move around the classroom together and take turns introducing each other to other classmates and the instructor. Each person should respond to the introduction appropriately.

Modelo: **Roberto, te presento a mi amiga Raquel. Raquel es de...**
             Profesor/a, le presento a...

Expresiones de cortesía (*Expressions of courtesy*)

Con permiso.	*Pardon me./Excuse me.* (*to seek permission to pass by someone or to leave*)
Perdón./Disculpe.	*Pardon me./Excuse me.* (*to get someone's attention or to seek forgiveness*)
Lo siento (mucho).	*I'm (so/very) sorry.*
Por favor.	*Please.*
(Muchas) Gracias.	*Thank you (very much).*
De nada.	*You're welcome.*

DICHOS

Cortesía y bien hablar (*talk*), cien puertas (*doors*) nos abrirán (*will open*).

¿Qué significa el dicho?

1-5 **¡Son muy corteses!** Write an appropriate expression from the box below under each drawing on pages 9 and 10.

Disculpe	Muchas gracias	Lo siento mucho
De nada	Con permiso	

1. El profesor Marín-Vivar a Natalia y Alfonso

Prof. Marín-Vivar is going to pass by Natalia and Alfonso. What does he say?

_____

2. Rubén a Camila

Rubén wants to speak to Camila, but she is talking with Carmen. What does Rubén say?

_____

3. Esteban a Inés y Pepita

4. Linda a Manuel
5. Manuel a Linda

Esteban drops his tray on Inés and Pepita!

Manuel gives Linda a gift. What does she say?

_____

_____

What does Manuel say to Linda?

_____

1-6 **Somos muy corteses también.** Look at the situations below and write what you would say in each case. Pretend you do not know any of these people, so you need to use formal forms.

1. You excuse yourself before you walk in front of someone.

_____

2. You lightly bump into someone and seek her/his forgiveness.

_____

3. You get someone's attention and ask the person her/his name and where she/he is from.

_____

4. You give someone something of yours, saying **Para usted** (_For you_). Expect a thank you and respond appropriately.

_____

Cultura: Greetings

In Spanish-speaking countries, women on a first-name basis will greet each other, and will also greet male friends, with a single light kiss on the right cheek, sometimes accompanied by a handshake. In Spain and some other countries, they will kiss once on each cheek. Men sometimes greet male friends and family with a short hug in addition to a handshake.

When the two people are in a last-name basis relationship, they will use a handshake only.

When people take leave of each other, they tend to repeat the same gestures as when they greeted each other.

How would the following Spanish-speakers probably greet and take leave from each other?

Susana and Antonio, Perú	One kiss	Two kisses	Handshake only
Juan and Alfonso, México	One kiss	Two kisses	Handshake only
Mr. González and Mrs. Burgos, Chile	One kiss	Two kisses	Handshake only
Elena and Linda, Spain	One kiss	Two kisses	Handshake only

Así se forma

Me llamo Pepita. Soy dinámica, atlética y extrovertida. Ah... y soy muy puntual.

Natalia y yo somos amigas.

Me llamo Natalia. Soy estudiante y soy de Nuevo México. Soy responsable, generosa y muy independiente.

1. Identifying and describing people: Subject pronouns and the verb *ser*

In the previous section you used some subject pronouns to address people (**usted, tú**) and forms of the verb **ser** (*to be*): **¿De dónde *es* usted? ¿De dónde *eres*? *Soy* de...** Here are some more subject pronouns and forms of **ser**.

Subject pronouns	Ser
yo (*I*)	**soy** estudiante
tú (*you, singular informal*)	**eres** inteligente
usted (Ud.) (*you, singular formal*)	**es** de Bolivia
él (*he*)/**ella** (*she*)	**es** profesor/profesora
nosotros/as (*we*)	**somos** estudiantes
vosotros/as (*you, plural informal*)	**sois** inteligentes
ustedes (Uds.) (*you, plural*)	**son** de Panamá
ellos (*they, masc.*)/**ellas** (*they, fem.*)	**son** profesores/profesoras

- **Vosotros/as** is used only in Spain. **Ustedes** is formal in Spain but both formal and informal in Hispanic America.

- Use subject pronouns only *to emphasize*, *to contrast*, or *to clarify*. Avoid them otherwise, since Spanish verb endings already indicate who the subject is.

Yo soy de Cuba y **él** es de Chile.	*I am from Cuba and **he** is from Chile.*
Soy de Cuba.	*I am from Cuba.*
Somos estudiantes.	*We are students.*

- Use the verb **ser** to tell who a person is, where a person is from, and what a person is like.

Natalia **es** estudiante.	*Natalia is a student.*
Es de Nuevo México.	*She is from New Mexico.*
Es muy independiente.	*She is very independent.*

Los cognados (*Cognates*)

Cognates are words that are identical or similar in two languages and have the same meaning. Cognates may be any type of word such as a noun, verb, adjective, etc. Below you have a list of adjectives (words we use to describe people and things) that are cognates. These adjectives are commonly used with **ser** to describe people.

Note that some adjectives may be used to describe males or females.

admirable	flexible	materialista	rebelde
arrogante	independiente	optimista	responsable
conformista	inteligente	paciente	sentimental
eficiente	irresponsable	pesimista	terrible
egoísta	liberal	puntual	tolerante

But other adjectives change **-o** to **-a** when referring to a female.

ambicioso/a	dinámico/a	introvertido/a	religioso/a
atlético/a	extrovertido/a	modesto/a	romántico/a
cómico/a	generoso/a	organizado/a	serio/a
creativo/a	impulsivo/a	práctico/a	tranquilo/a

To describe more than one person, add –s to adjectives that end in a vowel and –es to those ending in a consonant.

admirable   →   admirable**s**
sentimental   →   sentimental**es**

Since recognizing cognates is an important skill when learning a second language, new vocabulary consisting of cognates of English words will not be introduced with translation (but you can always find translations in the **Repaso de vocabulario** section at the end of each chapter).

NOTA DE LENGUA

To make a negative statement, place **no** before the verb.

    No soy estudiante.   I am not a student.

In answering yes/no questions, repeat the **no**.

    ¿Eres pesimista?   Are you a pessimist?

    ¡**No, no** soy pesimista!   No, I'm not a pessimist!

1-7 **¿Similares o diferentes?** Can you figure out what the title of this activity is? The words are cognates!

Paso 1. Read the following sentences and mark whether they are true (**cierto**) or false (**falso**) for you. Then add one more sentence using a different cognate from the box above.

		Cierto	Falso
1.	Soy optimista.	☐	☐
2.	Soy creativo/a.	☐	☐
3.	Soy serio/a.	☐	☐
4.	Soy responsable.	☐	☐
5.	Soy extrovertido/a.	☐	☐
6.	Soy paciente.	☐	☐
7.	_____	☐	☐

Paso 2. Work with a partner and compare your answers orally. Then write sentences about your differences.

Modelo: **Soy optimista, pero Kate no es optimista.**
Soy optimista y Kate es optimista también (*as well*).
No soy optimista y Kate no es optimista tampoco (*either*).

PALABRAS ÚTILES (*Useful Words*)

también	*also*
tampoco	*neither/not either*

NOTA CULTURAL

Una escritora chilena

Isabel Allende is a prolific Chilean author whose novels are bestsellers in many countries, including the United States. She was awarded Chile's National Literature Prize in 2010. Two of her novels, "**La casa de los espíritus**" ("*The House of the Spirits*") and "**De amor y de sombra**" ("*Of Love and Shadows*"), were made into movies starring actors like Javier Bardem, Benjamin Bratt, Meryl Streep, Glenn Close, Jeremy Irons, Winona Rider, Antonio Banderas y Vanessa Redgrave. Why don't you watch one of them and report back to the class?

1-8 **¿Cómo son?** Write the number of each sentence you hear next to the photo of the person/people it describes. You will hear two descriptions for each photo.

Jóvenes muralistas en Nueva York

____ y ____

Hombre indígena ecuatoriano

____ y ____

La novelista Isabel Allende

____ y ____

Chicas futbolistas

____ y ____

1-9 **Personas famosas.** Using adjectives from the following list, plus others that you can come up with, and the clues given in parentheses, tell a classmate about the following famous people and two more of your choice. Say what they do, where they are from, and use one or two adjectives to describe them.

Modelo: Penélope Cruz (actriz/España)
Penélope Cruz *es* actriz y *es* de España. Es muy bell*a* y dinámic*a*.

atlético/a	creativo/a	famoso/a	popular	bello/a (*beautiful*)
dinámico/a	fuerte (*strong*)	romántico/a	serio/a	rebelde(s)

1. Javier Bardem (actor/España)

2. Shakira (cantante/ Colombia)

3. Alberto Pujols (jugador de béisbol/ República Dominicana)

4. Jessica Alba (actriz/California)

5. ¿ ... ?

6. ¿ ... ?

1-10 **Mi personalidad.**

 Paso 1. In pairs, greet and introduce yourselves and talk about your origins. Then ask each other *yes/no* questions to determine your personality traits. Take notes, as you will need some of this information later.

Modelo: Estudiante A: **¿*Eres* (muy) extrovertid*o*/*a*?**
          Estudiante B: **Sí, *soy* muy extrovertid*o*/*a*. / No, no soy (muy) extrovertid*o*/*a*. ¿Y tú?**

 Paso 2. Walking around the classroom, introduce your classmate to three other students. Tell her/his name, origin, and two personality traits.

Modelo: **Mi amigo/a se llama... O, Te presento a mi amigo/a...**
          Es de...
          Es... y...

 Paso 3. Tell the class one difference between you and your classmate and two things you have in common. Remember to add -s or -es to the adjective to form the plural.

Modelo: **(*Partner's name*) es... y yo soy...**
          Él/Ella y yo somos... y...

Los números del 0 al 99

0 **cero**	10 **diez**	20 **veinte**	30 **treinta**
1 **uno**	11 **once**	21 **veintiuno**	31 **treinta y uno**
2 **dos**	12 **doce**	22 **veintidós**	32 **treinta y dos**
3 **tres**	13 **trece**	23 **veintitrés**	...
4 **cuatro**	14 **catorce**	24 **veinticuatro**	40 **cuarenta**
5 **cinco**	15 **quince**	25 **veinticinco**	50 **cincuenta**
6 **seis**	16 **dieciséis**	26 **veintiséis**	60 **sesenta**
7 **siete**	17 **diecisiete**	27 **veintisiete**	70 **setenta**
8 **ocho**	18 **dieciocho**	28 **veintiocho**	80 **ochenta**
9 **nueve**	19 **diecinueve**	29 **veintinueve**	90 **noventa**

- **Uno** is used for counting, but before a noun we use the indefinite article **un** (masculine)/**una** (feminine). The same holds true for **veintiuno**, **treinta y uno**, and so on.

  Un profesor, **una** profesora y **veintiún** estudiantes son de Texas.
  One (male) professor, one (female) professor, and twenty-one students are from Texas.

- The numbers from 16 to 29 are usually written as one word: **diecisiete**, **veinticuatro**. Those from 31 on are written as three words: **treinta y tres**; **cincuenta y seis**.

- Note the numbers that carry accent marks: **dieciséis**, **veintidós**, **veintitrés**, **veintiséis**.

numbers

1-11 ¿Correcto o incorrecto?

Paso 1. Listen to some math problems and decide whether the answer is correct (**correcto**) or incorrect (**incorrecto**).

	Correcto	Incorrecto
1.		
2.		
3.		
4.		
5.		

Paso 2. Now listen to a few more math problems. This time you have to provide the answers. Write them out in words in your notebook or on a sheet of paper.

1-12 Más matemáticas.
Write five simple math problems like the ones you just heard. In pairs, take turns reading your problems to your partner and writing out answers to hers/his. Then, check each other's answers.

Modelo: Estudiante A: **Diez y ocho son…**
         Estudiante B: **Dieciocho.**

1-13 Números de teléfono.
In Spanish, the digits of phone numbers are usually given in pairs and the article **el** (*the*) precedes the phone number: **"Es el 4-86-05-72."**

Paso 1. Listen as your instructor reads telephone numbers from the phone list on page 18. Raise your hand when you know whose number was read and tell whose number it is.

Modelo: **Es el número de Juan Millán.**

PALABRAS ÚTILES

C/ → Calle	*Street*
Avda. → Avenida	*Avenue*
Pl. → Plaza	*Square*

Paso 2. Now, in pairs, take turns reading phone numbers and identifying the person whose number it is.

Nombre	Dirección	Teléfono
		321.99.02
Antolín, Sonia	c/ Mayor, 34	844.93.15
Cruz, Ángel	Avda. de la Paz, 2	321.43.36
García, Ignacio	c/ Rivera, 20	423.15.90
Gregorio, Javier	c/ Roma, 12	655.76.91
Hernández, Alicia	c/ Aurelio Díaz, 11	251.90.02
Jiménez, Luis	Avda. de América, 43	630.18.54
Landa, Marina	Pl. Abril, 1	922.37.78
Martínez, Elena	c/ Luz, 77	794.47.20
Pérez, Félix	Avda. Juárez, 144	623.12.97
Schuhmacher, Elena	Avda. Pirineos, 22	777.85.32
Sanchez, Raquel	c/ Estrecho, 13	209.03.76
Yuster, Jorge	c/ Los Molinos, 27	

Así se dice

El alfabeto

The letters of the alphabet (**alfabeto** or **abecedario**) and their names follow.
Listen and repeat.

a (a)	**A**rgentina	**j** (jota)	**J**uárez	**r** (ere)	Puerto **R**ico
b (be)	**B**olivia	**k** (ka)	Nueva Yor**k**	**s** (ese)	**S**an **S**alvador
c (ce)	**C**uba, **C**iudad Real	**l** (ele)	**L**aredo	**t** (te)	**T**egucigalpa
d (de)	**D**allas	**m** (eme)	**M**anagua	**u** (u)	**U**ruguay
e (e)	**E**cuador	**n** (ene)	**N**icaragua	**v** (ve, uve)	**V**enezuela
f (efe)	**F**lorida	**ñ** (eñe)	Espa**ñ**a	**w** (doble ve, doble uve, uve doble)	**W**ashington
g (ge)	**G**uatemala, **G**erona	**o** (o)	**O**axaca	**x** (equis)	e**x**amen, Mé**x**ico
h (hache)	**H**onduras	**p** (pe)	**P**anamá	**y** (i griega)	**Y**ucatán
i (i)	**I**quitos	**q** (cu)	**Q**uito	**z** (zeta)	**Z**acatecas, Cu**z**co

1-14 **¿Cómo se escribe?** (*How do you spell it?*)

Paso 1. Listen to the spelling of the names of some Hispanic cities and write them down.

1. _____   4. _____

2. _____   5. _____

3. _____   6. _____

Paso 2. Choose three cities where Spanish is spoken (check the maps at the end of your textbook) and write them down. Now work with a partner. Taking turns, spell the names of your cities for your partner and write down the names of the cities she/he spells for you.

1-15 **Mi nombre y mi número de teléfono.** In groups, ask for and give each other your names, phone numbers, and e-mail addresses, spelling things out in Spanish. Write the information accurately, as it will be used later for a Class Directory.

Modelo:	Estudiante A:	**¿Cómo te llamas?**
	Estudiante B:	**Me llamo Mónica Smith: M–o–n...**
	Estudiante C:	**¿Cuál es tu número de teléfono?**
	Estudiante B:	**Es el cuatro ochenta y seis, cero, cinco, setenta y dos.**
	Estudiante D:	**¿Cuál es tu correo electrónico?**
	Estudiante B:	**Es monica3@dicho.com: d–i–c–h...**

PALABRAS ÚTILES

número de teléfono	*phone number*
correo electrónico	*e-mail address*
arroba	*@*
punto	*dot*

INVESTIG@ EN INTERNET

Look for an e-card to send to one of the classmates whose e-mail address you wrote down. Use a search engine to find free e-cards in Spanish!

Así se dice

WILEY PLUS Pronunciación:
Practice pronunciation of the chapter vocabulary and particular sounds of Spanish in *WileyPLUS*.

Los días de la semana y los meses del año

Days of the week and months of the year

¿Qué día es hoy?

¡Ay, es lunes!

septiembre

	lunes	martes	miércoles	jueves	viernes	sábado	domingo
						1	2
	3	4	5	6	7	8	9
	10	11	12	13	14	15	16
	17	18	19	20	21	22	23
	24	25	26	27	28	29	30

└ el **día** ┘   la **semana**   └ el **fin de semana** ┘

NOTA CULTURAL

Cinco de Mayo

September 16th is when Mexicans celebrate their independence from Spain in 1821. **Cinco de Mayo**, which is popular in the United States, is the celebration of an important victory against French invaders in Puebla, Mexico, in 1862.

- In Hispanic calendars, the week usually begins on Monday.

- The days of the week are not capitalized in Spanish.

- With the day of the week, the definite article **el** (singular) or **los** (plural) is used to indicate on.
  El sábado vamos a una gran fiesta.   *On Saturday* we are going to a big party.
  Los miércoles vamos al gimnasio.   *On Wednesdays* we go to the gym.

- The plural of **el sábado** and **el domingo** is **los sábados** and **los domingos**. The other days use the same form in the singular and in the plural:
  el lunes → los lunes.

1-16 **El mes de septiembre.** Listen to statements about what days of the week certain dates fall on, and mark whether the statements are true (**cierto**) or false (**falso**) based on the calendar on page 20.

	Cierto	Falso
1.		
2.		
3.		
4.		
5.		

1-17 **¿Qué día es?** In pairs, one of you will choose a day in the month of September from the calendar on page 20 and the other will indicate on what day of the week it falls. Take turns.

Modelo: Estudiante A: **¿Qué día es el catorce de septiembre?**
                      Estudiante B: **Es viernes.**

1-18 **¿Qué opinas? (*What do you think?*)** Complete the statements with the appropriate day(s). Then in groups, share your answers with your classmates. Are your opinions similar?

1. Mi día de la semana favorito es _____.
2. El peor (*worst*) día de la semana es _____.
3. Tengo (*I have*) muchas clases _____.
4. No tengo muchas clases _____.
5. Un día malo (*bad*) para exámenes es _____.
6. Un día bueno (*good*) para hacer fiestas es _____.

NOTA CULTURAL

El español en el mundo

Spanish is one of the five most spoken languages in the world and is the primary language in twenty countries: Argentina, Bolivia, Chile, Colombia, Costa Rica, Cuba, Dominican Republic, Ecuador, El Salvador, Guatemala, Honduras, Mexico, Nicaragua, Panama, Paraguay, Peru, Puerto Rico, Spain, Uruguay, Venezuela.

Spanish is widely spoken in the U.S., with large communities of Spanish speakers in and around New York, Miami, Los Angeles, and Chicago, and cities throughout the Southwest.

Spanish is also an official language in the African country of Equatorial Guinea and was an official language in the Philippines from the 16th century to 1987, although neither country is culturally Hispanic.

¿Cuál es la fecha de hoy?/ ¿Qué fecha es hoy?

What's today's date?

Pero Alfonso, mi cumpleaños es el 13 de agosto.

- To express what day of the month it is, use cardinal numbers (**dos, tres, cuatro, ...**). In Latin America, the first of the month is always expressed with **el primero**. In Spain, **el uno** is used.

  Hoy es (el)[1] cuatro de abril.
  Mañana es (el) primero de abril. (Latin America)
  Mañana es el uno de abril. (Spain)

- To express the month in a date, use **de** before the month. Months are not generally capitalized in Spanish.

  el 25 **de** diciembre   el diez **de** mayo

- When dates are given in numbers, the day precedes the month.

  4/7 = **el cuatro de julio**

Note the names of the months in this calendar.

2011

enero

L	M	M	J	V	S	D
					1	2
3	4	5	6	7	8	9
10	11	12	13	14	15	16
17	18	19	20	21	22	23
24	25	26	27	28	29	30
31						

febrero

L	M	M	J	V	S	D
	1	2	3	4	5	6
7	8	9	10	11	12	13
14	15	16	17	18	19	20
21	22	23	24	25	26	27
28						

marzo

L	M	M	J	V	S	D
	1	2	3	4	5	6
7	8	9	10	11	12	13
14	15	16	17	18	19	20
21	22	23	24	25	26	27
28	29	30	31			

abril

L	M	M	J	V	S	D
				1	2	3
4	5	6	7	8	9	10
11	12	13	14	15	16	17
18	19	20	21	22	23	24
25	26	27	28	29	30	

mayo

L	M	M	J	V	S	D
						1
2	3	4	5	6	7	8
9	10	11	12	13	14	15
16	17	18	19	20	21	22
23	24	25	26	27	28	29
30	31					

junio

L	M	M	J	V	S	D
	1	2	3	4	5	
6	7	8	9	10	11	12
13	14	15	16	17	18	19
20	21	22	23	24	25	26
27	28	29	30			

julio

L	M	M	J	V	S	D
				1	2	3
4	5	6	7	8	9	10
11	12	13	14	15	16	17
18	19	20	21	22	23	24
25	26	27	28	29	30	31

agosto

L	M	M	J	V	S	D
1	2	3	4	5	6	7
8	9	10	11	12	13	14
15	16	17	18	19	20	21
22	23	24	25	26	27	28
29	30	31				

septiembre

L	M	M	J	V	S	D
			1	2	3	4
5	6	7	8	9	10	11
12	13	14	15	16	17	18
19	20	21	22	23	24	25
26	27	28	29	30		

octubre

L	M	M	J	V	S	D
					1	2
3	4	5	6	7	8	9
10	11	12	13	14	15	16
17	18	19	20	21	22	23
24	25	26	27	28	29	30
31						

noviembre

L	M	M	J	V	S	D
	1	2	3	4	5	6
7	8	9	10	11	12	13
14	15	16	17	18	19	20
21	22	23	24	25	26	27
28	29	30				

diciembre

L	M	M	J	V	S	D
			1	2	3	4
5	6	7	8	9	10	11
12	13	14	15	16	17	18
19	20	21	22	23	24	25
26	27	28	29	30	31	

---

[1] A word in parentheses ( ) indicates that it is optional.

Los días feriados

Not all holidays are celebrated equally or on the same dates in different Hispanic countries. For example, Father's Day is celebrated on March 19 in Spain, but on the second Sunday in June in other countries. Also, Mother's Day is always on May 10 in México and May 27 in Bolivia. Three Kings Day, or **el Día de los Reyes Magos** (*Wise Kings*), is the celebration of the Epiphany, honoring the arrival of the Three Wise Men to Jerusalem: Melchior, Balthazar, and Caspar. It is celebrated twelve days after Christmas (the "twelfth day of Christmas" in the famous Christmas carol). In the Hispanic world, the Three Kings bring gifts to children on this day, although **Santa Clos/San Nicolás** is gaining in popularity in many areas. Children often leave clumps of grass or hay for the Kings' camels to eat after their long journey.

▲ Los Reyes Magos

INVESTIG@ EN INTERNET

Find out what a **Rosca de Reyes** is and what surprise is baked inside of it!

1-19 **Días feriados.** Match each of the following celebrations with the month when they are celebrated in the United States. For how many of them can you give the date as well, according to the calendar on page 22?

Modelo: **El Día de Navidad es en diciembre. Es el veinticinco de diciembre.**

1. La Nochebuena (*Christmas Eve*)
2. El Día de Acción de Gracias (*Thanksgiving Day*)
3. El Día de los Reyes Magos
4. El Día de los Enamorados (*Valentine's Day*)
5. El Día de las Madres (*Mother's Day*)
6. El Día de los Padres (*Father's Day*)
7. El Día de la Independencia
8. El Día del Trabajo (*Labor Day*)

a. enero
b. febrero
c. mayo
d. junio
e. julio
f. septiembre
g. noviembre
h. diciembre

DICHOS

En abril, aguas (*water*) mil.

¿Qué significa el dicho?

1-20 Los cumpleaños (*Birthdays*).

Paso 1. Write the date of your birthday on a small piece of paper using numbers (**día/mes**) and give it to your instructor.

 Paso 2. Your instructor will now give each student one of the pieces of paper. Move around the class to find the person whose birthday is written on it.

Modelo: Estudiante A: **¿Cuándo es tu cumpleaños?**
Estudiante B: **Mi cumpleaños es el ocho de octubre.**

 Paso 3. Tell the class the name of the student whose birthday information you have and when her/his birthday is.

Modelo: **El cumpleaños de Roberta es el ocho de octubre.**

NOTA CULTURAL

El día del santo

In most Hispanic countries, it is common to celebrate your birthday and also your saint's day (based on the Catholic tradition). If your parents named you after the saint honored on the day of your birth, then your birthday and your saint's day are the same. If they named you after a saint honored on a different day of the year, you have two celebrations! Observe the names of the saints on the January calendar.

ENERO

LUNES	MARTES	MIÉRCOLES	JUEVES	VIERNES	SÁBADO	DOMINGO
○ LUNA LLENA DIA 1 - 31	☾ C. MENGUANTE DIA 9	○ LUNA NUEVA DIA 17	☽ C. CRECIENTE DIA 24	**1** LA CIRCUNCISIÓN	**2** SAN BASILIO M.	**3** SAN ANTERO PAPA
4 SAN PRISCO	**5** S.TELESFORO	**6** LOS S. REYES EPIFANÍA	**7** SAN RAYMUNDO	**8** SAN APOLINAR	**9** SAN MARCELINO	**10** SAN GONZALO
11 S. HIGINIO PAPA	**12** S. ARCADIO M.	**13** S. HILARIO OB.	**14** SAN FÉLIX M.	**15** SAN MAURO ABAD	**16** SAN MARCELO	**17** SAN ANTONIO ABAD
18 STA. PRISCA V.	**19** SAN MARIO	**20** SAN FABIÁN	**21** SAN FRUCTUOSO	**22** SAN VICENTE M.	**23** SAN ALBERTO	**24** SAN FRANCISCO DE S.
25 STA. ELVIRA V.	**26** S. TIMOTEO OB.	**27** STA. ÁNGELA V.	**28** STO. TOMÁS DE A.	**29** SAN VALERIO	**30** STA MARTINA	**31** SAN JUAN BOSCO

1-21 El día del santo.
Look at the calendar page above and find what days these people are celebrating their saints' day. Can you find a saint's day for someone you know?

Modelo: Ángela
El santo de Ángela es el 27 de enero.

1. Elvira
2. Gonzalo
3. Martina
4. Tomás
5. Félix

Así se dice

Decir la hora

Telling time

In Spanish, trends in telling time have been affected by the popularity of digital watches and clocks. This presentation on telling time reflects these changes.

- When you want to know what time it is, ask **¿Qué hora es?** For telling time on the hour, use **es** for *one o'clock* only. Use **son** for all other times.

Es la una.

Son las ocho.[1]

- To state the number of minutes past the hour, say the name of that hour plus (**y**) the number of minutes.

Es la una **y** diez.

Son las cuatro **y** cuarto.
Son las cuatro **y** quince.

Son las diez **y** media.
Son las diez **y** treinta.

Son las once **y** cuarenta.

- To state the number of minutes before the coming hour, give the next hour less (**menos**) the number of minutes to go before that hour.

Es la una **menos** diez.

Son las nueve **menos** veinticinco.

- To differentiate between hours in the morning, afternoon, and evening, use the following expressions.

Son las seis **de la manaña.**

Son las seis **de la tarde.**[2]

Son las diez **de la noche.**

Es **mediodía.**

Es **medianoche.**

- To ask at *what time* a class or event takes place, use **¿A qué hora... ?**
  —**¿A qué hora** es la clase?
  —Es **a las 8:15** de la mañana.

---

[1]Note that this digital clock uses a 24-hour system. To convert from the 24-hour clock to a 12-hour clock, subtract 12. For example: 14:00 minus 12 equals 2:00 p.m. All a.m. times are the same in both systems.

[2]In most Spanish-speaking countries, **tarde** is used while there is still daylight, and thus may extend until 7:00 P.M. or even 8:00 P.M.

1-22 **¿Qué hora es?**

 Paso 1. Listen to the times given and identify the clock (**reloj**) that tells each time.

Modelo: You hear: Son las ocho y media de la mañana.

You say: **Reloj 3.**

1. 2. 3. 4.

5. 6. 7. 8.

Paso 2. With a classmate, one of you chooses a clock and tells the time on it. Then the other identifies the clock that tells that time.

Modelo: Estudiante A: **Son las once y cinco de la mañana.**

Estudiante B: **Reloj 3.**

1. 2. 3. 4.

5. 6. 7. 8.

1-23 **¿A qué hora?** (*At what time?*) In pairs, each student looks at one of the following TV guides. Ask each other at what time the programs indicated are featured.

Modelo: Estudiante A: **¿A qué hora es *NX clusiva*?**
Estudiante B: **A las ocho de la noche.**

Estudiante A	
Horario Univisión (Hora del este)	
En la mañana	
7:00am - 10:00am	Despierta América
10:00am - 11:00pm	Casos de familia
11:00am - 12:00pm	¿Quién tiene la razón?
En la tarde	
12:00pm - 1:00pm	Sueño con tu amor
1:00pm - 2:00pm	Mi vida eres tú
2:00pm - 3:00pm	El amor no tiene precio
3:00pm - 4:00pm	Rebelde
4:00pm - 5:00pm	El Gordo y la Flaca
5:00pm - 6:00pm	Primer impacto
6:00pm - 6:30pm	¡Qué locura!
6:30pm - 7:00pm	Noticiero Univisión
En la noche	
7:00pm - 8:00pm	Heridas de amor
8:00pm - 9:00pm	La fea más bella
9:00pm - 10:00pm	Mundo de fieras
10:00pm - 11:00pm	Historias para contar
11:00pm - 11:30pm	Primer impacto extra
11:30pm - 12:00am	Noticiero Univisión - Última hora

Estudiante B	
Horario Galavisión (Hora del este)	
En la mañana	
7:00 - 10:00	Primero noticias
9:00 - 12:00	Hoy
En la tarde	
12:00 - 13:30	Tiempo en casa
13:30 - 14:30	Al sabor del Chef
14:30 - 15:30	Vida salvaje
15:30 - 17:00	Noticiero con Lolita Ayala
17:00 - 18:00	¿Qué nos pasa?
18:00 - 20:00	NX clusiva
En la noche	
20:00 - 21:00	El rastro de un crimen
21:00 - 21:30	Diarios de un crimen
21:30 - 22:30	Las noticias por Adela
22:30 - 24:30	Noticiero con Joaquín López Dóriga

Estudiante A
Ask about Galavision´s schedule:

1. Vida salvaje
2. Hoy
3. ¿Qué nos pasa?
4. Diarios de un crimen
5. Noticiero con Joaquín López Doriga

Estudiante B
Ask about Univision's schedule:

1. Noticiero Univisión - Última hora
2. Historias para contar
3. Casos de familia
4. Mi vida eres tú
5. Despierta América

1-24 **El mundo hispano (*The Hispanic world*).** Times on the map below are given according to the 24-hour clock. Tell what time it is in the following cities according to the information on the map. What do these cities have in common?

Modelo: ¿Qué hora es en San Salvador, El Salvador?
  Son las 7:30. O, Son las 7 y media de la mañana.

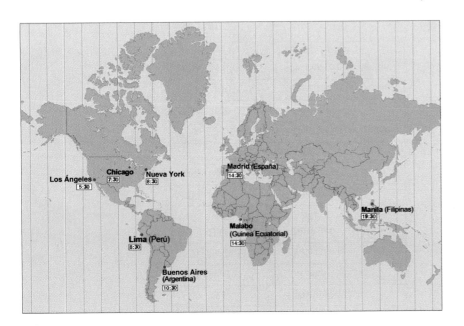

1. ¿Qué hora es en Lima?
2. ¿Qué hora es en Buenos Aires?
3. ¿Qué hora es en Los Ángeles?
4. ¿Qué hora es en Nueva York?
5. ¿Qué hora es en Madrid?
6. ¿Qué hora es en Chicago?
7. ¿Qué hora es en Manila?
8. ¿Qué hora es en Malabo?

1-25 **Las nacionalidades.** Work in pairs. Read to your partner the sentences on your list of nationalities of famous people. Your partner has to decide (or guess!) whether the statement is true (**cierto**) or false (**falso**). Then switch roles. Don't look at your partner's list.

Modelo: Estudiante A: **La artista Frida Kahlo es mexicana.**
       Estudiante B: **Es cierto.**

Estudiante A:

1. El cantante (*singer*) Marc Anthony es puertorriqueño.
2. Óscar Arias, Premio Nobel de la Paz, es costarricense.
3. La cantante Shakira es ecuatoriana.
4. La actriz Jennifer López es estadounidense.
5. La ex presidenta Michelle Bachelet es chilena.

Estudiante B:

6. La actriz Penélope Cruz es española.
7. La autora Isabel Allende es hondureña.
8. El escritor Gabriel García Márquez es colombiano.
9. Los jugadores de básquetbol Pau y Marc Gasol son españoles.
10. El jugador de béisbol Johan Santana es nicaragüense.

¿DE DÓNDE SON LOS HISPANOS?

When you travel to a Hispanic country, you will frequently be asked: **¿De dónde eres?** or **¿De dónde es usted?** If you are from the United States, your response would be: **Soy de Estados Unidos** or **Soy estadounidense.** Although we sometimes hear people from the U.S. referred to as **"americanos,"** in fact, **americano/a** can refer to anyone in North, Central, or South America.

Note that, as with some of the cognates above, several nationalities have two different forms: those ending in -**o** refer to a male, and those ending in -**a**, to a female, such as **mexicano** and **mexicana.** Other nationalities end in a consonant in the masculine form and -**a** in the female form, such as **español** and **española.** Others have only one form, -**e**, such as **estadounidense**.

Turn to the map of the Hispanic world on the back inside cover of your textbook, and become familiar with the names of the countries and their corresponding nationalities. Note that this includes the United States, where soon about 20 percent of the population will be of Hispanic origin![1]

Soy mexicana.

Soy español.

Soy cubano.

Soy estadounidense.

---

[1]*For a complete listing of nationalities from around the world, see **Apéndice 3**, page A-15.*

Repaso de vocabulario activo

Saludos y expresiones comunes *Greetings and common expressions*

Buenos días, señorita/señora/ señor.   *Good morning, Miss/Ma'am/ Sir.*

Buenas tardes.   *Good afternoon.*

Buenas noches.   *Good evening.*

¡Hola!   *Hello!/Hi!*

¿Cómo está usted? ¿Cómo estás?   *How are you?*

¿Qué tal?   *How is it going?*

Muy bien, gracias.   *Very well, thanks.*

Fenomenal.   *Great.*

Regular.   *OK./So-so.*

¿Qué pasa?   *What's happening?*

¿Qué hay de nuevo?   *What's new?*

Pues nada.   *Not much.*

Le presento a...   (formal) *I would like to introduce you to . . .*

Te presento a...   (informal) *I want to introduce you to . . .*

Mucho gusto.   *Nice meeting you.*

Encantado/a.   *Pleased to meet you.*

Igualmente.   *Nice meeting you too.*

El gusto es mío.   *The pleasure is mine.*

¿Cómo se llama usted? ¿Cómo te llamas?   *What's your name?*

Me llamo...   *My name is . . .*

¿De dónde es usted? ¿De dónde eres?   *Where are you from?*

Soy de...   *I am from . . .*

Perdón./Disculpe.   *Pardon me. Excuse me.* (≠ Con permiso.)

Lo siento (mucho).   *I am (very) sorry.*

Con permiso.   *Pardon me. Excuse me.* (≠ Perdón./Disculpe.)

Por favor.   *Please.*

(Muchas) gracias.   *Thank you (very much.)*

De nada.   *You're welcome.*

Adiós.   *Good-bye.*

Hasta luego.   *See you later.*

Hasta pronto.   *See you soon.*

Hasta mañana.   *See you tomorrow.*

Chao.   *Bye./So-long.*

Verbo

ser   *to be*

Los días de la semana *The days of the week*

lunes   *Monday*

martes   *Tuesday*

miércoles   *Wednesday*

jueves   *Thursday*

viernes   *Friday*

sábado   *Saturday*

domingo   *Sunday*

¿Qué día es hoy?   *What day is it?*

el día   *day*

la semana   *week*

el fin de semana   *weekend*

Los meses   *Months*

enero   *January*

febrero   *February*

marzo   *March*

abril   *April*

mayo   *May*

junio   *June*

julio   *July*

agosto   *August*

septiembre   *September*

octubre   *October*

noviembre   *November*

diciembre   *December*

¿Cuál es la fecha de hoy?/¿Qué fecha es hoy?   *What's the date today?*

¿Qué hora es?   *What time is it?*

la hora   *time/hour*

y/menos   *and/less*

cuarto/media   *quarter/half*

de la mañana/tarde/noche   *in the morning/afternoon/evening*

Es mediodía/medianoche.   *It's noon./ midnight.*

Autoprueba y repaso

I. Meeting and greeting each other. Complete the conversations. In some cases, there is more than one possible answer.

1. PROFESORA: Buenos días. ¿Cómo estás?

    PEPITA: _____. ¿Y usted?

    PROFESORA: _____.

2. PROFESORA: ¿_____?

    Pepita: Me llamo Pepita.

3. CARMEN: ¡Hola, Pepita! ¿_____?

    PEPITA: Regular. ¿Y tú?

    CARMEN: _____.

4. PEPITA: Profesora, le presento a Carmen Martínez.

    PROFESORA: _____.

    CARMEN: _____.

5. PEPITA: ¿Cómo te llamas?

    MANUEL: _____. ¿Y tú?

    PEPITA: _____.

    MANUEL: Encantado, Pepita.

    PEPITA: _____.

6. CARMEN: ¿_____?

    PEPITA: Son las 9:30.

    CARMEN: Pues, tengo una clase ahora. Hasta luego.

    PEPITA: _____.

II. Subject pronouns and the verb *ser*. Tell where the people are from. Write sentences using the correct form of the verb **ser**.

    Modelo: yo / de México; ella / de Panamá

        Yo soy de México pero (*but*) **ella es de Panamá.**

1. ellos / de Chile; nosotras / de México

2. tú / de Colombia; ustedes / de España

3. Luis / de El Salvador; Juan y Elena / de Honduras

III. Counting from 0 to 99. Tell how much each item costs. Write out the numbers ($ = **dólar/dólares**).

1. los jeans - $35.00

2. el suéter - $57.00

3. la chaqueta - $72.00

4. el sombrero - $26.00

5. el video - $15.00

6. el CD - $9.00

IV. Indicating dates. Write the dates in Spanish. Include only the day and the month.

    Modelo: 2/1/08 (día/mes/año)

        Es el dos de enero.

1. 14/2/11

2. 1/4/11

3. 4/7/12

4. 23/11/12

5. 25/12/10

V. Telling time. What time is it? Give both possible answers when it is a quarter after the hour, such as **Es la una y cuarto.** Or, **Es la una y quince.**

    Modelo: 1:10 P.M.

        Es la una y diez de la tarde.

1. 1:15 P.M.

2. 9:30 P.M.

3. 5:50 P.M.

4. 11:40 P.M.

5. 12:00 P.M.

VI. General review. Answer the questions in complete sentences.

1. ¿Cómo te llamas?

2. ¿Cómo estás?

3. ¿Eres inflexible y arrogante? ¿Eres responsable y generoso/a?

4. ¿De dónde eres?

5. ¿Cuál es la fecha de tu cumpleaños?

6. ¿Qué día es hoy?

7. ¿Qué hora es?

8. ¿A qué hora es la clase de español?

VII. *Cultura.* Answer the following questions.

1. How would a male and a female student greet each other in Argentina? And in Spain?

2. What is the Día de los Reyes Magos and when is it celebrated?

3. What is a person's Día del santo?

Answers to the *Autoprueba y repaso* are found in **Apéndice 2.**

La vida universitaria

Así se dice

La vida universitaria
  En el laboratorio
  En la clase
El campus universitario

Cultura

- Puerto Rico
- La vida universitaria en el mundo hispano

Así se forma

1. Nouns and articles
2. *Ir + a +* destination
  ¿Cuándo vamos?
  ¿Por cuánto tiempo?
  ¿Con qué frecuencia?
  ¿Tarde o temprano?
3. The present tense of regular *–ar* verbs
  Las actividades en la universidad
4. The present tense of regular *–er* and *–ir* verbs; *hacer* and *salir*
  Más actividades en la universidad

Dicho y hecho

Para leer: Salamanca: Un clásico

Para conversar: El fin de semana

Para escribir: ¿Soy un/a estudiante típico/a?

Para ver y escuchar: Una visita a la UNAM

By the end of this chapter you will be able to:

- Talk about computers, the language lab, and the classroom
- Talk about where you are going on campus
- Talk about your class schedule
- Talk about activities related to university life

ENTRANDO AL TEMA

1. Approximately what percent of students at your school live in campus dormitories?
2. **¿Cierto o falso?**
  a. Puerto Ricans are United States citizens.
  b. Salsa music originated in Puerto Rico.

If you are not sure about the answers to these questions, you will find out in this chapter.

Así se dice

La vida universitaria

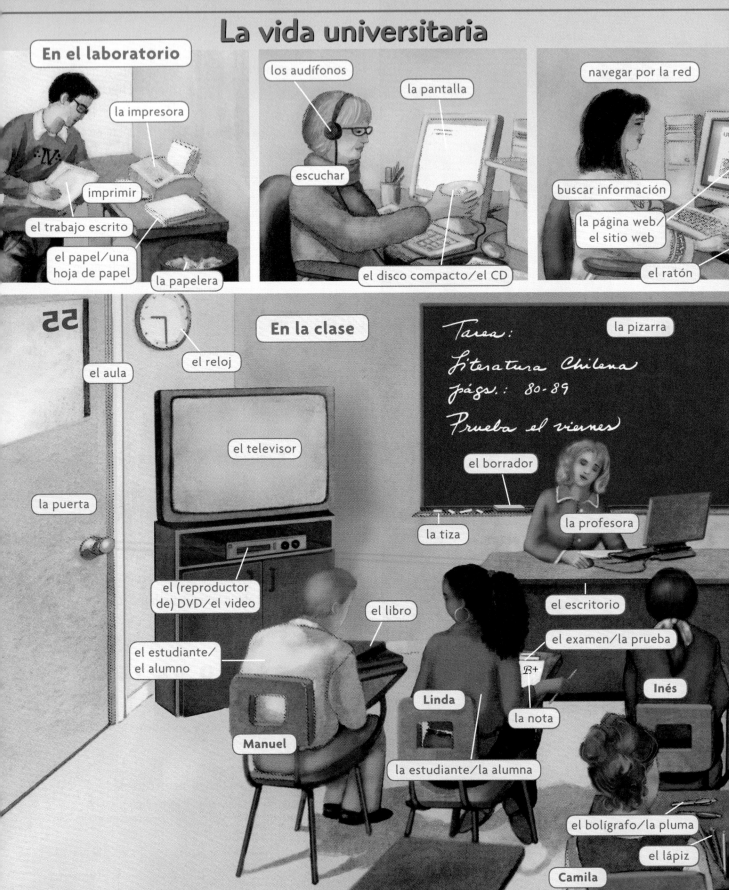

En el laboratorio

la impresora

imprimir

el trabajo escrito

el papel/una hoja de papel

la papelera

los audífonos

la pantalla

escuchar

el disco compacto/el CD

navegar por la red

buscar información

la página web/ el sitio web

el ratón

En la clase

la pizarra

Tarea:
Literatura Chilena
págs.: 80-89
Prueba el viernes

el aula

el reloj

el televisor

la puerta

el (reproductor de) DVD/el video

el estudiante/ el alumno

el borrador

la tiza

la profesora

el escritorio

el examen/la prueba

B+

el libro

Linda

Inés

la nota

Manuel

la estudiante/la alumna

el bolígrafo/la pluma

el lápiz

Camila

el correo electrónico

usar

la computadora

el teclado

enviar/mandar un mensaje electrónico

WILEY PLUS Pronunciación: Practice pronunciation of the chapter vocabulary and particular sounds of Spanish in *WileyPLUS*.

el aula	*the classroom*
buscar	*to look for*
enviar/mandar	*to send*
navegar por la red	*to surf the Web*
la pantalla	*screen (in tv, computer, movies)*
el papel (una hoja de papel)	*paper (a sheet of paper)*
la tarea	*homework*
el trabajo (escrito)	*an academic paper/essay*

New vocabulary is better learned when you make the connection between the thing or concept and the Spanish word directly, without an English translation. Therefore, we only include translations for new words when illustrations or context are not enough to figure out their meaning. All new words are translated in the section **Repaso de vocabulario activo** at the end of each chapter.

el mapa

la ventana

el diccionario

la calculadora

Esteban

la mesa

la silla

la mochila

el cuaderno

NOTA DE LENGUA

Hay means *there is* or *there are* in a statement, and *is there* or *are there* in a question. It is used with singular and plural forms.

Hay una ventana en el aula.	**There is** *a window in the classroom.*
Hay treinta pupitres.	**There are** *thirty desks.*
¿**Hay** mucha tarea?	**Is there** *a lot of homework?*

2-1 **¿Cuántos hay?**

Paso 1. Work with a partner. Look at the following chart and fill in how many of each item there are (**hay**) in your classroom. Fill in the last line of the chart with an item that you feel is important for a classroom to have.

En el aula hay...	(Número)
sillas	
ventanas	
televisores	
computadoras	
diccionarios	
pizarras	

Paso 2. Now decide how well-equipped (**equipada**) your classroom is. You can probably figure out the meanings of the cognates in two of the three options below.

☐ El aula está **muy bien** equipada.

☐ El aula está **adecuadamente** equipada.

☐ El aula está **insuficientemente** equipada.

2-2 **Asociación de palabras.** Indicate which word does not fit with the others, then add one that does.

1.	la impresora	el ratón	la computadora	la tiza	_____
2.	el bolígrafo	el lápiz	la pluma	el cuaderno	_____
3.	el alumno	la mesa	la ventana	la puerta	_____
4.	el reloj	el mapa	el borrador	la mochila	_____
5.	los audífonos	el papel	el cuaderno	el diccionario	_____
6.	navegar por la red	escuchar	la calculadora	imprimir	_____

NOTA CULTURAL

El coquí

There is a tiny tree frog in Puerto Rico called the **coquí**; its name is similar to the sound that it makes at night. The sound of **coquíes**, often very loud in the countryside, is dearly missed by many Puerto Ricans who are away from the island since the **coquí** is a beloved symbol of Puerto Rico. **Coquíes** brought to the mainland United States usually do not survive, although they have flourished in the state of Hawaii due to the tropical climate.

Así se forma

1. Identifying gender and number: Nouns and articles

All nouns in Spanish have two important grammatical features: gender (masculine and feminine) and number (singular and plural). Note that, although gender may reflect a biological distinction in some nouns referring to persons and animals, it is merely a grammatical feature in nouns that refer to nonliving things.

Masculine and Feminine Nouns

Los estudiant**es** están en clase. **Un** alumn**o** escribe en el cuaderno. Dos alumnos escriben en la pizarra. **La** profesor**a** conversa con **unas** alumn**as**.

Masculino	**Femenino**
• Most nouns referring to a male **el** estudiante **el** profesor **el** señor	• Most nouns referring to a female **la** estudiante **la** profesora **la** señora
• Most nouns that end in **–o** **el** escritori**o** **el** diccionari**o**	• Most nouns that end in –a[1] **la** impresor**a** **la** puert**a**
• Most nouns that end in **–r** or **–l** **el** televiso**r** **el** borrado**r** **el** pape**l**	• Almost all nouns ending in **–ón** and **–d** la informac**ión** la orac**ión** la actitu**d**
• BUT some nouns that end in **-a** are masculine. **el** mapa **el** día **el** problema **el** programa	• BUT some nouns that end in **–o** are feminine. **la** man**o** **la** radi**o**
• Finally, some nouns ending in **–e** and **–ista** can be either masculine or feminine **el** estudiante **el** turista **la** estudiante **la** turista	

PLUS Go to *WileyPLUS* and review the Animated Grammar Tutorial for this grammar point.

la estudiante   el estudiante

Number

- Singular nouns ending in a vowel form the plural by adding –**s**.
  un estudiante → dos estudiante**s**

- Nouns ending in a consonant add –**es**.
  un reloj → dos reloj**es**

- But nouns ending in –**z** change to –**ces**.
  un lápiz → dos lápi**ces**[2]

---

[1]**Aula** is feminine even though it uses the article **el**. The plural form is **las aulas**.
[2]Spanish-spelling rules disallow the combination **z** + **e**. Instead change the **z** to a **c**.

Definite and indefinite articles

The articles that accompany nouns must agree with respect to gender and number. Therefore, articles have masculine and feminine forms as well as singular and plural forms.

HINT

If you memorize the article when you learn a new noun, you will remember its gender. For example: **la** clas**e** (feminine), **el** pupitr**e** (masculine).

	Artículos definidos		**Artículos indefinidos**	
	the		*a/an; some*	
	singular	plural	singular	plural
masculino	**el** alumno	**los** alumnos	**un** alumno	**unos** alumnos
femenino	**la** alumna	**las** alumnas	**una** alumna	**unas** alumnas

- In general, definite articles indicate that the noun is specific or known.

  El libro de historia es fantástico.   *The history book is fantastic.*
  La puerta de **la** oficina está cerrada.   *The office door is closed.*

- Indefinite articles are used to refer to new information, and indicate that the noun is unspecified or unknown.

  Hay **un** libro en la mesa.   *There is **a** book on the table.*
  ¿Buscas **un** diccionario?   *Are you looking for **a** dictionary?*

NOTA DE LENGUA

Note that when talking about a group that includes both masculine and feminine nouns, we use the masculine plural.

dos chicos y tres chicas → un**os** chic**os**

2-3) **Vamos a comparar (*Let's compare*) mochilas.**

Paso 1. What is this student from the University of Puerto Rico putting in her backpack today? Mark the correct option in each sentence. Then in the second column, indicate whether you usually have these same items in your backpack.

Modelo: hay un   ☑ cuaderno   ☐ pluma

En la mochila de la estudiante de la Universidad de Puerto Rico...			**¿Hay eso en mi mochila también (*also*)?**	
1. hay unos	☐ lápices	☐ diccionario	Sí	No
2. hay una	☐ cuaderno	☐ pluma	Sí	No
3. hay unas	☐ hojas de papel	☐ trabajos escritos	Sí	No
4. hay un	☐ calculadora	☐ disco compacto	Sí	No
5. hay una	☐ pluma	☐ bolígrafo	Sí	No
6. hay unos	☐ calculadoras	☐ libros	Sí	No

Paso 2. Now work with a partner. Write down your guesses about the contents of your partner's backpack using the indefinite articles **un, unos, una, unas,** the vocabulary above, and some of the following words.

Modelo: **En la mochila de Karen hay unos discos compactos, una pluma, unos libros y unos cuadernos.**

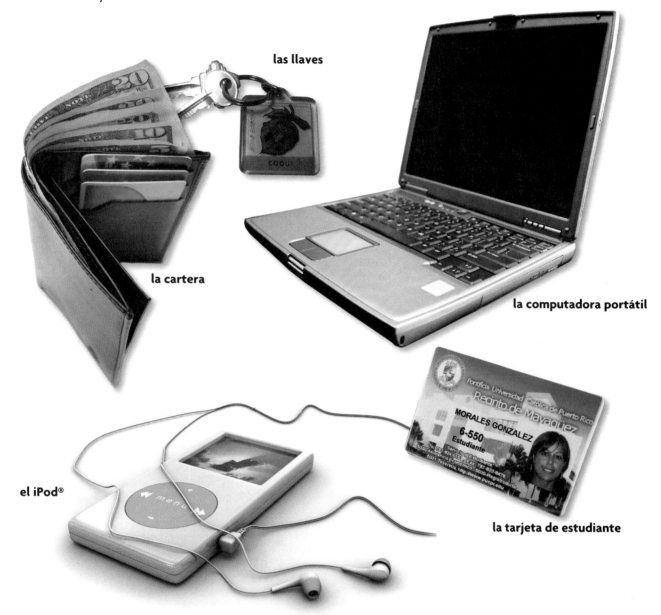

las llaves

la cartera

la computadora portátil

el iPod®

la tarjeta de estudiante

 Paso 3. Now read your guesses to each other and respond.

Modelo: [Karen may respond to the example above:]
Sí, en mi mochila hay una pluma y hay unos libros, pero no hay discos compactos o cuadernos.

Así se dice

El campus universitario

la residencia (estudiantil)

el apartamento

la casa

el cuarto

RESIDENCIA ESTUDIANT[IL]

la psicología

la sociología

las ciencias políticas

FACULTAD DE

FACULTAD DE CIENCIAS
SOCIALES Y POLÍTICAS

la biblioteca

MATEMÁTICAS
Y COMPUTACIÓN

la computación/la informática

el álgebra

el cálculo

el gimnasio

CENTRO ESTUDIANTIL

el arte

la música

FACULTAD DE ARTES

CAFETERÍA

WileyPLUS Pronunciación: Practice pronunciation of the chapter vocabulary and particular sounds of Spanish on *WileyPLUS*.

el alemán	*German*
la contabilidad	*accounting*
la facultad[1]	*school, department*
la informática	*computer science*
la química	*chemistry*

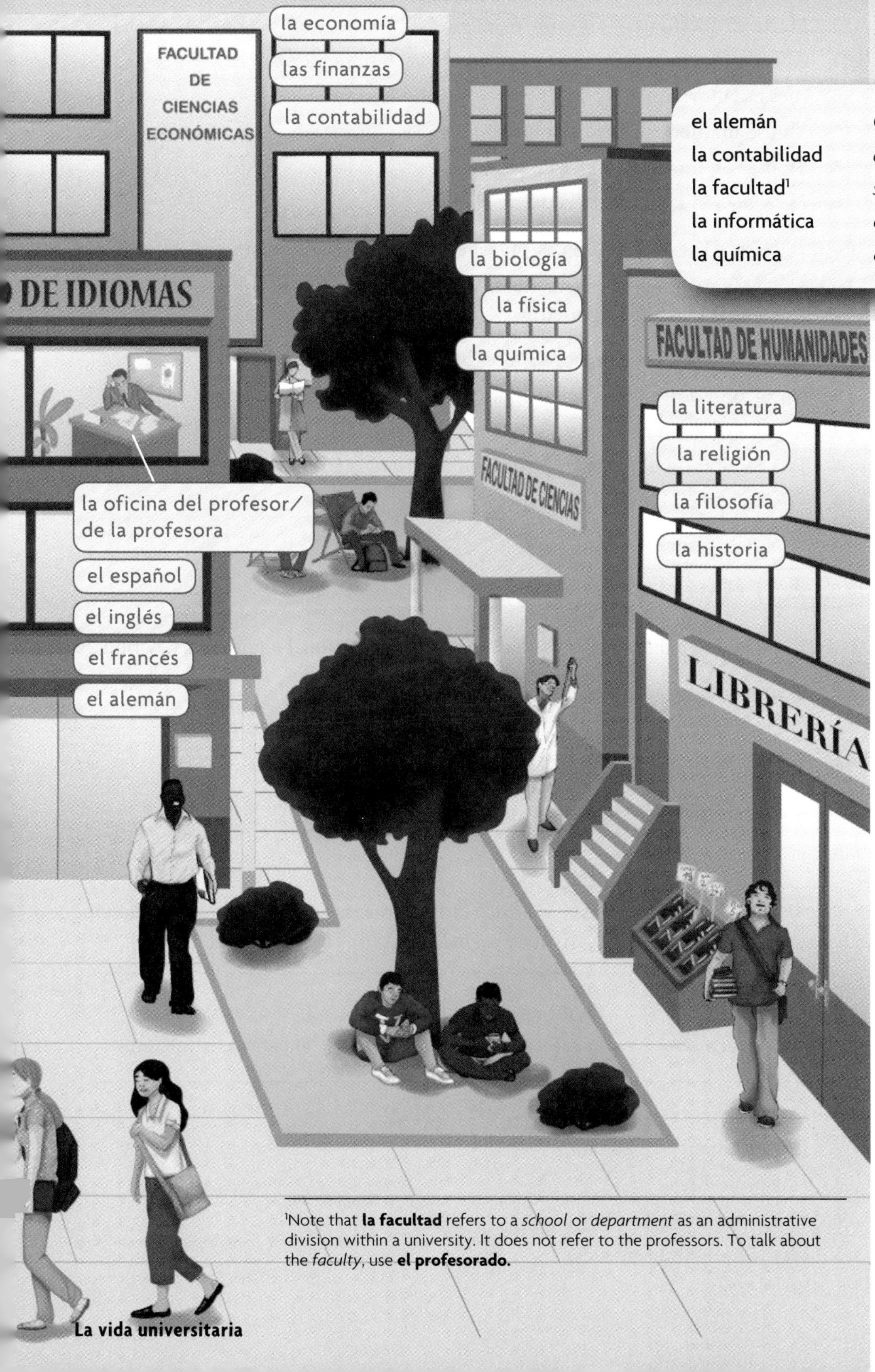

FACULTAD DE CIENCIAS ECONÓMICAS
la economía
las finanzas
la contabilidad
DE IDIOMAS
la oficina del profesor/ de la profesora
el español
el inglés
el francés
el alemán
la biología
la física
la química
FACULTAD DE CIENCIAS
FACULTAD DE HUMANIDADES
la literatura
la religión
la filosofía
la historia
LIBRERÍA

[1]Note that **la facultad** refers to a *school* or *department* as an administrative division within a university. It does not refer to the professors. To talk about the *faculty*, use **el profesorado.**

2-4 ¿Es lógico?

Paso 1. Listen to the statements and indicate whether they are logical or illogical, based on what the following individuals are using.

Modelo: You see: **Carmen usa un libro de español.**
You hear: **Es la clase de francés.**
You choose: **Ilógico.**

		Lógico	Ilógico
1.	Marta y Alberto usan unos microscopios.	☐	☐
2.	Alfonso usa un programa de cálculo para la computadora.	☐	☐
3.	Inés usa un violín.	☐	☐
4.	Yo uso un tubo con ácido sulfúrico.	☐	☐
5.	Tú usas un libro sobre Picasso.	☐	☐
6.	Natalia y Linda usan una copia de *Hamlet*.	☐	☐

Paso 2. Now, write sentences guessing where the following students are.

Modelo: Manuel usa una calculadora.
Es la clase de matemáticas.

1. Camila y Linda usan un libro sobre (*about*) Abraham Lincoln.
2. Nosotros usamos libros sobre Sigmund Freud.
3. Ustedes usan un libro sobre la Biblia y el Corán.
4. Tú necesitas un libro sobre el gobierno de Estados Unidos.
5. Yo necesito un libro sobre finanzas.

2-5 ¿Qué clase es...?

Paso 1. Write down the name of the class that, in your opinion, best fits each description.

1. Es muy interesante, pero difícil.
2. Es fascinante.
3. Es muy fácil (*easy*).
4. Es muy popular.
5. Es muy importante.

Paso 2. Now, in small groups, compare your answers. Do you agree in your opinions?

2-6 ¿Dónde? Indicate in which of these places you could find the following things, people and activities. Answers can include more than one place.

el gimnasio	la oficina del profesor	la residencia
la biblioteca	la cafetería	el centro estudiantil

1. Hay estudiantes. Duermen. (*They are sleeping*)
2. Hay estudiantes. Estudian.
3. Hay profesores.
4. Hay estudiantes. Comen. (*They're eating*)
5. Hay máquinas de ejercicio.

Así se forma

¿No vas a la biblioteca esta noche?

No, voy a una fiesta.

2. The present tense and talking about going places: *Ir + a* + destination

To state where you are going, use the verb **ir** (*to go*) + **a** (*to*) + destination.

WILEY **PLUS** Go to *WileyPLUS* and review the Verb Conjugator for this grammar point.

ir *to go*		
(yo)	**voy**	**Voy** a clase todos los días (*every day*).
(tú)	**vas**	¿**Vas** al teatro con frecuencia?
(usted, él, ella)	**va**	Ella **va** a la universidad.
(nosotros/as)	**vamos**	**Vamos** al restaurante.
(vosotros/as)	**vais**	¿**Vais** al café?
(ustedes, ellos/as)	**van**	Ellas **van** al gimnasio.

Observe the uses of the present tense as illustrated with examples of **ir** + **a** + destination. The Spanish present tense can be used to:

- talk about actions that occur in the present.
  Voy al gimnasio ahora.   ***I'm going*** *to the gym now.*

- talk about recurring or habitual actions.
  Voy al gimnasio todos los días.   ***I go*** *to the gym every day.*
  ¿**Vas** con frecuencia?   ***Do you go*** *frequently?*

- talk about actions in the near future when accompanied by phrases indicating the future.
  María **va** a una fiesta esta noche.   *María* ***will go/is going*** *to a party tonight.*

NOTA DE LENGUA

a (*to*) + **el** (*the*) = **al**	Vamos **al** cuarto de Anita.
a + **la, los, las** = *no change*	Vamos **a la** biblioteca.
de (*from, about, of*) + **el** = **del**	Vamos a la oficina **del** profesor.
de + **la, los, las** = *no change*	Vamos a la oficina **de la** profesora.

¿Cuándo vamos?

When do we go?

ahora	*now*
antes de/después de (clase)	*before/after* (class)
esta mañana/tarde/noche	*this morning/this afternoon/tonight*
más tarde	*later*
por/en la mañana/la tarde/la noche	*In the morning/afternoon/night*
todas la mañanas	*every morning*
todas las tardes	*every afternoon*
todos los días	*every day*
todos los fines de semana	*every weekend*

¿Por cuánto tiempo?

For how long?

toda la mañana	*all morning*
toda la tarde	*all afternoon*
todo el día	*all day*
todo el fin de semana	*all weekend*

¿Con qué frecuencia?

How often?

+					−
siempre	casi (*almost*) siempre	con frecuencia	a veces	casi nunca	nunca

¿Tarde o temprano?

Late or early?

Natalia llega **temprano**.

Pepita llega **a tiempo**.

Esteban llega **tarde**.

2-7 **¿Cuándo?** Read the sentences below and indicate whether they are referring to a current moment present (**ahora**) action, to habitual/recurrent (**habitual**) actions, or to an action in the near future (**futuro**).

		ahora	habitual	futuro
1.	¡Juan, espera (*wait*)! ¿Adónde vas?	☐	☐	☐
2.	A veces voy al gimnasio.	☐	☐	☐
3.	El sábado voy a una fiesta.	☐	☐	☐
4.	Ahora voy a la clase de inglés...	☐	☐	☐
5.	...y esta tarde voy a clase de historia.	☐	☐	☐
6.	Ustedes siempre van tarde a clase.	☐	☐	☐

2-8 **La vida universitaria.**

Paso 1. Indicate how often you go to the following places.

		(casi) todos los días	con frecuencia	a veces	casi nunca
1.	Voy a la biblioteca.	☐	☐	☐	☐
2.	Voy al laboratorio de computadoras.	☐	☐	☐	☐
3.	Voy a las horas de oficina de un profesor.	☐	☐	☐	☐
4.	Voy al centro estudiantil.	☐	☐	☐	☐
5.	Voy al gimnasio.	☐	☐	☐	☐
6.	Voy a la cafetería de la universidad.	☐	☐	☐	☐
7.	Voy a un restaurante.	☐	☐	☐	☐
8.	Voy a fiestas.	☐	☐	☐	☐

Paso 2. Now work with a classmate. Take turns restating the statements above as questions, remembering to use the **tú** form. Listen and note your partner's answers.

Modelo: Estudiante A: **¿Cuándo vas a la biblioteca?**
 Estudiante B: **Voy a la biblioteca a veces. / No voy casi nunca.**

Paso 3. Now tell your classmates what you and your partner have in common. Remember to use the **nosotros** form.

Modelo: **Pablo y yo casi nunca vamos...**

DICHOS

La vida es la mejor (*best*) escuela.

¿Qué significa el dicho?

2-9 **El horario (*Schedule*).** Work with a classmate (write her/his name in the chart below).

REMEMBER

¿Qué hora es? ≠ ¿A qué hora es (vas..., etc.)?

Paso 1. Give your classmate a list of your classes. Then, take turns asking each other the days and times of your classes and write them in the chart (use the last row for any classes or labs after 5:00 p.m.).

Modelo: Estudiante A: **¿Cúando vas a la clase de química?**
  Estudiante B: **Voy los martes y los jueves.**
  Estudiante A: **¿A qué hora vas?**

HINT

For additional course names, see **Apéndice 3**.

El horario de _____

	lunes	martes	miércoles	jueves	viernes
8:00 a.m.					
9:00 a.m.					
10:00 a.m.					
11:00 a.m.					
1:00 p.m.					
2:00 p.m.					
3:00 p.m.					
4:00 p.m.					
5:00 p.m.					

Paso 2. Now, compare your schedules. Are they similar or different? Write a short report and prepare to share it with the class.

Modelo: **Nuestros horarios son similares/diferentes: por las mañanas yo voy...
y/pero Jason va.../Jason y yo vamos...**

NOTA CULTURAL

Phosphorescent bay

There is a small island off the east coast of Puerto Rico called Vieques, which contains a mangrove swamp with special inhabitants: millions of tiny glowing organisms called *dinoflagellattes* (measuring 1/500 of an inch) that react to the slightest disturbance in the water. A fish, boat, or a hand causes them to emanate a blue-green light that traces the moving object. Tourists who take nighttime tours there are allowed to swim in the water. Few places in the world have such a high concentration of dinoflagellates. Go to *www. biobay.com* to see more pictures of the phosphorescent bays in Vieques.

2-10 ¿Adónde vas después de las clases?

Paso 1. In your notebook, complete the following sentences with information that is true for you. You can write more than one place for each sentence.

1. Por la mañana temprano, voy a…
2. Antes de esta clase voy a… y después de esta clase voy a…
3. Casi siempre voy a comer (*eat*) en…
4. Después de las clases casi siempre voy a… pero a veces voy a…
5. Esta tarde voy a…

 Paso 2. Now in small groups, compare your activities.

Modelo:	Estudiante A:	**Mike, ¿adónde vas después de las clases?**
	Estudiante B:	**Voy a la cafetería, ¿y ustedes?**
	Estudiante C:	**Yo voy a…**

2-11 ¿Estudiantes típicos?

Paso 1. Complete the left column indicating when or how frequently you think most students at your college do these things.

Los estudiantes típicos de esta universidad…

Mi opinión	La opinión del grupo
Modelo: Van a clase por <u>la mañana</u>.	… la mañana y por la tarde temprano.
Casi siempre van a clase (¿temprano, a tiempo…?) _____.	
Van a la oficina del profesor _____	
Van a la biblioteca _____.	
Estudian (*study*) en su cuarto _____.	
Trabajan (*work*) _____.	
Escuchan música _____.	
Navegan por la red _____.	
Mandan mensajes electrónicos _____.	
Van a fiestas _____.	

Paso 2. In groups, compare your sentences and try to agree on statements that describe what typical students do. Write those in the right column.

2-12 **La Universidad de Puerto Rico.** Imagine that you are studying abroad at the Río Piedras campus of the University of Puerto Rico (UPR). Using the campus map as a guide, answer the following questions.

1. ¿Adónde van los estudiantes para...

comer (*to eat*)?
comprar (*to buy*) libros?
ver arte?
obtener una fotografía para su tarjeta de identificación (*ID*)?

visitar al médico?
hablar con el decano (*dean*)?
estacionar el auto?
buscar libros?

2. ¿Cuántos (*how many*) estacionamientos hay? ¿Cuántas facultades?

3. ¿A qué facultad van los estudiantes para una clase de educación? ¿Y para una clase de biología?

4. En la UPR, ¿hay departamentos, facultades, etc. que no hay en tu universidad? ¿Cuáles? Da ejemplos.

5. ¿Hay residencias estudiantiles en la UPR?

Mapa del Recinto de Río Piedras de la Universidad de Puerto Rico

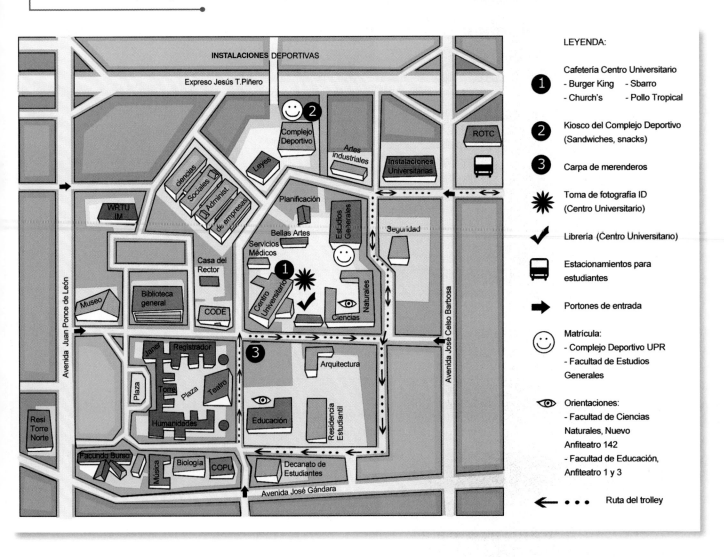

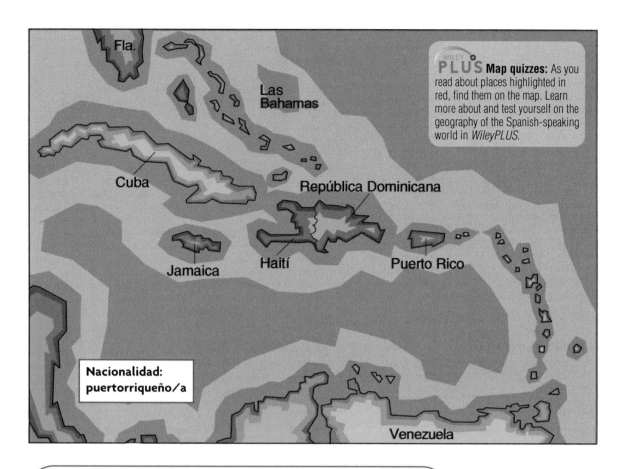

Fla.

Las Bahamas

PLUS Map quizzes: As you read about places highlighted in red, find them on the map. Learn more about and test yourself on the geography of the Spanish-speaking world in *WileyPLUS*.

Cuba

República Dominicana

Jamaica

Haití

Puerto Rico

Nacionalidad: puertorriqueño/a

Venezuela

Antes de leer

1. Locate the following countries on the map:
   Puerto Rico, Cuba, Jamaica, the Dominican Republic, Haiti

2. Puerto Rico is part of the archipelago known as las Antillas Mayores. What U.S. state is also an archipelago?

Puerto Rico es una isla relativamente pequeña (*small*) (de aproximadamente 100 millas de largo y 40 millas de ancho), pero con una historia rica. Sus primeros habitantes, los taínos, llaman a la isla *Borinquén* o *Tierra* (*Land*) *de los Grandes Señores.* Hoy, la palabra **boricua** designa a la gente de Puerto Rico.

LA HISTORIA

Cristóbal Colón desembarca en **Puerto Rico** en 1493, durante su segundo (*second*) viaje desde España, y la isla se incorpora al Imperio español. La población taína disminuye rápidamente, pero muchas palabras taínas pasan al idioma español. Por ejemplo:

hamaca	*hammock*
maracas	*maracas*
canoa	*canoe*
barbacoa	*barbecue*

▲ Un bohío (*hut*) taíno

▲ Pintura del **Paseo Boricua** (*Puerto Rican Promenade*) en Chicago.

▲ En 2008, eligen a Luis Fortuño gobernador del Estado Libre Asociado de Puerto Rico.

En 1898, después de la Guerra Hispano-Estadounidense, Puerto Rico se incorpora a Estados Unidos, y en 1917, los puertorriqueños reciben la nacionalidad estadounidense. En 1952, Puerto Rico se convierte en estado libre asociado (*Commonwealth*) con su propio (*own*) gobierno. Las leyes (*laws*) federales de Estados Unidos se aplican en Puerto Rico. No forma parte del territorio nacional estadounidense y no hay representante con derecho a voto en el Congreso. La isla tiene dos idiomas oficiales: español e inglés; pero el 70% de sus habitantes hablan principalmente español. Los 3.9 millones de residentes en la isla no votan en las elecciones estadounidenses, pero los 3.8 millones de puertorriqueños que viven en el resto del país sí pueden votar. La comunidad puertorriqueña representa el grupo hispano más grande de Estados Unidos continental, después de la población mexicana. Los puertorriqueños del continente viven principalmente en el este, en los estados de Nueva York, Florida, Nueva Jersey, Pennsylvania y Massachusetts. En los últimos (*last*) 30 años crecen (*grow*) significativamente las comunidades de puertorriqueños en Connecticut, Illinois, California, Ohio y Texas.

Después de leer

1. Many indigenous Taíno words made their way into Spanish. Do you know of any Native American words that made their way into U.S. English?

2. Like Puerto Rico, there are two U.S. states that have two legally recognized languages. Which are they?

3. Although Puerto Rican cooking is somewhat similar to that of Spain and some other Hispanic cuisines, it is a unique blend of influences. Look up *arroz con habichuelas* and *tostones*, two very popular items. If one or both appear appetizing to you, explain why.

El Viejo San Juan, distrito colonial de la capital de Puerto Rico. ▼

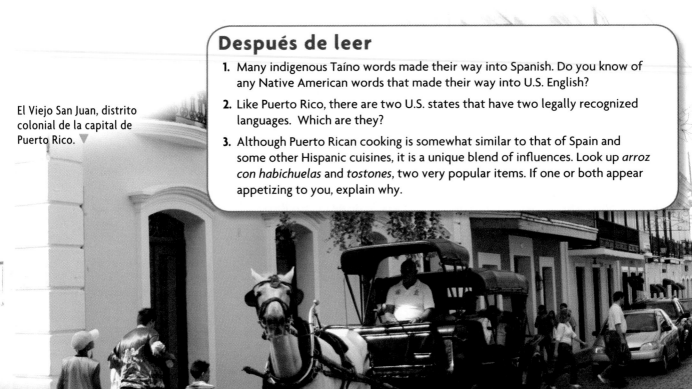

Así se forma

Alfonso, ¿estudias todas las noches?

¡Sí!

3. Talking about actions in the present: Regular -ar verbs

When you look up a Spanish verb in the dictionary, you will find the infinitive form, which in Spanish always ends in either **–ar**, **–er**, or **–ir**. It is important to notice which of these endings the infinitive has, because each type is conjugated in a different way.

In this section you will learn about regular **–ar** verbs.

Observe what happens when we use **hablar** to talk about the present (*I speak, he speaks, etc.*). Note that you drop the **–ar** from the infinitive and replace it with the endings indicated. The endings correspond to the subject of the verb.

WILEY PLUS Go to *WileyPLUS* and review the Animated Grammar Tutorial and Verb Conjugator for this grammar point.

hablar *to speak*	
hablar → habl-	
(yo)	habl**o**[1]
(tú)	habl**as**
(usted, él/ella)	habl**a**
(nosotros/as)	habl**amos**
(vosotros/as)	habl**áis**
(ustedes, ellos/as)	habl**an**

Camila

Natalia

Read about what Natalia and her friend Camila do.

Las actividades en la universidad

Natalia y Camila **llegan** a la universidad a las ocho de la mañana. Natalia **desayuna** en la cafetería de la universidad, pero Camila nunca **desayuna,** sólo (*only*) **compra** un té. Primero (*First*) van a la clase de psicología. Ahí (*There*) escuchan al profesor y **toman apuntes**. Luego van a la clase de español donde **practican**, **hablan** y **estudian** con los compañeros de clase. Por la tarde van a la biblioteca para **estudiar** y **preparar** sus lecciones. Son excelentes estudiantes. Generalmente **sacan** buenas notas en las pruebas y en los exámenes. Después de **cenar**, Camila **trabaja** tres horas en la biblioteca de la universidad. Natalia **regresa** temprano a su casa, **prepara** su trabajo para la clase de historia, **navega** por la red y **envía** mensajes electrónicos a sus amigos.

cenar	*to have dinner*	**regresar**	*to return, go back*
comprar	*to buy*	**sacar ... notas**	*to get . . . grades*
desayunar	*to have breakfast*	**tomar apuntes**	*to take notes*
llegar	*to arrive*	**trabajar**	*to work*

[1]Unlike nouns, Spanish verbs do not have gender: Both males and females say **hablo** (*I speak*).

2-13 Un día típico en la clase de español.

Paso 1. Read the statements below about Spanish class, and indicate whether they are true (**Sí**) or false (**No**) for you.

Yo	Sí/No	Mis compañeros de clase	Sí/No
Casi siempre llego a tiempo a clase.		Casi siempre llegan a tiempo a clase.	
Tomo apuntes en todas las clases.		Toman apuntes en todas las clases.	
Pregunto con frecuencia en clase.		Preguntan con frecuencia en clase.	
Casi nunca hablo inglés en la clase.		Casi nunca hablan inglés en la clase.	
Practico en el laboratorio o en la computadora casi todos los días.		Practican en el laboratorio o en la computadora casi todos los días.	
Preparo la lección siempre.		Preparan la lección siempre.	
Estudio y completo la tarea de español después de la clase.		Estudian y completan la tarea de español después de la clase.	

Paso 2. In groups of 5 or 6 students, share your answers and write the number of students who answered **Sí** in the right column. Then, answer the questions below.

Modelo: ¿Casi siempre llegan a tiempo a clase?

Respondan a las siguientes preguntas: En general, ¿son sus hábitos de estudio de español similares o diferentes? ¿Son ustedes estudiantes "ideales"?

PALABRAS ÚTILES

bailar	to dance
mirar	to watch
cocinar	to cook
descansar	to rest
viajar	to travel
limpiar	to clean
visitar	to visit

2-14 Imagina.

Paso 1. In pairs, select one person from the class to guess about. Write down five guesses about what you think that person does. Use verbs you have learned so far or from the **Palabras útiles** box.

Modelo: You select: Tina
You write: **Después de las clases, va a la biblioteca y estudia.**
Envía muchos mensajes electrónicos a sus amigos.
Después, mira la televisión en su cuarto. Baila todas las noches y regresa a su cuarto muy tarde…

Paso 2. Now, share some of your sentences with the class. The selected person will indicate whether your guesses are true (**cierto**) or false (**falso**).

Paso 3. Now, think about what a good student and a not-so-good student does during a typical week. Write at least four activities for each student.

Un estudiante bueno…
Un estudiante no tan bueno…

2-15 Las actividades de otras (*other*) personas.

Paso 1. Describe some daily activities of the following people. Form sentences using verbs you have learned so far or from the **Palabras útiles** box on page 52.

1. Mi compañero/a de cuarto/casa...

2. Mis amigos y yo...

3. Mi padre/madre...

4. Los estudiantes universitarios de Puerto Rico... (¡Usa tu imaginación!)

 Paso 2. Share your descriptions in small groups. Are your descriptions of these peoples' daily activities mostly similar or different?

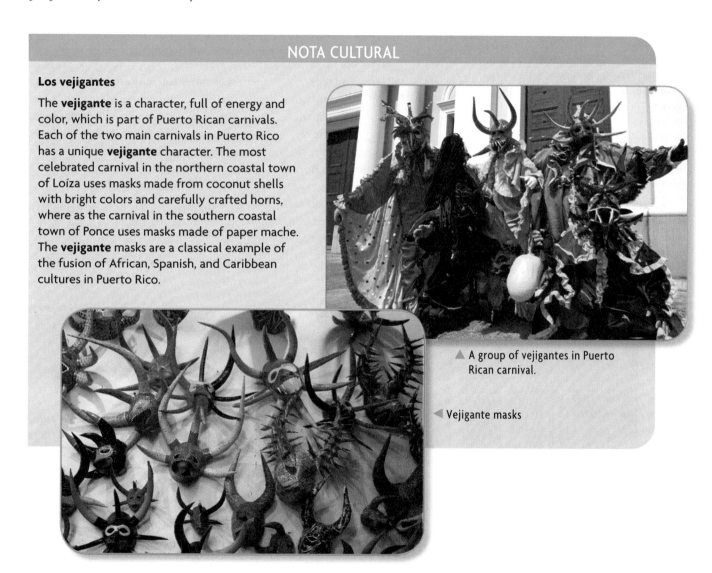

NOTA CULTURAL

Los vejigantes

The **vejigante** is a character, full of energy and color, which is part of Puerto Rican carnivals. Each of the two main carnivals in Puerto Rico has a unique **vejigante** character. The most celebrated carnival in the northern coastal town of Loíza uses masks made from coconut shells with bright colors and carefully crafted horns, where as the carnival in the southern coastal town of Ponce uses masks made of paper mache. The **vejigante** masks are a classical example of the fusion of African, Spanish, and Caribbean cultures in Puerto Rico.

▲ A group of vejigantes in Puerto Rican carnival.

◀ Vejigante masks

Cultura: La vida universitaria en el mundo hispano

Antes de leer

What are some of your favorite aspects about college so far?

- Ability to take a wide range of courses
- Living in a dorm
- Sports
- Other: _____

While reading the following, take note of aspects that are similar and different from what you've noted above.

INVESTIG@ EN INTERNET

You really want to learn more Spanish and start looking into Spanish language summer programs in Puerto Rico. Find a program you are interested in and print out or write down all the important information (dates, price, what is included in the program). Be ready to explain why you chose that program.

La mayoría de las universidades hispanas son instituciones públicas. En muchos países (*countries*) hispanos, el gobierno (*government*) financia el costo de la educación en la universidad; los estudiantes sólo compran los libros. Sin embargo (*however*), también existen universidades privadas. Los estudiantes universitarios normalmente viven con sus padres porque es más económico y porque, por lo general, no hay residencias estudiantiles.

Las clases son muy especializadas y los programas son muy rígidos. Un estudiante de medicina, por ejemplo, sólo toma cursos de medicina, no toma cursos en otras áreas. Por eso (*for this reason*) los estudiantes hispanos seleccionan una carrera (*major*) antes de comenzar sus estudios.

A diferencia de las universidades estadounidenses, no hay tantos equipos deportivos (*sports teams*) ni tampoco organizaciones como las fraternidades.

▲ Universidad de Puerto Rico en San Juan

▲ Biblioteca de la Universidad del País Vasco, España

Después de leer

1. Are the following common in universities in Latin America?

   a. Las residencias estudiantiles   ☐ Son comunes.   ☐ No son comunes.

   b. Los equipos deportivos   ☐ Son comunes.   ☐ No son comunes.

   c. Programas de estudio estructurados   ☐ Son comunes.   ☐ No son comunes.

2. Write two or three main differences between your college or university and Hispanic universities.

VideoEscenas: ¿Estudiamos o no?

▲ Jaime y Ana are meeting at the library to study together, but Ana is late.

Paso 1. Answer these questions before you watch the video.

1. Where do you usually study, in your room, at the library or in some other place?
2. Do you prefer to study on your own or with a friend?
3. When you go to class or other scheduled activities, are you punctual? How about when you are meeting friends?

Paso 2. Watch the video paying attention to the main ideas. Then choose the statement that best describes Ana.

☐ Ana es una excelente estudiante, saca buenas notas y es muy responsable.

☐ Ana es buena estudiante, pero hoy está cansada (*tired*).

☐ Ana no es buena estudiante y no es muy responsable.

Paso 3. Look at the statements below and watch the video again. This time focus on the specific information you need to complete each statement logically.

1. Ana llega (*arrives*)… ☐ temprano ☐ a tiempo ☐ tarde
2. Ana necesita (*needs*)… ☐ música ☐ una computadora ☐ café
3. A las once y media Jaime va… ☐ a la clase de álgebra ☐ al laboratorio ☐ a la biblioteca
4. Ana se va porque (*because*)… ☐ trabaja en la biblioteca ☐ llega tarde a la clase de matemáticas ☐ no tiene (*does not have*) el libro

Así se forma

WILEY PLUS Go to *WileyPLUS* and review the Animated Grammar Tutorial and Verb Conjugator for this grammar point.

Vivo para comer.

Como para vivir.

4. Talking about actions in the present: Regular *–er* and *–ir* verbs; *hacer* and *salir*

Regular *–er* and *–ir* verbs

Observe the forms for **comer** and **vivir** in the present tense. Note that you drop the **–er/–ir** from the infinitive and replace it with endings to agree with the subject of the verb. Note, also, that **–er** and **–ir** verbs have identical endings except in the **nosotros** and **vosotros** forms.

	comer *to eat* comer → com-	**vivir** *to live* vivir → viv-
(yo)	com**o**	viv**o**
(tú)	com**es**	viv**es**
(usted, él/ella)	com**e**	viv**e**
(nosotros/as)	com**emos**	viv**imos**
(vosotros/as)	com**éis**	viv**ís**
(ustedes, ellos/ellas)	com**en**	viv**en**

Hacer and *salir*

The verbs **hacer** (*to do, make*) and **salir** (*to leave, go out*) are irregular only in the **yo** form.

> **hacer:** **hago**, haces, hace, hacemos, hacéis, hacen
> **salir:** **salgo**, sales, sale, salimos, salís, salen

Hago la tarea todas las noches.   *I do homework every night.*
Salgo con mis amigos los fines de semana.   *I go out with my friends on weekends.*

Más actividades en la universidad

Read what Octavio has to say about his university life.

Soy de Mendoza, Argentina, y **asisto** a la Universidad Politécnica de California. **Vivo** en la residencia estudiantil. Tomo cursos de informática, de ciencias políticas y de literatura latinoamericana. En mis clases de ciencias políticas y literatura **leemos** y **escribimos** mucho y yo participo con frecuencia en las discusiones. En la clase de informática analizamos sistemas de computadoras y **aprendemos** a usar *software*. A veces no **comprendo** todo, pero mis compañeros de clase me explican los conceptos difíciles. Me gustan (*I like*) mucho mis clases. Al mediodía voy con mis compañeros a la cafetería de la universidad. Ahí **comemos**, **bebemos** y conversamos de mil cosas (*a thousand things*). La comida de la cafetería no es excelente pero tampoco (*neither*) es terrible. Los sábados por la mañana voy al gimnasio y por la noche **salgo** con mis amigos. No **hago** mucho los domingos.

aprender	*to learn*	**comprender**	*to understand*
asistir a	*to attend*	**escribir**	*to write*
beber	*to drink*	**leer**	*to read*

2-16 ¿En qué clase?

Paso 1. Indicate what classes you have this semester and mark which statements are true for each.

En mi clase de...	español	_____	_____	_____
1. aprendo cosas muy interesantes.				
2. hago mucha tarea.				
3. hablo y participo en clase.				
4. comprendo todo o casi todo.				
5. asisto a clase muchas horas por semana.				
6. miro películas (*films*).				
7. hago muchos exámenes.				
9. investigo (*I research*) en Internet.				
10. escribo muchos trabajos.				

Paso 2. In small groups, share your responses and listen to your classmates.

Paso 3. Of the classes you just heard about, which one would you like to take? Write briefly about why you would like to take that class.

Modelo: **Quiero (*I want to*) tomar la clase de _____ porque los estudiantes aprenden cosas interesantes.**

2-17 ¿Qué hacen los estudiantes en Puerto Rico?

As we saw in *Cultura* on page 54, there are several differences in university life between Latin America and the United States. From the list of phrases below, create sentences that describe what typical students in Puerto Rico do (and don't do).

1. asistir a eventos deportivos del campus
2. vivir en una residencia
3. aprender inglés
4. salir con amigos
5. unirse (*join*) a una fraternidad o hermandad (*sorority*)
6. hacer la tarea

SITUACIONES

Work in pairs. Both of you have a part-time job in the mornings, where you work together, and go to classes in the evenings. Your boss needs someone to cover for another employee on Thursday from 3:00 P.M. until 9:00 P.M. but both of you have extra-curricular activities or other plans for Thursday evening. Discuss your situation, explaining to each other why you cannot work on Thursday and trying to arrive to a solution.

PALABRAS ÚTILES

el bar	*bar*
el cine	*movie theater*
el teatro	*theatre*
la discoteca	*night club*
un partido deportivo	*sporting match, game*

2-18 ¿Qué hacemos en... ?

Paso 1. Write two or three activities that you do in the places below. Add one more place on campus you usually go to.

Modelo: En la biblioteca.
Voy a la biblioteca todos los días después de la clase de español; hago la tarea de cálculo y estudio filosofía. A veces leo o investigo para un trabajo escrito...

1. En la biblioteca...

2. En mi cuarto...

3. En la residencia/el laboratorio/el centro estudiantil...

 Paso 2. Interview a classmate about her/his activities in the places above. Take turns asking questions about the activities she/he does there, when she/he goes, etc.

Modelo: **¿Cuándo vas a la biblioteca?**
¿Estudias allí (*there*)?
¿Haces la tarea allí?

Now take a vote: Which is the class' favorite place (**el lugar favorito**)?

2-19 Sondeo (*Survey*): El tiempo libre (*Leisure time*).

Paso 1. Complete the first column in the chart below with what you like to do in your time off. Add one more activity of your choice at the end.

Paso 2. Walk around the classroom to find out who shares your preferences. Transform your statements into questions (see the example in parentheses) to ask your classmates. When someone answers affirmatively, write her/his name in the second column. How many affirmative answers can you get in ten minutes? Your professor may ask you to share your results with the class.

Actividades de tiempo libre		¿Quién?
Modelo: Asistir a . . .	Asisto a los conciertos de rock. (¿Asistes a los conciertos de rock?)	Megan
1. Asistir a...		
2. Ir a...		
3. Salir a... con...		
4. Hablar con...		
5. Comer... en...		
6. Mirar...		
7. Leer...		
8. ¿ ... ?		

2-20 El profesor. You have talked a lot about what you and other students do. What do you think your teachers do? Write a short paragraph describing what you imagine is a typical day for your Spanish teacher. Try to add details and be creative!

Dicho y hecho

ANTES DE LEER

If you were planning to spend a semester abroad, what criteria would be important to you, both in terms of the institution and the location?

ESTRATEGIA DE LECTURA

Skimming A common pitfall for students reading a text in Spanish is trying to understand every single word encountered. Skimming the text first, that is looking over it quickly to get a sense of the topic and main ideas, will help you focus on what is relevant when you read in more detail. When skimming, also pay attention to the title, introduction, and subtitles, since these often point at the key ideas.

A LEER

1. Skim over the text quickly and write down in a sentence or two what you think this text is about.

2. Now, read the text. Try to focus on the words you know and recognize and on getting the main ideas. Do not worry if you do not know some words or cannot understand every detail.

Segura, adaptable y cultural, Salamanca es una ciudad[1] ideal para los estudiantes de español. Sólo en 2007, recibió unos 26,000 estudiantes de español.

Una ciudad ideal Salamanca tiene 180,000 habitantes, incluyendo 35,000 estudiantes españoles universitarios. Su universidad, fundada en 1218, es una de las más antiguas de Europa y la responsable académica de los prestigiosos exámenes DELE (Diploma de Español como Lengua Extranjera[2]). Además, la Universidad Pontificia y numerosas escuelas privadas también ofrecen clases de español. Por tanto, hay opciones para todas las necesidades.

Una ciudad joven[3] Como ciudad, Salamanca es perfecta para estudiantes. Es pequeña[4] y manejable, con muchas actividades culturales y un ambiente muy joven. Muchos estudiantes de español prefieren Salamanca por su calidad de vida. Los estudiantes gastan[5] entre 500 y 700 euros al mes, algo que en Madrid, por ejemplo, es casi imposible. Los estudiantes que hacen un curso intensivo de seis semanas gastan aproximadamente 1,000 euros en total, con el curso y el alojamiento[6] incluidos. Además, el hecho de que muchos estudiantes españoles decidan estudiar su carrera[7] allí facilita la integración de los estudiantes foráneos, porque hay muchos apartamentos mixtos de españoles y extranjeros. Estina, una estudiante noruega, nos dice: "Es una ciudad muy viva[8], hay muchos estudiantes, se puede andar por todas partes[9]… Sí, me gusta[10] la gente[11] de aquí".

Texto y fotografía: Clara de la Flor / *Punto y coma*

---

[1] city, [2] foreign, [3] young, [4] small, [5] spend, [6] lodging, [7] university studies, [8] lively, [9] **se…** one can walk everywhere, [10] **me…** I like, [11] people

Dicho y hecho

▲ Vista de la Catedral Nueva de Salamanca

DESPUÉS DE LEER

1. Select the statement that best summarizes the text.

   ☐ Salamanca is an ideal city for students of Spanish because there are many young people and bars, so it is lively and fun.

   ☐ Salamanca is an ideal city for students of Spanish because there are many different Spanish programs, many Spanish and international students and a high quality of life.

2. Indicate which words are applicable for each statement, according to the text

a. En Salamanca hay muchos/as…

   ☐ estudiantes   ☐ residencias   ☐ bibliotecas   ☐ escuelas de español   ☐ bares

b. Es una ciudad…

   ☐ moderna   ☐ tradicional   ☐ antigua   ☐ cara (*expensive*)   ☐ viva

c. Hay estudiantes…

   ☐ universitarios españoles   ☐ universitarios extranjeros   ☐ de español

3. In small groups discuss whether you would like to study abroad. If so, share where you would like to go and why.

PARA CONVERSAR: El fin de semana

Talk with a classmate about what she/he typically does on campus or in town on weekends. Where does she/he go? What does she/he do there? Determine whether or not you are likely to run into each other over the weekend.

PALABRAS ÚTILES	
el cine	*the movie theater*
el bar	*the bar*
la discoteca	*the club*
el centro comercial	*the mall*
el supermercado	*the supermarket*
mirar la televisión/una película	*to watch TV/a movie*
descansar	*to rest*
hacer ejercicio	*to exercise, work out*
jugar al tenis/baloncesto/fútbol americano/béisbol	*to play tennis/basketball/ football/baseball*

ESTRATEGIA DE COMUNICACIÓN

Simplifying your expression As you begin sharing ideas in Spanish, you may feel you have a lot more you want to say than you can actually express. Avoid trying to translate complex sentences from English to Spanish, and instead try to formulate your ideas more simply in Spanish, using the vocabulary and structures you have learned. For example, instead of translating *I attend a regularly scheduled study group for my organic chemistry class on alternating Sunday afternoons,* you can say **A veces estudio con mis compañeros de la clase de química los domingos.**

PARA ESCRIBIR: ¿Soy un/a estudiante típico/a?

In this composition, you will describe your campus activities and argue either that you are a typical student or that you are an atypical student on your campus. The audience for this composition is a friend of yours who goes to a different school.

ESTRATEGIA DE REDACCIÓN

Generating ideas: Brainstorming The first stage of the writing process consists in generating ideas. A very effective way to do that is by brainstorming, jotting down any and all ideas that come to mind when thinking about your topic. The goal is to explore the topic, so do not worry about how those ideas connect, which would be better for your composition, grammar, spelling, etc. As much as possible, try to brainstorm in Spanish, recalling words you have already learned.

ANTES DE ESCRIBIR

Paso 1. Think about "typical" students on your campus. What do they do during an average school week? Jot down any ideas that come to mind in your notebook. You may refer to the paragraphs about Natalia and Camila (p. 51) and Octavio (p. 56) for ideas.

Durante la semana, los estudiantes típicos de mi campus….

Paso 2. Now, think about what *you* do during a typical school week. Write down your ideas in your notebook.

Durante la semana, yo…

Paso 3. Compare the activities you wrote for the **estudiante típico** in **Paso 1** to the ones you wrote for yourself in **Paso 2**. Are you a typical student, an atypical student, or a bit of both?

☐ Soy un/a estudiante totalmente típico/a.

☐ Soy un/a estudiante totalmente atípico/a.

☐ Bueno (*well*), soy un/a estudiante un poco típico/a pero un poco diferente también.

A ESCRIBIR

Write a composition in which you summarize this information. The following outline can help you organize your composition.

Párrafo (*paragraph*) 1: En esta composición, voy a (*I am going to*) comparar las actividades de los estudiantes típicos con mis actividades, para (*in order to*) determinar si soy típico/a o no.

Párrafo 2: Las actividades de los estudiantes típicos…

Párrafo 3: Mis actividades…

Párrafo 4: En conclusión…

PALABRAS ÚTILES

las mismas (*same*) actividades
actividades similares
actividades muy diferentes

Dicho y hecho

> **Para escribir mejor:** Here are a few more connecting words to add and contrast ideas:
>
> | | | |
> |---|---|---|
> | **también** | *also, as well* | Used at the beginning or end of a sentence. |
> | | **También** leo mucho. /Leo mucho **también.** | |
> | **además** | *besides, in addition* | Typically used at the beginning of a sentence. |
> | | **Además** leo mucho. | |
> | **aunque** | *although, even though* | Used at the beginning of a sentence. |
> | | **Aunque** no leo todos los días. | |

DESPUÉS DE ESCRIBIR

Revisar y editar: **El contenido.** Once you have generated a first draft of your composition, set it aside for at least one day. Return to it and review the content, that is, the ideas you included and whether they adequately address the topic. You may want to ask yourself questions such as:

☐ Are the main topic and purpose of my composition clear?

☐ Does it describe 4 or 5 activities that "typical" students do during the week?

☐ Does it describe 4 or 5 activities that I do during the week?

☐ Does it explain whether I consider myself a typical student or not?

☐ Are the ideas relevant and sufficiently developed for the purpose of the text?

☐ Will the intended reader understand what I am describing, or should I provide greater detail?

PARA VER Y ESCUCHAR: Una visita a la UNAM

ANTES DE VER EL VIDEO

Paso 1. In pairs, and before you watch the video, write a list of what you think would be important factors in choosing a location to study Spanish abroad. You may consider the following characteristics:

- class size
- city or small town
- opportunities to interact with other students
- cultural activities
- highly qualified teachers
- other _____

Paso 2. In the video segment, you will learn about classes for international students who wish to improve their Spanish at the National Autonomous University of Mexico (**Universidad Nacional Autónoma de México, or UNAM**). Several students will state their names and what countries they are from. Take a guess which countries will be mentioned from the following list:

☐ Haití	☐ Rusia	☐ Francia	☐ Estados Unidos
☐ Corea	☐ Japón	☐ Indonesia	☐ Brasil
☐ China	☐ Australia	☐ Marruecos	☐ Italia

ESTRATEGIA DE COMPRENSIÓN

Ignoring words you don't know Although ideally we strive to understand all words in a conversation or video that is presented to us, sometimes being overly concerned about every single word can actually be counterproductive. It may cause you to get caught up on one small portion and not allow your attention to continue to follow the action and the dialogue. Thus, it can sometimes be a better strategy to temporarily ignore words that you don't immediately understand. You can return to them later and replay the segment as many times as you like to get the full meaning. For now, see how much you can understand and what you may need to ignore the first time you listen.

A VER EL VIDEO

 Paso 1. View the video the first time without subtitles, and see how much you comprehend. Try not to get stuck on words that you don't immediately understand. In small groups, share what you understood.

Paso 2. Before you watch the video a second time, look at the statements below. After watching, state whether they are true or false. Rewrite the false statements to make them correct.

		Cierto	Falso
1.	Las clases son muy grandes.	☐	☐
2.	Los estudiantes trabajan mucho en grupos pequeños.	☐	☐
3.	Es una universidad muy ordenada.	☐	☐
4.	Los profesores no están muy motivados.	☐	☐
5.	No hay muchas oportunidades para practicar el español.	☐	☐

Paso 3. According to the young man from the United States, why is it important to study Spanish? Do you agree with him?

DESPUÉS DE VER EL VIDEO

At the end of the video, the viewer is asked, **¿Es la UNAM la universidad para ti?** In groups, tell your classmates whether you would answer "**Sí**" or "**No**" and why.

Repaso de vocabulario activo

Adverbios y expresiones adverbiales

ahora/más tarde *now/ later*

a tiempo/temprano/ tarde *on time/early/ late*

a veces *sometimes*

antes de/después de (clase) *before/after (class)*

casi nunca *rarely*

esta mañana/tarde/ noche *this morning/ afternoon/evening*

el fin de semana *weekend*

con frecuencia *frequently*

nunca *never*

por/en la mañana/tarde/ noche *in the morning/ afternoon/evening*

siempre *always*

toda(s) la(s) mañana(s)/ tarde(s)/noche(s) *every morning/afternoon/ evening*

todos los días *every day*

Sustantivos   *Nouns*

En la clase

el alumno/el estudiante *student (male)*

la alumna/la estudiante *student (female)*

los apuntes *notes*

el bolígrafo/la pluma *pen*

el borrador *eraser*

la calculadora *calculator*

el cuaderno *notebook*

el diccionario *dictionary*

el (reproductor de) DVD *DVD, DVD player*

el escritorio *desk*

el examen *exam*

la hoja de papel *sheet of paper*

el lápiz *pencil*

el libro *book*

el mapa *map*

la mesa *table*

la mochila *backpack*

la nota *grade*

la papelera *wastebasket*

la pizarra *blackboard*

el profesor *teacher/ professor (male)*

la profesora *teacher/ professor (female)*

la puerta *door*

el reloj *clock*

la silla *chair*

la tarea *homework*

la tiza *chalk*

el trabajo escrito *academic paper, essay*

la ventana *window*

En el laboratorio

los audífonos *headphones*

la computadora *computer*

el correo electrónico *e-mail address*

el disco compacto/el CD *compact disc*

la impresora *printer*

el mensaje electrónico *e-mail (message)*

la página web *Web page*

la pantalla *screen*

el ratón *mouse*

el sitio web *website*

el teclado *keyboard*

el televisor *television set*

La clase de...

alemán *German*

álgebra *algebra*

arte *art*

biología *biology*

cálculo *calculus*

ciencias políticas *political science*

computación/ informática *computer science*

contabilidad *accounting*

economía *economy*

español *Spanish*

filosofía *philosophy*

finanzas *finances*

física *physics*

francés *French*

historia *history*

inglés *English*

literatura *literature*

matemáticas *mathematics*

música *music*

psicología *psychology*

química *chemistry*

religión *religion*

sociología *sociology*

Lugares   *Places*

la casa *home/house*

el apartamento *apartment*

la biblioteca *library*

la cafetería *cafeteria*

el centro estudiantil *student center*

el cuarto *room*

la casa *home/house*

la facultad *school or department within a university*

el gimnasio *gymnasium*

la librería *bookstore*

la oficina *office*

la residencia estudiantil *student dorm*

el restaurante *restaurant*

la universidad *university*

Verbos y expresiones verbales

aprender *to learn*

asistir a *to attend*

beber *to drink*

buscar *to look for*

cenar *to have dinner*

comer *to eat, have lunch*

comprar *to buy*

desayunar *to have breakfast*

comprender *to understand*

enviar *to send*

escribir *to write*

escuchar *to listen to*

estudiar *to study*

hablar *to talk*

hacer *to do, make*

hay *there is, there are*

imprimir *to print*

ir *to go*

leer *to read*

llegar *to arrive*

mandar *to send*

navegar por la red *to surf the Web*

practicar *to practice*

preparar *to prepare*

regresar *to return, to go back*

salir *to go out*

ser *to be*

tomar (apuntes) *to take (notes)*

trabajar *to work*

usar *to use*

vivir *to live*

sacar una nota *to get a grade*

Palabras interrogativas

¿Cuándo? *When?*

¿Adónde? *Where to?*

Autoprueba y repaso

I. Nouns and definite and indefinite articles.

A. Professor B is more demanding than Professor A, and she always gives more homework. Complete each professor's assignment with the appropriate definite article (**el, la, los, las**). Change nouns to the plural when necessary.

Modelo: PROFESOR A: Contesten _____la_____ pregunta n° 1.

PROFESOR B: Contesten _las preguntas_ 1 a 10.

1. PROF. A: Escriban _____ ejercicio A.

PROF. B: Escriban _____ A y B.

2. PROF. A: Estudien _____ lección 1.

PROF. B: Estudien _____ 1 y 2.

3. PROF. A: Lean_____ página 40.

PROF. B: Lean _____ 40 y 41.

4. PROF. A: Completen _____ Capítulo 3.

PROF. B: Completen _____ 3 y 4.

B. Describe your school by completing the sentences with **un, una, unos,** or **unas**.

En la universidad hay _____ centro estudiantil con _____ librería grande. Tenemos _____ laboratorio con _____ impresora y _____ computadoras nuevas. Hay _____ biblioteca grande con _____ libros muy antiguos e interesantes.

II. *Ir + a* + destination. Tell where the following people go to carry out the indicated activities. Avoid subject pronouns.

Modelo: Esteban /estudiar
Va a la biblioteca.

1. yo / desayunar

2. nosotros / trabajar en la computadora

3. mis amigos y yo / hacer ejercicio

4. los estudiantes / hablar con el profesor

5. tú / comprar libros y cuadernos

6. Susana / tomar una siesta

III. The present tense of regular *–ar* verbs. Indicate or ask questions about what college students do. Change the verbs to correspond to the subjects given in parentheses. Avoid the use of subject pronouns.

Modelo: navegar por la red con frecuencia (yo)
Navego por la red con frecuencia.

1. comprar libros y cuadernos en la librería (yo)

2. llegar a clase a tiempo (todos los estudiantes)

3. ¿estudiar en la biblioteca por la tarde (tú)?

4. ¿trabajar por la noche (usted)?

5. usar el correo electrónico todos los días (nosotros)

6. escuchar música clásica por la noche (Ana)

IV. The present tense of regular *–er* and *–ir* verbs; *hacer* and *salir*. Indicate or ask questions about what college students do. Change the verbs to correspond to the subjects given in parentheses. Avoid the use of subject pronouns.

Modelo: hacer muchos exámenes y escribir muchas composiciones (ella)
Hace muchos exámenes y escribe muchas composiciones.

1. asistir a una universidad buena y aprender mucho (nosotros)

2. vivir en la residencia y estudiar en la biblioteca (yo)

3. comer en la cafetería y tomar café en el centro estudiantil (los estudiantes)

4. leer libros interesantes y escribir muchas composiciones (nosotros)

5. imprimir los trabajos y usar las computadoras en el laboratorio (tú)

6. hacer la tarea y después salir con mis amigos/as (yo)

V. *General review.*

1. ¿Vas a clase todos los días?

2. ¿A qué hora es tu primera (*your first*) clase?

3. ¿Cuántos estudiantes hay en la clase de español?

4. ¿Hay tarea todas las noches? ¿Mucha tarea?

5. ¿Escriben ustedes en el Cuaderno de ejercicios todas las noches?

6. ¿Adónde vas para comprar libros interesantes? ¿Y para usar las computadoras?

7. ¿Adónde vas a conversar con tus amigos?

8. ¿A qué hora cenas?

9. ¿Dónde comes normalmente?

VI. *Cultura.*

1. What are some of the principal differences between universities in the Spanish-speaking world vs. the United States?

2. What is the **coquí**?

Answers to the *Autoprueba y repaso* and are found in **Apéndice 2.**

Así es mi familia

Así se dice

Así es mi familia
  La familia, los parientes y
  los amigos
  Relaciones personales

Así se forma

1. *Tener* and *tener... años*
2. Descriptive adjectives
   Adjetivos descriptivos
   con *ser*. Los opuestos
3. Possessive adjectives and
   possession with *de*
4. *Estar* + location and
   condition
   ¿Dónde están?/¿Cómo
   están?

Cultura

- Los hispanos en Estados
  Unidos
- La familia hispana

Dicho y hecho

Para leer:
Enciclopedia del español en
los Estados Unidos

Para conversar:
Las personas especiales

Para escribir:
Retrato de familia

Para ver y escuchar:
Todo en familia

By the end of this chapter you will be able to:

- Talk about the family
- Tell age
- Indicate possession
- Describe people and things
- Indicate location
- Describe mental and physical conditions

ENTRANDO AL TEMA

1. How many relatives are there in your family? How about your extended family?

2. How many people of Hispanic origin live in your town/city (or the place where you are from)? Do you know what their countries of origin or heritage are?

Así se dice

Así es mi familia

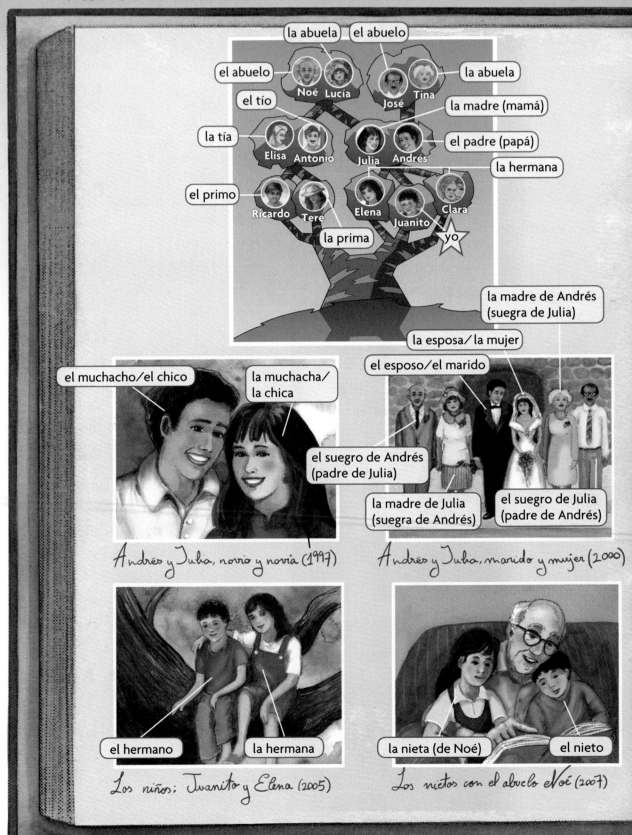

la abuela · el abuelo

el abuelo · Noé · Lucía

José · Tina · la abuela

el tío · la madre (mamá)

la tía · Elisa · Antonio · Julia · Andrés · el padre (papá)

la hermana

el primo · Ricardo · Tere · Elena · Juanito · Clara

la prima · yo

la madre de Andrés (suegra de Julia)

la esposa/ la mujer

el esposo/el marido

el muchacho/el chico · la muchacha/ la chica

el suegro de Andrés (padre de Julia)

la madre de Julia (suegra de Andrés) · el suegro de Julia (padre de Andrés)

Andrés y Julia, novio y novia (1997)

Andrés y Julia, marido y mujer (2000)

el hermano · la hermana

Los niños: Juanito y Elena (2005)

la nieta (de Noé) · el nieto

Los nietos con el abuelo Noé (2007)

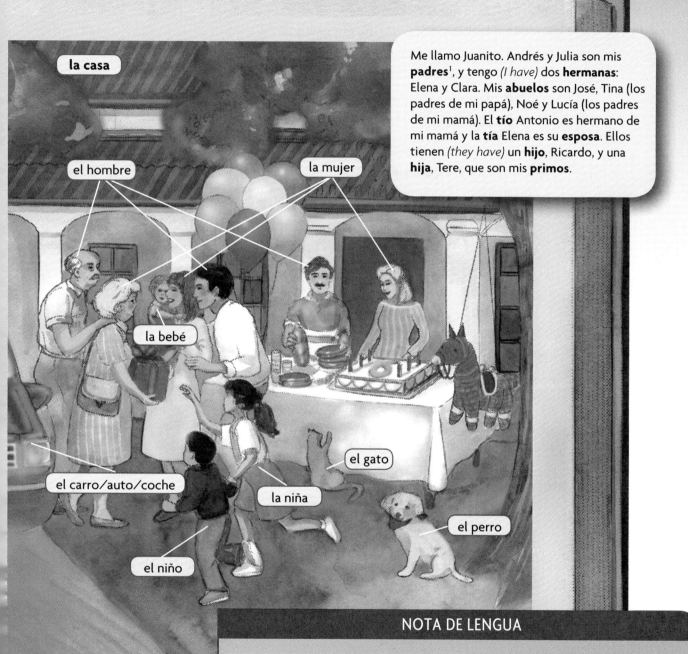

la casa

el hombre

la mujer

la bebé

el carro/auto/coche

la niña

el gato

el niño

el perro

Me llamo Juanito. Andrés y Julia son mis **padres**[1], y tengo *(I have)* dos **hermanas**: Elena y Clara. Mis **abuelos** son José, Tina (los padres de mi papá), Noé y Lucía (los padres de mi mamá). El **tío** Antonio es hermano de mi mamá y la **tía** Elena es su **esposa**. Ellos tienen *(they have)* un **hijo**, Ricardo, y una **hija**, Tere, que son mis **primos**.

El cumpleaños de Juanito (2008)

NOTA DE LENGUA

There are different terms to refer to a romantic partner: **esposo/a**, **marido/mujer** when married; **novio/a**, **enamorado/a** (parts of Lat. Am.) when dating, **prometido/a** when engaged. A general term that anyone can use is **pareja** *(partner, significant other)*.

[1]In Spanish, the masculine plural can refer to a group of both males and females. Examples: **padres** = *parents*, **abuelos** = *grandparents*, **tíos** = *aunts and uncles*, **hermanos** = *brothers and sisters (siblings)*.

3-1 **La familia: ¿cierto o falso?** **Paso 1.** Listen as your instructor or a classmate reads the sentences below. Decide whether they are true (**cierto**) or false (**falso**).

Modelo: El hijo de mis padres es mi hermano. ☑ Cierto ☐ Falso

	Cierto	Falso
1. La abuela de mi hermana es mi abuela.	☐	☐
2. La hermana de mi madre es mi tía.	☐	☐
3. Los hijos de mis tíos son mis nietos.	☐	☐
4. El padre de mi madre es mi tío.	☐	☐
5. Mi hermana es la hija de mi padre y mi madre.	☐	☐
6. El padre de mi padre es el suegro de mi madre.	☐	☐
7. Yo soy el nieto/la nieta de mis primos.	☐	☐

3-2 **¿Quién es?** Take turns with a classmate explaining and guessing who various family members are until you have each explained and guessed five different family members.

Modelo: Estudiante A: **Son los hijos de mi tía.**
          Estudiante B: **tus primos**

La familia, los parientes y los amigos

Camila tells us about her family, relatives, and friends.

INÉS: Camila, eres de la República Dominicana, ¿verdad?

CAMILA: Sí, pero mi familia y yo vivimos (*live*) en Nueva York. Mi familia es interesante porque mis padres son divorciados y ahora mi madre tiene (*has*) otro esposo: mi **padrastro**.

INÉS: Y, ¿**cuántos** hermanos tienes?

CAMILA: Bueno, aquí en Nueva York mi padrastro tiene dos hijos: mi **hermanastro** Pablo y mi **hermanastra** Mónica. Mi madre y su esposo no tienen hijos, por eso (*therefore*) no tengo (*have*) **medios hermanos**. Pero sí tengo un hermano **mayor**, Raúl, y una hermana **menor**, Paula.

INÉS: **¿Dónde** están?

CAMILA: Están en Santo Domingo, y también mi **cuñada** Marta, la esposa de mi hermano, y sus hijos, mis **sobrinos** Pablo y Martita.

INÉS: **¿Quién** más de tu familia está en Santo Domingo?

CAMILA: Están allá mi padre, mis cuatro abuelos, mi **bisabuela** (abuela de mi padre) y otros **parientes**. Mi **mejor amiga**, Pilar, es de Santo Domingo también. Sin embargo (*however*), ya (*already*) tengo excelentes amigos aquí en Estados Unidos.

el bisabuelo/la bisabuela	*great-grandfather/great-grandmother*
el hermanastro/la hermanastra	*stepbrother/stepsister*
el medio hermano/la medio hermana	*half-brother/half-sister*
mayor	*older*
el mejor amigo/la mejor amiga	*best friend (male/female)*
menor	*younger*
los parientes	*relatives*
¿Cuántos/Cuántas?	*How many?*
¿Quién/Quiénes?	*Who?*
¿Dónde?	*Where?*

DICHOS

De tal palo (*stick*), tal astilla (*splinter*).
De tal padre, tal hijo.

¿Cuál es el dicho equivalente en inglés? ¿Se aplica a tu familia? ¿Eres tú como (*like*) tu madre o como tu padre?

3-3 La familia de Camila.
Based on what you know about Camila's family, indicate the correct answers below.

1. ¿De dónde es Camila? ☐ de Nueva York ☐ de Santo Domingo
2. ¿Dónde vive (*lives*) Camila? ☐ en Nueva York ☐ en Santo Domingo
3. ¿Quién es su padrastro? ☐ el padre de su madre ☐ el esposo de su madre
4. ¿Es Raúl mayor que (*than*) Paula? ☐ Sí, Raúl es mayor. ☐ No, Raúl es menor.
5. ¿Quién se llama Marta? ☐ la cuñada de Camila ☐ la sobrina de Camila

Relaciones personales

See what an important role Carmen's family plays in her very busy lifestyle.

Carmen trabaja, estudia y es madre soltera (*single*). Sus hijas gemelas (*twins*), Tina y Mari, tienen tres años. Carmen **ama a** sus hijas con todo el corazón (*heart*). Cuando va al trabajo o a la universidad, su tía o la niñera (*babysitter*) **cuida a** las niñas. Todas las mañanas, al salir de la casa, Carmen **besa** y **abraza a** Tina y **a** Mari. Con frecuencia **llama a** sus padres y abuelos, que viven en Ponce, Puerto Rico. Ellos **visitan a** Carmen y **a** las nietas dos veces al año.

abrazar	*to hug*	**besar**	*to kiss*	**llamar**	*to call*
amar	*to love*	**cuidar**	*to take care of*	**visitar**	*to visit*

3-4 Tú y tu familia.

Paso 1. In the table below, answer the questions about you and your family (both immediate and extended) in the column "**Yo**".

Paso 2. Then ask the questions to a classmate and write down her/his answers in the column "**Mi compañero/a**". Can you find any similarities?

		Yo	Mi compañero/a
1.	¿A quién en tu familia amas mucho (*a lot*)?		
2.	¿A quién abrazas con frecuencia?		
3.	¿A quién besas?		
4.	¿A quién llamas por teléfono con frecuencia?		
5.	¿A qué parientes visitas con más frecuencia?		

NOTA DE LENGUA

La *a* personal

Observe the use of the word **a** in the above description of Carmen's life. It precedes a direct object that is a specific person (or persons). It is called **a personal** and there is no equivalent in English. Note that **a + el → al**.

— ¿**A** quién buscas?
Who(m) are you looking for?

— Busco **a** mi amigo/**al** profesor.
I am looking for my friend/the professor.

Note that when the direct object is not a person, there is no **a**.

— ¿Qué buscas?
What are you looking for?

— Busco su apartamento.
I am looking for his apartment.

Así se forma

WILEY PLUS Go to *WileyPLUS* and review the Verb Conjugator for this grammar point.

¡Tengo ochenta y un años!

Abuelo, ¿cuántos años tienes?

1. Indicating possession and telling age: The verb *tener* and *tener ... años*

The verb *tener*

You have already informally used **tener** (*to have*) to express possession, as in **tengo dos hermanos**. Now observe the following forms (note that **tener** is irregular in the present).

Tener (irreg.)		
(yo)	**tengo**	**Tengo** un hermano.
(tú)	**tienes**	¿**Tienes** bisabuelos?
(usted, él/ella)	**tiene**	Mi madre **tiene** cuatro hermanas.
(nosotros/as)	**tenemos**	Mi hermano y yo **tenemos** un perro.
(vosotros/as)	**tenéis**	¿**Tenéis** coche?
(ustedes, ellos/ellas)	**tienen**	Mis tíos **tienen** una casa nueva.

Tener ... años *(To be . . . years old)*

Whereas English uses *to be . . .* to tell age (*She is eighteen years old.*), Spanish uses **tener ... años.** To inquire about age, the question **¿Cuántos años... ?** (*How many years . . . ?*) is used with **tener.**

—¿**Cuántos años tiene él?**   *How old is he?*
—**Tiene veintiún años.**   *He is twenty-one years old.*

3-5 ¿Quién dice (*says*) esto? Based on the family pictures on p. 68, who is saying the following?

1. Tenemos dos primos.
   ☐ Ricardo y Tere   ☐ Elena y Juanito   ☐ Andrés y Julia

2. Tengo tres sobrinitos.
   ☐ Julia   ☐ Elisa   ☐ Tina

3. Mi hijo tiene dos hermanas.
   ☐ Andrés   ☐ José   ☐ Antonio

4. Mi suegro tiene dos nietos.
   ☐ Elisa   ☐ Tina   ☐ Julia

5. Tenemos cinco nietos.
   ☐ José y Tina   ☐ Noé y Lucía   ☐ Julia y Andrés

6. En este cumpleaños tengo seis años.
   ☐ Noé   ☐ Ricardo   ☐ Juanito

3-6 ¿Y tu (*your*) familia?

Paso 1. You are going to interview a classmate about her/his family using the following questions, but first you need to complete them with the correct form of **tener**.

Modelo: **¿Tienes** primos? ¿Cuántos años **tienen** tus primos?

1. ¿Cuántos años _____ (tú)?

2. ¿_____ (tú) hermanos o hermanas mayores? ¿Cómo se llaman y cuántos años _____?

3. ¿_____ (tú) hermanos o hermanas menores? ¿Cómo se llaman y cuántos años _____?

4. ¿Sabes (*do you know*) cuántos años _____ tus padres aproximadamente?

5. ¿_____ (tú) abuelos? ¿Cuántos años _____ tus abuelos?

6. ¿_____ (tú) bisabuelos? ¿Cuántos años _____ tu bisabuelo o tu bisabuela?

 Paso 2. Work with a partner and find out about her/his family members using the questions above. Jot down the answers.

Paso 3. Now write a short report, which you might be asked to share with the class. What do your families have in common, and what is different?

Modelo: **Ricardo tiene un hermano y yo tengo una hermana. Mi hermana tiene veinte años, pero el hermano de Ricardo tiene dieciocho años...**

3-7 Mi árbol genealógico (*My family tree*).
First, draw your family tree in your notebook. Then write a description of your family with additional details. You may be asked to share it with a classmate.

Modelo: **Tengo una tía y dos tíos. Mi tía se llama... y tiene... años. Es divorciada, pero vive con su novio en...**

Los Ángeles

NOTA CULTURAL

Los hispanos en las grandes ciudades (*cities*)
Look at the following table with data from the 2000 Census about the Latino populations in some large U.S. cities. How large is the Latino community where you live?

	Number of Latinos	Percent of the city's population that is Latino	Majority Latino group(s)
New York City	2,160,554	27%	Puerto Rican, Dominican
Los Ángeles	1,719,073	47%	Mexican
Chicago	753,644	26%	Mexican, Puerto Rican
El Paso	431,875	77%	Mexican
Miami	238,351	66%	Cuban

Miami

WILEY PLUS Cultura: Los hispanos en Estados Unidos

WILEY PLUS **Map quizzes:** As you read about places highlighted in red, find them on the map. Learn more about and test yourself on the geography of the Spanish-speaking world in *WileyPLUS.*

Map legend:
- Estados que tienen más del 15.1% de población hispana
- Estados que tienen 5.1-15.1% de población hispana
- Estados que tienen 2-5% de población hispana
- ★ Ciudades indicadas tienen más de 100.000 hispanos

Población hispana total en los Estados Unidos según el censo de 2000 = aproximadamente 35.3 millones

Antes de leer

1. Do you know (or can you guess) what percentage of the U.S. population is Hispanic?

2. Looking at the map above, is there anything you did not expect?

¿CUÁNTOS HISPANOS HAY?

¿Sabes que los hispanos representan aproximadamente el 15% (por ciento) de la población de Estados Unidos (EE.UU.)? La comunidad hispana es una de las más importantes del país. Aproximadamente el 70% de la población hispana se concentra en cuatro estados: California, **Texas,** Nueva York y Florida. Gran parte de esta población vive en ciudades como Los Ángeles, la Ciudad de Nueva York, Miami, Chicago, Washington, D.C. y **San Antonio.**

¿DE DÓNDE SON?

La mayoría de los hispanos en EE.UU. son de México (60+ %), Puerto Rico (10+ %) y Cuba (5+ %). Gran parte de los nuevos inmigrantes hispanos de los últimos *(last)* treinta años son de Centroamérica — salvadoreños, nicaragüenses, hondureños y guatemaltecos— y también de la República Dominicana.

La amistad *(friendship)* entre México y Estados Unidos se representa en la escultura *Torch of Friendship* en San Antonio, Texas. El escultor Sebastián es un famoso artista mexicano.

LA INFLUENCIA HISPANA

En algunas partes del país, como el suroeste y Florida, la presencia de la población hispana es anterior a la llegada (*arrival*) de la población angloparlante (*English-speaking*). Los **nombres** de varias ciudades y estados son la evidencia más notable de la presencia hispana en la historia del país. Por ejemplo, la ciudad más antigua en el territorio continental de EE.UU. tiene un nombre hispano—San Agustín, FL.

La **vida diaria** (*daily*) de EE.UU. integra numerosos elementos de las artes, la comida (*food*) y el idioma de la cultura hispana. Por ejemplo, hay muchísimos restaurantes y tiendas con productos hispanos y se puede escuchar el español en muchas partes.

Los hispanos también hacen contribuciones muy valiosas (*valuable*) a la **política**, **las ciencias** y **las artes** del país. Ellen Ochoa fue la primera mujer hispana astronauta en navegar en el espacio; Henry Cisneros sirvió en el gabinete del presidente Bill Clinton; Ana Castillo es una escritora muy famosa; y Sonia Sotomayor es juez de la Corte Suprema. La **economía** de los hispanos también es notable—el mercado hispano se estima en (*is estimated at*) un billón (*a trillion*)[1] de dólares.

▲ A partir de 1959, como resultado de la Revolución cubana, muchos cubanos inmigraron al sureste de EE.UU., especialmente a Florida. Hoy, medio millón de cubanos y cubanoamericanos viven en Miami.

---

[1]**Un billón** is the Spanish equivalent of *a trillion*. To say *a billion* in Spanish, use **mil millones**.

INVESTIG@ EN INTERNET

Learn about a prominent U.S. Hispanic in the areas of politics, business, science, journalism, or the arts. Be prepared to share your findings with the class.

Chicago

Después de leer

1. Based on what you read, match these ideas.

____ El 60% de los hispanos en los EE.UU. son...

____ La mayoría de los hispanos en la Florida son...

____ Colorado, San Francisco, Nevada y Arizona son...

____ Hay muchos puertorriqueños y dominicanos en...

____ Las enchiladas, las empanadas y los tacos son...

a. comida hispana.

b. mexicanos.

c. Nueva York.

d. cubanos.

e. nombres hispanos.

2. Is there a Hispanic community or influence where you live?

3. Can you name any influential Hispanics in the U.S. such as actors/actresses, singers, politicians, or athletes?

Hoy hay más de un millón de puertorriqueños en la ciudad de Nueva York. La comunidad dominicana más grande del país también reside en esta ciudad.

Así se forma

Soy muy artística, ¿no?

2. Describing people and things: Descriptive adjectives

Adjectives are words that modify nouns. Descriptive adjectives describe and express characteristics of nouns (*tall, funny, interesting . . .*). You have already learned some adjectives of nationality (**mexicano/a**) and some that are cognates (**romántico/a**).

Formation of adjectives

Adjectives in Spanish agree in gender (masculine or feminine) and number (singular or plural) with the nouns or pronouns they modify.

- Adjectives that end in **-o** have four possible forms (masculine/feminine, singular/ plural) to indicate agreement.

	Singular	Plural
masculine	Él es honest**o**.	Ellos son honest**os**.
feminine	Ella es honest**a**.	Ellas son honest**as**.

- Adjectives ending in **-e** or **-ista**, and most that end in a consonant, have only two possible forms: singular or plural. (Adjectives of nationality that end in a consonant are one exception. See page 29.)

Singular	Plural
Él/Ella es inteligent**e**.	Ellos/Ellas son inteligent**es**.
. . . idea**lista**.	. . . idea**listas**.
. . . sentiment**al**.	. . . sentiment**ales**.

- Adjectives ending in **-dor** add **-a** to agree with a feminine singular noun:
  trabajador → trabajador**a**   conservador → conservador**a**

- To make a singular adjective plural, add **-s** to the vowel or **-es** to the consonant, as is done with nouns.
  american**o** → american**os**   español → español**es**

Adjective position

- In contrast to English, Spanish descriptive adjectives usually follow the noun they describe.
  Marta es una **estudiante responsable**.   *Marta is a responsible student.*

- Adjectives of quantity (such as numbers) precede the noun, as in English.
  Tres estudiantes son de Nuevo México.
  Muchos estudiantes van al concierto.

- **Bueno/a** and **malo/a** may be placed either before or after a noun. When placed before a masculine singular noun, **bueno** becomes **buen**, and **malo** becomes **mal**.

Es un estudiante **bueno/malo**. Or,   Es un **buen/mal** estudiante.
Es una profesora **buena/mala**. Or,   Es una **buena/mala** profesora.

3-8 **¿Quién es?** Listen to Juanito talk about his family and decide whether each statement refers to his mother, father, sisters, or cousins. Note that some adjectives could refer to more than one category.

	la mamá	el papá	las hermanas	los primos
1.				
2.				
3.				
4.				
5.				
6.				
7.				
8.				

Adjetivos descriptivos con *ser*
Los opuestos

Observe how Pepita describes her cousins Luis and Alberto.

Tengo dos primos que **son** completamente **diferentes.** Luis **es moreno,** bajo, con unos kilos de más. Alberto **es rubio,** alto, delgado y guapo. Luis **es muy amable;** tiene un carácter agradable. **Es divertido** y **simpático.** Alberto no habla mucho; **es serio, un poco egoísta** y algo (*somewhat*) **aburrido.** La verdad es que a veces **es antipático.** Los dos son mis primos, ¡**pero** qué contraste!

aburrido/a	*boring*	muy	*very*
amable	*friendly, kind*	pero	*but*
antipático/a	*unpleasant, disagreeable*	un poco	*a bit, somewhat*
divertido/a	*amusing, fun, funny*		
moreno/a	*brunette, dark-skinned*		
rubio/a	*blond/e*		
simpático/a	*nice, likeable*		

Los opuestos

> **ser** + adjective agreeing with noun in gender and number

The following descriptive adjectives are most commonly used with the verb **ser** to indicate characteristics or qualities that are considered inherent or natural to the person or thing described. They indicate what the person or thing is *like*. Observe the following pairs of opposites.

alto/a ≠ bajo/a

fuerte ≠ débil

joven ≠ mayor[1]

tonto/a ≠ inteligente

perezoso(a)/irresponsable ≠ trabajador(a)/responsable/

difícil ≠ fácil

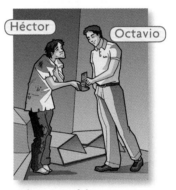

pobre ≠ rico(a)

bonito(a)/ hermoso(a)/ guapo(a) ≠ feo(a)

flaco(a)/ delgado(a) ≠ gordo(a)

malo(a) ≠ bueno(a)

pequeño(a) ≠ grande   **viejo(a) ≠ nuevo(a)**

---

[1]The plural of **joven** is **jóvenes.** Although the most common Spanish word for *old* is **viejo,** it is not polite to use it to describe people. Use **mayor** instead.

3-9 ¿Quién?

Paso 1. Answer the following questions with the names of famous people or fictional characters.

Modelo: ¿Quién es tonto?

Homer Simpson es tonto.

1. ¿Quién es feo?
2. ¿Quién es muy mala?
3. ¿Quién es rico?
4. ¿Quién es joven?
5. ¿Quiénes son guapas?

6. ¿Quién es divertido?
7. ¿Quién es simpática?
8. ¿Quiénes son muy inteligentes?
9. ¿Quién es antipático?
10. ¿Quién es un poco aburrido?

Paso 2. Now, write four sentences describing famous people or fictional characters. Then, in groups, you will read your sentences to your classmates, without mentioning who the person or character is. They will try to guess who you are talking about.

Modelo: Estudiante 1: **Es tonto, pero también es buen padre. Tiene un hijo y dos hijas. (Homer Simpson)**

Estudiante 2: **¿Es Homer Simpson?**

Estudiante 1: **Sí./No.**

NOTA DE LENGUA

You often use more than one adjective when describing a person. In doing so, note the following:

y (and) becomes **e** before words beginning with **i** or **hi**.
Mi madre es bonita **e** inteligente.

o (or) becomes **u** before words beginning with **o** or **ho**.
¿El presidente es deshonesto **u** honesto?

NOTA CULTURAL

El español en Estados Unidos

There are about 35 million Spanish speakers in the U.S., making it the country with the fifth largest Spanish-speaking population in the world. There are many Spanish language newspapers and television stations. In fact, in Miami and Los Angeles, the majority of people get their news in Spanish.

U.S. Spanish has some peculiar features brought about by its contact with English. For instance, many U.S. Spanish speakers adapt English vocabulary: they may say **aplicar** meaning to *apply*, while in Latin America and Spain, the word typically used is **solicitar**. It is also common to alternate in the use of English and Spanish. Contrary to popular belief, such alternation of languages is not random; it follows certain grammatical rules.

José: ¿Me das diez dólares *so I can buy lunch?* Se me olvidó la cartera.
Marta: Ahora no traigo dinero. *I'll give you some later.*

Así es mi familia

setenta y nueve   79

3-10 Los anuncios personales.

Paso 1. Read the personal ads and decide who would make a good couple.

1.
Soy una señorita enérgica, honesta y práctica. Tengo veintidós años y deseo conocer a un caballero romántico. En el futuro, quiero tener muchos hijos.

2.
¿Buscas a un hombre maduro y optimista? Tengo cuarenta y dos años, soy viudo (*widower*) y tengo una hija.

3.
Persona trabajadora y responsable busca a persona caribeña (*Caribbean*) tradicional y seria.

4.
Busco a una persona exótica y joven. Tengo veinticinco años y soy muy trabajador.

5.
Señorita dominicana de treinta años busca a un hombre inteligente y divertido. Soy muy religiosa.

6.
Tengo veinte años y trabajo en un estudio de tatuajes (*tattoos*). Busco a un hombre rico y guapo.

7.
Soy una madre divorciada. Tengo cuarenta años y tengo dos hijas. Quiero encontrar a un señor amable y responsable.

8.
Tengo treinta años y busco a una mujer enérgica y liberal. Soy muy romántico y tengo una familia grande.

 Paso 2. Share your matchmaking decisions with a partner. You might want to use these terms:

Modelo: Creo que la mujer (…) hace / no hace buena pareja (*makes a good couple*) con el hombre (…) porque… Tienen mucho en común / No tienen nada en común. Por ejemplo…

PALABRAS ÚTILES

Here are some more opposites and physical descriptions:

amable (*kind*)	grosero (*rude*)
honesto/a	deshonesto/a
conservador/a	liberal
moral	inmoral
egoísta	generoso/a
optimista	pesimista
enérgico/a	tranquilo/a
paciente	impaciente
exótico/a	ordinario/a
práctico	idealista
extrovertido/a	introvertido/a
serio/a	cómico/a
tolerante	intolerante

Tener pelo (*hair*) negro (*black*)/canoso (*grey*).
Ser pelirrojo (*redhead*).
Tener ojos (*eyes*) azules (*blue*)/verdes (*green*)/negros/café (*brown*).

3-11 Mi anuncio personal.

Paso 1. On a sheet of paper, write a short list of the traits that best describe you, both physically and in terms of personality.

(No) Soy…   (No) Tengo …

Paso 2. Now, write a description of yourself based on the list you wrote in **Paso 1,** and add other relevant details. Feel free to be either truthful or inventive. Write your name on the back and give it to your instructor, who will redistribute the descriptions.

Paso 3. Read the description you receive (but not the name of the student who wrote it) and write a personal ad that describes the perfect mate for your classmate. Do it on a piece of paper you can later give to her/him.

3-12 **Similares y diferentes.** In most families there are some people that are similar in some ways but very different in other ways. Can you think of two people in your family like this (you and a sibling, your parents, two grandparents, etc.)?

_____ **y** _____

Paso 1. First, write three sentences describing the similarities between the two family members.

Modelo: **Mi mamá y mi hermana son...** Or,

   Mi papá y yo somos...

1. _____
2. _____
3. _____

Now write three sentences describing their differences.

Modelo: **Mi mamá es... pero mi hermana es...** Or,

   Mi papá es... pero yo soy...

1. _____
2. _____
3. _____

 Paso 2. Now, you and a classmate share what you've written. Ask each other additional questions.

 3-13 **Adivinanzas (*Guessing game*).** One student will assume the role of a well-known celebrity but will not divulge her/his identity. The other students will ask questions to discover her/his identity. Use the adjectives you have studied in this chapter and from *Palabras útiles* on p. 80. The mystery celebrity may respond only with **Sí** or **No.**

Modelo: **¿Eres actor? ¿Eres joven/mayor? ¿Eres cómico/a?**

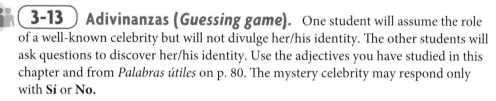 **3-14** **Amor y... menos amor (*Love and . . . less love*).** In pairs, take turns interviewing each other about each other's favorite person or least favorite person. Below are some questions to help you, but try to ask other questions for details. Pay attention and/or take notes on your partner's answers, as you may need this information later.

1. ¿Quién es tu persona favorita/menos favorita?
2. ¿Cómo es?
3. ¿Por qué (*Why*) es tu persona favorita/menos favorita?

SITUACIONES

Imagine you are a famous person (write the name on a piece of paper) and you have been unlucky in love lately, so you go to a speed-dating event in town. You have three minutes to talk to each eligible single, tell them about yourself and ask about them, but do not tell them who you are! Then, see if the classmates you spoke with can guess your identity.

Así es mi familia

Cultura: La familia hispana

Antes de leer

1. What family members live in a typical U.S. household? Do U.S. families tend to be nuclear or extended?

2. Think about events celebrated by many U.S. teenagers: Sweet 16, debutantes, bar/bat mitzvahs, etc. Describe who celebrates them and how.

Para la mayoría de los hispanos, la familia es una pequeña comunidad unida por la solidaridad y el cariño (*affection*). El concepto hispano de la familia incluye a los parientes más inmediatos (madre, padre, hijos, hermanos) y también a los abuelos, tíos, primos y numerosos otros parientes. En la familia tradicional, especialmente en las zonas rurales, es común tener muchos hijos. Esta tabla demuestra (*shows*) el tamaño promedio (*average*) de las familias de varios grupos en Estados Unidos.

Tamaño promedio de las familias (Censo de EE.UU. 2000)	
Hispanos	3.87
Asiáticos	3.80
Afroamericanos	3.00
Blancos	2.58

En los países hispanos, los padres, los hijos y los abuelos viven con frecuencia en la misma (*same*) casa. Los abuelos son muy importantes en la crianza (*raising*) de sus nietos y, por lo general, los cuidan cuando los padres salen. Tradicionalmente, el padre trabaja y la madre cuida de la casa y de los niños. Por lo general, los hijos solteros viven en la casa de sus padres mientras (*while*) asisten a la universidad o trabajan.

Sin embargo, hoy en día el concepto de la familia hispana está cambiando (*changing*). Dos de los cambios más notables son que la familia es más pequeña y que muchas mujeres trabajan fuera de (*outside*) casa.

Por lo general, la familia, ya sea tradicional o moderna, es el centro de la vida social. Abuelos, nietos, padres, tíos, padrinos (*godparents*) y primos se reúnen con frecuencia para celebrar los cumpleaños, bautizos (*baptisms*), quinceañeras, comuniones y otras fiestas. Las relaciones familiares ocupan un lugar (*place*) esencial en la sociedad hispana.

Una celebración hispana que es común en Estados Unidos es la fiesta de los quince años, que se llama **la quinceañera.** Por lo general, solamente las chicas celebran una quinceañera. Muchas veces hay una misa (*mass*) y después, una comida y baile. La quinceañera se viste de manera muy formal.

Después de leer

1. Fill in the diagram below with typical characteristics of Hispanic and U.S. families. Think about the following concepts:

   −Number of children

   −Who lives in the family household

   −Roles of the family members

   Traditional Hispanic families   **Typical U.S. Families**

   Both

2. How does the **quinceañera** celebration compare with a celebration typical of other U.S. teenagers that you're familiar with?

   Some good movies about Hispanic families are *Mi familia* (1995), *Real Women Have Curves* (2002), and *Under the Same Moon* (2008).

Así se forma

Ricardo y Tere son mis primos.

3. Indicating possession: Possessive adjectives and possession with *de*

Possessive adjectives

In addition to the verb **tener,** possession may also be expressed with possessive adjectives, which you have previously seen: *Mis* **abuelos viven en España.**
Possessive adjectives also show ownership (*my house*) or a relationship between people (*my boyfriend*).

<table>
<tr><td colspan="3" align="center">**Los adjetivos posesivos**</td></tr>
<tr><td>Singular</td><td>Plural</td><td></td></tr>
<tr><td>**mi** tío</td><td>**mis** tíos</td><td>*my*</td></tr>
<tr><td>**tu**[1] hermana</td><td>**tus** hermanas</td><td>*your (sing. informal)*</td></tr>
<tr><td>**su** abuelo</td><td>**sus** abuelos</td><td>*your (sing. formal), his, her, its*</td></tr>
<tr><td>**nuestro/a** amigo/a</td><td>**nuestros/as** amigos/as</td><td>*our*</td></tr>
<tr><td>**vuestro/a** primo/a</td><td>**vuestros/as** primos/as</td><td>*your (pl. informal, Spain)*</td></tr>
<tr><td>**su** abuelo</td><td>**sus** abuelos</td><td>*your (pl.), their*</td></tr>
</table>

The choice of pronoun (**mi** vs. **tu**) depends on the possessor. Note that the possessive adjective agrees in number (**mi** vs. **mis**) and sometimes gender (**nuestro** vs. **nuestra**) with the thing possessed or person related (not with the possessor).

Susana tiene **nuestros libros.**	*Susana has **our books.***
Mis padres y yo vivimos en **nuestra casa.**	*My parents and I live in **our house.***

Susana is a feminine singular noun, but **nuestros** (masc. pl.) agrees with **libro.**
Mis padres y yo is masculine plural, but **nuestra** (fem. sing.) agrees with **casa.**

(3-15) **Tu álbum de fotos.** You are preparing labels to put in your new family photo album, but the computer ruined your formatting. Match items in the left column with those in the right column to reconstruct your labels.

1. Esta foto es de mis	a. coche.
2. Mi mamá y sus	b. casa.
3. Aquí está mi hermana con su	c. abuelos maternos.
4. Esta es nuestra	d. gato.
5. Y este es nuestro	e. novio.
6. El animal de la casa: nuestro	f. hermanas (mis tías).

---

[1]**Tú** (with written accent) = *you;* **tu** (without written accent) = *your.* **Tú** tienes **tu** libro, ¿verdad? (*You have your book, right?*)

WILEY PLUS Go to *WileyPLUS* and review the Animated Grammar Tutorial for this grammar point.

Possession with *de*

Whereas English uses *'s* (or *s'*) + noun to indicate possession, Spanish uses **de** + noun.

Es la casa **de** mi abuela.	*It's my grandmother's house.*
Es la casa **de** mis abuelos.	*It's my grandparents' house.*
Las hijas **de** Carmen son simpáticas.	*Carmen's daughters are nice.*
Las fotos **del** señor Soto son interesantes.	*Mr. Soto's photos are interesting.*

HINT

de + el = del

- When ownership referred to by **su/sus** is not clear from the context, you may use this alternate form for clarity: **de** + pronoun or **de** + name.

  Es **su carro.**   Or,   Es el carro **de él/ella/usted/ellos/ellas/ustedes.**
                                 Es el carro de **Elena.**

- To express the equivalent of the English *Whose?*, Spanish uses **¿De quién?**

  — **¿De quién** es el álbum?   *Whose album is it?*
  — **Es de** Susana.   *It's Susana's.*

3-16   Nuestras fotos.

Paso 1. Write on a piece of paper what photos/posters you have in your room or on your computer. To get started, think about the following:

padres	hermano/a	actor/actriz	mejor amigo/a	perro/gato
parientes	casa	cantante/grupo favorito		lugar

Modelo: **Tengo una/s foto/s de mis padres.**
                    Tengo...

Paso 2. Now work in pairs and guess what photos your classmate has. Take notes and respond to her/him as well. Your instructor may ask you about your partner.

Modelo:	Estudiante A:	**¿Tienes una foto de tus padres?**
	Estudiante B:	**Sí, tengo una foto de mis padres en mi cuarto/mi computadora.** O, **No, no tengo fotos de mis padres.**

                Estudiante A escribe: **Sandra tiene una foto de sus padres en...**

3-17   Mis parientes favoritos. Describe to your classmate three of your
favorite relatives. Define the family relationship.

Modelo: **Mi abuelo favorito se llama... Tiene... años. Es de... Es muy inteligente... Es el padre de mi madre.**

You may be called upon to share information about your classmate with the class:

           El abuelo favorito de (*classmate's name*) se llama...

VideoEscenas: Mi cuñado favorito

▲ Ernesto receives a message from an online dating service he has signed up for.

Paso 1. Answer these questions before you watch the video.

1. Do you use social networking sites (e.g. Facebook)? What do you like or dislike about them?
2. Have you ever met a friend or boyfriend/girlfriend online?
3. What would you like to know about a person you meet online?

Paso 2. Watch the video paying attention to the main ideas. Then, indicate whether the following statements are true (**cierto**) or false (**falso**). Correct the statements that are false to make them true.

	Cierto	Falso
1. Románticos.com manda información a Ernesto sobre una chica.	☐	☐
2. La primera (*first*) chica no es una buena candidata para Ernesto.	☐	☐
3. La segunda (*second*) chica sí es buena candidata para Ernesto.	☐	☐

Paso 3. Look at the questions below and the options offered. You will have to mark all the options that apply. Then, watch the video again. This time focus on the specific information you need to answer the questions.

1. ¿Cómo es la primera chica?
   - ☐ fea
   - ☐ guapa
   - ☐ perezosa
   - ☐ baja
   - ☐ alta
   - ☐ trabajadora

2. ¿Por qué no es una buena candidata para Ernesto?
   - ☐ es de Colombia
   - ☐ es muy alta
   - ☐ es perezosa

3. ¿Cómo es la segunda chica?
   - ☐ fea
   - ☐ guapa
   - ☐ morena
   - ☐ rubia
   - ☐ alta
   - ☐ baja
   - ☐ mayor
   - ☐ joven

4. ¿Qué le sorprende (*surprises*) a Javier, el amigo de Ernesto, de la segunda chica?
   - ☐ es independiente
   - ☐ es su cuñada
   - ☐ es su hermana

Paso 4. Answer the following questions:

¿Te parece buena idea salir con el/la hermano/a de un amigo, o con un amigo de tu hermano/a? ¿Por qué?

Así se forma

4. Indicating location and describing conditions: The verb *estar*

Indicating location of people, places, and things

WILEY PLUS Go to *WileyPLUS* and review the Animated Grammar Tutorial and Verb Conjugator for this grammar point.

You have used the two Spanish verbs that mean *to be*: **ser** and **estar**. So far, you have used **ser** to tell origin, to indicate days of the week, dates, and time, and to describe inherent personality and physical characteristics. You have used **estar** with the expressions **¿Cómo está usted?** and **¿Cómo estás?** When **estar** is used with the preposition **en** (*in, at*), it indicates the location of people, places, or objects.

Study the forms of the present tense of the verb **estar** (*to be*), as well as the sample sentences.

estar (irreg.)		
(yo)	estoy	**Estoy** en la universidad.
(tú)	estás	**¿Estás** en casa?
(usted, él/ella)	está	Acapulco **está** en México.
(nosotros/as)	estamos	**Estamos** en clase.
(vosotros/as)	estáis	**¿Estáis** en el apartamento de Beatriz?
(ustedes, ellos/ellas)	están	Mis amigas **están** en clase.

¿Dónde están?

estar + **en** (*at*) + *location*

el campo	*country*
la ciudad	*city*
el colegio	*school (high school)*
la escuela	*school (elementary school)*
la montaña	*mountain*
la playa	*beach*
el trabajo	*work, workplace*

estar +

allí	*there*
aquí	*here*

HINT

Note that **en** = *in* or *at*;
a = *to*. **Vamos *a* la playa.**
Están *en* la playa.

▲ Mi prima Susana está en el colegio.[1]

◀ Mi hermano Ricardo está en la escuela.

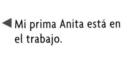

◀ Mi prima Anita está en el trabajo.

Mis tíos están en ▶ su casa.

▲ Mi primo y yo estamos en la playa.

▲ Aquí estoy en las montañas de Colorado.

▲ Estamos en la ciudad de Los Ángeles. ¡Hay mucho tráfico allí!

Estamos en el campo. ▶

---

[1]**El colegio, el liceo,** and **la preparatoria** (Mexico) are words to refer to primary or secondary school (varies by region). Use **universidad** for university or college.

(3-18) ¿Dónde están?

Paso 1. Guess where the following people are according to the information given.

Modelo: Juanito está en clase con su maestra. Tiene seis años.
Está en la escuela.

1. Sandra toma varias clases. Tiene muchos maestros.
2. Tenemos varios profesores. Somos adultos. Las clases son difíciles.
3. Trabajamos desde las 9:00 de la mañana hasta las 5:00 de la tarde.
4. Tomo una siesta. Miro la televisión. Hablo por teléfono.
5. Estás de vacaciones. El océano es muy bonito.
6. Estás de vacaciones. Usas tus suéteres y tus esquís.
7. Los González dicen (*say*) que hay mucho tráfico allí.
8. Los Martínez dicen que hay animales, flores y mucha tranquilidad allí.

 Paso 2. Now tell a classmate where some of the important people in your life are right now.

Modelo: **Mi pareja/Mi mejor amigo/a...**

 ## (3-19) ¿Dónde estás?

Paso 1 Complete the "**Yo**" column in the table below, writing where you are at the indicated times. Then, walk around the classroom asking your classmates where they normally are on these days and times. When someone is at the same place as you, write her/his name in the column labeled "**Mis compañeros**".

Paso 2. Report back to the class about what you found. Do you and your classmates have similar schedules?

Modelo: **Por lo general, ¿dónde estás los lunes a las ocho de la mañana?**

	Yo	Mis compañeros
lunes – 8:00 a.m.		
martes – 9:30 a.m.		
miércoles – 10:45 a.m.		
jueves – 1:30 p.m.		
viernes – 3:00 p.m.		
sábado – 10:00 p.m.		
domingo – 8:00 a.m.		

Describing conditions

Estar can also be used with descriptive words to indicate the mental, emotional, or physical condition in which the subject is found at a given time.

Estoy cansado/a.   *I'm tired.* (physical)
¿Estás preocupado?   *Are you worried?* (mental/emotional)
¡Carlos **está** furioso!   *Carlos is furious!* (emotional).

¿Cómo están?

Rubén

Camila

Octavio

Alfonso

Rubén está **aburrido.**

Camila está **enojada.**

Octavio está muy **cansado.**

¡Pobre Alfonso! Está **enfermo.**

Linda   Manuel

Natalia

Carmen

Linda está **contenta** y **bien.** Pero Manuel está **mal** y **triste.**

Natalia está **ocupada.**

Carmen está **nerviosa, preocupada** y **estresada.**

La puerta y el libro están **cerrados.** La ventana y el cuaderno están **abiertos.**

aburrido/a	*bored*	**mal**	*bad, badly, sick*
bien	*well*	**ocupado/a**	*busy*
contento/a	*happy*	**preocupado/a**	*worried*
enojado/a	*angry*	**triste**	*sad*

NOTA DE LENGUA

Bien and **mal** are adverbs and do not change in gender (masculine/feminine) or number (singular/plural) as adjectives do. **Bien** and **mal** are often used with **estar**. Note the difference between these examples:

Mis padres **están** muy **bien.**   *My parents are very well.*

Mis padres **son** muy **buenos.**   *My parents are very good (people).*

3-20 Condiciones. Read the descriptions below and indicate who they describe from the illustrations on page 90. Then comment on that person's current state.

Modelo: Está en una clase que no le gusta. No quiere prestar atención.
Es Rubén. Está aburrido.

1. Está en la cama. Tiene una temperatura de 102 grados.
2. Está en la oficina, habla por teléfono y toma notas.
3. Está en el gimnasio, juega al básquetbol.
4. Está en la universidad. Tiene un examen muy difícil.
5. Está en su casa. ¡Su novio llega una hora tarde!

3-21 ¿Qué o cuál?

Choose three of the adjectives you just learned in this section and think of a situation in which you would feel each one. Read your situations to a partner. Your partner will try to guess the appropriate adjective.

Modelo: Enojado
Mis amigos no me llaman en mi cumpleaños.

3-22 Nuestro amigo Javier. In small groups, describe what Javier is like (**ser** + *characteristics*) and/or imagine how he is feeling (**estar** + *condition*) according to the circumstances. Use the adjectives provided and others you think of.

cansado	contento	enfermo	estresado	fuerte
inteligente	ocupado	preocupado	trabajador	

Modelo: Javier juega al tenis toda la mañana.
No es perezoso, pero está muy cansado...

1. Saca buenas notas.
2. Va al gimnasio y levanta pesas.
3. Hoy está en la clínica.
4. Toma cinco clases, es voluntario y trabaja en el laboratorio por la noche.
5. Tiene dos exámenes mañana.
6. ¡Marlena, su mejor amiga, llega este fin de semana!

3-23 Así es mi familia. Imagine that a student from Mexico is going to spend a week with your family as part of a student exchange program. Write a letter to him describing your family. Include the family tree you did in Activity 3–7 and complete the information you wrote with more details to describe your family: what your parents, siblings, grandparents, and other relatives are like (**ser** + *characteristics*), as well as origin and nationality, profession, age, physical and personality traits, and any other interesting details. Talk about where they are now and how they are feeling (**estar** + *location/condition*). Conclude by writing about yourself. You might want to add some family photos. Your professor may ask for volunteers to present their work to the class.

> **HINT**
>
> To describe deceased relatives, use **era** (*she/he was*) or **eran** (*they were*). Refer to *Apéndice 3* for a listing of nationalities and professions.

Dicho y hecho

PARA LEER: Enciclopedia del español en los Estados Unidos

ANTES DE LEER

1. De los 45 millones de latinos en Estados Unidos, unos 34,500,000 hablan el español (*American Community Survey*, Censo 2007). Mira la lista a continuación y determina el número en la lista que ocupa Estados Unidos.

Poblaciones más grandes, países hispanohablantes:	
País	**Población**
México	103,263,388
España	45,989,016
Colombia	42,888,592
Argentina	40,134,425
Perú	28,220,764
Venezuela	26,814,843

En este momento, Estados Unidos es el país hispanohablante número _____ en el mundo.

2. Este artículo menciona unas predicciones para el futuro de la población hispanohablante en Estados Unidos. En tu opinión, en el futuro el número de hispanohablantes en este país…

☐ …va a ser **más grande**.

☐ …se va a **reducir**.

ESTRATEGIA DE LECTURA

Cognates are words that look very similar in English and Spanish and have the same meaning. For example, in this reading you will see cognates such as **ciencia** (*science*) and **extinción** (*extinction*). These words can help you significantly in understanding the meaning of the Spanish sentences in which they appear.

However, you have to watch out for false cognates (words that share a similar spelling but which actually mean different things). For example, **actual** in Spanish means *current* in English. Context will help you identify and sort out useful cognates from false cognates.

As you read the following article, circle the cognates you find to see how the English word's meaning can help you understand the Spanish.

A LEER

No es ciencia ficción ni un guión[1] del director Stanley Kubrick: si las predicciones son correctas, en el año 2050 Estados Unidos será el país con mayor número de hispanohablantes con cerca de 132 millones, aún más que el populoso México. En realidad, este país tiene ya un 15% de población latina (cerca de 45 millones) y un crecimiento[2] exponencial por la alta natalidad[3] y la llegada continua de inmigrantes.

Ante esta realidad, el Instituto Cervantes está haciendo un gran esfuerzo para comprender este fenómeno y sus repercusiones sociales y lingüísticas. Por ello[4], Carmen Cafarell, Directora del Instituto Cervantes, presentó en Nueva York la *Enciclopedia del español en los Estados Unidos,* un libro de más de 1,200 páginas.

La Sra. Carafell explicó que este trabajo no representa una oposición al inglés, es simplemente una herramienta[5] para comprender un fenómeno lingüístico apasionante de hoy: la expansión imparable[6] del español en este país[7].

El libro está dividido en 16 capítulos y contiene más de 80 artículos escritos[8] por cerca de 40 prestigiosos expertos. Explora el español en los Estados Unidos desde varias perspectivas: demográfica, legal y política, socio-lingüística, artística y comercial. Un capítulo interesante, por ejemplo, analiza los medios de comunicación, la producción cultural en español y el crecimiento de las compañías hispanas. Otros temas de especial relevancia son el fenómeno del *spanglish* y la existencia de una cultura latina propia de[9] los Estados Unidos – algunos estudiosos[10] consideran Nueva York como la capital cultural de Latinoamérica.

Texto: José Ángel Gonzalo / *Punto y coma*
Foto: Cortesía de Santillana

---

[1] screenplay, [2] growth, [3] birthrate, [4] Thus, [5] tool, [6] unstoppable, [7] country, [8] written, [9] particular to, [10] **algunos...:** some scholars

DESPUÉS DE LEER

1. Say whether the following statements about the *Enciclopedia del Español en los Estados Unidos* are **cierto** or **falso.**

	Cierto	Falso
a. No se opone al inglés.	☐	☐
b. Carmen Cafarell es la directora del libro.	☐	☐
c. Tiene contribuciones de aproximadamente 40 autores.	☐	☐
d. No menciona el *spanglish*.	☐	☐
e. Dice que Nueva York es la capital de Latinoamérica.	☐	☐

2. Match each of the perspectives from which the *Enciclopedia* looks at Spanish in the U.S. with the appropriate example of the type of topic an article might explore.

Perspectivas

_____ Demográfica

_____ Socio-lingüística

_____ Legal y política

_____ Artística

_____ Comercial

Temas

a. Las novelas escritas en español.

b. Las compañías quieren contratar (*hire*) a personas bilingües.

c. El número de hispanos en zonas urbanas vs. rurales.

d. Nuevo México tiene dos lenguas oficiales: el inglés y el español.

e. Las diferencias del español en México y Puerto Rico, por ejemplo.

3. Work with a partner. Choose two or three of the five *Perspectivas* in question 2, and come up with an interesting topic you would choose to explore from each of those perspectives if hired as the writing team for an article in the next edition of the *Enciclopedia.*

Dicho y hecho

PARA CONVERSAR: Las personas especiales

In pairs, you will share two (2) photos of family members, your partner, or friends, describe the people in them, and report to the class about one of your partner's photos.

Paso 1. Write two or three statements about each of your photos, in preparation for your partner's possible questions.

 Paso 2. Exchange your two photos with your partner. Study the photos and think of two or three questions you'd like to ask your partner about each photo. You may jot down quick notes about what you'd like to ask. Then, ask each other your questions, jotting down notes about the answers.

Paso 3. Now present one of your partner's photos to the rest of the class.

EXPRESIONES ÚTILES

¿A qué se dedica?
 What does she/he do?
¿Dónde vive?
¿Cuántos años tiene?
¿Quién es?
¿Qué le gusta hacer?
¿Por qué es especial
 para ti?

ESTRATEGIA DE COMUNICACIÓN

Predicting the type of information you will exchange How does the type of information you would expect to hear vary according to the topic of conversation? Before looking at your classmate's photos, think about how your questions will vary according to whether the photos are of family members, a partner, or friends. If your classmate shows you a photo of siblings, for example, you might want to know how old they are, whereas if your classmate shows you a photo of her/his partner, you might want to know how long they've been together. Based on the photos you are going to share, what questions do you think you can expect from your classmate?

PARA ESCRIBIR: Retrato de familia (*family portrait*)

In this writing assignment, you will produce a description of your family and family life for a distant relative who is doing a genealogy project and documenting your family tree.

ESTRATEGIA DE REDACCIÓN

Organizing: Idea maps Idea maps are also good ways to help you generate ideas and to start organizing your writing. Start by identifying the central topic or idea and placing it in the center of your page. Then, diagram related ideas in connected clusters. You can map out your ideas further by adding more clusters, indicating relationships between them, etc.

Mi familia

amable, divertido — Papá — Mamá

siempre está en su oficina ...

ANTES DE ESCRIBIR

Start your own idea map, in Spanish, with **Mi familia** in the center of the page. Add clusters for your direct relatives. You can also add other relatives you would like to talk about, or a pet. Extend your idea map adding something to say about each member of the family: age, physical descriptions, personality features, where they are, activities they do or you do with them, etc.

A ESCRIBIR

Decide what you would like to say about your family in this written portrait. In this composition, use your idea map as a source for ideas and organization. Try to make it personal and interesting, rather than a mere collection of facts about them. You might want to follow an outline similar to this:

Primer (*first*) párrafo: Introduce the topic by describing your family in one sentence, for instance:

Mi familia es … / Tengo una familia…

Párrafos centrales: Describe your relatives in one or more cohesive paragraphs, for instance:

Mis padres… Mi papá… Y mi mamá…

También tengo _____ hermano/a/os…

Y, para mí, es muy importante mi… porque…

Párrafo final: End your composition with a final thought that sums up who your family is, your feelings about them, etc. Recall that the purpose is to help a distant relative who is doing a genealogy project understand your family. You might begin with:

Por eso, mi familia…

Para escribir mejor:

Here are two connectors that will help you express relationships between ideas in your writing.

porque   *because* — expresses cause
Estoy estresado porque tengo dos exámenes hoy.

por eso   *for that reason, that's why, so* — expresses consequence
Hoy tengo dos exámenes, por eso estoy estresado.

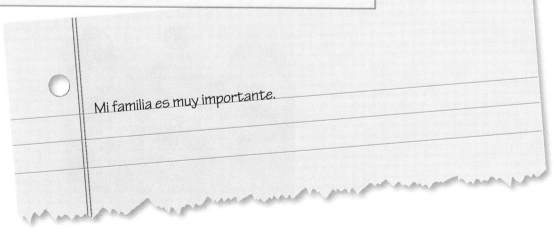

Mi familia es muy importante.

Así es mi familia

Dicho y hecho

Revisar y editar: La organización. Even if the ideas in your composition are interesting and well developed, you have to make sure you convey them clearly and your reader can follow what you are saying. In revising the organization of your composition, ask yourself these questions:

☐ Is my composition easy to read? Is there a logical sequence?

☐ Are the ideas well organized into paragraphs? Is there an appealing introduction? Does it have an effective conclusion?

☐ Do ideas flow easily within each paragraph? Are they well connected? Are there any ideas that should be linked with connecting words?

El contenido y la gramática. Revise your composition for content as well as for general organization. Pay some attention to the grammar you have learned already as well, especially, agreement between nouns, articles and adjectives, and between subjects and verbs, and the use of **ser** and **estar.**

PARA VER Y ESCUCHAR: Todo en familia

ANTES DE VER EL VIDEO

This clip explains the importance of the family in Latino communities, and shows Rocío and Rogelio watching their wedding video with Rocío´s parents. Before you watch it, think about the following questions and try to recall all the relevant vocabulary you know in Spanish.

- Do you spend time with your family? Do you plan family events? What kind of activities do you do together as a family? Who is usually present in those events or activities?

- What do you know about weddings in general? Who celebrates a wedding? Who is usually present in the celebration?

ESTRATEGIA DE COMPRENSIÓN

Using background knowledge to anticipate and interpret Most of the times that you listen to a conversation, lecture, watch TV, etc., you already know something about the topics mentioned and the context of the conversation. Consider what you know about a topic before listening, as well as while you are listening, in order to anticipate what might be mentioned, so that you can better interpret what you hear.

A VER EL VIDEO

Paso 1. Watch the video once, for now, focus on getting the gist of it. How many of the ideas you anticipated did you see or hear mentioned?

Paso 2 Before you watch the clip again, look at the following questions. If you can answer any now, do so. Then watch the clip checking your answers and completing them as needed.

1. ¿Cuántos hijos tienen ahora Rocío y Rogelio?
2. ¿Cómo se sienten los suegros de Rocío?
3. ¿De dónde son los tíos de Rogelio?
4. ¿Cuántos nietos tiene la abuela de Rocío? ¿Y cuántos bisnietos tiene?
5. ¿Cuántos hijos tiene la tía Graciela?

DESPUÉS DE VER EL VIDEO

 In small groups, write a list of the Hispanic celebrations you have learned about in this course as well as others you may know. Do they all have an equivalent in your culture(s)? For those that do, how are they similar or different in each culture?

NOTA CULTURAL

Los hispanos "mixtos"

Mixed Hispanics are common in Latino communities. Someone may have, for instance, a Mexican father and an Ecuadorian mother; a Dominican father and a Colombian mother; or an African American father and a Cuban mother. In Chicago and New York City, there are many *MexiRicans,* who typically have features from both Mexican and Puerto Rican cultures.

La bandera puertorriqueña y la mexicana.

Repaso de vocabulario activo

Adjetivos

abierto/a *open*

(estar) aburrido/a *to be bored*

alto/a *tall*

amable *friendly, kind*

antipático/a *unpleasant*

bajo/a *short*

bonito/a *good looking, pretty/handsome*

bueno/a *good*

cansado/a *tired*

cerrado/a *closed*

contento/a *happy*

débil *weak*

delgado/a *thin*

difícil *difficult*

divertido/a *amusing, fun*

enfermo/a *sick*

enojado/a *angry*

estresado/a *stressed*

fácil *easy*

feo/a *ugly*

flaco/a *skinny*

fuerte *strong*

gordo/a *fat*

grande *big*

guapo/a *good looking, pretty/handsome*

hermoso/a *good looking, pretty/handsome*

inteligente *intelligent*

joven *young*

malo/a *bad*

mayor *old/older*

menor *younger*

moreno/a *dark skinned*

nervioso/a *nervous*

nuevo/a *new*

ocupado/a *busy*

pequeño/a *small*

perezoso/a *lazy*

pobre *poor*

preocupado/a *worried*

responsable *responsible*

rico/a *rich*

rubio/a *blond/e*

simpático/a *nice*

serio/a *serious*

tonto/a *dumb, silly*

trabajador/a *hardworking*

triste *sad*

viejo/a *old*

Adverbios

allí *there*

aquí *here*

bien *well*

mal *badly*

muy *very*

un poco *a little*

Conjunciones

o/u *or*

pero *but*

y/e *and*

Sustantivos

La familia

el abuelo/la abuela *grandfather/grandmother*

los abuelos *grandparents*

el bisabuelo/la bisabuela *great-grandfather/great-grandmother*

el cuñado/la cuñada *brother-in-law/sister-in-law*

el esposo, el marido/la esposa *husband/wife*

el hermano/la hermana *brother/sister*

el hermanastro/la hermanastra *stepbrother/stepsister*

el hijo/la hija *son/daughter*

la madrastra *stepmother*

la madre (mamá) *mother (mom)*

el medio hermano/la media hermana *half-brother/half-sister*

el nieto/la nieta *grandson/granddaughter*

el padrastro *stepfather*

el padre (papá) *father (dad)*

los padres *parents*

el/la pariente *relative*

el primo/la prima *cousin (male/female)*

el sobrino/la sobrina *nephew/niece*

el suegro/la suegra *father-in-law/mother-in-law*

el tío/la tía *uncle/aunt*

Otras personas

el amigo/la amiga *friend (male/female)*

mi mejor amigo/a *my best friend*

el/la bebé *baby*

el chico/la chica *boy/girl*

el hombre *man*

el muchacho/la muchacha *boy/girl*

la mujer *woman*

el niño/la niña *boy/girl*

el novio/la novia *boyfriend/girlfriend*

mi pareja *my partner, significant other*

Las mascotas *Pets*

el gato *cat*

el perro *dog*

Las cosas y los lugares *Things and places*

el auto *car*

el campo *country, countryside*

el carro *car*

la ciudad *city*

el coche *car*

el colegio *school*

la escuela *school*

la montaña *mountain*

la playa *beach*

el trabajo *work*

Verbos y expresiones verbales

abrazar *to hug*

amar *to love*

besar *to kiss*

cuidar *to take care of*

estar (irreg.) *to be*

llamar *to call*

tener (irreg.) *to have*

tener... años *to be . . . years old*

¿Cuántos años tienes? *How old are you?*

visitar *to visit*

Palabras interrogativas

¿Cuántos/as? *How many?*

¿Dónde? *Where?*

¿Quién/es? *Who?*

Autoprueba y repaso

I. The verb *tener*. Use the correct form of **tener**.

1. Yo _____ tres hermanos.
2. Mi hermano mayor _____ 21 años.
3. Mis padres _____ 55 años.
4. Mi hermano menor y yo _____ un perro.
5. ¿Cuántos años _____ tú?

II. Possessive adjectives. Use possessive adjectives to explain what each person has.

Modelo: mi hermano / cuadernos
   Tiene sus cuadernos.

1. yo / fotos
2. ¿tú / libros?
3. José / diccionario
4. mi hermano y yo / televisor
5. ¿ustedes / calculadoras?

III. Possession with *de*. Indicate to whom each object belongs.

Modelo: la mochila / Juan
   Es la mochila de Juan.

1. la foto / Marta
2. los cuadernos / José
3. los exámenes / los estudiantes

IV. Descriptive adjectives. Complete the first sentence in each item with the correct form of the verb **ser**. Then complete the second sentence with the correct form of **ser** and the adjective of opposite meaning.

Modelo: Mi tío Paco **es** un poco gordo. Por el contrario, mi tía Lisa **es delgada.**

1. Yo _____ trabajador/a. Por el contrario, algunos de mis amigos _____.
2. Mis padres _____ muy altos. Por el contrario, mi hermano _____.
3. Nosotros no _____ antipáticos. Por el contrario, _____ muy _____.
4. Nuestra clase de español _____ fácil. Por el contrario, nuestras clases de ciencias _____.

V. *Estar* to indicate location. Tell where on campus the students are located according to the activity.

Modelo: Juana estudia mucho
   Está en la biblioteca.

1. Linda y Mónica compran lápices, bolígrafos y sus libros de texto.
2. Octavio y yo hacemos ejercicio.
3. Hablo con mis amigos y compro comida.
4. Mi amiga habla con la profesora Falcón. No están en el aula.

VI. *Estar* to indicate condition. React to the statements with forms of **estar** and appropriate adjectives.

Modelo: Tenemos un problema.
   Estamos preocupados.

1. Tengo un examen mañana.
2. Mis amigos tienen mucha tarea.
3. Sancho tiene apendicitis.
4. ¡Tenemos un día sin (*without*) preocupaciones! ¡No hay clases!

VII. General review. Answer the following questions.

1. ¿Cuántos años tienes?
2. ¿Cómo es tu madre/padre?
3. ¿Cómo son tus amigos/as?
4. ¿Cómo están tus amigos/as?
5. ¿Están tú y tus amigos preocupados por sus notas? ¿En qué materias (*subjects*)?
6. ¿Qué días tienen ustedes clases?
7. ¿Cómo son sus clases?

VIII. *Cultura*.

1. ¿Cuáles son algunas características de la familia tradicional hispana?
2. ¿Qué porcentaje de la población de Estados Unidos es de origen hispano? ¿En qué zonas vive la mayoría de ellos?

Answers to the *Autoprueba y repaso* are found in **Apéndice 2.**

¡A la mesa!

Así se dice

¡A la mesa!
Las comidas y las bebidas
   ¿Cuál es tu preferencia?
   Tengo hambre

Así se forma

1. The verb *gustar*
2. Stem-changing verbs
3. Counting from 100 and indicating the year
4. Interrogative words (A summary)

Cultura

- México
- Las comidas en el mundo hispano

Dicho y hecho

Para leer:
Pedro y la fábrica de chocolate

Para conversar:
¿Qué comemos?

Para escribir:
Comer en la universidad

Para ver y escuchar:
La comida hispana

By the end of this chapter you will be able to:

- Buy and talk about food in a market, restaurant, etc.
- Express likes and dislikes. Talk about actions, desires, and preferences in the present
- Express large quantities, prices, and dates
- Ask for specific information

ENTRANDO AL TEMA

1. Which factors do you think most strongly influence your eating habits in general: cost, time, flavor, health, family, etc?

2. What Hispanic foods or dishes have you tried? Have you heard of any that you would like to try?

Así se dice

¡A la mesa!

Mercado Central

Frutas

Mariscos

¿Cuánto **cuestan**?

¿Qué **desea**, señor?

Necesitamos fresas.
Vamos a **comprar** un kilo.

el pescado

las piñas

las bananas/
los plátanos

la langosta   los camarones

las manzanas

las uvas

las sandías

las naranjas

las peras

las fresas

los limones

las cerezas

los melocotones/
los duraznos

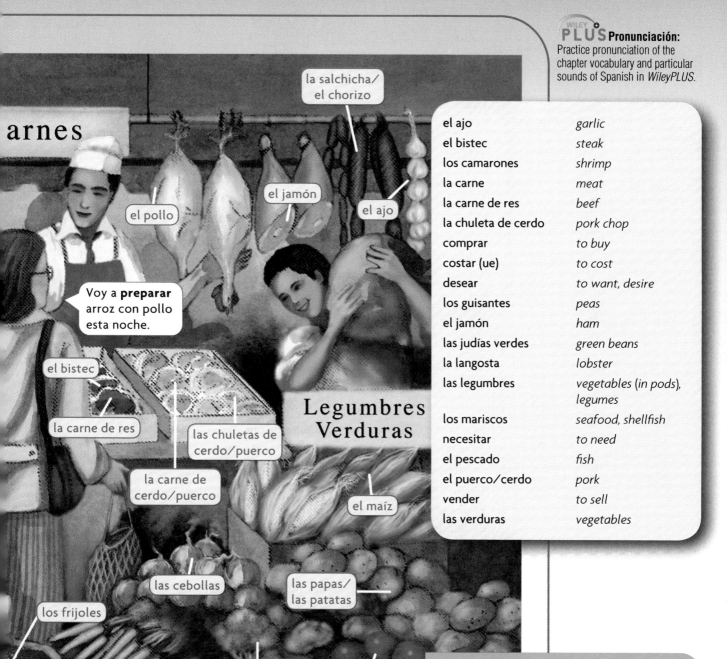

la salchicha/
el chorizo

arnes

el pollo

el jamón

el ajo

Voy a **preparar**
arroz con pollo
esta noche.

el bistec

la carne de res

las chuletas de
cerdo/puerco

la carne de
cerdo/puerco

Legumbres
Verduras

el maíz

las cebollas

las papas/
las patatas

los frijoles

las zanahorias

el brócoli

los tomates

las lechugas

el arroz

los guisantes

las judías verdes

el ajo	*garlic*
el bistec	*steak*
los camarones	*shrimp*
la carne	*meat*
la carne de res	*beef*
la chuleta de cerdo	*pork chop*
comprar	*to buy*
costar (ue)	*to cost*
desear	*to want, desire*
los guisantes	*peas*
el jamón	*ham*
las judías verdes	*green beans*
la langosta	*lobster*
las legumbres	*vegetables (in pods), legumes*
los mariscos	*seafood, shellfish*
necesitar	*to need*
el pescado	*fish*
el puerco/cerdo	*pork*
vender	*to sell*
las verduras	*vegetables*

NOTA CULTURAL

Las variaciones del español

There are many varieties of Spanish, and many words vary from one region to another. This variety is obvious, for instance, in the different words used for foods in different parts of the Hispanic world. Some examples from the vocabulary on the left are: **patatas** and **papas**; **plátano**, **banana** and **guineo**, but there are many more. Notice, for example, the many names for green beans in Spanish-speaking countries: **judías verdes**, **ejotes**, **habichuelas**, **chauchas**, and **porotos verdes**.

4-1 **¿Vegetariano o no?** Listen to the following food items and decide whether a vegetarian person would eat them or not. Write the names of the foods in the appropriate column.

NOTA CULTURAL

El vegetarianismo

While somewhere between 4 and 7% of people in the United States are vegetarians, with increasing access to animal-free products, such diets are not as common in Spanish-speaking countries.

	Sí, una persona vegetariana come esto.	No, una persona vegetariana no come esto.
1.	☐	☐
2.	☐	☐
3.	☐	☐
4.	☐	☐
5.	☐	☐
6.	☐	☐
7.	☐	☐
8.	☐	☐

4-2 **¿Cómo se dice?** Read these descriptions and identify the food they are referring to. Then indicate whether you like each one or not.

	Sí	No
1. Es una fruta ovalada muy grande, verde por fuera (*green outside*) y roja por dentro (*red inside*).	☐	☐
2. Son frutas pequeñas. Vienen en racimos (*bunches*) y son moradas (*purple*) o verdes.	☐	☐
3. Es de carne molida (*ground*) y tiene forma de cilindro.	☐	☐
4. Es una verdura de granos pequeños, generalmente amarillos (*yellow*) o blancos (*white*) y tiernos (*tender*).	☐	☐
5. Es una verdura blanca con sabor (*flavor*) muy fuerte que se usa para sazonar muchos platos.	☐	☐
6. Es un animal marino con tenazas (*pincers*). Su carne es cara.	☐	☐
7. Son granos pequeños y blancos. Son perfectos con frijoles.	☐	☐
8. Es una fruta cítrica pequeña, amarilla y ácida.	☐	☐

Ingredientes:
duraznos
judías verdes
pollo
fresas
uvas
cerezas
frijoles
zanahorias
pescado
carne de res
papas
peras
cebolla

4-3 **Una cena en casa.** You and your friend are going to a potluck party, and you need to prepare the following dishes. Decide who is going to prepare each one.

Una sopa de pollo   Una ensalada de frutas

Paso 1. Individually, write the ingredients you need for your dish. Then, read your list to your partner, who might offer other ideas. Use ingredients from the list on the left and any others you wih to add.

Una sopa de pollo

Una ensalada de frutas

Paso 2. Each of you has some ingredients at home, as described below. Underline any ingredients you can use for your dish.

Estudiante A: Tienes en casa cebolla, ajo, duraznos y cerezas.

Estudiante B: Tienes en casa fresas, uvas, pasta y papas.

Then write the ingredients you still need in the left column of the table. Finally, ask your friend whether s/he has them.

Modelo: Estudiante A: **¿Tienes zanahorias?**
Estudiante B: **No, no tengo zanahorias.**

Otros ingredientes que necesito	¿Mi amigo tiene este ingrediente?
	☐ Sí ☐ No
	☐ Sí ☐ No
	☐ Sí ☐ No

Are there any ingredients you need that neither you or your friend have? Write a shopping list of what you need to buy at the store.

NOTA CULTURAL

El mercado

While supermarkets and grocery stores are very common in Latin America and in Spain, some people still prefer to shop at traditional markets, or **mercados**.

4-4   Chef Merito.

Paso 1. Look at the image on page 107.

1. Based on its format and visuals, it probably is…
   - ☐ a scientific article.
   - ☐ a brochure.
   - ☐ an ad.
   - ☐ an excerpt from a novel.

2. It is probably about…
   - ☐ a restaurant.
   - ☐ healthy eating.
   - ☐ a brand of spices.
   - ☐ a supermarket.

Paso 2. Look for cognates in the text and write them down:

_____

Paso 3. Skim for general content focusing on cognates and other words you understand, and write a sentence to summarize the main idea in this ad.

Paso 4. Look at the tasks below and read the ad again. Then, write your answers where appropriate.

1. Identifica las carnes y las legumbres del anuncio.
2. Indica las cualidades de los productos de Chef Merito, según el anuncio (*according to the ad*).
   - ☐ Son baratos (*cheap*).
   - ☐ Son fáciles (*easy*) de usar.
   - ☐ Tienen garantía de calidad.
   - ☐ Son variados.
   - ☐ Son orgánicos.
   - ☐ Son auténticos.

Paso 5. ¿Y ustedes?

1. ¿Usan ustedes salsa picante? ¿En qué comidas?
2. ¿Qué sazonadores (*seasonings*) usan ustedes para preparar sus comidas favoritas? ¿Qué sazonadores del Chef Merito desean comprar?

INVESTIG@ EN INTERNET

Busca en Internet el sitio de Chef Merito. ¿Qué producto es nuevo para ti (*for you*)? ¿Qué producto deseas probar (*try*)?

El pollo, la carne, o el pescado más exquisito, Usted lo prepara con Chef Merito...

Con los productos **Chef Merito**, Usted no tiene que saber cocinar. Con recetas en cada frasco, **Chef Merito** le ayuda a preparar cualquier platillo. **Chef Merito** tiene un Sazonador para cada ocasión y la **mejor auténtica Salsa Picante.** Todos los productos **Chef Merito** tienen sellos protectores y fechas de expiración para garantizar el buen sabor y calidad. Recuerde...**con Chef Merito en la sartén, cualquiera cocina bien**.

Pídalo en su tienda favorita o llame al **800-MERITO-1** o visítenos en www.chefmerito.com.

▲ *CHEF MERITO INC. & CHEF MERITO* are Trademark owned by Chef Merito, Inc., a California Corp.

Así se forma

Sí, me gustan mucho.

¿Te gustan los plátanos?

Octavio

Inés

WILEY PLUS Go to *WileyPLUS* and review the Animated Grammar Tutorial and Verb Conjugator for this grammar point.

1. Expressing likes and dislikes: The verb *gustar*

Read the following dialog between Octavio and Inés. Pay attention to the forms of **gustar**.

INÉS: ¿**Te gusta** (*Do you like*) la comida de la cafetería de la universidad?

OCTAVIO: Sí, **me gusta** (*I like it*) mucho.

INÉS: ¿De veras? A mí **no me gusta** para nada y a mi compañera de cuarto **no le gusta** (*doesn't like it*) tampoco (*either*).

OCTAVIO: ¿Por qué no **les gusta**?

INÉS: No **nos gusta** porque no es nutritiva ni muy sabrosa (*tasty*).

OCTAVIO: Pero esta sopa de champiñones (*mushrooms*) está deliciosa. **Me gusta** muchísimo.

INÉS: Sí, está deliciosa y **me gustan** mucho los champiñones, pero el problema es ¡que no tiene champiñones!

OCTAVIO: ¡Qué horror! ¿Qué son entonces (*then*)?

INÉS: ¿Quién sabe (*knows*)?

Spanish expresses likes and dislikes with the verb **gustar**, which literally means *to be pleasing* (*to someone*).

Spanish expression with *gustar*	English equivalent	Literal Translation
Me gusta el helado.	I like ice cream.	Ice cream is pleasing to me.
¿Te gustan las fresas?	Do you like strawberries?	Are strawberries pleasing to you?
No le gusta tomar vino.	He doesn't like to drink wine.	Drinking wine is not pleasing to him.

As you can see in the examples, the subject pronouns (**yo, tú, él...**) are not used with **gustar**. To express who is doing the liking (or literally, to whom something is pleasing), the forms **me, te, le, nos, os,** and **les** are used[1]. The verb takes the singular form **gusta** when the thing that is pleasing is a single item and the plural form **gustan** when the thing liked is plural.

Person(s) who like	+	gusta(n)	+	thing(s) liked
me				el helado
te		gusta		la fruta
le				comer
nos				las uvas
os		gustan		las fresas
les				los camarones

---

[1] The indirect-object pronouns, meaning *to me, to you, to you/him/her, to us, to you, to you/them*, will be studied in detail in **Capítulo 7**.

TO like   possesive

me   MI
Te   +U
le   SU
nos   nuestro(a
les   SU

- The definite article is used with the thing/things liked:

  Me gusta **el** helado.   *I like ice cream.*
  Me gustan **las** fresas.   *I like strawberries.*

- If what is pleasing is an activity or a series of activities, use the singular form **gusta** with the infinitive (**–ar, –er, –ir** form) of the appropriate verb(s):

  Nos **gusta** <u>comer</u>.   *We like to eat.*

  Les **gusta** <u>cenar</u> en restaurantes y   *They like to have dinner in restaurants and*
  asistir a conciertos.   *attend concerts.*

- To clarify the meaning of **le** and **les**, add **a** + person: **a Pedro, a ella, a las niñas, a ellos,** etc.:

  Pedro y Ana toman el desayuno   *Pedro and Ana have breakfast together.*
  juntos.
  A **Pedro** <u>le</u> gusta tomar café, pero   *Pedro likes to drink coffee, but she likes tea.*
  a ella <u>le</u> gusta el té.

- For emphasis, add **a mí, a ti, a usted, a nosotros,** etc.:

  A mí no me gustan los camarones.   *I don't like shrimp.*
  A ti te gustan, ¿verdad?   *You like them, right?*

- To ask a follow-up question, use: **¿Y a ti? ¿Y a usted? ¿Y a él?**, etc.

(4-5) **¡Me gusta!** You will hear a series of statements. Decide which food item is being talked about in each one.

Modelo: You hear: Me gusta.
         You choose: ☐ los limones   ☒ el ajo

1. ☐ las zanahorias   ☐ el pescado
2. ☐ la lechuga   ☐ las fresas
3. ☐ las cerezas   ☐ el jamón
4. ☐ el bistec   ☐ las naranjas
5. ☐ las peras   ☐ la langosta
6. ☐ el pollo   ☐ los camarones

(4-6) **Y a ti, ¿te gusta?** Write sentences with information that is true for you, paying attention to the appropriate form of the verb.

Modelo: las peras
         Las peras me gustan muchísimo / no me gustan para nada / etc.

1. la sopa de verduras   5. la ensalada de frutas
2. los camarones   6. comer carne
3. beber agua   7. ir al mercado
4. el ajo   8. los guisantes

4-7 **¿A quién le gusta?** Read the following statements or questions and decide who is being referred to.

Modelo: Le gusta la langosta.
☐ A ellos   ☒ A ella

1. Te gustan los tomates.   ☐ A ti   ☐ A él
2. Les gusta mucho el pescado.   ☐ A Carmen y a Ana   ☐ A nosotros
3. Le gustan los plátanos.   ☐ A ustedes   ☐ A Jorge
4. Nos gusta la piña.   ☐ A nosotros   ☐ A ellos
5. ¿Le gusta el ajo?   ☐ A usted   ☐ A ti
6. Me gusta el maíz.   ☐ A Elena   ☐ A mí

4-8 **Una cena con los amigos.** You want to have your friends Luis, Óscar and Andrea over for a Mexican inspired dinner, so you call Luis to find out what they like. Complete the dialogue with the appropriate pronouns (**me/te/le/nos/os/les**) and **gustar** forms.

TÚ: Hola Luis, voy a preparar una cena para los amigos el sábado, y tengo algunas ideas. Por ejemplo, ¿a ti _____ los camarones?

LUIS: Sí, a mí los mariscos _____ mucho. Pero a Óscar no _____. Bueno, en realidad, tiene alergia.

TÚ: Uy, no, no, entonces el ceviche de mariscos no es buena idea. ¿Y a vosotros _____ la sopa de tortilla?

LUIS: Sí, a Óscar y a mí _____ mucho.

TÚ: Muy bien. ¿Y el pescado, _____?

LUIS: Bueno, creo que a Óscar y Andrea sí _____, pero a mí no _____ mucho. ¿Por qué no preparas pollo en mole? A Óscar y Andrea _____ muchísimo.

TÚ: Y a ti, ¿también (*also*) _____?

LUIS: Sí, sí, especialmente con arroz y frijoles.

TÚ: Bueno, a mí no _____ los frijoles mucho, pero no hay problema. Voy a preparar guacamole también. Y después, ¿crema de mango?

LUIS: ¡Uhm, delicioso! El mango _____ a todos.

▲ Ceviche de mariscos

▲ Pollo en mole

4-9 **En la universidad.**

Paso 1. First, answer the questions about yourself in the column **A mí** in the table on page 111 and fill in the last two questions about additional food items that you choose. Then, use the questions to interview a classmate. Ask for more details and take notes.

Modelo: Estudiante A: **¿Te gustan las clases este semestre?**
Estudiante B: **Sí.**
Estudiante A: **¿Qué clases tomas? ¿Te gustan todas?**
Estudiante B: **Casi todas. Me gustan las clases de español y biología, pero no me gusta mucho la clase de química.**

	A mí		A mi compañero/a _____	
1. ¿Te gusta la universidad?	☐ Sí	☐ No	☐ Sí	☐ No
2. ¿Te gustan las clases este semestre?	☐ Sí	☐ No	☐ Sí	☐ No
3. ¿Te gustan los profesores?	☐ Sí	☐ No	☐ Sí	☐ No
4. ¿Te gustan los edificios (*buildings*) de la universidad?	☐ Sí	☐ No	☐ Sí	☐ No
5. ¿Te gusta estudiar en la biblioteca?	☐ Sí	☐ No	☐ Sí	☐ No
6. ¿Te gusta aprender español?	☐ Sí	☐ No	☐ Sí	☐ No
7. ¿ _____ ?	☐ Sí	☐ No	☐ Sí	☐ No
8. ¿ _____ ?	☐ Sí	☐ No	☐ Sí	☐ No

Paso 2. How much do you have in common? Write a short paragraph comparing and contrasting your likes and dislikes. Don't forget the **a** where needed.

Modelo: **A nosotros nos gusta mucho la universidad. A Cristina le gustan las clases de español y biología. A mí también me gusta la clase de…**

4-10 Preguntas para tu profesor/a.

Paso 1. First, in pairs, make guesses about what your instructor likes to do in the column **A nuestro/a profesor/a…** in the chart. Add an item in the last row.

	A nuestro/a profesor/a…	Detalles (*Details*)
1.	Le gusta / No le gusta leer novelas.	¿Qué tipo? ¿Cuál es su novela favorita?
2.	Le gusta / No le gusta cenar en restaurantes.	¿Qué tipo de comida? ¿Cómo se llama su restaurante favorito?
3.	Le gusta / No le gusta mirar la televisión.	¿Qué tipos de programas mira? ¿Qué programa no le gusta?
4.	Le gusta / No le gusta asistir a conciertos.	¿Qué tipo de música? ¿Qué cantantes o grupos musicales son sus favoritos?
5.	Le gusta / No le gusta usar Internet.	¿Con mucha frecuencia? ¿Envía mensajes electrónicos, navega por Internet… ?
6.	Le gusta / No le gusta _____ .	¿ _____ ?

Paso 2. Now, take turns asking your instructor whether she/he likes to do those things and follow up with the questions in the column **Detalles** or others of your own. Be sure to note her/his answers. How well do you know your instructor? Did you guess correctly?

Modelo: **¿Le gusta leer novelas? ¿Qué tipo?**

Paso 3. In small groups, discuss how your instructor's likes and dislikes compare with your own.

Principales tipos de clima de México

- ☐ Cálido húmedo
- ■ Cálido subhúmedo
- ☐ Seco
- ☐ Muy seco
- ☐ Templado subhúmedo
- ■ Templado húmedo

Tijuana · Mexicali
Ciudad Juárez
Hermosillo
Chihuahua
Torreón · Monterrey
La Paz · Culiacán
MÉXICO
Golfo Mexicano
Durango · Ciudad Victoria
Mazatlán · Tampico
Océano Pacífico
Aguascalientes · San Luis Potosí
Cancún
Guadalajara
Mérida
México
Morelia · Veracruz
Netzahualcoyotl · Puebla
Villahermosa
Acapulco · Oaxaca

Nacionalidad: mexicano/a

Antes de leer

1. Which indigenous people lived in Mexico before the Spanish arrived?

   ☐ Mayans   ☐ Aztecs   ☐ Olmecs   ☐ All of these, plus many others

2. How many languages are spoken in Mexico today?

   ☐ One   ☐ Approximately 20   ☐ Approximately 60

3. True or false: Mexico's climate is very hot all year round.

   ☐ True   ☐ False

PLUS Map quizzes: As you read about places highlighted in red, find them on the map. Learn more about and test yourself on the geography of the Spanish-speaking world in *WileyPLUS*.

UN TERRITORIO DIVERSO

México es un país (*country*) muy diverso. En el norte del país, incluyendo a **Monterrey**, **Chihuahua** y **Hermosillo**, hace frío (*it's cold*) en invierno. El centro del país, que incluye **Aguascalientes**, **San Luís Potosí**, **Puebla** y **la Ciudad de México**, es una vasta región de valles, donde el clima no es muy frío (*cold*) ni muy caluroso (*warm*). La región centro-oeste, incluyendo **Guadalajara** y **Mazatlán**, es una zona muy fértil con mucha agricultura y ganadería (*cattle ranching*). En el sureste, por ejemplo en **Cancún**, hay mucho turismo.

Ciudad	enero		abril		julio		octubre	
	Máx	Min	Máx	Min	Máx	Min	Máx	Min
Acapulco	87	72	87	73	89	77	89	77
México, D.F.	66	42	77	51	73	53	70	50

Máx = temperatura máxima; Min = temperatura mínima.

LA HISTORIA

México tiene una de las poblaciones indígenas más numerosas de Latinoamérica. En el pasado, existían muchos grupos diversos como los olmecas, los totonacos, los mayas y los aztecas. Cada grupo hablaba un idioma diferente. Hoy, todavía (*still*) existen unos 60 de estos idiomas en el territorio mexicano.

Cuando llegaron los conquistadores españoles, los aztecas eran el grupo dominante. Controlaban 371 grupos indígenas diferentes en 33 provincias y todos hablaban la lengua náhuatl. La capital azteca, Tenochtitlán, era una ciudad de puentes (*bridges*) y canales en medio de un lago (*lake*). Tenía una población de 300,000 personas y era uno de los centros urbanos más grandes del mundo.

En el año 1500, las poblaciones aproximadas de estas ciudades eran:	
Beijing	600,000
El Cairo	400,000
Tenochtitlán	**300,000**
Constantinopla	200,000
París	200,000
Venecia	115,000
Londres	50,000

Cuando el español Hernán Cortés llegó a Tenochtitlán en 1519, el emperador era Moctezuma. Cortés era muy blanco y tenía barba (*beard*) y algunos historiadores imaginan que los aztecas identificaron a Cortés con el dios (*god*) llamado Quetzalcóatl, y le dieron una gran bienvenida (*welcome*). Pero Cortés conquistó a los aztecas en 1521 con la importante ayuda de La Malinche, quien sirvió de intérprete entre los españoles y los varios grupos indígenas.

◀ Moctezuma y Cortés

▲ La Malinche, intérprete y esposa de Cortés. Es considerada "la Madre del México moderno" porque sus hijos con Cortés representan la primera mezcla de españoles con indígenas.

Ciudad flotante de Tenochtitlán

Quetzalcóatl

LA CAPITAL

Hoy, el antiguo Tenochtitlán es todavía la capital del país, pero se llama la Ciudad de México, el Distrito Federal, el D.F., o simplemente México. Actualmente (*currently*) el D.F. tiene una población de 21 millones de personas y es la tercera (*third*) ciudad del mundo (*world*) en número de personas después de Tokio y Mumbai. La cultura indígena es visible en los murales que decoran la capital y en las caras (*faces*) de muchos de los habitantes. En las avenidas del centro de la ciudad hay tiendas (*stores*), restaurantes, teatros y hoteles elegantes.

▲ Paseo de la Reforma con vistas al Angel de la Independencia por la noche

Mural en el Palacio Nacional de la Ciudad de México, México – Tenochtitlán, capital azteca ▶

EL TURISMO

México tiene muchos lugares interesantes para visitar. Los pueblos coloniales como Taxco, Guanajuato y Cuernavaca conservan hermosos edificios del siglo XVI. También hay playas famosas como Cancún y Puerto Vallarta, y otras playas (*beaches*) espectaculares como Playa del Carmen, Ixtapa/Zihuatanejo y Huatulco.

▲ Antes, Tenochtitlán

Ahora, la Ciudad de México ▶

Taxco

LA ECONOMÍA

México es la tercera economía más importante de América, después de Estados Unidos y Brasil. El petróleo es la industria principal de México. El turismo es la segunda industria del país y la tercera fuente de ingresos (*income*) son las remesas: el dinero que envían (*send*) a México los mexicanos y mexicano-americanos que viven y trabajan en los Estados Unidos. En el año 2005, el total de las remesas fue de unos 18,000 millones[1] (*eighteen billion*) de dólares.

Con el Tratado de Libre Comercio entre Estados Unidos, México y Canadá (*NAFTA, 1994*), la frontera entre Tijuana y Matamoros es una región cada vez más (*increasingly*) fundamental para el comercio y la industria. Muchas fábricas maquiladoras (*assembly plants*) en las ciudades fronterizas con México emplean a un millón de mexicanos y millones de individuos vienen a buscar empleo en Estados Unidos. Mexicanos y estadounidenses cruzan los puentes fronterizos constantemente para ir de compras (*shopping*).

[1] **Mil millones** is *one billion* in Spanish.

▲ Paso entre Tijuana y San Diego

Después de leer

1. Go back to the questions in **Antes de leer**. Do you want to change any of your answers?

2. Put the following industries in the order of economic importance in Mexico today.

   _____ tourism
   _____ remittances from abroad
   _____ oil

3. Take a close look at the flag of Mexico. What animal does it contain that is also an important national symbol in the United States?

4. Consider the role of La Malinche (look up further details on the Internet if you wish). Do you know of an indigenous woman in United States history who also played an important role as a language interpreter?

La "Riviera maya"

VideoEscenas: ¿La nueva cocina?

▲ Paloma y Pedro pasean por la tarde, quieren tomar algo
y deciden entrar en un restaurante de "nueva cocina".

Paso 1. Answer these questions before you watch the video.

1. What types of cuisine and specific dishes do you like best when you eat out?
2. What is the strangest thing you have eaten?
3. What do you think "new cuisine" could be like?

Paso 2. Watch the video paying attention to the main ideas and indicate which of the following statements are true (**cierto**) or false (**falso**).

	Cierto	Falso
1. Paloma y Pedro quieren (*want*) cenar.	☐	☐
2. El restaurante sirve cocina tradicional.	☐	☐
3. A Paloma le gusta su postre.	☐	☐
4. Pedro piensa (*thinks*) que su helado va a ser muy bueno.	☐	☐

Paso 3. Look at the questions below and watch the video again. This time focus on the specific information you need to answer the questions. You may take notes as you listen.

1. ¿Qué quieren tomar Paloma y Pedro?
2. ¿Por qué quiere entrar Paloma en este restaurante?
3. ¿De qué manera son inusuales los postres de Paloma y Pedro?
4. ¿Cómo reacciona Pedro a la "nueva cocina" de este restaurante?

Paso 4. In small groups, share your opinions.

 ¿Quieres probar (*try*) este tipo de "nueva cocina"? ¿Por qué sí o por qué no?

Así se forma

2. Talking about actions, desires, and preferences in the present: Stem-changing verbs

Stem-changing (irregular) verbs have the same endings as regular –ar, –er, and –ir verbs. They differ from regular verbs in that a change occurs in the stem vowel (e→ie, o→ue, or e→i) in all persons except **nosotros** and **vosotros**. The stem is the part of the verb that remains after the –ar, –er, or –ir ending is removed.

Study the pattern of change in the following model verbs. Note that anytime a stem-changing verb is presented, the stem change will be listed in the entry in parenthesis, as in the examples below:

Rubén, ¿quieres cenar en un restaurante con nosotras esta noche?

Prefiero cenar solo, gracias.

¡Ay, ay, ay!

e → ie

querer *to want, to love* quer- → quier-	
qu**ie**ro	queremos
qu**ie**res	queréis
qu**ie**re	qu**ie**ren

querer (ie)	*to want, to love*	No **quiero** comer ahora.
preferir (ie)	*to prefer*	**Prefiero** comer más tarde.
entender (ie)	*to understand*	¿**Entienden** el problema?
pensar[1] (ie)	*to think*	¿**Piensas** que hay un problema?

WILEY **PLUS** Go to *WileyPLUS* and review the Animated Grammar Tutorial and Verb Conjugator for this grammar point.

o → ue

dormir *to sleep* dorm- → duerm-	
d**ue**rmo	dormimos
d**ue**rmes	dormís
d**ue**rme	d**ue**rmen

dormir (ue)	*to sleep*	¿**Duermes** bien?
almorzar (ue)	*to have lunch*	¿A qué hora **almuerzas**?
poder (ue)	*to be able*	¿**Puedes** cenar a las 7:00?
volver (ue)	*to return, go back*	¿A qué hora **vuelves** a la casa?

e → i

pedir *to ask for* ped- → pid-	
p**i**do	pedimos
p**i**des	pedís
p**i**de	p**i**den

pedir (i)	*to ask for, request, order*	Ella siempre **pide** pizza.
servir (i)	*to serve, to be good (for something)*	¿**Sirven** langosta aquí? Esta cebolla **sirve** para la sopa.

DICHOS

Querer es poder.

¿Puedes explicar este dicho en español?

[1]When seeking an opinion, ask **¿Qué piensas de... ?** (*What do you think about . . . ?*). When giving your opinion, say **Pienso que...** (*I think that . . .*).

4-11 La confesión de Esteban.

Paso 1. Read the following paragraph, paying special attention to the stem-changing verbs.

Sí, es verdad. Soy un poco glotón —bueno, muy glotón. Muchos estudiantes comen cereales por la mañana, pero yo pref**ie**ro tomar un desayuno más... tradicional, con huevos (*eggs*) y tocino (*bacon*). Por la tarde alm**ue**rzo una hamburguesa con papas y un refresco. Después v**ue**lvo a mi cuarto y d**ue**rmo la siesta. Antes de hacer la tarea, tomo café y unas galletas (*cookies*) para estar más despierto. No p**ue**do estudiar cuando no tomo un café, p**ie**nso que necesito tomar cafeína. Generalmente, ceno en la cafetería de la universidad. La comida no es muy variada pero siempre s**ir**ven pizza, pollo frito y p**ue**do comer todo lo que qu**ie**ro. Verdaderamente p**ie**nso que no está mal. No ent**ie**ndo a esas personas que siempre hacen dietas y p**ie**nsan en la nutrición todo el día y ¡no qu**ie**ren comer estas cosas tan buenas!

¿Cierto o falso? Cover the paragraph and decide whether the following statements are true or false. If they are false, correct them.

		Cierto	Falso
1.	Esteban pref**ie**re un desayuno ligero (*light*).	☐	☐
2.	Esteban alm**ue**rza comida rápida (*fast food*).	☐	☐
3.	Después de almorzar, v**ue**lve a la universidad.	☐	☐
4.	Esteban nunca d**ue**rme la siesta.	☐	☐
5.	P**ie**nsa que la cafeína es buena para él.	☐	☐

Paso 2. Complete what Esteban says using appropriate forms of the verbs provided. Use all the verbs at least once. You will have to use some verbs more than once.

almorzar	poder	preferir	servir
entender	pensar	volver	querer

Me gusta mucho comer y _____ en comer todo el tiempo (*all the time*). ¿Qué _____ hacer? Todos (nosotros) _____ la comida de nuestras madres, claro, pero a muchos estudiantes no les gusta la comida de la cafetería y no _____ comer allí. (Ellos) _____ que en la cafetería no _____ muchas verduras y frutas frescas. No _____ el problema, la pizza tiene tomate, ¿no? Y las hamburguesas también tienen tomate y lechuga y cebolla... Además, hay otras opciones diferentes. Por ejemplo, muchos estudiantes _____ en restaurantes de comida rápida. Si (tú) _____, _____ comer en uno diferente todos los días de la semana. En mi opinión, la comida en la universidad no está mal. Pero, la verdad, cuando _____ a mi casa, la comida me gusta mucho más.

Paso 3. Write a short paragraph comparing yourself to Esteban. Be careful to make the stem changes in the **yo** and **él** (Esteban) forms, but to keep the original vowel in the **nosotros** forms.

Modelo: **Esteban y yo somos (muy) similares/diferentes. Nosotros preferimos tomar un desayuno... / Él almuerza comida rápida y yo almuerzo en mi casa....**

4-12 Sondeo alimentario.

Paso 1. Answer the questions below about yourself.

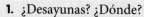

1. ¿Desayunas? ¿Dónde?
2. ¿Dónde almuerzas?
3. ¿Dónde prefieres cenar durante la semana?
4. ¿Qué piensas de las cafeterías y los restaurantes universitarios?
   a. son buenos
   b. son malos
   c. son mediocres
5. En general, ¿qué piensas de la "comida rápida" en el campus?
   a. es mala
   b. es buena
   c. es mediocre
6. ¿Qué restaurante prefieres para una comida rápida en el campus?
7. ¿Puedes cocinar (*cook*) en tu cuarto/apartamento?
8. ¿Qué platillos (*dishes*) sabes preparar?
9. Cuando vuelves a casa para visitar a tu familia, ¿qué comida pides?

 Paso 2. Now, in groups of four, share your answers and take notes of the group's answers as well. Be ready to report back to the class.

4-13 La comida de la universidad.
A student from Mexico is coming to your university next semester and he e-mails you asking about the university's food. Answer his questions.

Asunto : Recomendaciones para comer en el campus

¡Hola!

Voy a estudiar en tu universidad el próximo semestre y me gustaría saber un poco sobre la comida. Por lo general, ¿cómo es la comida que sirven en la universidad? ¿Sirven carne, pescado o mariscos con frecuencia? ¿Qué tipo de platillos hay? ¿Sirven ensalada y sopa todos los días? ¿Qué tipo? ¿Qué frutas sirven? ¿Hay frutas todos los días?

¿Qué otras opciones hay para comer? ¿Prefieren ustedes la comida de la universidad o la comida rápida?

Muchas gracias. Un saludo atento,
Pablo Morales

Así se dice

Las comidas y las bebidas

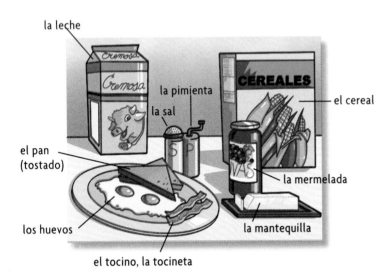

la leche

la pimienta

la sal

el pan (tostado)

los huevos

el tocino, la tocineta

CEREALES

el cereal

la mermelada

la mantequilla

el jugo, el zumo (España)

el azúcar

el café

el té

el refresco
el sándwich, el bocadillo (España)

la hamburguesa

las papas fritas

el aceite   el vinagre

las aceitunas

la sopa

la ensalada

el pastel

el queso

la torta

las galletas

el helado

el vino

la cerveza

el agua

el hielo

el aceite	*oil*	**la mermelada**	*jam*
la aceituna	*olive*	**el refresco**	*soft drink*

¿Cuál es tu preferencia?

Imagine that you are studying abroad in Mexico and staying with a Spanish-speaking family. Shortly after your arrival, your host mother (a great cook) has many questions for you. She aims to please!

Puedes tomar tres **comidas** en casa con nosotros: tomamos el **desayuno** a las ocho de la mañana, el **almuerzo** a las dos de la tarde y la **cena** a las ocho de la noche. En la mañana, ¿prefieres **tomar** una **bebida fría**, por ejemplo jugo, o una bebida **caliente** como café o té? ¿Prefieres jugo de naranja o jugo de piña? ¿Tomas el café **con** azúcar o **sin** azúcar? ¿Prefieres los huevos **fritos** o **revueltos**? Esta noche voy a preparar sopa, ensalada y pollo con papas fritas. ¿Prefieres el pollo **a la parrilla**, **frito** o **al horno**? ¿Comes **mucha** o **poca** carne? ¿Cuál es tu **postre** favorito? ¿Te gusta el pastel de tres leches? Como ves, ¡me gusta **cocinar**!

al horno	*baked*	**postre**	*dessert*
a la parrilla	*grilled*	**revuelto/a**	*scrambled*
cocinar	*to cook*	**mucho/a/os/as**	*much, a lot, many*
la comida	*food, meal, main meal*	**poco/a/os/as**	*little (quantity), few*
la bebida	*drink, beverage*	**con**	*with*
frito/a	*fried*	**sin**	*without*

NOTA DE LENGUA

- **Mucho** and **poco** do not change in gender and number when they modify verbs.

  Comemos **mucho/poco**.   *We eat a lot/little.*

  When they modify nouns, **mucho** and **poco** do change in gender and number to agree with the noun.

  Comemos **muchas** verduras y **poca** carne.

- Spanish uses the preposition **de** (*of*) to join two nouns for the purpose of description.

  helado **de** vainilla   *vanilla ice cream*

  jugo **de** naranja   *orange juice*

  How many combinations can you come up with?

DICHOS

Desayuna como un rey (*king*), almuerza como un burgués (*middle class person*) y cena como un mendigo (*beggar*).

¿Cómo puedes explicar este dicho?

4-14 **El menú.** You work at a café and the cook has just given you a list of the dishes available today. Post each item in the section it belongs to on the menu board. Some items could go into more than one section.

El desayuno	El almuerzo	La merienda¹	La cena	El postre

¹A late afternoon snack, usually consisting of a light sandwich or pastries.

1. pan tostado con mantequilla y mermelada
2. sopa y ensalada
3. pastel de manzana con helado de vainilla
4. un cóctel de camarones
5. huevos revueltos con tocino
6. jugo/zumo de naranja

7. unas galletas y leche
8. un sándwich/bocadillo de jamón y queso
9. arroz con pollo, pan y vino
10. café caliente con crema y azúcar
11. una hamburguesa con papas fritas
12. bistec a la parrilla con papas al horno y ensalada mixta

 4-15 **Asociaciones.**

Paso 1. Estudiante A and **Estudiante B** write a list of ideas that each associates with the words given on her/his list.

Modelo: el té
caliente, desayuno, mi mamá, bebida, azúcar

Estudiante A
1. las chuletas
3. el pan
5. el hielo

Estudiante B
2. los huevos
4. el postre
6. la sopa

Paso 2. Read your lists to your partner, who will try to identify the original words.

Modelo: Estudiante A: **Mi lista es: caliente, desayuno, mi mamá, bebida, azúcar.**

Estudiante B: **¿Piensas en el té?**

4-16 **Tu comida ideal.**

Paso 1. What would make an ideal day in terms of food for you? Include everything that you would like (beverages, sides, desserts, etc.) in a chart like this in your notebook.

Desayuno	Almuerzo	Merienda	Cena

 Paso 2. In small groups, compare your ideal meals.

Modelo: **Mi desayuno perfecto son dos huevos fritos, tostadas con mantequilla…**

4-17 **Consejos (*Advice*) de los nutricionistas.** Medical studies show that certain foods are beneficial and reduce the risk of cancer and other diseases. In pairs, compile two lists of foods for incoming first-year students: those they should consume a lot of (**mucho(s)/mucha(s)**) and those they should consume less of (**poco(s)/poca(s)**) to maintain optimum health.

¡Tengo hambre!

Pepita jogs every morning and leads a very active life. She also has a big appetite! Read the conversation between Pepita and the waiter at a local café.

MESERO: ¿Qué desea usted, señorita?

PEPITA: **¡Tengo mucha hambre! Quisiera** un sándwich de jamón y queso y **también** una ensalada.

MESERO: ¿Y para tomar?

PEPITA: Una limonada grande, por favor. **Tengo** mucha **sed.**

MESERO: A la orden (*at your service*), señorita.

(Pepita se lo come todo y decide que **todavía** tiene hambre. Pide **más** comida.)

MESERO: ¿Desea usted algo más?

PEPITA: Sí, **otro** sándwich, por favor, y otra limonada, pero con **menos** hielo.

MESERO: Con mucho gusto, señorita.

tener (mucha) hambre	*to be (very) hungry*
tener (mucha) sed	*to be (very) thirsty*
más/menos	*more/less, fewer*
quisiera	*I would like (polite)*
otro/a	*another*
también	*also*
todavía	*still, yet*

NOTA DE LENGUA

In Spanish, the verb **tener** has many uses. In **Capítulo 3** you learned the expression **tener... años** (to be ... years old). **Tener hambre** and **tener sed** follow the same pattern.

¡Tengo mucha hambre!   *I am very hungry.*

Also note that **otro/a** does not use the indefinite article **un/una.**

Quisiera otra limonada, por favor.   *I would like another lemonade, please.*

4-18 **¡Qué hambre tenemos!** Work in groups of three. Two of you have just run a marathon and you are famished and extremely thirsty. You are now at a restaurant where the third student is the waiter. Work together on a dialogue using the words and expressions in the box below. Be ready to act it out for the class.

tener hambre	otro/a	quisiera
tener sed	más	menos

Cultura: Las comidas en el mundo hispano

Antes de leer

1. At what time are breakfast, lunch, and dinner typically eaten in the United States? Which is usually the heaviest meal of the day?

2. Are you familiar with dishes consisting of a flour crust and meat filling, either fried or baked?

3. If you've tried both types, do you prefer corn or flour tortillas? Have you seen other types of tortillas, such as whole wheat?

▲ Una máquina para hacer tortillas

◀ ¿Quieres un pan dulce (*sweet*) de esta pastelería mexicana?

El desayuno hispano es normalmente entre las 6 y las 9 de la mañana. Comparado con el desayuno tradicional estadounidense, el desayuno hispano es muy ligero (*light*). Muchos españoles e hispanoamericanos desayunan una taza de café con leche y pan con mantequilla o mermelada o pan dulce.

El almuerzo, generalmente es entre la 1 y las 2 de la tarde y es la comida más fuerte (*largest*) del día. El almuerzo puede incluir una ensalada, sopa, arroz o verduras, carne o pescado y postre. En algunos países, a las 4 o a las 5 de la tarde es común comer la merienda, que consiste en café o té, leche, galletas, pastel o un bocadillo.

Generalmente los hispanos cenan más tarde que los estadounidenses, pero es una comida más ligera. La cena hispana típicamente es entre las 8 y las 9 de la noche, y en España puede ser incluso más tarde, entre las 10 y las 12 de la noche.

Una parte importante de la comida es **la sobremesa**. Este término se refiere a la charla (*chat, conversation*) después de la comida. Es cuando se toma el café, a veces seguido de (*followed by*) un licor, y se conversa de diferentes asuntos (*issues*).

ALGUNOS PLATOS (*DISHES*) TÍPICOS DEL MUNDO HISPANO

◀ La **empanada**: masa de harina rellena generalmente con carne, cebolla, huevo y aceituna, frita o al horno.

La **paella** (España): plato de arroz con pollo, mariscos y guisantes, sazonado con azafrán (*saffron*). ▼

▲ Las **quesadillas** (México): tortillas de maíz, fritas, con queso, pollo, champiñones y otros ingredientes al gusto. En el desayuno típico de la foto se sirven con frijoles, papaya, jugo de naranja y café con leche.

Los **churros**: una masa de ▶ harina cilíndrica y frita. Frecuentemente se sirven con café con leche o con chocolate caliente.

▲ Las **tortillas** que se comen en México y otras partes de Latinoamérica generalmente son de maíz o de harina. Son redondas y planas (*round and flat*).

La **tortilla española** está hecha de huevos, papas ▶ y cebolla. Se sirve con frecuencia a la hora de la merienda en los bares de España. También se come en casa para la cena.

▲ El **flan**: un postre hecho de huevos, leche, azúcar y vainilla, cocido en un molde al horno con almíbar (*syrup*) de caramelo.

Después de leer

1. Based on the text you have just read, determine whether the following meals are typical of the U.S., a Hispanic country, or both.
   a. desayuno con pan y café con leche
   b. almuerzo con sopa, carne, arroz y postre
   c. desayuno con cereales, huevos y tocino
   d. cena a la medianoche
   e. cena con una pizza y refresco
   f. merienda con leche y galletas
   g. almuerzo con un sándwich

2. Name two differences between *when* people eat in Hispanic countries and in the U.S.

3. What dishes mentioned in the text would you like to try? Which would you prefer not to try, and why?

4. If you were writing a textbook for students learning English, what foods would you include as "typical" of the United States?

SITUACIONES

In pairs or groups of three, you and your friend(s) are going out for dinner tonight but each one of you wants to go to a different restaurant. Try to persuade your friends to go to your favorite restaurant by telling them what type of food they serve, describing the dish(es) you think they would really like, what they have for dessert, etc. Make a decision and be ready to share it with the class.

Así se forma

ochocientos noventa y uno...

3. Counting from 100 and indicating the year

In *Capítulo 1*, you learned numbers up to 99. Here are the numbers over 100.

cien	100	ochocientos/as	800
ciento uno/a	101	novecientos/as	900
doscientos/as	200	mil	1,000
trescientos/as	300	dos mil	2,000
cuatrocientos/as	400	cien mil	100,000
quinientos/as	500	doscientos mil	200,000
seiscientos/as	600	un millón (de + *noun*)[1]	1,000,000
setecientos/as	700	dos millones (de + *noun*)	2,000,000

- **Cien** is used before a noun or as the number 100 when counting. **Ciento** is used with numbers 101 to 199.

  Hay **cien** estudiantes en la clase.　　**Cien, ciento uno...**
  Sólo tengo **cien** pesos.　　La torta cuesta **ciento un** pesos.

- In Spanish, there is no **y** between hundreds and a smaller number, although *and* is often used in English.

  205 (*two hundred and five*) = **doscientos cinco**
  　　　　　　　　　　　　　~~doscientos y cinco~~

- When the numbers 200–900 modify a noun, they agree in gender.

  trescient**os** alumnos y quinient**as** alumnas

- Years above 1000 are not broken into two-digit groups as they are in English.

  1971 (*nineteen seventy one*) = **mil novecientos setenta y uno**
  　　　　　　　　　　　　　　~~diecinueve setenta y uno~~

NOTA DE LENGUA

Marking thousands and decimals

Traditionally, Spanish and other romance languages use a dot (.) to mark thousands, and a comma (,) to mark decimals. Most Spanish speakers in the U.S. follow the English convention of marking thousands with a comma and decimals with a dot (or "point," or "period"). Usage varies in Spanish-speaking countries, but it is increasingly becoming commonplace to use the comma for thousands and the dot for decimals.

Las Américas　　　　　**Europa**
$ 121,250.50　　　　　$ 121.250,50

---

[1] When **millón/millones** is immediately followed by a noun, the word **de** must be used: **un millón de pesos, dos millones de euros**; but **un millón doscientos mil quetzales**.

4-19 **Los números.** Indicate which numbers you hear.

_____ **a.** 101 _____ **d.** 704

_____ **b.** 300,000 _____ **e.** 4,502

_____ **c.** 1987 _____ **f.** 2,000

4-20 **Datos sobre México.** Listen to the following numbers and write them down as numerals.

1. _____ la población aproximada de México (en 2010)
2. _____ la frontera entre Estados Unidos y México, en millas (*miles*)
3. _____ el año de la Independencia de México
4. _____ el número aproximado de hablantes de la lengua indígena Nahúatl
5. _____ el número de especies de reptiles que hay en México
6. _____ el año de nacimiento (*birth*) del volcán Paricutín, el más joven del mundo (*world*)

4-21 **¿En qué año?** Here is a list of some well-known restaurants with a long history. Listen and fill in the last column with the date that it opened.

¿Cuál es el restaurante más antiguo (*oldest*) de esta lista? ¿Sabes (*do you know*) cuál es el restaurante más antiguo de tu ciudad?

Nombre del restaurante	Año
La Diligencia, un antiguo hostal (*old guesthouse*) de Tarragona, España	
El Faro, primer restaurante español en Nueva York	
Hostería de Santo Domingo, primer restaurante de la Ciudad de México	
Venta de Aires, famoso por sus platos tradicionales, en Toledo, España	
Café Richmond, un elegante restaurante de Buenos Aires, Argentina	
Casa Botín, ¡el restaurante más antiguo del mundo![1](Madrid, España)	
Paladar La Guarida, famoso restaurante familiar, La Habana, Cuba	

[1]According to the Guinness Book of Records.

Casa Botín ▶

¡A la mesa!

4-22 **Más números.** In pairs, **Estudiante A** reads her/his numbers first, while **Estudiante B** determines which number was read. Then **Estudiante B** reads numbers while **Estudiante A** determines which was read.

Estudiante A lee	Estudiante A responde	
1. Doscientos mil	5. ☐ 400	☐ 104
2. Novecientos cuatro	6. ☐ 8,510	☐ 810
3. Tres mil ciento uno	7. ☐ 1,300,600	☐ 1,030,600
4. Mil ochocientos setenta y siete	8. ☐ 4,091	☐ 491

Estudiante B lee	Estudiante B responde	
5. Ciento cuatro	1. ☐ 200,000	☐ 2,000
6. Ocho mil quinientos diez	2. ☐ 94	☐ 904
7. Un millón trescientos mil seiscientos	3. ☐ 3,101	☐ 3,011
8. Cuatrocientos noventa y uno	4. ☐ 877	☐ 1,877

4-23 **¿Cuándo?** In pairs, determine in what year the following events took place, then write out the year in words, following the model.

Modelo: Estudiante A lee: El desastre del Challenger
Estudiante B dice: **1986** **Mil novecientos ochenta y seis**

1. ____ Los ataques terroristas en Nueva York   **a.** 1989 _____
2. ____ Los Juegos Olímpicos en México   **b.** 1945 _____
3. ____ Bomba atómica en Hiroshima   **c.** 2001 _____
4. ____ La caída del Muro (*wall*) de Berlín   **d.** 1968 _____
5. ____ Murió (*died*) Coretta Scott King.   **e.** 2006 _____

4-24 **Vamos a cambiar (*exchange*) dólares.** In pairs, one of you is a teller (**cajero/a**) at a money exchange booth at the Miami International airport and the other is a client travelling to Hispanic countries. Listen to the amount of dollars your client wants to exchange and tell her/him how much money that is in the currency of the countries she/he will be visiting. Use the exchange rates in the chart below.

País	1 dólar de EE.UU. son	
Bolivia	7	bolivianos
Colombia	1,982	pesos colombianos
Costa Rica	557	colones
Guatemala	8	quetzales
Honduras	19	lempiras
México	13	pesos mexicanos
Perú	3	nuevos soles
Venezuela	2	bolívares

Follow the model and use the information on page 129, each taking a turn as **cajero/a** and **cliente/a**.

Modelo: Cliente/a: **Buenos días, quiero cambiar doscientos dólares a pesos mexicanos, por favor.**

Cajero/a: **Aquí tiene, dos mil seiscientos pesos.**

Estudiante A: Eres el cliente, vas a visitar estos países. Cambia los dólares indicados y anota el dinero local recibido.

México	725 dólares	Son _____	pesos mexicanos.
Guatemala	425 dólares	Son _____	quetzales.
Honduras	350 dólares	Son _____	lempiras.
Costa Rica	600 dólares	Son _____	colones.

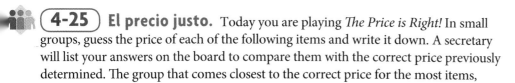

Estudiante B: Eres el cliente, vas a visitar estos países. Cambia los dólares indicados y anota el dinero local recibido.

Colombia	425 dólares	Son _____	pesos colombianos.
Venezuela	350 dólares	Son _____	bolívares.
Perú	600 dólares	Son _____	soles.
Bolivia	725 dólares	Son _____	bolivianos.

(4-25) El precio justo. Today you are playing *The Price is Right!* In small groups, guess the price of each of the following items and write it down. A secretary will list your answers on the board to compare them with the correct price previously determined. The group that comes closest to the correct price for the most items, without going over, wins. Remember: In this activity, the teacher is always right!

1. una cena elegante para dos en un restaurante de cinco estrellas (*stars*) en la Ciudad de Nueva York
2. una mansión en Beverly Hills, California
3. un televisor plasma de 37 pulgadas (*inches*)
4. una computadora portátil
5. una cámara digital de 14.1 MP (megapíxeles)
7. la matrícula de un año en la universidad
8. un carro híbrido nuevo

NOTA CULTURAL

La comida mexicana vs. la comida Tex-Mex

Tex-Mex is a term given to food, music, and other cultural products based on the combined cultures of Texas and Mexico. Many ingredients of Tex-Mex cooking are common in Mexican cuisine, although other ingredients are unknown in Mexico. Tex-Mex food encompasses a wide variety of dishes such as burritos, chimichangas, nachos, fajitas, tortilla chips with salsa, and chili con carne, all of which are usually not found in Mexico.

Así se forma

¿Con quién?
¿Cuándo?
¿Dónde?

PLUS Go to *WileyPLUS* and review the Animated Grammar Tutorial for this grammar point.

4. Asking for specific information: Interrogative words (A summary)

You have used some interrogative words to ask questions: **¿Cómo estás? ¿Qué pasa? ¿De dónde eres? ¿Adónde vas después de la clase? ¿Cuántos años tienes? ¿Cuánto cuesta?** Following are the most commonly used interrogative words in Spanish.

¿Qué?	*What?*	**¿Qué** frutas tienen hoy?
		¿Qué quiere usted?
¿Cómo?	*How?*	**¿Cómo** están las fresas hoy?
¿Cuándo?	*When?*	**¿Cuándo** llegan las piñas?
¿Por qué?	*Why?*	**¿Por qué** no hay cerezas?
¿Quién/Quiénes?	*Who?*	**¿Quién** vende/**Quiénes** venden mariscos?
¿De quién?	*Whose?*	**¿De quién** es?
¿Cuál/Cuáles?	*Which (one/ones)?*	**¿Cuál/Cuáles** prefieres?
¿Cuánto?	*How much?*	**¿Cuánto** es en total?
¿Cuántos/Cuántas?	*How many?*	**¿Cuántos** tomates/**Cuántas** peras quiere?
¿Dónde?	*Where?*	**¿Dónde** está el vendedor?
¿Adónde?	*(To) where?*	**¿Adónde** va?
¿De dónde?	*From where?*	**¿De dónde** es?

- Note the difference between **¿qué?** and **¿cuál?**:

  ¿Qué + noun? When followed by a noun, use **qué.**

  ¿Qué postre deseas? — *What (Which) dessert do you want?*

  ¿Qué/Cuál + ser? When followed by the verb **ser,** use **qué** to ask for a definition or explanation; use **cuál** to ask for specific data or a piece of information.

  ¿Qué es una dirección? — *What is an address?*

  An appropriate answer (definition) would be: It is the information about where a place is located or where somebody lives.

  ¿Cuál es tu dirección? — *What is your address?*
  An appropriate (specific information) answer would be: It is 34 Longwood Avenue.

  ¿Qué/Cuál + verb? When followed by a verb other than **ser,** use **qué** to ask about a general choice; use **cuál** to ask about a choice among given options.

  ¿Qué quieres comprar? — *What do you want to buy?*

  ¿Cuál quieres, el rojo o el azul? — *Which one do you want, the red one or the blue one?*

- Note that all the interrogative words above have written accents. When they appear without it, they connect two separate thoughts within a statement rather than ask a question.

que	*that, which, who*	En el mercado **que** está en la plaza se venden mariscos.
lo que	*what, that which*	Compro **lo que** necesito.
cuando	*when*	**Cuando** tengo hambre, voy a la cafetería.
porque	*because*	Quiero una pizza grande **porque** tengo mucha hambre.

4-26 **¿Qué palabra interrogativa?** Imagine that one classmate interviewed another for a class assignment. Match the questions with the appropriate answers.

1. ¿Cómo estás?
2. ¿A qué hora es tu primera clase?
3. ¿Dónde prefieres estudiar?
4. ¿Cuándo vas a dormir?
5. ¿Cuál es tu clase favorita?
6. ¿Qué clases tienes?
7. ¿Cuánto cuestan tus libros?
8. ¿A quién pides ayuda con los problemas?
9. ¿Cuántas horas estudias cada día?
10. ¿Cómo es la comida en la cafetería?
11. ¿Qué haces después de las clases?

a. ____ Tres o cuatro.
b. ____ Voy al gimnasio o a la biblioteca.
c. ____ Quinientos dólares más o menos.
d. ____ Muy bien, gracias.
e. ____ Español, historia y biología.
f. ____ A las 9 de la mañana.
g. ____ Buena... a mí me gusta.
h. ____ Normalmente, a medianoche.
i. ____ ¡Español, claro!
j. ____ A mi consejero (*advisor*).
k. ____ En mi cuarto.

4-27 **¿Qué o cuál?** Mark the correct interrogative word keeping in mind the given answers.

1. — ¿☐ Qué ☐ Cuál   es tu dirección de correo electrónico?
   — Es mar2@mail.com.
2. — ¿☐ Qué ☐ Cuál   es una manzana?
   — Es una fruta.
3. — ¿☐ Qué ☐ Cuál   estudias?
   — Estudio economía y finanzas.
4. — ¿☐ Qué ☐ Cuál   postre desea usted?
   — Quisiera un helado.
5. — ¿☐ Qué ☐ Cuál   prefiere, el helado de chocolate o el de vainilla?
   — El de chocolate.

4-28 **Vamos a ser honestos.** You and your classmate have been friends for a while, but have not always been honest with each other. Finally you decide to come clean. Take turns telling each other about your secrets and ask for the truth. Add one more secret of your own.

Modelo: Estudiante A: **La verdad (*truth*) es que tus raviolis no son mi plato favorito.**
         Estudiante B: **¿No? ¿Cuál es tu plato favorito?**
         Estudiante A: **Los tamales.**

Estudiante A
1. No me llamo...
2. No tengo... años.
3. No estudio...
4. Mi cantante (*singer*) favorito/a no es...
5. ...

Estudiante B
1. No soy de...
2. No vivo en una residencia estudiantil.
3. Después de las clases no voy a la biblioteca.
4. Mi película favorita no es...
5. ...

Dicho y hecho

ANTES DE LEER

What is your favorite food? Do you have a favorite dish or recipe that includes that food?

ESTRATEGIA DE LECTURA

Using text format and visuals Becoming familiar with the topic and main ideas of the text will greatly help you interpret it correctly when you read it in detail. Recognizing a particular text format and paying attention to any visuals and their captions can give you a good sense of what the text is about. For example, look at the selection that follows. Read the title and introduction to the text, look at the text format and pictures. Then answer the following questions:

- What food is this text going to talk about?
- There are two different types of text here, how would you categorize each of them?
- What cues in the title, introduction, format and visuals have you used to answer the questions above?

A LEER

"Desconfía[1] de las personas que no tienen vicios", dice mi abuela. En el caso del chocolate, dicen que hace mal a los dientes. Pues, mejor para mi dentista.

Soy un vicioso del chocolate, y en especial de uno "puro y con almendras", que tomo en dosis sensatas[2] pero constantes. Una tarde de domingo se me ocurrió escribir al director de la fábrica de mi chocolate, para agradecerle[3] la calidad, la constancia y el placer que me causa saborear cada día su golosina[4]. Para mi sorpresa, dos días después, a las diez de la mañana, suena el teléfono y la voz del otro lado me dice: "Buenos días, soy Pedro López, director general de Chocolates Valor. Acabo de leer su carta y le llamo para darle las gracias".

El bisabuelo Pedro López empezó en el negocio del chocolate a finales del siglo XIX, en 1881, por lo que Pedro convive con el chocolate desde el útero materno. Cuatro generaciones después, los métodos artesanos de su bisabuelo se han modificado. Su compañía cuenta con los mejores profesionales y un innovador laboratorio de I+D (investigación y desarrollo[5]). Pero para fabricar chocolate "es necesaria la calidez[6] y la frialdad". La calidez y la ilusión de un niño, y la cabeza fría del profesional. Pedro afirma también: "El chocolate es bonito de por sí y el estar en chocolate de alta gama, pues más todavía[7]".

---

[1]Be suspicious, [2]sensible, [3]to thank, [4]candy, sweet, [5]research and development, [6] warmth, [7]even more

RECETA DE TRUFAS DE CHOCOLATE

Ingredientes:
- Una tableta de ½ kilo de chocolate puro
- 50 gramos de mantequilla
- 2 huevos
- 5 galletas
- Una copita de coñac
- Fideos[8] de chocolate
- Moldes de papel para trufas

Elaboración

 Derretir[9] el chocolate y la mantequilla.

 En otro bol, batir[10] la yema de huevo[11] y mezclarla[12] con las galletas y el coñac.

 Por otro lado, batir la clara de huevo[13] a punto de nieve[14] y reservarla.

 Mezclar el chocolate y la mantequilla derretidos con la yema, las galletas y el coñac, y batirlo todo.

 Finalmente, incorporar la clara a punto de nieve a esta mezcla y batir de nuevo. La mezcla debe reposar en el congelador[15] durante una o dos horas.

 Después hacer bolitas con la mezcla, cubrirlas con los fideos de chocolate y ponerlas en los moldes de papel.

[8] sprinkles, [9] melt, [10] beat, [11] egg yolk, [12] mix, [13] egg white, [14] until stiff, [15] freezer

Texto: Luis de Benito / *Punto y coma*

DESPUÉS DE LEER

1. Answer the following questions about the text.

   a. ¿Por qué escribe el autor del artículo al director de la fábrica de chocolate?

   b. ¿Quién fundó la compañía de Chocolates Valor? ¿Cuándo?

   c. ¿Cómo se ha transformado la fabricación del chocolate Valor?

   d. ¿Qué dos cualidades son necesarias para fabricar chocolate, según (*according to*) el Sr. López?

2. The steps to make truffles got mixed up. Can you number them in the correct order below?

   1. Derretir chocolate y mantequilla

   ____ Enfriar.

   ____ Batir yema de huevo.

   ____ Bañar las bolitas con fideos de chocolate.

   ____ Batir la mezcla de chocolate (*chocolate mix*) y la mezcla de galletas.

   ____ Mezclar yema, galletas y coñac.

   ____ Incorporar la clara batida a la mezcla de chocolate.

   ____ Formar bolitas de chocolate.

   ____ Batir clara de huevo.

3. Are you a good cook or is microwave popcorn your highest achievement in the kitchen? In small groups, share the recipe for your specialty, in Spanish, using vocabulary you have learned in *Capítulo 4* and from reading the article above.

Dicho y hecho

EXPRESIONES ÚTILES

el mesero/la mesera
¿Qué desean ustedes?
¿Y para usted?
¿Qué desean tomar?
Les recomiendo
  (comidas/ bebidas)...
Nuestros (platos
  especiales/postres...)
  son exquisitos.

el/la cliente
Quisiera...
¿Cuál es la sopa del día?
¿Qué nos recomienda?
¿Sirven arroz y frijoles
  con todos los platos?
Podemos compartir
  el pollo.
Muchas gracias.
¡La cuenta (*check*) por
  favor!

PARA CONVERSAR: ¿Qué comemos?

Work in groups of three. Two of your friends and you are in the Cancún airport traveling back home from vacation. Two of you decide to eat in El Rincón, where traditional Mexican food is served. You are hungry and thirsty but you only have 200 pesos (about $15 dollars) left, so you might need to share some dishes. The third student will play the role of the server.

Paso 1. Individually, each of the traveling friends looks at the menu and decides what she/he would like to eat based on personal preferences and cost. Be prepared to explain your choices to your friend. Remember that prices are in **pesos** (1 dollar = 13 **pesos**, approximately). Meanwhile, the server studies the menu and comes up with two specials of the day. (Server: Write down what those specials are so that you can use them when you tell your customers about them.)

El Rincón – Almuerzo

Sopas
Consomé azteca (pollo, arroz, cilantro, cebolla y aguacate[1])	71
Sopa de tortilla (tortilla de maíz, tomate, chipotle[2], queso y aguacate)	67
Sopa de frijol	65
Sopa del día (pregunte a su mesero)	65

Ensaladas
	Mediana	Grande
El Rincón (lechuga, pollo, tortilla frita, jícama[3] y piña asada)	60	98
De toronja (lechuga, toronja[4], aguacate y cebollitas)	55	88

Enchiladas (de pollo o queso, con guarnición[5] de frijoles)
Rojas, verdes o chipotle	95
De mole[6] poblano (con salsa de chiles y chocolate)	98
Suizas (con espinacas y salsa de crema agria)	95

Especialidades El Rincón
Carne de res en salsa de tomate	115
Puerco en salsa verde (con tomatillos[7], chiles güeros[8] y papas)	105
Pollo en mole	110
Pescado a la Veracruzana (con tomate, aceitunas y alcaparras[9])	125
Chile relleno con queso	98

Bebidas
		Postres	
Jugos naturales (naranja, toronja o guanábana[10])	28	Flan	36
Coca-Cola, Fanta, Sprite, Fresca	17	Arroz con leche	32
Agua mineral	15	Helados	32

[1]avocado; [2]smoke-dried chili; [3]jicama – a crispy, sweet edible root; [4]grapefruit; [5]side dish, [6]Mexican sauce made with chili peppers, chocolate, and a variety of other ingredients; garnish; [7]green tomatoes; [8]banana peppers; [9]capers; [10]soursop – a tropical fruit.

Paso 2. It's time to order! First, look at the expressions in *Expresiones útiles* on page 134. They will help you order and also understand the server. Then, listen to the server and ask questions, discuss your options with your partner and order your food. The server will try to help by offering several suggestions. After your meal, ask for the check, pay your bill and let the waiter know how your meal was.

PARA ESCRIBIR: Comer en la universidad

In this chapter you will be able to choose among different writing options in order to describe your experiences eating on campus. You will choose one of the audiences below.

ANTES DE ESCRIBIR

 Paso 1. You will describe your eating experiences on your campus. In small groups, discuss how this composition would be different if you were writing for the following audiences. Consider:

- **Purpose:** What would be your goal in each of the following situations? Can you think of examples of how such purposes may affect your composition?

- **Content:** What would be the message that you are trying to convey? What type of information would be appropriate in each case? Can you think of anything that might be appropriate for one of the contexts and not for another?

- **Writing format:** How are the three types of writings described differently in what we expect them to contain?

- **Tone:** Would the language in each be formal or informal? What would the tone of each be like?

	Purpose	Content	Writing format	Tone
An e-mail to your uncle, who often sends you money for school				
An article for the student newspaper				
A report requested by the Director of Dining Services, who wishes to assess whether changes need to be made to campus dining options				

Dicho y hecho

Paso 2. Choose one of the three options described in **Paso 1** (the e-mail to your uncle, the article for the student newspaper or the report for the Director of Dining Services). Start planning your writing by brainstorming for a few minutes, writing down everything that comes to mind, or developing an idea map with sub-topics and clusters of ideas. Now, choose the three or four most important ideas that you want to develop in your composition. Each idea should form the topic sentence of a paragraph.

A ESCRIBIR

Write the letter of your choice from **Paso 1** making an effort to convey relevant, well-developed ideas in a logical, easy to follow sequence. Remember to write appropriately for your purpose and reader.

Para escribir mejor: How to use a bilingual dictionary

In general, you should try to generate your compositions entirely in Spanish, using the words and structures that you already know. However, you will probably want to use a dictionary occasionally to stretch your communicative abilities. Be aware that we often cannot generate word-for-word translations from one language into another.

When you look up a word in the dictionary, be sure to note whether it is a noun or a verb. Using the example "I can fly to New York", look up *can* and *fly* in the online dictionary www.wordreference.com, using the "English to Spanish" section, and write what you find:

can	noun =	_____
	verb =	_____
fly	noun =	_____
	verb =	_____

What is the correct translation of "I can fly to New York"?

_____

DESPUÉS DE ESCRIBIR

Revisar y editar: El contenido y la organización. Revise your composition for content and organization. Specifically ask yourself these questions:

☐ Does each paragraph contain one main idea? Is all of the other information in the paragraph related to that main idea?

☐ Is the tone appropriate for the type of audience I have selected? (uncle, newspaper, or Director of Dining Services)

☐ Have I provided enough details? Are there a few more details I could include?

PARA VER Y ESCUCHAR: La comida hispana

 ANTES DE VER EL VIDEO

In pairs, and before you watch the video, write a list of Hispanic dishes you know (include the ones you remember from this chapter and others you might have known before). Together, try to remember as much as you can about these dishes.

> ### ESTRATEGIA DE COMPRENSIÓN
>
> **Silent viewing.** Visual information can help us greatly when watching television or a video segment; we can learn about the context, events and people involved, and use this information to better comprehend what we hear in the segment. In order to get the most out of that visual information, view the segment without any sound first. This will allow you to focus on what you see and use that information to anticipate and interpret what is being said. This exercise will also help you train yourself to pay attention to all those visual cues when watching Spanish-language TV or movies.

A VER EL VIDEO

 Paso 1. In the video, you will hear about the foods served in two different restaurants. View the video once without sound and pay attention to the places, people and food you see. Then, in small groups, share all the ideas and details you remember. You can also guess what some things may be!

Paso 2. Before you watch the video again, look at the words in the box. After watching the video, now with sound, say whether the following statements are true or false. Rewrite the false statements to make them correct.

> ### PALABRAS ÚTILES
>
> aperitivo *appetizer*
> bacalao *cod*
> camarones
> = gambas (España) *shrimp*
> morcilla *blood sausage*
> jamón serrano *dry cured ham*
> pimientos *peppers*
> pulpo *octopus*

	Cierto	Falso
1. El restaurante Macitas sirve comida cubana.	☐	☒
2. Macitas sólo sirve cenas.	☐	☒
3. Macitas también vende comida para llevar a casa.	☒	☐
4. El restaurante Botín se especializa en tapas.	☐	☒
5. Los españoles salen de tapas con su familia.	☐	☐

Paso 3. You are going to choose some dishes to try from each of these restaurants later, so you have to pay attention to their offerings. Complete the following sentences with any information you might remember. Then, watch the video again to check and complete your answers.

1. En el restaurante Macitas el calentado es un desayuno típico, que consiste en

   _____.

2. En la panadería de Macitas venden _____.

3. Las empanadas de Macitas son de _____.

4. Se sirven con una salsa de _____.

5. La especialidad de Botín son las carnes asadas, pero también sirven distintas tapas. Algunas tapas populares en España son _____.

 DESPUÉS DE VER EL VIDEO

In groups, tell your classmates which food or dish you would like to try in Macitas and in Botín (assume they serve all the tapas mentioned in the video.)

¡A la mesa!

ciento treinta y siete   **137**

Repaso de vocabulario activo

Adjetivos y expresiones adjetivales

al horno *baked*
a la parrilla *grilled*
caliente *hot*
frío/a *cold*
frito/a *fried*
mucho/a/os/as *much, a lot, many*
otro/a/os/as *another/other*
poco/a/os/as *little (quantity), few*

Adverbios

más/menos *more/less*
mucho/poco *a lot/a little*
también *also*
todavía *still*

Conjunciones

cuando *when*
lo que *what (that which)*
porque *because*
que *that, which, who*

Palabras interrogativas

¿Adónde? *(To) where?*
¿Cómo? *How?*
¿Cuál/es? *Which (one/s)?*
¿Cuándo? *When?*
¿Cuánto/a/os/as? *How much?/How many?*
¿De dónde? *From where?*
¿De quién? *Whose?*
¿Dónde? *Where?*
¿Por qué? *Why?*
¿Qué? *What? Which?*
¿Quién/es? *Who?*

Preposiciones

con *with*
sin *without*

Sustantivos
Las comidas del día *Meals*

el almuerzo *lunch*
la cena *dinner*

el desayuno *breakfast*

Las legumbres y las verduras *Legumes and vegetables*

el brócoli *broccoli*
la cebolla *onion*
los frijoles *beans*
los guisantes *peas*
las judías verdes *green beans*
la lechuga *lettuce*
el maíz *corn*
la papa/la patata *potato*
las papas fritas *French fries*
el tomate *tomato*
la zanahoria *carrot*

Las frutas *Fruits*

la banana/el plátano *banana*
la cereza *cherry*
la fresa *strawberry*
el limón *lemon*
la manzana *apple*
el melocotón/el durazno *peach*
la naranja *orange*
la pera *pear*
la piña *pineapple*
la sandía *watermelon*
la uva *grape*

Las carnes, los pescados y los mariscos *Meat, fish, and seafood*

el bistec *steak*
el camarón/la gamba *shrimp*
la carne de cerdo/puerco *pork*
la carne de res *beef*
la chuleta de cerdo/puerco *pork chop*
la hamburguesa *hamburger*
el jamón *ham*
la langosta *lobster*
el pescado *fish*

el pollo *chicken*
la salchicha/el chorizo *sausage*
la tocineta/el tocino *bacon*

Las bebidas *Beverages*

el agua *water*
el café *coffee*
la cerveza *beer*
el jugo/el zumo *juice*
la leche *milk*
el refresco *soda drink*
el té *tea*
el vino *wine*

Los postres *Desserts*

la galleta *cookie*
el helado *ice cream*
el pastel *pie, pastry*
la torta *cake*

Otras comidas y condimentos *Other foods and condiments*

el aceite *oil*
la aceituna *olive*
el ajo *garlic*
el arroz *rice*
el azúcar *sugar*
el cereal *cereal*
la crema *cream*
la ensalada *salad*
el hielo *ice*
el huevo *egg*
los huevos revueltos/fritos *scrambled/fried eggs*
la mantequilla *butter*
la mermelada *jam*
el pan *bread*
el pan tostado *toast*
la pimienta *pepper*
el queso *cheese*
la sal *salt*
el sándwich/el bocadillo *sandwich*
la sopa *soup*
el vinagre *vinegar*

Verbos y expresiones verbales

almorzar (ue) *to have lunch*
cocinar *to cook*
comprar *to buy*
costar (ue) *to cost*
desear *to want, to wish*
dormir (ue) *to sleep*
entender (ie) *to understand*
gustar *to like*
necesitar *to need*
pedir (i) *to ask for, to order*
pensar (ie) *to think*
poder (ue) *to be able, can*
preferir (ie) *to prefer*
preparar *to prepare*
querer (ie) *to want, to love*
servir (i) *to serve*
tomar *to take, to drink*
vender *to sell*
volver (ue) *to return, to go back*
quisiera *I would like*
tener (irreg.) (mucha) hambre *to be (very) hungry*
tener (mucha) sed *to be (very) thirsty*

...eba y repaso

...rite questions according to ... answer them. Use the correct form of **gustar** and the appropriate corresponding pronoun.

Modelo: ¿A tu hermano / las legumbres?
> **¿A tu hermano le gustan las legumbres?**
> **Sí, le gustan las legumbres. O, No, no le gustan...**

1. ¿A tus padres / tomar café?
2. ¿A ustedes / la comida italiana?
3. ¿A ustedes / desayunar temprano?
4. ¿A tu abuela / los postres?
5. ¿A ti / los frijoles negros?

II. Stem-changing verbs.
Write questions to your friends using the **ustedes** form of the verb. Then write answers to the questions using the **nosotros** form.

Modelo: entender el ejercicio
> **¿Entienden el ejercicio?**
> **Sí, entendemos el ejercicio. O, No, no entendemos el ejercicio.**

1. poder cocinar
2. querer ir al supermercado
3. almorzar a las doce todos los días
4. preferir cenar en un restaurante o en la cafetería
5. normalmente pedir postres en los restaurantes

III. Counting from 100 and indicating the year.

A. Mr. Trompa, a very wealthy man, is going to buy everything his two daughters need to start college. How much money does he need to buy two of each of the following items? Follow the model and write out the numbers.

Modelo: Un libro de psicología cuesta $90.
> **Dos cuestan ciento ochenta dólares.**

1. Un libro de arte cuesta $125.
2. Una buena calculadora cuesta $170.
3. Una impresora cuesta $450.
4. Una computadora con teclado y monitor cuesta $1,400.
5. Un televisor para el cuarto cuesta $750.
6. Un coche nuevo cuesta $25,000.

B. Write out the following famous years.

1. Colón llega a las Américas: 1492
2. La creación de la Armada Invencible de España: 1588
3. La Declaración de Independencia de EE.UU.: 1776
4. La caída (*fall*) del Muro de Berlín: 1989
5. La caída de las Torres Gemelas: 2001

IV. Interrogative words.
Use various interrogative words to obtain more information.

Modelo: Ana no come en la cafetería.
> **¿Dónde come? O, ¿Por qué no come en la cafetería?**

1. Ana no bebe vino.
2. La sandía no es su fruta favorita.
3. No trabaja por la mañana.
4. No es de Buenos Aires.
5. No tiene veinte años.
6. No vive en la residencia estudiantil.
7. No va a la librería ahora.
8. No está enferma hoy.

V. General review.
Answer the following questions about yourself and your friends. Use complete sentences.

1. ¿Qué comes en el desayuno?
2. ¿Cuál es tu postre favorito?
3. ¿Qué frutas te gustan más?
4. ¿Dónde quieres cenar esta noche?
5. ¿Cuántas horas duermes (generalmente) por la noche?
6. Tú y tus amigos, ¿pueden estudiar toda la noche sin dormir?

VI. Cultura.

1. Name two or three differences between Hispanic cultures and your culture with regards to diet and eating habits.
2. Describe the difference between a **tortilla** made in México and a **tortilla** made in Spain.
3. What are some of the largest contributors to México's economy?

Answers to the *Autoprueba y repaso* are found in **Apéndice 2.**

Recreaciones y pasatiempos

Así se dice

Recreaciones y pasatiempos
   Los colores
   Más actividades y
   deportes
Preferencias, obligaciones
   e intenciones
El tiempo y las estaciones

Así se forma

1. Additional *yo*-irregular
   verbs; *saber* and *conocer*
2. *Ir + a* + infinitive
3. The present progressive
4. *Ser* and *estar* (A summary)

Cultura

- Cuba y la República
  Dominicana
- El fútbol: Rey de los
  deportes

Dicho y hecho

Para leer:
La realidad virtual

Para conversar:
Un día sin clases

Para escribir:
Tu tiempo libre en la
universidad

Para ver y escuchar:
¡Feliz fin de semana!

By the end of this chapter you will be able to:

- Talk about hobbies, pastimes, and activities
- Talk about the weather and the seasons
- Express future actions
- Describe an action in progress

ENTRANDO AL TEMA

1. What is the most popular sport in the Spanish-speaking world—that is, the one with the greatest number of players and fans?

2. Can you name three Spanish-speaking countries located in the Caribbean?

Así se dice

Recreaciones y pasatiempos

el lago

esquiar

las hojas

Juanito

el árbol

nadar

jugar (ue) al voleibol

tomar el sol

la pelota

Natalia

Inés

tocar (la guitarra)

cantar

Rubén

pintar (un cuadro)

caminar (por el parque)

Camila

dar un paseo

las flores

Linda

Manuel

WILEY
PLUS **Pronunciación:**
Practice pronunciation of the
chapter vocabulary and particular
sounds of Spanish in *WileyPLUS*.

cantar	*to sing*
dar un paseo	*to take a walk, stroll*
descansar	*to rest*
ganar	*to win*
hacer ejercicio	*to exercise*
el lago	*lake*
el partido	*game, match*
perder (ie)	*to lose*
practicar	*to practice*
tomar el sol	*to sunbathe*

Javier

jugar (ue) al
básquetbol/
baloncesto

Esteban

jugar (ue) al tenis

el partido (de tenis)

Octavio

Alfonso

levantar pesas

hacer ejercicio

correr

fumar

Pepita

montar en bicicleta

Elena

descansar

Héctor

Remember that the letters in
parenthesis following a verb, for
example, **perder (ie)**, **jugar (ue)**,
indicate a stem change in the
present tense.

Recreaciones y pasatiempos

5-1 ¿Somos sedentarios o activos?

Paso 1. Put the following activities into the correct column based on whether they are sedentary or active.

nadar	tomar el sol	jugar al voleibol	levantar pesas
esquiar	cantar	pintar un cuadro	tocar la guitarra
fumar	descansar	montar en bicicleta	jugar al tenis
correr	caminar	jugar al baloncesto	hacer ejercicio

Actividades sedentarias	Actividades físicas

Paso 2. Now write sentences that say how often you do each activity, using the following terms of frequency.

con frecuencia	a veces	casi nunca	nunca

Modelo: **Nado con frecuencia.**
No monto en bicicleta nunca.

Paso 3. Now, share your answers in small groups and together discuss the following question: **En general, ¿son ustedes sedentarios o activos?**

5-2 ¿Qué me recomiendas?
In pairs, take turns telling your partner what you want to accomplish and suggesting appropriate actitivities to each other. Can you recommend more than one activity? Be prepared to tell the class whether you agree with your partner's suggestions.

Modelo: Estudiante A reads: Me gustan las actividades rápidas (*fast*).
Estudiante B suggests: **Te recomiendo jugar al baloncesto y correr.**

Estudiante A:
1. Quiero expresarme artísticamente.
2. Quiero practicar un deporte con otra persona.
3. Quiero estar al aire libre (*outdoors*), pero no puedo correr.
4. Me gusta mucho el agua.

Estudiante B:
1. Quiero estar más fuerte.
2. Quiero reducir el estrés.
3. Quiero hacer actividades con mi perro.
4. Soy muy competitivo/a.

5-3) ¿Qué te gusta hacer?

Paso 1. You and a classmate will interview each other in depth about activities that you engage in frequently. Be sure to ask follow-up questions to get more details.

Modelo: Estudiante A **¿Qué te gusta hacer en tu tiempo libre *(leisure time)*?**
   Estudiante B: **Me gusta nadar.**
   Estudiante A **¿Nadas con frecuencia? ¿Prefieres nadar en un lago, una piscina *(pool)* o en el océano?**

PALABRAS ÚTILES

jugar al ajedrez	*to play chess*
jugar al golf	*to play golf*
jugar a los videojuegos	*to play videogames*
patinar (sobre ruedas)	*to skate (rollerblade)*
practicar yoga	*to practice yoga*

Paso 2. Write a short paragraph describing your classmate's activity.

Modelo: **A Ana le gusta nadar. Ella nada con frecuencia. Prefiere nadar en una piscina.**

Los colores

Camila enjoys painting in the park. Observe the colors on her palette.

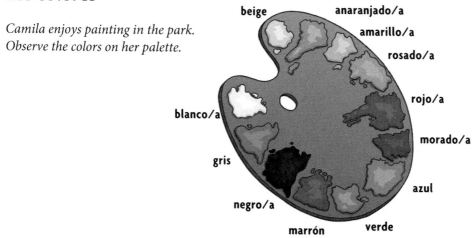

beige anaranjado/a amarillo/a rosado/a rojo/a morado/a azul verde marrón negro/a gris blanco/a

WILEY PLUS Pronunciación: Practice pronunciation of the chapter vocabulary and particular sounds of Spanish in *WileyPLUS*.

NOTA DE LENGUA

All of the colors shown are adjectives. Those that end in *–o* change to reflect both gender and number: **blanco, blanca, blancos, blancas.** Those that end in *–e* (**verde**) or a consonant (**gris, marrón, azul**) have two forms: singular and plural (**verde, verdes**).

Las flores son azules y amarillas.

5-4 **¿Cuáles son tus colores?** Sports teams' uniforms and their colors are important symbols for a team. Sports commentators even refer to teams by the colors of their jerseys: **"los blancos ganan el partido"** (*the white team wins the game*).

Paso 1. Listen to the descriptions of the jerseys of five popular soccer teams. Identify the jersey that corresponds to the description and write its letter by the team name.

PALABRAS ÚTILES	
béisbol	*baseball*
camiseta	*t-shirt, jersey*
fútbol	*soccer*
fútbol americano	*football*
raya	*stripe*

____ Real Betis   ____ Peñarol   ____ Club América

____ Boca Juniors   ____ River Plate

Paso 2. Now in small groups, describe the colors of a well-known sports team to your classmates. If they have trouble guessing, help by telling them which sport they play.

Modelo: **Su camiseta (*t-shirt*) es… Juegan baloncesto/béisbol…**

a.

b.

NOTA CULTURAL

El fútbol

Soccer, called **fútbol** in Spanish, is by far the most popular sport in the Spanish-speaking world. You will read more about **el fútbol** in this chapter. However, baseball is the preferred sport in several Caribbean countries, including Puerto Rico, the Dominican Republic, Venezuela, and Cuba. Can you name famous baseball players from these places?

What is called football in the United States is **fútbol americano** in Spanish.

INVESTIG@ EN INTERNET

Find out which cities and countries are home to the teams mentioned in Exercise 5-4. Then choose one of those teams (or a different one you have heard about) and learn more about it. Your instructor may ask you to share your findings in class.

Más actividades y deportes

Manuel and Linda have been dating for a while, although they seem to have somewhat different interests. Here are some of their answers to a compatibility survey.

¡Quiero ver el fútbol!

¡Pues yo prefiero la telenovela!

Cuestionario de compatibilidad

	Nombre: Linda	**Nombre:** Manuel
1. ¿Qué le gusta hacer en su tiempo libre (*leisure time*)?	Me *encanta*[1] pasear y salir con mis amigos, y me gusta *bailar* merengue.	Me gusta ir a fiestas o a la discoteca y bailar con Linda.
2. ¿Le gusta **ver la televisión**? ¿Qué tipo de programas ve?	Sí, veo partidos de tenis; también me gustan las telenovelas (*soap operas*).	Me gusta ver la tele, especialmente los deportes: **fútbol, béisbol,** torneos de **golf**...
3. ¿Qué hace los fines de semana?	Generalmente *limpio* mi cuarto y *voy de compras*. A veces cocino para mis amigos.	Me encanta *manejar*[2] mi carro nuevo y casi siempre llevo a Linda cuando va de compras.
4. ¿Practica algún **deporte** con regularidad?	Mi deporte favorito es el **fútbol americano**, pero juego al tenis.	Sí, juego al baloncesto. Mi deporte favorito es el fútbol, pero en Estados Unidos no es muy popular...
5. ¿Cuál es su equipo favorito?	Mi equipo son los Celtas.	Mi equipo favorito son los Padres.
6. ¿Escucha música? ¿De qué tipo?	Sí, en casa casi siempre escucho música y me gusta toda la música.	Sí, siempre escucho música en casa, en el carro, con mi iPod. Me gusta el rock latino: Maná, Los Jaguares y Café Tacuba.
7. ¿Qué hace para relajarse?	Casi siempre doy un paseo y, a veces, leo un libro.	¿Relajarme? No tengo tiempo para eso.
8. ¿Le gusta **viajar**? ¿Adónde?	Me encantan los viajes a lugares exóticos, pero casi nunca hago viajes porque no tengo dinero.	No, nunca viajo si no es necesario. En las vacaciones prefiero descansar en casa.

bailar	*to dance*	**limpiar**	*to clean*
encantar	*to love*	**manejar**	*to drive*
equipo	*team*	**ver la tele**	*to watch TV*
ir de compras	*to go shopping*	**viajar**	*to travel*

[1]Note that **encantar** has a similar structure to that of **gustar:**
Me *gusta* bailar / Me *encanta* bailar. Me *gustan* los deportes / Me *encantan* los deportes.

[2]**Manejar = conducir** in Spain. Present tense: **conduzco, conduces, conduce, conducimos, conducís, conducen.**

5-5) Compatibilidad.

Paso 1. Listen to the following statements and decide whether they refer to Linda, Manuel, or both (in which case, mark both columns).

Paso 2. Now work in small groups to answer the following questions.

¿Tienen Linda y Manuel muchos intereses y hábitos en común? ¿Son muy similares o diferentes? ¿Piensas que son compatibles?

	Manuel	Linda
1.	☐	☐
2.	☐	☐
3.	☐	☐
4.	☐	☐
5.	☐	☐
6.	☐	☐
7.	☐	☐
8.	☐	☐

5-6) Mis hábitos.
In pairs, talk about how often you do the following activities, using terms of frequency. (Review *Capítulo 2* if needed.) Then, determine whether you could be compatible as roommates. You may not agree! Be ready to explain your decision to the class.

Modelo: Estudiante A: **Nunca manejo para ir a clase.**
Estudiante B: **Yo tampoco, pero a veces monto en bicicleta para
ir a clase.**
(…)
Estudiante A: **Cristina y yo (no) somos compatibles como compañeras
de cuarto/apartamento porque...**

1. Manejar para ir a clase.
2. Bailar en fiestas o en una discoteca (*club*).
3. Ver telenovelas o programas *reality* como Gran Hermano (*Big Brother*) o Sobrevivientes (*Survivor*).
4. Ver partidos de fútbol/básquetbol/tenis/béisbol en la tele.
5. Hacer ejercicio por la mañana/tarde/noche.
6. Ir de compras los fines de semana.
7. Limpiar mi cuarto/apartamento.
8. Escuchar música rock/pop/country a un volumen alto en mi cuarto.
9. Fumar.

5-7) Mis pasatiempos favoritos.

Paso 1. Individually, make a list of your favorite pastimes, adding details such as how often you do each activity, when, where, etc.

Paso 2. In groups, share your lists and ask for more details regarding pastimes you find interesting. Take notes.

Paso 3. Select a pastime from your classmates' lists that you want to try or you think is interesting. Be prepared to report back to the class.

Modelo: **Quiero tocar la guitarra, como (*like*) Roberto, porque...** Or,
Roberto toca la guitarra. Es interesante porque...

Cultura: Cuba y la República Dominicana

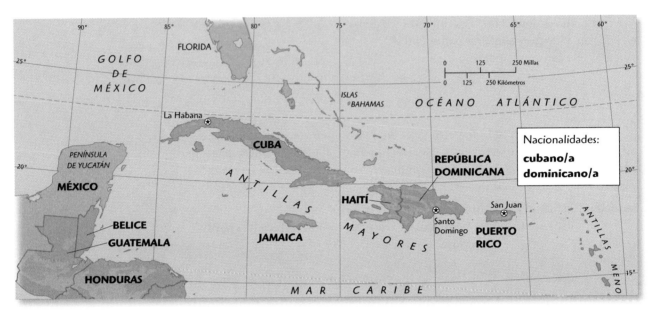

Antes de leer

1. Notice which of the islands in the Greater Antilles is closest to Florida. Do you know how many miles away it is?

2. Do you know anyone, famous or otherwise, from Cuba or the Dominican Republic?

PLUS Map quizzes: As you read about places highlighted in red, find them on the map. Learn more about and test yourself on the geography of the Spanish-speaking world in *WileyPLUS*.

Las **Antillas Mayores,** situadas entre el océano Atlántico y el mar Caribe, incluyen tres países de habla hispana: **Cuba, Puerto Rico** y **la República Dominicana.** La República Dominicana ocupa gran parte de la isla La Española, nombrada así por Cristóbal Colón en su primera visita a las Américas. Las Antillas son territorios muy importantes por su posición como "puerta" al continente americano.

La caña de azúcar, el tabaco, las frutas tropicales y el ron (*rum*) han sido (*have been*) las principales industrias de estas islas durante siglos (*centuries*). Hoy, por su clima y belleza natural, estas islas atraen un gran número de turistas.

La música y las danzas de estas islas son una expresión cultural importante de sus habitantes. Los bailes como la salsa, el mambo, el bolero y el merengue tienen influencia española en sus melodías, pero en los ritmos es evidente la influencia africana. De hecho, la herencia africana está muy presente hoy en los rasgos (*traits*) físicos de los habitantes del Caribe.

El deporte nacional de Cuba, Puerto Rico y la República Dominicana es el béisbol, o como se dice en estos países, la pelota. Hay muchos peloteros talentosos en estos países y ¡muchos juegan en equipos de Estados Unidos!

▲ Manny Ramírez

CUBA

Cuba fue una colonia de España desde principios del siglo XVI hasta 1898. Después de la guerra entre Estados Unidos y España, Cuba pasó a ser un protectorado de EE.UU. Cuba se independizó en 1902, pero su economía siguió dependiendo de EE.UU. La revolución de 1959 instituyó una dictadura marxista y, bajo (*under*) Fidel Castro, Cuba empezó a depender económicamente de la Unión Soviética.

El embargo de Estados Unidos (1962) y la disolución de la Unión Soviética (1991) contribuyeron a la crisis económica en Cuba. A consecuencia de graves problemas de salud, Fidel instaló a su hermano Raúl como jefe del gobierno en 2006. Parte del plan de recuperación económica consiste en la construcción y restauración de hoteles para atraer el turismo.

▲ Playa Varadero, un ejemplo de un lugar turístico que ofrece playas magníficas y otras atracciones naturales.

▲ **Celia Cruz** (1924–2003) fue la cantante cubana más famosa del mundo. Más de 20 de sus discos ganaron premios de oro con canciones de rumba, salsa, boleros y otros géneros. Su frase famosa, que decía con frecuencia en sus canciones, era "¡Azúcar!" (*Sugar*)

LA REPÚBLICA DOMINICANA

En 1496, los españoles fundaron **Santo Domingo,** la primera ciudad de origen europeo en América. Los franceses establecieron una colonia, Haití, al oeste de la colonia española, en la misma isla. Después de años de guerra —¡contra los españoles, los franceses y los haitianos!— la República Dominicana se independizó en 1865.

En 1927, después de una ocupación estadounidense, el general Rafael Trujillo tomó el poder. Su dictadura fue totalitaria y terminó con su asesinato en 1961. Un libro famoso sobre esta época, de Julia Álvarez, se titula *En el tiempo de las mariposas* (*butterflies*). Hoy la República Dominicana es una democracia.

La República Dominicana tiene las construcciones coloniales más antiguas del continente, como la catedral de Santo Domingo, la primera de las Américas. También tiene 300 millas de playas que atraen el turismo.

▲ **Julia Álvarez** es una autora dominicana prolífica. ¿A qué crees que se refiere el título de su libro *En el tiempo de las mariposas*? a) A unas mariposas que migran cada año a la República Dominicana; b) A tres hermanas que organizaron una resistencia a la dictadura de Trujillo.

Después de leer

1. To which country of the Greater Antilles does each of the following statements pertain?

Cuba   República Dominicana

☐   ☐   a. Comparte La Española con otra nación.
☐   ☐   b. Es la isla más grande de las Antillas.
☐   ☐   c. Su gobierno no es democrático.
☐   ☐   d. La primera catedral de las Américas está situada en su capital.

2. Look for the video of any Celia Cruz song by visiting *YouTube.com* or another source. Describe the song, the year it was from, and Celia's outfit. Did she shout "**¡Azúcar!**" during the song? Does she remind you of any other singers you know?

3. Refer back to what you learned in *Capítulo 2*. What do Cuba and the Dominican Republic have in common with their neighbor Puerto Rico? How are they different?

Así se forma

> Conozco a María, el amor de mi vida, pero ella ni sabe mi nombre...

WILEY PLUS Go to *WileyPLUS* and review the Animated Grammar Tutorial and Verb Conjugator for this grammar point.

1. Talking about activities in the present: Additional *yo*-irregular verbs

Saber and *conocer*

These verbs both mean *to know*, but have very different uses. First, observe their forms and note the irregular **yo** form in their conjugations.

saber	
sé	sabemos
sabes	sabéis
sabe	saben

conocer	
conozco	conocemos
conoces	conocéis
conoce	conocen

- **Saber** means *to know* facts, information, and *to know how to* do things. That is, it describes the kind of knowledge that one learns, such as a piece of information, and skills that can be demonstrated.

  Sé dónde vive Inés.   *I know where Inés lives.*
  Ella **sabe** tocar el piano.   *She knows how to play the piano.*

  Notice that when **saber** means *to know how to* it is followed by an infinitive.

  Sé bailar salsa.   *I know how to dance salsa.*

- **Conocer** means *to know* in the sense of being acquainted or familiar with persons, places, or things. It also means *to meet* for the first time.

  Conozco a Carmen.   *I know Carmen.*
  Ella **conoce** bien la ciudad de Ponce.   *She knows the city of Ponce well.*
  Quiero **conocer** a Marta Uribe.   *I want to meet Marta Uribe.*
  ¿**Conoce** usted la poesía de Guillén?   *Are you familiar with Guillén's poetry?*

  Notice that when **conocer** means *to know* a person, it is followed by "*a personal*".

  Conozco a la profesora Ruiz.   *I know Professor Ruiz.*

Notice the difference between these two sentences:

Sé quién es el profesor Velasco.   *I know who Professor Velasco is.*
Conozco al profesor Velasco.   *I know Professor Velasco.*

PALABRAS ÚTILES

Instrumentos musicales: el piano, el violín, la guitarra, la trompeta, el saxofón, el clarinete. Idiomas: italiano, francés, ruso, japonés, alemán.

5-8 **¿Qué sabemos hacer?** Moving about the classroom, find out who knows how to do each of the things in the chart on page 153. If she/he says "**Sí**", jot down her/his name by the activity and ask a follow-up question. Be prepared to report back to the class. Take notes.

Modelo: Estudiante A: **¿Sabes esquiar?**
             Estudiante B: **Sí, sé esquiar.**
             Estudiante A: **¿Esquías con frecuencia? ¿Dónde esquías?**

	Nombre	Detalles
1. esquiar		
2. jugar un deporte		
3. montar en bicicleta		
4. cocinar		
5. tocar un instrumento musical		
6. hablar otro idioma		

 5-9 **Deportistas famosos.** Work in pairs. Ask each other if you know who these athletes are. Use the categories in the box.

Modelo: Mia Hamm

Estudiante A: **¿Sabes quién es Mia Hamm?**

Estudiante B: **Sí, sé quién es. Ella jugaba fútbol.** Or, **No, no sé quién es.**

¿Sabes quién es…?

1. Tiger Woods
2. Albert Pujols
3. Rafael Nadal
4. David Beckham
5. Pau Gasol
6. Lance Armstrong

PALABRAS ÚTILES

ciclista
futbolista
jugador de básquetbol/
        béisbol/golf
tenista

▲ Pau Gasol

▲ Rafael Nadal

5-10 **¿Quieres conocerlos?** In small groups, imagine you have won a Spanish spelling contest and your prize is to meet the famous people of your choice, with whom you will share a day in a city of your choice where you have never been before. But you all have to agree in order to get the prize.

Use the pronouns **lo** (to refer to males, like *him*) and **la** (to refer to females, like *her*) as in the *Modelo*. (You will learn more about these pronouns in *Capítulo 6*). If you don't know who the person is, just say: **No sé quién es.**

Modelo: Estudiante A: **Yo quiero conocer La Habana / a Jennifer López porque…**

Estudiante B: **Sí, la quiero conocer también / No, no la quiero conocer porque…**

5-11 **¿Saber o conocer?** Celia has questions for Antonio about a restaurant near his house. Complete their conversation with the correct forms of **saber** or **conocer,** according to context.

CELIA: Antonio, ¿_____ cómo se llama el restaurante cubano de tu calle?

ANTONIO: Sí, claro que lo _____: se llama Café Oriental. Además, lo _____ muy bien. Comemos allí frecuentemente porque mis padres _____ a los dueños (*owners*).

CELIA: Y ¿ _____ qué platos típicos sirven?

ANTONIO: Tienen *moros y cristianos,* y también sirven un *ajiaco* buenísimo.

CELIA: ¿Ajiaco? No lo _____. ¿Qué es?

ANTONIO: Bueno, es una sopa de carne y verdura, pero no _____ todos los ingredientes.

5-12 **¿Lo/La conoces bien?**

Paso 1. Individually, fill in the blanks for *Estudiante A* in the conversation that follows with **sabes** or **conoces,** as appropriate.

Paso 2. In pairs, interview your partner about one of your other classmates using the conversation as a guide. Then reverse roles to ask about a different classmate.

Estudiante A:

¿A quién de la clase _____ bien?

¿_____ dónde vive?

¿_____ su número de teléfono o su correo electrónico?

¿_____ cuántos años tiene?

¿_____ qué actividades le gustan?

¿_____ a los amigos de él/ella?

Estudiante B:

_____ bien a _____.

Sí, vive en.../No lo sé.

...

...

...

...

Sí, los/No, no los _____.

NOTA CULTURAL

Buena Vista Social Club

The Buena Vista Social Club in Havana, Cuba, held dances and concerts during the 1940s. In the 1990s, it inspired a recording made by Cuban musician Juan de Marcos González and American guitarist Ry Cooder, using some of the original 1940s musicians. The recording, titled *Buena Vista Social Club,* became an international success, and Wim Wenders's documentary of the same name won numerous accolades. The success of both the album and film sparked a revival of international interest in traditional Cuban music and Latin American music in general.

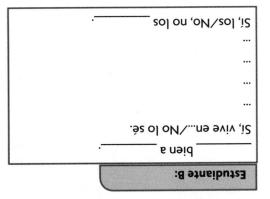

◀ Buena Vista Social Club

Additional verbs with an irregular *yo* form

In *Capítulo 2* you learned two verbs with an irregular **yo** form: **salir** and **hacer.** Review them, and then observe the verbs that follow.

salir (de)	hacer	traer	poner	oír	ver	dar
to leave, go out	*to do, make*	*to bring*	*to put, place*	*to hear*	*to see*	*to give*
salgo	**hago**	**traigo**	**pongo**	**oigo**	**veo**	**doy**
sales	haces	traes	pones	**oyes**	ves	das
sale	hace	trae	pone	**oye**	ve	da
salimos	hacemos	traemos	ponemos	oímos	vemos	damos
salís	hacéis	traéis	ponéis	oís	veis[1]	dais[1]
salen	hacen	traen	ponen	**oyen**	ven	dan

HINT

Think of the following verbs as the "**yo-go** verbs"—verbs whose **yo** forms end in **–go**: salir, **hacer, traer, poner, oír, tener, venir, and decir.**

- **Salir** is followed by **de** when the subject is leaving a stated place.

  Salen del gimnasio.　　vs.　　Salen con sus amigos.

- When **hacer** is used in a question, it does not necessarily require a form of **hacer** in the answer. This is also true in English of the verb *to do.*

  — ¿Qué haces normalmente por la tarde?　　*What do you usually do in the afternoon?*

  — Voy a la biblioteca, hago la tarea y después, trabajo en la librería.　　*I go to the library, I do my homework and later, I work at a book store.*

Like **tener**, which you learned in *Capítulo 3*, the verbs **venir** and **decir** have irregular **yo** forms in addition to stem changes.

tener (ie)	*to have*	venir (ie)	*to come*	decir (i)	*to say, tell*
tengo		**vengo**		**digo**	
tienes		**vienes**		**dices**	
tiene		**viene**		**dice**	
tenemos		venimos		decimos	
tenéis		venís		decís	
tienen		**vienen**		**dicen**	

---

[1]Note there is no accent on **veis** or **dais**.

5-13 ¿Qué hace tu profesor/a?

Paso 1. Read the following sentences about your instructor and decide whether they are true (cierto) or false (falso).

Cierto   Falso

☐ ☐   **1.** Salgo de mi casa a las 6 de la mañana.

☐ ☐   **2.** Oigo las noticias (*news*) en el carro.

☐ ☐   **3.** Traigo comida a la clase de español.

☐ ☐   **4.** Digo "Buenos días" cuando entro a la clase.

☐ ☐   **5.** Doy mucha tarea de español los viernes.

☐ ☐   **6.** Tengo cinco hijos.

Paso 2. Now ask your professor whether she/he does the things you marked **cierto.** Who guessed most accurately? Who knows the professor best?

5-14 ¿Qué hace Pepita?

Paso 1. Look at what Pepita does on a typical weekday. Can you put the illustrations in chronological order, numbering them from 1–8, and use the verbs below to describe what she does?

decir	hacer	llegar	llevar	oír	ver	salir

_____

_____

_____

_____

_____   _____   _____   _____

 Paso 2. Now, with a partner, interview each other about your typical day. You may use Pepita's activities from *Paso 1* as a guide.

Modelo: Estudiante A: **¿A qué hora oyes el despertador por las mañanas?**

Estudiante B: **Por las mañanas, oigo el despertador a las siete y media. ¿A qué hora oyes tú el despertador?**

(5-15) ¿Lo hago o no?

Paso 1. Create six sentences about yourself using the verbs below. Three sentences should be true and three should be false.

| poner | ver | oír | hacer | decir | dar |

 Paso 2. In groups of three, read each statement to your partners, who will guess whether it is true or not.

(5-16) ¿Qué hacemos los sábados?

Paso 1. In three minutes, write a list as long as you can of the things you do yourself on Saturdays.

Modelo: **Los sábados yo tomo el desayuno tarde, llamo a mis padres, me baño, salgo…**

Paso 2. Work in small groups and compare your list with your classmates' lists. Write another list of the things most or all of you have in common using the **nosotros** form. The class will then share lists to see which group's members have the most in common.

Modelo: **Los sábados nosotros tomamos el desayuno tarde, nos bañamos…**

DICHOS

Decir y hacer son dos cosas, y la segunda es la dificultosa.
¿Puedes explicar este dicho?

Así se dice

Esteban

Alfonso

Preferencias, obligaciones e intenciones

Read the conversation between Esteban and Alfonso to find out about their preferences, obligations, and intentions.

ESTEBAN: Esta noche voy con mis amigos a la discoteca. Y tú, ¿tienes planes para esta noche? ¿Qué **piensas hacer**?

ALFONSO: Tengo un examen de química mañana, **tengo que estudiar** mucho.

ESTEBAN: ¡Qué aburrido! ¿No quieres salir conmigo? ¿No **tienes ganas de venir** con nosotros a la discoteca?

ALFONSO: No puedo, **debo estudiar** química. Además, ¡a mí no me gusta bailar!

Note the meaning of these expressions in the chart below. What other verbs and expressions do you already know that you can add to the table?

Preferencia, deseo (*desire*)	Obligación	Intención, planes
tener ganas de + *infinitivo* preferir querer desear	tener que + *infinitivo* deber + *infinitivo*	pensar + *infinitivo*

NOTA DE LENGUA

The expression *to need to* is often used to express obligation in English, but in Spanish, **necesitar** is generally not used with this meaning. The preferred forms to express obligation are **tener que** or **deber**.

Tengo que/Debo estudiar esta noche.   *I need to study tonight.*

5-17 **¿Preferencias u obligaciones?** Tell whether the characters have to do or feel like doing the activities depicted in the drawings on page 159.

Modelo: Esteban
Creo que Esteban tiene ganas de/ tiene que...

1. Esteban

2. Inés

3. Javier

4. Camila

5. Natalia

6. Rubén

7. Pepita

8. Octavio

5-18 **Obligaciones, preferencias y planes.**

Paso 1. In groups of four, read the statements and decide on at least two activities that you have to do, feel like doing, or plan/intend to do in response to each circumstance. Appoint a secretary to record the information. For item 5, the group should invent a new circumstance.

| tener que... | deber... | tener ganas de... | pensar... |

Modelo: Estamos muy preocupados/as porque tenemos examen mañana.
Tenemos que estudiar mucho esta noche; no debemos ver la tele...

1. Estamos muy ocupados/as esta semana.
2. Estamos aburridos/as con la vida social de la universidad.
3. Estamos un poco estresados/as porque tenemos una presentación mañana.
4. ¡No tenemos que estudiar ni hacer tarea este fin de semana!
5. _____

Paso 2. The group secretary reads two activities aloud and the rest of the class must decide whether the circumstances are **una obligación, una preferencia,** or **un plan**.

SITUACIONES

Estudiante A: Tu compañero/a de cuarto te invita a una fiesta con sus amigos, pero sus amigos no te gustan mucho y no tienes ganas de ir con ellos. Inventa excusas.
Estudiante B: Vas a una fiesta con tus amigos. Invitas a tu compañero/a de cuarto pero es tímido/a y piensas que no quiere ir porque tiene vergüenza (*is embarrassed*). Insiste.

EXPRESIONES ÚTILES

¿Sabes?	*You know, . . . ?*
¡Vamos!	*Come on!*
(Verás), es que . . .	*(You see/Well), the thing is . . .*

Así se forma

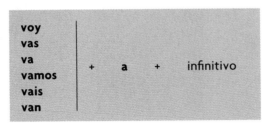

Voy a impresionar a Pepita con mis músculos.

WILEY PLUS Go to *WileyPLUS* and review the Animated Grammar Tutorial and Verb Conjugator for this grammar point.

2. Making future plans: *Ir* + *a* + infinitive

To talk about plans and actions yet to occur, use
ir + **a** + infinitive

voy vas va vamos vais van	+ a + infinitivo

Vamos a jugar al básquetbol.
Inés **va a tocar** el piano esta noche.
Y tú, ¿qué **vas a hacer** mañana por la tarde?

We are going to play basketball.
Inés *is going to play* the piano tonight.
And you, what are you going to do tomorrow afternoon?

The following expressions are useful to talk about the future.

En el futuro	
el mes/año/verano que viene	*next month/year/summer*
el próximo mes/año/verano	*next month/year/summer*

5-19 ¿Qué voy a hacer?

Paso 1. Read the statements below and describe the circumstances in which you would say them.

Modelo: "Voy a dormir".
              Son las dos de la mañana. Tengo sueño (*I'm sleepy*).

1. "Voy a correr en el parque."   _____

2. "Voy a llamar a mi mamá."   _____

3. "Voy a comer un sándwich."   _____

4. "Voy a ver la tele."   _____

5. "Voy a tomar un vaso de agua."   _____

6. "Voy a comprar tortillas."   _____

7. "Voy a ir a la biblioteca."   _____

8. "Voy a estudiar."   _____

Paso 2. In the column **Yo**, write what you are going to do in response to the following situations. When you finish writing, ask a classmate and fill in her/his answers in the column **Mi compañero/a**. Are they similar or different? Be ready to share with the class.

Modelo: El día está bonito.
   Estudiante A: **¿Qué vas a hacer?**
   Estudiante B: **Voy a dar un paseo.**

	Yo	Mi compañero/a
¡Tengo un billete de lotería premiado (*a winning lottery ticket*)!	Voy a…	Va a…
Mis padres vienen de visita este fin de semana.		
Tenemos un mes de vacaciones.		
Necesito dinero.		

5-20 **El grupo de estudio.** You have formed a study group with three or four classmates to prepare for a Spanish test.

Paso 1. Fill in the agenda schedule pages below with your activities for today (**hoy**) and tomorrow (**mañana**).

Paso 2. Now, talk with your classmates and try to find a 1–2 hour slot when you can meet at the library. Use the model below to structure your answers about what you will be doing.

Modelo: Estudiante A: **¿Pueden ir a la biblioteca esta tarde a las 2?**
   Estudiante B: **No, voy a estar en mi clase de química.**
   Estudiante C: **Y yo voy a jugar al fútbol de 1:30 a 3.**

Hoy	Mañana
8:00 A.M.	8:00 A.M.
9:00 A.M.	9:00 A.M.
10:00 A.M.	10:00 A.M.
11:00 A.M.	11:00 A.M.
12:00 P.M.	12:00 P.M.
1:00 P.M.	1:00 P.M.
2:00 P.M.	2:00 P.M.
3:00 P.M.	3:00 P.M.
4:00 P.M.	4:00 P.M.
5:00 P.M.	5:00 P.M.
6:00 P.M.	6:00 P.M.
7:00 P.M.	7:00 P.M.
8:00 P.M.	8:00 P.M.

VideoEscenas: Un fin de semana en Sevilla

▲ Rocío y Carmen se encuentran (*run into each other*) en el Parque del Retiro, en Madrid (España).

 Paso 1. Make a list of activities that would make an ideal weekend, and then share it with a classmate.

Paso 2. Watch the video once and select the statement that best describes the main idea.

☐ Rocío y Carmen hacen planes para el fin de semana.
☐ Rocío y Carmen hablan sobre sus planes para el fin de semana.

Paso 3. Watch the video again, this time pay attention to the details and mark all the options that are true for each statement. Look at the statements and options now so you know what you need to watch and listen for.

1. Rocío va a…
   ☐ ver la tele.
   ☐ salir con su novio.
   ☐ ver un partido de fútbol.
   ☐ jugar un partido de fútbol.
   ☐ ir de compras.

2. Carmen va a…
   ☐ visitar a su prima.
   ☐ ir a todos los parques.
   ☐ pasear por Sevilla.
   ☐ montar en bicicleta.

3. Rocío piensa que Carmen…
   ☐ tiene que ir al Parque María Luisa.
   ☐ debe ir a Sevilla en primavera.
   ☐ tiene que montar en bicicleta.

 Paso 4. In small groups, imagine that Carmen is coming to town for the weekend, what would you suggest she does?

Modelo: **Tiene que visitar… Puede ir a …**

Así se dice

El tiempo y las estaciones
(The weather and the seasons)

Hace buen tiempo. Hace fresco y **está nublado** (hay **nubes**). **Es primavera.**

Llueve todas las tardes. Ahora también **está lloviendo**. Dicen que después de **la lluvia** sale **el sol**.

Hace sol y **hace** (mucho) **calor.** Octavio **tiene calor.** Es **verano.**

Hace mal tiempo. Hace viento. Es **otoño.**

Hace frío. Esteban **tiene frío.** Es **invierno.**

Aquí, en el invierno, **nieva** casi todos los días. **Está nevando** ahora. ¡Me encanta **la nieve!**

El tiempo		Las estaciones	Las personas
hace	(muy) buen/mal tiempo	primavera	tener calor/frío
	sol	verano	
	fresco	otoño	
	(mucho) calor	invierno	
	(mucho) frío		
	(mucho) viento		
llover (ue) →	la lluvia		
nevar (ie) →	la nieve		

To ask what the weather is like, say: **¿Qué tiempo hace?**

clima	*climate*	**nublado**	*cloudy*
fresco	*cool*	**el sol**	*sun*
la nube	*cloud*	**el viento**	*wind*

Notice that **el tiempo** can either refer to time or weather (context will help you interpret it correctly):

—¿Qué hora es?
—Son las 4:00. ¿Tienes tiempo para tomar café?

—What time is it?
—It's 4 o'clock. Do you have time for coffee?

—¿Qué tiempo hace?
—Hace frío.

—What's the weather like?
—It's cold.

NOTA CULTURAL

Grados Fahrenheit vs. grados centígrados (Celsius)

Most Spanish-speaking countries measure air temperature in degrees Celsius rather than in degrees Fahrenheit. Here is the formula for converting from one to the other.

To convert from °F to °C
__ °C = (__ °F − 32) ÷ 1.8

To convert from °C to °F
__ °F = 1.8 x (__ °C) + 32

The thermometer reads 50°F. What's the temperature in degrees Celsius? If the temperature is 40°C, is it really hot or really cold?

(5-21) Por aquí y por allá

Paso 1. Por aquí. Fill in the following chart with details about each month where you live.

Mes	Tiempo
enero	
abril	
julio	
octubre	

 Paso 2. Por el mundo hispano. In pairs and taking turns, one of you will select one of the photos below, describe what the weather is like and identify the season of the year. The other identifies the location being described.

Modelo: Estudiante A: **Hace frío y hay mucha nieve. Es invierno.**[1]
Estudiante B: **Es el Parque Nacional Los Glaciares, Argentina.**

▲ Parque Nacional Los Glaciares, Argentina

▲ Huracán Georges, Puerto Rico

▲ Playa Manuel Antonio, Costa Rica

[1]The seasons of the year are reversed in the northern and southern hemispheres; for example, when it is winter in Argentina, it is summer in the United States and Canada.

▲ Resort de esquí, Chile

▲ Maestrazgo, España

▲ Tres Piedras, Nuevo México

5-22 El clima y las estaciones.

Paso 1. A prospective student from the Dominican Republic wants to come to the United States for a semester and she wants to know a bit more about the weather in the places she is considering and what people do in different seasons. Read her e-mail and talk about her questions with a classmate.

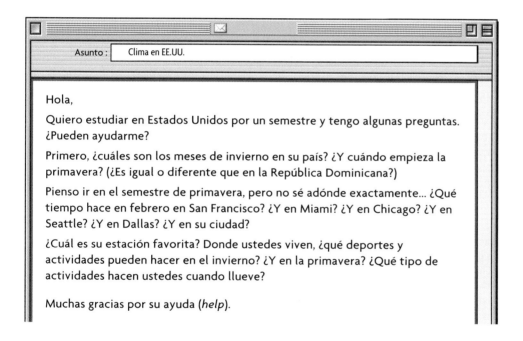

Asunto: Clima en EE.UU.

Hola,

Quiero estudiar en Estados Unidos por un semestre y tengo algunas preguntas. ¿Pueden ayudarme?

Primero, ¿cuáles son los meses de invierno en su país? ¿Y cuándo empieza la primavera? (¿Es igual o diferente que en la República Dominicana?)

Pienso ir en el semestre de primavera, pero no sé adónde exactamente... ¿Qué tiempo hace en febrero en San Francisco? ¿Y en Miami? ¿Y en Chicago? ¿Y en Seattle? ¿Y en Dallas? ¿Y en su ciudad?

¿Cuál es su estación favorita? Donde ustedes viven, ¿qué deportes y actividades pueden hacer en el invierno? ¿Y en la primavera? ¿Qué tipo de actividades hacen ustedes cuando llueve?

Muchas gracias por su ayuda (*help*).

Paso 2. Now, reply to her message. Be sure to answer all of her questions, and offer your recommendation on which city you think she should choose, and why.

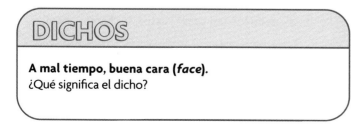

DICHOS

A mal tiempo, buena cara (*face*).
¿Qué significa el dicho?

Cultura: El fútbol:
Rey de los deportes

▲ En 2010, España ganó la Copa Mundial.

Antes de leer

1. Are you a sports fan? Of which sport(s)?

2. What do "average" and "extreme" fans do to support their teams?

3. Do you know where the latest World Cup soccer event took place?

Muchos jóvenes aspiran a ▶ ser futbolistas famosos.

▲ Carlos Bocanegra, capitán del equipo nacional de Estados Unidos en la Copa Mundial de 2010.

Para los dominicanos, los puertorriqueños, los cubanos y los venezolanos, el béisbol es el deporte más importante. Sin embargo, para gran parte del mundo hispano, y la mayor parte de la gente del planeta, el fútbol es el rey de los deportes. En muchos países hispanos, el fútbol es más que un deporte. ¡Es una forma de vida!

Los aficionados (*fans*) hacen de este deporte casi una religión. Ver un partido importante, en el estadio o por televisión, es una obligación.

La pasión por el fútbol aumenta al máximo cada cuatro años con la celebración de la Copa Mundial. Durante la competencia, los aficionados no se pierden (*don't miss*) ni un solo partido. El fútbol no respeta horarios (*schedules*) ni lugares: en muchos países los empleados ponen televisores en sus lugares de trabajo para ver jugar a sus equipos favoritos. Los futbolistas talentosos son auténticos héroes nacionales y mundiales.

▲ Lionel Messi (Argentina)

Brandy Chastain cuando Estados Unidos derrotó (*defeated*) a China en la Copa Mundial Femenina en 1991. Esta Copa se creó en 1991 y hoy el equipo de Estados Unidos es uno de los mejores (*best*) del mundo. ▼

Después de leer

1. Although the U.S. launched Major League Soccer in 1996 and soccer is one of the most commonly played sports by children in the country, which sports are generally the most popular here? Do you think they have as strong a following as soccer does in Latin America?

2. How much do you know about how soccer is played? If you don't know the following terms, look up what they refer to:

   yellow & red card   assist   charge   wall

INVESTIG@ EN INTERNET

¿Cuándo empieza (*begin*) y termina (*end*) la Liga de Fútbol en España? ¿Y en Argentina? ¿Sabes por qué?

Así se forma

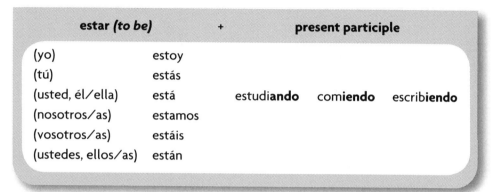

3. Emphasizing that an action is in progress: The present progressive

To indicate and emphasize that an action is in progress, Spanish uses **estar** + *present participle* (**–ndo**) (the present progressive). The present participle always ends in **–ndo**: It does not change to agree with the subject. **Estar,** however, always changes to agree with the subject.

estar *(to be)*		+	present participle		
(yo)	estoy				
(tú)	estás				
(usted, él/ella)	está		estudi**ando**	com**iendo**	escrib**iendo**
(nosotros/as)	estamos				
(vosotros/as)	estáis				
(ustedes, ellos/as)	están				

PLUS Go to *WileyPLUS* and review the Verb Conjugator for this grammar point.

Elena **está estudiando** para un examen.
Nosotros **estamos comiendo** galletas.

*Elena **is studying** for an exam.*
*We **are eating** cookies.*

Note how the present participle is formed.

	stem	+	ending	=	present participle
–ar verbs	**estudi**ar		**–ando**		**estudiando**
–er verbs	**com**er		**–iendo**		**comiendo**
–ir verbs	**escrib**ir		**–iendo**		**escribiendo**

All –ir verbs with a stem change, also have stem changes in the present participle, sometimes that stem change is the same as in the simple present tense, but other times it is different:

pedir (i, i[1])   **pidiendo**   preferir (ie, i)   **prefiriendo**
dormir (ue, u)   **durmiendo**

A few other present participle forms are irregular. You will have to learn these individually.

leer (irreg.)   **leyendo**   oír (irreg.)   **oyendo**

Unlike in English, the present progressive in Spanish emphasizes that the action is in progress at the moment. It is generally not used to talk about habitual and repeated actions, nor is it used to talk about the future.

¿Ustedes todavía **están comiendo**?   ***Are you** still **eating**?*

Salgo en una hora.   ***I am leaving** in an hour.*
~~Estoy saliendo en una hora.~~

---

[1] Lists and glossary entries of stem changing verbs will show the stem changes in parentheses. When two changes are shown, the second is the present participle change, for example: pensar (ie) p**ie**nso, pensando; dormir (ue, u) d**ue**rmo, d**u**rmiendo.

NOTA DE LENGUA

Note that there are important differences between Spanish and English regarding the use of the present participle. Remember, for instance, that we use the infinitive and not the present participle with **gustar**. *(See Capítulo 4.)*

No me gusta **correr** en el parque.
I don't like running in the park.

~~No me gusta corriendo en el parque.~~

5-23 ¿Qué están haciendo?

 Paso 1. As you listen, write the number of each sentence underneath its corresponding drawing.

Paso 2. With a partner, add two additional activities that each of these people is doing at the same time as the activities shown. Then share your ideas with the whole class.

Modelo: Javier está estudiando.

Está leyendo un libro de química y está pensando en su examen de mañana.

5-24 Probablemente.
Work with a partner. First, in the **Yo** column, write two things you would probably be doing in each situation or location. Then, in the **Tú** column, write two things your partner would probably be doing in each situation or location. Finally, ask each other and see if you guessed correctly. How much do you have in common?

Modelo: En un concierto de salsa

Estudiante 1: **En un concierto de salsa, ¿estás bailando y cantando?**

Estudiante 2: **Sí, estoy bailando, pero no estoy cantando.**

	Yo	Tú
En el gimnasio	1. Estoy… 2. Estoy…	1. Estás… 2. Estás…
En la Playa Varadero	1. 2.	1. 2.
En un restaurante cubano	1. 2.	1. 2.
En tu cuarto	1. 2.	1. 2.

5-25 Actores y actrices.
 Eight volunteers dramatize an activity in front of the class. The rest of the class indicates what each actor is doing. Close your textbooks!

Modelo: Profesor/a: ¿Qué está haciendo José?

Estudiantes: **Está caminando por el salón.**

Así se forma

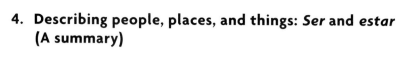

Lisa, ¿quieres conocer a Martín?

Pues, ¿cómo es? ¿De dónde es?

4. Describing people, places, and things: *Ser* and *estar* (A summary)

To indicate that an action is in progress (present progressive), Spanish uses **estar** + *present participle* (**-ndo**). The present participle always ends in **-ndo**: It does not change to agree with the subject. **Estar,** however, always changes to agree with the subject.

WILEY PLUS Go to *WileyPLUS* and review the Animated Grammar Tutorial and Verb Conjugator for this grammar point.

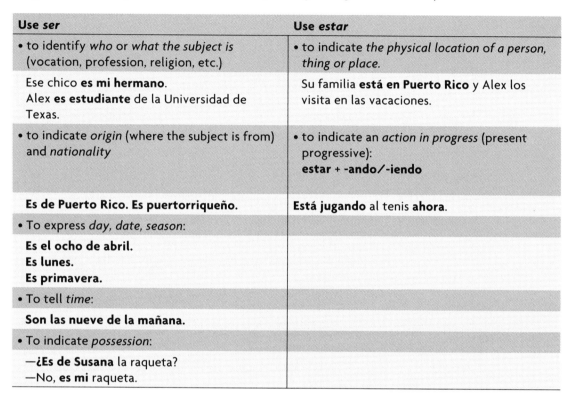

Use *ser*	Use *estar*
• to identify *who* or *what the subject is* (vocation, profession, religion, etc.)	• to indicate *the physical location* of a person, thing or place.
Ese chico **es mi hermano**. Alex **es estudiante** de la Universidad de Texas.	Su familia **está en Puerto Rico** y Alex los visita en las vacaciones.
• to indicate *origin* (where the subject is from) and *nationality*	• to indicate an *action in progress* (present progressive): **estar + -ando/-iendo**
Es de Puerto Rico. Es puertorriqueño.	**Está jugando** al tenis **ahora**.
• To express *day, date, season*:	
Es el ocho de abril. Es lunes. Es primavera.	
• To tell *time*:	
Son las nueve de la mañana.	
• To indicate *possession*:	
—**¿Es de Susana** la raqueta? —No, **es mi** raqueta.	

Ser + adjectives	Estar + adjectives
• to indicate *what the subject is like* —inherent or essential traits or qualities, both physical and in personality.	• to indicate *physical* or *emotional state*, *condition* or *traits not inherent* to the thing or person —often a change from the usual.
Es alto, simpático y **muy inteligente**. Alex **es nervioso**. La nieve **es fría**. Adela **es muy guapa** (*is very pretty*).	Ahora **está un poco enfermo**. Alex **está nervioso** porque tiene un examen. Esta sopa **está fría**. Adela **está muy guapa** (*looks very pretty*) hoy.
Therefore, **ser** is the only option with adjectives that can only express inherent qualities.	**Estar**, on the other hand, is the only option with adjectives that can only express states.
Santiago **es inteligente** y **trabajador**. ~~Santiago está inteligente y trabajador.~~	Santiago **está bien/mal/cansado** (*tired*). ~~Santiago es bien/mal/cansado.~~

Some adjectives are used with either **ser** or **estar**, and express a different meaning according to which verb they are used with. Sometimes the difference in meaning is just a nuance, other times it is more significant.

With *ser*		With *estar*	
ser bonito/a	*to be handsome/pretty*	**estar bonito/a**	*to look handsome/pretty*
Ana **es** muy **bonita.**		Ana **está** muy **bonita.**	
Ana is very pretty.		*Ana looks very pretty.*	
ser aburrido	*to be boring*	**estar aburrido**	*to be bored*
Esa clase **es aburrida.**		Siempre **estoy aburrido** en esa clase.	
That class is boring.		*I am always bored in that class.*	
ser cansado	*to be tiring*	**estar cansado**	*to be tired*
Correr **es cansado.**		Hoy **estoy muy cansado.**	
Running is tiring.		*Today I am very tired.*	

5-26 **¿Quieres salir con él/ella?** Work with a classmate. One of you wants to arrange a blind date for the other. Complete the conversation with forms of **ser** or **estar**.

ESTUDIANTE A: ¿Cómo se llama tu amigo/a?

ESTUDIANTE B: _____. _____ de la Ciudad de Nueva York.

ESTUDIANTE A: ¿ _____ estudiante?

ESTUDIANTE B: Sí, de esta (*this*) universidad. Y también _____ atleta. Le gusta jugar al tenis y al básquetbol, montar en bicicleta, levantar pesas...

ESTUDIANTE A: Pues, ¿cómo _____? Descríbemelo/la.

ESTUDIANTE B: _____ una persona muy buena, muy amable.

ESTUDIANTE A: ¿_____ guapo/a?

ESTUDIANTE B: Sí, _____ muy guapo/a y muy divertido/a (*fun*). ¿Quieres conocerlo/la?

ESTUDIANTE A: Sí, ¡por supuesto (*of course*)! ¿Dónde _____ ahora?

ESTUDIANTE B: Creo que _____ en el laboratorio de biología. Seguro que _____ trabajando ahora porque _____ asistente del profesor.

ESTUDIANTE A: No importa. ¡Vamos al laboratorio!

PALABRAS ÚTILES

callado/a	*quiet*
enojado/a	*angry*
grosero/a	*rude*
impaciente	*impatient*
tranquilo/a	*calm*

5-27 **Sugerencias (*Suggestions*).** Make a three-column chart with the names of three or four people that you know in the left column. In the middle column, write what each person is *normally* (**Generalmente es...**) like. In the left column, indicate a *change* (**Ahora está...**) in her/his disposition. Take turns sharing your concerns with your partner, who will ask the reason for the change. After you respond, she/he will offer a suggestion about what she/he should do. Be ready to report to the class and explain whether you agree with the advice or not.

Modelo: Estudiante 1: **Generalmente, mi hermano es muy enérgico, pero ahora está cansado porque está en el equipo de fútbol y practica todos los días.**

Estudiante 2: **Debe/Tiene que descansar los domingos.**

Dicho y hecho

PARA LEER: La realidad virtual

ANTES DE LEER

1. What are the most popular channels in the U.S. on which to watch sports games? Do you prefer some of these channels over others? Why?

2. Which sports channels and events are televised for free, and which do you have to pay for? Do you expect more from sports events that you pay to watch?

ESTRATEGIA DE LECTURA

Reading to identify the main idea

Particularly as readings become more difficult, it's important not to get hung up on deciphering every single idea a text develops. Instead, try to identify and follow the main idea of each paragraph. Often, the main idea is expressed in the first sentence, but sometimes it can be embedded deeper in the paragraph. As you read the selection that follows, pause after each paragraph and jot down what you understood as its main idea before continuing to the next paragraph. For example, read the first paragraph and determine which of these is the main idea:

☐ In Argentina, there are two channels that televise soccer games in very different ways.

☐ In Argentina, many soccer fans become hypnotized while watching games on television.

Jot down the main idea of the other paragraphs in your notebook. Read through your notes in sequence to get a sense of the article's overall message.

A LEER

Durante un reciente viaje a Argentina me llamó la atención algo curioso. Los grandes partidos de fútbol se televisan de dos maneras: en una se ve el partido, y en la otra no. En un canal (*TyC Sports*) las cámaras enfocan la cancha[1], y en el otro canal (*Fox*) sólo enfocan las gradas[2]. En el primero pagas[3] por ver a los jugadores, y en el segundo te conformas[4] mirando a los aficionados[5]. Lo sorprendente es que muchas personas se quedan hipnotizadas en los bares, imaginando el partido en las caras de los aficionados de su equipo. Se puede decir entonces que los aficionados argentinos han logrado algo impensable[6]: sustituir al espectáculo al que asisten, proyectando un partido virtual.

Un domingo de abril, noté en un bar la perplejidad[7] de unos turistas extranjeros, que miraban fijamente el televisor esperando que en algún momento las cámaras mostraran ese partido que rugía[8], cantaba y corría fuera de la pantalla. Durante una hora y media vi pasar por las mesas a franceses, mexicanos y japoneses. Todos entraban atraídos por el ruido[9] del estadio, se sentaban interesadísimos, pedían una bebida y después de unos minutos comenzaban a mirar a su alrededor, incómodos[10]. Miraban las caras de los otros parroquianos[11], tratando de leer en sus caras qué demonios[12] era lo que miraban con tanta atención. A mí me pareció un momento de tremendo gozo[13]: yo contemplaba divertido a los turistas extranjeros, ellos observaban cada vez más confundidos a los parroquianos del bar, estos miraban la pantalla, y en la pantalla miles de caras desconocidas miraban el partido que nosotros no podíamos ver. Ustedes que leen esta escena continúan la historia.

Esta manera absurda de seguir partidos invisibles por la tele me hace pensar seriamente en la vida moderna. Somos cada vez más[14] espectadores de la realidad por la televisión. Y, en tiempos de elecciones, los políticos nos tratan como consumidores de promesas, compradores de programas. Pero toda realidad es virtual mientras no se demuestre lo contrario[15]. Y muy pocas veces el control remoto está en nuestras manos.

Texto: Andrés Neuman / *Punto y coma*
Fotografía: Por cortesía de FC Barcelona

---

[1] playing field, [2] stands, bleachers, [3] you pay, [4] you settle for, [5] fans, [6] unthinkable, [7] perplexity, bewilderment, [8] was roaring, [9] noise, [10] uncomfortable, [11] regular customer, local patron, [12] what the devil, [13] enjoyment, [14] more and more, [15] until proven otherwise

Dicho y hecho

Después de leer

1. Compare your notes about the main ideas of the text with a classmate, are they similar? If not, try to work together to determine the main point or points the article makes.

2. Answer the following questions about the text.

    a. Cuando el canal Fox en Argentina televisa un partido de fútbol, ¿cómo saben los espectadores qué ocurre?

    b. ¿Por qué están perplejos los turistas que el autor del artículo encuentra en el bar?

3. If you were a soccer fan in Argentina, would you watch games on *Fox,* or would you pay to watch them on *TyC Sports*? Discuss your answers in Spanish, in small groups.

PARA CONVERSAR: Un día sin clases

Imagine that it is early in the morning on a day with no classes. You are going to spend your free day with a couple of classmates. Plan an outing or day trip. Talk about:

- el tiempo (para determinar el destino/las actividades/etc.)
- lo que tienen ganas de hacer y adónde tienen ganas de ir
- lo que piensan comer, a qué hora y dónde

ESTRATEGIA DE COMUNICACIÓN

Begin prepared to compromise You and your classmates may have very different ideas about what makes for an enjoyable outing, where you'd like to stop and get something to eat, etc. Before engaging in conversation to make your plans, think of a couple of possibilities for something to do in the morning, a couple of possible places to stop for lunch, and a couple of potential afternoon activities. This way you will have alternatives to suggest to each other and more readily plan an outing you'll all enjoy.

DICHOS

El ocio es la madre de todos los vicios.

¿Qué significa este dicho? ¿Estás de acuerdo?

PARA ESCRIBIR: Tu tiempo libre en la universidad

You will write a brochure that your college wants to include in the informational packets for prospective students and their parents. This brochure should present the town or area where your campus is located, focusing on local recreational and cultural activities.

ANTES DE ESCRIBIR

Paso 1. Start by having a very clear idea of the purpose and audience for this piece of writing. In your notebook, answer these questions: What is the purpose of this brochure? Who is its intended audience?

ESTRATEGIA DE REDACCIÓN

Generating details *Capítulo 3* discussed how to use idea maps to generate and start organizing ideas in clusters. Now we will consider how to generate greater details for each of your ideas. For example, if one of your ideas is **"Deportes"**, you may wish to talk about your school's football team. But instead of simply mentioning them, you could look up their win-loss record for the past three years and include this detail.

Paso 2. Now, complete an idea map like the one below with activities of interest to prospective students that are available in your area. You can also add more categories.

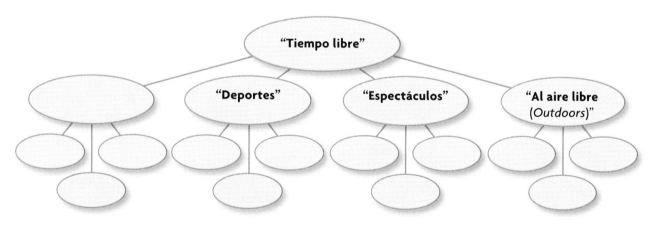

Paso 3. Generate at least two specific details for each idea in your brochure. These could describe the place or event, what one can do there, etc.

Main idea:	Two specific details:
	1. 2.
	1. 2.
	1. 2.

After you have decided what your plans are, share them with another pair of students.

Dicho y hecho

A ESCRIBIR

Now, write your brochure describing the main attractions in the area. Since your purpose is to attract students and their families, be sure to use positive adjectives and an upbeat tone. You may also want to use **ir a**+ *infinitive* when describing activities, to make them more vivid.

Modelo: **En el Centro Deportivo, vas a poder jugar al baloncesto, nadar, tomar clases de yoga…**

Para escribir mejor: As you are writing, you might want to give examples or explain what you mean. These connectors will be useful:

por ejemplo *for example, for instance*
Hay muchos parques para pasear o descansar. **Por ejemplo,** el Parque Lincoln está cerca del campus, pero es muy tranquilo.

como *as, such as*
Hay importantes eventos culturales durante el otoño, **como** el Festival de Cine Latinoamericano.

DESPUÉS DE ESCRIBIR

Revisar y editar: Formas correctas. A good use of grammar in writing consists in using the forms and structures that best convey your ideas. After revising your composition for content and organization, review the grammar in your composition, ask yourself these questions:

☐ Do all your sentences have the necessary elements (e.g. subject, verb, necessary articles, etc.)?

☐ Are you using the forms that best convey your ideas? For instance, be sure to use the right type of word (such as the adjective **bueno/a** to describe a person or thing, or the adverb **bien** to describe an event or condition.)

☐ Check for accuracy in your grammar, especially irregular verb forms and the use of **ser** and **estar**.

 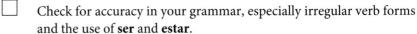
PARA VER Y ESCUCHAR: ¡Feliz fin de semana!

ANTES DE VER EL VIDEO

In pairs or small groups, think about activities people do on the weekends within each of these categories: **Solo/a** (*Alone*), **Con amigos, Con la familia.** Make a chart with your group's conclusions.

ESTRATEGIA DE COMPRENSIÓN

Listening for the main idea When you listen to Spanish, you might want to understand everything that is said. However, the main objective when you watch a video segment should be getting the gist or main ideas. Concentrating on the words that you know and ignoring those that you don't will help you focus on the essence of what is being said.

A VER EL VIDEO

Paso 1. Watch the video segment once and complete the following sentences summing up what you heard.

En los fines de semana los hispanos _____.

Casi siempre hacen estas actividades con _____.

Paso 2. Before you watch the video again, complete the table with any activities mentioned that you might remember for each category. Then, watch to check and complete your answers.

Deportes	Juegos (*Games*)	Entretenimiento (*Entertainment*)	Otras

DESPUÉS DE VER EL VIDEO

 In groups, answer the following questions.

1. ¿Qué actividades mencionadas en el video haces los fines de semana? ¿Con quién?
2. ¿Qué actividades haces con tu familia en tu tiempo libre?

Repaso de vocabulario activo

Adjetivos

amarillo/a   *yellow*

anaranjado/a   *orange*

azul   *blue*

beige   *beige*

blanco/a   *white*

gris   *grey*

marrón   *brown*

morado/a   *purple*

negro/a   *black*

rojo/a   *red*

rosado/a   *pink*

verde   *green*

Adverbios y expresiones adverbiales

el mes/año/verano que viene   *next month/year/summer*

el próximo mes/año/verano   *next month/year/summer*

Las estaciones   *The seasons*

el invierno   *winter*

el otoño   *fall*

la primavera   *spring*

el verano   *summer*

El tiempo   *The weather*

Está (muy) nublado.   *It's (very) cloudy.*

Hace buen/mal tiempo.   *The weather is nice/bad.*

Hace (mucho) calor.   *It's (very) hot.*

Hace fresco.   *It's cool.*

Hace (mucho) frío.   *It's (very) cold.*

Hace sol.   *It's sunny.*

Hace viento.   *It's windy.*

Llueve./Está lloviendo.   *It's raining.*

la lluvia   *rain*

Nieva./Está nevando.   *It's snowing.*

la nieve   *snow*

las nubes   *clouds*

¿Qué tiempo hace?   *What's the weather like?*

Sustantivos
Los deportes   *Sports*

el baloncesto/el básquetbol   *basketball*

el béisbol   *baseball*

el ejercicio   *exercise*

el equipo   *team*

el fútbol   *soccer*

el fútbol americano   *football*

el golf   *golf*

el partido   *game, match*

la pelota   *ball*

el tenis   *tennis*

el voleibol   *volleyball*

En el parque   *At the park*

el árbol   *tree*

la flor   *flower*

la hoja   *leaf*

el lago   *lake*

Verbos y expresiones verbales

bailar   *to dance*

caminar   *to walk*

cantar   *to sing*

conocer (irreg.)   *to meet, know*

correr   *to run*

dar (irreg.)   *to give*

dar un paseo   *to take a walk, stroll*

deber + infinitivo   *should + verb*

decir (irreg.)   *to say*

descansar   *to rest*

encantar   *to delight*

esquiar   *to ski*

fumar   *to smoke*

ganar   *to win*

hacer (irreg.) ejercicio   *to exercise*

ir de compras   *to go shopping*

jugar (ue)   *to play*

  jugar al...   *to play a sport*

levantar pesas   *to lift weights*

limpiar   *to clean*

llover (ue)   *to rain*

manejar   *to drive*

me encanta(n)   *I really like it (them)*

montar en bicicleta   *to ride a bicycle*

nadar   *to swim*

nevar (ie)   *to snow*

oír (irreg.)   *to hear*

pensar (ie) + infinitivo   *to think about doing something*

perder (ie)   *to lose*

pintar   *to paint*

poner   *to put*

practicar   *to practice*

saber   *to know*

salir (irreg.) (de)   *to leave*

tener (irreg.) calor   *to be hot*

tener frío   *to be cold*

tener ganas de + infinitivo   *to feel like + infinitive*

tener que + infinitivo   *to have to + infinitive*

tocar   *to touch*

tocar (instrumento musical)   *to play an instrument*

tomar el sol   *to sunbathe*

traer (irreg.)   *to bring*

venir (irreg.)   *to come*

ver   *to see*

ver la tele(visión)   *to watch TV*

viajar   *to travel*

Autoprueba y repaso

I. Saber and conocer. Complete the dialogue with the correct form of the appropriate verb.

Marta: ¿_____ (tú) tocar la guitarra? Necesito encontrar un guitarrista para nuestra fiesta.

Pablo: No _____ tocar la guitarra, pero (yo) _____ a una persona que sabe tocarla muy bien.

Marta: ¿_____ (tú) dónde vive?

Pablo: No _____. Pero podemos buscar su dirección (*address*) y número de teléfono en la guía telefónica y llamarlo. Podemos ir en mi coche a su casa. (Yo) _____ bien la ciudad y puedo acompañarte.

Marta: ¡Gracias!

II. Additional *yo*-irregular verbs. What do perfect students do?

Modelo: tener interés en la clase (Juan, yo)
Juan tiene interés en la clase.
Yo tengo interés en la clase también.

1. venir a clase todos los días (tú, yo)
2. decir *hola* a los estudiantes al entrar en la clase (nosotros, yo)
3. traer la tarea a clase (ellas, yo)
4. poner la tarea en el escritorio del profesor (Ana, yo)
5. saber todo el vocabulario (nosotros, yo)
6. hacer preguntas en clase (ustedes, yo)
7. no salir de clase temprano (ella, yo)

III. *Ir + a* + infinitive. What is happening tomorrow?

Modelo: Lisa / estudiar
Lisa va a estudiar.

1. Marta / jugar al tenis
2. Luisa y Alberto / montar en bicicleta
3. (yo) / ver un partido de fútbol
4. (tú) / preparar una paella
5. nosotros / ir a la playa

IV. The present progressive. What is happening right now?

Modelo: Llueve.
Está lloviendo.

1. Nieva.
2. El niño duerme.
3. Leo una novela.
4. Vemos la tele.
5. Mis hermanos preparan la cena.

V. Ser and estar. What is happening right now?

Luisa Pereira _____ mexicana. _____ de la ciudad de México, pero ahora _____ en Guadalajara. _____ abogada y _____ una mujer inteligente y dinámica. Hoy _____ preocupada porque tiene un caso importante en la corte municipal.

VI. General review. Answer with complete sentences.

1. ¿Qué estás haciendo en este momento?
2. ¿Qué vas a hacer esta noche?
3. ¿Qué haces los fines de semana?
4. ¿Qué tienes que hacer mañana?
5. ¿Qué tienes ganas de hacer ahora?
6. ¿A quién conoces muy bien en la clase de español?
7. ¿Qué traes a la clase?
8. ¿Cuál es tu estación favorita? ¿Por qué?
9. ¿Qué tiempo hace hoy?

VII. Cultura.

1. Regarding sports, in what way are the Spanish-speaking nations of the Caribbean different from other Hispanic nations?
2. What is the novel *En el tiempo de las mariposas* about?
3. How is the African influence in the Dominican Republic and Cuba present today?

Answers to the *Autoprueba y repaso* are found in **Apéndice 2**.

La vida diaria

Así se dice

La vida diaria
  Por la mañana
  Por la noche
Algunas profesiones
  El trabajo

Así se forma

1. Reflexive verbs
2. Reciprocal constructions
3. The preterit of regular verbs and *ser/ir*
4. Direct object pronouns

Cultura

• España
• Los días festivos

Dicho y hecho

• **Para leer:**
  Vivir a la española
• **Para conversar:**
  ¿Somos compatibles?
• **Para escribir:**
  Un día inolvidable
• **Para ver y escuchar:**
  La feria de San Isidro

By the end of this chapter you will be able to:

• Talk about daily routines
• Describe how actions take place
• Talk about actions in the past
• Talk about job-related issues

ENTRANDO AL TEMA

1. Do you know the name of the currency used in Spain? *Hint:* It is the same as in the rest of the EEC (European Economic Community).

2. Which group lived in Spain for almost 800 years and exerted tremendous cultural influence?

☐ Arabs   ☐ Germans   ☐ Chinese

Así se dice

La vida diaria

Por la mañana

Camila

despertarse (ie)

Celia

la cama

el reloj despertador

sonar (ue)

vestirse (i, i)

Alex

Tomás

ponerse (los zapatos, la ropa, etc.) (irreg.)

lavarse (la cara, las manos, etc.)

Cristina

bañarse

Rosa

secarse

el secador de pelo

cortarse (el pelo, las uñas, etc.)

Natalia

las tijeras

Sonia

cepillarse el pelo/el cabello

maquillarse

el cepillo

Lupe

peinarse

Pepita

el maquillaje

el peine

Inés

Alfonso

Pedro

el champú

el gel

ducharse

la toalla

el jabón

el papel higiénico

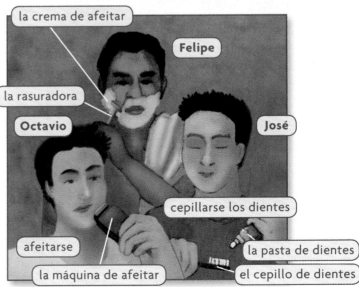

la crema de afeitar

Felipe

la rasuradora

Octavio

José

cepillarse los dientes

afeitarse

la pasta de dientes

la máquina de afeitar

el cepillo de dientes

Por la noche

dormirse (ue)

Pepe

Esteban

la compañera de cuarto

tener sueño

Alicia

Luisa

acostarse (ue)

quitarse (la ropa, los zapatos, etc.)

Leo

Ariel

relajarse

el profesor Marín-Vivar

Carmen

Divertirse (ie, i)

Javier

Marlena

Rubén

Linda

Manuel

acostarse (ue)	*to go to bed*
despertarse (ie)	*to wake up*
divertirse (ie, i)	*to have a good time*
dormirse (ue, u)	*to fall asleep, to go to sleep*
el compañero/la compañera de cuarto	*roommate*
levantarse	*to get up, arise*
quitarse (la ropa)	*to take off (one's clothes, etc.)*
secarse (el pelo, las manos, etc.)	*to dry (one's hair, hands, etc.)*
sonar (ue)	*to ring, sound*
tener sueño	*to be sleepy*
vestirse (i, i)	*to get dressed*

6-1) La rutina diaria.

Paso 1. Organiza estas actividades en orden cronológico, según (*according to*) tu rutina diaria personal. Numéralas del 1 al 15.

_____ acostarse   _____ estudiar

_____ bañarse/ducharse   _____ levantarse

_____ cenar   _____ peinarse

_____ cepillarse los dientes   _____ quitarse la ropa

_____ desayunar   _____ secarse

_____ despertarse   _____ vestirse/ponerse la ropa

_____ dormirse   _____ ver la tele

_____ ir a clase

Paso 2. Ahora compara tu lista con la lista de un/a compañero/a (*classmate*). ¿Son sus rutinas similares o diferentes?

6-2) Nuestras actividades diarias. ¿Qué actividades asocias con los siguientes objetos? Intenta (*try*) pensar en el mayor (*largest*) número posible.

Modelo: el reloj despertador
              despertarse, levantarse, sonar . . .

1. la ropa   5. el peine   9. el desodorante
2. el champú   6. la pasta de dientes   10. la cama
3. el pelo   7. el maquillaje   11. la toalla
4. las tijeras   8. el jabón   12. el cepillo

6-3) ¡Adivina! (*Guess!*) En parejas, uno de ustedes va a leer las descripciones 1–5 mientras (*while*) el otro escucha (¡con el libro cerrado!) e intenta adivinar (*tries to guess*) las actividades o cosas descritas. Después, el Estudiante B lee las descripciones 6-10 y el Estudiante A adivina. ¿Quién puede identificar más cosas o acciones?

Estudiante A:
1. Un líquido para lavarse en la ducha.
2. Un objeto para cepillarse los dientes. Pones la pasta de dientes en él.
3. Una máquina para despertarse por la mañana. Suena mucho.
4. La acción de quitarse pelo con una rasuradora o con una máquina.
5. Después de la ducha o después de lavarse. Se hace con una toalla.

Estudiante B:
6. Un objeto para cortarse el pelo o las uñas, para cortar papel, etc.
7. Un producto para lavarse la cara, las manos.
8. Ir a la cama para dormir.
9. Las chicas usan esto para estar guapas.
10. Un producto para lavarse el pelo.

6-4 Colgate Total.

Paso 1. Mira el anuncio (*ad*) de abajo. ¿Qué está anunciando?

a. un cepillo de dientes   **b.** un desodorante   **c.** una pasta de dientes

Protege tu boca aún cuando no te estás cepillando.

¡La nueva COLGATE TOTAL, con su avanzada fórmula de acción prolongada sigue trabajando después de cepillarte y te ayuda a proteger tu boca contra las caries, el sarro, la placa, la gingivitis y el mal aliento, hasta por doce horas! Colgate Total es una pasta tan avanzada que sigue trabajando entre cepilladas mientras te diviertes, mientras trabajas y hasta cuando duermes. ¡Hora tras hora tras hora!

Visite nuestro website http://www.colgate.com

La cepillada tan avanzada que trabaja entre cepilladas.

Paso 2. Lee las preguntas de abajo (*below*). Después lee el anuncio otra vez (*again*) y contesta las preguntas.

1. ¿Contra qué protege Colgate?

2. ¿Cuándo sigue (*does it continue*) trabajando?

Paso 3. En grupos pequeños, comenten las siguientes (*following*) preguntas sobre sus preferencias respecto a los productos de higiene personal.

1. ¿Qué marca (*brand*) de pasta de dientes usas?

2. Respecto a productos de higiene personal, ¿tienes marcas preferidas? ¿Hay marcas que no te gustan para nada (*at all*)?

3. ¿Qué factor es más importante cuando compras estos productos? ¿Cuánto cuestan? ¿El olor (*scent*) o el sabor (*taste*)? ¿Prefieres los productos clásicos o los nuevos?

Así se forma

Pero mamá, no quiero bañarme. Quiero jugar.

WILEY PLUS Go to WileyPLUS and review the Animated Grammar Tutorial and Verb Conjugator for this grammar point.

1. Talking about daily routines: Reflexive verbs

These verbs combine with reflexive pronouns (**me, te, se, nos, os, se**) to show that the person is doing the action to herself/himself. Note the differences in form and meaning in the following examples.

Carlos **baña** a su hermanito.　　　　*Carlos **bathes** his little brother.* (nonreflexive)
Carlos **se baña**.　　　　　　　　　　*Carlos **bathes himself**.* (reflexive)

Vamos a **vestir** a los niños.　　　　*We're going **to dress** the children.* (nonreflexive)
Vamos a **vestirnos**.　　　　　　　　*We're going **to get dressed**.* (reflexive)

Some verbs have a reflexive form but do not have a reflexive meaning:

Nunca **me duermo** en clase.　　　　*I never **fall asleep** in class.*
Mis amigos **se divierten**.　　　　　*My friends **have fun**.*

Formation of reflexive verbs

There are a few important things to consider:

1. Which reflexive pronoun to chose? The reflexive pronoun and the subject of the verb refer to the same person, so they agree with each other.

vestirse			
(yo)	**me** vist**o**	(nosotros/as)	**nos** vest**imos**
(tú)	**te** vist**es**	(vosotros/as)	**os** vest**ís**
(usted, él/ella)	**se** vist**e**	(ustedes, ellos/ellas)	**se** vist**en**

2. Where to place the reflexive pronoun? This depends on the sentence structure:

   • Immediately before a conjugated verb.

   Me despierto a las seis.　　　　*I wake up at six.*
   No **nos** acostamos tarde.　　　　*We don't go to bed late.*

   • If a conjugated verb is followed by an infinitive or present participle (–**ando**/–**iendo** form), place the reflexive pronoun either *immediately before the conjugated verb* <u>or</u> *after and attached to the infinitive or present participle.*

   Me tengo que levantar temprano.　⎤
   Tengo que levantar**me** temprano.　⎦ —— *I have to get up early.*

   Linda **se** está divirtiendo.　　　⎤
   Linda está divirtiéndo**se**.　　　⎦ —— *Linda is having a good time.*

   • Note that when the reflexive pronoun is attached to a present participle, we need to add a written accent on the vowel that carries the emphasis.

   Linda esta divirti**é**ndose.
   Estoy bañ**á**ndome.

NOTA DE LENGUA

With reflexive verbs, the *definite article* (not possessive adjectives) is normally used to refer to parts of the body or articles of clothing.

Voy a cepillarme **los** dientes.
~~Voy a cepillarme **mis** dientes.~~ }———— *I am going to brush **my** teeth.*

¿Vas a ponerte **el** suéter?
~~¿Vas a ponerte **tu** suéter?~~ }———— *Are you going to put on **your** sweater?*

6-5 **La rutina de Camila e Inés.**

Paso 1. Escucha estos enunciados (*statements*) que describen la rutina matutina (*morning*) de Camila e Inés y escribe el número apropiado debajo de cada ilustración.

Camila   Inés

9:30   7:00

La vida diaria

Paso 2. Ahora indica quién crees que hace estas actividades. Para el número 8, añade (*add*) una actividad que, en tu opinión, hacen las dos chicas.

	Camila	Inés
1. Se quita la ropa y la pone en el piso (*on the floor*).	☐	☐
2. Se acuesta a las 2:00 de la mañana.	☐	☐
3. Se corta el pelo¹ en un salón de belleza (*beauty shop*) muy elegante.	☐	☐
4. Nunca se pone camisas o pantalones de vestir (*dressy*).	☐	☐
5. Se despierta temprano los sábados.	☐	☐
6. Se divierte viendo una película extranjera (*foreign movie*).	☐	☐
7. Se duerme mientras estudia.	☐	☐
8. ...	☒	☒

6-6 **La rutina de Pepe.** Pepe, un estudiante español, va a describir su rutina en el *Colegio Mayor* (una residencia de estudiantes).

Paso 1. Observa la tabla y complétala con las actividades del cuadro, indicando si piensas que Pepe las hace por la mañana, por la noche o en las dos (*both*). Después escucha a Pepe hablar de su rutina y comprueba (*check*) tus respuestas en el cuadro (*chart*).

levantarse	peinarse	divertirse	cepillarse los dientes	lavarse la cara
dormirse	despertarse	ducharse	acostarse afeitarse	vestirse

Por la mañana	Por la noche	Las dos
se levanta		

Paso 2. Con un/a compañero/a, comenten la rutina de Pepe y si (*if*), en su opinión, es común o no.

Modelo: **Pepe se cepilla los dientes...**
Pienso que es/no es común.

---

¹**Cortarse el pelo** is a peculiar reflexive verb in that it does not necessarily mean that one cuts her/his own hair. Often, it means: *to get/have a haircut.*

Paso 1. Lee las siguientes (*following*) preguntas sobre actividades diarias. En la columna *Tú*, decide si las oraciones son ciertas (**sí**) o falsas (**no**) para ti.

Por las mañanas...	Tú		Tu compañero/a	
	Sí	No	Sí	No
¿te despiertas con un reloj despertador?	☐	☐	☐	☐
¿te levantas antes de las 8 de la mañana?	☐	☐	☐	☐
¿te duchas en 5 minutos o menos (*less*)?	☐	☐	☐	☐
¿te cepillas los dientes antes de desayunar?	☐	☐	☐	☐
¿te afeitas o te maquillas?	☐	☐	☐	☐

Por las noches...	Tú		Tu compañero/a	
	Sí	No	Sí	No
¿te diviertes con tus amigos?	☐	☐	☐	☐
¿te duermes cuando ves la televisión?	☐	☐	☐	☐
¿te bañas para relajarte?	☐	☐	☐	☐
¿te peinas o cepillas el pelo?	☐	☐	☐	☐
¿te acuestas después de las 12 de la noche?	☐	☐	☐	☐

Paso 2. Ahora, en parejas, entrevisten (*interview*) a su compañero/a con las preguntas del Paso 1. Pidan (*ask for*) y ofrezcan más detalles. Tomen nota de las respuestas de su compañero/a en la columna correspondiente. Después, expliquen a la clase si sus rutinas son similares o diferentes, dando ejemplos.

Modelo: Estudiante A: **Por las mañanas, ¿te despiertas con un despertador?**
 Estudiante B: **No, no necesito un despertador porque mi compañero de cuarto siempre pone la televisión.**

6-8 ¿Qué prefieres? Ahora vas a averiguar (*find out*) algunos detalles sobre la rutina de tu compañero/a.

Paso 1. Escoge (*Select*) tus preferencias entre las opciones de abajo (*below*). Después escribe oraciones (*sentences*) imaginando las preferencias de tu compañero/a. Inventa una nueva actividad para el número 5.

Modelo: **Yo me ducho, pero creo que Pedro se baña.**
 Yo me ducho y creo que Pedro se ducha también.

1. ducharse vs. bañarse
2. ducharse/bañarse por la mañana vs. por la noche
3. usar gel (de ducha) vs. jabón
4. secarse el pelo con secador vs. con toalla
5. ¿ ... ?

Paso 2. Túrnense (*take turns*) para hablar de sus preferencias y sus hipótesis del Paso 1. Añadan detalles si es posible.

Modelo: Estudiante A: **Yo me ducho, pero creo que tú te bañas.**
 Estudiante B: **No, yo me ducho también.**
 Estudiante A: **¿Usas gel o jabón?/¿Qué marca de champú usas?**

NOTA DE LENGUA

Los adverbios

Adverbs are words that tell *how, how much, how often, when, why,* or *where* an action takes place. You know some already: **bien, mal, ahora, hoy, mañana, a veces, nunca, tarde, aquí, allí,** and **siempre.** Other adverbs are formed by adding **–mente** (equivalent to the English *–ly*) to an adjective.

- Add **–mente** to adjectives ending in **–e** or a consonant.

posible	→	**posiblemente**
general	→	**generalmente**

- Add **–mente** to the feminine singular form of adjectives ending in **–o/–a**.

rápido	→	rápida	→	**rápidamente**
tranquilo	→	tranquila	→	**tranquilamente**

- Adjectives with written accents maintain the written accent in the adverbial form.

rápido	→	**rápidamente**
fácil	→	**fácilmente**

6-9) **Los estudiantes en general.**

Paso 1. Decide cuáles (*which*) de las siguientes afirmaciones probablemente son ciertas para la mayoría (*most*) de los estudiantes universitarios. Inventa tres afirmaciones más.

		Cierto	Falso
1.	Normalmente nos levantamos muy temprano.	☐	☐
2.	Desayunamos todos los días.	☐	☐
3.	Generalmente nos vestimos de manera muy informal.	☐	☐
4.	Nos afeitamos o nos maquillamos para ir a clase frecuentemente.	☐	☐
5.	A veces no nos quitamos el pijama para ir a clase.	☐	☐
6.	Nos divertimos mucho en la clase de español.	☐	☐
7.	Usualmente nos acostamos después de las 12:00 de la noche.	☐	☐
8.	...	☐	☐
9.	...	☐	☐
10.	...	☐	☐

Paso 2. En grupos, compartan (*share*) sus respuestas. ¿Están de acuerdo (*do you agree*) en la mayoría de los casos? Deben estar listos (*ready*) para compartir sus ideas con el resto de la clase más tarde.

NOTA CULTURAL

Tú y usted

In Spain, the form **usted** is generally used less than in Latin America, but teachers and professors expect their students to use **usted**. Does your Spanish instructor prefer that students use **tú** or **usted** when addressing her/him?

6-10) Los instructores.

Paso 1. Piensa ahora sobre (*about*) tus profesores. Escoge la opción que, en tu opinión, describe mejor a la mayoría de ellos. Inventa dos afirmaciones más.

1. Se levantan	☐ antes de las 7 de la mañana.	☐ entre las 7 y las 8 de la mañana.	☐ después de las 8 de la mañana.
2. Se afeitan (ellos) o se maquillan (ellas)	☐ todos los días.	☐ con frecuencia.	☐ a veces.
3. Se visten de manera	☐ informal.	☐ formal.	☐ muy formal.
4. Van a la universidad	☐ a pie (*by foot*) o en bicicleta.	☐ en coche.	☐ en autobús.
5. Se divierten en clase	☐ siempre.	☐ con frecuencia.	☐ a veces.
6. Se acuestan	☐ antes de las 12 de la medianoche.	☐ entre las 12 y la 1 de la mañana.	☐ después de la 1 de la mañana.
7. ...			
8. ...			

 Paso 2. En parejas, comparen sus respuestas. Después, pregunten a su instructor sobre algunas de sus actividades.

Modelo: **¿A qué hora se levanta usted?**

6-11) En la escuela secundaria y en la universidad. ¿Es la vida universitaria muy diferente de la vida durante la escuela secundaria?

 Paso 1. Con un compañero/a, escribe dos actividades habituales para estudiantes universitarios, dos actividades habituales para estudiantes de escuela secundaria y tres que son habituales para los dos grupos de estudiantes.

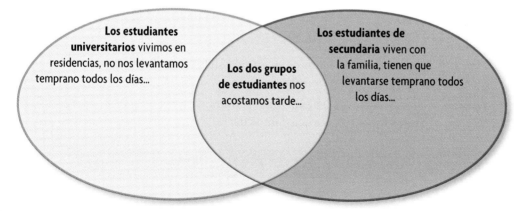

Los estudiantes **universitarios** vivimos en residencias, no nos levantamos temprano todos los días...

Los dos grupos de estudiantes nos acostamos tarde...

Los estudiantes de **secundaria** viven con la familia, tienen que levantarse temprano todos los días...

 Paso 2. En grupos pequeños, compartan sus ideas y decidan: ¿Qué prefieren, la rutina de la escuela secundaria o la rutina de la vida universitaria?

6-12 **Hábitos diarios.** Muchos estudiantes universitarios se quejan (*complain*) de sentirse (*feel*) cansados y de enfermarse (*get sick*) con frecuencia. El Departamento de Salud (*health*) de tu universidad quiere investigar la causa de este problema y tú vas a colaborar en este estudio.

Paso 1. Responde a las preguntas 1–7. Después, anota otros datos relevantes sobre tu estilo de vida, por ejemplo, ejercicio físico, hábitos alimenticios (*eating habits*), etc.

Departamento de Salud
Estudio: Hábitos de vida

1. ¿Tienes sueño ahora?   ☐ Sí   ☐ Un poco   ☐ No

2. ¿A qué hora te levantas los días de clase? _____

3. ¿A qué hora te acuestas normalmente? _____

4. ¿Te duermes cuando estudias o ves la televisión?   ☐ Siempre   ☐ A veces   ☐ Nunca

5. ¿Necesitas un reloj despertador para despertarte?   ☐ Siempre   ☐ A veces   ☐ Nunca

6. ¿Cuántas tazas de café o té tomas cada día? _____

7. ¿Desayunas antes de ir a clase?   ☐ Siempre   ☐ A veces   ☐ Nunca

Otra información: _____
_____
_____
_____

 Paso 2. En grupos de tres o cuatro personas, compartan sus respuestas y tomen notas.

 Paso 3. Compartan las respuestas de su grupo con la clase. ¿Pueden hacer alguna generalización sobre los hábitos de la clase?

Modelo: **Dos de nosotros tenemos sueño ahora.**
              Todos nosotros nos acostamos tarde.

PALABRAS ÚTILES

el estrés	*stress*
estar estresado/a	*to be stressed*
tomar una siesta	*to take a nap*

6-13 **Consejos (Advice).** Tu compañero/a y tú quieren ayudar a otros estudiantes a tener un estilo de vida más saludable (*healthy*). Por eso quieren ser voluntarios en la campaña (*campaign*) del Departamento de Salud. Como parte de su entrenamiento (*training*), van a participar en algunas dramatizaciones (*role-plays*).

Paso 1. Tomen turnos para indicar qué tipo de problema tienen y escuchen los consejos (*advice*) de su compañero/a.

Modelo: Estudiante A: **Siempre tengo sueño.**
           Estudiante B: **Debes acostarte/tomar una siesta** (*take a nap*)**.**

Estudiante A:
1. Siempre llego tarde a clase.
2. Siempre estoy débil.
3. Estoy estresado porque trabajo y estudio mucho todos los días.

Estudiante B:
1. Me canso mucho (*I get very tired*) cuando camino a mis clases.
2. No puedo levantarme por la mañana.
3. Me duermo en la clase de Contabilidad.

Paso 2. Ustedes quieren colaborar en la creación del folleto (*brochure*) del Departamento de Salud. Piensen y escriban juntos (*together*) los tres consejos más importantes que tienen para los estudiantes universitarios.

NOTA CULTURAL

En la universidad

There are some significant differences between higher education in Spain and the United States. In Spain, it is typical for college students to go to universities in their own cities or nearby, and live with their parents while they attend college. When studying in a different city, it is much more common to rent apartments than to stay in a dorm.

In terms of academics, Spaniard college students choose their field of specialization (*carrera*) before they begin their studies, and follow a 3 or 5 year program of courses designed specifically for that major, with no required courses in unrelated areas. Many college courses are extremely demanding, and it is not uncommon to receive a failing grade. When students fail a course required for their specialization, they have to retake it until they pass, so it is not uncommon for students to drop out of college or graduate in their late 20s.

Until recently, many academic institutions in the U.S. considered the degree awarded after a typical five-year course of study in Spain as the equivalent of a master's degree rather than as the equivalent of a bachelor's degree.

INVESTIG@ EN INTERNET

Una de las universidades más antiguas de España (¡y del mundo!) es la **Universidad de Alcalá de Henares.** Imagina que quieres estudiar allí el próximo año. Visita su página web www.uah.es, busca un curso que quieras estudiar (**Departamentos → Asignaturas**), y escribe en un papel la información que encuentres (**profesorado, bibliografía, evaluación,** etc.).

Cultura: España contemporánea

MAR CANTÁBRICO

FRANCIA

La Coruña
Santander
San Sebastián

Santiago
Bilbao

ANDORRA

León
PIRINEOS

Burgos

Río Duero
Río Ebro

Barcelona

PORTUGAL

Segovia
Salamanca

Ávila · Madrid

E S P A Ñ A

Río Tajo
Toledo

Valencia

MENORCA

MALLORCA

IBIZA

ISLAS BALEARES

Lisboa

Río Guadiana

Río Guadalquivir
Córdoba

Sevilla
Granada
SIERRA NEVADA

MAR MEDITERRÁNEO

Cádiz
Málaga

Estrecho de Gibraltar
Algeciras

Nacionalidad: español/a

OCÉANO

ATLÁNTICO

MARRUECOS

ARGELIA

0   100   200 Millas
0   100   200 Kilómetros

Antes de leer

1. ¿Cuáles de estas personas son de España?

   ☐ Penélope Cruz, actress

   ☐ Antonio Banderas, actor

   ☐ Miguel de Cervantes, author of the book *Don Quijote de la Mancha*

   ☐ Pedro Almodóvar, film director

   ☐ Pablo Picasso, painter

2. ¿Cuáles de estas cosas se encuentran en España?

   ☐ olive oil

   ☐ flamenco music and dance

   ☐ a Guggenheim museum

WILEY PLUS Map quizzes: As you read about places highlighted in red, find them on the map. Learn more about and test yourself on the geography of the Spanish-speaking world in *WileyPLUS.*

LA HERENCIA (*HERITAGE*)

Por toda España se observa la herencia de varias culturas y civilizaciones, una de las cuales es la árabe. Los árabes vivieron en España durante casi 800 años (711–1492). La Alhambra, gran palacio y fortaleza situada en **Granada,** es un exquisito ejemplo de la belleza arquitectónica de esta cultura. Algunas de las múltiples atracciones de su decoración interior son el uso de diseños geométricos y el uso de azulejos (*ceramic tiles*) de colores vivos. ¿Qué contraste ves entre el interior y el exterior de la Alhambra?

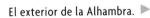

▲ Patio de los Leones en la Alhambra.

El exterior de la Alhambra. ▶

▲ El Rey Juan Carlos de España y su esposa, la Reina Doña Sofía.

▲ El Príncipe Felipe y su esposa, Doña Letizia.

LA FAMILIA REAL

¡En España hay reyes, príncipes y princesas! Sí, la familia real es muy querida por los españoles. El Rey Don Juan Carlos de Borbón tuvo un importante papel en la transición que llevó la democracia a España después de las 40 años de dictadura militar del General Francisco Franco. Ahora su papel es simbólico.

Un aspecto interesante sobre la familia real es su relación con los deportes: varios miembros de la familia real han participado en competiciones deportivas internacionales, incluyendo los Juegos Olímpicos en campeonatos de vela (*sailing*).

INVESTIG@ EN INTERNET

¿Qué sabes sobre la familia real española? Busca los nombres del rey y la reina, sus hijos/as y sus nietos/as, y cualquier (*any*) otra información de interés que puedas averiguar (*find out*) sobre ellos. Además, descubre quién será el sucesor del trono.

- Lope de Vega, un escritor español del siglo XVII, escribió más de 1,500 obras de teatro.
- Miguel de Cervantes, el autor del famoso libro *Don Quijote de la Mancha*, murió exactamente el mismo día que William Shakespeare—el 23 de abril de 1616.

◄ España tiene la cuarta universidad más antigua de Europa, en Salamanca. Fue fundada en el año 1218.

◀ El euro

La Unión Europea

LA MODERNIDAD

En España podemos visitar el pasado y vivir las innovaciones del presente al mismo tiempo. España es parte de la Unión Europea, un conjunto (*group*) de organizaciones creadas entre (*among*) la mayoría de los países de la Europa Occidental.

La Unión tiene el objetivo de articular la cooperación económica, política y social entre los países participantes. En el año 2002 entró en circulación en España el euro, la moneda usada en toda la Unión Europea.

Las playas, las montañas y los numerosos lugares históricos hacen de España uno de los destinos turísticos más populares de Europa. Por ejemplo, se puede esquiar en **los Pirineos,** y las playas de **las Islas Baleares** son muy famosas. **Madrid,** la capital del país, ofrece muchos museos internacionalmente famosos y **Barcelona** es conocida por las grandes obras de arquitectura de la ciudad, entre ellas la Sagrada Familia, del arquitecto Antoni Gaudí.

◀ Pedro Almodóvar es un famoso director de cine español. ¿Has visto alguna de sus películas?

La piel que habito (2011)
Los abrazos rotos (2009)
Volver (2006)
La mala educación (2004)
Hable con ella (2002)
Todo sobre mi madre (1999)
Átame (1990)
Mujeres al borde de un ataque de nervios (1989)

Hay un musical de Broadway basado en una de ellas. ¿Sabes cuál es?

Madrid

Barcelona

Las varias regiones de España constituyen diferentes zonas culturales con sus propios bailes, comidas, vestidos (*attire*) típicos, música, etc. El baile flamenco es típico de Andalucía, región del sur de España donde se encuentra Sevilla. ¿Hay bailes típicos en la región donde vives tú?

Las aceitunas, el aceite de oliva y las naranjas de Valencia son famosos en todo el mundo. ▼

España tiene cuatro idiomas oficiales: el castellano (variedad del español hablado en el centro de la península ibérica), el catalán, el gallego y el vasco. Mira las diferencias entre estos cuatro idiomas.

inglés	Madrid castellano (español)	Barcelona catalán	La Coruña gallego	Bilbao vasco
dog	perro	gos	can	txakurra
water	agua	aigua	auga	ur
sister	hermana	germana	irma	arreba

En la España contemporánea, se crea una vigorosa cultura que combina la herencia de un pasado brillante con las nuevas posibilidades del futuro. La arquitectura futurista del Museo Guggenheim en Bilbao refleja la vitalidad de la vida cultural de España.

◀ El Museo Guggenheim, Bilbao

▲ Hay diferentes recetas para la paella, pero todas usan arroz y casi todas, azafrán (*saffron*) y mariscos.

Después de leer

1. En tu opinión, ¿cuáles pueden ser dos buenos símbolos de la herencia y la modernidad de España?

2. Compara el número de años de diferencia.

Estados Unidos	España	Hay _____ años de diferencia
Mi universidad se fundó en el año _____.	La Universidad de Salamanca se fundó en el año _____.	
Estados Unidos ha existido (*has existed*) por _____ años.	Los moros (árabes) vivieron en España durante _____ años.	

3. Vuelve a mirar las fotos de la Alhambra y del Museo Guggenheim. ¿Qué arquitectura te interesa más? ¿Por qué?

Así se forma

2. Talking about each other: Reciprocal constructions

English uses the phrases *each other* and *one another* to express reciprocal actions: *They love each other/one another*. Spanish uses the pronouns **nos** and **se**, accompanied by the corresponding verb forms, to express reciprocal or mutual actions.

Siempre nos ayudamos con la tarea.

WILEY PLUS Go to *WileyPLUS* and review the Animated Grammar Tutorial for this grammar point.

Linda y Manuel **se** llaman mucho.
Claudia, Juana y yo **nos** conocemos bien.

*Linda and Manuel call **each other** a lot.*
*Claudia, Juana, and I know **one another** well.*

6-14 **¿Amigos o colegas?** Lee los siguientes enunciados y decide si probablemente lo dicen los amigos, los colegas o los dos.

	Amigos	Colegas	Los dos
1. Nos ayudamos con la tarea.	☐	☐	☐
2. Nos consultamos en los negocios importantes.	☐	☐	☐
3. Nos abrazamos frecuentemente.	☐	☐	☐
4. Casi todos los días nos llamamos.	☐	☐	☐
5. A veces nos prestamos (*lend*) ropa.	☐	☐	☐
6. Nos encontramos los fines de semana.	☐	☐	☐

6-15 **Un/a buen/a amigo/a.**

Paso 1. Piensa en un/a amigo/a y contesta las siguientes preguntas sobre ese/a amigo/a y tú.

Modelo: ¿Se llaman por teléfono todos los días?
              Sí, nos llamamos una o dos veces (*times*) todos los días.

1. ¿Cómo se comunican? ¿Se llaman por teléfono? ¿Se mandan correos electrónicos o mensajes de texto por teléfono?
2. ¿Se encuentran frecuentemente? ¿Dónde?
3. ¿Se cuentan (*tell*) sus problemas? ¿Se cuentan secretos?
4. ¿Se ayudan con los estudios?
5. ¿Qué cosas se prestan? ¿Dinero, ropa, CD...?
6. ¿Se hacen reír (*make each other laugh*)?
7. ¿Se enojan (*get upset*) a veces también?

 Paso 2. Comparte con un/a compañero/a tus respuestas sobre tu amigo/a y tú. Pídele (*ask her/him*) más detalles sobre sus respuestas y elabora tus respuestas también.

Modelo: Estudiante A: **Mi amigo Dan y yo no nos llamamos todos los días, pero nos mandamos correos electrónicos.**

              Estudiante B: **Mi amiga Julia y yo nos escribimos en Facebook, ¿ustedes también?**

Antes de leer

¿Hay celebraciones donde vives tú que no se celebran en otras partes del país? ¿Cuáles son y cómo se celebran?

Los días festivos marcan un cambio en la rutina diaria hispana. Usualmente, estas festividades son de dos tipos: religiosas o cívicas. Las fiestas religiosas celebran las tradiciones de la religión católica y las cívicas, los hechos (*events*) históricos. Cada país tiene sus propias (*their own*) fiestas, pero hay muchas que todos los hispanos conmemoran.

◄ Semana Santa en Sevilla, España

La celebración religiosa hispana más popular es la Semana Santa (*Holy Week*). Muchos participan en procesiones por las calles, llevando imágenes de Cristo o de la Virgen María, y se hacen representaciones de escenas bíblicas. Las actividades culminan el sábado y el domingo con bailes y fuegos artificiales (*fireworks*), para celebrar la resurrección de Cristo.

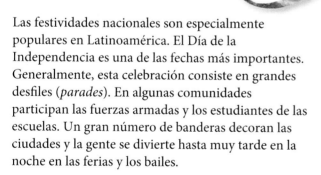

Las festividades nacionales son especialmente populares en Latinoamérica. El Día de la Independencia es una de las fechas más importantes. Generalmente, esta celebración consiste en grandes desfiles (*parades*). En algunas comunidades participan las fuerzas armadas y los estudiantes de las escuelas. Un gran número de banderas decoran las ciudades y la gente se divierte hasta muy tarde en la noche en las ferias y los bailes.

Otras festividades religiosas honran al santo patrón de una ciudad o de un país. Durante la fiesta de San Fermín, en Pamplona, España, ¡sueltan (*set free*) toros por algunas calles (*streets*)! Los habitantes de la ciudad y una enorme cantidad de turistas se visten de blanco con pañuelos (*kerchiefs*) y cinturones (*sashes*) rojos y corren detrás (*behind*) o delante (*in front of*) de los toros. La fiesta atrae a 1.5 millones de turistas todos los años.

Después de leer

1. ¿Hay celebraciones en Estados Unidos que se consideran peligrosas, como los San Fermines en Pamplona?

2. Completa el cuadro siguiente con algunos ejemplos específicos.

	Fiestas cívicas	Fiestas religiosas
España/Latinoamérica		
Estados Unidos		

Así se dice

Algunas profesiones

el señor Vega

el **abogado**/la **abogada**

la señora Vega

la **mujer de negocios**/
el **hombre de negocios**

el Dr. López

el **médico**/la **médica**
el **doctor**/la **doctora**

la señorita Rojas

la **enfermera**/
el **enfermero**

la señora Ruiz

la **programadora de computadoras**/
el **programador de computadoras**

el señor Gómez

el **contador**/
la **contadora**

la señorita Cortés

la **maestra**/el **maestro**

la señora Casona

el **ama de casa**/
el **amo de casa**/

El trabajo

El **trabajo** es una de las actividades más importantes de nuestra vida. Muchos adultos tienen un trabajo **a tiempo completo** y trabajan todo el día, pero otros, por ejemplo muchos estudiantes, tienen trabajos **a tiempo parcial** y trabajan menos horas. No todos los trabajos compensan igual: los doctores, los abogados y otros, generalmente **ganan** mucho **dinero**, pero los maestros y las secretarias normalmente ganan poco. Algunas personas prefieren trabajar para una **compañía** grande, como una multinacional; otras personas prefieren **empresas** pequeñas o familiares. Hay personas que trabajan en una oficina, otras en una escuela o en una universidad, en una **tienda** o en un centro comercial, o por toda la ciudad, como los policías. Otros son **empleados** de una **fábrica**, de un restaurante o de un supermercado. ¿Qué tipo de trabajo prefieres tú?

Carmen es **secretaria**
y **recepcionista**.

Linda es **dependienta**
en una tienda de
ropa.

Alfonso es **mesero** en un restaurante y Natalia es **cajera**.

Octavio es **periodista**. Escribe para el periódico (*newspaper*) de la universidad.

el/la amo/ama de casa	*home maker*	el/la empleado/a	*employee*
el/la cajero/a	*cashier*	la empresa	*firm*
el/la dependiente/a	*salesclerk*	la fábrica	*factory*
la compañía	*company*	ganar	*to earn (money); to win*
el/la contador/a	*accountant*	el/la periodista	*journalist*
el dinero	*money*		
la tienda	*store*	a tiempo completo/parcial	*full-time/ part-time*

NOTA DE LENGUA

Many feminine nouns that start with a stressed **a** require the article **el** in the singular. It is easier to link **el** to the noun than **la**. However, in the plural, **las** is used rather than **los**.

el **a**ma de casa   BUT   **las** amas de casa

el **a**ula   BUT   **las** aulas

NOTA DE LENGUA

When stating a person's profession or vocation without further qualifiers or description, the indefinite article **un** or **una** is not used. When an adjective is added, the indefinite article is used.

Mi madre es **abogada**.   BUT   Mi madre es **una abogada** excelente.
~~Mi madre es **una** abogada.~~

6-16   **¿Sí o no?** Escucha los siguientes enunciados y decide si son lógicos (**sí**) o ilógicos (**no**).

1. ☐ Sí ☐ No	**3.** ☐ Sí ☐ No	**5.** ☐ Sí ☐ No
2. ☐ Sí ☐ No	**4.** ☐ Sí ☐ No	**6.** ☐ Sí ☐ No

6-17 **¿Quién es? ¿Y cuál es su profesión?** Identifica a cada (*each*) persona y su profesión en las páginas 198–199. En la última columna, si conoces a alguien (*someone*) con esa profesión o una profesión similar, escribe su nombre.

Actividad	Persona	Profesión	También tiene esta profesión o una similar
Modelo: Trabaja con computadoras.	**Es la señora Ruiz.**	**Es programadora.**	**Mi tío Ernesto es programador.**
1. Trabaja en un hospital y cuida a los pacientes día y noche.			
2. Escribe informes sobre la situación económica de una compañía.			
3. Vende ropa y complementos en el centro comercial.			
4. Trabaja para una compañía grande, recibe visitas, contesta el teléfono, etc.			
5. Defiende a los inocentes.			
6. Pasa el día en la sala de clase de una escuela primaria. Tiene muchos alumnos.			
7. Trabaja en una clínica o en el hospital. Diagnostica y cura a muchos pacientes.			
8. Sirve comida en un restaurante.			
9. Trabaja en casa.			
10. Informa sobre las noticias y hace entrevistas.			

6-18) La vida profesional.

Paso 1. Elige (*choose*) una de las profesiones nombradas anteriormente y escribe un párrafo corto sobre un día en la vida de una persona con esa profesión.

Modelo: **Cada mañana esta persona se levanta a las...**

 Paso 2. En grupos, compartan sus descripciones y adivinen (*guess*) a qué profesión se refiere cada descripción.

SITUACIONES

One of you will play the role of a career advisor and the other will be herself / himself seeking advice to plan for a professional career. Decide now who is going to play each role.

Career advisor:
1. You are going to interview the student, asking the questions below and two more questions that you think will be relevant. (Write them now.) Listen and take notes.
2. Based on your partner's answers, suggest a profession that would be good for her/him and explain why she/he would like it.

Student: Close your book for this part. In this conversation you are going to:
1. Listen to the questions the career advisor is going to ask you and respond truthfully and with as many details as you can.
2. Listen to the suggestion of the career advisor, tell her/him whether you agree with her/his choice or not, explaining why.

Cuestionario de orientación profesional. Nombre: _____

_____

1. ¿Trabajas? (Si respondes "No", salta (*skip*) al número 5.) _____

2. ¿Qué tipo de trabajo tienes? _____

3. ¿Qué aspectos de tu trabajo te gustan? _____

4. ¿Qué aspectos no te gustan? _____

5. ¿Qué estudias? _____

6. ¿Cuáles son tus clases favoritas? _____

7. ¿Dónde quieres trabajar? En una oficina, en un hospital... _____

8. ¿Es importante para ti ganar mucho dinero? _____

9. ¿ ... ? _____

10. ¿ ... ? _____

Así se forma

WILEY **PLUS** Go to *WileyPLUS* and review the Animated Grammar Tutorial and Verb Conjugator for this grammar point.

¿Saliste con José anoche?

Sí, fuimos al cine.

¿A qué hora regresaron?

3. Talking about actions in the past: The preterit of regular verbs and *ser/ir*

The preterit tense is used to talk about *actions in the past we view/perceive as complete*, or *past actions with a specific beginning, end, or both.*

Me levanté a las ocho y **desayuné**.	*I got up at eight and had breakfast.*
—¿Cuándo **volviste**?	—*When did you return?*
—**Volví** a la una.	—*I returned at one.*
Estudié en la biblioteca por dos horas.	*I studied at the library for two hours.*
Comencé a estudiar a las tres.	*I began to study at three.*
Terminé a las cinco.	*I finished at five.*

Preterit form of regular verbs

		estudiar	**volver** (*to return*)	**salir** (*to leave*)
(yo)		estud**ié**	volv**í**	sal**í**
(tú)		estud**iaste**	volv**iste**	sal**iste**
(usted, él/ella)		estud**ió**	volv**ió**	sal**ió**
(nosotros/as)		estud**iamos**[1]	volv**imos**	sal**imos**
(vosotros/as)		estud**iasteis**	volv**isteis**	sal**isteis**
(ustedes, ellos/ellas)		estud**iaron**	volv**ieron**	sal**ieron**

- Note that **–er/–ir** preterit verb endings are identical.

- In the preterit tense, **–ar** and **–er** verbs never change their stems[2]. (See **volver** above.)

Other preterit forms

- **Ser** and **ir** have identical irregular preterit endings; the context clarifies which verb is used.

ser/ir	**fui, fuiste, fue, fuimos, fuisteis, fueron**	
(ir)	**Fueron** a la playa ayer.	*They went to the beach yesterday.*
(ser)	**Fue** un día extraordinario.	*It was an extraordinary day.*

- There are other irregular forms. Form example, **leer** (*to read*) and **oír** (*to hear*) change the **i** of the third-person singular and plural endings to **y** (**–ió** → **–yo**; **–ieron** → **–yeron**).

leer	leí, leíste, **leyó**, leímos, leísteis, **leyeron**
ser/ir	oí, oíste, **oyó**, oímos, oísteis, **oyeron**

---

[1] The **nosotros** form of **-ar** and **-ir** verbs in the preterit are the same as their respective present-tense forms. [2] You will learn about preterit forms of **–ir** stem-changing verbs in *Capítulo 7*.

Note that verbs ending in **–gar, –car,** and **–zar** have spelling changes in the preterit in order to maintain their pronunciation in the **yo** form.

–gar $g \rightarrow gu$	jugar	yo **jugué**, tú jugaste,...
	llegar	yo **llegué**, tú llegaste,...
–car $c \rightarrow qu$	tocar	yo **toqué**, tú tocaste,...
	buscar	yo **busqué**, tú buscaste,...
–zar $z \rightarrow c$	abrazar	yo **abracé**, tú abrazaste,...
	almorzar	yo **almorcé**, tú almorzaste,...

NOTA CULTURAL

Los calendarios

In many Spanish-speaking countries, calendars begin with Monday, not Sunday. And the "bad luck" day is Tuesday the 13th, not Friday the 13th.

Here are some adverbs and other expressions commonly used with the preterit.

anteayer	ayer	hoy	
12 lunes	13 martes	14 miércoles	15 jueves
Tarea de español	9:00 a.m. – Examen de química	¡Descansar!	
	anoche		
	8:00 p.m. – Trabajar en el restaurante		

primero	*first*
después	*afterwards*
la semana/el mes/el año pasado/a, etc.	*last week/month/year, etc.*
entonces	*then*
luego	*then, later*
ya	*already*

DICHOS

El martes trece, ni te cases, ni te embarques.

¿Qué significa este dicho? Y tú, ¿eres supersticioso?

6-19 ¿Cómo fue tu día ayer?

Paso 1. Lee las siguientes oraciones y, si son ciertas para ti, escribe *Sí.* Si no, reescríbelas para que sean (*are*) ciertas para ti.

1. ____ Me levanté temprano.
2. ____ Fui al gimnasio.
3. ____ Desayuné en la cafetería de la universidad.
4. ____ Llegué temprano a mis clases.
5. ____ Mis amigos y yo comimos juntos.
6. ____ Estudié en la biblioteca.
7. ____ Mi amigo/a y yo fuimos a cenar a un restaurante.
8. ____ Leí una novela en mi cuarto.
9. ____ Me acosté a las 11 de la noche.

Paso 2. Ahora, usa las oraciones del Paso 1 y añade más detalles sobre lo que hiciste ayer. Usa por lo menos (*at least*) tres de las siguientes expresiones:

primero	después	entonces	luego

6-20　Actividades del pasado.

Paso 1. En la columna izquierda (*left*), escribe preguntas para tus compañeros de clase sobre si hicieron estas actividades en el pasado o no. Después añade una actividad original.

Modelo:　comprar un coche nuevo
　　　　　　¿Compraste un coche nuevo?

	El año pasado	Firma
1. viajar a un lugar exótico	¿ _____? ¿Dónde?	
2. ver una película extranjera (*foreign*)	¿ _____? ¿Cuál?	
3. hablar con alguien famoso	¿ _____? ¿Quién?	
4. probar (*to try*) una comida nueva	¿ _____? ¿Cuál?	
5. ir con tus amigos a un sitio peligroso (*dangerous*)	¿ _____? ¿Dónde?	
6. leer un libro escandaloso	¿ _____? ¿Cuál?	
7. estudiar algo nuevo	¿ _____? ¿Qué?	
8. ¿...?	¿ _____?	

 Paso 2. Ahora, hazles las preguntas a tus compañeros. Cuando un/a compañero/a responda "Sí," pídele que firme (*sign*) en la columna *Firma,* y pídele también más detalles, usando las preguntas del cuadro.

 Paso 3. Comenten lo que descubrieron. ¿Quién tuvo el año más interesante?

6-21　La semana de la profesora Rodríguez.

Tu amiga está hablando sobre su profesora de español. Algunas de las oraciones se refieren a cosas que siempre hace y otras se refieren a cosas que hizo específicamente la semana pasada. ¿Puedes distinguir entre las dos? Vas a escuchar cada oración dos veces.

	Siempre	La semana pasada		Siempre	La semana pasada
1.	☐	☐	6.	☐	☐
2.	☐	☐	7.	☐	☐
3.	☐	☐	8.	☐	☐
4.	☐	☐	9.	☐	☐
5.	☐	☐	10.	☐	☐

PALABRAS ÚTILES

enseñar	*to teach*
ayudar	*to help*

Paso 2. Ahora que sabes un poco más sobre las actividades de la profesora Rodríguez la semana pasada, escribe cuatro oraciones más sobre otras actividades que probablemente hizo. Usa los verbos del cuadro.

salir	cenar	acostarse	ver

6-22 El sábado pasado.
Escucha varias oraciones sobre lo que Javier y su hermano menor, Samuel, hicieron el sábado. Escribe el número de cada oración al lado del dibujo apropiado.

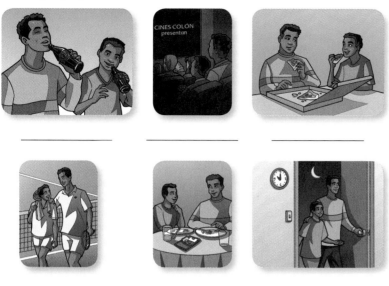

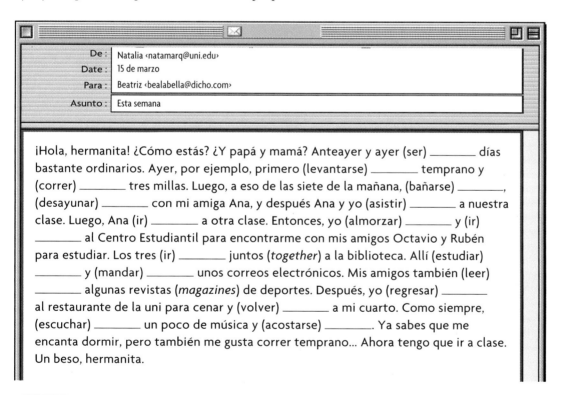

6-23 Un día normal.
Lee el mensaje que Natalia le envió a su hermana ayer y completa los espacios con la forma apropiada de cada verbo.

De : Natalia ‹natamarq@uni.edu›
Date : 15 de marzo
Para : Beatriz ‹bealabella@dicho.com›
Asunto : Esta semana

¡Hola, hermanita! ¿Cómo estás? ¿Y papá y mamá? Anteayer y ayer (ser) _____ días bastante ordinarios. Ayer, por ejemplo, primero (levantarse) _____ temprano y (correr) _____ tres millas. Luego, a eso de las siete de la mañana, (bañarse) _____, (desayunar) _____ con mi amiga Ana, y después Ana y yo (asistir) _____ a nuestra clase. Luego, Ana (ir) _____ a otra clase. Entonces, yo (almorzar) _____ y (ir) _____ al Centro Estudiantil para encontrarme con mis amigos Octavio y Rubén para estudiar. Los tres (ir) _____ juntos (together) a la biblioteca. Allí (estudiar) _____ y (mandar) _____ unos correos electrónicos. Mis amigos también (leer) _____ algunas revistas (magazines) de deportes. Después, yo (regresar) _____ al restaurante de la uni para cenar y (volver) _____ a mi cuarto. Como siempre, (escuchar) _____ un poco de música y (acostarse) _____. Ya sabes que me encanta dormir, pero también me gusta correr temprano... Ahora tengo que ir a clase. Un beso, hermanita.

6-24 Un fin de semana interesante.

Paso 1. Escribe un párrafo con muchos detalles sobre lo que hiciste el sábado pasado. No escribas tu nombre en el papel.

Paso 2. Cuando toda la clase haya acabado (has finished), el instructor va a repartir (distribute) todas las historias. Lee la historia que te da y adivina quién la escribió.

VideoEscenas: La rosa sevillana

▲ En el Capítulo 5 Rocío y Carmen hablaron de sus planes para el fin de semana. Carmen fue a visitar a una amiga en Sevilla. Ahora ya está en Madrid y habla con Rocío otra vez.

 Paso 1. Antes de (*before*) ver el video, di (*tell*) a un/a compañero/a dónde fuiste este fin de semana. Escucha a tu compañero/a también y toma apuntes. ¿Fueron a algún lugar (*any place*) similar?

Paso 2. Mira el video prestando atención a las ideas principales. Después, indica si estas afirmaciones son ciertas o falsas.

		Cierto	Falso
1.	Carmen no fue a Sevilla.	☐	☐
2.	Carmen visitó muchos lugares (*places*) interesantes.	☐	☐
3.	Carmen bailó flamenco.	☐	☐
4.	Un chico le regaló una rosa a Carmen.	☐	☐

Paso 3. Lee las oraciones a continuación y mira el video otra vez. Ahora, presta atención a la información específica que necesitas para completar estas oraciones.

1. Anoche Carmen _____.

2. Carmen _____ a un parque, un museo y una catedral.

3. Por la noche Carmen _____ a un chico fantástico y ahora está enamorada (*in love*).

Así se forma

Felipe, mi amiga Rosa quiere conocerte.

¿Rosa? La vi ayer en la cafetería.

La conozco. ¡Es muy simpática!

4. Direct object pronouns

A **direct object** is the person or thing that directly receives the action of the verb. It answers the question *Who/Whom?* or *What?*

(What?)	Compré **el carro**.	→	**Lo** compré.
	*I bought **the car**.*		*I bought **it**.*
(Who/Whom?)	Vi **a Laurie**.	→	**La** vi.
	*I saw **Laurie**.*		*I saw **her**.*

WILEY **PLUS** Go to *WileyPLUS* and review the Animated Grammar Tutorial for this grammar point.

In the examples above, *the car* and *Laurie* are <u>direct object nouns</u>. When a direct object has been previously mentioned and we want to avoid redundancy we use <u>direct object pronouns</u>. In the sentences above; *it* and *her* are the direct object (DO) pronouns.
Important! When the direct object noun is a person, it requires the personal **a** (observe the contrast in the examples above).

Pronombres de objeto directo

me	Carlos no **me** llamó.	*Carlos did not call **me**.*
te	¿**Te** llamó Carlos?	*Did Carlos call **you**?*
lo	No **lo** conozco. (a Juan/a usted, *m.*)	*I don't know **him/you** (m.).*
	No **lo** tengo. (el libro)	*I don't have **it** (m.).*
la	Juan **la** conoce. (a Lola/a usted, *f.*)	*Juan knows **her/you** (f.).*
	Juan **la** come. (la fruta)	*Juan eats **it** (f.).*
nos	Laurie **nos** visitó anoche.	*Laurie visited **us** last night.*
os	¿Quién **os** visitó?	*Who visited **you** (pl.)?*
los	Voy a llamar**los**. (a ellos/a ustedes, *m.*)	*I am going to call **them/you** (m.).*
	Voy a preparar**los**. (los cafés)	*I am going to prepare **them** (m.).*
las	Pedro **las** admira. (a ellas/a ustedes, *f.*)	*Pedro admires **them/you** (f.).*
	Pedro **las** va a preparar. (las bebidas)	*Carlos is going to prepare **them** (f.).*

• Direct object pronouns must agree with the nouns they replace or refer to.

—¿Compraste **la pasta de dientes**?	*Did you buy **the toothpaste**?*
—Sí, **la** compré.	*Yes, I bought **it**.*
—¿Usaste **el nuevo jabón**?	*Did you use **the new soap**?*
—Sí, **lo** usé.	*Yes, I used **it**.*

NOTA DE LENGUA

Note that the pronoun *it* can only be translated as **lo/la** when it functions as a direct object. The English *it* subject pronoun is usually omitted in Spanish.

I ate it.	→	**Lo comí.**	
			We didn't write it. → **No lo escribimos.**

BUT

It is expensive.	→	**Es caro.**	
			It opens at 8 A.M. → **Abre a las 8 de la mañana.**

Position of direct object pronouns

- The direct object pronoun is placed immediately before a conjugated verb.

Lo compré.   *I bought **it**.*

- If a conjugated verb is followed by an infinitive or present participle (**-ando/-iendo** form), place the direct object pronoun either immediately before the conjugated verb or after and attached to the infinitive or present participle[1]. It cannot be placed between both forms.

Voy a invitar**la**.	*o* **La** voy a invitar.	*I am going to invite **her**.*
Estoy llamándo**la**.	*o* **La** estoy llamando.	*I am calling **her**.*

6-28 **De compras.** Estás en la farmacia para comprar algunas cosas que necesitan tú y tu compañera de cuarto. Eres un poco despistada (*absent-minded*) así que tu compañera te llama para asegurarse (*make sure*) de que no olvidas nada. Escucha y elige la respuesta correcta.

1.	□ Sí, lo voy a comprar.	□ Sí, la voy a comprar.	□ Sí, los voy a comprar.	□ Sí, las voy a comprar.
2.	□ Sí, lo tengo.	□ Sí, la tengo.	□ Sí, los tengo.	□ Sí, las tengo.
3.	□ Sí, lo busqué.	□ Sí, la busqué.	□ Sí, los busqué.	□ Sí, las busqué.
4.	□ No, no lo tengo.	□ No, no la tengo.	□ No, no los tengo.	□ No, no las tengo.
5.	□ No, no lo tengo.	□ No, no la tengo.	□ No, no los tengo.	□ No, no las tengo.
6.	□ No, no lo puedo comprar.	□ No, no los puedo comprar.	□ No, no la puedo comprar.	□ No, no las puedo comprar.

6-29 **¿Quién tiene mis tijeras?** Los estudiantes frecuentemente se prestan cosas. En parejas, imaginen que viven en la residencia de las páginas 180–181 y no encuentran algunas cosas. Primero, el Estudiante A le pregunta al Estudiante B sobre las cosas que no encuentra (1–5) y el Estudiante B explica *quién* tiene cada cosa y *para qué* la están usando, según la ilustración. Luego, el Estudiante B pregunta sobre sus cosas (6–10) y el Estudiante A contesta.

Modelo: tijeras

    Estudiante A: **¿Quién tiene mis tijeras?**

    Estudiante B: **Natalia *las* tiene. *Las* está usando para cortarse el pelo.**

Cosas del Estudiante A:
1. secador de pelo
2. peine
3. cepillo
4. maquillaje
5. champú

Cosas del Estudiante B:
6. máquina de afeitar
7. pasta de dientes
8. despertador
9. desodorante
10. guitarra

---

[1]In other instances, you must attach the pronoun to the infinitive or the **–ando/–iendo** form.
Voy al laboratorio para ver**lo**.
Aprendo los verbos practicándo**los**.

6-30 **Cosas (*Things*) para vender.** En grupos pequeños, imaginen que son estudiantes universitarios en España. Necesitan dinero y quieren vender algunas cosas que ya no usan.

Paso 1. Individualmente, selecciona cuatro cosas de la lista que quieres vender. Decide en qué condición está cada cosa (**nuevo, casi nuevo, usado, muy usado**) y escribe el precio en euros que quieres por cada cosa. ¡No dejes que tus compañeros lo vean!

Modelo: ☑ un refrigerador pequeño   *casi nuevo*_____ € _39_

☐ una máquina de afeitar   _____ € _____

☐ un radio-despertador   _____ € _____

☐ un teléfono celular   _____ € _____

☐ unos libros de psicología   _____ € _____

☐ una impresora a color   _____ € _____

☐ un sofá   _____ € _____

☐ un televisor muy grande   _____ € _____

☐ una computadora portátil   _____ € _____

☐ unos CDs de música clásica   _____ € _____

Paso 2. Tomen turnos para vender sus cosas. Es posible que tengan que negociar los precios. Toma nota de todo el dinero que ganas (*earn*). Si quieres rechazar algo, piensa en una excusa. Si a una persona no le interesa uno de tus objetos, intenta vendérselo a otra persona. ¿Cuánto dinero ganaste?

Modelo:
Estudiante A: **Tengo un refrigerador pequeño para vender. Está casi nuevo.**
Estudiante B: **¿Cuánto cuesta?**
Estudiante A: **Cuesta treinta y nueve euros. ¿Quieres comprarlo?**
Estudiante B: **Sí, lo compro./ No gracias. Es un poco caro (*expensive*)...**

> **INVESTIG@ EN INTERNET**
>
> Desde que España es miembro de la Unión Europea, ha adoptado el euro (€) en lugar de (*instead of*) su divisa (*currency*) tradicional, la **peseta**. ¿Recuerdas las divisas de otros países hispanos?

6-31 **La telenovela *Un día de la vida*.** Van a hacer una prueba (*audition*) para los papeles de Aurora y Anselmo, dos personajes de una telenovela cursi (*cheesy*): ***Un día de la vida.*** Primero, completen el diálogo con los objetos directos **me, te** o **lo**. Después, léanlo muy dramáticamente. ¡Realmente quieren obtener los papeles!

Anselmo: Mi amor, estás muy triste. ¿Qué pasa?... _____ amas, ¿verdad?

Aurora: _____ amo con todo mi corazón, pero tengo que ser muy franca. También adoro a Rafael y sé que él _____ adora a mí.

Anselmo: Pero yo también _____ adoro. Eres el amor de mi vida. _____ necesitas, ¿verdad?

Aurora: Claro que _____ necesito, pero no puedo imaginar mi vida sin Rafael. También _____ necesito a él. _____ extraño (*miss*) mucho.

Anselmo: Mi cielo, tú sabes muy bien que no va a volver, y tú sabes que yo estoy aquí y que _____ quiero.

Aurora: (*Ella solloza* [sobs].) Pero él es único. Yo no _____ quiero a ti como _____ quiero a él.

Anselmo: (*También solloza.*) Tengo que reconocer (*admit*) que también _____ quiero. Yo también _____ extraño.

Aurora: Nunca vamos a encontrar otro perro como él.

Dicho y hecho

PARA LEER: Vivir a la española

ANTES DE LEER

1. Lee el título del texto, observa su formato y escoge (*select*) una de estas descripciones.

   ☐ Un informe sobre los hábitos de los españoles.
   ☐ Un artículo de opinión comparando España con otros países.
   ☐ Entrevistas (*interviews*) sobre la vida diaria en España.

2. ¿Qué ideas asocias con la vida en España? Piensa en costumbres, hábitos, tradiciones, cultura, etc.

ESTRATEGIA DE LECTURA

Activate your background knowledge After you get an idea of the topic and main ideas in a text by looking at the title, headings and visuals, and skimming over it, it is a good idea to think about what you know about the topic before you start to read. Applying that knowledge, you'll be better able to interpret the text. Keep the ideas you came up with in question 2 above, and anything else you may have learned about Spain in mind as you read the selection that follows.

A LEER

El tópico[1] relaciona a España con los toros[2], el flamenco, la juerga[3] y el sol. Cierto o no, entrevistamos a dos jóvenes extranjeros[4] que viven aquí y les preguntamos sobre su vida en nuestro país.

ALBERTA ARVALLI 25 años, Padua (Italia)

No es la primera vez[5] que Alberta vive en España. En esta segunda etapa vive en Madrid y trabaja como arquitecto.

¿Por qué decidiste volver?

Porque, bueno, España me encanta por la manera que tienen los españoles de vivir y Madrid es una ciudad preciosa que ya conocía y, nada, porque encontré al final trabajo aquí.

¿Crees que hay diferencia entre la gente[6] española y la gente italiana?

Yo creo que la gente del sur de España es más parecida[7] a la gente del sur de Italia. La gente del norte de España, más parecida a la del norte de Italia. La cultura (es) un poco diferente, pero yo creo que en Europa, ahora mismo, la gente es muy similar.

Has mencionado la cultura española, ¿qué piensas de ella?

A mí me encanta. A mí me encanta leer y creo que hay muchos libros, mucha literatura española que la gente tiene que leer porque España tiene una cultura muy amplia.

PHILLIP STARK 28 años, Toledo (Ohio)

Llegó a Bilbao hace seis años y desde entonces vive en España. Empezó trabajando como profesor de inglés y hoy en día dirige una revista[8], tiene un negocio en Internet y realiza documentales.

¿Por qué decidiste venir a España?

Pues… yo había visto un folleto[9] para estudiar español en el extranjero y me parecía muy interesante Bilbao. Entonces, pues nada, fui a Bilbao y lo pasé genial[10], y me dije "yo me quedo aquí para siempre".

¿Para ti qué es lo mejor que tiene España?

A ver… lo mejor que tiene España… España, no sé, es otra cultura, una cultura muy tranquila, gente tranquila, las cosas van un poco más, no sé, lentas. Me gusta la comida, me gusta Madrid porque es como vivir en Nueva York pero sin tanta locura.

Y ahora que vives en Madrid, ¿para ti cómo es un día ideal en esta ciudad?

¿En Madrid? Pues un día ideal es irme a un bar de viejos, hablar con el camarero un poquito, tomarme una cañita[11] y una tapa y ya está, no me hace falta más.

Texto: Elena Giménez / *Punto y coma*

---

[1] cliché, [2] bullfighting, [3] partying, [4] foreign, [5] time, occasion, [6] people, [7] similar, [8] magazine, [9] brochure, [10] I had a great time, [11] draft beer

1. ¿Menciona el texto algunas ideas que tú y tus compañeros tenían sobre la vida en España antes de leer el texto? ¿Cuáles?

2. Escoge la opción más apropiada de acuerdo con las opiniones de los entrevistados.

   a. Los españoles son parecidos a/ diferentes de/ más lentos que otros europeos.

   b. La literatura española es muy famosa / excesiva / extensa.

   c. Madrid es similar a Nueva York porque es una ciudad tranquila/ es una ciudad loca/ ofrece variedad de eventos culturales.

3. Imagina que eres el periodista que entrevistó a Alberta y Phillip. ¿Qué otras preguntas tienes para ellos?

PARA CONVERSAR: ¿Somos compatibles?

 Tres amigos/as y tú están pensando en alquilar (*to rent*) un apartamento juntos, pero sólo hay dos dormitorios (*bedrooms*) y un cuarto de baño (*bathroom*).

Paso 1. Descríbeles a tus compañeros/as tus actividades en un día normal. En particular, incluye las cosas que haces en casa y cuándo. También debes escuchar las descripciones de ellos/ellas y hacer preguntas.

Paso 2. Decidan como grupo si son compatibles o no. Deben decidir si son compatibles para compartir el apartamento, quiénes van a compartir dormitorio y cómo van a organizar el uso del baño y la cocina.

ESTRATEGIA DE COMUNICACIÓN

Establishing timeframe and sequence Giving structure to your description of the events of a regular day will make your message easier for your listener to understand. Organize the events into morning events **(Por la mañana...)**, and afternoon events **(Por la tarde...)**, and within each timeframe, use expressions to mark sequence such as the following.

Primero...	*First...*	**Después...**	*Afterwards...*
Luego...	*Then...; Later...*	**Finalmente...**	*Finally..., Lastly...*

PARA ESCRIBIR: Un día inolvidable (*unforgettable*)

Vas a describir un día que fue inolvidable por alguna razón, usando verbos en el pretérito. Tu lector/a (*reader*) es una persona que va a escribir una biografía sobre tu vida.

ANTES DE ESCRIBIR

Paso 1. ¿Qué día quieres describir?

☐ el mejor (*best*) día de mi vida   ☐ el día más triste de mi vida

☐ el día más feliz de mi vida   ☐ el día más extraño de mi vida

☐ _____

Dicho y hecho

Paso 2. ¿Qué pasó ese día? Ahora piensa en por lo menos cuatro eventos que ocurrieron ese día. Escríbelos en tu cuaderno usando los verbos en el pretérito.

Modelo: El despertador no **funcionó** y **me desperté** tarde. **Perdí** (*I missed*) el tren. **Llegué** tarde al trabajo…

A ESCRIBIR

Escribe un primer borrador (*draft*) que describa este día en tu vida. Usa los eventos que mencionaste en el Paso 2 de *Antes de escribir* como las oraciones temáticas de tus párrafos.

Para escribir mejor: Estas palabras de conexión probablemente te pueden ayudar a escribir mejor al igual que en la conversación.

primero	*first*	**finalmente**	*finally*
segundo	*second*	**por último**	*lastly*
después	*next/then*	**además**	*in addition*

En tu conclusión, puedes usar frases como estas:

No quiero tener otro día como este nunca.

Este día fue realmente fantástico.

DESPUÉS DE ESCRIBIR

Revisar y editar: Después de escribir el primer borrador de tu composición, déjalo a un lado (*put it aside*) por un mínimo de un día sin leerlo. Cuando vuelvas (*you return*) a leerlo, corrige la organización, el contenido, la gramática y el vocabulario. Hazte (*ask yourself*) estas preguntas:

☐ ¿Tiene cada párrafo una oración temática?

☐ ¿Tiene cada idea, en cada párrafo, relación con la oración temática?

☐ ¿Describí los cuatro eventos con suficientes detalles?

☐ ¿Usé palabras de conexión entre los eventos?

☐ Subraya (*underline*) cada verbo. ¿Usé correctamente el pretérito?

☐ ¿Usé correctamente los pronombres de objeto directo?

PARA VER Y ESCUCHAR: La feria de San Isidro

ANTES DE VER EL VIDEO

Piensa en las celebraciones típicas de Estados Unidos. ¿Cómo se festejan (*are they celebrated*)?

La gente...	Celebraciones
... se pone ropa especial.	
...come algo en particular.	
...toca música.	
...va a un servicio religioso.	

ESTRATEGIA DE COMPRENSIÓN

Taking notes When listening to a lecture, instructions or whenever you need to recall specific information, it is useful to take notes. It is key to keep in mind your purpose (are you interested in the main ideas or specific details?) so that you can focus on taking notes that are relevant.

A VER EL VIDEO

1. Mira el video concentrándote en las ideas generales. Puedes tomar notas breves de ideas o palabras clave. Después, escribe un resumen de las ideas principales del video.

   La Feria de San Isidro es…
   Algunas actividades típicas durante la feria son…

2. Lee las siguientes preguntas. Después mira el video otra vez y toma nota de los detalles relevantes para responder a las preguntas.

   a. ¿Cuándo y dónde se celebra el día de San Isidro?

   b. ¿Qué hace la gente en la iglesia de San Isidro?

   c. Después van a la Plaza Mayor, ¿qué hacen allí?

   d. ¿Cuántos tipos de rosquillas hay? ¿Cómo son diferentes?

   e. ¿Qué tipos de música y baile se escuchan y ven durante esta fiesta?

DESPUÉS DE VER EL VIDEO

¿Tiene algo en común la Feria de San Isidro con alguna celebración que conoces en Estados Unidos?

Repaso de vocabulario activo

Adverbios y expresiones adverbiales

el (año/mes/verano, etc.) pasado   *last (year/month/summer)*

anoche   *last night*

anteayer   *the day before yesterday*

ayer   *yesterday*

después   *later*

entonces   *then*

el fin de semana pasado   *last weekend*

luego   *later, then*

más tarde   *later*

primero   *first*

la semana pasada   *last week*

ya   *already*

Sustantivos
La rutina diaria   *Daily routine*

la cama   *bed*

el cepillo (de dientes)   *(tooth)brush*

el champú   *shampoo*

la crema de afeitar   *shaving cream*

el desodorante   *deodorant*

el gel (de ducha)   *(shower) gel*

el jabón   *soap*

el maquillaje   *makeup*

la máquina de afeitar   *electric shaver*

el papel higiénico   *toilet paper*

la pasta de dientes   *toothpaste*

el peine   *comb*

la rasuradora   *razor*

el reloj despertador   *alarm clock*

el secador de pelo   *hair dryer*

las tijeras   *scissors*

la toalla   *towel*

El trabajo   *Work*

la compañía   *company*

el dinero   *money*

la empresa   *a business, company*

la fábrica   *factory*

la tienda   *store, shop*

de ropa   *clothing store*

el trabajo   *work*

a tiempo completo/parcial   *full-time/part-time*

Más personas y profesiones

el/la abogado/a   *lawyer*

el/la amo/a de casa   *homemaker*

el/la cajero/a   *cashier*

el/la compañero/a de cuarto   *roommate*

el/la contador/a   *accountant*

el/la dependiente/a   *salesclerk*

el/la empleado/a   *employee*

el/la enfermero/a   *nurse*

el hombre/la mujer de negocios   *businessperson*

el/la maestro/a   *teacher*

el/la médico/a   *doctor*

el/la mesero/a   *waiter/waitress*

el/la periodista   *journalist*

el/la programador/a de computadoras   *computer programmer*

el/la recepcionista   *receptionist*

el/la secretario/a   *secretary*

Verbos y expresiones verbales

acostarse (ue)   *to go to bed*

afeitarse   *to shave*

bañarse   *to take a bath*

cepillarse los dientes/el pelo   *to brush one's teeth/hair*

cortarse el pelo/las uñas/el dedo   *to cut one's hair/nails/a finger*

despertarse (ie)   *to wake up*

divertirse (ie, i)   *to have fun*

dormirse (ue, u)   *to sleep*

ducharse   *to take a shower*

ganar   *to earn, make (money)*

lavarse las manos/la cara, etc.   *to wash one's hands/face, etc.*

levantarse   *to get up*

maquillarse   *to put on makeup*

peinarse   *to comb one's hair*

ponerse los zapatos/la ropa, etc. (irreg.)   *to put on one's shoes/clothes, etc.*

quitarse (la ropa)   *to take off (one's clothes)*

relajarse   *to relax*

secarse   *to dry (oneself)*

tener (irreg.) sueño   *to be sleepy, tired*

trabajar para...   *to work for*

sonar (ue)   *to ring, sound*

vestirse (i, i)   *to get dressed*

Autoprueba y repaso

I. Reflexive verbs. Son las ocho de la mañana en la residencia estudiantil. Indica qué pasa.

Modelo: Alfonso / levantarse
Alfonso se levanta.

1. mi compañero/a de cuarto / despertarse
2. yo / levantarse
3. tú / bañarse
4. Pepita / cepillarse los dientes
5. nosotros / ponerse suéteres porque hace frío
6. Octavio y Manuel / vestirse

II. Reciprocal constructions. Imagina que estás contando cómo se conocieron tus papás. Usa el pretérito o el presente de acuerdo a la situación.

Modelo: conocerse en la universidad.
Mis padres se conocieron en la universidad.

1. gustarse inmediatamente
2. darse los números de teléfono ese mismo día
3. verse todos los días
4. aún hoy, después de veinticinco años, quererse mucho

III. The preterit of regular verbs and *ser/ir*.

A. Indica qué pasó esta mañana antes del trabajo.

Modelo: yo / levantarse temprano
Me levanté temprano.

1. yo / ducharse
2. Pepita / peinarse
3. tú / lavarse la cara
4. nosotros / afeitarse
5. ellos / cepillarse los dientes

B. Indica qué pasó durante la jornada laboral.

Modelo: yo / desayunar en Starbucks
Desayuné en Starbucks.

1. yo / llegar al trabajo a las nueve
2. dos colegas / leer las noticias (*news*) del día
3. mi colega y yo / mandar un correo electrónico al presidente de la compañía
4. tú / escribir un memo muy importante
5. nosotros / ir a un restaurante chino para almorzar
6. en la tarde, mi colega / llamar a varios de nuestros clientes
7. ella / resolver un problema serio
8. nosotros / salir del trabajo a las cinco de la tarde

IV. Direct object pronouns.

A. Camilia va a invitar a su fiesta a todos los que deseen ir.

Modelo: Elena quiere ir a la fiesta.
Pues, Camila va a invitarla.

1. Yo quiero ir.
2. Nosotros queremos ir.
3. Ustedes quieren ir.
4. Mis hermanas quieren ir.
5. Mis hermanos quieren ir.
6. Pepita quiere ir.
7. Tú quieres ir.

B. Contesta la pregunta con el pronombre de objeto directo apropiado.

Modelo: ¿Quieres conocer al presidente de la universidad?
Sí, quiero conocerlo./Sí, lo quiero conocer. O,
No, no quiero conocerlo./No, no lo quiero conocer.

1. ¿Quieres ver a tus amigos/as hoy?
2. ¿Vas a llamar a tus padres esta noche?
3. ¿Estás haciendo la tarea para la clase de español ahora?
4. ¿Completaste todos los ejercicios del Capítulo 6?
5. ¿Vas a estudiar todo el vocabulario?

V. *Repaso general.* Contesta cada pregunta con tantas actividades como sea posible.

1. ¿Qué haces por la mañana después de levantarte?
2. ¿Qué haces antes de acostarte?
3. ¿Adónde fuiste ayer? ¿Qué más ocurrió ayer?
4. ¿Qué pasó el fin de semana pasado?
5. ¿Llamaste a tu mejor amigo/a la semana pasada? ¿De qué hablaron?

VI. *Cultura.*

1. Nombra dos cosas que has aprendido sobre la historia de España.
2. Nombra dos cosas que has aprendido sobre la España moderna.
3. Explica qué son los **azulejos** y cómo llegaron a España.

Las respuestas de *Autoprueba y repaso* se pueden encontrar en el **Apéndice 2.**

Por la ciudad

Así se dice

Por la ciudad
  En el centro de la ciudad
En correos y en el banco
  En la oficina de correos
  El dinero y los bancos

Así se forma

1. Prepositions
2. Demonstrative adjectives and pronouns
3. The preterit of *hacer* and stem-changing verbs
4. Indirect object pronouns

Cultura

- Argentina y Chile
- La plaza en el mundo hispano

Dicho y hecho

Para leer:
El Tortoni: Café con historia

Para conversar:
¿Qué compramos?

Para escribir:
Tres días en Santiago o en Buenos Aires

Para ver y escuchar:
La plaza: Corazón de la ciudad

By the end of this chapter you will be able to:

- Talk about places and things in the city
- Carry out transactions at the post office and the bank
- Talk about actions in the past
- Talk about to whom or for whom something is done

ENTRANDO AL TEMA

1. La ciudad de esta foto es la capital de Chile. ¿Sabes cómo se llama?

2. ¿Sabes cuál es la ciudad más austral (*southernmost*) del planeta?

3. Chile y Argentina forman parte de América del Sur. Otro nombre para esta zona es:
   ☐ El Medio Oeste   ☐ El Cono Sur   ☐ Tierra Caliente

Así se dice

Por la ciudad

el rascacielos

el edificio

el banco (*bank*)

ALMACÉN TORRES

el almacén

Banco Central

el centro comercial

la pastelería

Pastelería Colón

la pizzería

Pizzería Roma

EL MESÓN

la película

EL H ARA

la joyería

CALLE 3

Zapatería Colón

La Perla

la calle

la zapatería

el restaurante/el café

el autobús

AVE. COLÓN

PARADA

el taxi

la avenida

la parada de autobús

la estatua

la plaza

el metro

METRO Plaza Colón

Cristóba

WILEY
PLUS **Pronunciación:**
Practice pronunciation of the
chapter vocabulary and particular
sounds of Spanish in *WileyPLUS*.

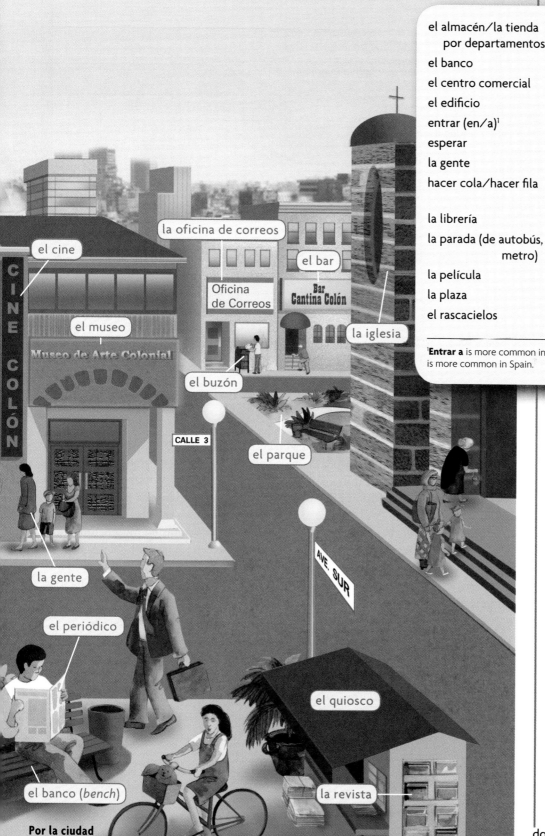

el almacén/la tienda por departamentos	*department store*
el banco	*bank; bench*
el centro comercial	*shopping center, mall*
el edificio	*building*
entrar (en/a)[1]	*to enter, go in*
esperar	*to wait for*
la gente	*people*
hacer cola/hacer fila	*to get/stand/wait in line*
la librería	*bookstore*
la parada (de autobús, metro)	*(bus, subway) stop*
la película	*film, movie*
la plaza	*town square*
el rascacielos	*skyscraper*

[1]**Entrar a** is more common in Latin America, while **entrar en** is more common in Spain.

el cine

la oficina de correos

el bar

Oficina de Correos

Bar Cantina Colón

C I N E   C O L Ó N

el museo

Museo de Arte Colonial

la iglesia

el buzón

CALLE 3

el parque

AVE. SUR

la gente

el periódico

el quiosco

el banco (*bench*)

la revista

Por la ciudad

7-1 **En mi ciudad.** Indica si la comunidad donde vives tiene estos lugares. Si respondes *Sí*, escribe el nombre de uno específico.

	Sí, (escribe el nombre de uno)	No
Modelo: un banco	**Sí, el American Trust**	
1. un parque		
2. un café		
3. una zapatería		
4. una estatua		
5. un rascacielos		
6. una avenida		
7. un quiosco		
8. una iglesia		
9. un cine		
10. una parada de metro		

7-2 **¿Dónde?** Escucha varias actividades que vas a hacer. ¿Dónde haces cada actividad?

Modelo: Oyes: Quieres comprar una pizza.
Escribes: **Voy a una pizzería.**

En el centro de la ciudad

Mi amigo y yo vamos a **pasar** el día en el centro porque allí encontramos los **lugares** más interesantes de la ciudad. Primero tenemos que saber a qué hora **abren** las tiendas y los museos, y a qué hora **cierran**. También queremos preguntar dónde podemos comprar **entradas** para una **obra de teatro**, y a qué hora **empieza** la representación. Por la mañana, queremos ir de compras en las tiendas pequeñas y también en el centro comercial. Después podemos visitar un museo, tomar algo y luego pasar la tarde en un parque o dar un paseo en un jardín botánico o el zoológico. El **mejor** restaurante también está en el centro y quiero **invitar**[1] a mi amigo a cenar allí. Después de ir al **teatro** y **terminar** las actividades de un largo día, podemos regresar a casa tomando el metro o un taxi.

abrir	*to open*	**el/la mejor**	*the best*
cerrar (ie)	*to close*	**la obra (de teatro)**	*play*
empezar (ie)	*to start, begin*	**pasar (tiempo)**	*to spend (time)*
la entrada	*ticket*	**terminar**	*to finish, end*
el lugar	*place*		

[1]**Invitar** requires the preposition **a** when followed by the infinitive: **Me invitó *a* cenar.**

7-3) ¿Qué pueden hacer?

En parejas, el Estudiante A explica sus problemas al Estudiante B, que ofrece
sugerencias, y viceversa. Toma nota de las sugerencias de tu compañero/a. Cada
estudiante debe también inventar un problema nuevo.

Estudiante A
Problemas
1. Tenemos hambre, pero no queremos salir de casa para ir a un restaurante.
2. Mi amigo quiere leer un periódico o una revista, pero no encuentra un quiosco.
3. Jesús va a la joyería para comprarle un regalo a su novia Ana, pero dejó su dinero en casa.
4. Mis amigos y yo queremos ir a una obra de teatro en el centro de la ciudad, pero hay mucho tráfico.
5. ¿ ?
Sugerencias para tu compañero/a
• ¿Por qué no vas al centro comercial?
• Te recomiendo el restaurante El Mesón, que tiene excelente comida argentina.
• Pueden tomar una excursión con guía (*guided tour*).
• Hay un buzón en la avenida Sur.
• ¿ ?

Estudiante B
Problemas
1. Necesito enviar esta carta, pero no hay ninguna oficina de correos cerca.
2. Quiero ir de compras y ver muchas tiendas, pero hace frío para pasear en la calle.
3. Mis padres quieren ir al mejor restaurante de la ciudad para celebrar su aniversario.
4. Queremos ver el edificio más bonito, el mejor museo y la iglesia más vieja de la ciudad.
5. ¿ ?
Sugerencias para tu compañero/a
• Puede ir a la librería.
• ¿Por qué no toman el metro?
• Pueden pedir comida en un restaurante con entrega a domicilio (*home delivery*).
• Hay un banco muy cerca de allí.
• ¿ ?

7-4) Nuestras actividades comunes.

Paso 1. ¿Con qué frecuencia haces estas actividades? Indícalo en las columnas bajo *Yo*.

	Yo			Mi compañero/a		
	Mucho	A veces	Nunca	Mucho	A veces	Nunca
1. leer el periódico						
2. ver una obra de teatro						
3. ir a una iglesia, una mezquita (*mosque*) o un templo						
4. tomar el autobús						
5. ver una exposición en un museo						
6. ir al cine						
7. invitar a un/a amigo/a a cenar en un restaurante						
8. pasar todo el día con amigos						

Paso 2. Ahora pregunta a un/a compañero/a con qué frecuencia hace estas actividades e
indícalo en las columnas bajo *Mi compañero/a*.

Modelo:	Estudiante A:	**¿Con qué frecuencia vas al cine?**
	Estudiante B:	**Voy al cine mucho. / No voy al cine nunca.**

Así se forma

¿Sabes dónde está el apartamento de Carmen?

Sí. Está en la avenida Sur cerca del museo y frente al parque.

1. Indicating relationships: Prepositions

Prepositions of location and other useful prepositions

Go to *WileyPLUS* and review the Animated Grammar Tutorial for this grammar point.

Prepositions are words that express a relationship between nouns (or pronouns) and other words in a sentence. You have already learned some prepositions such as: **a** (*to, at*), **en** (*in, on, at*), **de** (*from, of, about*), **con** (*with*), and **sin** (*without*). Below are some additional prepositions to describe location and movement through a place.

Preposiciones de lugar		
cerca de	*near*	El almacén Torres está **cerca de** la Plaza Colón.
lejos de	*far from*	Los rascacielos están **lejos de** la Plaza Colón.
dentro de	*inside*	Hay muchas oficinas **dentro del** Banco Central.
fuera de	*outside*	Hay un buzón **fuera de** la oficina de correos.
debajo de	*beneath, under*	La estación de metro está **debajo de** la plaza.
encima de	*on top of, above*	Hay apartamentos **encima de** la pastelería.
detrás de	*behind*	El niño corre **detrás de** su perro.
delante de	*in front of*	El perro corre **delante del** niño.
enfrente de, frente a	*in front of, opposite*	El banco está **frente al** quiosco.
al lado de	*beside, next to*	El Museo de Arte Colonial está **al lado del** cine.
sobre, en	*on*	Hay periódicos **sobre el** suelo, al lado del quiosco.
entre	*between, among*	La joyería está **entre** la zapatería y el mesón.
por	*by, through, alongside, around*	La niña pasea en bicicleta **por** la plaza.
		El autobús pasa **por** la avenida Colón.

Otras preposiciones útiles		
antes de	*before*	Quiero leer el menú **antes de** pedir la comida.
después de	*after*	Podemos tomar un café **después de** comer.
en vez de	*instead of*	Yo quiero té **en vez de** café.
para + *infinitive*	*in order to (do something)*	Necesito dinero **para tomar** un taxi.
al + *infinitive*	*upon (doing something)*	Tienes que levantar la mano **al pedir** un taxi.

¡Importante! In Spanish a verb following a preposition is always in the infinitive (–**ar**, –**er**, –**ir**) form. In contrast, English uses the –*ing* form.

Antes de ir al teatro, vamos a cenar.
~~Antes de yendo al teatro...~~

Before going to the theater, we're going to have dinner.

7-5 **¿Cierto o falso?** Tu amigo/a dice que conoce esta ciudad (en las páginas 218–219) perfectamente, pero en realidad está un poco confundido/a. Lee sus comentarios, decide si son ciertos o falsos y, si son falsos, corrígelos (*correct them*).

Modelo: La pizzería está al lado de la joyería.
No, la pizzería está al lado de la pastelería.

1. El buzón está detrás de la oficina de correos, ¿verdad?
2. Y el cine Colón está entre el restaurante El Mesón y el Museo de Arte Colonial.
3. El autobús pasa por la avenida Sur, junto a la Plaza Colón, ¿no?
4. Creo que el Museo de Arte Colonial está cerca del Almacén Torres.
5. El Banco Central está delante de la zapatería y de la joyería.
6. En la Plaza Colón, hay un banco enfrente del quiosco, ¿verdad?
7. Todas las mesas de El Mesón están dentro del restaurante, ¿verdad?
8. No hay ningún rascacielos cerca de la Plaza Colón, ¿verdad?
9. Y hay un parque enfrente de la iglesia, ¿no?
10. En la Plaza Colón hay una estatua de Hernán Cortés muy bonita delante del cine, ¿verdad?

7-6 **¿Qué o quién es?**

Paso 1. Escoge cuatro objetos o personas que ves en la clase y escribe oraciones describiendo dónde están.

Modelo: **Esta persona/cosa está entre la puerta y Sara.**
Está detrás de Tom y al lado de...

Paso 2. En parejas, lee tus oraciones a tu compañero/a. Él/Ella va a intentar (*try*) identificar a la persona o cosa a la que te refieres.

7-7 **Nuestros lugares interesantes.** Un estudiante de Chile acaba de llegar a estudiar en tu universidad. ¿Qué lugares interesantes del campus o de la ciudad puedes recomendarle?

Paso 1. Escribe una lista de cinco lugares y explica dónde están con el mayor detalle posible (*with as much detail as possible*). Usa las preposiciones de lugar.

Paso 2. En grupos pequeños, comparen sus listas y escojan los diez lugares más interesantes.

7-8) Tus hábitos.

Paso 1. Completa estas oraciones pensando en tus hábitos y preferencias.

Modelo: Casi nunca llevo **ropa formal** para **ir a clase.**

1. Casi siempre voy _____ para _____.
2. Siempre necesito _____ para _____.
3. No me gusta _____ sin _____.
4. Me gusta _____ antes de _____.
5. A veces _____ en vez de _____.
6. Nunca, nunca _____ después de _____.

 Paso 2. Ahora, en grupos pequeños, comparte esta información con tus compañeros/as y pregunta si ellos/as también lo hacen.

Modelo:
Estudiante A: **Casi nunca llevo ropa formal para ir a clase, ¿y ustedes?**
Estudiante B: **Yo llevo ropa formal a veces, por ejemplo, cuando hago una presentación.**
Estudiante C: **No, yo tampoco llevo ropa formal casi nunca.**

Pronouns with prepositions

The pronouns that follow prepositions (**pronombres preposicionales**) are the same as subject pronouns except for **yo** and **tú,** which become **mí** and **ti.**

WILEY **PLUS** Go to *WileyPLUS* and review the Animated Grammar Tutorial for this grammar point.

—¿Es este cuadro para **mí?**   *Is this painting for **me?***
—Sí, es para **ti.**   *Yes, it's for **you.***

Pronombres preposicionales (*a, de, para, por, sin,* etc.)

para **mí**	para **nosotros/as**
para **ti**	para **vosotros/as**
para **usted**	para **ustedes**
para **él/ella**	para **ellos/ellas**

The combination of **con** + **mí** or **ti** becomes **conmigo** (*with me*) or **contigo** (*with you*), respectively.

—¿Quieres ir **conmigo?**   *Do you want to go **with me?***
—¡Sí! Voy **contigo.**   *Yes! I'll go **with you.***

NOTA DE LENGUA

Note the accent on **mí** (*me*) to differentiate from **mi** (*my*) and avoid ambiguity.

Mi hijo hizo un dibujo (*drawing*) para **mí.**

7-9 **¿Te gusta o no te gusta?**

Paso 1. Si tu pareja (novio/a, esposo/a) te dice estas cosas, ¿te gusta o no te gusta?

	Sí, a mí me gusta.	No, a mí no me gusta.
1. Quiero ir de compras **contigo.**	☐	☐
2. Quiero estar siempre **cerca de ti.**	☐	☐
3. Estas flores son **para ti.**	☐	☐
4. No puedo vivir **sin ti.**	☐	☐
5. ¿Quieres viajar a Hawái **conmigo?**	☐	☐
6. Nunca hablo de ti con mis **amigos/as.**	☐	☐
7. No puedo estudiar **contigo.**	☐	☐
8. Nunca tienes tiempo **para mí.**	☐	☐
9. Tengo un regalo **para ti.**	☐	☐

Paso 2. En grupos, comparen y expliquen sus respuestas usando **gustar** y otras expresiones como **sorprender, parecer bien/mal/normal,** etc..

Modelo: **A mí me sorprende mucho cuando mi novio dice: "Quiero ir de compras contigo", porque a mi novio no le gusta nada ir de compras.**

> **HINT**
>
> Remember that with verbs like **gustar, a** + *prepositional pronoun* is sometimes used for emphasis or clarification.
>
> **A él** no **le** gustó la película.
> *He didn't like the movie.*
> **A mí** tampoco **me** gustó.
> *I didn't like it either.*

PLUS Go to *WileyPLUS* and review the Animated Grammar Tutorial for this grammar point.

7-10 **Linda y Manuel.** En parejas, lean y dramaticen la conversación, completándola con los pronombres apropiados.

Linda está sentada en un sofá en la sala de su casa. Habla por teléfono con su novio, Manuel.

MANUEL: Linda, ¿quieres salir con _____ esta noche? Me muero (*I'm dying*) por verte.

LINDA: Sí, mi amor. Voy con _____ a donde quieras.

MANUEL: Pues, te voy a llevar a un lugar muy especial y… ¡tengo una sorpresa maravillosa para _____!

LINDA: ¿Para _____? ¡Eres un ángel, Manuel! A _____ me encantan las sorpresas. Yo también tengo una sorpresa para _____.

MANUEL: ¿Ah, sí? ¿Cuál es?

LINDA: Pues, no vamos a estar solos esta noche porque mi hermanito menor tiene que venir con _____.

MANUEL: ¿Con _____? ¿No pueden quedarse (*stay*) tus padres con _____?

LINDA: Manuelito, sé (*be*) flexible. ¿No quieres hacerlo por _____?

MANUEL: Bueno, está bien.

LINDA: ¡Gracias, mi amor! Por cierto, ¿qué sorpresa tienes para _____?

NOTA CULTURAL

Benito Quinquela Martín

Benito Quinquela Martín (1890–1977) was an Argentine painter famous for depicting the port of Buenos Aires and the nearby area known as La Boca. La Boca is known for its numerous brightly painted houses.

Cultura: Argentina y Chile

Antes de leer

1. ¿Cuál es la capital de Argentina? ¿Con qué países tiene frontera (*border*) Argentina? Localiza Las Pampas y la Patagonia en el mapa.

2. ¿Cuál es la capital de Chile y cómo se llama el desierto que está en el norte de Chile?

3. ¿Cómo se llama la cordillera (*mountain range*) que pasa por Chile y Argentina?

PLUS **Map quizzes:** As you read about places highlighted in red, find them on the map. Learn more about and test yourself on the geography of the Spanish-speaking world in *WileyPLUS*.

Nacionalidades:
argentino/a
chileno/a

DOS COLOSOS DEL CONO SUR

Chile y Argentina son dos países con fuerte influencia europea. Esta influencia es aparente en su cultura y en su población.

ARGENTINA

Argentina es el país hispano más grande del mundo. El 86% de los argentinos se identifican con ascendencia europea. Se estima que hasta un 60% de la población del país tiene ascendencia italiana.

Argentina tiene varias regiones diferentes. Al noreste encontramos las planicies (*flatlands*) del río Paraná, donde está la jungla; al sur está **la Patagonia**, una llanura (*plain*) rica en petróleo. A pesar de la gran extensión del territorio de Argentina, la vida se centra en su capital, **Buenos Aires**, llamada el "París de las Américas". Más del 30% de la población de Argentina vive en el área de Buenos Aires y se les llama "porteños" (del puerto).

La Avenida 9 de Julio, una de las más anchas (*wide*) del mundo, y el Obelisco, que conmemora la fundación de la ciudad, son símbolos famosos de Buenos Aires. ¿Cuántos carriles (*lanes*) tiene esta avenida?

¡EVITA, EVITA!

¿Conoces la obra musical *Evita* y la canción "No llores por mí, Argentina"? Pues este musical es sobre la vida de Eva Perón, esposa del dictador Juan Perón (1895–1974), quien fue presidente hasta 1955, cuando los militares lo obligaron a abandonar el poder. Después de una serie de dictaduras militares, en 1983, Argentina volvió a un sistema democrático. En 2007, Cristina Fernández fue elegida presidenta, siendo la primera mujer elegida democráticamente para ocupar dicho cargo.

INVESTIG@ EN INTERNET

Manu Ginóbili es un jugador de básquetbol argentino. Busca información en Internet sobre él y otros jugadores argentinos que juegan en Estados Unidos. Imprime o anota los datos interesantes para compartirlos con tus compañeros/as de clase.

UN ESCRITOR EXCEPCIONAL

Jorge Luis Borges (1899–1986), gigante de la literatura latinoamericana, es el escritor más célebre y más estudiado de la literatura argentina. Como quedó ciego (*blind*) a los 55 años, tuvo que dictar sus últimas (*last*) creaciones literarias a una secretaria.

El espectacular Teatro Colón de la capital presenta conciertos, óperas, recitales y espectáculos de variedades. Atrae a músicos y artistas del mundo entero. ¿Cuántas gradas (*tiers*) hay en el teatro? ▼

◄ En esta fascinante ciudad de tiendas elegantes, restaurantes y una intensa vida nocturna, las artes son muy importantes. En Buenos Aires nació el tango, el apasionado baile que todo el mundo asocia con Argentina. ¿Sabes bailar tango?

Las pampas, una extensa llanura dedicada en gran parte a la ganadería (*cattle ranching*), ocupan la zona central del país. La pampa es la tierra del gaucho argentino —el prototipo del jinete (*rider*) solitario e independiente que recorre la pampa en su caballo (*horse*). ¿Cuál es el equivalente al gaucho en la historia estadounidense?

Los Andes están al oeste del país y es aquí donde está el pico más alto de América del Sur: el Aconcagua, de aproximadamente 22,835 pies de altura (*feet high*). ¿Te gustaría escalar (*to climb*) esta montaña?

CHILE

Chile tiene una configuración geográfica única: es una larga franja (*strip*) de tierra que va desde Bolivia hasta la punta sur del continente y desde los Andes en el este hasta el océano Pacífico en el oeste. El país tiene 2,690 millas de largo y solamente 291 millas de ancho. Es el país más largo (*long*) del mundo. En Chile, es posible practicar esquí acuático en el mar por la mañana y esquiar en la nieve de las montañas por la tarde. Por estar en el "Anillo de Fuego," desafortunadamente Chile ha sufrido varios terremotos. Uno reciente, en marzo de 2010, midió un 8.8 en la escala Richter. Perdieron la vida unas 520 víctimas, y los sismólogos estiman que fue tan poderoso (*powerful*) que movió el eje (*axis*) de la Tierra 8 centímetros.

Se ha estimado que la población chilena es de un 53% de ascendencia europea y de un 44% mestiza (mezcla de indígena y europeo). Hay una comunidad alemana numerosa y unos 200,000 chilenos que hablan el alemán hoy en día. En 1970 los chilenos eligieron (*elected*) al primer presidente socialista del continente, Salvador Allende; pero en 1973 Augusto Pinochet dio un golpe (*coup*) de estado y estableció una dictadura militar. En 1989 Chile tuvo elecciones libres y hoy en día continúa siendo un país democrático. En 2006, Michelle Bachelet se convirtió en la primera mujer en ser electa presidente de Chile.

¿TE GUSTA ESQUIAR?

La superficie esquiable más grande del hemisferio sur está al este de **Santiago,** la capital. La región conocida como "los Tres Valles de los Andes" tiene un total de 10,700 hectáreas y montañas que sobrepasan los 5,000 metros (16,404 pies) de altura.

Al norte de Chile está el desierto de Atacama, ¡el lugar más seco del mundo! En esta región hay muchas minas de cobre (*copper*), un metal que Chile exporta a muchas partes del mundo. ¿Te gustaría pasar unos días explorando este desierto?

▲ El centro de Chile es una zona fértil de clima moderado donde vive la mayoría de la población y en la que se cultivan muchas frutas y verduras. En esta zona está la capital, Santiago, una ciudad cosmopolita, moderna y de aspecto europeo.

Los 1,100 km de la Carretera Austral cruzan los lugares más atractivos del sur de Chile, con sus montañas, parques nacionales, fiordos, termas (*hot springs*), ríos y lagos, ideales para la pesca (*fishing*) deportiva. El Parque Nacional Torres del Paine es uno de los más espectaculares del país. ¿Te gustaría visitar esta región? ¿Hay glaciares en alguna región de tu país? ¿Dónde? ▶

¡PRIMER PREMIO NOBEL EN LA LITERATURA LATINOAMERICANA!

◀ En 1945, la poeta chilena Gabriela Mistral (1889–1957) fue la primera persona latinoamericana en ganar el Premio Nobel de Literatura.

¿Sabías que muchas de las uvas ▶ que compramos son importadas de Chile? Los vinos chilenos también son muy conocidos.

INVESTIG@ EN INTERNET

Imagina que vas a pasar unas cortas vacaciones en Santiago de Chile y quieres organizarlo todo antes de (*before*) llegar. Busca un hotel cerca del (*near*) centro y planifica actividades para cinco días, incluyendo detalles sobre el transporte, los lugares que quieres visitar, algunos restaurantes donde te gustaría comer, etc. Calcula aproximadamente cuánto dinero vas a necesitar.

Después de leer

1. Un estudio fonético reveló que el ritmo y la entonación del español de Buenos Aires tiene más en común con la lengua napolitana de Italia que con cualquier otra lengua. ¿Por qué crees que puede ser?

2. ¿Has probado un vino chileno o argentino? ¿Te gustó?

3. ¿Qué región de los Estados Unidos también produce vino y sufre de terremotos? ¿Qué otros rasgos (*features*) tiene en común esa región con Chile?

Así se forma

¿Quién es ese muchacho que está con Inés?

¿Ese? Es su amigo de Madrid.

PLUS Go to *WileyPLUS* and review the Animated Grammar Tutorial for this grammar point.

2. Demonstrative adjectives and pronouns

Demonstrative adjectives

Demonstrative adjectives point out the location of nouns (such as objects and people) with respect to the speaker. Like all adjectives, demonstratives agree in gender and number with the noun they refer to. The demonstrative adjective to use depends upon how close the speaker is to the item being pointed out.

Adjetivos demostrativos		
close to speaker	*at a short distance*	*at a great distance*
este bar **esta** calle	**ese** bar **esa** calle	**aquel** bar **aquella** calle
estos bares **estas** calles	**esos** bares **esas** calles	**aquellos** bares **aquellas** calles

Me gusta **este** parque.
Vamos a visitar **esos** museos.
Aquella tienda tiene cuadernos.

*I like **this** park.*
*We are going to visit **those** museums.*
That store (over there) has notebooks.

Demonstrative pronouns

Demonstrative pronouns are pronounced and spelled like demonstrative adjectives, but while adjectives usually precede the noun, pronouns replace it to avoid repetition. Observe in the following examples the use of both demonstrative adjectives and pronouns.

Compramos en **esta** tienda y en **aquella**.
     (adjective)   (pronoun)

*We shop in **this** store and **that one**.*

— ¿Te gustan **estos** zapatos?
     (adjective)

*Do you like **these** shoes?*

— No. Prefiero **esos**.
      (pronoun)

*No. I prefer **those**.*

NOTA DE LENGUA

The demonstratives **esto** (*this*) and **eso** (*that*) are neutral in gender (neither masculine nor feminine) because they refer to an idea, situation or statement, or to an object that has not yet been identified.

— ¿Qué es **esto?**
— ¡No sé!

What is this?
I don't know!

— No quiere pagar la cuenta.
— ¡**Eso** es ridículo!

He doesn't want to pay the bill.
That's ridiculous!

7-11 **¿Dónde está?** Estás paseando por la ciudad con una amiga. Escucha las oraciones que dice y decide si los lugares que menciona están cerca, un poco lejos o muy lejos. ¡Presta atención al adjetivo demostrativo que menciona tu amiga!

Modelo: Me gusta este parque. ☑ Está cerca.
Vamos a comer en aquella pizzería. ☑ Está muy lejos.

1. ☐ Está cerca. ☐ Está un poco lejos. ☐ Está muy lejos.
2. ☐ Está cerca. ☐ Está un poco lejos. ☐ Está muy lejos.
3. ☐ Está cerca. ☐ Está un poco lejos. ☐ Está muy lejos.
4. ☐ Está cerca. ☐ Está un poco lejos. ☐ Está muy lejos.
5. ☐ Está cerca. ☐ Está un poco lejos. ☐ Está muy lejos.

7-12 **Soy un guía turístico.** Imagina que trabajas para una agencia de turismo en Buenos Aires y le muestras (*show*) la ciudad a un grupo de visitantes. Usa adjetivos demostrativos para simplificar las oraciones.

Modelo: La iglesia que (*that*) está un poco lejos es del período colonial.
Esa iglesia es del período colonial.

1. El rascacielos que está muy lejos es el más moderno de la ciudad.
2. La estatua que está un poco lejos es del presidente.
3. La estación del metro que está cerca fue la primera (*the first*) de la ciudad.
4. El parque que está un poco lejos es muy famoso.
5. Las ceremonias importantes se celebran en la iglesia que está muy lejos.
6. Los almacenes que están cerca venden de todo.
7. El restaurante que está un poco lejos sirve parrilladas (*barbecue*) y otros platos argentinos.

DICHOS

De aquellos polvos vienen estos lodos.

¿Qué significa este dicho? ¿Estás de acuerdo?

NOTA CULTURAL

El mate

Mate is a tea-like beverage consumed mainly in Argentina, Chile, Uruguay, Paraguay, and southern Brazil. The name *mate* derives from the word for the gourd that is traditionally used to drink the infusion. Mate is sipped using a metal or wood decorative straw and filter called **bombilla.** Sharing a cup of mate among close friends and family, using the same *bombilla*, is a sign of acceptance and friendship. More than a drink, mate has become a cultural phenomenon. In Buenos Aires, some people carry their mate with them throughout the day.

7-13 **¡Tengo hambre! ¿Cuánto cuestan?** Después del paseo por Buenos Aires, tienes hambre y vas a la Pastelería Río de la Plata. Trabaja con un compañero/a, que va a ser el/la dependiente/a. Pregunta los precios de los productos, el/la dependiente/a contesta consultando los precios de la lista.

Modelo: Cliente/a: **¿Cuánto cuesta este pastel de limón?**

Dependiente/a: **Ese cuesta dos pesos, cincuenta y cinco centavos.**

Al final, decide qué vas a comprar y completen la transacción.

Cliente/a: **Voy a comprar ese/esa… y …**

Dependiente/a: **Muy bien, son… pesos.**

PALABRAS ÚTILES

empanada *turnover*
medialuna *croissant*

Río de la Plata

galletas de chocolate	– $4.75 la docena
de azúcar	– $4.00 la docena
pastel de manzana	– $2.50 (el pedazo)
de limón	– $2.75 (el pedazo)
torta de chocolate	– $12.95
de fresa	– $13.25
pan de queso	– $2.25
de aceitunas	– $2.60
empanada de carne	– $1.60 cada una
vegetariana	– $1.15 cada una
medialuna de jamón y queso	– $1.90 cada una
de chocolate	– $1.80 cada una

Cultura: La plaza en el mundo hispano

Antes de leer

¿Cuál es el lugar público más importante de tu ciudad o pueblo? ¿Qué pasa (*happens*) allí?

La plaza es el corazón (*heart*) de las ciudades y los pueblos hispanos. Generalmente, se encuentra en la parte más vieja de la ciudad o del pueblo y es el centro político, religioso, social y comercial de una ciudad. En la plaza hay mercados al aire libre y se celebran festivales y ceremonias importantes.

Una plaza típica está rodeada de (*surrounded by*) una iglesia, edificios públicos, cafés, tiendas y bares. Generalmente, en el centro hay una estatua o un monumento y, en muchas ocasiones, también hay fuentes (*fountains*) y jardines. Las plazas aún (*still*) tienen mucha importancia para los habitantes de una comunidad. Durante el día la gente camina, conversa, lee o juega a las cartas o al dominó. Por la noche, los jóvenes se reúnen para verse y charlar (*chat*).

▲ Plaza de Mayo, Buenos Aires, Argentina

La Plaza de Mayo en Buenos Aires es un lugar donde los argentinos celebran actividades sociales y políticas. Está rodeada por la catedral, el cabildo (*city/town hall*) y la Casa Rosada, el equivalente de la Casa Blanca en Washington, D.C. Otras plazas famosas son la Plaza Mayor en Madrid, la Plaza del Zócalo en la Ciudad de México y la Plaza de Armas en Chile.

Después de leer

1. Nombra tres cosas que generalmente se encuentran en las plazas hispanas.

2. ¿Es la función social de las plazas latinoamericanas comparable a la de los centros comerciales en Estados Unidos? Menciona similitudes y diferencias.

Plaza de Armas, Santiago, Chile

Así se forma

WILEY
PLUS Go to *WileyPLUS* and review the Animated Grammar Tutorial and Verb Conjugator for this grammar point.

3. Talking about actions in the past: The preterit of *hacer* and stem-changing verbs

Hacer

The verb **hacer** is irregular in the preterit. Note that the stem (**hic–**) is constant and that **c → z** before **o**. Also observe the special preterit endings **–e** and **–o**.

hice	**hic**imos
hiciste	**hic**isteis
hizo	**hic**ieron

—¿Qué **hiciste** anoche?   *What **did** you **do** last night?*
—Fui al gimnasio e **hice ejercicio**.   *I went to the gym and **worked out**.*

Remember that you do not always use **hacer** to answer **hacer** questions.

—¿Qué **hicieron** ustedes ayer?   *What **did** you **do** yesterday?*
—**Fuimos** al centro y **vimos** una película.   *We **went** downtown and **saw** a movie.*

7-14 Los sábados de Javier. Escucha las siguientes oraciones e indica si Javier se refiere a los sábados en general (verbo en presente) o al sábado pasado (verbo en pasado).

Modelo:	Juan hizo una fiesta.	**Los sábados**	**El sábado pasado**
		☐	☑

	Los sábados	**El sábado pasado**
1.	☐	☐
2.	☐	☐
3.	☐	☐
4.	☐	☐
5.	☐	☐
6.	☐	☐

7-15 El sábado pasado.

Paso 1. Lee la descripción que hace Javier de sus sábados en la página 235. Basándote en esto, ¿qué hizo Javier el sábado pasado? Cambia los verbos en **negrita** (*boldface*) al pretérito.

¿Qué **hago** los sábados? Pues, **me levanto** un poco tarde y **desayuno** en casa. A las diez de la mañana **juego** al tenis con mi hermanito Samuel y luego **hacemos** una visita a los abuelos. Me gusta mucho visitarlos y mi abuela siempre **hace** chocolate caliente para merendar. Por la tarde, **hago** algunas compras en el centro con mi amiga Nidia. Más tarde, **salimos** con nuestros amigos, **cenamos** en algún restaurante y **vamos** al cine. **Volvemos** a casa bastante tarde. Claro, después **llego** a casa tan cansado… que los domingos ¡no hago nada!

HINT

Before doing Exercise 7-15, review the preterit of regular verbs and of **ser** and **ir** (pp. 202–203).

Modelo: ¿Qué **hice** el sábado pasado? Pues…

Paso 2. Ahora escribe un párrafo comparando tu sábado pasado con el de Javier.

Modelo: **Javier se levantó tarde, pero yo me levanté a las 6:00 de la mañana…**

Stem-changing verbs

- Note that **–ir** verbs with a stem change in the present tense (**o → ue, e → ie, e → i**) also change in the preterit[1].

- The stem change in the preterit is the same that takes place in the present participle (**–ando/–iendo** form), but it only occurs in the third-person singular (**usted/él/ella**) and the third-person plural (**ustedes/ellos/ellas**) forms.

¿Quién pidió los espaguetis?

dormir (ue, **u**[2]) **du**rmiendo → **du**rmió/**du**rmieron
pedir (i, **i**) **pi**diendo → **pi**dió/**pi**dieron

dormir (o → u)	
dormí	dormimos
dormiste	dormisteis
durmió	**du**rmieron

pedir (e → i)	
pedí	pedimos
pediste	pedisteis
pidió	**pi**dieron

HINT

First, review the present tense stem-changing verbs on page 117. Then practice the preterit tense of the verbs presented in this section.

Note the pattern of change in the following model verbs.

o → ue; u	**morir** (ue, u)	*to die*	Pablo Neruda **murió** en 1973.
e → ie; i	**preferir** (ie, i)	*to prefer*	Las chicas **prefirieron** no hablar del incidente.
	divertirse (ie, i)	*to have a good time*	¿**Se divirtieron** en el restaurante anoche?
e → i; i	**pedir** (i, i)	*to ask for, request*	Tina **pidió** una paella de mariscos.
	servir (i, i)	*to serve*	¿Qué más **sirvieron**?
	repetir (i, i)	*to repeat*	El mesero **repitió** la lista de postres.
	vestirse (i, i)	*to get dressed*	Más tarde **se vistieron** y fueron a un baile.

---

[1]Remember that **–ar** and **–er** stem-changing verbs never have a stem change in the preterit or present participle (see p. 202.) For example: pensar (ie) pienso pensando pensó
[2]Remember that stem changes are indicated in parenthesis, the first (and sometimes only) change shows present simple changes and the second one shows present participle/preterit changes.

7-16 Las actividades de Alicia. ¿Qué hizo Alicia ayer? Relaciona las actividades de la columna A con las actividades correspondientes de la columna B.

A

_____ **1.** Por la tarde hizo su tarea de francés y escuchó el audio del Capítulo 7.

_____ **2.** Luego, para descansar un poco, buscó un periódico.

_____ **3.** A las siete de la tarde, ella y dos de sus amigas cenaron en un restaurante.

_____ **4.** El mesero les sirvió tres postres diferentes.

_____ **5.** Después de cenar, estudió casi toda la noche en la biblioteca.

B

a. Las chicas prefirieron la torta de chocolate.

b. Todas pidieron pasta con camarones y ensalada.

c. No durmió mucho.

d. Leyó que tres personas murieron en un accidente. ¡Qué triste!

e. Repitió las palabras del vocabulario.

7-17 El día de Jaime. Primero, imagina el orden cronológico de las actividades de Jaime. Luego, escribe lo que hizo usando el pretérito.

Modelo: **Se levantó a las siete de la mañana. Luego,...**

_____ irse al trabajo

_____ bañarse

_____ desayunar en un café

_____ salir con sus amigos

_1_ levantarse a las siete

_____ vestirse

_____ pedir café con leche y pan

_____ acostarse a medianoche

_____ dormirse

_____ cenar en casa

_____ divertirse mucho

_____ regresar a casa después del trabajo

7-18 Y tú, ¿qué hiciste?

EXPRESIONES ÚTILES

¿Sí?/¿De verdad?
These expressions look for confirmation (similar to *Really?*).

No me digas.
This expresses disbelief/surprise and encouragement to continue (as in *No way!*).

Yo también/tampoco.
This expresses agreement (equivalent to *Me too/neither.*).

Paso 1. Piensa en lo que hiciste ayer y completa la columna *Yo* con tus actividades.

	Yo	Mi compañero/a _____
por la mañana temprano		
a media mañana (*midmorning*)		
al mediodía (*noon*)		
por la tarde		
por la noche		

Paso 2. Ahora entrevista a un/a compañero/a. Haz preguntas sobre los detalles: ¿Dónde? ¿Con quién? ¿Qué? (¿Qué película viste? ¿Qué comiste?). Anota sus respuestas. Túrnense. ¿Quién tuvo el día más interesante?

Modelo: Estudiante A: **¿Qué hiciste ayer por la mañana temprano?**

Estudiante B: **Bueno, me levanté a las ocho de la mañana, me duché y tomé el desayuno.**

Estudiante A: **¿Sí? ¿Qué tomaste? (¿Dónde? ¿Fuiste con alguien? ...)**

7-19 ¿Qué hizo el/la profesor/a?

Paso 1. En grupos pequeños, imaginen qué hizo su profesor/a de español ayer, incluyendo algunos detalles. ¡Sean creativos!

Modelo: El profesor Redondo se levantó a las siete de la mañana, se duchó, se afeitó y preparó el desayuno para la familia...

	El/La profesor/a...
por la mañana temprano	
a media mañana	
al mediodía	
por la tarde	
por la noche	

Paso 2. Hagan preguntas a su profesor/a para confirmar sus ideas.

Modelo: ¿Se levantó a las siete de la mañana?

7-20 El fin de semana.

Paso 1. Escribe oraciones sobre tus actividades del fin de semana pasado en la columna *Yo*. Añade otras dos actividades que hiciste.

Modelo: leer
Leí una novela muy interesante en mi cuarto.

	Yo	Mis compañeros/as
1. leer (¿Qué? ¿Dónde?)		
2. hacer ejercicio/jugar un deporte (¿Dónde? ¿Con quién?)		
3. estudiar (¿Qué? ¿Dónde?)		
4. comer (¿Qué? ¿Dónde?)		
5. ir de compras (¿Dónde? ¿Con quién? ¿Qué?)		
6. ver la tele/una película (¿Cuál? ¿Dónde?)		
7. comprar (¿Qué? ¿Dónde?)		
8. ir a...		
9. ¿...?		
10. ¿...?		

Paso 2. En grupos, hablen de las cosas que hicieron y tomen apuntes en la columna *Mis compañeros/as.*

Modelo: Estudiante A: **Yo leí un libro de poesía de Borges y ustedes, ¿leyeron algo?**
Estudiante B: **Sí, yo leí unos artículos de *Newsweek* en la biblioteca.**
Estudiante C: **Pues yo leí mis libros de texto y una revista.**

Paso 3. Ahora comenten las cosas que averiguaron (*you found out*).

Modelo: **Todos leímos algo, pero leímos cosas diferentes...**

7-21   **Muy responsable.** Hoy le pediste algunas cosas a tu compañero/a de clase. Ahora lo/la llamas para preguntar si hizo lo que pediste. Escucha también sus preguntas y responde afirmativamente, como en el modelo.

Modelo: Estudiante A: **¿Llevaste el libro a la biblioteca?**
            Estudiante B: **Sí , lo acabo de llevar a la biblioteca.**

Estudiante A:
1. pedir a Laura su número de teléfono.
2. anotar las horas de oficina del profesor.
3. hacer tu parte del proyecto para clase.

Estudiante B:
1. leer mi mensaje electrónico.
2. ir a la librería.
3. comprar unos bolígrafos para mí.

NOTA CULTURAL

Los mapuches de Chile

The Mapuche, or "people of the earth", are the most numerous indigenous group in Chile and the only one to have successfully resisted attacks from both the Incas and the Spaniards. After Chile gained its independence from Spain in 1818, a long armed conflict between the government and the Mapuche led to a significant reduction in the Mapuche territory. As a result, many Mapuches moved to urban areas. However, in central and southern Chile, the Mapuches still maintain a strong cultural identity. Their ancestral beliefs are traditionally passed on by women in Mapundungun, the Mapuche language.

VideoEscenas: Y ¿luego fueron al cine?

▲ Álvaro le cuenta a María lo que hizo ayer.

Paso 1. Responde a estas preguntas antes de ver el video.

1. ¿Con quién sales los fines de semana?
2. ¿Adónde van tú y tus amigos cuando salen?

Paso 2. Mira el video prestando atención (*paying attention*) a la idea principal. Después, resume (*summarize*) lo que hizo Álvaro completando estas oraciones.

Álvaro _____ con sus amigos para _____.

Ellos _____ muchas cosas, pero no _____.

Paso 3. Lee las siguientes preguntas. Si sabes algunas respuestas (*answers*), puedes escribirlas ahora. Después, mira el video otra vez para comprobar (*check*) y completar tus respuestas.

1. ¿Cómo se divirtieron Álvaro y sus amigos?
2. ¿Adónde fueron los chicos primero y para qué?
3. ¿Adónde fueron después y para qué?
4. ¿Adónde fueron más tarde y para qué?
5. ¿Adónde fueron los chicos finalmente y por qué?

Así se dice

En correos y en el banco

En la oficina de correos

Quiero **mandar/
enviar** esta tarjeta
postal a mi amigo.

Recibí una **carta**
de mi amiga.

Quiero **contestar**
inmediatamente.
Escribo la **dirección**
en el **sobre**.

Necesito comprar
una **estampilla/**un
sello.

¿Para quién es este
paquete?

enviar	*to send*
recibir	*to receive*
contestar	*to answer*

 (7-22) La historia de una carta

Paso 1. En parejas, determinen el orden cronológico de estas actividades. ¿Qué pasó
primero? ¿Y después?

____ buscar el buzón

____ mi amigo / contestarme

    inmediatamente

____ enviar la carta

____ escribir la dirección en el sobre

____ ir a la oficina de correos

____ mi amigo / abrirla y leerla

____ comprar un sello de 80 centavos

____ mi amigo / recibir la carta

____ escribir la carta

Paso 2. Ahora narren la historia cronológicamente, cambiando los verbos al pretérito.

Modelo: **Primero, escribí la carta.**

7-23 ¿Correo tradicional o correo electrónico?

Paso 1. Trabajen con un/a compañero/a. Ustedes son defensores del correo electrónico o del correo tradicional (su instructor/a les asignará uno). Escriban una lista de razones para justificar su preferencia.

Paso 2. Ahora, busquen una pareja que prefiere el otro tipo de correo y debatan el tema.

Modelo: PAREJA A: **El correo electrónico es más rápido.**
          PAREJA B: **Sí, pero con el correo tradicional no necesitas tener una computadora.**

El dinero y los bancos

Nicolás **cuenta** su dinero.

Cuando tiene suficiente dinero, lo **gasta** en una tienda.

Nicolás también **gana** dinero trabajando por las tardes.

Por fin decide **abrir una cuenta** en un banco para **ahorrar** su dinero.

¿Qué más podemos hacer con el dinero?

cambiar	*to change, exchange*	**invertir (ie, i)**	*to invest*
contar (ue)	*to count*	**perder (ie)**	*to lose*
depositar	*to deposit*	**pagar (la cuenta)**	*to pay (for) (the bill, check)*
encontrar	*to find*	**retirar**	*to withdraw*

¿Cómo pagamos? ¿Cómo recibimos dinero?

el cajero automático	*ATM machine*
el cambio	*change, small change, exchange*
el cheque	*check*
el cheque de viajero	*traveler's check*
cobrar	*to cash; to charge*
el efectivo	*cash*
firmar (un cheque)	*to sign (a check)*
la moneda	*currency, money, coin*
la tarjeta de crédito/débito	*credit/debit card*

NOTA DE LENGUA

Note the difference between the use of **gastar** (dinero/energía) vs. **pasar** (tiempo)

Gastamos mucho **dinero** en libros.   *We spend a lot of money on books.*
Jorge **pasa** bastante **tiempo** estudiando.   *Jorge spends a lot of time studying.*

7-24 **Organizar el dinero.** En parejas, imaginen que están de vacaciones en Santiago de Chile. Decidan qué tienen que hacer en las siguientes situaciones.

Modelo: Ya no tienen efectivo, pero necesitan más.
Tenemos que buscar un cajero automático.

1. No pueden encontrar los cheques de viajero que quieren usar.
2. Quieren comprar algo en una tienda, pero no aceptan tarjetas de crédito.
3. No saben cuánto cobra el banco por cambiar sus dólares.
4. Tienen muchas monedas, pero ya no las quieren llevar en los bolsillos.
5. No encuentran un cajero automático.

7-25 **Tus finanzas.**

Paso 1. Marca tus respuestas a esta encuesta (*survey*) sobre tus hábitos financieros.

Usted y el dinero	
¿Va usted a hacerse rico o tendrá problemas económicos?	
1. Casi siempre pago...	☐ con efectivo ☐ con tarjeta de débito ☐ con tarjeta de crédito
2. Intento ahorrar...	☐ un 10% de mi salario ☐ un 25% de mi salario ☐ No ahorro nada.
3. Cuando tengo monedas...	☐ las uso ☐ no las quiero ☐ las ahorro y luego las llevo al banco
4. Reviso mis gastos...	☐ cada semana ☐ cada mes ☐ nunca
5. Cuando viajo...	☐ uso cheques de viajero ☐ uso la tarjeta de crédito
6. Mis tarjetas de crédito...	☐ tienen un saldo (*balance*) pequeño ☐ tienen un saldo grande ☐ ¿Qué tarjetas de crédito?
7. Invierto...	☐ en la bolsa (*stock market*) ☐ No invierto en nada. ☐ en productos seguros (*safe*)
8. Pago mis cuentas a tiempo...	☐ siempre ☐ a veces ☐ casi nunca

Paso 2. Ahora, compara tus respuestas con las de un/a compañero/a y respondan las siguientes preguntas:

- ¿Tienen hábitos similares o diferentes?
- ¿Piensan que sus hábitos son típicos entre estudiantes?
- ¿Qué hábitos les gustaría cambiar?

 Paso 3. En grupos, escriban una pequeña *Guía de consejos financieros para estudiantes.*

 7-26 **Una visita al banco.** En grupos pequeños, tienen cinco minutos para describir la escena ilustrada en el dibujo. Mencionen lo que está pasando, lo que pasó y lo que va a pasar. Un/a estudiante sirve de secretario/a y apunta las ideas. ¡Usen su imaginación! ¿Qué grupo puede escribir la descripción más completa?

PALABRAS ÚTILES

se escapa	*escapes*
recoger	*to pick up*
suelo	*floor*

SITUACIONES

Estás en el aeropuerto y decides tomar un taxi con una persona que no conoces, y compartir el precio del viaje para llegar al centro. Cuando llegas a tu destino, ¡descubres que no tienes tu billetera (*wallet*)! ¿Qué dices? ¿Cómo reacciona el otro pasajero? Intenten llegar a una solución. Las expresiones útiles a continuación les pueden ayudar.

Estudiante A: No tienes dinero para pagar el taxi. Debes pedir disculpas y proponer alternativas al otro pasajero hasta encontrar una solución.

Estudiante B: Tu compañero/a de taxi dice que no tiene dinero. Estás enojado y, por supuesto (*of course*), no quieres pagarlo todo tú. Defiende tu postura hasta llegar a una solución justa.

EXPRESIONES ÚTILES

¡Ay, Dios mío!	*Oh, my God!*
¡Lo siento muchísimo!	*I am very sorry!*
¿Qué le parece si... ?	*What do you think about . . . ?*
(No) Me parece bien/mal...	*I (do not) think it's okay/not okay . . .*

Así se forma

WILEY PLUS Go to *WileyPLUS* and review the Animated Grammar Tutorial for this grammar point.

Ya es tarde para tomar el metro.

¿Te llamo ese taxi?

HINT

Review direct object pronouns in *Capítulo 6*, p. 207. Remember to ask the questions *Who(m)?* or *What?* to identify the direct object.

4. Indicating to whom or for whom something is done: Indirect object pronouns

An indirect object identifies the person *to whom* or *for whom* something is done. Thus, this person receives the action of the verb *indirectly*.

To whom?	*I gave the package **to her**. / I gave **her** the package.*
For whom?	*I bought some tea **for him**. / I bought **him** some tea.*

In contrast, remember that the direct object indicates who or what directly receives the action of the verb.

Who(m)?	*I saw **her** yesterday.*
What?	*Did you buy **the newspaper**?*

Indirect object nouns are generally introduced by **a.**

Dimos una sorpresa **a Juan.**
 (OD)   (OI)

Pronombres de objeto indirecto

You already know the indirect object pronouns: they are the forms used with the verb **gustar** to indicate *to whom* something is pleasing.

A Carlos **le** gustó mucho la plaza.   *Carlos liked the plaza very much.*
 (OI)   (S)

me	me (to/for me)	José **me** dio una foto de los mapuches.
te	you	¿**Te** dio una carta?
le	you (formal) him her	Él quiere dar**le** un libro a usted. Yo quiero dar**le** un libro a él. Quiero dar**le** un libro a ella también.
nos	us	Nuestros amigos **nos** compraron chocolates.
os	you	¿**Os** pidieron algo?
les	you/them	¿Ellos **les** mandaron tarjetas postales **a ustedes**?

Position of indirect object pronouns

The indirect object pronoun, like the direct object pronoun and reflexive pronoun, is placed immediately before a conjugated verb, but may be attached to an infinitive or a present participle.

Me dijeron que esa película es muy buena.
They told me that that movie is really good.

¿Vas a comprar**me** esa revista?
¿**Me** vas a comprar esa revista?
Are you going to buy me that magazine?

Estoy dándo**le** mi tarjeta de crédito.
Le estoy dando mi tarjeta de crédito.
I'm giving her/him my credit card.

- **Redundancy.** Even though it may sound redundant, third-person indirect object pronouns **(le/les)** are generally used in conjunction with the indirect object noun.

  Les escribí **a mis primos.**
  *I wrote **to my cousins.***
  También **le** escribí **a Mónica.**
  *I wrote **to Mónica** too.*

- **Le** and **les** are often clarified with the preposition **a** + *pronoun.*
  Le escribí a **ella** anoche.
  *I wrote **to her** last night.*

  It is also common to use the forms **a mí, a ti, a usted, a él, a ella, a nosotros/as, a vosotros/as, a ustedes, a ellos, a ellas** with the indirect object pronoun for emphasis.

  Sancho **me** mandó el paquete **a mí.**
  *Sancho sent the package **to me.** (not to someone else)*

Dar and other verbs that frequently require indirect object pronouns

The verb **dar** (*to give*) is almost always used with indirect objects. Review its present tense conjugation and study the preterit.

dar			
Presente		**Pretérito**	
doy	damos	di[1]	dimos
das	dais	diste	disteis
da	dan	dio	dieron

[1]Note that in the preterit **dar** uses **−er/−ir** endings, but with no written accent.

- Some verbs that frequently have indirect objects are **contestar, decir, enviar, escribir, mandar,** and **pedir** as one generally tells, sends, or asks for something (OD) to someone (OI).

Here are some new verbs that frequently have indirect objects:

contar (ue)	*to tell, narrate (a story or incident)*	**preguntar**	*to ask*
devolver (ue)	*to return (something)*	**prestar**	*to lend*
explicar	*to explain*	**regalar**	*to give (as a gift)*
mostrar (ue)	*to show*		

7-27 **¿Qué hice o qué voy a hacer?** Relaciona las declaraciones de la columna A con las actividades correspondientes de la columna B. Lee las oraciones relacionadas.

<table>
<tr><td align="center">**A**</td><td align="center">**B**</td></tr>
<tr><td>____ **1.** Mis abuelos siempre quieren saber lo que estoy haciendo en la universidad.</td><td>**a.** Voy a prestarle mi carro.</td></tr>
<tr><td>____ **2.** Es el cumpleaños de mi madre.</td><td>**b.** Le di una de mis calculadoras.</td></tr>
<tr><td>____ **3.** Fui al banco ayer y abrí una cuenta para mi sobrino.</td><td>**c.** Voy a pedirte la dirección.</td></tr>
<tr><td>____ **4.** Mi amiga Natalia no tiene medio de transporte y necesita ir al centro.</td><td>**d.** Le conté toda la historia (*story*).</td></tr>
<tr><td>____ **5.** Quiero ir al restaurante argentino esta noche. Tú sabes dónde está, ¿verdad?</td><td>**e.** Le deposité $100 para empezar a ahorrar.</td></tr>
<tr><td>____ **6.** Mi hermana quería saber lo que pasó. anoche</td><td>**f.** Voy a escribirles una carta.</td></tr>
<tr><td>____ **7.** ¿No entendiste los pronombres?</td><td>**g.** Le mandé un regalo.</td></tr>
<tr><td>____ **8.** Camila tiene problemas con las matemáticas.</td><td>**h.** Voy a ir para darles apoyo (*support*).</td></tr>
<tr><td>____ **9.** Rubén y Oscar van a tocar en un concierto este fin de semana.</td><td>**i.** Te voy a explicar las ideas más importantes.</td></tr>
</table>

7-28 **Sondeo: Cuestiones personales.** Casi todos tenemos buenas relaciones con nuestros padres, hermanos, mejores amigos, etc., pero ¿hasta qué punto?

Paso 1. Indica tus respuestas a las siguientes preguntas.

	padre	madre	hermanos/as	mejor amigo/a	pareja	otros
¿A quién...						
...le pides consejo?						
...le cuentas todo?						
...le dices tus notas?						
...le prestas tus apuntes de clase?						
...le prestas libros, discos, etc.?						
¿Quién...						
...te pide consejo?						
...te cuenta todo?						
...te dice sus notas?						
...te presta sus apuntes de clase?						
...te presta libros, discos, etc.?						

Paso 2. Ahora, en grupos, hablen sobre sus respuestas y discutan las posibles diferencias personales.

Modelo: **Yo les pido consejo a mi madre y a mi padre porque... pero no les pido consejo a mis hermanos porque...**

(7-29) La tarjeta perdida (*lost*). Completa las oraciones. Usa los pronombres **lo/la** (directos) o **le** (indirecto) según la situación.

Ayer Manuel _____ pidió un favor a su novia Linda._____ dio su tarjeta del cajero automático y_____ dijo: "¿Puedes ir al cajero esta tarde y sacar_____ $100?" Cuando Linda llegó al cajero y buscó la tarjeta ¡no_____ pudo encontrar! _____ buscó en su mochila y en los bolsillos (*pockets*). ¿Quizá _____ dejó en su cuarto? Llamó a su compañera y _____ preguntó: "¿Hay una tarjeta en mi escritorio?" Su compañera _____ respondió que no. Pero unos segundos después, dijo "¡ _____ encontré! Está al lado de la puerta!" Cuando por fin Linda _____ llevó el dinero a Manuel, no _____ contó nada de la tarjeta perdida

(7-30) Un paseo por la ciudad.

Paso 1. Tienes unos amigos que viven en Santiago, Chile. Fuiste a visitarlos y te divertiste mucho. Ahora dile a un/a compañero/a lo que hicieron tus amigos para ti durante tu visita a Santiago. Aquí tienes algunas ideas.

organizar una fiesta   llevar por toda la ciudad   comprar cosas en un
llevar a una plaza   invitar al teatro   centro commercial
cocinar algo especial   presentar (*introduce*) a sus amigos   sacar fotos en el museo

Modelo: **Mis amigos me...**

Paso 2. ¿Cuál fue tu mejor (*best*) visita a unos amigos? ¿Y la peor (*worst*)? Cuéntaselo a tu compañero/a y explica por qué una visita te gustó y la otra no.

NOTA CULTURAL

Pablo Neruda

Pablo Neruda (1904-1973) was Chilean, but spent a good part of his adult life in various countries in Asia and Europe. Neruda is among the most distinguished Latin American poets of the twentieth century. His prolific writing, considered exceptional, lead him to winning the Nobel Prize for Literature in 1971. He died with eight books still unpublished.

▲ Pablo Neruda acepta el Premio Nobel del rey de Suecia.

Dicho y hecho

PARA LEER: El Tortoni: Café con historia

ANTES DE LEER

1. ¿Conoces un restaurante o café al que va mucha gente famosa? ¿Cuál es y dónde está? Si no, ¿hay algún café o restaurante donde vives que tiene mucha historia?

2. Intenta emparejar las personas siguientes con su descripción.

___ Jorge Luis Borges   a. cantante de tango argentino
___ Carlos Gardel   b. actor italiano
___ Vittorio Gassman   c. escritor argentino
___ Alfonsina Storni   d. director de cine estadounidense
___ Federico García Lorca   e. escritor español
___ Francis Ford Coppola   f. poeta argentina
___ Arthur Rubinstein   g. pianista estadounidense

ESTRATEGIA DE LECTURA

Writing down unfamiliar words As you read through a text for the first time, write down unfamiliar words that seem important in understanding the overall meaning. Note: This does not mean that you should write down every word you don't understand. As you read each paragraph, focus on new words that seem key in understanding its message. Often you will find that as you read further, context will help you understand some of these key words and, as your comprehension of the text's overall message develops from one paragraph to another, you may decide some of the words you've written down aren't so important after all.

As you read the article about el *Café Tortoni* through for the first time, write down two or three unfamiliar words in each paragraph. Then, as you read each paragraph more closely a second time, decide which of the words you've written down still seem key to unlocking its meaning and go ahead and look those up.

A LEER

Pocos son los turistas que visitan Buenos Aires y no se acercan a conocer el célebre Café Tortoni. A lo largo de sus 150 años de vida, ha formado una parte importante en la historia de la ciudad, y su nombre está asociado al tango y la literatura, al jazz y la pintura, la política y las artes plásticas[1]. Sus mesas de mármol[2] fueron frecuentadas por figuras tan relevantes como Jorge Luis Borges, Carlos Gardel, Vittorio Gassman, Juan Manuel Fangio, Federico García Lorca o Francis Ford Coppola, otorgándole[3] un aura de leyenda y fama internacional.

Origen

Fundado en 1858 por el francés Jean Touan, el primer emplazamiento[4] del Café fue en la esquina de las calles Rivadavia y Esmeralda, llamándose "Tortoni" en referencia a un local de París, en el Boulevard des Italiens, donde se reunía la élite de la cultura parisina en el siglo XIX. Es en 1880 cuando el Tortoni se traslada[5] a su lugar actual, teniendo su entrada por la calle Rivadavia hasta 1898. A partir de entonces, la entrada principal se ubicó[6] en la Avenida de Mayo. También por esta época, el local cambió de dueño, pasando a ser propiedad de otro francés, Celestino Curtuchet, que habitaba en los altos[7] del Café.

Pasado y presente

En 1926, un grupo de clientes habituales autodenominado[8] "Agrupación Gente de Artes y Letras" pero popularmente conocidos como La Peña[9], piden permiso al dueño del establecimiento para reunirse en la bodega[10]. Son un grupo de pintores, escritores, periodistas y músicos que se dedica a la difusión de la cultura mediante conciertos, recitales, conferencias, etc.

---

[1]visual arts, fine arts [2]marble [3]bestowing upon it [4]location, site [5]moves [6]was located [7]above [8]self-proclaimed [9]club [10]wine cellar, store room

Entre los asistentes figuraban celebridades de todas las disciplinas, desde Ortega y Gasset hasta Albert Einstein, pasando por Alfonsina Storni y Arthur Rubinstein. La Peña funcionaría hasta 1943, cuando se cierra la bodega donde se reunían y el grupo se disolvió. Ahora la "Asociación Amigos del Café Tortoni" continúa con la labor de La Peña.

En la actualidad, el propietario es el Touring Club Argentino y la bodega es escenario habitual para artistas de distinto género. El tango, por ejemplo, siempre tuvo un sitio preferente en el Café Tortoni, y en la primera planta del mismo edificio, tiene su sede la Academia Nacional del Tango. Otras actividades incluyen presentaciones de libros, concursos de poesía y exposiciones de pintura.

Texto: Carlos Paredes / Punto y coma
Fotografía: Beatrice Murch

DESPUÉS DE LEER

1. Indica si estas afirmaciones son **ciertas** o **falsas** según lo que leíste.

	Cierto	Falso
a. El Café Tortoni está en el lugar donde se fundó en 1858.	☐	☐
b. El grupo de intelectuales La Peña organizó muchos eventos culturales en el Café Tortoni.	☐	☐
c. Actualmente hay espectáculos de tango en el café.	☐	☐

2. De todos los personajes famosos mencionados en la lectura, ¿a quién te gustaría conocer? ¿Por qué?

3. ¿Crees que un grupo artístico como "La Peña" o la "Asociación Amigos del Café Tortoni" podría formarse en un café de cadena (*chain*) como Starbucks? ¿Por qué sí o no?

4. En tu ciudad, ¿hay grupos de artistas que se reúnen regularmente? ¿Dónde?

Dicho y hecho

PARA CONVERSAR: ¿Qué compramos?

En parejas, imaginen que son hermanos de visita en Buenos Aires, pero pronto vuelven a casa. Tienen $250 pesos argentinos (ARS), que es aproximadamente el equivalente a $60 dólares estadounidenses, y quieren gastarlos antes de irse. Cada uno (*Each one*) de ustedes quiere comprar un recuerdo (*souvenir*), pero también quieren llevar regalos a sus padres.

PALABRAS ÚTILES

A mí me gusta más....
Yo prefiero....
(No) Me parece buena idea...

caro/a	*expensive*
barato/a	*inexpensive, cheap*
un buen precio	*a good price*

ESTRATEGIA DE COMUNICACIÓN

Expressing emphatic reaction You and your classmate may not agree on how to spend all of your money. Look at the list of items available to get a sense of what things you think are well priced and what things you think are too expensive. Think about what things are useful, practical, etc. and which might be frivolous (to you). As you discuss what to buy with your classmate, react emphatically to her/his suggestions when you don't agree. Here are some useful expressions.

¡(Pero) hombre/mujer...!	(roughly equivalent to *Come on now!*)
¿Cómo?	*What!?*
¡Ay no!	*No way!*
¡Ni pensarlo!	*Don't even think about it!; Not a chance!*

Dos libras (*pounds*) de mate y una bombilla	$ 97	ARS
Una cartera de cuero (*leather*)	$116	ARS
Una botella de vino de Mendoza	$ 77	ARS
Un CD de tango	$ 77	ARS
Una camiseta del grupo de rock Los Piojos	$ 96	ARS
Un libro de recetas de comida argentina	$ 58	ARS

PARA ESCRIBIR: Tres días en Santiago o en Buenos Aires

Vas a preparar una propuesta (*proposal*) para un itinerario de tres días en una capital de América del Sur: Santiago, Chile, o Buenos Aires, Argentina. Tú propuesta está dirigida a una agencia de viajes que va a regalar un viaje al autor del mejor itinerario.

ANTES DE ESCRIBIR

Elige la ciudad que "visitaste" y cuándo (elige un mes):

☐ Santiago, Chile en _____ (mes)

☐ Buenos Aires, Argentina en _____

Haz un mapa de ideas con la información que aprendiste sobre la ciudad en este capítulo. También busca detalles adicionales en Internet. Nota: Es muy importante que consideres cómo es el tiempo en América del Sur en el mes de tu itinerario. Por ejemplo, recuerda que el verano allá es de noviembre a enero.

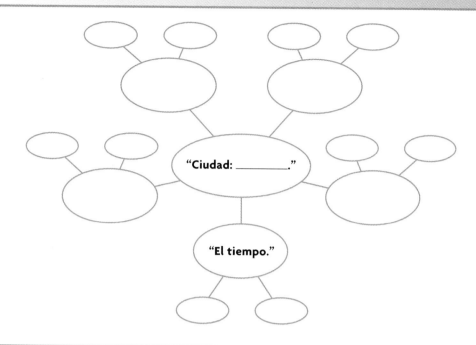

"Ciudad: _____."

"El tiempo."

ESTRATEGIA DE REDACCIÓN

Outlines In *Capítulo 3* you learned how to use idea maps to generate concepts. Once you have a number of good ideas, it's necessary to organize them in a clear and logical way. An outline helps you determine the best order in which to present and develop your ideas. What order is best depends on the type of writing you are doing—a narrative, for example, often uses chronological order to sequence the events of its plot.

It is important to remember that outlines are tools to help you get started, but that they shouldn't limit or restrict you! As part of the writing process, we often change our ideas, and can simply go back and change the outline. Don't be afraid to change your outline as your ideas develop!

Choose one of the models below, or your own thoughts about organization, to outline the ideas you will develop to describe your imagined trip.

Modelo 1	Modelo 2
Párrafo 1: La ciudad que elegí es _____ porque _____. Ahora voy a describir mi propuesta para un itinerario de tres días en esta ciudad.	**Párrafo 1:** La ciudad que elegí es _____ porque _____. Ahora voy a describir mi propuesta para un itinerario de tres días en esta ciudad.
Párrafo 2: Eventos culturales (días 1 y 3): Qué museos visitar, cuánto cuestan las entradas, etc.	**Párrafo 2:** Día 1: Todo lo que quiero hacer.
Párrafo 3: Eventos deportivos (día 2)	**Párrafo 3:** Día 2: Todo lo que quiero hacer.
Párrafo 4: De compras (días 2 y 3): Lo que voy a comprar, dónde, etc.	**Párrafo 4:** Día 3: Todo lo que quiero hacer.
Conclusión: Mi itinerario es fantástico porque...	**Conclusión:** Mi itinerario es muy original porque...

Dicho y hecho

A ESCRIBIR

Escribe un primer borrador que describa tu itinerario con muchos detalles. ¡La agencia de viajes va a pagar un viaje de verdad para la descripción más detallada y entusiasta!

Para escribir mejor: Estas formas de enfatizar adjetivos te pueden ayudar.

muy + adjetivo	*very + adjective*	muy bello
adjetivo + -ísimo/a	*very + adjective*	bellísimo
tan + adjetivo	*so + adjective*	tan bello
realmente + adjetivo	*really + adjective*	realmente bello
enormemente + adjetivo	*greatly + adjective*	enormemente bello

Aquí tienes otras palabras útiles.

incomparable	*incomparable*
impresionante	*impressive, stunning*
extraordinario	*outstanding*

DESPUÉS DE ESCRIBIR

Revisar y editar: El vocabulario. Al escribir es importante escoger palabras y expresiones apropiadas y que expresen nuestras ideas de forma precisa. Presta especial atención al uso de falsos cognados y, si usas un diccionario, comprueba que escoges palabras correctas. También debes evitar la repetición e intentar usar el vocabulario que estás aprendiendo. Hazte (*ask yourself*) estas preguntas:

☐ ¿Uso vocabulario preciso y apropiado?

☐ ¿Uso vocabulario variado? ¿Demuestra el texto el vocabulario que sé en español?

☐ ¿Estoy seguro/a (*sure*) de que no hay falsos cognados o expresiones traducidas (*translated*) literalmente del inglés?

La organización y el contenido. Después de escribir el primer borrador de tu composición, no lo leas (*do not read it*) al menos por un día. Cuando vuelvas (*you return*) a leerlo, corrígelo en términos de contenido, organización y gramática. Después, revisa también el uso de vocabulario con las preguntas de arriba. Además, hazte estas preguntas:

☐ ¿Está clara la organización?

☐ ¿Hay suficientes detalles?

☐ ¿Comunica entusiasmo la composición? ¿Es apropiada para competir por un premio?

☐ ¿Es correcta la gramática? ¿Usé correctamente los verbos en pretérito?

PARA VER Y ESCUCHAR: La plaza: Corazón de la ciudad

ANTES DE VER EL VIDEO

 En parejas o grupos pequeños, respondan a estas preguntas.

1. ¿Qué lugares o áreas son importantes en esta ciudad? ¿Por qué?
2. ¿Hay alguna plaza en esta ciudad? ¿Qué hace la gente allí?

ESTRATEGIA DE COMPRENSIÓN

Repeated viewing and pausing When you view and/or listen to recorded materials, you can play the video/audio several times. Focus on the main ideas first, and listen for details later. When listening for specific information, you can also use the pause function to take notes of each idea you heard so that you can concentrate on the next segment. Although you might not have a pause or replay option in a conversation in Spanish, you can also ask your interlocutor to repeat (**¿Perdón?** or **¿Puede repetir, por favor?**) or pause (**Un momento, por favor.**)

A VER EL VIDEO

Paso 1. Mira el video y responde a estas preguntas.

1. ¿Cuál era la función original de las plazas?
2. ¿Qué función tienen ahora las plazas?

Paso 2. Observa la siguiente tabla y presta atención a la información que debes obtener. Vas a escuchar el video dos veces (*twice*). La primera vez, usa la pausa después de cada sección para tomar notas. La segunda vez, intenta completar tus notas sin usar la pausa.

Plazas que vemos en el video	Eventos en las plazas actuales	Actividades y entretenimiento

DESPUÉS DE VER EL VIDEO

 En grupos pequeños, respondan a estas preguntas.

1. ¿En qué son similares y diferentes las plazas hispanas y las de tu comunidad?
2. ¿Hay otros lugares en tu comunidad que tienen una función similar a la plaza hispana?

Repaso de vocabulario activo

Adjetivo

el mejor   *the best*

Preposiciones

al lado de   *beside, next to*

antes de   *before*

cerca de   *near, close to*

debajo de   *beneath, under*

delante de   *in front of*

dentro de   *inside*

después de   *after*

detrás de   *behind*

en   *in, on*

encima de   *on top of, above*

enfrente de   *opposite, facing*

entre   *between, among*

en vez de   *instead of*

frente a   *opposite, facing*

fuera de   *outside*

lejos de   *far from*

para + infinitivo   *in order to + do something*

por   *by, through, alongside, around*

sobre   *on*

Sustantivos

En el banco   In the bank

el cajero automático   *ATM machine*

el cambio   *change, small change, exchange*

el cheque   *check*

el cheque de viajero   *traveler's check*

la cuenta   *account*

el efectivo   *cash*

la moneda   *currency, money, coin*

la tarjeta de crédito/débito   *credit/debit card*

En la ciudad   In the city

el almacén/la tienda por departamentos   *department store*

el autobús   *bus*

la avenida   *avenue*

el banco   *bank; bench*

el bar   *bar*

el café   *café, coffee shop*

la calle   *street*

el centro comercial   *shopping center, mall*

el cine   *movie theater, cinema*

el edificio   *building*

la entrada   *entrance; ticket*

la estatua   *statue*

la gente   *people*

la iglesia   *church*

la joyería   *jewelry store*

la librería   *bookstore*

el lugar   *place*

el metro   *metro, subway*

el museo   *museum*

las noticias   *news*

la obra de teatro   *play (theater)*

la parada de autobús   *bus stop*

el parque   *park*

la pastelería   *pastry shop, bakery*

la película   *film, movie*

el periódico   *newspaper*

la pizzería   *pizzeria*

la plaza   *plaza, town square*

el quiosco   *kiosk, newsstand*

el rascacielos   *skyscraper*

el restaurante   *restaurant*

la revista   *magazine*

el taxi   *taxi*

el teatro   *theater*

la zapatería   *shoe store*

En la oficina de correos
In the post office

el buzón   *mailbox*

la carta   *letter*

la dirección   *address*

la estampilla/el sello   *stamp*

el paquete   *package*

el sobre   *envelope*

la tarjeta postal   *postcard*

Verbos y expresiones verbales

abrir   *to open*

ahorrar   *to save*

cambiar   *to change, exchange*

cerrar (ie)   *to close*

cobrar   *to cash; to charge*

contar (ue)   *to count*

contestar   *to answer, reply*

depositar   *to deposit*

empezar (ie)   *to start*

encontrar (ue)   *to find*

entrar (en/a)   *to enter, go in*

enviar   *to send*

esperar   *to wait (for)*

firmar   *to sign*

gastar   *to spend (money)*

hacer cola/fila   *to be in line*

invertir (ie, i)   *to invest*

invitar   *to invite*

morir (ue, u)   *to die*

pagar   *to pay (for)*

pasar   *to pass, go by; to spend (time)*

perder (ie)   *to lose*

recibir   *to receive*

repetir (i, i)   *to repeat*

retirar   *to withdraw (money)*

terminar   *to finish*

Autoprueba y repaso

I. Prepositions of location. Todas las oraciones siguientes son falsas. Para corregirlas, cambia las preposiciones.

> **Modelo:** El buzón está detrás de la oficina de correos.
> **El buzón está *delante* de la oficina de correos.**

1. La gente está fuera del cine.
2. La iglesia está enfrente del banco.
3. La estatua está lejos del centro de la ciudad.
4. En el quiosco, las revistas están debajo de los periódicos.

II. Pronouns with prepositions. Termina las oraciones con los pronombres preposicionales correctos.

1. ¿Quieres ir con (*me*)?
2. Lo siento; no puedo ir con (*you, fam., s.*).
3. El pastel es para (*them*).
4. Y, ¿qué tienes para (*us*)?

III. Demonstrative adjectives and pronouns.

A. Indica qué lugares vas a visitar. Usa adjetivos demostrativos según las indicaciones.

> **Modelo:** Voy a visitar el museo. (cerca)
> **Voy a visitar este museo.**

1. Voy a visitar la iglesia. (un poco lejos)
2. Voy a visitar el museo. (cerca)
3. Quiero ver las obras de arte. (cerca)
4. Queremos ver los rascacielos. (muy lejos)

B. Contesta con un pronombre demostrativo.

> **Modelo:** ¿Te gusta este almacén?
> **No, prefiero ése.**

1. ¿Te gustan estas tiendas?
2. ¿Te gustan estos zapatos?
3. ¿Te gusta este restaurante?
4. ¿Te gusta esta pizzería?

IV. The preterit of *hacer* and stem-changing verbs. Hoy tú eres el/la profesor/a. Usando el pretérito, hazles preguntas a las personas indicadas. Imagina que ellos responden. Escribe las preguntas y las respuestas.

> **Modelo:** repetir los ejercicios / Ana
> Profesor/a: **Ana, ¿repetiste los ejercicios?**
> Ana: **Sí, los repetí.**

1. pedir ayuda a un tutor / Carlos y Felipe
2. dormir bien después de volver del centro / Alberto
3. hacer algo interesante en el centro / Linda y Celia
4. divertirse / Linda y Celia
5. preferir la ópera o el ballet / el director de la escuela (Sr. Sancho)

V. Indirect objects and indirect object pronouns. El tío Pedro acaba de regresar de Argentina. ¿Qué les trajo (*brought*) a ti y tu familia?

> **Modelo:** a mí / comprar / una mochila de cuero.
> **Me compró una mochila de cuero.**

1. a mí / dar / unos CD de rock argentino.
2. a mi hermana / regalar / un DVD para aprender a bailar tango.
3. a mis hermanos / comprar / camisetas de la selección argentina de fútbol.
4. a nosotros / mandar / muchas tarjetas postales desde lugares diferentes.
5. a ti / prestar / su cámara

VI. *Repaso general.* Contesta con oraciones completas.

1. ¿A qué hora abren los bancos en tu ciudad? ¿Y los almacenes?
2. ¿Gastaste mucho dinero en restaurantes el mes pasado? ¿Qué pediste?
3. Ayer fuiste a un café con tus amigos/as. ¿Qué pidieron ustedes?
4. ¿Fueron tú y tus amigos/as al centro el sábado por la noche? ¿Para qué?
5. ¿Cuántas horas dormiste anoche?
6. ¿Qué hiciste anoche?
7. ¿Qué hicieron tú y tus amigos/as el fin de semana pasado?
8. ¿Le diste la tarea para hoy a la profesora/al profesor?

VII. *Cultura.*

1. ¿Cuáles son los dos países más grandes del Cono Sur?
2. ¿Cuáles fueron los grupos europeos más numerosos que inmigraron a Buenos Aires?
3. Explica quiénes son tres de las siguientes personas o grupos: Salvador Allende, Augusto Pinochet, Juan Perón, los mapuches, Benito Quinquela Martín, los gauchos, Jorge Luis Borges, Gabriela Mistral.

Las respuestas de *Autoprueba y repaso* se pueden encontrar en el **Apéndice 2.**

8

WILEY PLUS

De compras

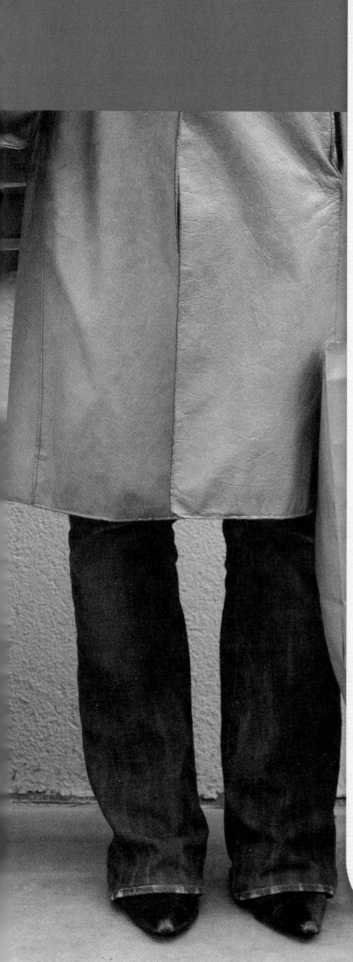

Así se dice

De compras
    La transformación de Carmen

Así se forma

1. Possessive adjectives and pronouns
2. The preterit of irregular verbs
3. Direct and indirect object pronouns combined
4. Indefinite words and expressions

Cultura

- Perú, Ecuador y Bolivia
- La ropa tradicional

Dicho y hecho

Para leer:
Peseta: La democratización de lo exclusivo

Para conversar:
El equipaje perdido

Para escribir:
La ropa aquí y allá

Para ver y escuchar:
El arte del tejido: Una tradición viva

By the end of this chapter you will be able to:

- Talk about and purchase clothing
- Indicate and emphasize possession
- Talk about actions in the past
- Express negation

ENTRANDO AL TEMA

1. ¿Sabes cuál es la moneda oficial de Ecuador?
   ☐ el peso   ☐ el sucre   ☐ el dólar

2. ¿En qué tipo de compras se puede regatear (*bargain*) el precio en Estados Unidos? ¿Con qué cosas o en qué lugares no se puede regatear?

Así se dice

De compras

La Única ROPA PARA DAMAS

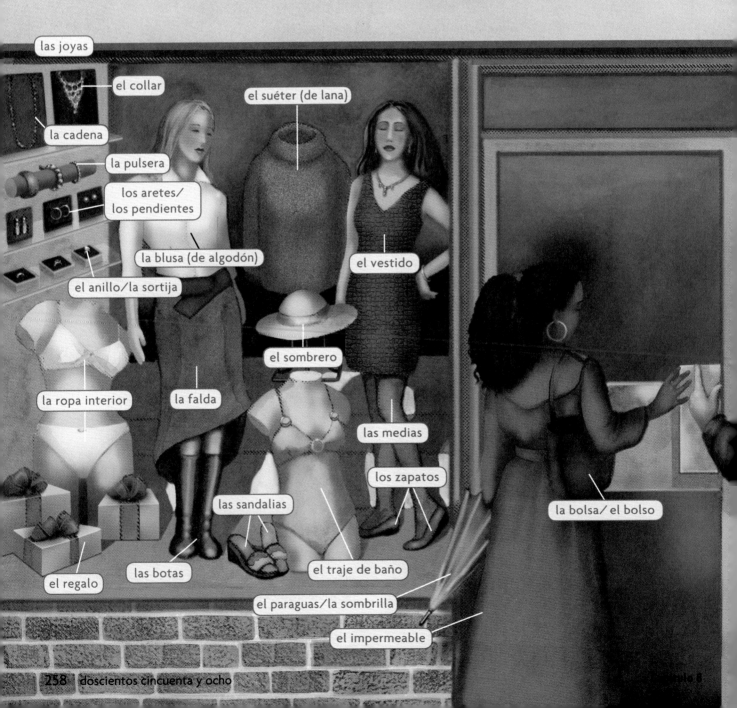

las joyas

el collar

la cadena

el suéter (de lana)

la pulsera

los aretes/
los pendientes

la blusa (de algodón)

el vestido

el anillo/la sortija

el sombrero

la ropa interior

la falda

las medias

los zapatos

las sandalias

la bolsa/ el bolso

las botas

el traje de baño

el regalo

el paraguas/la sombrilla

el impermeable

Y CABALLEROS

WILEY PLUS Pronunciación: Practice pronunciation of the chapter vocabulary and particular sounds of Spanish in *WileyPLUS*.

el algodón	cotton
el calzado	footwear
el cuero	leather
la lana	wool
la seda	silk
llevar	to wear
las joyas	jewelry

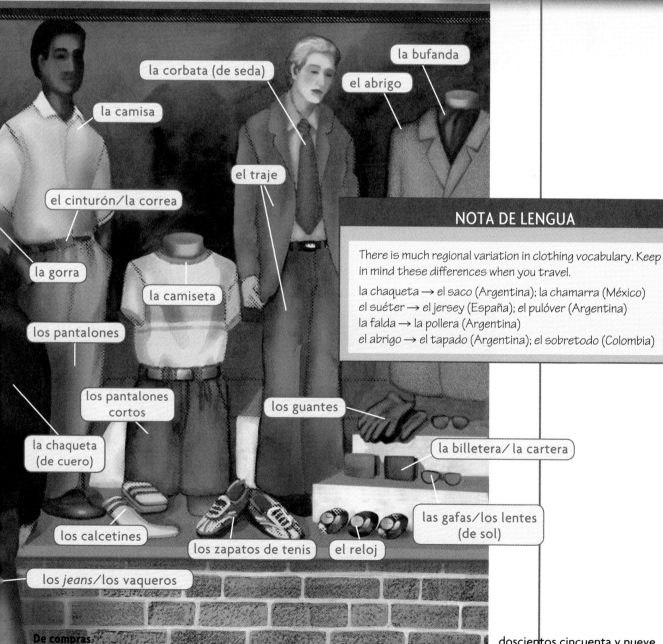

la corbata (de seda)

la camisa

el abrigo

la bufanda

el traje

el cinturón/la correa

la gorra

la camiseta

los pantalones

NOTA DE LENGUA

There is much regional variation in clothing vocabulary. Keep in mind these differences when you travel.

la chaqueta → el saco (Argentina); la chamarra (México)
el suéter → el jersey (España); el pulóver (Argentina)
la falda → la pollera (Argentina)
el abrigo → el tapado (Argentina); el sobretodo (Colombia)

los pantalones cortos

los guantes

la chaqueta (de cuero)

la billetera/ la cartera

los calcetines

los zapatos de tenis

el reloj

las gafas/los lentes (de sol)

los *jeans*/los vaqueros

8-1 **¿Dónde los encontramos?** Primero, empareja cada artículo con su nombre. Después, indica en qué departamento(s) de la tienda podemos encontrar cada uno.

a.

b.

c.

d.

e.

f.

g.

h.

	Departamentos			
	Accesorios	**Zapatos**	**Damas**	**Caballeros**
__ las corbatas	☐	☐	☐	☐
__ la falda	☐	☐	☐	☐
__ el bolso	☐	☐	☐	☐
__ la chaqueta	☐	☐	☐	☐
__ las camisas	☐	☐	☐	☐
__ los guantes	☐	☐	☐	☐
__ los tenis[1]	☐	☐	☐	☐
__ el reloj	☐	☐	☐	☐

[1]**Los tenis** is a common way of referring to **los zapatos de tenis.**

8-2 **¿Para damas o caballeros?** Escucha la mención de varios artículos de ropa y decide si cada uno normalmente se asocia con las damas, los caballeros o los dos.

	Las damas	Los caballeros	Los dos
1.	☐	☐	☐
2.	☐	☐	☐
3.	☐	☐	☐
4.	☐	☐	☐
5.	☐	☐	☐
6.	☐	☐	☐
7.	☐	☐	☐
8.	☐	☐	☐
9.	☐	☐	☐
10.	☐	☐	☐

8-3 **¿De quién es?** Tus amigos olvidaron (*forgot*) algunas cosas en tu cuarto.

Paso 1. Lee las siguientes oraciones y completa el cuadro para deducir quién olvidó cada prenda de vestir (*article of clothing*).

1. La bolsa es negra.
2. Sandra no tiene prendas o accesorios de cuero.
3. La gorra es de algodón.
4. Una prenda es de seda, otra es blanca y roja.
5. Raquel no olvidó una gorra.
6. La corbata es azul con lunares blancos.
7. Óscar olvidó una prenda de algodón.
8. Una chica olvidó su bolsa de cuero.
9. La bufanda es de rayas verdes y blancas.
10. La prenda de Sandra es de lana.

PALABRAS ÚTILES	
de/a rayas	*striped*
lunares	*dots*

Amigo/a	Prenda	Material	Color
		algodón	
			rayas verdes y blancas
	una bolsa		
Alberto			

Paso 2. Ahora, usa tu imaginación y escribe cuatro oraciones para describir las prendas que tus amigos/as olvidaron.

Modelo: **Andrea olvidó una blusa de algodón amarilla.**

8-4 ¿Qué combina mejor?

Paso 1. Empareja los artículos de ropa de la columna A y la columna B, especificando un color para la ropa de la columna B.

A

____ **1.** Una chaqueta gris

____ **2.** Unos vaqueros

____ **3.** Un vestido blanco

____ **4.** Un traje azul

____ **5.** Un abrigo marrón

____ **6.** Un impermeable rosa

____ **7.** Una blusa/camisa blanca

B

a. con una camiseta _____

b. con unos zapatos _____

c. con una corbata _____

d. con una falda/unos pantalones cortos _____

e. con unas botas _____

f. con unas sandalias _____

g. con unos pantalones _____

 Paso 2. Compara tus respuestas con las de un/a compañero/a y después, con la clase.

8-5 ¿Qué ropa es apropiada?

Paso 1. Escucha las siguientes descripciones e indica en qué ocasión es apropiado llevar esta ropa. (Algunas opciones pueden ser apropiadas para más de una ocasión.)

____ para ir a la playa

____ para ir a una entrevista de trabajo (*job interview*)

____ para correr en el parque

____ para ir a clase

____ para ir a una cena formal

____ para ir a la discoteca

Paso 2. En tu cuaderno, describe un atuendo (*outfit*) para un hombre y para una mujer para cada ocasión del Paso 1. Puedes repetir prendas y accesorios.

Paso 3. En grupos pequeños, cada estudiante lee una de sus descripciones. El resto del grupo debe identificar la ocasión y si el atuendo es para un hombre o para una mujer.

8-6 El color perfecto para cada ocasión.

Paso 1. Antes de leer.

¿Cuál es tu color favorito? ¿Qué características asocias con ese color?

Paso 2. Lee el texto de la página 263 y contesta las preguntas que siguen.

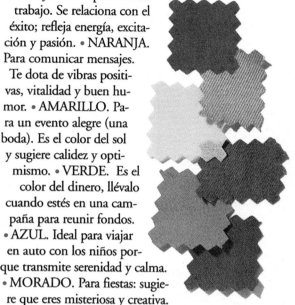

El color perfecto para cada ocasión

• ROJO. Ideal para buscar trabajo. Se relaciona con el éxito; refleja energía, excitación y pasión. • NARANJA. Para comunicar mensajes. Te dota de vibras positivas, vitalidad y buen humor. • AMARILLO. Para un evento alegre (una boda). Es el color del sol y sugiere calidez y optimismo. • VERDE. Es el color del dinero, llévalo cuando estés en una campaña para reunir fondos. • AZUL. Ideal para viajar en auto con los niños porque transmite serenidad y calma. • MORADO. Para fiestas: sugiere que eres misteriosa y creativa.

1. ¿Qué color simboliza energía? ¿Y calma? ¿Y misterio?

2. ¿Qué colores se llevan[1] con frecuencia cuando hace mucho calor? ¿Y cuando hace frío?

3. ¿Qué colores asocias con una persona que suele estar (*usually is*) contenta? ¿Y con una persona que está triste?

4. Según (*According to*) el texto, ¿qué es lo que se asocia con tu color favorito? ¿Crees que estas características describen tu personalidad correctamente? Si el artículo no menciona tu color favorito, ¿qué color es? ¿Y qué crees tú que puede sugerir?

Paso 3. Basándote en el texto *El color perfecto para cada ocasión,* ayuda a estas personas a escoger ropa apropiada para las siguientes ocasiones.

Modelo: Rosa quiere pedir un aumento (*raise*) en el trabajo.
Puede llevar un traje negro porque es elegante y profesional, y una blusa verde para atraer (*attract*) el dinero.

1. El Sr. Donoso va a comer con un cliente importante.

2. Pedro va a trabajar cuidando a niños esta noche.

3. Bernardo tiene una cita (*a date*) esta noche.

4. Andrea va a hacer una presentación en la clase de historia mañana.

5. Leo va a visitar a su abuela en el hospital.

---

[1] The word **se** placed before the verb slightly alters the meaning of the verb. Here, **se llevan** = *are worn;* **llevan** = *they, you (pl.) wear.*

La transformación de Carmen

Antes

Carmen nos habla de su pequeña transformación.

"Para empezar, fui a visitar al oftalmólogo y como resultado de la visita cambié mis gafas por **lentes de contacto,** algo que cambió mi vida radicalmente porque ahora me siento (*I feel*) más joven, más **a la moda.** Luego, organicé mi **ropero:** eliminé varias **cosas,** lavé toda la ropa **sucia** y ahora todo está **limpio** y ordenado. Por supuesto, mi amiga Irene y yo vamos a tener que ir de compras. Quiero comprar una falda **corta** para salir, una falda **larga** para el trabajo, unos pantalones negros, una blusa **de manga corta** y otra de **manga larga.** También voy a comprar unos aretes, un collar y tal vez unos anillos de fantasía (*costume*) porque las joyas de **oro** o **plata** son muy **caras** y yo no tengo mucho dinero. ¡El **precio** siempre es importante para una madre soltera! La verdad es que no sé cuánto va a **costar** todo esto, pero Irene me dice que en el **centro comercial** hay unas tiendas donde venden ropa de moda **barata**

Después

porque ahora tienen **rebajas.** Además, primero vamos a **mirar** en varias tiendas y a comparar precios. ¡Ah! Y en cuanto a (*as for*) la **talla,** voy a arreglar (*fix*) ese problemita porque me voy a poner a dieta y todo me va a quedar (*fit*) perfecto".

corto/a	*short*	**el oro**	*gold*
la cosa	*thing*	**la plata**	*silver*
costar (ue)	*cost*	**las rebajas**	*sales*
largo/a	*long*	**el ropero**	*closet*
limpio/a	*clean*	**sucio/a**	*dirty*
de manga (corta)	*(short-)sleeved*	**la talla**	*size*
la moda[1]	*fashion, style*		

NOTA CULTURAL

La formalidad de la ropa

In most United States colleges and universities, it is acceptable for students to attend class in informal clothing such as sweatpants and baseball caps. However, in many Spanish-speaking countries, such attire would be viewed as inappropriate. People tend to dress less informally for school, or to go out in general.

---

[1] While **ir/estar a la moda** is used to refer to people (to dress with style), **estar de moda** is used to talk about a particular article of clothing, color, etc. that is in fashion: **El negro está de moda.**

8-7 ¿Qué puedes ponerte?

Paso 1. Indica las prendas y los accesorios que son apropiados para estos lugares y situaciones.

	Las clases	Una cena formal	La oficina	El cine	El centro comercial	Una fiesta
joyas de oro						
una camiseta vieja						
una bolsa elegante						
una corbata						
una gorra						
sandalias						
jeans						
pantalones cortos						
zapatos de tenis						
una falda corta						
un vestido largo						

 Paso 2. En grupos pequeños, comparen sus respuestas. ¿Tienen opiniones similares?

 Paso 3. En sus grupos, escriban una lista de ropa o accesorios que consideren inapropiados para cada ocasión.

 ## 8-8 Un gran contraste. En parejas, tomen turnos para describir el aspecto y la ropa de Esteban y Octavio. Un/a estudiante dice una oración y el otro/la otra adivina (*guesses*) si se refiere a Esteban o a Octavio.

Modelo: Estudiante A: **Lleva una camiseta limpia.**

Estudiante B: **Es Octavio.**

¿Qué impresiones tienen sobre los tipos de cosas y actividades que Esteban y Octavio prefieren hacer según su modo de vestir?

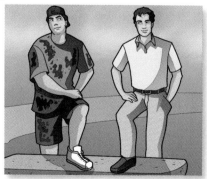

Esteban   Octavio

8-9 ¿Qué prefieres?

Paso 1. Indica tus preferencias respecto a la ropa y las compras y responde a las preguntas de abajo.

1. los suéteres   ☐ de lana   ☐ de algodón   ☐ de seda
2. las camisas   ☐ de manga larga   ☐ de manga corta
3. los pantalones   ☐ cortos   ☐ largos   ☐ los *jeans*
4. el calzado   ☐ los zapatos   ☐ las sandalias   ☐ las botas
5. para los ojos   ☐ gafas   ☐ lentes de contacto
6. la ropa   ☐ elegante   ☐ de calidad   ☐ de moda
   ☐ cómoda (*comfortable*)
7. comprar en   ☐ el almacén   ☐ el centro comercial   ☐ Internet
8. ¿Vas de compras frecuentemente? ¿Vas solamente cuando buscas algo específico o para mirar?
9. ¿Cuáles son tus marcas favoritas? ¿Qué tiendas o almacenes prefieres para comprar ropa?

Paso 2. En grupos, comparen sus preferencias: ¿son similares o diferentes?

8-10 El precio correcto.

Trabajan en el Almacén Galerías de la Moda y deben poner las etiquetas de precios en estos artículos. Pero, ¿dónde está la lista de precios? En parejas, decidan qué precio corresponde a cada artículo.

Modelo: Estudiante A: **Yo creo que el reloj cuesta 370 dólares.**

Estudiante B: **¿Tú crees? Me parece un precio barato.**

Estudiante A: **Pero no es de oro, ¿verdad?...**

$3,450

$2,500

$25

$6

$10

$175

$125

$36

$65

NOTA DE LENGUA

While shopping, one usually looks for, looks at, and sees various items. Observe the differences between the verbs **buscar** (*to look for*), **mirar** (*to look at*), and **ver** (*to see*). Natalia y Camila…

buscan un regalo,
   are looking for a gift,
miran varias gafas de sol
   look at various sunglasses,
y **ven** las que quieren comprar.
   and see the ones they want to buy.

EXPRESIONES ÚTILES

¿Tú crees?
   Do you think so?
¿Estás seguro/a?
   Are you sure?
¿Qué te parece?
   What do you think?
Me parece (caro/barato)
   It seems (expensive/ cheap)

NOTA DE LENGUA

The prepositions **por** and **para** can be problematic for English speakers because they both can be equivalent to *for*. Which one is used depends on the meaning we want to convey. You have already studied some uses of **por** and **para** (*Capítulo 7*). Additional uses are:

Para + *person/thing* = *for* + *the recipient/beneficiary of something*

Esta blusa es **para** mi novia.   *This blouse is **for** my girlfriend.*
Necesita una silla **para** su oficina.   *He needs a chair **for** his office.*

Por + *an amount* = *for, in exchange for*

Pagué $200 **por** el collar.   *I paid $200 **for** the necklace.*
~~Pagué $200 **para** el collar.~~

8-11 **Regalos para todos.** El Almacén Galerías de la Moda tiene rebajas y ustedes compran muchos regalos para su familia y sus amigos. Habla con tu compañero/a y dile qué compraste, para quién es cada regalo y cuánto dinero gastaste. Haz preguntas y comentarios sobre sus compras. Túrnense.

EXPRESIONES ÚTILES

¡Qué barato/caro!
How cheap/expensive!
¡No me digas!
Really?/Seriously?/No way!

Modelo: Estudiante A: **Estos guantes son para mi hermana. Los compré por cuatro dólares.**

Estudiante B: **¡Qué baratos! Pero ahora no hace mucho frío.**

Estudiante A: **No, pero mi hermana siempre tiene frío.**

8-12 **¿Qué necesitamos?**

Paso 1. El próximo año vas a estudiar en Ecuador y estás pensando en lo que necesitas para el viaje. ¿Qué ropa y accesorios vas a necesitar para ir a los siguientes lugares? En la sección de cultura sobre Ecuador, en las páginas 270–271, vas a encontrar información interesante sobre su clima.

Las playas de Guayaquil (agosto)	Volcán Chimborazo (noviembre)	Selva amazónica (septiembre)	Cena en la Embajada de EE.UU. en Quito (octubre)

Paso 2. ¡Qué casualidad! Tu compañero/a también va a ir a Ecuador. Comparen sus listas y expliquen por qué van a llevar estas cosas. ¿Quieres eliminar, añadir (*add*) o cambiar algo en tu lista?

Así se forma

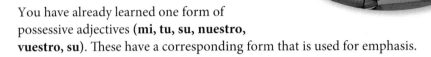

PLUS Go to *WileyPLUS* and review the Animated Grammar Tutorial for this grammar point.

1. Emphasizing possession: Possessive adjectives and pronouns

You have already learned one form of possessive adjectives (**mi, tu, su, nuestro, vuestro, su**). These have a corresponding form that is used for emphasis.

Es **mi** bolsa.	*It's **my** purse.*
Esa bolsa es **mía.**	*That purse is **mine.***

These emphatic possessive forms are also adjectives and therefore agree in gender (masculine/feminine) and number (singular/plural) with the thing possessed.

Los posesivos enfáticos

mío/a, míos/as	*mine*	Esa chaqueta es **mía.**
tuyo/a, tuyos/as	*yours*	¿Los guantes azules son **tuyos?**
suyo/a, suyos/as[1]	*his*	Pepe dice que esa gorra es **suya.**
	hers	Ana dice que esas botas son **suyas.**
	yours (usted)	¿El bolso de cuero es **suyo?**
nuestro/a, nuestros/as	*ours*	Esa casa es **nuestra.**
		Esos dos gatos son **nuestros.**
vuestro/a, vuestros/as	*yours*	¿Es **vuestro** ese carro?
		¿Son **vuestras** las bicicletas?
suyo/a, suyos/as	*theirs*	Ana y Tere dicen que esas cosas son **suyas.**
	yours (ustedes)	Señoras, ¿son **suyos** estos paraguas?

They follow either a form of the verb **ser** to indicate *mine, yours,* etc., or a noun to indicate *of mine, of yours,* etc.

Esas botas son **mías.**	*Those boots are **mine.***
Pero un amigo **mío** dice que son **suyas.**	*But a friend of **mine** says that they are **his.***

---

[1]As with **su/sus**, if the context does not clearly indicate who **suyo/a/os/as** refers to, you may use an alternate form for clarity.

Es **su** ropa.	Or,	Es la ropa **de él/ella/usted.**
Esa ropa es **suya.**	Or,	Esa ropa es **de ellos/ellas/ustedes.**

Possessive pronouns are used when the possessed object has been mentioned before, to avoid repetition. Their form is similar to that of emphatic possessive adjectives but they require the use of definite articles (**el, la, los, las**).

—Tengo mi suéter. ¿Tienes el **tuyo**?   *I have my sweater. Do you have **yours**?*
—Sí, tengo el **mío**.   *Yes, I have **mine**.*

8-13 **En la lavandería (*laundromat*).** Alfonso y Rubén están en la lavandería y usan la misma (*same*) secadora. Ahora cada uno busca su ropa.

Paso 1. Presta atención a lo que dicen e indica a qué prendas se refieren.

Alfonso   Rubén

Rubén dice:

1. Esta es mía.   **a.** la chaqueta   **b.** los pantalones   **c.** el suéter
2. Este es mío.   **a.** los calcetines   **b.** el suéter   **c.** la camiseta

Alfonso dice:

3. Estos son míos.   **a.** la chaqueta   **b.** la camisa   **c.** los pantalones cortos
4. Estas son mías.   **a.** las camisas   **b.** los jeans   **c.** el impermeable

WILEY
PLUS Go to *WileyPLUS* and review the Animated Grammar Tutorial for this grammar point.

Paso 2. Ahora, completa estas oraciones indicando de quién es cada prenda.

1. Rubén dice que **la chaqueta es…**
2. Alfonso dice que…
3. Rubén dice que…
4. Alfonso dice que…

8-14 **¡Un ladrón o una ladrona (*robber, thief*) en la clase!** ¡Cierren los ojos! (El/La profesor/a va a caminar por la clase "robando" algunos de los artículos de los/as estudiantes para ponerlos sobre su escritorio.) Luego, abran los ojos y contesten las preguntas del/de la profesor/a.

Modelo: Profesor/a: Señor/Señorita, ¿es suyo este reloj?
        Estudiante: No, no es **mío**.
        Profesor/a a la clase: Pues, ¿de quién es?
        Un/a estudiante indica: Es **suyo**. O, Es **de Lisa**.

DICHOS

Se cree el ladrón que todos son de su condición.

¿Qué significa el dicho? ¿Estás de acuerdo?

Cultura: Perú, Ecuador y Bolivia

WILEY PLUS **Map quizzes:** As you read about places highlighted in red, find them on the map. Learn more about and test yourself on the geography of the Spanish-speaking world in *WileyPLUS*.

Antes de leer

1. ¿Cuáles son las capitales de estos tres países? ¿Qué país tiene dos capitales?

2. ¿Qué tienen Ecuador y Perú que no tiene Bolivia?

   ☐ costa (*coast*)　　☐ frontera con otro país　　☐ montañas

3. ¿Sabes por qué es famoso Machu Picchu?

4. ¿Cómo se llama el lago que está en la frontera entre Perú y Bolivia?

EL GRAN IMPERIO INCA

Ecuador, Perú y Bolivia están situados en el corazón (*heart*) de los Andes y formaban parte del antiguo Imperio inca llamado Tahuantinsuyo. Con una extensión de 3,000 millas de norte a sur, la zona está caracterizada por espectaculares picos nevados, impresionantes volcanes y el inmenso **lago Titicaca.** Los emperadores incas gobernaron durante casi 400 años. Bajo su gobierno a nadie le faltó (*no one lacked*) comida ni ropa y después de conquistar a otras tribus, los incas incorporaban a los líderes conquistados en su gobierno. El último emperador inca fue Atahualpa y fue capturado en 1532 por Francisco Pizarro cuando los españoles conquistaron la región. Durante este periodo la ciudad peruana de **Lima** se convirtió en el centro colonial más importante de América del Sur.

Los incas perfeccionaron el cultivo de la papa y el cuidado del ganado (*livestock*) de los Andes, como las llamas y las alpacas. Muchos indígenas todavía llevan la ropa tradicional andina: sarapes, ponchos y sombreros hechos de lana de alpaca. Después del español, el quechua es la lengua más hablada entre los indígenas de la zona andina. Las siguientes palabras proceden del quechua: *cóndor*, *puma* y *papa*. Aunque es una lengua minoritaria, el quechua es uno de los idiomas oficiales de Ecuador.

▲ Plaza de la Independencia, Quito, Ecuador

ECUADOR

La línea ecuatorial que pasa por el norte de **Quito** le dio su nombre al país. Ecuador es un país pequeño, pero de grandes contrastes geográficos. En sus costas cálidas y secas hay playas excelentes. En la región oriental está la zona amazónica, donde el clima es caliente y húmedo y existe una gran variedad de flora y fauna. El área andina, con impresionantes volcanes, tiene un clima frío y seco.

Quito, la capital de Ecuador, tiene una zona antigua de gran belleza con numerosos ejemplos de arte y arquitectura coloniales. Por eso, muchas personas la llaman "la cara de Dios (*the face of God*)". En la foto se ve la Plaza de la Independencia. El 10 de agosto de 1809 el primer grito (*cry*) de independencia de América Latina se dio en Quito. En 1822, Ecuador se independizó de España y se incorporó a la Gran Colombia. En 1830 se convirtió en una república independiente. En el año 2000, Ecuador adoptó el dólar de Estados Unidos como moneda nacional.

Hoy en día, muchas de las flores y plantas que se venden en las floristerías de Estados Unidos y Europa provienen de Ecuador.

Las islas Galápagos, donde Darwin desarrolló muchas de sus teorías, son un verdadero tesoro ecológico. Estas islas, cuyo nombre oficial es "Archipiélago de Colón", quedan a unas 600 millas de la costa ecuatoriana. En ellas coexisten especies de reptiles, aves (*birds*) y plantas únicas en el mundo. Las tortugas (*turtles*) de las Galápagos pueden vivir sin comer un año, llegar a pesar 500 libras y vivir hasta 100 años.

Tortuga Galápago ▶

PERÚ

Perú es el tercer país más grande de América del Sur. La costa árida del Pacífico (donde están Lima y el puerto principal, **El Callao**) es la región más dinámica del país, pero el área andina, con montañas muy elevadas, domina su geografía. La influencia indígena en Perú es muy marcada. En la foto, la calle de Cuzco muestra la fusión de las culturas indígena y española. Los incas construyeron el muro de piedra (*stone wall*) y los españoles construyeron la parte superior del edificio. Los idiomas oficiales de Perú son el español y un gran número de lenguas indígenas, entre las que destacan el quechua y el aimara.

▲ Cuzco, Peru

◄ Ciudad de Machu Picchu, Perú

Cerca de Cuzco, Perú, a más de 8,000 pies de altura, los incas construyeron la ciudad de **Machu Picchu.** Esta ciudad refleja el alto nivel de tecnología del Imperio inca. Los españoles no sabían de la existencia de Machu Picchu y, después de la conquista, el sitio se perdió durante siglos. Sus ruinas fueron redescubiertas en 1911 por el arqueólogo estadounidense Hiram Bingham.

Mario Vargas Llosa es un famoso escritor peruano. Fue parte del *boom* literario latinoamericano y alcanzó la fama en la década de 1960 con novelas como *La ciudad y los perros* (1963) y *La casa verde* (1965). A lo largo de su carrera; ha recibido numerosas distinciones, entre ellas el Premio Rómulo Gallegos (1967) el Premio Cervantes (1994) y el Premio Nobel de Literatura (2010). Entre sus obras cabe señalar *Pantaleón y las visitadoras* (1973), *La tía Julia y el escribidor* (1977), *Lituma en los Andes* (1993) y *La fiesta del Chivo* (2000). En 1990, Vargas Llosa se presentó a la presidencia de Perú, pero perdió frente a Alberto Fujimori.

En 1999, en las afueras de Lima, Perú, se descubrió un cementerio inca con una extensión aproximada de 20 acres. Esta zona se conoce con el nombre de Puruchuco-Huaquerones. Hasta el momento más de 2,200 momias envueltas en bultos de tela (*bundles of cloth*) han sido exhumadas (*have been exhumed*) de este sitio arqueológico. Estos bultos pueden llegar a pesar (*weigh*) hasta 500 libras y contienen cuerpos (*bodies*) y los artefactos que los difuntos (*dead*) usaron durante su vida.

En la frontera entre Bolivia y Perú, a unos 12,500 pies de altura, está el lago Titicaca, que es el segundo más grande de América del Sur (mide más de 3,000 millas cuadradas) y el lago navegable más alto del mundo. En esta foto, se cruza el lago en una canoa de totora (*cattail plant*).

Lago Titicaca, Perú ▷

BOLIVIA

El nombre de este país rinde homenaje a Simón Bolívar, el héroe de las guerras de independencia de Hispanoamérica. Bolivia fue parte de Perú durante casi toda la época colonial. Las minas de plata de **Potosí** fueron la atracción principal para los españoles y en tiempos coloniales Potosí llegó a ser la ciudad más poblada de las Américas. Bolivia se independizó en 1825.

Sucre es la capital constitucional de Bolivia. **La Paz,** la capital administrativa, es la sede del gobierno. Con sus casi 13,000 pies de altura, es famosa por ser una de las ciudades más altas del mundo. De hecho, debido a la altura y a la poca cantidad de oxígeno, en La Paz es muy difícil encender (*light*) y mantener un fuego. Por eso hay muy pocos incendios (*fires*).

▲ La Paz, Bolivia

Al igual que en Perú y Ecuador, la presencia indígena es muy visible en Bolivia. Sólo la mitad de los bolivianos hablan español como primera lengua. Además del español, Bolivia tiene más de treinta lenguas oficiales, entre ellas el quechua, el aimara y el guaraní.

Después de leer

1. ¿Dónde se encuentra el lago Titicaca y por qué es famoso? ¿Conoces alguna atracción turística natural situada en la frontera entre Estados Unidos y otro país?

2. ¿Qué hacían los incas después de conquistar otra tribu?

3. ¿A qué país o países se refieren las siguientes oraciones?

	Ecuador	Perú	Bolivia
Las islas Galápagos pertenecen a (*belong to*) este país.	☐	☐	☐
Tiene playas, selva tropical, volcanes y zonas frías.	☐	☐	☐
El quechua es una lengua oficial de este país.	☐	☐	☐
Su capital es una de las ciudades más altas del mundo.	☐	☐	☐
Exporta muchas rosas.	☐	☐	☐

4. El presidente de Ecuador, Rafael Correa, sabe hablar quechua. ¿Algún presidente de Estados Unidos hablaba una lengua indígena?

Así se forma

WILEY PLUS Go to *WileyPLUS* and review the Animated Grammar Tutorial and Verb Conjugator for this grammar point. Consult the verb charts in *Apéndice 1* at the end of your book for additional verbs with irregular preterit forms.

2. The preterit of irregular verbs: Expressing actions in the past

In *Capítulo 7*, you learned the irregular preterit forms of the verb **hacer**. The following verbs also have one consistent preterit stem and the same endings as **hacer**.

estar **estuv-**	tener **tuv-**	poder **pud-**	poner **pus-**	saber **sup-**	venir **vin-**	querer **quis-**	traer **traj-**	decir **dij-**
estuve	tuve	pude	puse	supe	vine	quise	traje	dije
estuviste	tuviste	pudiste	pusiste	supiste	viniste	quisiste	trajiste	dijiste
estuvo	tuvo	pudo	puso	supo	vino	quiso	trajo	dijo
estuvimos	tuvimos	pudimos	pusimos	supimos	vinimos	quisimos	trajimos	dijimos
estuvisteis	tuvisteis	pudisteis	pusisteis	supisteis	vinisteis	quisisteis	trajisteis	dijisteis
estuvieron	tuvieron	pudieron	pusieron	supieron	vinieron	quisieron	trajeron	dijeron

No **tuve** que trabajar anoche.	*I didn't have to work last night.*
Algunos amigos **vinieron** a visitarme.	*Some friends came to visit me.*
Rubén **trajo** su guitarra.	*Rubén brought his guitar.*

- Notice the difference in the **ellos, ellas,** and **ustedes** endings (-**ieron** and -**eron**) between the two groups of verbs above. Verbs whose stems end in **j** add -**eron** instead of -**ieron**.

- The verbs **saber, querer,** and **poder** convey a slightly different meaning in the preterit than in the present.

saber	**Supe** hacerlo.	*I found out/figured out how to do it.*
querer	**Quise** hablar con ella.	*I tried to speak with her.*
no querer	Ella **no quiso** hablar conmigo.	*She refused to speak with me.*
poder	**Pude** terminar el proyecto.	*I managed to finish the project.*
no poder	**No pude** encontrar al profesor.	*I didn't manage to find the professor.*

8-15 ¿Qué hicieron el fin de semana pasado (*last weekend*)?

Paso 1. Indica qué oraciones de la columna *El fin de semana pasado yo...* en la página 275 son ciertas para ti. Añade una oración original al final.

 Paso 2. Ahora, comparte (*share*) tus respuestas con un/a compañero/a añadiendo (*adding*) más detalles. Anota sus respuestas en la columna *El fin de semana pasado mi compañero/a....*

Modelo:	Estudiante A:	**El sábado hice ejercicio. Fui al gimnasio y monté en bicicleta. ¿Y tú?**
	Estudiante B:	**No, este fin de semana no hice ejercicio.**

El fin de semana pasado yo...	El fin de semana pasado mi compañero/a...
☐ hice ejercicio o practiqué un deporte.	☐ hizo ejercicio o practicó un deporte.
☐ tuve que estudiar mucho.	☐ tuvo que estudiar mucho.
☐ estuve en el centro comercial.	☐ estuvo en el centro comercial.
☐ traje comida a mi cuarto/apartamento.	☐ trajo comida a su cuarto/apartamento.
☐ fui a la biblioteca.	☐ fue a la biblioteca.
☐ me divertí mucho.	☐ se divirtió mucho.
☐ me puse algo especial para salir.	☐ se puso algo especial para salir.
☐ pude dormir mucho.	☐ pudo dormir mucho.
☐ dije chistes (*jokes*).	☐ dijo chistes.
☐ _____	☐ _____

Paso 3. Responde a las siguientes preguntas. Después, compara tus repuestas con las de tu compañero/a.

- ¿Quién tuvo el fin de semana más relajado?
- ¿Quién tuvo el fin de semana más divertido?

8-16 **La fiesta de cumpleaños.** Este fin de semana fue el cumpleaños de Carmen y todos fueron a su fiesta.

Paso 1. Escucha las siguientes descripciones y escribe el número correspondiente debajo del dibujo que describe la actividad.

_____

_____

_____

_____

_____

_____

Paso 2. Ahora, en parejas, organicen las actividades de la página 275 en orden cronológico y escriban una descripción de cada actividad. Pueden inventar más detalles. Si no recuerdan (*remember*) las palabras exactas que oyeron, usen su creatividad. Aquí tienen unos verbos útiles.

comprar	traer	hacer	abrir	irse	poner

 8-17 **Excusas.** Tu compañero/a y tú iban a (*were going to*) cenar juntos/as ayer, pero ¡los/as dos lo olvidaron (*forgot*)! Siguiendo el modelo, inventen excusas para explicar su ausencia y pregúntenle a su compañero/a sobre las suyas. Túrnense.

EXPRESIONES ÚTILES

¿De verdad?
¡Ah!, ¿sí?   } *Oh, really?*
¡No me digas!

Modelo: Estudiante A: **Lo siento, Pete, pero ayer tuve un laboratorio de química.**

Estudiante B: **¿De verdad? ¿A qué hora fue? ¿Dónde?...**

Estudiante A:

1. no poder salir del cuarto/apartamento

2. tener que ayudar a un/a amigo/a

3. sustituir a un/a compañero/a en el trabajo

4. ...

Estudiante B:

1. no saber llegar al restaurante

2. querer llamar por teléfono y no poder

3. estar enfermo/a

4. ...

8-18 **Mi aventura.**

Paso 1. Escribe un párrafo (cinco o seis oraciones) describiendo una aventura (real o imaginaria). ¿Adónde fuiste? ¿Cuánto tiempo estuviste allí? ¿Tuviste alguna experiencia interesante? ¿Qué hiciste? ¿Hay algo que quisiste hacer pero no pudiste?

 Paso 2. En grupos de cuatro, cada estudiante lee su aventura a los/as demás y éstos/as hacen preguntas sobre los detalles. Si tu aventura es imaginaria, ¡invéntalos! El resto del grupo intenta adivinar si las aventuras de sus compañeros/as son reales o imaginarias.

Cultura: La ropa tradicional

Antes de leer

¿Se lleva ropa tradicional actualmente en algunas regiones de tu país? ¿Dónde? ¿Puedes describir un ejemplo?

▲ Bailarines vestidos con ropa tradicional mexicana

La ropa tradicional de España y de Hispanoamérica es muy variada. En las ciudades sólo se usa la ropa tradicional en los días de fiesta nacional. En los desfiles (*parades*) cívicos, los niños, jóvenes y adultos se visten con la ropa típica de las diferentes regiones de su país y bailan música tradicional. Las compañías nacionales de danza también usan ropa típica. Gracias al flamenco, los trajes típicos del sur de España se conocen en todo el mundo.

Sin embargo, los indígenas de las zonas rurales de muchos países, como Bolivia, Ecuador, Guatemala y México, usan ropa típica todos los días. En la península mexicana de Yucatán las mujeres usan el huipil, un vestido (o una blusa) de origen maya con un bordado (*embroidery*) de flores de colores vivos (*bright*). Por el tipo de diseño del huipil que viste la mujer se distingue la región en la que vive.

Las polleras de las panameñas son verdaderos tesoros: estas prendas están decoradas con finos encajes (*lace*) y bordadas con hilos (*threads*) de oro. En las regiones costeras, sobre todo en el Caribe, es común ver a hombres con guayaberas: camisas de telas livianas (*light fabrics*), bordadas en colores claros, que son perfectas para el clima caliente de la zona.

En el pueblo de Otavalo, en la región andina de Ecuador, las mujeres llevan una falda negra con bordados de colores, una blusa blanca bordada de encajes, muchos collares y pulseras de cuentas (*beads*) rojas y doradas (*golden*) y un turbante en la cabeza. Por lo general, los hombres de esta región llevan un poncho de lana sobre una camisa, pantalones blancos con alpargatas (*rope-soled sandals*) blancas y un sombrero negro.

▲ La pollera panameña

▲ Una guayabera

▲ Familia indígena ecuatoriana

Después de leer

Empareja estos artículos de ropa con los lugares en los que se usan:

a. los huipiles ___ Panamá

b. la pollera ___ el Caribe

c. el poncho de lana ___ Ecuador

d. la guayabera ___ Yucatán

¿Cuál te gusta más?

Así se forma

> ¿Quién te mandó las flores?

> Me las mandó Manuel. Y a ti, ¿quién te las mandó?

WILEY PLUS Go to *WileyPLUS* and review the Animated Grammar Tutorial for this grammar point.

3. Direct and indirect object pronouns combined

When both the indirect and direct object are replaced with pronouns, the indirect object pronoun is always placed first: OI + OD.

La profesora **me lo** prestó.　　*The professor lent **it to me**.*
　　(OI)(OD)

Placement rules stay the same: before conjugated verbs and attached to infinitives and the **–ndo** form. In a negative statement, **no** precedes both objects.

¿Pedro no **te lo** explicó?　　*Didn't Pedro explain **it to you**?*
No, Carlos va a explicár**melo**/　　*No, Carlos is going to explain **it to me**.*
Carlos **me lo** va a explicar.

When both the indirect and direct object pronouns refer to the third person and they are used together, the indirect object pronoun **le** or **les** changes to **se.**

		lo		se lo
le or **les**	**+**	**los**	**=**	**se los**
		la		**se la**
		las		**se las**

Se lo expliqué a ellas.　　*I explained **it to them**.*

Estoy explicándo**selo**./　　*I am explaining **it to her/him/you**.*
Se lo estoy explicando.

—¿**Le** diste **la foto** a Linda?　　—*Did you give the photo to Linda?*
—Sí, **se la** di.　　—*Yes, I gave **it to her**.*

Note that when two pronouns are added to the infinitive or present participle, a written accent is added to preserve the original stress pattern:

Va a **mostrármelo.**
Está **mostrándoselo.**

SITUACIONES

Vas de compras al almacén *La Única* (págs. 258-259) con un/a compañero/a de clase porque los/las dos tienen que comprarles regalos a varios amigos o familiares. Cuando llegan al almacén, se separan y hacen sus compras por separado. Después, se reúnen en la cafetería del almacén para tomar un café. Háganse preguntas sobre qué le compraron a quién.

8-19 **¡Nos encantan los regalos!** Octavio fue a Ecuador y les trajo varios regalos a sus amigas. Observa los dibujos para ver qué regalos trajo y para quién.

Natalia / la camiseta

Pepita / el póster

Carmen e Inés / las toallas de playa

Camila y Linda / los collares y los pendientes

Paso 1. Estas son las reacciones de las chicas. Identifica el dibujo correspondiente y responde a estas preguntas.

	¿Quién lo dice?	¿De qué regalo habla/n?
a. ¡Impresionante! Octavio me lo regaló.	_____	_____
b. ¡Nos encantan! Octavio nos las regaló.	_____	_____
c. ¡Qué bonitos son! Octavio nos los regaló.	_____	_____
d. ¡Me encanta! Octavio me la regaló.	_____	_____

Paso 2. En parejas, una persona explica qué regalo le dio Octavio a una de sus amigas. El/La compañero/a tiene que confirmar o negar la información sustituyendo los objetos por pronombres.

Modelo: ESTUDIANTE A: **Octavio le dio la camiseta a Natalia.**
ESTUDIANTE B: **Sí,** *se la* **dio a Natalia.** O, **No,** *se la* **dio a...**

8-20 **Las compras.** Tú y tu compañero/a fueron hoy de compras: uno/a fue al supermercado y el/la otro/a fue a la librería. Tú le pediste a tu compañero/a algunas cosas. Pregúntale si te las compró. Responde también a sus preguntas.

Modelo: ESTUDIANTE A: **¿Me compraste los bolígrafos?**
ESTUDIANTE B: **Sí, te los compré.**

Estudiante A:

Pediste a tu compañero/a:
bolígrafos
un cuaderno
una regla (*ruler*)

Compraste para tu compañero/a:
leche
tortillas

Estudiante B:

Pediste a tu compañero/a:
pan
tortilla
leche

Compraste para tu compañero/a:
bolígrafos
una regla

8-21 **¿Quién te lo dio?** Cada estudiante le da a un/a compañero/a de clase un artículo (reloj, tarjeta de crédito, gorra, bolígrafo, etc.). Los/as estudiantes caminan por la clase, haciéndoles preguntas a cinco o seis compañeros/as diferentes.

Modelo: ESTUDIANTE A: **Melvin, ¿quién te dio ese reloj?**
ESTUDIANTE B: **Carla me lo dio. Y ¿quién te dio esos bolígrafos?**
ESTUDIANTE A: **Cliff me los dio.**

¡No olvides devolverle el artículo a tu compañero/a de clase!

8-22 **El amigo invisible.** Van a jugar al amigo invisible (*Secret Santa*) en su clase. Lean las instrucciones con atención.

Paso 1.

a. Escribe tu nombre en un pedazo de papel y dáselo al/a la profesor/a.

b. Ahora, toma un papel y mira el nombre.

c. Piensa en un regalo perfecto para esta persona y escríbelo en la parte de atrás (*back*) del papel. Dale el papel al/a la profesor/a otra vez.

d. El/La profesor/a va a leer los nombres y distribuir los "regalos".

Paso 2. Cada estudiante cuenta a la clase lo que le regalaron, si el regalo le gusta o no y por qué. Después, pregunta quién le hizo este regalo. El/La estudiante responsable responde y explica sus razones.

Modelo: ESTUDIANTE A: **Me regalaron un/a..., (no) me gusta porque...**
PROFESOR/A (A LA CLASE): **¿Quién se lo regaló?**
ESTUDIANTE B: **Yo se lo regalé porque...**

NOTA CULTURAL

Los mercados y el regateo (*bargaining*)

It is common to see various types of merchants in Spanish-speaking countries, including street vendors, merchants in open-air markets, modern indoor shopping malls, specialty stores, etc. Normally a degree of bargaining is expected with street vendors and in markets, particularly for arts and crafts, clothing, and jewelry. When bargaining, never insult the quality of the item or the vendor. Simply suggest a lower price than the one that is offered, and be prepared to meet somewhere in the middle. Bargain only for items that you intend to purchase. Shopping malls and department stores almost always have fixed prices, so bargaining is inappropriate there.

VideoEscenas: ¿Qué le compro?

▲ Álvaro y María van de compras.

Paso 1. ¿Cuáles de estos te parecen buenos regalos para un/a amigo/a? Añade otro más.

	Un amigo	Una amiga
1. un libro	☐	☐
2. un CD	☐	☐
3. una pulsera	☐	☐
4. unas flores	☐	☐
5. unos zapatos	☐	☐
_____	☐	☐

Paso 2. Mira el video e indica si estas afirmaciones son ciertas o falsas. Corrige las oraciones falsas.

	Cierto	Falso
1. Álvaro olvidó el cumpleaños de Marisol.	☐	☐
2. María le compró unos zapatos a Marisol.	☐	☐
3. A María no le gusta llevar pulseras.	☐	☐
4. María sugiere comprar flores.	☐	☐

Paso 3. Lee las siguientes preguntas. Después, mira el video otra vez y responde.

1. ¿Por qué no fue Álvaro a la fiesta de Marisol?
2. ¿Qué le regaló María a Marisol?
3. ¿Por qué no es buena idea comprarle una pulsera?
4. ¿Por qué no le compran los aretes?
5. ¿Por qué piensa María que las rosas son un buen regalo?

Paso 4. En grupos de tres o cuatro, respondan a estas preguntas:

¿Cuál fue el mejor regalo que te hicieron? ¿Cuál fue el peor? Explica por qué y escucha las experiencias de tus compañeros. ¿Quién recibió el mejor regalo del grupo? ¿Y el peor?

Así se forma

WILEY **PLUS** Go to *WileyPLUS* and review the Animated Grammar Tutorial for this grammar point.

4. Indefinite words and expressions

You have previously used some indefinite and negative Spanish words, such as **siempre**, **a veces**, and **nunca**. Here are some additional indefinite and negative words.

Cierto, no hay nadie como ella.

Es para alguien muy especial.

Palabras indefinidas y negativas

todo/a	everything, every			
algo	something, anything (interrogative)	→	nada	nothing, (not) anything
alguien	someone, anyone (interrogative)	→	nadie	no one, nobody
alguno/a/os/as	any, some, someone	→	ninguno/a	no, none, no one
también	also	→	tampoco	neither, not either
o	or	→	ni	nor, not even
o . . . o	either . . . or	→	ni . . . ni	neither . . . nor

- Note that, in Spanish, negation must be expressed before the verb. We may use the negative expressions above preceding the verb.

> negative word + verb

—**Nunca** llevo corbata.   *I **never** wear a tie.*
—Yo **tampoco** (llevo corbata).   *I don't (wear a tie) **either**.*

- If we use the negative expression after the verb, no must precede the verb in a double negative construction.

> no + verb + negative word

Hoy **no** compré **nada.**   *I didn't buy anything today.*
¿**No** hay **nadie** en ese taxi?   *Isn´t there anyone in that taxi?*
Nunca quiere llevar corbata.
No quiere llevar corbata **nunca.**   *He **never** wants to wear a tie.*

- The forms **alguno** and **ninguno** become **algún** and **ningún** before a masculine singular noun.

¿Tienen **algún** reloj de oro?   *Do you have **any** gold watches?*

- Notice that the words **ninguno/a** mean *not a single* and consequently do not have a plural form.

Tengo **algunos** vestidos negros, pero no tengo **ningún** vestido azul.

*I have **some** black dresses, but I don't have **any** blue dresses.*

Ninguno de mis vestidos es azul tampoco.

***None** of my dresses is blue either.*

- When **alguien** and **nadie** are direct objects, they are preceded by the **personal a** (review in *Capítulo 3*).

—¿Viste **a alguien** de la clase en el centro comercial?
—No, no vi **a nadie.**

8-23 El centro comercial. Tu amiga y tú van visitar Lima y quieres ir de compras al centro comercial Plaza. Lee la descripción de este centro. Después, escucha las preguntas de tu amiga y escoge la respuesta correcta.

El centro PLAZA es una propuesta moderna donde puede realizar sus compras, comer, entretenerse, relajarse, cuidar su imagen o simplemente pasear. Le ofrecemos 180 locales comerciales que incluyen tiendas de moda y accesorios, zapaterías, joyerías, salones de belleza, un *spa* y muchísimo más. Después de un largo día de compras, puede disfrutar de deliciosos momentos en alguno de los restaurantes o cafés en nuestro patio de comidas y, por que no, de una película en una de nuestras 14 salas de cine.

Otros servicios a su disposición son: servicio de información y atención al cliente, centro financiero con oficinas bancarias y cajeros automáticos, café Internet con Wi-Fi gratuito, sillas de ruedas (*wheelchairs*) y coches de niños (*strollers*), servicio de taxis.

Nuestro horario es de 10:00 a.m. a 10:00 p.m. todos los días.

1. ☐ Sí, hay alguna. ☐ Sí, hay alguno. ☐ No, no hay ninguna. ☐ No, no hay ninguno.
2. ☐ Sí, hay algunas. ☐ Sí, hay algunos. ☐ No, no hay ninguna. ☐ No, no hay ninguno.
3. ☐ Sí, hay algunas. ☐ Sí, hay algunos. ☐ No, no hay ninguna. ☐ No, no hay ninguno.
4. ☐ Sí, hay algunas. ☐ Sí, hay algunos. ☐ No, no hay ninguna. ☐ No, no hay ninguno.
5. ☐ Sí, cuesta algo. ☐ No, no cuesta nada.
6. ☐ Sí, hay alguien. ☐ No, no hay nadie.

8-24 ¿Qué hay en el centro comercial?

Antes de ir al centro comercial Plaza, tu amiga llama al servicio de atención al cliente. Completa su conversación con las palabras indefinidas y negativas del siguiente cuadro.

siempre	nunca	algún/a/os/as	ningún/a	alguien	ni … ni

TU AMIGA: Perdón, señor. ¿Hay _____ estación de metro cercana?

TELEFONISTA: Lo siento mucho, señora, no hay _____. Pero sí hay _____ autobuses que vienen desde el centro de la ciudad.

TU AMIGA: Bueno… ¿Y tienen _____ restaurante de comida tradicional peruana?

TELEFONISTA: Claro, hay _____ en el patio de comidas.

TU AMIGA: ¡Qué bien! Y, ¿hay _____ en la oficina de atención al cliente a todas horas? Es por si tengo _____ pregunta más…

TELEFONISTA: Sí, señora, _____ hay _____.

TU AMIGA: Y, para estar segura, no cierran temprano ____ los sábados ____ los domingos, ¿verdad?

TELEFONISTA: No, _____ cerramos antes de las 10 de la noche.

8-25 ¿Eres un buen testigo (witness)?

Paso 1. Mira los dibujos de abajo durante un minuto y después cúbrelos (cover them) con la mano o una hoja de papel.

 Paso 2. Ayer fuiste testigo de un robo a un banco (bank robbery) y ahora la policía te hace preguntas sobre el ladrón y lo que sucedió. Lee las instrucciones y preguntas de la policía y anota tus respuestas en una hoja. Luego, compara tus respuestas con las de un/a compañero/a.

INVESTIG@ EN INTERNET

Investiga sobre dónde realizar compras en tu ciudad. ¿Hay algún centro comercial? ¿Cuántos? ¿Conoces algún mercado callejero (flea market)? ¿Qué tipo de productos venden? Pregunta a tus amigos o familiares cuántos centros comerciales había cuando ellos eran jóvenes y dónde realizaban sus compras.

Informe policial

Imagine usted que está viendo todo en este momento y conteste:

1. Cuando llega el ladrón, ¿hay alguien en el banco? ¿Cuántos empleados y clientes hay? ¿Dónde están?

2. ¿El ladrón entra solo o con alguien?

3. Describa al ladrón: ¿cómo es? ¿Qué ropa lleva? ¿Lleva algo en la cabeza o la cara?

4. ¿Lleva algo en las manos cuando entra?

5. ¿Habla con alguien? ¿Dice algo?

6. ¿Qué hacen los empleados? ¿Qué hacen los demás (*the rest*)?

7. Cuando el ladrón sale, ¿hay algo en su bolsa (*bag*)? ¿Qué?

8. ¿Llama alguien a la policía?

9. ¿Recuerda algún otro detalle?

 8-26 Sospechoso (*suspect*). ¡Tu compañero/a de clase sospecha que tú eres el ladrón! Y la verdad es que tú también tienes sospechas (*suspicions*) sobre él/ella. Haz y responde a las siguientes preguntas y piensa en otras preguntas para hacerle a tu compañero/a. Contesta con oraciones completas.

1. ¿Estudiaste con alguien ayer por la tarde? (¿Con quién? ¿Desde qué hora? ¿Hasta qué hora?)

2. ¿Hablaste con alguien por teléfono? (¿Con quién? ¿Cuánto tiempo?)

3. ¿Fuiste a clases después de almorzar? (¿Qué clases? ¿Quién es el/la profesor/a?)

4. ¿Fuiste a la biblioteca o al laboratorio? (¿A qué hora? ¿Solo/a o con alguien?)

5. ¿A qué hora fuiste a tu cuarto? ¿Viste a tu compañero/a de cuarto?

6. ¿...?

8-27 ¿Cierto o falso? Observa el aula de español o el lugar donde estás. ¿Son las siguientes declaraciones ciertas o falsas? Responde y da ejemplos. Si son falsas, corrígelas usando palabras indefinidas y negativas.

Modelo: Nadie tiene mochila.
Cierto, nadie tiene mochila. O, **Falso. Alguien tiene mochila. Algunas personas tienen mochila. Por ejemplo, Ben.**

1. Alguien está escribiendo.

2. Hay algo en la mesa.

3. No hay nadie aburrido.

4. No hay tizas. Tampoco hay papelera.

5. No hay nada en la pared (*wall*).

6. Algunos estudiantes están hablando.

7. No hay ningún libro cerrado.

8. Hay alguien descansando.

Dicho y hecho

ANTES DE LEER

1. ¿Qué tipo de accesorios o complementos usas habitualmente?
2. ¿Qué es más importante para ti en tu ropa y accesorios: calidad, moda o función?

ESTRATEGIA DE LECTURA

Guessing meaning from context When reading in Spanish you will encounter many unfamiliar words. While some can be ignored, others are important to understanding the message of the text. You can often approximate the meaning of a new word by (1) paying attention to the overall meaning of the sentence (as we often do in our first language), (2) thinking of any similar words that you may know, and (3) recognizing whether a word is a noun, adjective, verb, etc. For instance, if a word is preceded by an article, you can be sure it is a noun; if you can recognize a verb ending, then it must be a verb, etc. Take these steps in trying to interpret unfamiliar words as you read the selection that follows.

A LEER

Si te encantan los estampados[1], si te mueres por los complementos[2] y si quieres ir a la moda, está claro: tú necesitas un Peseta. Bolsos, llaveros, bolsitas, mochilas o carteras son sólo algunas de las delicias que Peseta nos ofrece cada temporada[3]. Cada pieza tiene su nombre particular y su correspondiente tarjeta, que anuncia el origen de los materiales, la fecha y el lugar de creación. El encanto de Peseta es que para cada complemento intenta "buscarle como la gracia". Busca desarrollar nuevos formatos, cambiar telas[4] y formas sin estar limitada a estrictas colecciones temporales e inspirándose en todo lo que le rodea. Como ya le decía un buen amigo: "Peseta, es que tú eres transversal[5] a la moda".

Los complementos de esta marca se rigen por dos principios básicos: la necesidad y la multifuncionalidad. Son necesarios porque lo básico se convierte en esencial y multifuncionales porque nunca sabes lo que te espera dentro: bolsos-mochilas que se transforman a tu gusto, llaveros o bolsitas que puedes ajustar de tantas formas como la imaginación te permita. "Me mola[6] la versatilidad", comenta la diseñadora. En cada pieza también se mezclan[7] flores, estrellas, patos, galletas, rayas o cuadros sin la más mínima estridencia. "Lo que más me gusta es jugar con las telas y crear nuevas cosas, nuevos productos". A Peseta le gusta lo que hace, quizá por eso ha conseguido encontrarle el lado emocional a este negocio de la moda. "Se trata de hacer cosas que la gente tenga y que lo disfrute[8] y sienta el amor que yo le pongo al hacerlo".

La nueva colección de Peseta llega llena de sorpresas, como la bolsaukelele, de la que hizo una edición limitada para Marc Jacobs. Y eso no es todo, ya que también hay espacio para sus inconfundibles clásicos básicos. Las telas son de nuevo[9] ingrediente fundamental. "¡Tengo unas telas esta vez, que es que yo estoy como sufriendo porque lo quiero todo!". Así que no te lo pienses[10], ¡corre y consigue un Peseta ya!

▲ Una selección de Pesetas

Texto: Elena Giménez / *Punto y coma*
Fotografía: Peseta

---

[1]patterned prints, [2]accessories, [3]season, [4]fabrics, [5]oblique, perpendicular, [6]I like (slang), [7]mix, [8]enjoy, [9]again, [10]don't think twice about it

1. Ahora, responde a las siguientes preguntas sobre el texto.

    a. ¿Cómo son diferentes los productos de Peseta?

    b. ¿Qué dos principios guían el diseño de estos complementos?

    c. ¿Qué reacción busca la diseñadora en sus clientes?

2. Escoge los adjetivos de la lista que pueden aplicarse para describir los objetos de Peseta. Después compara tu lista con la de un/a compañero/a y justifica tu selección basándote en el texto.

3. ¿Te gustaría tener alguno de los accesorios de Peseta? ¿Cuál? ¿Por qué sí o no? Puedes visitar su tienda en Internet en http://www. peseta.org para ver los últimos diseños.

| artesanal | creativo | convencional | divertido (fun) | lujoso (luxurious) | práctico |

PARA CONVERSAR: **El equipaje perdido**

 Acaban de llegar al aeropuerto Mariscal Sucre de Quito, pero su equipaje no ha llegado y probablemente ¡está perdido! Van a estar en Ecuador una semana, visitando la costa y la capital, pero no tienen nada. La línea aérea les da $250 a cada uno/a como compensación por su pérdida.

Paso 1. Algunos estudiantes son turistas, otros son dependientes en tiendas o mercados callejeros. Individualmente, los turistas hacen una lista de los productos y ropa que necesitan, mientras los dependientes hacen inventario de sus productos y sus precios.

ESTRATEGIA DE COMUNICACIÓN

Being specific If you are a tourist, you know that you will be going to both to the mountains and to beach. When coming up with your shopping list, think about what you will need for a week (which items of personal hygiene and clothing, how many, what fabric or material, etc.) Salespeople have to come up with a list of items they sell (with details such as size, material, and number of each item in stock) and their prices, consistent with the store or market stall they have.

Paso 2. Los turistas visitan varias tiendas e intentan comprar todo lo que necesitan. Tanto los compradores como los vendedores deben intentar ser específicos (inventen los detalles que no habían anticipado). Hagan listas con sus compras y ventas, incluyendo los precios pagados.

Dicho y hecho

PARA ESCRIBIR: La ropa aquí y allá

Vas a describir brevemente el valor y la función de la ropa en Estados Unidos. El público estará compuesto por (*will be comprised of*) los miembros de un grupo indígena de América Latina, que usan ropa tradicional para indicar la región en la que viven y, a veces, la tribu a la que pertenecen. Seguramente, estos grupos tradicionales van a pensar que nuestra forma de vestir (*way of dressing*) es muy diferente a la suya (*theirs*).

ANTES DE ESCRIBIR

Paso 1. Piensa en la ropa y contesta estas preguntas:

1. Mira la ropa que tienes puesta en este momento. ¿Sabes de qué material está hecha? ¿Sabes dónde se fabricó? Si no, mira las etiquetas (*labels*). ¿Es importante para ti conocer el material y el origen de la ropa?

2. Mira a varias personas y analiza la ropa que llevan puesta. ¿Qué nos puede indicar la ropa que lleva una persona sobre la vida de esa persona?

3. ¿Hay alguna ocasión en que llevas ropa especial? Descríbela.

Paso 2. Ahora, debes hacer las mismas tres preguntas a dos personas diferentes que conoces. Si no hablan español, les puedes preguntar en inglés. Trata de escribir todo lo que dicen en sus respuestas.

ESTRATEGIA DE REDACCIÓN

Incorporating survey data In this composition, you are going to answer three questions about clothing. You are also going to conduct a survey of two people you know, asking each the same three questions. There are various ways of incorporating and presenting the data you gather in your composition. For example, you might organize the data by person:

Persona 1 (yo): Mis respuestas a las tres preguntas.
Persona 2: Sus respuestas a las tres preguntas.
Persona 3: Sus respuestas a las tres pregunras.

Or, you might organize your data by question:

Pregunta 1: Las respuestas de la Persona 1 (yo); las de la Persona 2; las de la Persona 3.
Pregunta 1: Las respuestas de la Persona 1 (yo); las de la Persona 2; las de la Persona 3.
Pregunta 1: Las respuestas de la Persona 1 (yo); las de la Persona 2; las de la Persona 3.

Choose whichever option you think is best suited to the ideas you want to express along with the basic data of your survey. Both offer a clear and organized way of presenting the data.

A ESCRIBIR

Escribe un primer borrador que resuma (*summarizes*) las respuestas de tu encuesta. Debes usar la opción 1 o la opción 2 de la sección *Estrategia de redacción* para organizar tu composición.

Para escribir mejor

Estas frases para expresar opiniones pueden ayudarte.

opinar que	*to be of the opinion that*
sentir que	*to feel that*
alegar que	*to claim that*

En tu conclusión, puedes usar frases como éstas:
En general, entre mis amigos, es importante/no es importante _____.
Algunos de mis amigos opinan _____, pero otros dicen que _____.

DESPUÉS DE ESCRIBIR

Revisar y editar: La organización. Después de escribir el primer borrador de tu composición, déjalo a un lado por un mínimo de un día sin leerlo. Cuando vuelvas a leerlo, corrígelo en términos de (*in terms of*) organización y contenido, además de gramática y vocabulario. Hazte estas preguntas:

☐ ¿Seguí bien la opción 1 o la opción 2 en términos de organización?

☐ ¿Está clara la conclusión?

☐ ¿Tuve en cuenta que el público de esta composición son grupos indígenas con ropa tradicional?

 PARA VER Y ESCUCHAR: **El arte del tejido: Una tradición viva**

ESTRATEGIA DE COMPRENSIÓN

Categorizing information As you are listening to a presentation of information in Spanish, you can try to identify the kinds of information being delivered and develop different categories for each kind of information. This can help you process the information more accurately. In this video, you will be asked to pay attention to four different categories of information.

ANTES DE VER EL VIDEO

1. ¿Qué animales nos dan lana (*yarn*) para fabricar la tela (*fabric*) que usamos en la ropa?

2. ¿Tienen alguna idea de cómo se fabrica la tela en las fábricas (*factories*) modernas?

A VER EL VIDEO

Mira el video e intenta completar la tabla.

Colaboradores		
___ comunidades	___ adultos	___ niños y jóvenes
Tres animales cuyas (*whose*) fibras se usan		
Fuentes (*sources*) de los tintes (*dyes*)		
Ropa tradicional que se usa		
Mujeres	**Hombres**	

DESPUÉS DE VER EL VIDEO

En grupos pequeños, respondan a estas preguntas.

1. Según el video, los tejedores sienten mucho orgullo por la ropa que crean. ¿Conoces a alguna otra persona que siente orgullo por la ropa que crea?

2. ¿En qué son similares y diferentes los métodos modernos y tradicionales de fabricación de telas?

Repaso de vocabulario activo

Adjetivos

barato/a   *cheap, inexpensive*

caro/a   *expensive*

corto/a   *short*

largo/a   *long*

limpio/a   *clean*

sucio/a   *dirty*

Palabras indefinidas y negativas

algo   *something, anything (interrogative)*

alguien   *someone, anyone (interrogative)*

alguno/a/os/as   *any, some, someone*

nada   *nothing*

nadie   *no one, nobody*

ni   *nor, not even*

ni...ni   *neither...nor*

ninguno/a   *no, none, no one*

o   *or*

o...o   *either...or*

también   *also*

tampoco   *neither, not either*

todo/a   *everything, every*

Sustantivos

La ropa   *Clothes/Clothing*

el abrigo   *coat*

el algodón   *cotton*

la blusa   *blouse*

   de manga corta/larga   *short/long sleeved*

las botas   *boots*

la bufanda   *scarf*

los calcetines   *socks*

la camisa   *shirt*

la camiseta   *T-shirt*

la chaqueta   *jacket*

el cinturón/la correa   *belt*

la corbata   *tie*

el cuero   *leather*

la falda   *skirt*

la gorra   *cap*

los guantes   *gloves*

el impermeable   *raincoat*

los *jeans*/los vaqueros   *jeans*

la lana   *wool*

las medias   *stockings, hose*

los pantalones   *pants*

los pantalones cortos   *shorts*

la ropa interior   *underwear*

las sandalias   *sandals*

la seda   *silk*

el sombrero   *hat*

el suéter   *sweater*

los (zapatos de) tenis   *tennis shoes, sneakers*

el traje   *suit*

el traje de baño   *bathing suit*

el vestido   *dress*

los zapatos   *shoes*

Las joyas   *Jewelry*

el anillo/la sortija   *ring*

los aretes/los pendientes   *earrings*

la cadena   *chain*

el collar   *necklace*

de oro/plata   *gold/silver*

la pulsera   *bracelet*

el reloj   *watch*

Otras palabras útiles

la billetera/la cartera   *wallet*

el bolso/la bolsa   *purse, bag*

el centro comercial   *shopping mall*

la cosa   *thing*

las gafas/los lentes (de sol)   *glasses/sunglasses*

los/las lentes de contacto   *contact lenses*

la moda   *fashion*

el paraguas/la sombrilla   *umbrella*

el precio   *price*

las rebajas   *sales*

el regalo   *gift*

el ropero/el clóset   *closet*

la talla   *size*

Verbos

contar (ue)   *tell*

devolver (ue)   *return (something)*

explicar   *explain*

llevar   *wear, carry, take*

mirar   *look at*

mostrar (ue)   *show*

preguntar   *ask*

prestar   *lend*

regalar   *give (a gift)*

Autoprueba y repaso

I. Possessive adjectives and pronouns.

A. Tú y tus amigos tienen su ropa en la residencia estudiantil. Indica de quién es la ropa.

Modelo: yo: calcetines, impermeable, chaqueta
Los calcetines son míos. El impermeable es mío. La chaqueta es mía.

1. yo: abrigo, botas, guantes, gorra
2. nosotros: ropa interior, *jeans,* corbatas
3. tú: blusa, vestido, camiseta, medias
4. Ana y Elena: ropa de verano, faldas, trajes de baño

B. Indica con quiénes van las personas a la fiesta. Sigue el modelo.

Modelo: yo / un amigo
Voy con un amigo mío.

1. mi primo / unos amigos
2. Viviana / un amigo
3. mi hermana y yo / un amigo
4. yo / unos amigos

II. The preterit of irregular verbs. Di quién hizo las siguientes cosas.

Modelo: hacer la torta para la fiesta (yo)
Hice la torta para la fiesta.

1. traer las decoraciones (Natalia y Linda)
2. poner las flores en la mesa (nosotros)
3. querer venir pero no poder (Javier)
4. venir (casi todos los estudiantes)
5. estar en la fiesta por cuatro horas (tú)
6. tener que salir temprano (yo)

III. Direct and indirect object pronouns combined. Forma oraciones en el pasado usando el verbo *regalar* y pronombres de objeto directo e indirecto.

Modelo: yo / unas gafas de sol / a Luisa
Se las regalé.

1. nosotros / un televisor pequeño / a los abuelos
2. mi hermano / una mochila nueva / a su prima
3. mis hermanas / joyas / a mamá
4. yo / una chaqueta de cuero / a mi hermano
5. mi madre / un perrito / a nosotras

IV. Indefinite and negative words. Contesta con oraciones negativas.

Modelo: ¿Compraste algo en el centro comercial recientemente?
No, no compré nada.

1. ¿Le prestas ropa a alguien?
2. Yo no me visto muy formal para ir a clase. ¿Y tú?
3. ¿Hay alguien elegante en la clase de español?
4. ¿Te pones algo especial cuando sales los fines de semana?

V. *Repaso general.* Contesta con oraciones completas.

1. ¿Qué ropa llevan las mujeres a un restaurante elegante? ¿Y los hombres?
2. ¿Qué ropa debes llevar a Alaska? ¿Y a Florida?
3. ¿Fuiste de compras el fin de semana pasado? (¿Adónde?) (¿Qué compraste?)
4. ¿Dónde estuviste anoche? ¿Y qué hiciste? (Menciona varias cosas.)
5. ¿Qué trajiste a clase hoy/ayer/anteayer?

VI. *Cultura.*

1. Nombra tres cosas que tienen en común Ecuador, Perú y Bolivia.
2. Nombra y describe tres artículos de ropa tradicional que se usan en estos países.

Las respuestas de *Autoprueba y repaso* se pueden encontrar en el **Apéndice 2.**

La salud

Así se dice

La salud
  El cuerpo humano
Una visita al consultorio

Así se forma

1. *Usted/Ustedes* commands
  ¿Qué nos dice la médica?

2. The imperfect

3. The imperfect vs. the preterit

Cultura

- Colombia y Venezuela
- Remedios caseros del mundo hispano

Dicho y hecho

Para leer:
Ayurveda: La ciencia de la vida

Para conversar:
En la sala de urgencias

Para escribir:
Lo que me pasó

Para ver y escuchar:
La medicina moderna y tradicional

By the end of this chapter you will be able to:

- Talk about health and related ailments
- Identify parts of the body
- Use commands in formal situations
- Talk about and describe persons, places, and actions in the past

ENTRANDO AL TEMA

1. ¿Conoces alguna expresión en inglés que incluya una parte del cuerpo? Por ejemplo: *Putting your foot in your mouth* o *Gut feeling*.

2. ¿Usas algún remedio casero (*home remedy*)? ¿Cuál?

Así se dice

La salud

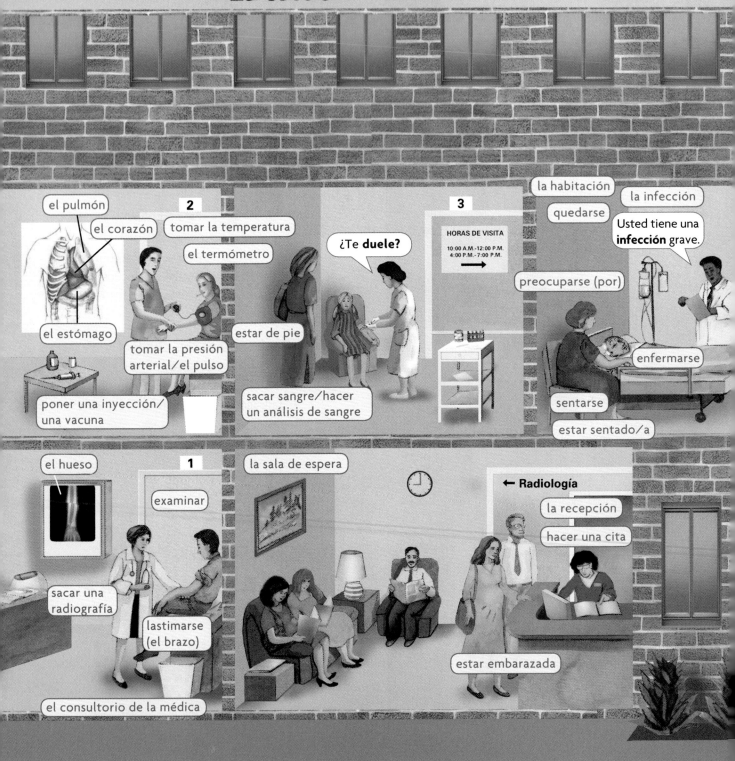

el pulmón

el corazón

el estómago

2

tomar la temperatura

el termómetro

tomar la presión arterial/el pulso

poner una inyección/ una vacuna

estar de pie

sacar sangre/hacer un análisis de sangre

¿Te **duele**?

3

HORAS DE VISITA

10:00 A.M.-12:00 P.M.
4:00 P.M.- 7:00 P.M.

la habitación

quedarse

la infección

Usted tiene una **infección** grave.

preocuparse (por)

enfermarse

sentarse

estar sentado/a

el hueso

1

examinar

la sala de espera

← **Radiología**

la recepción

hacer una cita

sacar una radiografía

lastimarse (el brazo)

estar embarazada

el consultorio de la médica

el análisis (de sangre)	*a (blood) test*
el consultorio	*doctor's office*
doler (ue)	*to be hurting, to hurt*
enfermarse	*to get/become sick*
estar de pie	*to stand*
estar sentado/a	*to be seated*
fracturarse	*to break (a bone)*
la habitación	*room*
hacer una cita	*to make an appointment*
la herida (grave)	*(serious) wound*
lastimarse	*to hurt oneself*
preocuparse por	*to worry about*
quedarse	*to stay*
sacar sangre	*to draw blood*
sacar una radiografía	*to take an X-ray*
la sala de espera	*waiting room*
sentarse (ie)	*to sit down*
torcerse (ue) el tobillo	*to sprain one's ankle*
el yeso	*cast*
la vacuna	*vaccine*

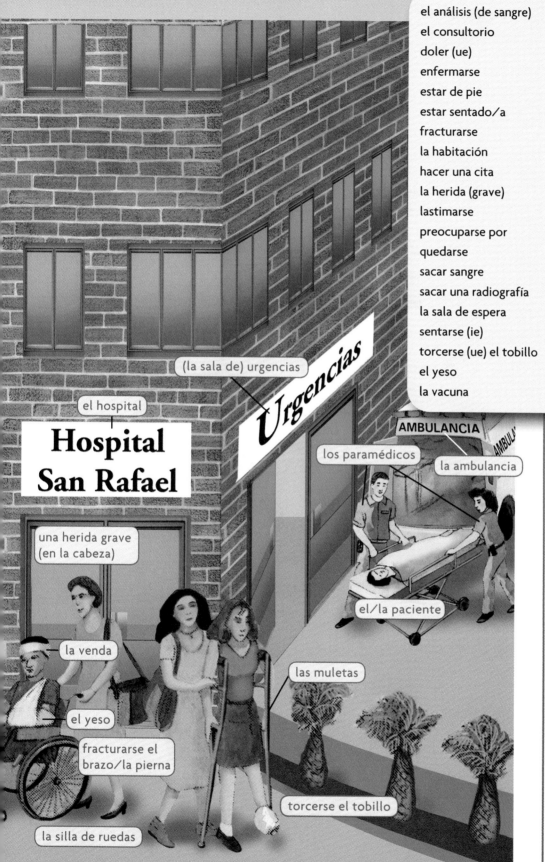

(la sala de) urgencias

el hospital

Hospital San Rafael

Urgencias

AMBULANCIA

los paramédicos

la ambulancia

una herida grave (en la cabeza)

el/la paciente

la venda

el yeso

las muletas

fracturarse el brazo/la pierna

torcerse el tobillo

la silla de ruedas

La salud

El cuerpo humano

la cabeza

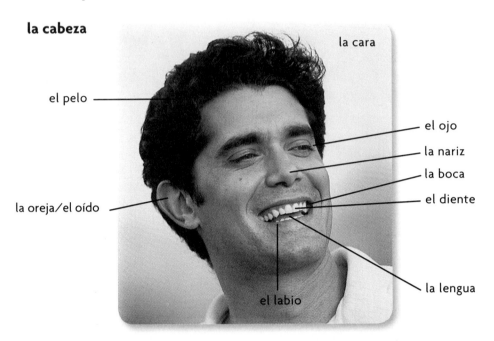

la cara

el pelo

el ojo

la nariz

la boca

el diente

la oreja/el oído

la lengua

el labio

el cuerpo

el cuello

la mano

el hombro

el dedo

la uña

el pecho

el brazo

la espalda

la pierna

el pie

Pobre Octavio.

Primero, conjuga los verbos entre paréntesis en el pretérito. Después, determina el orden cronológico de lo que le pasó a Octavio y lee la narración completa.

_____ La médica le _____ (poner) un yeso.

_____ Octavio _____ (salir) del hospital en una silla de ruedas.

_____ Octavio _____ (ir) a la sala de urgencias.

__1__ Octavio _____ (fracturarse) la pierna esquiando.

_____ Octavio _____ (empezar) a caminar con muletas.

_____ La médica le _____ (examinar) la pierna.

_____ Varias semanas más tarde, la médica le _____ (quitar) el yeso.

_____ La médica le _____ (sacar) una radiografía.

_____ Octavio _____ (empezar) un programa de terapia física.

_____ La médica le _____ (dar) medicamentos para el dolor (*pain*).

9-2 **¿Qué partes del cuerpo usamos?** Miren las actividades a continuación. En parejas, un/a estudiante elige una actividad sin nombrarla y describe para su compañero/a las partes del cuerpo que se usan para esa actividad. El/la compañero/a trata de adivinar qué actividad es.

manejar	escuchar música
leer	nadar
comer	tocar el piano
besar	cocinar

Modelo: Estudiante A: **Usamos los brazos, los hombros y las piernas.**
Estudiante B: **Esquiar**

DICHOS

El español, como muchas lenguas, tiene frases que incluyen partes del cuerpo. Trata de emparejar (*match*) estas frases con sus traducciones.

_____ **tener buen diente**   **a.** *to be cheap*
_____ **no tener pelos en la lengua**   **b.** *to not mince words*
_____ **ser codo (*elbow*)**   **c.** *to have a good appetite*

9-3 **¡Los extraterrestres (aliens)!** Un grupo de extraterrestres está visitando la ciudad, ¡y tú viste a uno ayer!

Paso 1. Inventa cómo es el extraterrestre que viste y dibújalo. Luego, descríbeselo a un/a compañero/a, que lo va a dibujar ¡sin mirar tu dibujo! Después, tú vas a dibujar al extraterrestre que tu compañero/a te describa.

 Paso 2. En parejas, comparen los dibujos. ¿Son similares el dibujo original y el dibujo del/de la compañero/a?

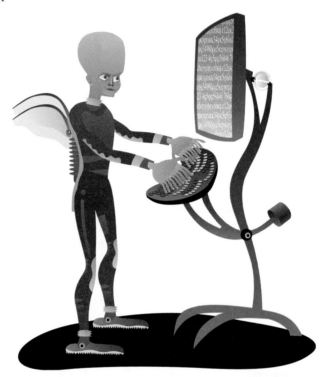

NOTA CULTURAL

La palabra *hispano*

The word *hispanic* is often used in the U.S. to refer to ethnicity and is usually identified with such traits as having dark hair and eyes and an olive complexion. However, Hispanics have many different faces and ethnic makeups: European, African, Asian, Native American, as well as other origins. The ethnicity of most people from Latin America combines different traits from various origins. Such is the case of people considered **mestizos** (of European and Native American origins) and **mulatos** (of European and African origins). Ethnic makeup differs from region to region. There are many unmixed Europeans in Argentina, Chile, and Uruguay. There are also unmixed Native Americans in the Andes and parts of Mexico and Central America, and a great range of mixed populations in the Caribbean region. Here are, as an example, some statistics about Colombia and Venezuela.

Colombia: 58% mestizo, 20% European, 14% mulatto, 4% African, 3% African and Native American, 1% Native American
Venezuela: 67% mestizo and mulatto, 21 % European, 10 % African, 2% Native American

Así se forma

1. Giving direct orders and instructions to others: *Usted/Ustedes* commands

WILEY **PLUS** Go to *WileyPLUS* and review the Animated Grammar Tutorial and Verb Conjugator for this grammar point.

Spanish has different command forms, depending on who is being addressed. In this chapter, you will learn to form command forms to use with a person that you would address formally (**usted**). You will also learn to form the command used to address more than one person (**ustedes**). You have already seen **ustedes** commands when instructions were given to more than one student (**cierren el libro, lean la oración**).

Regular forms

All **usted/ustedes** regular –**ar** verb commands end in –**e**/–**en**; all regular –**er**/–**ir** verb commands end in –**a**/–**an**. The appropriate ending is attached to the verb stem.

	esperar	**beb**er	**escrib**ir
usted	(no) esper**e**	(no) beb**a**	(no) escrib**a**
ustedes	(no) esper**en**	(no) beb**an**	(no) escrib**an**

Por favor, no se levante hoy. Descanse todo el día.

Object and reflexive pronouns *are attached* to the end of all *affirmative* commands. Note that a written accent is often added[1].

| Béba**lo**. | *Drink it.* |
| Siénte**se**, por favor. | *Please, sit down.* |

But they *precede* the verb in all *negative* commands.

| **No lo** beba. | *Don't drink it.* |
| **No se** siente todavía, por favor. | *Do not sit down yet, please.* |

Stem-changing and *yo*-irregular forms

Stem-changing and **yo**-irregular verbs delete the final -**o** from the **yo** form of the present tense and add the indicated endings. The verb **ir** has an irregular command form (not based on the present tense **yo**).

Infinitivo	Presente (yo)	Mandato
decir	dig~~o~~	diga/digan
hacer	hag~~o~~	haga/hagan
repetir	repit~~o~~	repita/repitan
encontrar	encuentr~~o~~	encuentre/encuentren
dormir	duerm~~o~~	duerma/duerman
ir	voy	vaya/vayan

---

[1]The emphasis in command forms with more than one syllable is on the second-to-last syllable (**tome, beba**), so these do not need an accent mark. When adding an extra syllable, the stressed syllable becomes third-to-last, and therefore it needs an accent mark.

¿Qué nos dice la médica?

Nos da instrucciones para hacer un examen físico.

Después de examinarnos, nos da consejos.

---

[1] Verbs ending in **–car**, are not really irregular in their command forms but they do have a spelling change: **sacar → saque, saques, saque, …**

9-4 **¿Usted o ustedes?** Escucha estas instrucciones. Decide si esta persona le habla a *usted* o a *ustedes*.

	Usted	Ustedes
1.	☐	☐
2.	☐	☐
3.	☐	☐
4.	☐	☐
5.	☐	☐

NOTA DE LENGUA

La forma *usted* en Colombia

In Colombia, the form **usted** is often used when the **tú** form is used in many other countries. It is common to hear friends, sisters and brothers, and wives and husbands use **usted** with each other. A similar phenomenon happened in English over 500 years ago, when the informal *thou* was eventually replaced by the formal *you*.

9-5 **¿Qué dice un/a doctor/a responsable?**

Paso 1. Decide si un/a doctor/a dice estas frases a sus pacientes.

		Sí	No
1.	Coma muchas frutas y verduras.	☐	☐
2.	No haga ejercicio nunca.	☐	☐
3.	Duerma ocho horas cada noche.	☐	☐
4.	Tome vitaminas.	☐	☐
5.	No fume.	☐	☐
6.	Si tiene náuseas, corra cinco millas.	☐	☐

Paso 2. En parejas, inventen dos oraciones para cada verbo: una la dice un/a doctor/a responsable y otra la dice un/a doctor/a irresponsable. Lean sus oraciones a otro grupo para ver si pueden adivinar quién las dice.

> comer   ir   beber   tomar

NOTA CULTURAL

El pabellón criollo

Venezuela's national dish, **pabellón criollo**, consists of shredded beef, rice, black beans, cheese, and fried plantain. **Pabellón** means *flag*, and **pabellón criollo** is a creole dish in which the ingredients are arranged in a way to resemble the tricolor flag of Venezuela. Others say the colors of the dish are meant to represent the different ethnic groups present in Venezuela. Many restaurants serve this dish for 4,000 **bolívares** (around $2.00 U.S. dollars).

9-6 **¿Puedo pedirlo?** Una persona con colesterol alto está en un restaurante cubano de Miami, pero no sabe qué puede comer y llama a su doctor.

Paso 1. Empareja las preguntas del paciente y las respuestas del doctor. Presta atención al uso de pronombres de objeto directo.

Paciente

1. ¿Puedo pedir sopa de pollo? ____
2. ¿Y los chicharrones de pollo? ____
3. ¿Puedo pedir masas de puerco? ____
4. ¿Y sorbete de guanábana? ____
5. ¿Y el flan de leche? ____

Doctor/a

a. No, no lo pida. Tiene mucho huevo.
b. Sí, pídalo. Es de fruta y no tiene grasa.
c. No, no los pida. Son fritos.
d. Sí, pídala. Tiene verduras y poca grasa.
e. No, no las pida. Son fritas.

 Paso 2. En parejas, uno de ustedes es el/la doctor/a y el/ otro es el/la paciente. Teniendo en cuenta los problemas de salud del/de la paciente, el/la doctor/a responde sus preguntas sobre lo que puede comer. Usen las preguntas y respuestas del Paso 1 como modelo. Después, intercambien los papeles (*reverse roles*).

Larios

SOPAS
SOUPS

SOPA DEL DÍA SOUP OF THE DAY	$3.75
SOPA DE POLLO CHICKEN SOUP	$3.50
SOPA DE FRIJOLES NEGROS BLACK BEAN SOUP	$3.50

TORTILLAS
OMELETTES

TORTILLA ESPAÑOLA *CON ARROZ Y PLÁTANOS* SPANISH OMELETTE, RICE & PLANTAINS	$6.75
TORTILLA DE PLÁTANO *CON ARROZ Y FRIJOLES NEGROS* PLANTAIN OMELETTE WITH RICE & BEANS	$5.95

ENSALADAS
SALADS

ENSALADA MIXTA HOUSE SALAD	$4.75
ENSALADA DE SARDINAS SARDINE SALAD	$6.95
ENSALADA DE TOMATE TOMATO SALAD	$3.50
SERRUCHO EN ESCABECHE PICKLED KINGFISH	$8.25
PLATO DE FRUTAS FRUIT PLATTER	$4.95

POLLO
CHICKEN

PECHUGA DE POLLO A LA PLANCHA BONELESS GRILLED CHICKEN BREAST	$8.25
POLLO ASADO ROASTED CHICKEN	$7.95
CHICHARRONES DE POLLO DEEP FRIED CHICKEN CHUNKS	$7.95
ARROZ CON POLLO CHICKEN AND YELLOW RICE	$6.95
PECHUGA DE POLLO RELLENA *CON CAMARONES* CHICKEN BREAST STUFFED WITH SHRIMP	$8.95

PESCADOS
FISH

PESCADO EMPANIZADO BREADED FISH	$9.95
PESCADO A LA PLANCHA GRILLED FISH	$9.75
BROCHETA DE CAMARONES SHRIMP KABOB	$11.75
CAMARONES EMPANIZADOS BREADED SHRIMP	$12.25
CAMARONES AL AJILLO SHRIMP IN GARLIC	$12.25
LANGOSTA ENCHILADA LOBSTER CREOLE	$20.50

Para regular el colesterol
EVITE alimentos fritos o con mucha grasa.
TOME alimentos lácteos desnatados (*skim*) o bajos en grasa.
CONSUMA alimentos altos en colesterol (huevos, camarones, etc.) con moderación.
COMA más frutas y verduras.
COMA más pan integral, cereales, frijoles y arroz.

9-7 ¿El/La doctor/a o los padres?

Lee los siguientes mandatos y decide si estas instrucciones son de un/a doctor/a a sus pacientes o de unos padres a sus hijos.

		Doctor	Padres
1.	Saquen la lengua.	☐	☐
2.	Péinense.	☐	☐
3.	Respiren profundamente.	☐	☐
4.	Digan "¡Aaah!"	☐	☐
5.	Lávense las manos.	☐	☐
6.	Hagan gárgaras (*gargle*) con sal.	☐	☐
7.	Quítense los zapatos en la casa.	☐	☐
8.	Tomen una pastilla cada dos horas.	☐	☐

9-8 ¿Quién manda?

Paso 1. El/La profesor/a manda. Forma oraciones con mandatos que dice el/la profesor/a a sus estudiantes.

Modelo: hacer

Hagan la tarea.

1. no hablar

2. llegar

3. traer

4. no usar

5. leer

Paso 2. Ustedes mandan. Imaginen que, sólo por un día, pueden dar instrucciones u órdenes a sus padres y a sus profesores. En parejas, escriban mandatos afirmativos y negativos en los cuadros.

	Mandatos afirmativos	Mandatos negativos
A los profesores	1. 2. 3.	1. 2. 3.
A los padres	1. 2. 3.	1. 2. 3.

Paso 3. Compartan sus ideas con otro grupo y escojan el mandato más razonable (*sensible*), el más atrevido (*daring*) y el más divertido de todos.

DICHOS

Ajo, cebolla y limón, y déjese de inyección.

¿Qué significa el dicho? ¿Es verdad?

Antes de leer

1. ¿En qué país es posible visitar las playas del Pacífico y también las del mar Caribe?

2. ¿Con qué países tiene frontera Colombia?

3. ¿Cuál es la capital de Colombia? Indica dos ciudades importantes en la costa.

4. ¿Cuál es el río principal que pasa por Venezuela y Colombia?

5. ¿Cuál es la capital de Venezuela?

COLOMBIA

Los españoles escucharon la leyenda de El Dorado (*the Golden One*) sobre un rey cubierto en oro que vivía en una ciudad llena de oro (*gold*). Lo buscaron durante 200 años. Por fin, descubrieron un grupo de indígenas en **Colombia** que celebraban una ceremonia en la que cubrían a su líder con polvo (*powder*) de oro, pero no había ninguna ciudad de oro.

Nacionalidades:
colombiano/a
venezolano/a

PLUS **Map quizzes:** As you read about places highlighted in red, find them on the map. Learn more about and test yourself on the geography of the Spanish-speaking world in *WileyPLUS.*

▲ Esmeraldas

Durante la época colonial, Colombia era parte de la Nueva Granada, que incluía los territorios que hoy son Panamá, Ecuador y Venezuela. Pero la Nueva Granada se independizó de España en 1810 y el líder Simón Bolívar creó la Federación de la Gran Colombia. Después, Ecuador, Venezuela y Panamá se separaron de esta Federación.

Hoy en día, Colombia es el principal productor de esmeraldas del mundo y el primer productor de oro de América del Sur. **Bogotá,** la capital de Colombia, está en un valle central. Tiene más de siete millones de habitantes y es una ciudad moderna, llena de rascacielos, tiendas de moda y grandes avenidas. Pero en esta ciudad también existen barrios (*neighborhoods*) muy pobres que contrastan con el lujo (*luxury*) de otras áreas.

▲ El espíritu del pueblo colombiano se ve en su música, sus bailes y sus diversiones populares. La cumbia y el vallenato son ritmos musicales de origen colombiano muy famosos en todo el mundo. Busca en Internet "vallenato colombiano" para escuchar un ejemplo.

Breve diccionario cafetómano latinoamericano

- **AMERICANO** (México, Miami): café aguado, en taza grande.
- **CAFÉ** (todos los países): cualquier cosa, pida más información.
- **CAFÉ-CAFÉ** (Chile): café de grano, normalmente en taza chica.
- **CAFÉ COMÚN** (Argentina): café aguado, en taza grande.
- **CAFÉ CON LECHE** (todos los países): autoexplicativo, pero la proporción leche/café es variable.
- **CAFÉ DOBLE** (Argentina): café cargado, en taza grande.
- **CAPUCHINO** (todos los países): un tercio de café, une tercio de leche, un tercio de espuma de leche. En Chile lleva además crema batida.
- **CAPUCCINO** (Argentina, Colombia): capuchino.
- **CARIOCA** (Brasil): café aguado, en taza chica.
- **CORTADO** (Chile, Argentina): café cargado con un toque de leche.
- **CORTADITO** (Miami): ídem.
- **CUBANO** (Miami): café muy cargado, muy dulce y muy "tacaño": menos de la mitad de una taza chica.
- **CURTO** (Brasil): café cargado en taza chica.
- **EXPRESO** (varios países): café concentrado especial en taza chica.
- **EXPRESSO** (Miami): expreso.
- **EXPRESS** (Chile): expreso.
- **GRANIZADO** (Colombia): café helado, con hielo picado, en vaso.
- **GUAYOYO** (Venezuela): café negro suave, hecho en colador de tela.
- **MARRÓN** (Venezuela): café cargado con toque de leche.
- **NEGRITO** (Venezuela): café sin leche en taza chica.
- **NEGRO** (varios países): café sin leche ni azúcar.
- **PERICO** (Colombia): café cargado con un toque de leche.
- **PINGADO** (Brasil): café con leche en taza grande.
- **TETERO** (Venezuela): leche caliente con un poco de café.
- **TINTO** (Colombia): café relativamente suave, en taza chica.

INVESTIG@ EN INTERNET

¿Sabes quién es Shakira? Es de Barranquilla, Colombia. En 2007, colaboró en la banda sonora de una película que hemos mencionado hace poco. ¿Sabes cuál es? ¿Para qué evento compuso la canción oficial en 2010? Busca información sobre Shakira en Internet y compártela con tus compañeros de clase.

◀ Colombia es el segundo productor de café del mundo, después de Brasil. Según el *Breve diccionario cafetómano latinoamericano*, ¿qué tipos de café son populares en Colombia? ¿Cuál es tu café favorito?

VENEZUELA

En Venezuela, los españoles encontraron fabulosas riquezas de oro, plata (*silver*) y perlas. El nombre del país significa "pequeña Venecia (*Venice*)". ¿Por qué? Porque a principios del siglo XVI, los españoles se encontraron con unos habitantes indígenas, los guajiros, que vivían en chozas (*huts*) suspendidas sobre unas islas muy pequeñas en el **lago Maracaibo,** que les recordaban (*reminded them*) los edificios de la famosa ciudad italiana de Venecia.

Caracas, la capital, está cerca de la costa y es una de las ciudades más cosmopolitas del continente. Los caraqueños son amantes del arte y tienen un admirable Museo de Bellas Artes y una magnífica Orquesta Sinfónica. Caracas también cuenta con (*has*) uno de los servicios de metro más sofisticados del mundo.

Caracas

▲ El "oro negro", o petróleo, es la mayor riqueza del país. La explotación de los grandes depósitos petrolíferos en el lago Maracaibo comenzó a principios del siglo XX. La industria petrolera generó mucha prosperidad en el país y su población se cuadruplicó.

◀ En Venezuela está el Salto Ángel, ¡la cascada más alta del mundo (3,281 pies/979 metros)!

Después de leer

1. ¿A qué país se refiere cada oración?

	Colombia	Venezuela
a. Es el primer productor de esmeraldas del mundo.	☐	☐
b. Los indios guajiros vivían en chozas suspendidas en un lago.	☐	☐
c. La cumbia y el vallenato son dos ritmos típicos.	☐	☐
d. La capital cuenta con un sofisticado sistema de transporte metropolitano.	☐	☐

2. ¿Con qué ciudades de Estados Unidos crees que se pueden comparar Bogotá y Caracas? ¿Por qué? Considera los siguientes detalles:

	Está/Tiene...	Una ciudad similar en Estados Unidos es...
Bogotá	• en un valle rodeado de montañas. • 7,300,000 habitantes. • muchos sitios para tomar café.	
Caracas	• en la costa. • 2,000,000 habitantes. • un sistema de metro muy sofisticado.	

Bogotá

Embajada

Parque Nacional Olaya Herrera

★ Museo Nacional

★ Museo de Arte Moderno

★ Villa de Simón Bolívar

★ Museo del Oro

★ La Catedral

3. Mira el siguiente mapa de Bogotá. Elige tres lugares que te gustaría visitar y di por qué.

Así se dice

Una visita al consultorio

Estás muy enfermo/a. Antes de ver al médico necesitas completar el siguiente cuestionario para pacientes.

Cuestionario sobre la salud

		Sí	No
1.	¿Le **duele la cabeza** con frecuencia?	☐	☐
2.	¿Tiene **dolor de estómago**?	☐	☐
3.	¿Tiene mucha **tos/Tose** mucho?	☐	☐
4.	¿Tiene **fiebre**?	☐	☐
5.	¿Tiene **diarrea**?	☐	☐
6.	¿Tiene **resfriados** o **gripe** con frecuencia?	☐	☐
7.	¿Tiene **alergias**?	☐	☐
8.	¿Tiene **congestión nasal**? ¿**Estornuda** mucho?	☐	☐
9.	¿Le **duele la garganta** con frecuencia?	☐	☐
10.	¿Tiene **vómitos/Vomita**?	☐	☐
11.	¿Tiene **náuseas**?	☐	☐
12.	¿Tiene **escalofríos**?	☐	☐
13.	¿**Se cansa** con frecuencia?	☐	☐
14.	¿Duerme bien?	☐	☐
15.	¿**Se siente deprimido/a**?	☐	☐

Otros síntomas _____

---

cansarse	*to get tired*	**la gripe**	*flu*
el resfriado	*cold*	**la salud**	*health*
el escalofrío	*chill*	**sentirse (ie, i)**	*to feel*
estornudar	*to sneeze*	**la tos**	*cough*
la garganta	*throat*	**toser**	*to cough*

NOTA DE LENGUA

To express aches, pains, and how you feel, use the following verbs and expressions:

doler (like **gustar**): *indirect object* + **doler (ue)** + **el/la/los/las** + *body part*
Me **duelen** las piernas. *My legs hurt.*
¿Te **duele** el estómago? *Do you have a stomachache?*

tener dolor de + *body part*
Tengo dolor de espalda. *I have a backache.*

sentirse (ie, i) + *adjective*
Se sintió/ Se siente bien, mal, enfermo/a, *She/He felt/feels . . .*
triste, cansado/a, etc.

9-9 ¿De quién es el diagnóstico y el tratamiento?

Paso 1. Mientras estudias en Venezuela, tus amigos Jorge, Pedro, Alberto y Daniel se enferman y van al médico. Escúchalos describir sus síntomas e indica a quién le pertenece cada diagnóstico y tratamiento.

DIAGNÓSTICO:	Otitis (infección de oído)
TRATAMIENTO:	<u>Tomar</u> antibióticos cada (*every*) 6 horas. <u>Aplicar</u> calor seco (*dry*) para aliviar el dolor.

1. Es de ☐ Jorge ☐ Pedro ☐ Alberto ☐ Daniel

DIAGNÓSTICO:	Alergia al polen
TRATAMIENTO:	<u>Cerrar</u> las ventanas. <u>Tomar</u> *Allegra* antes de salir a la calle.

2. Es de ☐ Jorge ☐ Pedro ☐ Alberto ☐ Daniel

DIAGNÓSTICO:	Gastroenteritis
TRATAMIENTO:	<u>Tomar</u> líquidos para evitar (*avoid*) la deshidratación y <u>descansar</u> mucho. No necesita medicina.

3. Es de ☐ Jorge ☐ Pedro ☐ Alberto ☐ Daniel

DIAGNÓSTICO:	Gripe
TRATAMIENTO:	<u>Tomar</u> aspirinas, líquidos y <u>descansar</u>.

4. Es de ☐ Jorge ☐ Pedro ☐ Alberto ☐ Daniel

Paso 2. Ahora, convierte las recomendaciones del médico (los verbos subrayados) en mandatos con la forma *usted*.

Modelo: **Tome antibióticos cada 6 horas.**

NOTA CULTURAL

Ayuda médica

There are different resources for medicine and healing in Latin America. Public health systems are the main providers of health care, with many well-equipped hospitals and highly trained doctors. For minor health issues, many people rely on their pharmacist, with whom a personal relationship is often developed. The pharmacist offers advice and provides over-the-counter medication. **Herbolarios**, where plants and homeopathic remedies are sold, are also common. Spiritual healers such as **curanderos** (*folk healer*) and **chamanes** heal through the use of medicinal plants and religious rituals.

DICHOS

El amor y la tos no pueden ocultarse (*hide*).

¿Por qué no pueden ocultarse ni el amor ni la tos?

9-10 ¿Qué me pasa, doctor? Ahora tú te sientes enfermo/a también y vas al consultorio.

Paso 1. Piensa en algunos síntomas y escríbelos en una hoja con el mayor detalle posible.

Paso 2. En parejas, túrnense en los papeles de paciente y doctor/a.

Paciente: Describe tus síntomas al doctor/a la doctora y responde sus preguntas (puedes improvisar). Después de escuchar su diagnóstico y recomendaciones, haz una o dos preguntas sobre qué cosas puedes o no puedes hacer.

Doctor/a: Escucha al/a la paciente y hazle algunas preguntas más sobre sus síntomas. Después, haz un diagnóstico y recomienda un tratamiento según el cuadro (*chart*). Responde a las preguntas del/ de la paciente.

Modelo:
PACIENTE: **Buenas tardes, doctor/a... Tengo muchos problemas. Estoy... / Me siento...**
MÉDICO/A: **A ver, ¿le duele(n)... ? ¿Tiene usted... ? Tengo varias recomendaciones: Primero... / Tome...**
PACIENTE: **¿Puedo... ? / ¿Tengo que... ?**

DIAGNÓSTICO	TRATAMIENTO
gripe	tomar aspirinas, líquidos, descansar
mononucleosis	tomar ibruprofeno, líquidos, descansar mucho
acidez de estómago	tomar un líquido contra la acidez
infección de...	tomar antibióticos
resfriado	tomar muchos líquidos, descansar
bronquitis	tomar jarabe para la tos y un expectorante
depresión	ir a ver a un psicólogo o psiquiatra

NOTA CULTURAL

Juanes

The musician Juan Esteban (nicknamed Juanes) Aristizábal Vásquez was born in 1972 in Antioquía, Colombia. He has sold more than fifteen million albums and has won seventeen Latin Grammys, more than any other artist, and one Grammy Award. Juanes is also known for his humanitarian work, especially with the aid he has provided Colombian mine victims. See if you can determine the meaning of these lyrics from his 2007 album *La vida es un ratico* (a short while).

La vida es un ratico, un ratico nada más
no dejemos que se nos acabe
que vienen tiempos buenos y los malos
ya se van, se van, se van.

Así se forma

> Era medianoche y hacía mucho viento. Los niños caminaban por la calle desierta...

2. The imperfect: Descriptions in the past

Spanish has two simple past tenses: the preterit and the imperfect. You have already learned to use the preterit to talk about past actions perceived as complete and past actions within a specific time frame (yesterday, last night, etc.).

Use of the imperfect

Like the preterit, the imperfect tense also expresses actions or events that took place in the past, but the imperfect does not focus on the completion of the action. It does not express beginning and/or end; it just views an action as something that was in place or in progress. It is used primarily:

- to describe in the past (background, weather, ongoing conditions, persons, places, things, etc.).

Hacía sol.	It **was** sunny.
La playa **era** hermosa.	The beach **was** beautiful.
El mar **estaba** muy tranquilo.	The sea **was** very tranquil.
Los niños **llevaban** trajes de baño y camisetas.	The children **were wearing** bathing suits and T-shirts.
Estaban muy contentos.	They **were** very happy.

- to indicate that past actions were in progress, ongoing, or habitual.

Un niño **jugaba** en el agua.	One child **was playing** in the water.
Otro **construía** un castillo.	Another **was building** a castle.
A otros siempre **les gustaba** jugar con una pelota.	Others always **liked** to play with a ball.

- Like **hay, había** denotes existence, but in the past.

Había tres pacientes en la sala de espera.	*There were* three patients in the waiting room.

Note that, although most of these actions and conditions surely started and finished at some point, we do not "perceive" a beginning or end in the examples above.

The imperfect tense can be translated with the English forms below, depending on the actual meaning expressed:

Mientras **esperaba** al médico, leyó un artículo en una revista.	*While she **was waiting/waited** for the doctor, she read an article in a magazine.*
El doctor la **examinaba** una vez al año.	*The doctor **used to/would examine** her once a year.*

Forms of the imperfect

To form the imperfect in regular verbs, delete the **–ar, –er,** or **–ir** from the infinitive and add the endings indicated below. Note that the imperfect **–er/–ir** endings are identical.

	examinar	toser	salir
(yo)	examin**aba**	tos**ía**	sal**ía**
(tú)	examin**abas**	tos**ías**	sal**ías**
(Ud., él/ella)	examin**aba**	tos**ía**	sal**ía**
(nosotros/as)	examin**ábamos**	tos**íamos**	sal**íamos**
(vosotros/as)	examin**abais**	tos**íais**	sal**íais**
(Uds., ellos/ellas)	examin**aban**	tos**ían**	sal**ían**

Irregular verbs

Only three verbs are irregular in the imperfect:

ser		ir		ver	
era	éramos	iba	íbamos	veía	veíamos
eras	erais	ibas	ibais	veías	veíais
era	eran	iba	iban	veía	veían

(9-11) En la época de nuestros bisabuelos.

Paso 1. El mundo era diferente en asuntos de salud cuando nuestros bisabuelos eran jóvenes. Indica si estas afirmaciones son ciertas o falsas y escribe otra afirmación cierta para el número 10.

Cuando mis bisabuelos eran jóvenes...	Cierto	Falso
1. Los doctores recetaban muchos antibióticos.	☐	☐
2. Muchas personas consumían comida rápida.	☐	☐
3. Casi todos consumían comida muy saludable (*healthy*).	☐	☐
4. El SIDA (*AIDS*) era una enfermedad peligrosa.	☐	☐
5. Todos conocían los efectos negativos de fumar.	☐	☐
6. Las personas no tenían mucho estrés.	☐	☐
7. Los jóvenes no eran activos; pasaban muchas horas sentados.	☐	☐
8. Había muchos problemas con las drogas.	☐	☐
9. Muchas personas usaban remedios caseros.	☐	☐
10. …	☑	☐

Paso 2. En parejas, contrasten el pasado (usando **antes**) y el presente (usando **ahora**). Incluyan sus afirmaciones originales.

Modelo: Los doctores recetaban muchos antibióticos.
Antes los doctores no recetaban muchos antibióticos, pero ahora sí lo hacen.

9-12 ¿Mejora la salud?

Paso 1. Una persona está tratando de mejorar su salud y te pide tu opinión. Primero quieres saber más sobre sus hábitos pasados y actuales (*current*). Escucha sus descripciones e indica si habla de los pasados (**Antes**) o los actuales (**Ahora**).

		Antes	Ahora
1.	tomar mucha cerveza los fines de semana	☐	☐
2.	comer pocas ensaladas y fruta	☐	☐
3.	ver la televisión dos o tres horas por la noche	☐	☐
4.	no tomar desayuno	☐	☐
5.	dormir menos de seis horas	☐	☐
6.	fumar bastante	☐	☐
7.	tomar mucho café todos los días	☐	☐
8.	ser poco activo	☐	☐
9.	ir al gimnasio una vez por semana	☐	☐

Paso 2. Tu amigo/a todavía tiene algunos hábitos poco saludables. Tú también hacías cosas similares antes, pero ahora tienes costumbres más sanas y ¡te sientes mucho mejor! Explícaselo en una breve carta.

Modelo: Hola Andrés:

Ya veo que tienes algunos buenos hábitos, pero todavía puedes mejorar otras cosas. ¡Vale la pena! (*It's worth it!*) Antes yo tampoco tomaba desayuno, pero ahora como cereal todas las mañanas y tengo mucha energía…

9-13 Cuando teníamos diez años.

Paso 1. Escribe oraciones describiendo cómo eras y qué hacías cuando tenías diez años.

1. ser (tímido/a; perezoso/a; trabajador/a…)
2. estudiar (¿Cuánto? ¿Dónde? ¿Con quién?)
3. hacer (deporte/actividades extraescolares…)
4. ver la tele (¿Cuánto? ¿Qué programas?)
5. leer (¿Qué revistas/libros/cómics?)
6. escuchar música (¿Qué tipo de música/cantante/grupo?)
7. hablar mucho por teléfono (¿Con quién?)
8. salir con mis amigos/as (¿Adónde? ¿Con qué frecuencia?)
9. trabajar (¿Dónde? ¿Con quién?)
10. querer tener o hacer… (¿Qué?)

Paso 2. Ahora, en parejas, haz preguntas a tu compañero/a sobre diferentes aspectos de su infancia (*childhood*). ¿Eran ustedes similares o diferentes cuando tenían diez años?

Modelo: ¿Cuánto estudiabas? ¿Dónde preferías estudiar?
¿Qué materia te gustaba estudiar?

9-14) Los hábitos diarios.

Paso 1. Escribe párrafos breves comparando tus hábitos relacionados con las siguientes actividades cuando tenías quince años y ahora.

Modelo: dormir

Me acostaba a las diez de la noche y me levantaba a las siete de la mañana entre semana (*on weekdays*). Los fines de semana me acostaba tarde, pero no me levantaba hasta las once... ¡Dormía mucho! Ahora me acuesto...

1. dormir
2. comer
3. beber
4. ejercicio/deporte
5. tiempo libre

 Paso 2. En grupos pequeños, compartan y comparen sus ideas. ¿Eran sus hábitos más saludables antes o lo son ahora?

SITUACIONES

Estudiante A: Eres estudiante de primer año. Estás cansado/a y te enfermas con frecuencia. Además engordaste (*gained*) 5 libras y estás estresado/a porque los exámenes son la próxima semana... pero te encanta tu nueva "libertad" (*freedom*) y quieres disfrutarla (*enjoy it*).

Estudiante B: Tu amigo/a está cometiendo muchos errores: no come bien, no hace ejercicio, sale con los amigos/as durante la semana y duerme poco. Tú ya tienes más experiencia; habla con él/ella y ofrécele algunos consejos (*advice*).

EXPRESIONES ÚTILES

Debes + infinitivo...
You ought to/ should/must...
Tienes que + infinitivo...
You have to/must...
Puedes + infinitivo...
You can...
¿Por qué no + presente...?
Why don't you...?

NOTA CULTURAL

Gabriel García Márquez

Gabriel García Márquez was born in 1927. He is a Colombian writer and journalist. He won international acclaim in 1967 with his masterpiece, *One Hundred Years of Solitude*, a defining classic of 20th century literature. He was awarded the Nobel Prize for Literature in 1982. His journalistic work includes 1996's *News of a Kidnapping*, which details the events that followed some notorious kidnappings committed by the Colombian drug cartels. Film adaptations of his novels *Love in the Time of Cholera* and *Of Love and Other Demons* were released in 2007 and 2010 respectively.

Cultura: Remedios caseros del mundo hispano

Antes de leer

1. ¿Usan remedios caseros en tu familia? ¿Cuáles? ¿Son efectivos?

2. ¿Prefieres usar remedios caseros o farmacéuticos?

Desde que (*since*) el ser humano se dio cuenta de (*realized*) que podía aliviar sus dolencias (*aches and pains*) con la ayuda de hierbas y plantas medicinales, toda una tradición de remedios se transmitió de generación en generación. Cada cultura, cada país, cada región tiene sus propias curas. A continuación vas a encontrar algunas de las tradiciones médicas populares del mundo hispano. Recuerda que no debes tomar remedios caseros ni farmacéuticos sin consultar con tu médico/a.

▲ Un té de tilo es bueno para calmar el estrés.

▲ La flor del naranjo, los azahares.

HIPO (*HICCUPS*)

Una vez más, los consejos son múltiples. Se recomienda poner jugo de limón en la lengua o tomar sorbos (*sips*) de agua. Otros creen que se debe asustar (*scare*) al paciente. En México, las abuelitas les ponen un hilo (*string*) rojo en la frente (*forehead*) a los bebés para detener el hipo.

RESFRIADO/GRIPE/CATARRO

Todos los remedios comienzan con una limonada caliente. Lo que cambia de receta a receta son los ingredientes que se agregan (*are added*). Algunos ponen miel (*honey*) en la limonada, mientras que otros ponen ron o whisky.

ORZUELOS (*STYES*)

Se recomienda hervir (*boiling*) unos clavos de olor (*cloves*) en agua y, cuando está tibia (*lukewarm*), aplicarla al orzuelo. Según los costarricenses, es un remedio seguro. Otros afirman que lo mejor es aplicar miel. Algunos orzuelos son infecciones y, si no desaparecen por su cuenta, deben ser tratadas con antibióticos.

DOLOR DE OÍDO

Se recomienda dorar (*browning*) un ajo al fuego, ponerlo en un algodón y colocarlo en la entrada del oído.

NERVIOSISMO/ESTRÉS

Las flores del naranjo, los azahares, hervidas en agua, tienen propiedades sedantes. Un té de tilo, otra hierba medicinal, también ayuda a calmar la ansiedad.

DOLOR DE PIES

Para relajar los pies y aliviar el cansancio se deben poner en agua de sal tibia. Un masaje con una crema hidratante también hace maravillas.

La próxima vez que le preguntes a un hispanoparlante sobre remedios caseros, prepárate: quizás recibas muchos consejos (*advice*) y respuestas.

Después de leer

Empareja los siguientes remedios con los problemas que curan.

_____ limonada caliente   **a.** el estrés

_____ los azahares   **b.** el resfriado

_____ el ajo   **c.** el dolor de oído

VideoEscenas: Un deporte peligroso

▲ Jaime le cuenta a Ana su accidente deportivo.

Paso 1. Indica si los siguientes deportes son peligrosos o no. Después, compara tu lista con la de un/a compañero/a. ¿Están de acuerdo (*do you agree*) en todo?

	¿Es peligroso?	
	Sí.	**No.**
1. el fútbol	☐	☐
2. el tenis	☐	☐
3. el fútbol americano	☐	☐
4. el esquí	☐	☐
5. el esquí acuático	☐	☐
6. el boxeo	☐	☐

Paso 2. Mira el video prestando atención a las ideas principales. Después, indica si las siguientes afirmaciones son ciertas o falsas.

	Cierto	**Falso**
1. Jaime jugó al futbol con sus amigos el sábado.	☐	☐
2. Después del partido, los amigos de Jaime se enfermaron.	☐	☐
3. Jaime tuvo un accidente jugando al fútbol.	☐	☐
4. Jaime no va a clase porque está enfermo.	☐	☐

Paso 3. Todos los amigos de Jaime tuvieron problemas de salud la semana pasada. Mira el video otra vez e indica qué le pasaba a cada uno.

Miguel: _____

José Mari: _____

Juan: _____

Germán: _____

Así se forma

Los niños caminaban por la calle desierta cuando de repente, ¡vieron un fantasma!

WILEY PLUS Go to *WileyPLUS* and review the Animated Grammar Tutorial and Verb Conjugator for this grammar point.

3. Talking about and describing persons, things, and actions in the past: The imperfect vs. the preterit

Although both the preterit and the imperfect tenses refer to the past, they convey different meanings. The difference is not one of time (when the event took place) but of aspect (how the event is perceived or what parts of it the focus is on). The main contrast is that, while the preterit presents the event as a complete one from beginning to end, or expresses its beginning or end points, the imperfect presents an action or event in the past with no reference to its beginning and/or end. Because it is sometimes difficult to make concrete decisions based on this general concept, here are more specific guidelines to help you decide which tense to use.

HINT

Review the preterit tense of regular, stem-changing, and irregular verbs in *Capítulos 6, 7,* and *8.*

The imperfect . . .	The preterit . . .
1. Describes the *middle* of a past action, state, or condition; indicates that it was *in progress*, with no emphasis on the beginning or end. Juan **estaba** enfermo. No **quería** comer. Sólo **dormía** y veía la tele.	1. Focuses on a past action or condition with an evident *beginning, end,* or *time frame.* Anita **se enfermó** el sábado. **Estuvo** enferma toda la semana. **Salió** del hospital ayer. **Pasó** tres días allí. **Se recuperó** completamente.
2. Describes a past action that was *repeated* or *habitual* over an indefinite period of time. La enfermera **visitaba** a sus pacientes todas las noches. A veces les **llevaba** jugo de naranja.	2. Indicates a *single past action*, generally quickly completed, or a *series of actions* in the past. El paciente **entró** en el consultorio. El enfermero le **tomó** la temperatura, le **explicó** el problema y le **puso** una inyección.

In addition, when narrating an incident or telling a story we use . . .

The imperfect . . .	The preterit . . .
1. To set the stage, give background information: • The date, the season **Era** el 12 de diciembre. **Era** invierno. • What time it was **Era** la medianoche. • The weather **Hacía** frío y **nevaba**. • A description of the setting La casa **era** muy vieja y **tenía** un árbol muy grande enfrente. • A description of the people involved, both their physical and personality traits, and also their age La abuela **era** bonita y muy amable. **Tenía** ochenta años. 2. To indicate people's emotional/physical state or condition. **Estaba** contenta, pero **tenía** hambre. 3. To describe ongoing actions. Ella **leía** un libro.	1. To express an event that interrupts an ongoing (imperfect) action. Mientras ella **leía** el libro, **sonó** el teléfono. 2. To narrate sequential events; moves the story forward, telling what happened **Se levantó, contestó** el teléfono y **salió** de la casa inmediatamente.

Some time expressions convey the idea of a state or repetition and are commonly used with the imperfect. Similarly, time expressions that refer to a particular point in the past or a delimited past time are often associated with the preterit.

IMPERFECTO		PRETÉRITO	
muchas veces	*many times, often*	**una vez**	*once, one time*
todos los días	*every day*	**ayer**	*yesterday*
mientras	*while*	**el verano pasado**	*last summer*
con frecuencia	*frequently*	**de repente**	*suddenly*
siempre/generalmente	*always/generally*	**anoche**	*last night*

<u>Todos los veranos</u> **íbamos** a la playa, pero <u>el verano pasado</u> **fuimos** a las montañas.

Note, however, that these are just tendencies and these expressions do not require the use of one tense or the other. The main criteria to choose a past tense should always be the speaker´s perspective, what she/he wants to convey.

Cuando estaba en el hospital, mi tío **vino** a verme **todos los días**.

When I was in the hospital, my uncle came to see me every day.

El verano pasado íbamos mucho a la playa.

Last summer we used to go to the beach a lot.

9-15) Nuestro gato Rodolfo.

Paso 1. Lean esta historia sobre lo que le pasó al gato.

Ayer, nuestro gato Rodolfo **se enfermó**. No **quería** comer y **tenía** diarrea. ¡Pobrecito! Por supuesto, todos **estábamos** muy preocupados. Elena y yo lo **llevamos** al veterinario y **nos sentamos** en la sala de espera, donde **había** muchos animales. Rodolfo **estaba** en una caja de cartón (*cardboard box*) y, por supuesto, no **estaba** nada contento. ¡**Tuvimos** que esperar por una hora! Por fin, el veterinario lo **examinó, descubrió** que el pobre Rodolfo **tenía** una infección intestinal y le **recetó** un antibiótico. **Volvimos** a casa e inmediatamente le **dimos** su medicamento. En poco tiempo, **se recuperó**. ¡Qué suerte! (*What luck!*)

Paso 2. Para cada verbo, indica si expresa una acción (A), o una descripción/un estado (*state*) (D/E).

1. **se enfermó**
2. no **quería** comer
3. **tenía** diarrea
4. **estábamos** preocupados
5. lo **llevamos** al veterinario
6. **nos sentamos** en la sala de espera
7. **había** muchos animales
8. Rodolfo **estaba** en una caja

9. no **estaba** nada contento
10. el veterinario lo **examinó**
11. **descubrió**
12. Rodolfo **tenía** una infección
13. le **recetó** un antibiótico
14. **volvimos** a casa
15. le **dimos** su medicamento
16. **se recuperó**

9-16 **¡Pobre Rodolfo!** La familia llevó a Rodolfo al veterinario porque notaron varios cambios en el pobre gato. En parejas, escriban oraciones sobre lo que Rodolfo hacía *casi todos los días* y lo que hizo *ayer*. ¡Usen la imaginación!

Modelo: pasear por el jardín por las noches
Siempre paseaba por el jardín por las noches, pero ayer no salió de la casa.

Casi todos los días...	pero ayer...
1. comer toda la comida de su tazón	…
2. descansar junto a la chimenea	…
3. pelear con Teo, el perro	…
4. jugar con Elena y Juanito	…
5. dormir una siesta por la tarde	…
6. ¿…?	…

9-17 **Más sobre nuestro gato Rodolfo.** Describan al gato Rodolfo y algunas de sus aventuras juveniles. Usen el pretérito o el imperfecto según el caso.

Es verdad que Rodolfo es un gato único. Cuando _____ (tener) dos años y _____ (llegar) a nuestra casa, _____ (ser) gordo y bonito. _____ (Poder) correr muy rápido y aún subir a los árboles, donde le _____ (encantar) observar los pájaros (*birds*). Año tras (*after*) año nos _____ (dar) sorpresas. Por ejemplo, normalmente _____ (tomar) agua de su tazón, pero un día ¡la _____ (tomar) del inodoro (*toilet*)! Casi siempre _____ (dormir) en el sótano, en el sofá, pero una noche _____ (dormir) afuera, en el jardín. Allí _____ (conocer) a Gitana (*Gypsy*), su gata favorita. Unos días más tarde, nos _____ (dar) otra sorpresa: ¡_____ (Comerse) el jamón de mi sándwich! Cuando yo _____ (entrar) en la cocina y lo _____ (descubrir), ¡el "delincuente" _____ (salir) corriendo de la casa! Allí _____ (ver) a Gitana y los dos _____ (escaparse). _____ (Regresar) a casa ¡tres días más tarde! Ahora tenemos una pareja de gatos durmiendo junto a la chimenea y probablemente una familia por venir.

9-18 **Martes trece.** No eres supersticioso/a, pero ayer fue martes, día 13, y ¡todo salió mal (*went wrong*)!

Paso 1. Mira la tabla de la página 319. Decide qué acciones de la primera columna hacías cuando sucedieron los eventos de la segunda columna. Escribe el número de la primera frase al lado de la segunda frase.

Paso 2. Usando las ideas del Paso 1, explica lo que hacías y lo que pasó. Luego continúa la historia contando dos cosas que pasaron por la noche.

Modelo: **Por la mañana, mientras me duchaba, se terminó el agua caliente...**

Mientras...			
1.	ducharse	_____	encontrar un pelo en la sopa
2.	desayunar	_____	empezar a llover
3.	hacer un examen	_____	congelarse (*freeze*) la computadora
4.	comer en la cafetería	_____	acabarse (*run out*) el agua caliente
5.	escribir un trabajo	_____	sonar mi teléfono celular
6.	volver a mi cuarto	_____	derramar (*spill*) café en mi camisa

(9-19) El accidente de Martín un martes trece. Narra la historia en pasado. Cambia los verbos al pretérito o al imperfecto según el caso. Debes estar preparado para explicar las razones de tus decisiones a la clase.

Martín **maneja** muy contento. No **ve** el alto (*stop sign*) y **choca** (*crashes*) con otro coche que **viene** en la dirección opuesta. Al otro conductor no le **pasa** nada, pero el pobre Martín **se lastima**. **Llega** la policía y una ambulancia que lo **lleva** al hospital. La pierna le **duele** mucho. El médico lo **examina** y lo **manda** a radiología. **Es** un mal día para Martín. **Se fractura** la pierna y **sale** del hospital en muletas. **Es** un martes trece y como dice el dicho: "Martes trece, ni te cases ni te embarques, ni de tu casa te apartes".

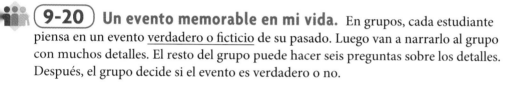

(9-20) Un evento memorable en mi vida. En grupos, cada estudiante piensa en un evento <u>verdadero o ficticio</u> de su pasado. Luego van a narrarlo al grupo con muchos detalles. El resto del grupo puede hacer seis preguntas sobre los detalles. Después, el grupo decide si el evento es verdadero o no.

(9-21) ¡Una noche increíble! En grupos, inventen la historia de una noche increíble. Pueden usar una de las ideas de abajo o una diferente. Un/a secretario/a escribe la historia para leérsela a la clase más tarde. Presten atención al uso del pretérito y del imperfecto.

Temas posibles:
1. una noche en la Ciudad de Nueva York
2. una noche en la sala de urgencias de un hospital
3. un sábado por la noche en una fiesta de la universidad
4. una noche viajando en autobús en Colombia o Venezuela
5. una noche en casa de los Simpson

Incluyan:
- referencia a la fecha, el día, la hora y el lugar donde estaban
- descripción del tiempo, del lugar y de las personas
- descripción de lo que pasaba en ese lugar (acciones en progreso, etc.)
- lo que pasó
- final de la historia

SITUACIONES

Estudiante A: Anoche fuiste a una fiesta fantástica, pero tu amigo/a no fue. Llámalo/a para preguntarle por qué no fue y hazle preguntas sobre su situación. También cuéntale sobre la fiesta: dónde era, qué música había, qué comida o bebidas tenían, quiénes estaban y qué hicieron tú y tus amigos. Al final, cuenta a tu amigo/a algo sorprendente que ocurrió.

Estudiante B: Anoche querías ir a una fiesta con tus amigos, pero te enfermaste y te sentías muy mal. Explícale a tu amigo/a por qué no fuiste, describiendo tus síntomas. Hazle también preguntas sobre la fiesta.

Dicho y hecho

PARA LEER: Ayurveda: La ciencia de la vida

ANTES DE LEER

1. El término *ayurveda* viene del idioma sánscrito: *ayus* = vida, *veda* = ciencia. Probablemente se refiere a:

   ☐ Películas de ciencia ficción hechas en la India.

   ☐ Un sistema de medicina tradicional.

2. Lee las tres descripciones a continuación y decide cuál te describe mejor.

   ☐ Individuo nervioso, de carácter activo; esbelto (*svelte*), pelo y piel (*skin*) secos.

   ☐ Individuo visceral, de carácter decidido; figura proporcionada; buen apetito.

   ☐ Individuo emocional, de carácter pacífico; figura grande, con tendencia a ganar peso.

ESTRATEGIA DE LECTURA

Scanning for details In *Capítulo 2* you practiced skimming a text to get the main idea(s). Sometimes getting the general idea of a text fulfills your purpose in reading it. Other times, you may be reading a text with a more focused purpose. Scanning consists in reading quickly over a text with the purpose of finding the specific information you are interested in or need to find. When scanning for specific details, run your eye over the text looking for key words that will lead you to the information you need. Look at the first paragraph of the article that follows, for example. If your purpose is to find specific information about where this particular form of medicine originated, you would scan until seeing **origen**, read more closely, and determine that its origins are in southern India. If your purpose were to determine the role the patient plays, you would scan until seeing **paciente** and **activo**. Read the following article first for the purpose of general understanding. You will practice scanning for specific information in *Después de leer*.

A LEER

El *ayurveda* no es solamente una medicina, es algo que te ayuda a conocerte mejor a ti mismo. El paciente tiene un papel[1] activo dentro de la terapia; es decir, cada uno debe aprender a ser su propio médico. Es la medicina tradicional más antigua de la historia, y sus conocimientos aparecen en textos de más de 5,000 años. Tiene su origen en el sur de la India y se basa en un sistema medicinal global e integral[2].

El estilo de vida de moda

El ayurveda se identifica con un estilo de vida que intenta ser beneficioso para la salud y para la belleza, mejorando la calidad de la piel y el cabello y ayudando a prevenir el envejecimiento[3]. En Occidente[4] es su perspectiva estética la que se ha puesto de moda y se ha introducido en *spas* y salones de belleza por sus buenos resultados. Incluso personajes como Madonna utilizan prácticas ayurvédicas para mantenerse sanos y jóvenes.

Sin embargo, esta ciencia ancestral no está limitada a lo estético. Abarca[5] los principales campos médicos como medicina interna completa, cirugía[6] general y específica, pediatría, ginecología, gerontología, toxicología y psiquiatría. Además, está reconocida por la Organización Mundial de la Salud.

Basándose en el estudio de los *doshas*, se trata al paciente como un individuo único, creando remedios y terapias específicos para cada persona.

---

[1] plays a role, [2] holistic, [3] aging, [4] the Western World, [5] covers, [6] surgery

Doshas o tipologías de las personas

Los *doshas* son los responsables de los cambios psico-biológicos y psico-patológicos de nuestro organismo. Existen tres *doshas*: *vata* (controla el sistema nervioso), *pitta* (responsable de las funciones digestivas y del hígado[7]) y *khapa* (controla las emociones).

Analizando las características fisiológicas, la constitución y el metabolismo, podemos reconocer cuáles son los *doshas* dominantes en cada persona:

Vata: Individuos nerviosos, de carácter activo; esbeltos, con tendencia a tener el pelo y la piel secos.

Pitta: Individuos viscerales, de carácter decidido; figura media y proporcionada y con tendencia a tener buen apetito.

Kapha: Individuos emocionales, de carácter pacífico; figura grande, con tendencia a ganar peso.

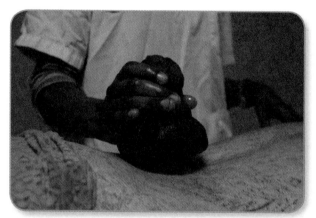

La clave para estar sanos es lograr el equilibrio entre los *doshas*, pues según el ayurveda, los desequilibrios son la causa de toda enfermedad. Observando los desequilibrios y el estado de los *doshas* se pueden determinar las causas de distintas enfermedades, curarlas y prevenirlas. También se tienen en cuenta[8] los siete tejidos del cuerpo (plasma, sangre, músculo, grasa, hueso, nervio y tejido reproductivo) y los tres desechos[9] principales que son las heces[10], la orina y el sudor[11]; en ellos se pueden encontrar signos de disfunciones o irregularidades del organismo. Además, se presta especial atención a la influencia del *agni*, que es la energía implicada en los procesos del metabolismo.

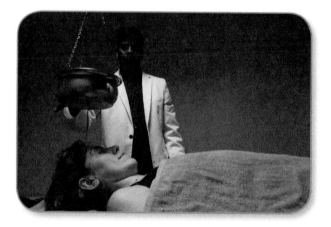

La enfermedad es una consecuencia de la falta de armonía en cualquiera de estos factores. "El ayurveda tiene tres pilares muy importantes: el primero es la dieta; el segundo, el estilo de vida; y el tercero es, si hay una enfermedad, tratarla", explica Deva Paksha, investigadora ayurvédica y terapeuta, además de fundadora de la asociación Shankha Ayurveda.

Los tratamientos

Los tratamientos ayurvédicos incluyen masajes terapéuticos, uso de aceites, ungüentos[12] e infusiones y un control de la dieta. Lo que caracteriza a los productos que se utilizan en el ayurveda es que todos parten de una base natural de plantas medicinales. Los tratamientos más conocidos del ayurveda se ocupan de la desintoxicación del organismo para limpiar el sistema nervioso y circulatorio y equilibrar el cuerpo.

El ayurveda es una alternativa para tratar diversos problemas de salud y mejorar nuestra calidad de vida y aspecto físico. Si logramos estar en equilibrio y armonía con nuestro organismo, estaremos sanos y, por consecuencia, más guapos y jóvenes.

Texto y fotografía: Rebeca Arnal / *Punto y coma*

---

[7] liver, [8] are taken into account, [9] waste, [10] feces, [11] sweat, [12] ointment

Dicho y hecho

DESPUÉS DE LEER

1. Indica si las siguientes afirmaciones son ciertas o falsas según el texto.

Cierto	Falso	
☐	☐	**a.** El ayurveda es una de las medicinas más modernas de la historia.
☐	☐	**b.** Es una ciencia ancestral reconocida por prestigiosos organismos internacionales.
☐	☐	**c.** Con esta ciencia se pueden mejorar el pelo, la piel y retrasar el envejecimiento.
☐	☐	**d.** La salud se alcanza logrando el equilibrio y la armonía en nuestro organismo.
☐	☐	**e.** Esta medicina se basa en controlar lo que comemos y cómo vivimos, pero no hay tratamientos o curas directas de las enfermedades.

2. Practica la estrategia de "*scanning*" para emparejar cada uno de estos términos con su significado.

___ dosha   **a.** La energía metabólica.
___ agni   **b.** La combinación del sistema nervioso, digestivo y emocional.
___ ayurveda   **c.** *Dosha* responsable de la digestión e hígado.
___ pitta   **d.** Un sistema de salud global que tiene más de 5,000 años.

3. Escanea el texto para buscar la información necesaria para contestar estas preguntas:

   a. ¿Qué campos de la medicina tradicional incluye el ayurveda?

   b. ¿Cuál es la causa de todas las enfermedades, según el ayurveda?

   c. Además de estudiar los *doshas* de cada persona, ¿qué otras partes del cuerpo se consideran en un diagnóstico del ayurveda?

   d. ¿De qué se componen los productos ayurvédicos?

4. ¿Has probado el ayurveda o estarías dispuesto/a (*willing*) a probarlo? Explica tu respuesta.

PARA CONVERSAR: En la sala de urgencias

 Imaginen que tres de ustedes están en la sala de urgencias de la clínica de la universidad. Cada uno/a le explica al/a la recepcionista por qué necesita ver al/a la doctor/a. El/La recepcionista les hace preguntas para determinar quién va primero.

Posibilidades:

- Estabas corriendo, te caíste (*fell*) y ahora…
- Comiste unos mariscos y ahora…
- Piensas que tienes la gripe.
- Tienes bronquitis.

ESTRATEGIA DE COMUNICACIÓN

Taking Risks Many adults can feel apprehensive about speaking a second language because they do not feel they are as convincing or authoritative as they are in their first language. But sometimes it is important to just jump in and take risks when speaking a second language without worrying too much about how you sound to the listeners. A very important part of a successful communication is a positive attitude and persistence. When carrying out this activity, try your best to communicate your needs so that you will be attended to in the emergency room.

PARA ESCRIBIR: Lo qué me pasó

Esta vez vas a contar una historia sobre una enfermedad o una visita médica. Puede ser cierta o ficticia, realista o imaginativa, sobre ti o sobre otros. ¿Qué historia vas a contar? Puedes contar una historia sobre una vez que estuviste enfermo/a o tuviste un accidente, una estadía en el hospital o una visita médica. Recuerda que la historia puede ser real o ficticia, seria o cómica, etc.

ANTES DE ESCRIBIR

- Escribe un bosquejo de los eventos en orden cronológico. ¿Qué pasó? ¿Cuándo?

- Escribe una lista de los lugares donde ocurrió la historia, y algunos detalles para describirlos. Piensa en estas preguntas: ¿En qué lugar estuve? ¿Cómo eran esos lugares? ¿Qué había? ¿Cómo era el ambiente (*atmosphere*)?

- Escribe una lista de personajes relevantes, incluyendo características importantes para la historia. Puedes pensar en preguntas como: ¿Qué personas fueron relevantes para la historia? ¿Cómo eran? ¿Qué hicieron? ¿Por qué?

ESTRATEGIA DE REDACCIÓN

Narrating There are many ways to tell a story. While you're learning Spanish, here are a few ideas that may help you.

- In terms of content, think of the events and the people that are important to the story. To add details, think of questions like *What? When? Where? Who? How? Why?* and choose details (answers to those questions) that are important or will make your story more interesting.
- Tell the story in chronological order and use connecting words that will help the reader follow the sequence of actions.
- Pay attention to your use of verb tenses. Remember to use the preterit to talk about completed actions and the imperfect to describe the scene and situation, the people, the atmosphere, etc.

A ESCRIBIR

Narra la historia incorporando información sobre la situación y los personajes cuando sea apropiado. Si quieres, puedes añadir otros detalles al escribir para dar interés y emoción (*excitement*) a tu historia. Puedes seguir esta estructura general:

Primer párrafo: Comienza con una oración introductoria seguida de oraciones atractivas o misteriosas para interesar al lector. Después describe la situación y el ambiente.

Modelo: **Era la noche del jueves y estaba en mi cuarto, haciendo la tarea de español, como todos los jueves…**

Párrafos centrales: Narra la acción y los eventos de la historia, introduciendo descripciones de personajes y lugares, o añadiendo otros detalles sobre la situación cuando sea apropiado.

Modelo: **…cuando llegué al hospital, la recepcionista me miró alarmada…**

Último párrafo: Como conclusión, ofrece un desenlace (*closure*) y una reflexión final.

Modelo: **… al día siguiente no recordaba nada. Aprendí algo importante esa noche…**

Dicho y hecho

> **Para escribir mejor:** Estos conectores ayudan a marcar la secuencia cronológica de una narración.
>
> | | |
> |---|---|
> | **al final** | *at the end* |
> | **al principio** | *at the beginning* |
> | **al cabo de (un mes/dos días)** | *(a month/two days) later* |
> | **de repente** | *suddenly* |
> | **después de (una hora)** | *after (an hour)* |
> | **después, luego, más tarde** | *later* |
> | **en ese momento/instante** | *at that time/moment* |
> | **entonces** | *then* |
> | **mientras (+ imperfecto)** | *while (+ imperfect)* |
> | **mientras tanto** | *in the meantime* |

DESPUÉS DE ESCRIBIR

Revisar y editar: El contenido, la organización, la gramática y el vocabulario.

Después de escribir el primer borrador de tu composición, déjalo a un lado por un mínimo de un día. Cuando vuelvas (*you return*) a leerlo, corrige el contenido, la organización, la gramática y el vocabulario. Además, hazte (*ask yourself*) estas preguntas:

- [ ] ¿Está clara la historia? ¿Es interesante? ¿Hay suficientes detalles sobre los personajes, lugares y situaciones?

- [ ] ¿Está clara la secuencia de eventos? ¿Usé la estructura sugerida en el Paso 3? ¿Usé conectores apropiados para indicar el orden cronológico y para mejorar la fluidez (*improve the flow*)?

- [ ] ¿Usé el pretérito y el imperfecto correctamente para describir y narrar en el pasado?

 ## PARA VER Y ESCUCHAR: La medicina moderna y tradicional

ANTES DE VER EL VIDEO

Empareja los tratamientos de enfermedades o dolencias (*ailments*) con las descripciones que les correspondan.

1. ___ acupuntura	**a.**	Uso de hierbas y productos comunes.
2. ___ quiropráctica	**b.**	Tratamiento de manipulación manual del sistema músculo-esqueletal.
3. ___ homeopatía	**c.**	Inserción y manipulación de agujas (*needles*) en el cuerpo.
4. ___ remedios naturales/caseros	**d.**	Uso de sustancias que provocan una reacción similar a la enfermedad, diluídas (*diluted*) al extremo.

INVESTIG@ EN INTERNET

¿Estás familiarizado con los remedios naturales? ¿Conoces los beneficios de alguna planta medicinal? Investiga en la Internet cuáles son los beneficios de la menta y coméntalo con el resto de la clase. Pregunta a tus familiares si alguna vez han usado alguna hierba medicinal como remedio casero y busca sus propiedades.

Paso 1. Mira el video una vez concentrándote en la idea principal. Resúmelo en una o dos oraciones.

ESTRATEGIA DE COMPRENSIÓN

Listening for a purpose, focusing on specific information If there is a particular goal for your listening (e.g. finding out what gate your plane leaves from in an airport) or you know ahead of time what specific information you need to gather from a spoken text, focusing your attention on that purpose will help you focus on the relevant information.

Paso 2. En este video, un herbolario mexicano nos explica los beneficios del uso de hierbas medicinales tradicionales. Antes de ver otra vez el video, lee las preguntas a las que vas a responder.

1. Según el video, ¿chocan (*clash*) en América Latina la medicina moderna y la tradicional, que usa hierbas medicinales?

2. ¿Por qué cree el herbolario que las hierbas medicinales son más seguras?

3. El herbolario menciona tres productos de su tienda. Anota <u>dos</u> problemas o enfermedades que trata cada uno.
   La menta:
   La caña de jabalí:
   El compuesto de hierbas:

4. ¿En qué casos puede ser peligroso (*dangerous*) el uso de hierbas medicinales?

DESPUÉS DE VER EL VIDEO

Contesten estas preguntas en grupos:

1. ¿Conocen a alguien que haya usado alguna de las terapias mencionadas en el video? ¿Sabes cómo fue su experiencia?

2. ¿Están dispuestos/as (*willing*) a usar alguna de esas terapias u otras diferentes? ¿Cuáles? ¿Por qué?

Repaso de vocabulario activo

Adjetivos

deprimido/a   *depressed*
embarazada   *pregnant*

Adverbios

cada   *each*
de repente   *all of a sudden, suddenly*
mientras   *meanwhile/while*
por fin   *finally*
una vez/muchas veces   *once/many times*

Expresiones sobre la salud

hacer un análisis de sangre/ sacar sangre   *to do a blood test/to draw blood*
hacer una cita   *to make an appointment*
poner una inyección/una vacuna   *to give a shot/vaccination*
sacar una radiografía   *to take an X-ray*
tener dolor de (cabeza/estómago)   *to have a (head/stomachache)*
tener náuseas/ escalofríos/ vómitos   *to have nausea/chills/to be vomiting*
tomar la temperatura/la presión arterial/el pulso   *to take one's temperature/blood pressure/pulse*

Órdenes que nos da un/a doctor/a   *Things the doctor tells us to do*

Abra la boca.   *Open your mouth.*
Descanse.   *Rest.*
Diga "¡Aaah!"   *Say "¡Aaah!"*
Lleve la receta a la farmacia.   *Take the prescription to the pharmacy.*
Respire profundamente.   *Take a deep breath.*
Saque la lengua.   *Stick out your tongue.*
Tome aspirinas/las pastillas/las cápsulas.   *Take aspirin/the pills/the capsules.*
Tome líquidos.   *Take liquids.*
Vaya a la farmacia.   *Go to the pharmacy.*

Sustantivos

Algunos problemas de salud

la alergia   *allergy*
la congestión nasal   *nasal congestion*
la diarrea   *diarrhea*
la fiebre   *fever*
la gripe   *flu*
la herida (grave)   *(serious) wound*
la infección   *infection*
el resfriado   *cold (illness)*
la tos   *cough*

El cuerpo humano

la boca   *mouth*
el brazo   *arm*
la cabeza   *head*
la cara   *face*
el corazón   *heart*
el cuello   *neck*
el dedo   *finger*
el diente   *tooth*
la espalda   *back*
el estómago   *stomach*
la garganta   *throat*
el hombro   *shoulder*
el hueso   *bone*
el labio   *lip*
la lengua   *tongue*
la mano   *hand*
la nariz   *nose*
el oído   *ear (inner)*
el ojo   *eye*
la oreja   *ear (outer)*
el pecho   *chest*
el pelo   *hair*
el pie   *foot*
la pierna   *leg*
el pulmón   *lung*
el tobillo   *ankle*
la uña   *nail*

En el hospital

la ambulancia   *ambulance*
la camilla   *gurney*

el consultorio del médico/de la médica   *doctor's office*
la habitación   *room*
el hospital   *hospital*
la inyección   *shot, injection*
las muletas   *crutches*
el/la paciente   *patient*
el/la paramédico   *paramedic*
la recepción   *reception desk*
el/la recepcionista   *receptionist*
la receta   *prescription*
la sala de espera   *waiting room*
la sala de urgencias   *emergency room*
la silla de ruedas   *wheelchair*
el termómetro   *thermometer*
la vacuna   *vaccine*
la venda   *bandage*
el yeso   *cast*

Verbos

cansarse   *to get tired*
doler (ue)   *to hurt/be hurting*
enfermarse   *to get sick*
estornudar   *to sneeze*
examinar   *to examine*
fracturar(se)   *to break (one's arm)*
lastimarse   *to hurt oneself*
preocuparse   *to worry*
quedarse   *to stay*
sentarse (ie)/estar sentado/de pie   *to seat/to be seated/to be standing*
sentirse (ie, i)   *to feel*
torcer(se) (ue)   *to sprain (one's ankle)*
toser   *to cough*
vomitar   *to vomit*

Autoprueba y repaso

I. *Usted/Ustedes* **commands.** Da mandatos afirmativos y negativos para *usted* y *ustedes*.

    Modelo: traerlo

        Tráigalo. / No lo traiga.
        Tráiganlo. / No lo traigan.

1. traérmelos
2. examinarla
3. descansar más
4. estudiar las palabras
5. leer el libro

II. The imperfect. Di cómo eran estas personas y lo que hacían cuando eran niños/as.

    Modelo: yo / ser muy obediente
        Era muy obediente.

1. mis hermanos y yo / ser niños muy buenos
2. nosotros / ir a una escuela pequeña
3. yo / escuchar a mis maestras
4. José / jugar al voleibol durante el recreo
5. Ana y Tere / ver la tele por la tarde
6. tú / comer galletas todos los días

III. The imperfect and the preterit. Lee la historia y luego decide si los verbos entre paréntesis deben estar en el imperfecto o el pretérito.

    Modelo: Roberto no **se sentía** (sentirse) nada bien.

1. Por eso _____ (llamar) al consultorio de su doctor y _____ (hablar) con la recepcionista.
2. Roberto le _____ (explicar) que _____ (estar) enfermo.
3. La recepcionista le _____ (preguntar) qué _____ (tener).
4. Él le _____ (explicar) que le _____ (doler) todo el cuerpo y que _____ (tener) fiebre, dolor de cabeza y escalofríos.
5. Ella también _____ (querer) saber si _____ (estar) muy congestionado.
6. Roberto _____ (contestar) afirmativamente.
7. La recepcionista le _____ (decir) que le _____ (poder) dar una cita para las dos de la tarde.
8. Roberto la _____ (aceptar) y le_____ (dar) las gracias.
9. Como era temprano y _____ (sentirse) mal, _____ (dormirse) otra vez.

IV. *Repaso general.* Contesta con oraciones completas.

1. ¿Qué síntomas tenías la última vez que fuiste al médico?
2. ¿Quién y cómo era tu maestro/a preferido/a en la escuela primaria?
3. ¿Recuerdas tu primera clase en la universidad? ¿Qué clase era, quién la enseñaba? ¿Qué otros detalles recuerdas?
4. ¿Qué hiciste durante tu primer día en la universidad? ¿Cómo te sentiste?

V. *Cultura.* Contesta con oraciones completas.

1. Nombra por lo menos un país que tiene frontera con Colombia y otro que tiene frontera con Venezuela.
2. ¿De dónde proviene el nombre de Venezuela?
3. Describe por lo menos un remedio casero que sea común en América Latina.
4. ¿Quién es Gabriel García Márquez?

Las respuestas de *Autoprueba y repaso* se pueden encontrar en el **Apéndice 2.**

Así es mi casa

Autoprueba y repaso

I. The subjunctive with time expressions.
Completa las oraciones con la frase entre paréntesis.
Usa el subjuntivo o el pretérito según la situación.

1. (yo / recibir el dinero) Te llamé tan pronto como…
Te voy a llamar tan pronto como…

2. (tú / darme el número de teléfono del hotel) Haré
las reservaciones cuando…Hice las reservaciones
cuando…

3. (tú / llamarme) Fui a la agencia de viajes después de
que…Iré a la agencia de viajes después de que…

4. (nosotros / regresar de la luna de miel) No
anunciaré nuestro matrimonio hasta que…No
anuncié nuestro matrimonio hasta que…

II. The present perfect subjunctive. ¿Cómo te
sientes acerca de los siguientes acontecimientos?

> **Modelo:** el crimen / aumentar este año
> **Siento / Es una lástima que el crimen
> haya aumentado este año.**

1. el empleo / mejorar

2. nosotros / ser aceptados en un programa de
voluntariado en Nicaragua

3. tú / votar en las elecciones generales

4. la drogadicción / desaparecer

5. los astronautas / tener un accidente

III. *Si* clauses. Haz oraciones indicando la condición
(Si…) y el resultado.

> **Modelo:** encontrar un trabajo mejor / ganar
> más dinero
> **Si encontrara un trabajo mejor, ganaría
> más dinero.**

1. ganar más dinero / ahorrarlo

2. ahorrarlo / tener mucho dinero

3. tener mucho dinero / comprar un coche

4. comprar un coche / hacer un viaje

5. hacer un viaje / ir a Puerto Vallarta

6. ir a Puerto Vallarta / quedarme allí dos meses

7. quedarme allí dos meses / perder mi trabajo

8. perder mi trabajo / no tener dinero

IV. *Repaso general.* Contesta con oraciones
completas.

1. ¿Cuáles son algunos de los problemas más serios de
nuestro país hoy en día?

2. Si pudieras cambiar una cosa de nuestro mundo,
¿qué cambiarías? ¿Por qué?

3. Cuando estabas en la escuela secundaria, ¿te
preocupabas por algún problema mundial?
(¿Cuáles?) ¿Te preocupabas por otros problemas?
(¿Cuáles?)

4. ¿Qué harás cuando te gradúes?

V. *Cultura.* Contesta con oraciones completas.

1. ¿Cómo se llaman las dos emisoras televisivas
hispanas más grandes en Estados Unidos?

2. ¿En qué se diferencian las típicas telenovelas en
español de las *soap operas* en inglés?

3. ¿Quiénes son Cristina Saralegui y Don Francisco?

Las respuestas de *Autoprueba y repaso* se pueden encontrar
en el **Apéndice 2.**

Apéndice 1: *Verbos*

Regular Verbs: *Simple Tenses*

Infinitive / Present Participle / Past Participle	Indicative					Subjunctive		Imperative (commands)
	Present	Imperfect	Preterit	Future	Conditional	Present	Imperfect	
hablar *to speak* / hablando / hablado	hablo	hablaba	hablé	hablaré	hablaría	hable	hablara	habla/ no hables
	hablas	hablabas	hablaste	hablarás	hablarías	hables	hablaras	hable
	habla	hablaba	habló	hablará	hablaría	hable	hablara	hablemos
	hablamos	hablábamos	hablamos	hablaremos	hablaríamos	hablemos	habláramos	hablad/ no habléis
	habláis	hablabais	hablasteis	hablaréis	hablaríais	habléis	hablarais	hablen
	hablan	hablaban	hablaron	hablarán	hablarían	hablen	hablaran	
comer *to eat* / comiendo / comido	como	comía	comí	comeré	comería	coma	comiera	come/ no comas
	comes	comías	comiste	comerás	comerías	comas	comieras	coma
	come	comía	comió	comerá	comería	coma	comiera	comamos
	comemos	comíamos	comimos	comeremos	comeríamos	comamos	comiéramos	comed/ no comáis
	coméis	comíais	comisteis	comeréis	comeríais	comáis	comierais	coman
	comen	comían	comieron	comerán	comerían	coman	comieran	
vivir *to live* / viviendo / vivido	vivo	vivía	viví	viviré	viviría	viva	viviera	vive/ no vivas
	vives	vivías	viviste	vivirás	vivirías	vivas	vivieras	viva
	vive	vivía	vivió	vivirá	viviría	viva	viviera	vivamos
	vivimos	vivíamos	vivimos	viviremos	viviríamos	vivamos	viviéramos	vivid/ no viváis
	vivís	vivíais	vivisteis	viviréis	viviríais	viváis	vivierais	vivan
	viven	vivían	vivieron	vivirán	vivirían	vivan	vivieran	

Regular Verbs: *Perfect Tenses*

Indicative				Subjunctive	
Present Perfect	Past Perfect	Future Perfect	Conditional Perfect	Present Perfect	Past Perfect
he hablado	había hablado	habré hablado	habría hablado	haya hablado	hubiera hablado
has comido	habías comido	habrás comido	habrías comido	hayas comido	hubieras comido
ha vivido	había vivido	habrá vivido	habría vivido	haya vivido	hubiera vivido
hemos	habíamos	habremos	habríamos	hayamos	hubiéramos
habéis	habíais	habréis	habríais	hayáis	hubierais
han	habían	habrán	habrían	hayan	hubieran

Stem-changing -ar and -er Verbs: e → ie; o → ue

Infinitive Present Participle Past Participle	Indicative						Subjunctive		Imperative (commands)
	Present	Imperfect	Preterit	Future	Conditional		Present	Imperfect	
pensar (ie) *to think*	**pienso**	pensaba	pensé	pensaré	pensaría		**piense**	pensara	**piensa**/ no **pienses**
pensando	**piensas**	pensabas	pensaste	pensarás	pensarías		**pienses**	pensaras	**piense**
pensado	**piensa**	pensaba	pensó	pensará	pensaría		**piense**	pensara	pensemos
	pensamos	pensábamos	pensamos	pensaremos	pensaríamos		pensemos	pensáramos	pensad/ no penséis
	pensáis	pensabais	pensasteis	pensaréis	pensaríais		penséis	pensarais	**piensen**
	piensan	pensaban	pensaron	pensarán	pensarían		**piensen**	pensaran	
volver (ue) *to return*	**vuelvo**	volvía	volví	volveré	volvería		**vuelva**	volviera	**vuelve**/ no **vuelvas**
volviendo	**vuelves**	volvías	volviste	volverás	volverías		**vuelvas**	volvieras	**vuelva**
vuelto (irreg.)	**vuelve**	volvía	volvió	volverá	volvería		**vuelva**	volviera	volvamos
	volvemos	volvíamos	volvimos	volveremos	volveríamos		volvamos	volviéramos	volved/ no volváis
	volvéis	volvíais	volvisteis	volveréis	volveríais		volváis	volvierais	**vuelvan**
	vuelven	volvían	volvieron	volverán	volverían		**vuelvan**	volvieran	

Other verbs of this type are:

e → ie: cerrar, despertarse, empezar, entender, nevar, pensar, perder, preferir, querer, recomendar, regar, sentarse

o → ue: acordarse de, acostarse, almorzar, costar, encontrar, jugar, mostrar, poder, recordar, resolver, sonar, volar, volver

Stem-changing -ir Verbs: e → ie, i; e → i, i; o → ue, u

Infinitive Present Participle Past Participle	Indicative						Subjunctive		Imperative (commands)
	Present	Imperfect	Preterit	Future	Conditional		Present	Imperfect	
sentir (ie, i) *to feel,*	**siento**	sentía	sentí	sentiré	sentiría		**sienta**	sintiera	**siente**/ no **sientas**
to regret	**sientes**	sentías	sentiste	sentirás	sentirías		**sientas**	sintieras	**sienta**
sintiendo	**siente**	sentía	**sintió**	sentirá	sentiría		**sienta**	sintiera	**sintamos**
sentido	sentimos	sentíamos	sentimos	sentiremos	sentiríamos		**sintamos**	sintiéramos	sentid/ no **sintáis**
	sentís	sentíais	sentisteis	sentiréis	sentiríais		**sintáis**	sintierais	**sientan**
	sienten	sentían	**sintieron**	sentirán	sentirían		**sientan**	sintieran	
pedir (i, i) *to ask (for)*	**pido**	pedía	pedí	pediré	pediría		**pida**	pidiera	**pide**/ no **pidas**
pidiendo	**pides**	pedías	pediste	pedirás	pedirías		**pidas**	pidieras	**pida**
pedido	**pide**	pedía	**pidió**	pedirá	pediría		**pida**	pidiera	**pidamos**
	pedimos	pedíamos	pedimos	pediremos	pediríamos		**pidamos**	pidiéramos	pedid/ no **pidáis**
	pedís	pedíais	pedisteis	pediréis	pediríais		**pidáis**	pidierais	**pidan**
	piden	pedían	**pidieron**	pedirán	pedirían		**pidan**	pidieran	

Stem-changing -ir Verbs: e → ie, i; e → i, i; o → ue, u *(continued)*

Infinitive Present Participle Past Participle	Indicative					Subjunctive		Imperative (commands)
	Present	Imperfect	Preterit	Future	Conditional	Present	Imperfect	
dormir (ue, u) *to sleep* **durmiendo** dormido	**duermo** **duermes** **duerme** dormimos dormís **duermen**	dormía dormías dormía dormíamos dormíais dormían	dormí dormiste **durmió** dormimos dormisteis **durmieron**	dormiré dormirás dormirá dormiremos dormiréis dormirán	dormiría dormirías dormiría dormiríamos dormiríais dormirían	**duerma** **duermas** **duerma** **durmamos** **durmáis** **duerman**	**durmiera** **durmieras** **durmiera** **durmiéramos** **durmierais** **durmieran**	**duerme**/ no **duermas** **duerma** **durmamos** dormid/ no **durmáis** **duerman**

Other verbs of this type are:

e → ie, i: divertirse, invertir, preferir, sentirse, sugerir

e → i, i: conseguir, despedirse de, reírse, repetir, seguir, servir, vestirse

o → ue, u: morir(se)

Verbs with Spelling Changes

1. c → qu: tocar (model); buscar, explicar, pescar, sacar

Infinitive Present Participle Past Participle	Indicative					Subjunctive		Imperative (commands)
	Present	Imperfect	Preterit	Future	Conditional	Present	Imperfect	
tocar *to play* *(musical instr.),* to *touch* tocando tocado	toco tocas toca tocamos tocáis tocan	tocaba tocabas tocaba tocábamos tocabais tocaban	**toqué** tocaste tocó tocamos tocasteis tocaron	tocaré tocarás tocará tocaremos tocaréis tocarán	tocaría tocarías tocaría tocaríamos tocaríais tocarían	**toque** **toques** **toque** **toquemos** **toquéis** **toquen**	tocara tocaras tocara tocáramos tocarais tocaran	toca/ no **toques** **toque** **toquemos** tocad/ no **toquéis** **toquen**

2. z → c: abrazar; Also almorzar (ue), cruzar, empezar (ie)

Infinitive Present Participle Past Participle	Present	Imperfect	Preterit	Future	Conditional	Present	Imperfect	Imperative (commands)
abrazar *to hug* abrazando abrazado	abrazo abrazas abraza abrazamos abrazáis abrazan	abrazaba abrazabas abrazaba abrazábamos abrazabais abrazaban	**abracé** abrazaste abrazó abrazamos abrazasteis abrazaron	abrazaré abrazarás abrazará abrazaremos abrazaréis abrazarán	abrazaría abrazarías abrazaría abrazaríamos abrazaríais abrazarían	**abrace** **abraces** **abrace** **abracemos** **abracéis** **abracen**	abrazara abrazaras abrazara abrazáramos abrazarais abrazaran	abraza/ no **abraces** **abrace** **abracemos** abrazad/ no **abracéis** **abracen**

3. g → gu: pagar; Also **apagar, jugar (ue), llegar**

	Present	Imperfect	Preterite	Future	Conditional	Present Subjunctive	Imperfect Subjunctive	Commands
pagar *to pay (for)*	pago	pagaba	**pagué**	pagaré	pagaría	**pague**	pagara	
pagando	pagas	pagabas	pagaste	pagarás	pagarías	**pagues**	pagaras	paga/ no **pagues**
pagado	paga	pagaba	pagó	pagará	pagaría	**pague**	pagara	**pague**
	pagamos	pagábamos	pagamos	pagaremos	pagaríamos	**paguemos**	pagáramos	**paguemos**
	pagáis	pagabais	pagasteis	pagaréis	pagaríais	**paguéis**	pagarais	pagad/ no **paguéis**
	pagan	pagaban	pagaron	pagarán	pagarían	**paguen**	pagaran	**paguen**

4. gu → g: seguir (i, i); Also **conseguir**

	Present	Imperfect	Preterite	Future	Conditional	Present Subjunctive	Imperfect Subjunctive	Commands
seguir (i, i) *to follow*	**sigo**	seguía	seguí	seguiré	seguiría	**siga**	**siguiera**	
siguiendo	sigues	seguías	seguiste	seguirás	seguirías	**sigas**	**siguieras**	sigue/ no **sigas**
seguido	sigue	seguía	**siguió**	seguirá	seguiría	**siga**	**siguiera**	**siga**
	seguimos	seguíamos	seguimos	seguiremos	seguiríamos	**sigamos**	**siguiéramos**	**sigamos**
	seguís	seguíais	seguisteis	seguiréis	seguiríais	**sigáis**	**siguierais**	seguid/ no **sigáis**
	siguen	seguían	**siguieron**	seguirán	seguirían	**sigan**	**siguieran**	**sigan**

5. g → j: recoger; Also **escoger, proteger**

	Present	Imperfect	Preterite	Future	Conditional	Present Subjunctive	Imperfect Subjunctive	Commands
recoger *to pick up*	**recojo**	recogía	recogí	recogeré	recogería	**recoja**	recogiera	
recogiendo	recoges	recogías	recogiste	recogerás	recogerías	**recojas**	recogieras	recoge/ no **recojas**
recogido	recoge	recogía	recogió	recogerá	recogería	**recoja**	recogiera	**recoja**
	recogemos	recogíamos	recogimos	recogeremos	recogeríamos	**recojamos**	recogiéramos	**recojamos**
	recogéis	recogíais	recogisteis	recogeréis	recogeríais	**recojáis**	recogierais	recoged/ no **recojáis**
	recogen	recogían	recogieron	recogerán	recogerían	**recojan**	recogieran	**recojan**

6. i → y: leer; Also **caer, oír.** Verbs with additional **i → y** changes (see below): **construir;** Also **destruir**

	Present	Imperfect	Preterite	Future	Conditional	Present Subjunctive	Imperfect Subjunctive	Commands
leer *to read*	leo	leía	leí	leeré	leería	lea	**leyera**	
leyendo	lees	leías	leíste	leerás	leerías	leas	**leyeras**	lee/ no leas
leído	lee	leía	**leyó**	leerá	leería	lea	**leyera**	lea
	leemos	leíamos	leímos	leeremos	leeríamos	leamos	**leyéramos**	leamos
	leéis	leíais	leísteis	leeréis	leeríais	leáis	**leyerais**	leed/ no leáis
	leen	leían	**leyeron**	leerán	leerían	lean	**leyeran**	lean
construir *to construct, to build*	**construyo**	construía	construí	construiré	construiría	**construya**	**construyera**	
construyendo	**construyes**	construías	construiste	construirás	construirías	**construyas**	**construyeras**	**construye**/ no **construyas**
construido	**construye**	construía	**construyó**	construirá	construiría	**construya**	**construyera**	**construya**
	construimos	construíamos	construimos	construiremos	construiríamos	**construyamos**	**construyéramos**	**construyamos**
	construís	construíais	construisteis	construiréis	construiríais	**construyáis**	**construyerais**	construid/ no **construyáis**
	construyen	construían	**construyeron**	construirán	construirían	**construyan**	**construyeran**	**construya**

Irregular Verbs

Infinitive Present Participle Past Participle	Indicative Present	Imperfect	Preterit	Future	Conditional	Subjunctive Present	Imperfect	Imperative (commands)
caer *to fall* **cayendo** caído	**caigo** caes cae caemos caéis caen	caía caías caía caíamos caíais caían	caí caíste **cayó** caímos caísteis **cayeron**	caeré caerás caerá caeremos caeréis caerán	caería caerías caería caeríamos caeríais caerían	caiga caigas caiga caigamos caigáis caigan	cayera cayeras cayera cayéramos cayerais cayeran	cae/ no caigas caiga caigamos caed/ no caigáis caigan
conocer *to know, to be acquainted with* conociendo conocido	**conozco** conoces conoce conocemos conocéis conocen	conocía conocías conocía conocíamos conocíais conocían	conocí conociste conoció conocimos conocisteis conocieron	conoceré conocerás conocerá conoceremos conoceréis conocerán	conocería conocerías conocería conoceríamos conoceríais conocerían	conozca conozcas conozca conozcamos conozcáis conozcan	conociera conocieras conociera conociéramos conocierais conocieran	conoce/no conozcas conozca conozcamos conoced/no conozcáis conozcan
conducir *to drive* conduciendo conducido	**conduzco** conduces conduce conducimos conducís conducen	conducía conducías conducía conducíamos conducíais conducían	**conduje** **condujiste** **condujo** **condujimos** **condujisteis** **condujeron**	conduciré conducirás conducirá conduciremos conduciréis conducirán	conduciría conducirías conduciría conduciríamos conduciríais conducirían	conduzca conduzcas conduzca conduzcamos conduzcáis conduzcan	condujera condujeras condujera condujéramos condujerais condujeran	conduce/no conduzcas conduzca conduzcamos conducid/no conduzcáis conduzcan
dar *to give* dando dado	**doy** das da damos dais dan	daba dabas daba dábamos dabais daban	**di** **diste** **dio** **dimos** **disteis** dieron	daré darás dará daremos daréis darán	daría darías daría daríamos daríais darían	**dé** **des** **dé** **demos** **deis** **den**	diera dieras diera diéramos dierais dieran	da/no des **dé** demos dad/no déis den
decir *to say, to tell* **diciendo** **dicho**	**digo** **dices** **dice** decimos decís **dicen**	decía decías decía decíamos decíais decían	**dije** **dijiste** **dijo** **dijimos** **dijisteis** **dijeron**	**diré** **dirás** **dirá** **diremos** **diréis** **dirán**	**diría** **dirías** **diría** **diríamos** **diríais** **dirían**	diga digas diga digamos digáis digan	dijera dijeras dijera dijéramos dijerais dijeran	di/no digas diga digamos decid/no digáis digan

Infinitive / Present Participle / Past Participle	Present	Imperfect	Preterite	Future	Conditional	Present Subjunctive	Imperfect Subjunctive	Commands
estar *to be*	**estoy**	estaba	**estuve**	estaré	estaría	**esté**	estuviera	
estando	**estás**	estabas	**estuviste**	estarás	estarías	**estés**	estuvieras	**estés**/ no estés
estado	**está**	estaba	**estuvo**	estará	estaría	**esté**	estuviera	esté
	estamos	estábamos	**estuvimos**	estaremos	estaríamos	**estemos**	estuviéramos	estemos
	estáis	estabais	**estuvisteis**	estaréis	estaríais	**estéis**	estuvierais	estad/ no estéis
	están	estaban	**estuvieron**	estarán	estarían	**estén**	estuvieran	estén
haber *to have*	**he**	había	**hube**	**habré**	**habría**	**haya**	hubiera	
habiendo	**has**	habías	**hubiste**	**habrás**	**habrías**	**hayas**	hubieras	
habido	**ha**	había	**hubo**	**habrá**	**habría**	**haya**	hubiera	
	hemos	habíamos	**hubimos**	**habremos**	**habríamos**	**hayamos**	hubiéramos	
	habéis	habíais	**hubisteis**	**habréis**	**habríais**	**hayáis**	hubierais	
	han	habían	**hubieron**	**habrán**	**habrían**	**hayan**	hubieran	
hacer *to do, to make*	**hago**	hacía	**hice**	**haré**	**haría**	haga	hiciera	
haciendo	haces	hacías	**hiciste**	**harás**	**harías**	hagas	hicieras	**haz**/ no hagas
hecho	hace	hacía	**hizo**	**hará**	**haría**	haga	hiciera	haga
	hacemos	hacíamos	**hicimos**	**haremos**	**haríamos**	hagamos	hiciéramos	hagamos
	hacéis	hacíais	**hicisteis**	**haréis**	**haríais**	hagáis	hicierais	haced/ no hagáis
	hacen	hacían	**hicieron**	**harán**	**harían**	hagan	hicieran	hagan
ir *to go*	**voy**	**iba**	**fui**	iré	iría	**vaya**	fuera	**ve**/ no vayas
yendo	**vas**	**ibas**	**fuiste**	irás	irías	**vayas**	fueras	vaya
ido	**va**	**iba**	**fue**	irá	iría	**vaya**	fuera	vayamos
	vamos	**íbamos**	**fuimos**	iremos	iríamos	**vayamos**	fuéramos	id/ no vayáis
	vais	**ibais**	**fuisteis**	iréis	iríais	**vayáis**	fuerais	vayan
	van	**iban**	**fueron**	irán	irían	**vayan**	fueran	
oír *to hear*	**oigo**	oía	oí	oiré	oiría	oiga	oyera	oye/ no oigas
oyendo	**oyes**	oías	**oíste**	oirás	oirías	oigas	oyeras	oiga
oído	**oye**	oía	**oyó**	oirá	oiría	oiga	oyera	oigamos
	oímos	oíamos	**oímos**	oiremos	oiríamos	oigamos	oyéramos	oíd/ no oigáis
	oís	oíais	**oísteis**	oiréis	oiríais	oigáis	oyerais	oigan
	oyen	oían	**oyeron**	oirán	oirían	oigan	oyeran	

Irregular Verbs (continued)

Infinitive Present Participle Past Participle	Indicative						Subjunctive		Imperative (commands)
	Present	Imperfect	Preterit	Future	Conditional		Present	Imperfect	

Infinitive Present Participle Past Participle	Present	Imperfect	Preterit	Future	Conditional	Present	Imperfect	Imperative (commands)
poder (ue) to be able, can podiendo podido	**puedo** **puedes** **puede** podemos podéis **pueden**	podía podías podía podíamos podíais podían	**pude** **pudiste** **pudo** **pudimos** **pudisteis** **pudieron**	**podré** **podrás** **podrá** **podremos** **podréis** **podrán**	**podría** **podrías** **podría** **podríamos** **podríais** **podrían**	pueda puedas pueda podamos podáis puedan	pudiera pudieras pudiera pudiéramos pudierais pudieran	
poner to put, to place poniendo **puesto**	**pongo** pones pone ponemos ponéis ponen	ponía ponías ponía poníamos poníais ponían	**puse** **pusiste** **puso** **pusimos** **pusisteis** **pusieron**	**pondré** **pondrás** **pondrá** **pondremos** **pondréis** **pondrán**	**pondría** **pondrías** **pondría** **pondríamos** **pondríais** **pondrían**	ponga pongas ponga pongamos pongáis pongan	pusiera pusieras pusiera pusiéramos pusierais pusieran	**pon**/ no pongas ponga pongamos poned/ no pongáis pongan
querer (ie) to wish, to want, to love queriendo querido	**quiero** **quieres** **quiere** queremos queréis **quieren**	quería querías quería queríamos queríais querían	**quise** **quisiste** **quiso** **quisimos** **quisisteis** **quisieron**	**querré** **querrás** **querrá** **querremos** **querréis** **querrán**	**querría** **querrías** **querría** **querríamos** **querríais** **querrían**	quiera quieras quiera queramos queráis quieran	quisiera quisieras quisiera quisiéramos quisierais quisieran	quiere/ no quieras quiera queramos quered/ no queráis quieran
saber to know sabiendo sabido	**sé** sabes sabe sabemos sabéis saben	sabía sabías sabía sabíamos sabíais sabían	**supe** **supiste** **supo** **supimos** **supisteis** **supieron**	**sabré** **sabrás** **sabrá** **sabremos** **sabréis** **sabrán**	**sabría** **sabrías** **sabría** **sabríamos** **sabríais** **sabrían**	**sepa** **sepas** **sepa** **sepamos** **sepáis** **sepan**	supiera supieras supiera supiéramos supierais supieran	sabe/ no sepas sepa sepamos sabed/ no sepáis sepan
salir to leave, to go out saliendo salido	**salgo** sales sale salimos salís salen	salía salías salía salíamos salíais salían	salí saliste salió salimos salisteis salieron	**saldré** **saldrás** **saldrá** **saldremos** **saldréis** **saldrán**	**saldría** **saldrías** **saldría** **saldríamos** **saldríais** **saldrían**	salga salgas salga salgamos salgáis salgan	saliera salieras saliera saliéramos salierais salieran	sal/ no salgas salga salgamos salid/ no salgáis salgan

Infinitive Present participle Past participle	Present	Imperfect	Preterite	Future	Conditional	Present subjunctive	Imperfect subjunctive	Commands
ser *to be* **siendo** **sido**	soy eres es somos sois son	era eras era éramos erais eran	fui fuiste fue fuimos fuisteis fueron	seré serás será seremos seréis serán	sería serías sería seríamos seríais serían	sea seas sea seamos seáis sean	fuera fueras fuera fuéramos fuerais fueran	sé/ no seas sea seamos sed/ no seáis sean
tener *to have* teniendo tenido	tengo tienes tiene tenemos tenéis tienen	tenía tenías tenía teníamos teníais tenían	tuve tuviste tuvo tuvimos tuvisteis tuvieron	tendré tendrás tendrá tendremos tendréis tendrán	tendría tendrías tendría tendríamos tendríais tendrían	tenga tengas tenga tengamos tengáis tengan	tuviera tuvieras tuviera tuviéramos tuvierais tuvieran	ten/ no tengas tenga tengamos tened/ no tengáis tengan
traer *to bring* **trayendo** traído	traigo traes trae traemos traéis traen	traía traías traía traíamos traíais traían	traje trajiste trajo trajimos trajisteis trajeron	traeré traerás traerá traeremos traeréis traerán	traería traerías traería traeríamos traeríais traerían	traiga traigas traiga traigamos traigáis traigan	trajera trajeras trajera trajéramos trajerais trajeran	trae/ no traigas traiga traigamos traed/ no traigáis traigan
venir *to come* **viniendo** venido (also **prevenir**)	vengo vienes viene venimos venís vienen	venía venías venía veníamos veníais venían	vine viniste vino vinimos vinisteis vinieron	vendré vendrás vendrá vendremos vendréis vendrán	vendría vendrías vendría vendríamos vendríais vendrían	venga vengas venga vengamos vengáis vengan	viniera vinieras viniera viniéramos vinierais vinieran	ven/ no vengas venga vengamos venid/ no vengáis vengan
ver *to see* **viendo** **visto**	veo ves ve vemos veis ven	veía veías veía veíamos veíais veían	vi viste vio vimos visteis vieron	veré verás verá veremos veréis verán	vería verías vería veríamos veríais verían	vea veas vea veamos veáis vean	viera vieras viera viéramos vierais vieran	ve/ no veas vea veamos ved/ no veáis vean

Apéndice 2: *Respuestas para las autopruebas*

Capítulo 1

I.
1. PEPITA: (Muy) Bien, gracias.
   PROFESORA: (Muy) Bien, gracias.
2. PROFESORA: ¿Cómo te llamas?
3. CARMEN: ¿Cómo estás? (¿Qué tal?)
   CARMEN: Muy bien, gracias. (Regular.)
4. PROFESORA: Mucho gusto. (Encantada.)
   CARMEN: El gusto es mío. (Igualmente.)
5. MANUEL: Me llamo Manuel.
   PEPITA: Me llamo Pepita.
   PEPITA: Igualmente.
6. CARMEN: ¿Qué hora es?
   PEPITA: Hasta luego. (Hasta pronto. Chao. Adiós.)

II.
1. Ellos son de Chile pero nosotras somos de México.
2. Tú eres de Colombia pero ustedes son de España.
3. Luis es de El Salvador pero Juan y Elena son de Honduras.

III.
1. (Los jeans cuestan) treinta y cinco dólares.
2. (El suéter cuesta) cincuenta y siete dólares.
3. (La chaqueta cuesta) setenta y dos dólares.
4. (El sombrero cuesta) veintiséis dólares.
5. (El video cuesta) quince dólares.
6. (El CD cuesta) nueve dólares.

IV.
1. Es el catorce de febrero.
2. Es el primero de abril.
3. Es el cuatro de julio.
4. Es el veintitrés de noviembre.
5. Es el veinticinco de diciembre.

V.
1. Es la una y cuarto (la una y quince) de la tarde.
2. Son las nueve y media (las nueve y treinta) de la noche.
3. Son las seis menos diez (las cinco y cincuenta) de la mañana.
4. Son las doce menos veinte (las once y cuarenta) de la noche.
5. Es (el) mediodía.

VI.
1. Me llamo...
2. Muy bien, gracias. (Regular.)
3. Sí, (No, no) soy inflexible y arrogante. Sí, (No, no) soy responsable y generoso/a.
4. Soy de...
5. Es el... de...
6. Es lunes, etc.
7. Son las... (Es la...)
8. Es a las...

VII.
1. With a light kiss on the right cheek in Argentina. With one kiss on each cheek in Spain.
2. It is the celebration of the Epiphany, on January 6th.
3. It is the day when the saint with your name is honored.

Capítulo 2

I. A.
1. el, los ejercicios
2. la, las lecciones
3. la, las páginas
4. el, los Capítulos

   B. un, una, un, una, unas, una, unos

II.
1. Voy a la cafetería (al centro estudiantil).
2. Vamos al laboratorio (a la residencia estudiantil/al cuarto).
3. Vamos al gimnasio.
4. Van a la oficina del profesor.
5. Vas a la librería.
6. Va al cuarto (a la residencia estudiantil/a casa/al apartamento).

III.
1. Compro...
2. Llegan...
3. ¿Estudias...?
4. ¿Trabaja...?
5. Usamos...
6. Escucha...

IV.
1. Asistimos... aprendemos...
2. Vivo... estudio...
3. Comen... toman...
4. Leemos... escribimos...
5. Imprimes... usas...
6. Hago... salgo...

V.
1. Sí, (No, no voy) a clases todos los días.
2. Mi primera clase es a la (las)...
3. Hay... estudiantes en la clase de español.
4. Sí, (No, no) hay (mucha) tarea todas las noches.
5. Sí, (No, no) escribimos en el *Cuaderno de ejercicios* todas las noches.
6. Voy a la librería. Voy al laboratorio (al centro de computadoras).
7. Voy a...
8. Ceno a las...
9. Como en casa (en la cafetería/en mi apartamento/en un restaurante).

VI.
1. Most universities in Spanish-speaking countries are public and financed by the government so students only have to pay for their books and supplies. Programs of study are very rigid and specialized.
2. It is a small tree frog found in Puerto Rico and a symbol of the country.

Capítulo 3

I.
1. tengo
2. tiene
3. tienen
4. tenemos
5. tienes

II.
1. Tengo mis fotos.
2. ¿Tienes tus libros?
3. Tiene su diccionario.
4. Tenemos nuestro televisor.
5. ¿Tienen (ustedes) sus calculadoras?

III.
1. Es la foto de Marta.
2. Son los cuadernos de José.
3. Son los exámenes de los estudiantes.

IV.
1. soy, son perezosos
2. son, es bajo
3. somos, somos... simpáticos
4. es, son difíciles

V.
1. Están en la librería.
2. Estamos en el gimnasio.
3. Estoy en la cafetería (en el centro estudiantil).
4. Está en la oficina de la profesora Falcón.

VI.
1. Estoy nervioso/a (preocupado/a).
2. Están (muy) ocupados.
3. Está (muy) enfermo.
4. Estamos contentos/as.

VII.
1. Tengo... años.
2. Mi madre es simpática, etc. o Mi padre es alto, etc.
3. Mis amigos/as son simpáticos/as, etc.
4. Mis amigos/as están bien (contentos/as), etc.
5. Sí, estamos preocupados/as por nuestras notas en la clase de... o No, no estamos preocupados/as por nuestras notas.
6. Tenemos clases los lunes, etc.
7. Nuestras clases son difíciles, etc.

VIII.
1. Traditional families have more children and the family includes grandparents (often they live with their children and grandchildren) uncles, cousins, etc.
2. Approximately 15% of the population in the USA is Hispanic. Most of them live in California, Texas, New York, and Florida.

Capítulo 4

I.
1. ¿A tus padres les gusta tomar café? Sí, (No, no) les gusta tomar café.
2. ¿A ustedes les gusta la comida italiana? Sí, (No, no) nos gusta la comida italiana.
3. ¿A ustedes les gusta desayunar temprano? Sí, (No, no) nos gusta desayunar temprano.
4. ¿A tu abuela le gustan los postres? Sí, (No, no) le gustan los postres.
5. ¿A ti te gustan los frijoles negros? Sí, (No, no) me gustan los frijoles negros.

II.
1. ¿Pueden cocinar? Sí, (No, no) podemos cocinar.
2. ¿Quieren ir al supermercado? Sí, (No, no) queremos ir al supermercado.
3. ¿Almuerzan a las doce todos los días? Sí, (No, no) almorzamos a las doce todos los días.
4. ¿Prefieren cenar en un restaurante o en la cafetería? Preferimos cenar en un restaurante (en la cafetería).
5. ¿Normalmente piden postres en los restaurantes? Sí, normalmente pedimos postres en los restaurantes. o No, normalmente no pedimos...

III. A.
1. Dos cuestan doscientos cincuenta dólares.
2. Dos cuestan trescientos cuarenta dólares.
3. Dos cuestan novecientos dólares.
4. Dos cuestan dos mil ochocientos dólares.
5. Dos cuestan mil quinientos dólares.
6. Dos cuestan cincuenta mil dólares.

B.
1. mil cuatrocientos noventa y dos
2. mil quinientos ochenta y ocho
3. mil setecientos setenta y seis
4. mil novecientos ochenta y nueve
5. dos mil uno

IV.
1. ¿Qué bebe? o ¿Por qué no bebe vino?
2. ¿Cuál es su fruta favorita?
3. ¿Cuándo trabaja? o ¿Qué hace por la mañana?
4. ¿De dónde es?
5. ¿Cuántos años tiene?
6. ¿Dónde vive?
7. ¿Adónde va? o ¿Cuándo va?
8. ¿Cómo está?

V.
1. Como huevos, etc.
2. Mi postre favorito es el helado, etc.
3. Me gustan más las manzanas, etc.
4. Quiero cenar en...
5. Generalmente duermo... horas.
6. Sí, (No, no) podemos estudiar toda la noche sin dormir.

VI.
1. (*Answers may vary.*)
2. A Mexican tortilla is a thin corn or flour bread, while Spanish tortilla is an omelet typically made with potato, onion and eggs.
3. Oil, tourism, and money sent back by emigrants. There is also developing industry and trade in the areas near the U.S. border.

Capítulo 5

I.
MARTA: Sabes
PABLO: sé, conozco
MARTA: Sabes
PABLO: sé, conozco

II.
1. Tú vienes a clase todos los días. Yo vengo...
2. Nosotros decimos "hola" a los estudiantes al entrar en la clase. Yo digo "hola"...
3. Ellas traen la tarea a clase. Yo traigo...
4. Ana pone la tarea en el escritorio del profesor. Yo pongo...
5. Nosotros sabemos todo el vocabulario. Yo sé...
6. Ustedes hacen preguntas en clase. Yo hago...
7. Ella no sale de clase temprano. Yo no salgo...

III.
1. Marta va a jugar al tenis.
2. Luisa y Alberto van a montar en bicicleta.
3. Voy a ver un partido de fútbol.
4. Vas a preparar la paella.
5. Vamos a ir a la playa.

IV.
1. Está nevando.
2. El niño está durmiendo.
3. Estoy leyendo una novela.
4. Estamos viendo la tele.
5. Mis hermanos están preparando la cena.

V. es, Es, está, Es, es, está

VI. (*Answers may vary.*)
1. Estoy escribiendo los ejercicios de la *Autoprueba*.
2. Voy a estudiar, etc.
3. Hago tarea para la clase de..., salgo con mis amigos, etc.
4. Tengo que estudiar, etc.
5. Tengo ganas de dormir, etc.
6. Conozco muy bien a...
7. Traigo mis libros, etc.
8. Mi estación favorita es la primavera (el verano, etc.) porque...
9. Hace calor (buen tiempo/frío/viento/etc.)

VII.
1. In Caribbean countries baseball is more popular than soccer.
2. The story of a family during Rafael Trujillo's dictatorship in the Dominican Republic.
3. The islands' African heritage is present in the racial makeup of their inhabitants. There is also African influence in the music and dance of Dominicans and Cubans.

Capítulo 6

I.
1. Mi compañero/a de cuarto se despierta.
2. Me levanto.
3. Te bañas.
4. Pepita se cepilla los dientes.
5. Nos ponemos suéteres porque hace frío.
6. Octavio y Manual se visten.

II.
1. Mis padres se gustaron inmediatamente.
2. Mis padres se dieron los números de teléfono ese mismo día.
3. Mis padres se ven todos los días.
4. Mis padres, aún hoy, después de 25 años, se quieren mucho.

III. A.
1. Me duché.
2. Pepita se peinó.
3. Te lavaste la cara.
4. Nos afeitamos.
5. Ellos se cepillaron los dientes.

B.
1. Llegué al trabajo a las nueve.
2. Dos colegas leyeron las noticias del día.
3. Mi colega y yo mandamos un mensaje...
4. Escribiste un memo muy importante.
5. Fuimos a un restaurante chino para almorzar.
6. En la tarde, mi colega llamó a varios de nuestros clientes.
7. Ella resolvió un problema serio.
8. Salimos del trabajo a las cinco de la tarde.

IV. A. 1. Pues, Camila va a invitarme. *o* Camila me va a invitar.
2. Pues, Camila va a invitarnos. *o* Camila nos va a invitar.
3. Pues, Camila va a invitarlos/las. *o* Camila los/las va a invitar.
4. Pues, Camila va a invitarlas. *o* Camila las va a invitar.
5. Pues, Camila va a invitarlos. *o* Camila los va a invitar.
6. Pues, Camila va a invitarla. *o* Camila la va a invitar.
7. Pues, Camila va a invitarte. *o* Camila te va a invitar.

B. 1. Sí, (No, no) quiero verlos/las. *o* Sí, (No, no) los/las quiero ver.
2. Sí, (No, no) voy a llamarlos. *o* Sí, (No, no) los voy a llamar.
3. Sí, (No, no) estoy haciéndola ahora. *o* Sí, (No, no) la estoy haciendo ahora.
4. Sí, (No, no) los completé.
5. Sí, (No, no) voy a estudiarlo. *o* Sí, (No, no) lo voy a estudiar.

V. 1. Por la mañana después de levantarme, me ducho, etc.
2. Antes de acostarme, me cepillo los dientes, etc.
3. Ayer fui a... También...
4. El fin de semana pasado...
5. Sí, lo/la llamé. Hablamos de... *o* No, no lo/la llamé.

VI. 1. Posibles respuestas: Los árabes vivieron en España durante casi 800 años y dejaron huella en muchos aspectos de la cultura española. Hubo una dictadura durante 40 años. Tiene un rey, Juan Carlos I.
2. Posibles respuestas: España pertenece a la Unión Europea. La divisa española es el euro. Los Juegos Olímpicos de 1992 fueron en Barcelona. España se compone de diferentes regiones con su propia identidad cultural. Hay cuatro lenguas oficiales en España.
3. Los azulejos son baldosas de cerámica, traídas originalmente por los árabes cuando se asentaron en la península.

Capítulo 7

I. 1. La gente está dentro del cine (en el cine).
2. La iglesia está detrás del banco.
3. La estatua está cerca del centro de la ciudad.
4. En el quiosco, las revistas están encima de los periódicos.

II. 1. conmigo
2. contigo
3. ellos/ellas
4. nosotros

III. A. 1. Voy a visitar esa iglesia.
2. Voy a visitar este museo.
3. Quiero ver estas obras de arte.
4. Queremos ver aquellos rascacielos.

B. 1. No, prefiero ésas (aquéllas).
2. No, prefiero ésos (aquéllos).
3. No, prefiero ése (aquél).
4. No, prefiero ésa (aquélla).

IV. 1. Carlos y Felipe, ¿pidieron ustedes ayuda a un tutor? Sí, (No, no) la pedimos.
2. Alberto, ¿durmió usted bien después de volver del centro? Sí, (No, no) dormí bien después de volver del centro.
3. Linda y Celia, ¿hicieron ustedes algo interesante en el centro? Sí, hicimos algo interesante. *o* No, no hicimos nada interesante.
4. Linda y Celia, ¿se divirtieron ustedes? Sí, (No, no) nos divertimos.
5. Sr. Sancho, ¿prefirió el director de la escuela la ópera o el ballet? El director de la escuela prefirió la ópera (el ballet).

V. 1. A mí me dio unos CD de rock argentino.
2. A mi hermana le regaló un DVD para aprender a bailar tango.
3. A mis hermanos les compró camisetas de la selección argentina de fútbol.
4. A nosotros nos mandó muchas tarjetas postales desde lugares diferentes.
5. A ti te prestó su cámara.

VI. 1. Los bancos abren a las... de la mañana. Los almacenes abren a las...
2. Sí, gasté mucho dinero en restaurantes el mes pasado. Pedí... *o* No, no gasté...

3. Pedimos...
4. Sí, fuimos al centro para... *o* No, no fuimos al centro...
5. Dormí... horas.
6. Anoche estudié, etc. *o* No hice nada anoche.
7. El fin de semana pasado fuimos..., etc. *o* No hicimos nada.
8. Sí, le di la tarea al profesor. *o* No, no le di la tarea al profesor.

VII. 1. Argentina, Chile
2. Los grupos europeos más numerosos que emigraron a Buenos Aires fueron grupos españoles, italianos, alemanes y armenios.
3. Salvador Allende (primer presidente socialista de Chile), Pinochet (dictador chileno), Juan Perón (dictador argentino), los mapuches (grupo indígena de Chile), Benito Quinquela Martín (pintor argentino), los gauchos (rancheros argentinos), Jorge Luis Borges (escritor argentino), Gabriela Mistral (Premio Nóbel de Literatura)

Capítulo 8

I. A. 1. El abrigo es mío. Las botas son mías. Los guantes son míos. La gorra es mía.
2. La ropa interior es nuestra. Los jeans son nuestros. Las corbatas son nuestras.
3. La blusa es tuya. El vestido es tuyo. La camiseta es tuya. Las medias son tuyas.
4. La ropa de verano es suya. Las faldas son suyas. Los trajes de baño son suyos.

B. 1. Mi primo va con unos amigos suyos.
2. Viviana va con un amigo suyo.
3. Mi hermana y yo vamos con un amigo nuestro.
4. Voy con unos amigos míos.

II. 1. Natalia y Linda trajeron las decoraciones.
2. Pusimos las flores en la mesa.
3. Javier quiso venir pero no pudo.
4. Casi todos los estudiantes vinieron.
5. Estuviste en la fiesta por cuatro horas.
6. Tuve que salir temprano.

III. 1. Se lo regalamos.
2. Se la regaló.
3. Se las regalaron.
4. Se la regalé.
5. Nos lo regaló.

IV. 1. No, no le presto la ropa a nadie.
2. No, yo tampoco me visto muy formal para ir a clase.
3. No, no hay nadie elegante en la clase de español.
4. No, no me pongo nada especial cuando salgo los fines de semana.

V. 1. Las mujeres llevan vestido, etc. Los hombres llevan chaqueta y corbata, etc.
2. Debo llevar mi abrigo, mis suéteres, etc. a Alaska. Debo llevar mi traje de baño, mis pantalones cortos, etc. a la Florida.
3. Sí, fui de compras el fin de semana pasado a Sears. Compré zapatos de tenis, etc. *o* No, no fui de compras...
4. Estuve en casa (en una fiesta, etc.). Estudié, etc.
5. Traje mis libros, etc.

VI. 1. Los tres están situados en el corazón de los Andes. Forman parte del antiguo imperio inca llamado Tahuantinsuyo. La zona está caracterizada por espectaculares picos nevados e impresionantes volcanes.
2. Muchos indígenas todavía llevan la ropa tradicional andina: sarapes, ponchos y sombreros hechos de lana de alpaca.

Capítulo 9

I.
1. Tráiganmelos./No me los traigan.
2. Examínela./No la examine.
3. Descanse más./No descanse más.
4. Estudie las palabras./No estudie las palabras.
5. Lea el libro./No lea el libro.

II.
1. Mis hermanos y yo éramos niños muy buenos.
2. Íbamos a una escuela pequeña.
3. (Yo) Escuchaba a mis maestras.
4. José jugaba al voleibol durante el recreo.
5. Ana y Tere veían la tele por la tarde.
6. Comías galletas todos los días.

III.
1. llamó, habló
2. explicó, estaba
3. preguntó, tenía
4. explicó, dolía, tenía
5. quería, estaba
6. contestó
7. dijo, podía
8. aceptó, dio
9. se sentía, se durmió

IV.
1. La última vez que fui al medico tenía fiebre (*dolor de cabeza, ect.*).
2. En la escuela primaria mi maestro/a preferido/a era (*nombre*). Era muy simpático/a, inteligente,...
3. Mi primera clase en la universidad fue difícil (*divertida, interesante, ect.*). Fue de biología (*matemáticas, literatura, ect.*). El profesor se llamaba (*nombre*).
4. Mi primer día en la universidad fue importante (*complicado, aburrido, ect.*). Fui a clase y conocí a mis compañeros. Fui a la oficina del profesor. Me sentí feliz (*triste, preocupado, ect.*).

V.
1. Frontera con Colombia: Ecuador, Brasil, Panamá, Perú, Venezuela; Frontera con Venezuela: Colombia, Brasil, Guyana.
2. Venezuela significa "pequeña Venecia" porque en el año 1500 los españoles encontraron allí a los indios guajiros, que vivían en chozas suspendidas sobre unas islas muy pequeñas en el Lago Maracaibo.
3. Posibles respuestas de remedios caseros: limonada caliente con ron, whisky o miel para los resfriados o la gripe; hervir clavos de olor en agua para los orzuelos; dorar un ajo al fuego y aplicar al oído con un algodón para el dolor de oídos; asustar, poner jugo de limón en la lengua, poner un hilo rojo en la frente para el hipo; té de flores de naranjo, té de tilo para el nerviosismo; poner los pies en agua de sal tibia para el dolor de pies.
4. Gabriel García Márquez es un autor y periodista colombiano que ganó el Premio Nóbel de Literatura en 1982.

Capítulo 10

I.
1. Beatriz, ¡haz la cama!
2. María, ¡pasa la aspiradora!
3. Luis, ¡devuelve los libros!
4. Laila, ¡pon la mesa!
5. Juanito, ¡saca la basura!

II.
1. No prendas el estéreo, por favor.
2. No uses mi computadora, por favor.
3. No toques mis cosas, por favor.
4. No me digas mentiras, por favor.
5. No te preocupes, por favor.

III.
1. La abuela ha trabajado en el jardín.
2. Todos hemos lavado y secado la ropa.
3. Papá ha limpiado el garaje.
4. Mi hermana ha salido dos veces a bailar.

IV.
1. Había apagado la computadora.
2. Habías imprimido tu trabajo escrito.
3. Habíamos hecho la tarea para la clase de español.
4. Linda y Teresa habían leído la novela para la clase de inglés.

V.
1. Los profesores son tan simpáticos como los estudiantes. *o* Los estudiantes son tan simpáticos como los profesores.
2. Susana tiene tanta paciencia como Ana. *o* Ana tiene tanta paciencia como Susana.
3. Su hermano compró tantos libros como Alberto. *o* Alberto compró tantos libros como su hermano.

VI. A.
1. El reloj Rolex es más caro que el reloj Timex. *o* El reloj Timex es menos caro que el reloj Rolex.
2. Ir de vacaciones a la playa es mejor que ir de vacaciones a las montañas. *o* Ir de vacaciones a las montañas es mejor que ir de vacaciones a la playa.
3. Limpiar la casa es menos divertido que ver la tele. *o* Ver la tele es más divertido que limpiar la casa.

B.
1. Bill Gates es el hombre más rico de los tres.
2. El Honda (el Ford/el Subaru) es el mejor coche de los tres.
3. La revista *National Geographic* (*Newsweek/Movie Line*) es la más interesante de las tres. *o National Geographic* (*Newsweek/Movie Line*) es la revista más interesante de las tres.

VII.
1. Mi casa/apartamento es grande, luminoso y bonito (*pequeño, barato, ect.*).
2. Tengo tantas clases como mi mejor amigo/a. *o* Tengo más/menos clases que mi mejor amigo/a. Yo estudio más/menos que él/ella. *o* Yo estudio tanto como él/ella.
3. La mejor película que he visto últimamente se llama (*nombre*). La película más cómica que he visto últimamente se llama (*nombre*).

VIII.
1. La población de Paraguay es diversa (inmigrantes europeos y 25 tribus indígenas; el 95% de la población es de origen mestizo), mientras que la población de Uruguay es uniforme (casi un 90% desciende de inmigrantes europeos).
2. Cristina Peri Rossi es una escritora uruguaya.
3. El patio es un elemento representativo de muchas casas hispanas y tiene varias funciones importantes, como recibir visitas o dar una pequeña fiesta.

Capítulo 11

I.
1. Quiere que estudiemos más. Quiere que Ana y Linda estudien más.
2. Quiere que Esteban haga la tarea. Quiere que hagamos la tarea.
3. Quiere que Juan vuelva pronto. Quiere que volvamos pronto.
4. Quiere que me divierta en clase. Quiere que nos divirtamos en clase.
5. Quiere que los estudiantes sean puntuales. Quiere que seas puntual.
6. Quiere que (yo) vaya a la biblioteca. Quiere que todos los estudiantes vayan a la biblioteca.

II.
1. Es mejor que vayan durante el invierno.
2. Les recomiendo que exploren las playas remotas.
3. Deseo que se diviertan mucho durante su visita a San Juan.
4. Les sugiero que visiten el bosque pluvial.
5. Es importante que hablen en español todo el tiempo.
6. Les pido a todos que me compren un regalo.

III.
1. Me alegro de que tengamos una cita esta noche.
2. Me gusta que me lleve a un buen restaurante.
3. Temo que llegue un poco tarde.
4. Es increíble que quiera salir conmigo.
5. Espero que no se olvide de la cita.
6. Ojalá que podamos comunicarnos bien.

IV. A.
1. Lidia romperá con su novio.
2. Yo saldré con más frecuencia.
3. Nosotros visitaremos algunos países hispanos.
4. Tú tendrás nuevos amigos.
5. Jorge y Tomás viajarán a Panamá.

B.
1. Yo eliminaría las clases los viernes.
2. Pedro abriría el centro estudiantil las 24 horas.
3. Tú pondrías un límite de tres clases por estudiante por semestre.
4. Linda y Martina hablarían con el decano todas las semanas.
5. Nosotros haríamos cambios en la biblioteca y en la cafetería.

V.
1. La etapa que me parece más interesante es la infancia (la adolescencia, la vejez, ect.) porque...La etapa que me parece menos interesante es.... porque... Normalmente, la gente en esas etapas...
2. Me llevo muy bien con mi mejor amigo (hermano/a, primo/a, novio/a, ect.). De estas personas, me gusta...
3. Sí, hago muchas llamadas de larga distancia. o No, no hago muchas llamadas de larga distancia. Uso un teléfono celular (público, de casa, ect.). Llamo a mi familia (a mi novio/a, a mi amigo/a, ect.). Hablo de...
4. Quiero que mis amigos.... No quiero que mis amigos...
5. Prefiero que la persona con quien vivo (mi compañero/a de piso, mi familia, ect.)... Prefiero que la persona con quien vivo no...
6. Me molesta que mis profesores.... Me gusta que mis profesores... Espero que... Quiero que...

VI.
1. Las dos monedas oficiales de Panamá son el dólar estadounidense y el balboa panameño.
2. El Canal de Panamá es el mayor canal navegable del continente con 82.6 kilómetros (50 millas) de largo. Su construcción comenzó en 1902. En 1999 los EE.UU. le entregaron el canal a los panameños.
3. Los "sombreros de Panamá" se fabrican en Ecuador.

Capítulo 12

I.
1. Trabajé para poder ir a Costa Rica.
2. Salí para Costa Rica el 6 de agosto.
3. Estuve allí por un mes.
4. Viajé por todo el país.
5. Compré un libro sobre los bosques nubosos para mi madre.
6. Lo compré por tres mil colones.

II. A.
1. No creo que ustedes encuentren el remo.
2. Es posible que el guía no sepa hablar español.
3. Dudo que los kayaks lleguen a tiempo.
4. No estoy seguro/a de que estemos remando bien.
5. No creo que puedas ir con nosotros.

B.
1. Pienso que cuesta más de doscientos dólares.
2. No creo que haya un problema serio.
3. Dudo que sea muy larga.
4. Es probable que sean buenos.
5. Estoy seguro/a de que vienen con nosotros.

III.
1. En Centroamérica se come arroz y frijoles.
2. En Argentina se baila tango.
3. En México se hablan muchas lenguas indígenas.
4. En Puerto Rico se baila bomba.
5. En Cuba se producen muchas frutas tropicales.
6. En Centroamérica se cultiva café de gran calidad.

IV.
1. Me interesan más...
2. No creo que pueda pasar unas buenas vacaciones en... porque...
3. Sí, he viajado mucho. o No, no he viajado mucho. He viajado a... Fui a... para... Quiero ir a... Es posible que en el futuro vaya a...
4. Sí, creo que estamos haciendo suficiente para proteger el medio ambiente. o No, no creo que estemos haciendo suficiente para proteger el medio ambiente. Es importante que...
5. Creo que en 10 años la situación del medio ambiente será... Es probable que... Es posible que... Es imposible que...

V.
1. Los ticos son personas costarricenses de ascendencia española. También se usa "ticos" para describir a los costarricenses. Se dice que esta palabra viene del diminutivo y que se usa porque las personas en Costa Rica suelen usar mucho el diminutivo.
2. El "ecoturismo" se practica mucho en Costa Rica. Es el turismo a áreas naturales en las que se conserva el medio ambiente a la vez que se apoya a los residentes locales.
3.
- Las esferas de piedra constituyen un misterio arqueológico de Costa Rica. Se han encontrado más de 300 en el país. Sus medidas varían desde algunos centímetros hasta los 2 metros de diámetro. Hoy en día se usan como decoraciones en edificios de gobierno, hospitales y escuelas, y también como símbolo de estatus en las casas de algunas personas ricas y poderosas.
- Irazú es uno de los cuatro volcanes que rodean a San José. En ocasiones está activo. Mide 3,432 metros de altura y desde él se pueden ver las costas del océano Pacífico y el mar Caribe al mismo tiempo.
- "La negrita" es el apodo con el que se conoce a la santa patrona de Costa Rica, la Virgen de Los Ángeles, debido al color de su piel.

Capítulo 13

I. 1. Es una lástima que el avión llegue tarde.
2. Es bueno que tenga todo el equipaje.
3. Es urgente que vayamos a la aduana.
4. Es horrible que no pueda encontrar el boleto.
5. Es extraño que no haya asistentes de vuelo.
6. Es cierto que no me gusta/guste volar.

II. A. 1. Necesito una habitación que esté en la planta baja.
2. Prefiero un cuarto que tenga camas sencillas.
3. Quiero un baño que sea más grande.
4. Necesito una llave que abra el mini-bar.

B. 1. tenga, tiene
2. esté, est
3. sea, sean
4. sirva, sirve

III. A. *(Answers may vary.)*
1. Hace... que estoy en clase.
2. Hace... que estudio español.
3. Hace... que conozco al/la profesor/a de español.
4. Hace... que vivo en la misma casa o apartamento.
5. Hace... que tengo licencia de conducir un auto.

B. *(Answers may vary.)*
1. Hace... que hablé con su familia.
2. Hace... que compré un regalo para alguien.
3. Hace... que me hice un examen médico.
4. Hace... que visité un museo.
5. Hace... que llegué a la universidad.

IV. 1. Encontramos las horas de las salidas y llegadas de los vuelos.
2. Muestran sus pasaportes, facturan su equipaje, consiguen sus tarjetas de embarque, etc. Compran un boleto, están en el andén, ect.
3. Busco un hotel que tenga... *o* Busco un hotel que sea...
4. Sí, conozco algún lugar que es económico. *o* No, no conozco ningún lugar que sea económico.
5. La última vez fue hace...

V. 1. Tres cosas que tienen en común: 1. Tienen frontera con Honduras; 2. La capital tiene un nombre igual o muy similar al nombre del país; 3. Se habla español; Tres cosas que los hacen diferentes: 1. Guatemala tiene frontera con Belice, El Salvador no; 2. Guatemala es más grande que El Salvador; 3. Guatemala tiene costa con el Océano Pacífico y el Mar Caribe, El Salvador tiene costa sólo con el Océano Pacífico.
2. La pupusa es el plato nacional de El Salvador. Son dos tortillas de maíz rellenas de carne, frijoles y, a veces, queso.
3. Los paradores son un tipo de alojamiento común en el mundo hispano. Son edificios históricos, como monasterios, castillos o palacios, normalmente ubicados en parajes pintorescos, de excepcional belleza.

Capítulo 14

I. 1. Levantémonos a las diez. No nos levantemos...
2. Salgamos para el centro. No salgamos...
3. Vamos (Vayamos) por la ruta más directa. No vayamos...
4. Paremos en el supermercado. No paremos...
5. Crucemos el nuevo puente. No crucemos...
6. Sigamos recto por cuatro cuadras. No sigamos recto...
7. Exploremos el sector histórico de la ciudad. No exploremos...

II. 1. ...me llame.
2. ...la sepa (la tenga).
3. ...me ayudes (me des papel, etc.).
4. ...tenga(s) veintiún años, licencia de conducir y tarjeta de crédito. *o* ...haya uno disponible.
5. ...tenga que trabajar (estudiar, etc.). *o* ...llueva, etc. *o* ...mi(s) padre(s) (esposo/a) insista(n) que yo...

III. A. 1. Quería que limpiara mi cuarto/ fuera al supermercado/ llamara a mis abuelos/ reparara el control remoto.

2. Nos sugirió que escribiéramos los ejercicios del manual/ llegáramos a clase temprano/ hiciéramos los ejercicios del laboratorio/ participáramos en clase.
3. Esperaban que los llamara (llamáramos) para Navidad/ les escribiera (escribiéramos) un mensaje electrónico/ los visitara (visitáramos) en verano/ les regalara una cámara de video.

B. 1. Ojalá (que) mi computadora funcionara.
2. Ojalá (que) comprara un coche híbrido.
3. Ojalá (que) viera más películas 3D pronto.
4. Ojalá (que) la universidad tuviera muchas computadoras nuevas.

IV. *(Answers may vary.)*

V. 1. Es un grupo étnico que llegó a Honduras en el siglo XVIII huyendo de la esclavitud en las colonias inglesas del Caribe. Viven en la costa caribeña de Honduras.
2. Es una forma distinta de conjugar los verbos, empleando la forma *vos* en vez de *tú*. El vos se usa de diferentes maneras en varios países, y está presente en Honduras, Nicaragua, Argentina, Chile y Uruguay.
3. *(Answers may vary.)*

Capítulo 15

I. 1. ...recibí el dinero., ...reciba el dinero.
2. ...me des el número de teléfono del hotel., ... me diste el número de teléfono del hotel.
3. ...me llamaste (llamaras), ...me llames.
4. ...regresemos de la luna de miel., ... regresamos de la luna de miel.

II. *(Answers may vary.)*
1. Dudo que el empleo haya mejorado.
2. Es estupendo que hayamos sido aceptados en un programa de voluntariado en Nicaragua.
3. Es importante que hayas votado en las elecciones generales.
4. Es increíble que la drogadicción haya desaparecido.
5. Siento que los astronautas hayan tenido un accidente.

III. 1. Si ganara más dinero, lo ahorraría.
2. Si lo ahorrara, tendría mucho dinero.
3. Si tuviera mucho dinero, compraría un coche.
4. Si comprara un coche, haría un viaje.
5. Si hiciera un viaje, iría a Puerto Vallarta.
6. Si fuera a Puerto Vallarta, me quedaría allí dos meses.
7. Si me quedara allí dos meses, perdería mi trabajo.
8. Si perdiera mi trabajo, no tendría dinero.

IV. 1. (En mi opinión,) Algunos de los problemas más serios son...
2. Cambiaría... porque...
3. Sí, me preocupaba por... *o* No, no me preocupaba por los problemas del mundo/ otros problemas.
4. (Cuando me gradúe,) Trabajaré, haré un viaje, etc.

V. 1. Univisión y Telemundo.
2. Las telenovelas duran entre ocho y doce meses, mientras que las *soap operas* pueden durar años. Las telenovelas se televisan a la hora punta, por las noches, mientras que las *soap operas* se televisan por la mañana o por la tarde.
3. Cristina Saralegui es la anfitriona del Show de Cristina; Don Francisco es el presentador de Sábado Gigante, el show de variedades de más duración en la historia de la televisión.

Países

Afganistán (el) – afgano/a
Albania – albanés, albanesa

Alemania – alemán, alemana
Andorra – andorrano/a
Angola – angoleño/a
Antigua y Barbuda – antiguano/a
Arabia Saudí o Arabia Saudita – saudí
Argelia – argelino/a
Argentina (la) – argentino/a
Armenia – armenio/a
Australia – australiano/a
Austria – austriaco/a
Azerbaiyán – azerbaiyano/a

Bahamas (las) – bahameño/a
Bahréin – bahreiní
Bangladesh – bengalí
Barbados – barbadense
Bélgica – belga
Belice – beliceño/a
Benín – beninés, beninesa
Bielorrusia – bielorruso/a
Bolivia – boliviano/a
Bosnia-Herzegovina – bosnio/a
Botsuana – bostuano/a
Brasil (el) – brasileño/a
Brunéi Darussalam – bruneano/a
Bulgaria – búlgaro/a
Burkina Faso – burkinés, burkinesa
Burundi – burundés, burundesa
Bután – butanés, butanesa

Cabo Verde – caboverdiano/a
Camboya – camboyano/a
Camerún (el) – camerunés, camerunesa
Canadá (el) – canadiense
Chad – (el) – chadiano/a
Chile – chileno/a
China – chino/a
Chipre – chipriota
Ciudad del Vaticano – vaticano/a
Colombia – colombiano/a
Comoras – comorense/a
Congo (el) – congoleño/a
Corea del Norte – norcoreano/a
Corea del Sur – surcoreano/a
Costa Rica – costarricense
Costa de Marfil – marfileño/a
Croacia – croata
Cuba – cubano/a

Dinamarca – danés, danesa
Dominica – dominiqués/dominiquesa

Ecuador (el) – ecuatoriano/a
Egipto – egipcio/a
Emiratos Árabes Unidos (los) – emiratense
Eritrea – eritreo/a

Eslovaquia – eslovaco/a
Eslovenia – esloveno/a
España – español/a
Estados Unidos de América (los) – estadounidense
Estonia – estonio/a
Etiopía – etíope

Filipinas – filipino/a
Finlandia – finlandés, finlandesa
Francia – francés, francesa
Fiyi – fiyiano/a

Gabón (el) – gabonés, gabonesa
Gambia – gambiano/a
Georgia – georgiano/a
Ghana – ghanés, ghanesa
Granada – granadino/a
Grecia – griego/a
Guatemala – guatemalteco/a
Guinea – guineano/a
Guinea-Bissáu – guineano/a
Guinea Ecuatorial (la) – guineano, ecuatoguineano/a
Guyana – guyanés, guyanesa

Haití – haitiano/a
Honduras – hondureño/a
Hungría – húngaro/a

India (la) – indio/a
Indonesia – indonesio/a
Irán – iraní
Iraq – iraquí
Irlanda – irlandés, irlandesa
Islandia – islandés, islandesa
Islas Cook (las) – cookiano/a
Islas Marshall (las) – marshalés, marshalesa
Islas Salomón (las) – salomonense
Israel – israelí
Italia – italiano/a

Jamaica – jamaicano/a
Japón (el) – japonés, japonesa
Jordania – jordano/a

Kazajstán – kazako/a
Kenia – keniata
Kirguistán – kirguís
Kiribati – kiribatiano/a
Kuwait – kuwaití

Laos – laosiano/a
Lesotho – lesothense
Letonia – letón, letona
Líbano (el) – libanés, libanesa
Liberia – liberiano/a
Libia – libio/a
Liechtenstein – liechtensteiniano/a
Lituania – lituano/a
Luxemburgo – luxemburgués, luxemburguesa

Macedonia – macedonio/a
Madagascar – malgache
Malasia – malayo/a

Malawi – malawiano/a
Maldivas – maldivo/a
Malí – malí
Malta – maltés, maltesa
Marruecos – marroquí
Mauricio – mauriciano/a
Mauritania – mauritano
México – mexicano/a
Micronesia – micronesio/a
Moldavia – moldavo/a
Mónaco – monegasco/a
Mongolia – mongol/a
Montenegro – montenegrino/a
Mozambique – mozambiqueño/a
Myanmar – birmano/a

Namibia – namibio/a
Nauru – nauruano/a
Nepal – nepalés, nepalesa
Nicaragua – nicaragüense
Níger – nigerino/a
Nigeria – nigeriano/a
Noruega – noruego/a
Nueva Zelanda o Nueva Zelandia – neozelandés, neozelandesa

Omán – omaní

Países Bajos (los) – neerlandés, neerlandesa
Pakistán (el) – pakistaní
Paláu – palauano/a
Panamá – panameño/a
Papúa Nueva Guinea – papú
Paraguay (el) – paraguayo/a
Perú (el) – peruano/a
Polonia – polaco/a
Portugal – portugués, portuguesa
Puerto Rico – puertorriqueño/a

Qatar – catarí

Reino Unido – británico/a
República Centroafricana (la) – centroafricano/a
República Checa (la) – checo/a
República Democrática del Congo (la) – congoleño/a
República Dominicana (la) – dominicano/a
Ruanda – ruandés, ruandesa
Rumania o Rumanía – rumano/a
Rusia – ruso/a

Salvador (el) – salvadoreño/a
Samoa – samoano/a
San Cristóbal y Nieves – sancristobaleño/a
San Marino – sanmarinense
Santa Lucía – santalucense
Santo Tomé y Príncipe – santotomense/a
San Vicente y las Granadinas – sanvicentino/a
Senegal (el) – senegalés, senegalesa
Serbia – serbio/a
Seychelles – seychellense
Sierra Leona – sierraleonés, sierraleonesa
Singapur – singapurense
Siria – sirio/a

Somalia – somalí
Sri Lanka cingalés, cingalesa
Suazilandia – suazi
Sudáfrica – sudafricano/a
Sudán (el) – sudanés, sudanesa
Suecia – sueco/a
Suiza – suizo/a
Surinam – surimanés, surimanesa

Tailandia – tailandés, tailandesa
Tanzania – tanzaniano/a
Tayikistán – tayiko/a
Togo (el) – togolés, togolesa
Tonga – tongano/a
Trinidad y Tobago – trinitense
Túnez – tunecino/a
Turkmenistán – turcomano/a
Turquía – turco/a
Tuvalu – tuvaluano/a

Ucrania – ucraniano/a
Uganda – ugandés, ugandesa
Uruguay (el) – uruguayo/a
Uzbekistán – uzbeko/a

Vanuatu – vanuatuense
Vaticano – vaticano/a
Venezuela – venezolano/a
Vietnam – vietnamita

Yemen (el) – yemení
Yibuti – yibutano/a

Zambia – zambiano/a
Zimbabue – zimbabuense

Más profesiones

actor   *actor m*
actress   *actriz f*
administrator   *administrador/a*
ambassador   *embajador/a*
anchorperson   *presentador/a (de radio y televisión)*
artist   *artista m/f*
astrologer   *astrólogo/a*
astronaut   *astronauta m/f*
astronomer   *astrónomo/a*
baker   *panadero/a*
barber   *barbero m*
bodyguard   *guardaespaldas m/f*
bricklayer   *albañil m*
butler   *mayordomo m*
captain   *capitán/a*
carpenter   *carpintero/a*
cartographer   *cartógrafo/a*
chauffeur   *chofer*
consultant, advisor   *consejero/a (en asuntos técnicos)*
cook   *cocinero/a*
counselor   *consejero/a (en asuntos personales)*
dancer   *bailarín m/ f*
dentist   *dentista m/f*

designer   diseñador/a
diplomat   diplomático/a
dishwasher   lavaplatos
electrician   electricista m/f
engineer   ingeniero/a
farmer   agricultor/a
firefighter   bombero/a
fisherman, fisherwoman   pescador/a
flight attendant   azafata f, sobrecargo m/f
florist   florista m/f
flower grower   floricultor/a
foreman, forewoman   capataz/a
forest ranger   guardabosque m/f
gardener   jardinero/a
geographer   geógrafo/a
geologist   geólogo/a
governor   gobernador/a
hairdresser   peluquero/a
historian   historiador/a
janitor   conserje m/f
jeweler   joyero/a
journalist   periodista m/f
judge   juez m/f
laborer, worker   obrero/a
librarian   bibliotecario/a
maid   sirvienta f
make-up artist   maquillador/a
male nurse, nurse   enfermero/a
manager   gerente m/f
manufacturer   fabricante m
masseur, masseuse   masajista m/f
mathematician   matemático/a
mayor, mayoress   alcalde/sa
mechanic   mecánico/a
miner   minero/a
minister   ministro/a
musician   músico/a
notary (public)   notario/a
novelist   novelista m/f
office worker   oficinista m/f
painter   pintor/a
parking attendant   guardacoches m/f
pastry cook   pastelero/a
philosopher   filósofo/a
photographer   fotográfo/a
pianist   pianista m/f
pilot   piloto m/f
playwright, dramatist   dramaturgo/a
plumber   plomero, fontanero m
poet, female poet   poeta/isa
police superintendent   comisario/a
policeman, policewoman   policía m/f
politician   político/a
priest   sacerdote m
psychiatrist   psiquiatra m/f
psychologist   psicólogo/a
radio announcer   locutor/a
real estate agent   agente de bienes raíces
    m/f

sailor   marinero/a
sculptor, sculptress   escultor/a
shopkeeper   tendero/a
singer   cantante m/f
soldier   soldado/mujer soldado
tailor   sastre/a
technician   técnico/a
teller   cajero/a (en banco)
tour guide   guía m/f turístico
tradesman, tradeswoman   comerciante m/f
translator   traductor/a
truck driver   camionero/a
veterinarian   veterinario/a
warder, jailer   carcelero/a
wrestler   luchador/a
writer   escritor/a

Otras materias académicas

anatomy   anatomía
anthropology   antropología
architecture   arquitectura
Arabic (language)   árabe
astronomy   astronomía
biochemistry   bioquímica
botany   botánica
business administration   administración
    de empresas
Chinese (language)   chino
civil engineering   ingeniería civil
computer science   computación
creative writing   escritura creativa
dramatic arts   teatro, artes dramáticas
drawing   dibujo
electrical engineering   ingeniería
    eléctrica
film   cine
finance   finanzas
genetics   genética
geography   geografía
geology   geología
geometry   geometría
gymnastics   gimástica
Hebrew (language)   hebreo
industrial engineering   ingeniería
    industrial
Italian (language)   italiano
Japanese (language)   japonés
journalism   periodismo
jurisprudence   derecho
Latin (language)   latin
law   derecho
linguistics   lingüística
mechanical engineering   ingeniería
    mecánica
microbiology   microbiología
nursing   enfermería
nutrition   nutrición

obstetrics   obstetricia
painting   pintura
pharmacology   farmacología
philology   filología
physical education   educación física
physiology   fisiología
Russian (language)   ruso
sculpture   escultura
social work   trabajo social
statistics   estadística
swimming   natación
theology   teología
zoology   zoología

Vocabulario: *Spanish-English*

A

a at, to 2
a veces sometimes 2
abierto/a open 3
abogado/a *m/f* lawyer 6
aborto *m* abortion 15
abra la boca open your mouth 9
abrazar to hug 3
abrigo *m* coat 8
abril April 1
abrir to open 7
abrocharse el cinturón to fasten one's seat belt 13
abuela *f* grandmother 3
abuelo *m* grandfather 3
abuelos *m, pl.* grandparents 3
aburrido/a bored 3; boring 3
acampar to camp 12
accidente *m* accident 14
aceite *m* oil 4
aceituna *f* olive 4
aconsejar to advise 11
acordarse (ue) de to remember 11
acostarse (ue) to go to bed 6
acuerdo *m* **de paz** *f* peace agreement 15
adiós good-bye 1
adicto/a *m/f* addicted 14
adolescencia adolescence 10
adolescentes *m, pl.* adolescents 10
¿adónde? (to) where? 2
aduana *f* customs 13
adultos *m, pl.* adults 11
aerolínea *f* airline 13
aeropuerto *m* airport 13
afeitarse to shave 6
afiche *m* poster 10
afinar el motor tune the motor 14
agosto August 1
agua *f (but el agua)* water 4
ahora now 2
ahorrar to save (money) 7
aire acondicionado air conditioning 13
aire libre *m* outdoors 12
ajo *m* garlic 4
al + *infinitivo* upon (doing something) 7
al lado de beside 7
alegrarse (de) to be glad (about) 11
alemán *m* German (language) 2
alergia *f* allergy 9
alfombra *f* rug, carpet 10
álgebra *f (but el álgebra)* algebra 2
algo anything, something 8
algodón *m* cotton 8
alguien anyone, someone, somebody 8
algún (alguno/a/os/as) any, some, someone 8
allí there 3
almacén *m* department store 7
almohada *f* pillow 13
almorzar (ue) to have lunch 4

almuerzo *m* lunch 4
alpinismo/el andinismo *m* mountain climbing 12
alquilar to rent 10
alto/a tall 3
alumno/a *m/f* student 2
amo/a *m/f* **de casa** homemaker 6
amable friendly, kind 3
amar to love 3
amarillo/a yellow 5
ambulancia *f* ambulance 9
amigo/a *m/f* friend 3
amistad *f* friendship 11
amor *m* love 11; **amor a primera vista** love at first sight 11
anaranjado/a orange (color) 5
ancianos *m/***la anciana** *f /***el anciano** *m pl.* elderly 11
andén *m* platform 13
andinismo *m,* **alpinismo** *m* mountain climbing 11
anillo *m* ring 8
animal *m* animal 11
año *m* year 4; **tener… años** to be … years old 3
anoche last night 6
anteayer day before yesterday 6
antes de (clase) *prep.* before (class) 2; **antes de que** *conj* before 15
antipático/a disagreeable, unpleasant (persons) 3
apagar to turn off 10
aparato *m* device, appliance, machine 14
apartamento *m* apartment 2
apoyar to support (a candidate/cause) 15
aprender to learn 2
apuntes *m, pl.* notes 2
aquel/aquella *adj.* that 6; **aquél/ aquélla** *pron* that one 6
aquellos/as *adj.* those 6; **aquéllos/as** *pron* those 6
aquí here 3
araña *f* spider 12
árbol *m* tree 5
arena *f* sand 12
aretes *m, pl.* earrings 8
argentino/a *m/f, n., adj* Argentinian 1
arma *f* weapon 15
arroz *m* rice 4
arte *m (but las artes)* art 2
ascensor *m* elevator 13
aseos *m, pl.* restroom 13
asiento *m* seat 13
asistente de vuelo *m/f* flight attendant 13
asistir (a) to attend 2
aterrizar to land 13
audífonos *m, pl.* headphones 2
aula *f (but el aula)* classroom 1
auricular *m* earphone 14
auto *m* car 3

autobús *m* bus 7; **parada** *f* **de autobús** bus stop 7
autopista *f* highway 14
¡Auxilio! Help! 14
avenida *f* avenue 7
aventura *f* adventure 12
averiguar to find out, inquire 6
avión *m* airplane 13
ayer yesterday 6
ayudar (a) to help 10
azúcar *m* sugar 4
azul blue 5

B

bailar to dance 5
bajar to go down 10; **bajarse de** to get off, to get out of . . . 13
bajo/a short 3
baloncesto *m* basketball 5
balsa *f* raft 12
balsismo *m* rafting 12
banana *f* banana 4
bañarse to take a bath, bathe 6
banco *m* bank 7; bench 7
bañera *f* bathtub 10
baño *m* bathroom 10, restroom 14; **baño privado** private bath 13
bar *m* bar 7
barato/a inexpensive 8
barco *m* boat 12
básquetbol *m* basketball 5
basura *f* garbage 12
bebé *m/f* baby 3
beber to drink 2
bebida *f* drink, beverage 4
beige beige 5
béisbol *m* baseball 5
besar to kiss 3
biblioteca *f* library 2
bicicleta *f* bicycle 5
bien fine 1; well 3
bienvenido/a welcome 13
billete *m* ticket 13; **billete de ida y vuelta** round trip ticket 13, **de ida/ sencillo** one-way ticket 13
billetera/la cartera *f* wallet 8
biología *f* biology 2
bisabuela *f* great-grandmother 3
bisabuelo *m* great-grandfather 3
bistec *m* steak 4
blanco/a white 5
blusa *f* blouse 8
boca *f* mouth 9
bocadillo *m* sandwich 4
boda *f* wedding 11
boleto *m* ticket 13; **boleto de ida y vuelta** round trip ticket 13; **boleto de primera/ segunda clase** *m* first/ second class ticket 13
bolígrafo *m* pen 2
boliviano/a *m/f, n., adj* Bolivian 1

bolso/a *m* purse, bag 8
bomba bomb 15
bonito/a good-looking, pretty 3
borrador *m* eraser 2
bosque *m* forest 12
botas *f, pl.* boots 8
bote *m* boat (small) 12; **bote de basura** *m* garbage can 10
botones *m* bellhop 13
brazo *m* arm 9
brócoli *m* broccoli 4
bucear to scuba dive, skin dive 12
bueno/a good 3; **es bueno** it's good 13
bufanda *f* scarf 8
buscador *m* search engine 14
buscar to look for 2
buzón *m* mailbox 7

C

caballo *m* horse 12
cabeza *f* head 9; **dolor** *m* **de cabeza** headache 9
cable *m* cable 14
cada each, every 9
cadena *f* chain 8
café *m* coffee 4; coffee place 7
cafetería *f* cafeteria 2
cajero *m* **automático** ATM machine 7
cajero/a *m/f* cashier 6
calcetines *m, pl.* socks 8
calculadora *f* calculator 2
cálculo *m* calculus 2
calefacción *f* heating 13
calentamento global *m* global warming 12
caliente hot (temperature, not spiciness) 5
calle *f* street 7
cama *f* bed; **cama doble** double bed; **cama sencilla** single bed 6, 13
cámara *f* camera 12
cámara (de video) *f* (video) camera 14
camarera *f* maid (hotel) 13
camarón *m* shrimp 4
cambiar to change, exchange 7
cambio *m* change, small change, exchange 7
camilla *f* gurney 9
caminar to walk 5
camino *m* road 14
camión *m* truck 14
camisa *f* shirt 8
camiseta *f* T-shirt, undershirt 8
campamento *m* camp 12
campo *m* country 3
cáncer *m* cancer 15
candidato/a *m/f* candidate 15
cansado/a tired 3
cansarse to get tired 9
cantar to sing 5
capa *f* **de ozono** ozone layer 12

capítulo *m* chapter 2
cara *f* face 9
¡Caramba! Oh my gosh! 14
cariñoso/a affectionate 11
carne *f* meat, beef 4; **carne de cerdo/ puerco** pork 4; **carne de res** beef 4
caro/a expensive 8
carretera *f* road 14
carro *m* car 3
carta *f* letter 7
cartera *f* wallet 8
casa *f* home, house 2; **amo/a** *m/f* **de casa** homemaker 6; **en casa** at home 3
casado/a married 11; **recién casados** *m, pl.* newlyweds 11
casarse (con) to get married (to) 11
cascada *f* waterfall 12
casi almost; **casi nunca** rarely; **casi siempre** almost always 2
castillo de arena *m* sand castle 12
catarata *f* waterfall 12
causa (a causa de) because of 12
CD *m* CD, compact disk 2
cebolla *f* onion 4
celoso/a jealous 11
cena *f* supper, dinner 3
cenar to have dinner 2
centro comercial mall, shopping center 7; **centro estudiantil** student center 2
cepillarse el pelo to brush one's hair 6; **cepillarse los dientes** to brush one's teeth 6
cepillo *m* brush 6; **cepillo de dientes** toothbrush 6
cerca de near 7
cerdo *m* pig 12; **chuleta** *f* **de cerdo** pork chop 4; **carne** *f* **de cerdo** pork 4
cereal *m* cereal 4
cereza *f* cherry 4
cerrado/a closed 3
cerrar (ie) to close 7
cerveza *f* beer 4
champú *m* shampoo 6
chao bye, so-long 1
chaqueta *f* jacket 8
cheque *m* check 7; **cheque de viajero** traveler's check 7
chica *f* girl 3
chico *m* boy 3
chileno/a *m/f, n., adj* Chilean 1
chimenea *f* fireplace, chimney 10
chocar to crash, collide 14
choque *m* crash 14
chorizo *m* sausage 4
chuleta *f* **de cerdo/puerco** pork chop 4
ciclismo *m* **de montaña** mountain biking 12
cielo *m* sky 12
ciencias *f, pl.* **políticas** political science 2

cierto: es . . . it's true, correct 13
cine *m* movie theater, cinema 7
cinturón *m* belt 8; **abrocharse el cinturón** to fasten one's seat belt 13
cita *f* date, appointment 11
ciudad *f* city 3
ciudadano/a *m/f* citizen 15
¡Claro! Of course! 14
clase *f* class 2
clima *m* weather 5
clóset *m* closet 8
cobija *f* blanket 13
cobrar to cash, to charge 7
coche *m* car 3
cocina *f* kitchen 10
cocinar to cook 4
código *m* **de área** area code 11
cola *f* line (of people or things) 7
colegio *m* high school 3
colina *f* hill 12
collar *m* necklace 8
colombiano/a *m/f, n., adj* Colombian 1
comedor *m* dining room 10
comer to eat 2
comida *f* food, main meal 3
¿cómo? how? 4; **¿Cómo está usted?** How are you? (*formal*) 1; **¿Cómo estás?** How are you? (*informal*) 1; **¿Cómo se llama usted?** What's your name (*formal*)? 1; **¿Cómo te llamas?** What's your name? (*informal*) 1
cómoda *f* bureau 10
cómodo/a comfortable 14
compañero/a *m/f* **de cuarto** roommate 6
compañía *f* company 6
comprar to buy 2
comprender to understand 2
comprensivo/a understanding 11
comprometerse (con) to get engaged (to) 11
computación *f* computer science 2
computadora *f* computer 2; **computadora portátil** laptop/ notebook computer) 13
computadora portátil *f* laptop 14
comunicarse to communicate 11
con with 4; **con permiso** pardon me, excuse me 1; **con tal (de) que** provided that 14
con . . . de anticipación . . . ahead of time 13
conducir to drive 14
conductor/a driver 14
conexión *f* connection 14
congestión *f* **nasal** nasal congestion 9
conocer to meet, know, be acquainted with 5
conservar to save, conserve 12
constantemente constantly 6
control remoto *m* remote control 14

construir construct 15

consultorio *m* **del médico/de la médica** doctor's office 9

contabilidad *f* accounting 2

contador/a *m/f* accountant 6

contaminación *f* pollution 12

contar (ue) to count, tell, narrate (a story or incident) 7, 8

contento/a happy 3

contestar to answer 7

contestador automático *m* answering machine 11

continuar to continue 14

contribuir (y) to contribute 12

copa *f* goblet 10

corazón *m* heart 9

corbata *f* tie 8

correo electrónico *m* e-mail 2

correr to run 5

corrupción *f* corruption 15

cortar: . . . **el césped** to cut the lawn 10; **cortarse** to cut oneself 5; **cortarse el pelo/ las uñas/ el dedo** to cut one's hair/nails/a finger 6

cortina *f* curtain 10

corto/a short 8; de manga corta short-sleeved 8

cosa *f* thing 8

costar (ue) to cost 4

costarricense *m/f, n., adj.* Costa Rican 1

creer to believe 11

crema *f* cream 4; **crema de afeitar** shaving cream 6

crucero *m* cruise ship 12

cruzar to cross 14

cuaderno *m* notebook 2

cuadra *f* (city) block 14

cuadro *m* picture, painting 4

¿cuál? which (one)? 4

¿cuáles? which (ones)? 4

cuando when 4; **¿cuándo?** when? 2

¿cuánto/a? how much? 4

¿cuántos/as? how many? 3

cuarto a quarter 1

cuarto *m* room 2; **cuatro de estar** *m* living room/family room 10

cuarto/a fourth 12

cubano/a *m/f, n., adj.* Cuban 1

cubo *m* **de la basura** trash can 10

cuchara *f* spoon 10

cucharita *f* teaspoon 10

cuchillo *m* knife 10

cuello *m* neck 9

cuenta *f* bill, check 7; account 7

cuero *m* leather 8

cuerpo *m* body 9

cuidar to take care of 2

cumpleaños *m* birthday 2

cuñada *f* sister-in-law 3

cuñado *m* brother-in-law 3

cura *f* cure 15

D

dar to give 5; **dar a luz** to give birth 11

dar de comer to feed 15

dar un paseo to take a walk/stroll 5; **dar una caminata** to take a hike 12

de *prep* of, from 1; **de repente** suddenly 9

debajo de beneath, under 7

deber + *infinitive* ought to, should (do something) 5

débil weak 3

décimo/a tenth 14

decir (i) to say, tell 5

dedo *m* finger 9

desforestación *f* deforestation 12

dejar to leave 13; **dejarse** to leave behind 13; **dejar un mensaje** to leave a message 11

delante de in front of 7

delgado/a thin 3

delincuente *m* delinquent, offender, criminal 15

delito *m* misdemeanor, crime 15

demasiado *adv.* too, too much 14

demora *f* delay 13

dentro de inside 7

dependiente/a *m/f* store clerk 6

deporte *m* sport 5

depositar to deposit 7

deprimido/a depressed 9

derecha: a la ... to the right 14

derecho straight, straight ahead 14

derechos *m, pl.* **humanos** human rights 15

desafortunadamente unfortunately 6

desamparados *m, pl.* homeless people 15

desayunar to have breakfast 2

desayuno *m* breakfast 3

descansar to rest 5; **descanse** rest 9

desear want, wish 4

desempleo *m* unemployment 15

desierto *m* desert 12

desinflado/a flat, deflated (tire) 14

desodorante *m* deodorant 6

despedirse (i, i) to say good-bye 13

despegar to take off 13

desperdiciar to waste 12

despertador *m* alarm clock 6

despertarse (ie) to wake up 6

después de (clase) after (class) 2; afterwards, later 7; **después de** *prep* after 7; **después de que** *conj* after 15

destruir (y) destroy 12

destrucción *f* destruction 12

detrás de behind 7

devolver (ue) to return (something) 8

día *m* day 1; **buenos días** good morning 1

diarrea *f* diarrhea 9

diccionario *m* dictionary 2

diciembre December 1

diente *m* tooth 9

digital digital 14

difícil difficult, hard 3

Diga ¡ah! Say ah! 9

dinero *m* money 6

dirección address 7; **dirección** *f* **electrónica** e-mail address 2

disco compacto *m* CD, compact disk 2

discriminación *f* discrimination 15

Disculpe I am sorry. 1

disfrutar de to enjoy (something) 13

divertido/a *m/f* amusing, fun 3

divertirse (ie) to have a good time 6

divorciado/a divorced 11

divorciarse to get divorced 11

divorcio divorce 11

doblar to turn 14

doctor/a *m/f* doctor 2

dolor *m* **de cabeza** *f* headache 9; **dolor de estómago** *m* stomachache 9

dolor de garganta *f* sore throat 9

domingo *m* Sunday 1

dominicano/a *m/f n., adj* Dominican 1

¿dónde? where 3; **¿adónde?** (to) where? 2; **¿de dónde...?** from where? 4

dormir (ue) to sleep 4; **dormirse (ue)** to go to sleep, to fall asleep 6

dormitorio *m* bedroom 10

drogadicción *f* drug addiction 15

drogas *f, pl* drugs 15

ducha *f* shower 10

ducharse to take a shower 6

dudar to doubt 12

durazno *m* peach 4

E

echar gasolina to put gas (in the tank) 14

economía *f* economics 2

ecuatoriano/a *m/f, n., adj* Ecuadorian 1

edificio *m* building 7

efectivo *m* cash 7

ejercicio *m* exercise 2; **hacer ejercicio** to exercise, to do exercises 5

ejército *m* army 15

el *m, definite article* the 2

él *m, subj* he 1; *obj. prep. pron.* him 6

elección *f* election 15

eliminar to eliminate 15

ella *f, subj* she 1; *obj. of prep.* her 6

ellas *f, subj* they 1; *obj. of prep.* them 6

ellos *m, subj* they 1; *obj. of prep.* them 6

embarazada pregnant 9

emergencias emergency f, pl. 9

emocionante exciting 12

empacar to pack 13

empezar (ie) (a) to begin 7

empleado/a *m/f* employee 6

empleo *m* job 15

empresa *f* business 6

en in, at 2; on 7; **en caso de que** in case 14

en vez de instead of 7
enamorarse (de) to fall in love (with) 11
encantado/a delighted (to meet you) 1
encantar to really like, love 5; to delight, to enchant 11
encima de on top of, above 7
encontrar (ue) to find 7; **encontrarse (ue) (con)** to meet up (with) (by chance) 11**enero** January 1
enfermarse to get/become sick 9
enfermero/a m/f nurse 6
enfermo/a sick 3
enfrente de in front of, opposite 7
enlace m link 14
enojado/a angry 11
enojarse to get angry 11
ensalada f salad 4
entender (ie) to understand 4
entonces then 6
entrada f (admission) ticket 7
entrar (en/a) to enter, go into 7
entre between, among 7
entrevista f interview 15
enviar to send 2
equipaje m luggage 13
equipo m team 5
escalar (la montaña) to climb (the mountain) 12
escalera f stairs 10
escalofrío m chill 9
escoger to choose 15
escribir to write 2
escritorio m (teacher's) desk 2
escuchar to listen to 2
escuela f elementary school 3
ese/a adj. that 6; **ése/a** pron. that one 6
esos/as adj. those 6; **ésos/as** pron. those 6
espalda f back 9
español m Spanish (language) 2
español/a m/f, n., adj. Spanish 1
especie animal f animal species 12
espejo m mirror 10
esperar to wait (for) 7; to hope, expect 11
esposa f wife 3
esposo m husband 3
esquiar to ski 5
esquina f (street) corner 14
esta this, that 6; **esta mañana** this morning 2; **esta noche** tonight 2; **esta tarde** this afternoon 2
estación f season 4; **estación de autobuses** bus station 14
estación de servicio/la gasolinera service/gas station 14
estación de ferrocarril railroad station 14
estacionamiento m parking 14
estacionar to park 14

estadounidense m/f, n., adj American (from the United States) 1
estampilla f stamp 7
estante m bookshelf, shelf 10
estar to be 3; **estar a favor de** to be in favor of 15
estar casado/a (con) to be married (to) 11
estar comprometido/a to be engaged 11
estar de pie to be standing 8
estar de vacaciones f, pl. to be on vacation 12
estar embarazada to be pregnant 11
estar enamorado/a de to be in love (with) 11
estar en contra de to be against 15
estar juntos/as to be together 11
estar listo to be ready 12
estar prometido/a to be engaged 11
estar seguro/a (de) to be sure of 12
estar sentado/a to be seated 9
estatua f statue 7
este/a adj. this 6; **éste/a** pron. this one 6
estéreo m stereo 10
estómago m stomach 9; **dolor** m **de estómago** stomachache 9
estornudar to sneeze 9
estos/as adj. these 6; **estos/as** pron. these 6
estrella f star 12
estresado/a stressed 3
estudiante m/f student 2
estudiar to study 2
estufa f stove 10
etapas f, pl. **de la vida** stages of life 11
evitar to avoid 12
examen m exam 2
examinar to examine 9
explicar to explain 8
exploración f **del espacio** (outer) space exploration 15
explosión f explosion 15
extinción f extinction 12
extrañar to miss 11
extraño: es . . . it's strange 13

F

fábrica f factory 6
fácil easy 3
fácilmente easily 6
facturar to check (baggage) 13
falda f skirt 8
familia f family 2
farmacia f pharmacy 9
fascinar to be fascinating to, to fascinate 11
favor (por favor) please 1
febrero February 1
fecha f date 1
felicidades f congratulations 11

fenomenal terrific 1; **es fenomenal** it's wonderful 13
feo/a ugly 3
fiebre f fever 9
fiel faithful 11
fiesta f party 2
fila f line (of people or things) 7
filosofía f philosophy 2
fin m **de semana** weekend 2; **fin de semana pasado** last weekend 6; **por fin** finally 9
finanzas f, pl finances 2
firmar to sign 7
física f physics 2
flaco/a skinny 3
flores f, pl flowers 5
fogata f campfire 12
fracturar(se) (el brazo/ la pierna) to break one's (arm/leg) 9
francés m French (language) 2
frecuentemente frequently 6; **con frecuencia** frequently 2
fregadero m sink (kitchen) 10
frenos m, pl. brakes 14
frente a in front of, opposite, facing 7
fresa f strawberry 4
frijoles m, pl beans 4
frío/a cold 5; **hace (mucho) frío** it's (very) cold 5
frito/a fried 4
frontera f border 15
fruta f fruit 3
fuego m fire 12
fuera de outside 7
fuerte strong 3
fumar to smoke 5
funcionar to run, work, function (machine) 14
fútbol m soccer 5; **fútbol americano** football 5

G

gafas f, pl. eyeglasses 8; **gafas de sol** sunglasses 8
galleta f cookie 4
gallina f chicken 12
gamba f shrimp 4
ganar to win 5; to earn, make money 6
garaje m garage 10
garganta f throat 9; **dolor** m **de garganta** sore throat 9
gasolina f gas 14
gasolinera f gas station 14
gastar to spend 7
gato m cat 3
gel m gel 6
generalmente generally 6
gente f people 7
gerente m/f manager 15
gimnasio m gym, gymnasium 2
gobierno m government 15

golf *m* golf 5
gordo/a fat 3
gorra *f* cap 8
gracias thank you/thanks 1
grande big, large 3
granja *f* farm 12
gratis free of charge 14
gripe *f* flu 9
gris gray 5
guantes *m, pl.* gloves 8
guapo/a good-looking, pretty/ handsome 3
guardar to keep 10, to save 14
guatemalteco/a *m/f, n., adj.* Guatemalan 1
guerra *f* war 15
guía *f* **telefónica** phone book 11
guisante *m* pea 4
guitarra *f* guitar 4
gustar to like 4; **el gusto es mío** the pleasure is mine 1

H

habitación *f* room 10
habitación doble double room 13
habitación sencilla single room 13
hablar to speak 2
hace buen/mal tiempo the weather is nice/bad 5
hace (mucho) calor/fresco/frío/sol/ viento it's (very) hot/cool/cold/ sunny/windy 5
hace sol it's sunny 5
hacer to do, make 2
hacer la cama to make the bed 10
hacer cola to get (stand) in line 7
hacer ejercicio to exercise, work out, do exercises 5
hacer escala to have a layover 13
hacer *esnórquel* to go snorkeling 12
hacer fila to get (stand) in line 6
hacer las maletas to pack 13
hacer reservaciones/reservas to make reservations 14
hacer *surf* to surf 12
hacer un análisis de sangre do a blood test 9
hacer un viaje en crucero/en barco to go on a cruise, take a trip on a ship/ boat/cruise ship 12
hacer una cita to make an appointment 9
hambre *f* (*but el* **hambre**) hunger 15
hamburguesa *f* hamburger 4
hasta: hasta mañana see you tomorrow. 1; **hasta pronto** see you soon 1; **hasta que** until 15
hay there is/are 2
helado *m* ice cream 4
herida *f* **grave** serious wound 9
hermana *f* sister 3

hermanastra *f* stepsister 3
hermanastro *m* stepbrother 3
hermano *m* brother 2
hermoso/a good-looking, pretty/ handsome 3
híbrido *m* hybrid 14
hielo *m* ice 4
hierba *f* grass 12
hija *f* daughter 3
hijo *m* son 3
historia *f* history 2
hoja *f* **de papel** sheet of paper 2; **hojas** *f, pl.* leaves 5
hola hello/hi 1
hombre *m* man 3; **hombre de negocios** businessman 6
hombro *m* shoulder 9
hondureño/a *m/f, n., adj* Honduran 1
hora *f* time 1
horario *m* schedule 13
horno *m* oven 10; **al horno** baked 4
horrible: es . . . it's horrible 13
hospital *m* hospital 9
hostal *m* hostel 13
hotel *m* hotel 13
hoy today 1
hueso *m* bone 9
huésped/a *m/f* guest 13
huevo *m* egg 4; **huevos fritos** fried eggs 4; **huevos revueltos** scrambled eggs 4

I

iglesia *f* church 7
igualdad *f* equality 15
igualmente nice meeting you too 1
impermeable *m* raincoat 8
importante: es . . . it's important 13
importar to be important to, to matter 12
imposible: es . . . it's impossible 13
impresora *f* printer 2
imprimir to print 2
improbable: es . . . it's improbable 13
incendios *m, pl.* **forestales** forest fires 12
infancia *f* infancy 11
infección *f* infection 9
informar/reportar to inform 15
informática *f* computer science 2
inglés *m* English (language) 2
inmediatamente immediately 6
inodoro *m* toilet 10
improbable: es . . . it's improbable 13
insectos *m, pl.* insects 12
insistir (en) to insist (on) 11
inteligente intelligent 3
intentar to try 14
interesante: es . . . it's interesting 13
interesar to be interesting to, to interest 12
invertir (ie, i) to invest 7
investigación *f* research 15

invierno *m* winter 5
invitar (a) to invite 7
inyección *f* injection 9
ir to go 2
ir de compras to go shopping 5
ir(se) de vacaciones to go on vacation 12
irse leave, depart, to go away 11
isla *f* island 12
italiano *m* Italian (language) 5
izquierda *f*: **a la...** to the left 14

J

jabón *m* soap 6
jamón *m* ham 4
japonés *m* Japanese (language) 5
jardín *m* garden 10
jeans *m, pl.* jeans 8
jefa *f* boss 15
jefe *m* boss 15
joven young 3
jóvenes *m, pl.* **/los adolescentes** young people, adolescents 11
joyas *f, pl.* jewelry 8
joyería *f* jewelry shop 7
judía *f* **verde** green bean 4
jueves *m* Thursday 1
jugar (ue) to play 5; **jugar al (deporte)** to play (sport) 5
jugo *m* juice 4
julio July 1
junio June 1
juntos/as: estar ... to be together 11
justicia *f* justice 15
justo fair 13; **no es . . .** it's unfair 13
juventud *f* youth 11

K

kayak *m* kayak 12
kilómetro *m* kilometer 14

L

la *f, definite article* the 2; *dir. obj.* her, you (f), it (f) 5
labio *m* lip 9
laboratorio *m* laboratory 2
lado: al . . . de beside 7
lago *m* lake 5
lámpara *f* lamp 10
lana *f* wool 8
langosta *f* lobster 4
lápiz *m* pencil 2
largo/a long 8; **de manga larga** long- sleeved 8
las *dir. obj.* them (f), you (f, pl.) 5
las *f, pl. definite article* the 2
lástima: es una ... it's a shame 13
lastimarse to hurt oneself 9
lavabo *m* sink (bathroom) 10
lavadora *f* washer 10
lavamanos *m* bathroom sink 10

lavaplatos *m* dishwasher 10

lavar: . . . los platos to wash the dishes 10

lavarse to wash oneself 5; **lavarse las manos/la cara** to wash one's hands/face 6

le *ind. obj.* you, him, her (to/for . . .) 8

lección *f* lesson 2

leche *f* milk 4

lechuga *f* lettuce 4

lector electrónico *m* electronic reading device 14

leer to read 2

legalizar to legalize 15

legumbre *f* vegetable 3

lejos de far from 7

lengua *f* tongue 9

lento/a slow 14

lentamente slowly 6

lentes *m* **de contacto** contact lenses 8

les *ind. obj.* you, them (to/for you, them) 8**levantar pesas** to lift weights 5

levantarse to get up 6

ley *f* law 15

libertad *f* freedom 15

librería *f* bookstore 2

libro *m* book 2

licencia *f* **de conducir** driver's license 14

líder *m/f* leader 15

límite de velocidad *m* speed limit 14

limón *m* lemon 4

limpiar to clean 5

limpio/a clean 8

línea está ocupada the line is busy 11

listo/a: estar . . . to be ready 11

literatura *f* literature 2

llamada *f* **telefónica** telephone call 11; **llamada de larga distancia** long distance call 11

llamar to call 3

llanta *f* tire 14; **llanta desinflada** flat tire 14

llave *f* key 13

llegada *f* arrival 13

llegar to arrive 2

llenar (el tanque) to fill (the tank) 14

llevar to wear 8

llevarse bien/mal to get along well/badly 11

Lleve la receta a la farmacia. Take the prescription to the pharmacy. 9

llorar to cry 11

llover (ue) to rain 5; **está lloviendo** it's raining 5; **llueve** it's raining, it rains 5

lluvia *f* rain 5; **lluvia ácida** acid rain 12

lo *dir. obj. m* him, you, it 5; **lo que** what, that which 4; **lo siento (mucho)** I'm (so) sorry 1

los *m, dir. obj.* them, you 6; *m, pl., definite article* the 2

los aseos/el servicio *m* bathroom 14

Lo siento mucho. I'm very sorry. 14

luchar (por) to fight (for) 15

luego then 6

lugar *m* place 7

luna *f* moon 12; **luna de miel** honeymoon 11

lunes *m* Monday 1

luz *f* light 10

M

madrastra *f* stepmother 3

madre *f* mother 3

madurez *f* adulthood, maturity 11

maestro/a *m/f* teacher 2

maíz *m* corn 4

mal bad, badly 3

maleta *f* suitcase 13

maletero *m* trunk 14

maletín *m* briefcase, carry-on bag 13

malo/a bad 3

mañana tomorrow, morning *f* 1; **de la mañana** A.M. (in the morning) 1; **hasta mañana** see you tomorrow 1; **por/en la mañana** in the morning 2

mandar to send 2

manejar to drive 5

manga *f* sleeve 8; **de manga larga/corta** long-/short-sleeved 8

mano *f* hand 9

manos libres *m* handsfree 14

manta *f* blanket 13

mantequilla *f* butter 4

manzana *f* apple 4

mapa *m* map 2

maquillaje *m* makeup 6

maquillarse to put on makeup 6

máquina *m* **de afeitar** electric shaver 6

mar *m* sea 12

marido *m* husband 3

mariposa *f* butterfly 12

marisco *m* seafood 3

marrón brown 5

martes *m* Tuesday 1

marzo March 1

más more 4; **más tarde** later 2

matar to kill 11

matemáticas *f, pl* mathematics 2

mayo May 1

mayor old (elderly) 3; older 3

me *dir. obj.* me 5; *ind. obj.* me (to/for me) 8; *refl. pron.* myself 5; **me llamo . . .** my name is . . . 1

media *f* half 1; **media hermana** half-sister 3; **mi media naranja** my soul mate, other half 11

medias *f, pl.* stockings, hose, socks 8

medianoche *f* midnight 1

médico/a *m/f* doctor 2

medicina *f* medicine 15

medio hermano *m* half-brother 3

medio *m* **ambiente** environment 12

mediodía *m* noon 1

mejor best 7; **mejor amigo/a** *m/f* best friend 3; **es mejor** it's better 13

melocotón *m* peach 4

menor younger 3

menos less 4; **a menos (de) que** unless 14

mensaje de texto *m* text message 14

mensaje *m* **electrónico** e-mail message 2

mentir to lie 11

mercado *m* market 3

merienda *f* snack 3

mermelada *f* jam 4

mes *m* month 1

mesa *f* table 2

mesero/a *m/f* waiter/waitress 6

mesita *f* **de noche** nightstand 10

metro *m* metro, subway 7

mexicano/a *m/f, n., ad.j* Mexican 1

mí *obj. prep. pron.* me 6; **¡Ay de mí!** Poor me! (What am I going to do?) 14

mi/mis my 2

microondas *m* microwave 10

mientras while 9

miércoles *m* Wednesday 1

mío/a/os/as (of) mine 7; **el gusto es mío** the pleasure is mine 1

mirar to look at 8

mochila *f* backpack 2

moda *f* fashion; **a la moda** in style 8

molestar to be annoying to, to bother 11

moneda *f* currency, money, coin 7

monitor *m* monitor 14

montañas *f, pl.* mountains 3

montar a caballo to ride horseback 12

morado/a purple 5

moreno/a brunette, dark-skinned 3

morir (ue, u) to die 7

mosca *f* fly 12

mosquito *m* mosquito 12

mostrar (ue) to show 8

motocicleta *f* motorcycle 14

motor *m* motor 14; **afinar el motor** to tune the motor 14

mover(se) (ue) to move (oneself) 10

muchacha *f* girl 3

muchacho *m* boy 3

mucho *adv.* much, a lot 4; **mucho/a/os/as** *m/f adj* much, a lot 4; **(muchas) gracias** thank you (very much) 1; **muchas veces** *f pl.* many times, often 8; **mucho gusto** pleased to meet you 1

mudarse to move (from house to house) 10

muebles *m, pl.* furniture 10

muerte *f* death 11; **pena de muerte** death penalty 15

mujer *f* woman, wife 3; **mujer de negocios** businesswoman 6
mujer policía policewoman 14
muletas *f, pl.* crutches 9
multa *f* fine, ticket 14
mundo *m* world 12
museo *m* museum 7
música *f* music 2
muy very 3; **muy bien** very well 1

N

nacer to be born 11
nacimento *m* birth 11
nada nothing 8; **de nada** you're welcome 1
nadar to swim 12
nadie no one, nobody 8
naranja *f* orange (fruit) 4
narcotráfico *m* drug trafficking 15
nariz *f* nose 9
naturaleza *f* nature 12
náuseas *f, pl.* nausea 8
nave *f* **espacial** space ship 15
navegador *m* browser 14
navegar por la red to surf the Web 2
necesario: es . . . it's necessary 13
necesitar to need 4
negro/a black 5
nervioso/a nervous 3
nevar (ie) to snow 5; **está nevando** it's snowing 5
ni not, not even 8
ni... ni neither . . . nor 8
nicaragüense *m/f, n., ad.j* Nicaraguan 1
nieta *f* granddaughter 3
nieto *m* grandson 3
nieva it's snowing 5
nieve *f* snow 5
ningún (ninguno/a) no, none, no one 8
niña *f* child 3
niñez childhood 11
niño *m* child 3
niños *m, pl.* children 11
noche *f* night 1; **buenas noches** good evening/night 1; **de la noche** p.m. (in the evening, at night) 1; **por/en la noche** in the evening, at night 2
normalmente normally 6
nos *dir. obj.* us 5; *ind. obj.* us (to/for us) 7; *refl. pron.* ourselves 5
nosotros/as *m/f, subj. pron.* we 1; *obj. prep.* us 6
nota *f* grade, score 2
noticias *f, pl.* news 7
noticiero *m* newscast 15
noveno/a ninth 14
novia *f* girlfriend 3
noviembre November 1
novio *m* boyfriend 3
nube *f* cloud 5

nublado cloudy 5; **está (muy) nublado** it's (very) cloudy 5
nuestro/a/os/as our 2;(of) ours 8
nuevo/a new 3
nunca never 2

O

o or 8; **o . . . o** either . . . or 8
obra *f* **de teatro** play 7
obvio: es . . . it's obvious 13
océano *m* ocean 12
octavo/a eighth 14
octubre October 1
ocupado/a busy 3
oficina *f* office 2; **oficina de correos** post office 8
ojo *m* eye 9
oído *m* ear (inner) 9
oír to hear 5
ojalá que . . . I hope 11
ola *f* wave 12
olvidar to forget 11; **olvidarse de** to forget 11
ordenar (el cuarto) to tidy (the room) 10
oreja *f* ear (outer) 9
oro *m* gold 8
os *dir. ob.j* you (pl.) 5; *ind. obj.* you (to/for you) 7; *refl. pron.* yourselves 5
otoño *m* autumn, fall 5
otro/a another 4
otros/as other 4

P

paciente *m/f* patient 9
padrastro *m* stepfather 3
padre *m* father 2
padres *m, pl.* parents 3
pagar to pay (for) 7
página *f* page 2; **página web** Web page 2
país *m* country 13
pájaro *m* bird 12
pan *m* **(tostado)** bread (toast) 4
pantalla *f* screen 2
pantalones *m, pl* pants 8; **pantalones cortos** shorts 8
papa *f* potato 4; **papas fritas** french fries 4
papel *m* paper 2; **papel higiénico** toilet paper 6
papelera *f* wastebasket 2
paquete *m* package 7
para for, in order to, toward, by 12; **para que** so that, in order that 14; **para + *infinitivo*** in order to (do something) 7
parabrisas *m* windshield 14
parada *f* **de autobús** bus stop 7
paraguas *m* umbrella 8
paramédicos *m, pl.* paramedics 9
parar to stop (movement) 14

parece que it seems that . . . 13
pared *f* wall 10
pareja *f* partner, significant other 3; couple 11
pariente *m* relative 3
parque *m* park 7
parrilla (a la parrilla) grilled 4
partido *m* game, match 5
pasado: el año/ mes/ verano . . . last year/ month/ summer 6
pasajero/a *m/f* passenger 13
pasaporte *m* passport 13
pasar to spend (time), to happen, pass, 7
pasar la aspiradora to vacuum 10
pasillo *m* aisle (between rows of seats) 13
pasta *f* **de dientes** toothpaste 6
pastel *m* pie, pastry 4
pastelería *f* pastry shop, bakery 7
patata *f* potato 4
paz *f* peace 15
pedir (i, i) to ask for, request, order 4
pecho *m* chest, breast 9
peinarse to comb one's hair 6
peine *m* comb 6
película *f* film, movie 7
peligroso/a dangerous 12
pelo *m* hair 9; **secador** *m* **de pelo** hair dryer 6
pelota *f* ball 5
pendientes *m, pl* earrings 8
pensar (ie) to think 4; **pensar (ie) + *infinitivo*** to intend/plan (to do something) 5; **pensar (ie) en** to think about (someone or something) 11
peor worse 10
pequeño/a small, little 3
pera *f* pear 4
perder (ie) to lose 7; **perder el tren** to miss the train 13
perdón pardon me, excuse me 1
perezoso/a lazy 3
periódico *m* newspaper 7
periodista *m/f* journalist 6
pero but 3
perro *m* dog 3
personalmente personally 6
pescado *m* fish 4
pescar to fish 12
pesticida f tóxico poisonous pesticide 12
pez *m* **(los peces)** fish 12
pie *m* foot 9; **estar de pie** to be standing 9
pierna *f* leg 9
piloto/a *m/f* pilot 13
pimienta *f* pepper 4
piña *f* pineapple 4
pintar to paint 5
piscina *f* swimming pool 13
piso *m* floor (of a building) 10
pizarra *f* chalkboard, board, blackboard 2
pizzería *f* pizzeria 7

planeta *m* planet 12
planta *f* plant 12
planta baja main floor 13
plata *f* silver 8
plátano *m* banana 4
plato *m* dish, course 3; plate 10
playa *f* beach 3
plaza *f* plaza, town square 7
pluma *f* pen 2
pobre poor 3
pobreza *f* poverty 15
poco *adv.* little 4; **un poco** *adv* a bit, a little, somewhat 3
poco/a *m/f, adj.* little (quantity) 4; **pocos/ as** *m/f, adj.* few 4
poder (ue) to be able, can 4
policía *m* policeman 14
política *f* **mundial** world politics 15
pollo *m* chicken 4
poner to put, place 5; **poner la mesa** to set the table 10
poner una inyección/una vacuna to give a shot/vaccination 9
ponerse (los zapatos, la ropa, etc.) to put on (shoes, clothes, etc.) 6
por for, down, by, along, through 7
por favor please 1
por fin finally 9
por la mañana in the morning 2
por la noche in the evening, at night 2
por la tarde in the afternoon 2 **¿por qué?** why? 4
¡Por supuesto! Of course! 14
porque because 4
posible: es . . . it's possible 13
posiblemente possibly 6
póster *m* poster 10
postre *m* dessert 3
practicar to practice 2
practicar el descenso de ríos to go white-water rafting 12
practicar el *parasail* to go parasailing 12
precio *m* price 8
preciso: es . . . it's necessary 13
preferir (ie, i) to prefer 4
pregunta *f* question 2
preguntar to ask 8
prejuicio *m* prejudice 15
prender to turn on 10
preocupado/a worried 3
preocuparse (por) to worry (about) 9
preparar to prepare 2
prestar to lend 8
prevenir to prevent 12
primavera *f* spring 5
primer first 14; **primer piso** *m* first floor, 10
primero *adv.* first 6; **primero/a** first 14; **de primera clase** first class 14
primo/a *m/f* cousin 3
probable: es . . . it's probable 13

probablemente probably 6
problema *m* problem 12
profesor/a *m/f* professor 2
programa (de computadora) *m* software 14
programador/a *m/f* computer programmer 2
prohibir to prohibit 15
propina *f* tip 13
proteger to protect 12
próximo/a next 5; **el próximo mes/ año / verano** next month/year/ summer 5
prueba *f* quiz 2
psicología *f* psychology 2
puente *m* bridge 14
puerta *f* door 2; **puerta de salida** gate 13
puerto (USB) *m* (USB) port 14
puertorriqueño/a *m/f, n., adj* Puerto Rican 1
pues well 1
pues nada *(informal)* not much 1
pulmón *m* lung 9
pulsera *f* bracelet 8
pupitre *m* (student) desk 2

Q

que that 4; **lo que** what, that which 4; **¿qué?** what?, which? 4; **¿qué hay de nuevo?** what's new? *(informal)* 1; **¿qué pasa?** what's happening? *(informal)* 1; **¿qué tal?** how are you? *(informal)* 1
¡Qué barbaridad! How awful! 14
¡Qué lástima! What a shame! 14
¡Qué lío! What a mess! 14
¡Qué suerte! What luck!/ How lucky! 14
quedarse to stay 9
quejarse de to complain about 11
querer (ie) to want, love 4
queso *m* cheese 4
¿quién/quiénes? who? 3; **¿de quién?** whose? 4
química *f* chemistry 2
quinto/a fifth 14
quiosco *m* newsstand 7
quisiera I would like 4
quitar: . . . la mesa to clear the table 10
quitarse la ropa to take off (clothes, etc.) 6

R

rafting: **practicar el . . .** to go white-water rafting 12
rápidamente rapidly 6
rápido/a fast 14
rascacielos *m* skyscraper 7
rasuradora *f* razor 6
ratón *m* mouse 2
rebajas *f* sales 8
recámara *f* bedroom 10

recepción *f* reception, front desk 9
recepcionista *m/f* receptionist 13
receta *f* prescription 9
recibir to receive 7
reciclar to recycle 12
recientemente recently 6
reclamo de equipajes *m, pl.* baggage claim 13
recoger to pick up, gather 12
recomendar (ie) to recommend 11
recordar (ue) to remember 11
recursos *m, pl.* **naturales** natural resources 12
red social *f* social network 14
reducir to reduce 12
refresco *m* soft drink 4
refrigerador *m* refrigerator 10
regalar to give (as a gift) 8
regalo *m* gift 8
registrarse to register 13
regresar to return 2
regular OK, so-so 1
reírse (de) to laugh at 11
relámpago *m* lightning 12
religión *f* religion 2
reloj *m* clock 2; watch 8
remar to row 12
reparar to repair 14
repente all of a sudden, suddenly 9
repetir (i, i) to repeat 7
reportar to report 15
reportero/a reporter 15
reproductor de DVD *m* DVD player 2
reservación *f* reservation 13
resfriado *m* cold 9
residencia *f* **estudiantil** student dorm 2
resolver (ue) to solve/resolve 10
Respire profundamente. Take a deep breath. 7
responsable responsible 3
respuesta *f* answer 2
restaurante *m* restaurant 2
retirar take out, to withdraw 7
reunirse (con) to meet, get together 11
revisar to check over 14
revista *f* magazine 7
rico/a rich 3
ridículo: es . . . it's ridiculous 13
río *m* river 15
robar to rob, steal 15
rojo/a red 5
romper to break 10; **romper (con)** to break up (with) 11; **romperse** to get broken 14
ropa *f* clothes, clothing 8; **ropa** *f* **interior** underwear 8
ropero/clóset *m* closet 8
rosado/a pink 5
rubio/a blonde 3
ruido *m* noise 10
ruso *m* Russian (language) 5

rutina *f* routine 6

S

sábado *m* Saturday 1
sábana *f* sheet 13
saber to know (facts, information) 5; to know how to (skills) 5
sacar fotos *f, pl.* to take photos 11
sacar la basura to take out the garbage 10
sacar los pasaportes to get passports 13
sacar una nota to get a grade 2
sacar una radiografía to x-ray 9
sacar sangre to draw blood 9
saco *m* **de dormir** sleeping bag 12
sal *f* salt 4
sala *f* living room 10; **sala de espera** waiting room 9; **sala de urgencias** emergency room 9
salchicha *f* sausage 4
salida *f* departure 13
salir to leave, go out 2; **salir (con)** to go out (with), date 11
salud *f* health 8
saltar en paracaídas to go parachute jumping 12
sandalias *f, p.l* sandals 8
sandía *f* watermelon 4
sándwich *m* sandwich 4
Saque la lengua. Stick out your tongue. 9
satélite *m* satellite 14
se *reflex. pron.* yourself, himself, herself, themselves 5
secador *m* **de pelo** hair dryer 6
secadora *f* dryer 10
secar: . . . los platos to dry the dishes 9; **secarse** to dry (oneself) 6
secretario/a *m/f* secretary 6
seda *f* silk 8
seguir (i, i) to continue, follow 14
segundo/a second 14; **de segunda clase** second class 14
segundo piso second floor 10
seguro *m* insurance 14
seguro/a safe 14
sello *m* stamp 7
selva *f* jungle 12
semáforo *m* traffic light 14
semana *f* week 1; **semana** *f* **pasada** last week 6
sentarse (ie, i) to sit down 9
sentir (ie, i) to be sorry, regret 11; **lo siento (mucho)** I'm (so) sorry 1; **sentirse (ie, i)** to feel 9
señal *f* sign 14
separarse (de) to separate 11
septiembre September 1
séptimo/a seventh 14
sequía *f* drought 12
ser to be 2
serio/a serious, dependable 3

serpiente *f* snake 12
servicio de habitación room service 13
servilleta *f* napkin 10
servir (i, i) to serve 4
sexto/a sixth 14
SIDA *m* AIDS 15
silla *f* chair 2; **silla de ruedas** wheel chair 9
sillón *m* easy chair 10
simpático/a nice, likeable 3
sin without 4
sincero/a honest, sincere 11
sistema GPS *f* GPS 14
sitio web *m* Web site 2
sobre on 7; **sobre** *m* envelope 7
sobrepoblación *f* overpopulation 15
sobrina *f* niece 3
sobrino *m* nephew 3
sociedad *f* society 15
sociología *f* sociology 2
¡Socorro! ¡Help! 14
sofá *m* sofa 10
sol *m* sun 12
solicitar to apply for (job) 15
solicitud *f* application 15
soltero/a single 11
sombrero *m* hat 8
sombrilla *f* umbrella 8
sonar (ue) to ring, to sound 6
sopa *f* soup 4
sortija *f* ring 8
sótano *m* basement 10
su/sus his, her, its, your (*formal*), their 2
subir to go up 10; **subirse a** to get on, board 13
sucio/a dirty 8
suegra *f* mother-in-law 3
suegro *m* father-in-law 3
suelo *m* floor 10
suéter *m* sweater 8
sufrir to suffer 15
sugerir (ie, i) to suggest 11
suyo/a/os/as (of) his, (of) hers, (of) theirs, (of) yours (*formal*) 8

T

talla *f* size (clothing) 8
taller *m* **mecánico** shop 14
también also 8
tampoco neither, not either 8
tan: tan . . . como as . . . as 9; **tan pronto como** as soon as 15
tanque *m* tank 14
tanto: tanto como as much as 10; **tanto/a/os/as . . . como** as much/ many . . . as 10
taquilla *f* ticket window 13
tarde *f* afternoon 1; **buenas tardes** good afternoon 1; **de la tarde** P.M. (in the afternoon) 1; **por/en la tarde** in the afternoon 2

tarea *f* homework, assignment, task 2
tarjeta *f* card; **tarjeta de crédito/ débito** credit/debit card 7
tarjeta de embarque boarding pass 13
tarjeta postal post card 7
tarjeta telefónica calling card 11
taxi *m* taxi 7
taza *f* cup 10
te *dir. obj.* you (*informal*) 5; *ind. obj.* you (to/for you) (*informal*) 8; **¿Te duele?** Does it hurt? 9
te presento (*informal*) I want to introduce . . . to you 1; *reflex. pron.* yourself (*informal*) 5
té *m* tea 4
teatro *m* theater 7
techo *m* roof 10
teclado *m* keyboard 2
teléfono *m* **celular** cell phone 15
televisor *m* television set 2
temer to fear, be afraid of 11
temprano early 2
tenedor *m* fork 10
tener calor/frío to be hot/cold 5
tener celos to be jealous 11
tener cuidado to be careful 14
tener éxito to be successful 15
tener ganas de + *infinitivo* to feel like (doing something) 5
tener hambre/sed to be hungry/thirsty 4
tener miedo to be afraid 12
tener prisa to be in a hurry 13
tener que + *infinitivo* to have to . . . (do something) 5
tener sueño to be sleepy, tired 6
tenis *m* tennis 5
tercero/a third 14
terminar to finish 7
termómetro *m* thermometer 9
terrorismo *m* terrorism 15
ti *obj. prep* you (*informal*) 6
tía *f* aunt 3
tiempo m weather 5; **a tiempo** on time 2
tienda *f* store, shop 6; **tienda de campaña** tent 12
tienda *f* **de ropa** clothing store 5
tienda por departamentos *f* department store 8
tierra *f* earth, land 12
tijeras *f, pl* scissors 6
tío *m* uncle 3
tiza *f* chalk 2
toalla *f* towel 6
tobillo *m* ankle 9
tocar to play (instruments) 5
tocineta *f* bacon 4
tocino *m* bacon 4
todo *adj., m* everything 8

todo/a/os/as *adj.* **toda la mañana** all morning 2; **toda la noche** all night 2; **toda la tarde** all afternoon 2; **todas las mañanas** every morning 2; **todas las noches** every evening, night 2; **todas las tardes** every afternoon 2; **todo el día** all day 2; **todos los días** every day 2

todavía still, yet 4

tomar to take, drink 4; **tomar apuntes** *m, pl.* to take notes 2; **tomar el sol** to sunbathe 5; **tomar fotos** *f, pl.* to take photos 12

tomar la temperatura to take one's temperature 9; **tomar la presión arterial** to take one's blood pressure 9; **tomar el pulso** to take one's pulse 9

tomate *m* tomato 4

Tome aspirinas/las pastillas/las cápsulas. Take aspirin/the pills/the capsules. 9

Tome líquidos. Take liquids. 9

tonto/a dumb, silly 3

torcer(se) (ue) to sprain (one's ankle) 9

tormenta *f* storm 12

torta *f* cake 4

tos *f* cough 9

toser to cough 9

trabajador/a hardworking 3

trabajar to work 2; **trabajar para . . .** to work for 6

trabajo *m* work 6; **trabajo** *m* **a tiempo completo** full-time job 5; **trabajo a tiempo parcial** part-time job 5; **trabajo** *m* **escrito** paper (academic) 2; **trabajo voluntario** *m* volunteer work 15; **en el trabajo** at work 3

traer to bring 5

tráfico *m* traffic 14

traje *m* suit 8; **traje de baño** bathing suit 8

tranquilamente calmly 6

tránsito *m* traffic 14

tratar de + *infinitivo* to try to (do something) 14

tren *m* train 14

triste sad 3

tú *subj. pron.* you (*informal*) 1**tu/tus** your (*informal*) 2

tutor/a tutor 15

tuyo/a/os/as (of) yours (*informal*) 7

U

un/uno/una a 2; one 1; **un poco** *adv.* a bit, a little, somewhat 3; **una vez** once, one time 9

ura lástima: es . . . it's a pity 13

unos/unas some 2

universidad *f* college/university 2

uña *f* fingernail 9

urgente: es . . . it's urgent 13

uruguayo/a *m/f, n., adj.* Uruguayan 1

usar to use 2

usted *subj. pron.* you (*formal*) 1; *obj. prep.* you (*formal*) 6

ustedes *subj. pron.* you (*pl.*) 1; *obj. prep.* you (*pl.*) 6

uva *f* grape 4

V

vaca *f* cow 12

vacaciones *f, pl.* vacation 12

vacuna *f* vaccination 9

valle *m* valley 12

vaqueros *m, pl.* jeans 8

vaso *m* glass (drinking) 10

Vaya a la farmacia. Go to the pharmacy. 9

VCR *m* VCR, video 2

vecino/a *m/f* neighbor 10

vejez old age 11

velocidad *f* speed 14

venda *f* bandage 9

vender to sell 4

venir (ie) to come 5

ventana *f* window 2

ventanilla *f* window (airplane, train, car) 13

ver to see 5; **ver la tele(visión)** to watch TV 5

verano *m* summer 5

verdad: es . . . it's true 13

verde green 5

verdura *f* vegetable 3

vestido *m* dress 8

vestirse (i) to get dressed 6

viajar to travel 5

viaje *m* a trip 14

víctima *f* victim 15

vida *f* life 11

videoconsola *f* video game playing device 14

videojuego *m* video game 14

viejo/a old 3

viernes Friday 1

vinagre *m* vinegar 4

vino *m* wine 4

violencia *f* violence 15

visitar to visit 3

viudo/a *m/f* widower/widow 11

vivir to live 2

volante *m* steering wheel 14

volar (ue) to fly 13

voleibol *m* volleyball 5

voluntario/a *m/f* volunteer 15

volver (ue) to return, to go back 4

vomitar to vomit 9

vómito *m* vomit 9

vosotros/as *m/f, subj.* you (*informal, pl., Sp.*) 1; *obj. prep.* you (*informal, pl., Sp.*) 6

votar (por) to vote (for) 15

vuelo *m* flight 13

vuestro/a/os/as your (*informal*) 2; (of) yours (*informal*) 7

Y

y and 3

ya already 6

yeso *m* cast 9

yo *subj. pron.* I 1

Z

zanahoria *f* carrot 4

zapatería *f* shoe store 7

zapatos *m, pl.* shoes 8; **zapatos de tenis** tennis shoes 8

zumo *m*, juice 4

Vocabulario: *English–Spanish*

A

a bit, a little, somewhat un poco *adv.* 3
a quarter cuarto 1
a trip viaje *m* 14
A.M. (in the morning) de la mañana 1
a; one un/uno/una 1; 2
abortion aborto *m* 15
accident accidente *m* 14
accountant contador/a *m/f* 6
accounting contabilidad *f* 2
acid rain lluvia ácida 12
addicted adicto/a *m/f* 14
address dirección 7
admission ticket entrada *f* 7
adolescence adolescencia 10
adolescents adolescentes *m, pl.* 10
adulthood, maturity madurez *f* 11
adults adultos *m, pl.* 11
adventure aventura *f* 12
affectionate cariñoso/a 11
after después de que *conj* 15
after (class) después de (clase) 2
afternoon tarde *f* 1
afterwards, later después de *prep.* 7
ahead of time con... de anticipación 13
AIDS SIDA *m* 15
air conditioning aire acondicionado 13
airline aerolínea *f* 13
airplane avión *m* 13
airport aeropuerto *m* 13
aisle (between rows of seats) pasillo *m* 13
alarm clock despertador *m* 6
algebra álgebra *f (but el* álgebra) 2
all afternoon toda la tarde 2
all day todos los días 2
all morning todo/a/os/as *adj.*: toda la mañana 2
all night toda la noche 2
all of a sudden, suddenly repente 9
allergy alergia *f* 9
(almost) always (casi) siempre 2
already ya 6
also también 8
ambulance ambulancia *f* 9
American (from the United States) estadounidense *m/f, n., adj.* 1
amusing, fun divertido/a *m/f* 3
and y 3
angry enojado/a 11
animal animal *m* 11
animal species especie animal *f* 12
ankle tobillo *m* 9
another otro/a 4
answer respuesta *f* 2
answering machine contestador automático *m* 11
any, some, someone algún (alguno/a/os/as) 8
anyone alguien 8
anything algo, nada 8

apartment apartamento *m* 2
apple manzana *f* 4
application solicitud *f* 15
April abril 1
area code código *m* de área 11
Argentinian argentino/a *m/f, n., adj.* 1
arm brazo *m* 9
army ejército *m* 15
arrival llegada *f* 13
art arte *m (but las* artes) 2
as . . . as tan: tan... como 9
as much as tanto: tanto como 10
as much/ many . . . as tanto/a/os/as... como 10
as soon as tan pronto como 15
at home en casa 6
at work en el trabajo 3
at, to a 2
ATM machine cajero *m* automático 7
August agosto 1
aunt tía *f* 3
autumn, fall otoño *m* 5
avenue avenida *f* 7

B

baby bebé *m/f* 3
back espalda *f* 9
backpack mochila *f* 2
bacon tocineta *f* 4
bacon tocino *m* 4
bad malo/a 3
bad, badly mal 3
baggage claim reclamo de equipajes *m, pl.* 13
baked al horno 4
ball pelota *f* 5
banana banana *f* 4
banana plátano *m* 4
bandage venda *f* 9
bank; bench banco *m* 7
bar bar *m* 7
baseball béisbol *m* 5
basement sótano *m* 10
basketball baloncesto *m* 5
basketball básquetbol *m* 5
bathing suit traje de baño 8
bathroom baño *m* 10
bathroom los aseos/el servicio *m* 14
bathtub bañera *f* 10
beach playa *f* 3
beans frijoles *m, pl.* 4
because porque 4
because of causa (a causa de) 12
bed cama *f* 6
bedroom dormitorio *m* 10
bedroom recámara *f* 10
beer cerveza *f* 4
before antes de que *conj* 15
before (class) antes de (clase) *prep* before 2
behind detrás de 7

beige beige 5
bellhop botones *m* 13
belt cinturón *m* 8
beneath, under debajo de 7
beside al lado de 7
beside lado: al... de 7
best mejor 7
best friend mejor amigo/a *m* 3
between, among entre 7
bicycle bicicleta *f* 5
big, large grande 3
bill, check; account cuenta *f* 7
biology biología *f* 2
bird pájaro *m* 12
birth nacimento *m* 11
birthday cumpleaños *m* 2
black negro/a 5
blanket cobija *f* 13
blanket manta *f* 13
blonde rubio/a 3
blouse blusa *f* 8
blue azul 5
boarding pass tarjeta de embarque 13
boat barco *m* 12
boat (small) bote *m* 12
body cuerpo *m* 9
Bolivian boliviano/a *m/f, n., adj.* 1
bomb bomba 15
bone hueso *m* 9
book libro *m* 2
bookshelf, shelf estante *m* 10
bookstore librería *f* 2
boots botas *f, pl.* 8
border frontera *f* 15
bored/boring aburrido/a 3
boss jefe/a *m/f* 15
boy chico *m* 3
boy muchacho *m* 3
boyfriend novio *m* 3
bracelet pulsera *f* 8
brakes frenos *m, pl.* 14
bread (toast) pan *m* (tostado) 4
breakfast desayuno *m* 3
bridge puente *m* 14
briefcase, carry-on bag maletín *m* 13
broccoli brócoli *m* 4
brother hermano *m* 2
brother-in-law cuñado *m* 3
brown marrón 5
browser navegador 14
brunette, dark-skinned moreno/a 3
brush cepillo *m* 6
building edificio *m* 7
bureau cómoda *f* 10
bus autobús *m* 7
bus station estación de autobuses 14
bus stop parada *f* de autobús 7
business empresa *f* 6
businessman hombre de negocios 6
businesswoman mujer de negocios 6
busy ocupado/a 3

but pero 3
butter mantequilla f 4
butterfly mariposa f 12
bye, so-long chao 1

C

cable cable m 14
cafeteria cafetería f 2
cake torta f 4
calculator calculadora f 2
calculus cálculo m 2
calling card tarjeta telefónica 11
calmly tranquilamente 6
camera cámara f 12
camp campamento m 12
campfire fogata f 12
cancer cancer m 15
candidate candidato/a m/f 15
cap gorra f 8
car auto m 3
car carro m 3
car coche m 3
card tarjeta f 7
carne de cerdo carne f de cerdo 4
carrot zanahoria f 4
cash efectivo m 7
cashier cajero/a m/f 6
cast yeso m 9
cat gato m 3
cathedral catedral f 7
CD, compact disk CD m 2
CD, compact disk disco compacto m 2
cell phone teléfono m celular 15
cereal cereal m 4
chain cadena f 8
chair silla f 2
chalk tiza f 2
chalkboard, board, blackboard pizarra f 2
change, small change, exchange
    cambio m 7
chapter capítulo m 2
check cheque m 7
cheese queso m 4
chemistry química f 2
cherry cereza f 4
chest, breast pecho m 9
chicken gallina f 12
chicken pollo m 4
child niña f 3
child niño m 3
childhood niñez 11
children niños m, pl. 11
Chilean chileno/a m/f, n., adj. 1
chill escalofrío m 9
church iglesia f 7
citizen ciudadano/a m/f 15
city ciudad f 3
city block cuadra f 14
class clase f 2
classroom aula f (but el aula) 1
clean limpio/a 8

clock; watch reloj m 2; 8
closed cerrado/a 3
closet clóset m 8
closet ropero/clóset m 8
clothes, clothing ropa f 8
clothing store tienda f de ropa 5
cloud nube f 5
cloudy está (muy) nublado 5
coat abrigo m 8
coffee; coffee place café m 4
cold frío/a 5
cold resfriado m 9
college/university universidad f 2
Colombian colombiano/a m/f, n., adj. 1
comb peine m 6
comfortable cómodo/a 14
company compañía f 6
computer computadora f 2
computer programmer programador/a
    m/f 2
computer science computación f 2
computer science informática f 2
congratulations felicidades f 11
connection conexión f 14
constantly constantemente 6
construct construir 15
contact lenses lentes m de contacto 8
cookie galleta f 4
corn maíz m 4
corruption corrupción f 15
Costa Rican costarricense m/f, n., adj. 1
cotton algodón m 8
cough tos f 9
country campo m 3
country país m 13
cousin primo/a m/f 3
cow vaca f 12
crash choque m 14
cream crema f 4
credit/debit card tarjeta de crédito/
    débito 7
crime delito m 15
cruise ship crucero m 12
crutches muletas f, pl. 9
Cuban cubano/a m/f, n., adj. 1
cup taza f 10
cure cura f 15
currency, money, coin moneda f 7
curtain cortina f 10
customs aduana f 13

D

dangerous peligroso/a 12
date fecha f 1
date, appointment cita f 11
daughter hija f 3
day día m 1
day before yesterday anteayer 6
death muerte f 11
death penalty pena de muerte 15
December diciembre 1

deforestation desforestación f 12
delay demora f 13
delighted (to meet you) encantado/a 1
delinquent, offender, criminal
    delincuente m 15
deodorant desodorante m 6
department store tienda por
    departamentos f 7
departure salida f 13
depressed deprimido/a 9
desert desierto m 12
dessert postre m 3
destroy destruir (y) 12
destruction destrucción f 12
device aparato m 14
diarrhea diarrea f 9
dictionary diccionario m 2
difficult, hard difícil 3
dining room comedor m 10
dirty sucio/a 8
disagreeable, unpleasant (persons)
    antipático/a 3
discrimination discriminación f 15
dish, course, plate plato m 3, 10
dishwasher lavaplatos m 10
divorce divorcio 11
divorced divorciado/a 11
do a blood test hacer un análisis de
    sangre 9
doctor doctor/a m/f 2
doctor médico/a m/f 2
doctor's office consultorio m del
    médico/de la médica 9
Does it hurt? ¿Te duele? 9
dog perro m 3
Dominican dominicano/a m/f n., adj. 1
door puerta f 2
double bed cama doble 6
double room habitación doble 13
dress vestido m 8
drink, beverage bebida f 4
driver conductor/a 14
driver's license licencia f de conducir 14
drought sequía f 12
drug addiction drogadicción f 15
drug trafficking narcotráfico m 15
drugs drogas f, pl. 15
dryer secadora f 10
dumb, silly tonto/a 3
DVD player el (reproductor) de DVD 2

E

each, every cada 9
ear (inner) oído m 9
ear (outer) oreja f 9
early temprano 2
earphone auricular m 14
earrings aretes m, pl. 8
earrings pendientes m, pl. 8
earth, land tierra f 12

easily fácilmente 6
easy fácil 3
easy chair sillón *m* 10
economics economía *f* 2
Ecuadorian ecuatoriano/a *m/f, n., adj.* 1
egg/fried eggs/scrambled eggs huevo *m*/huevos fritos/huevos revueltos 4
eighth octavo/a 14
either...or o...o 8
elderly ancianos *m pl.*/ la anciana *f* /el anciano *m* 11
election elección *f* 15
electric shaver máquina *m* de afeitar 6
electronic reading device lector electrónico *m* 14
elementary school escuela *f* 3
elevator ascensor *m* 13
e-mail correo *m* electrónico 2
e-mail address dirección *f* electrónica 2
e-mail message mensaje *m* electrónico 2
emergency *f, pl.* emergencias 9
emergency room *f, pl.* sala de urgencias 9
exciting emocionante 12
employee empleado/a *m/f* 6
English (language) inglés *m* 2
envelope sobre *m* 7
environment medio *m* ambiente 12
equality igualdad *f* 15
eraser borrador *m* 2
every afternoon todas las tardes 2
every day todo el día 2
every evening, night todas las noches 2
every morning todas las mañanas 2
everything todo *adj.* 8
exam examen *m* 2
exciting emocionante 12
exercise ejercicio *m* 2
expensive caro/a 8
explosion explosión *f* 15
extinction extinción *f* 12
eye ojo *m* 9
eyeglasses gafas *f, pl.* 8

F

face cara *f* 9
factory fábrica *f* 6
fair justo 13
faithful fiel 11
family familia *f* 2
family room la sala/el cuarto de estar *f/m* 10
far from lejos de 7
farm granja *f* 12
fashion moda *f* 8
fast rápido/a 14
fat gordo/a 3
father padre *m* 2
father-in-law suegro *m* 3
February febrero 1
fever fiebre *f* 9

few pocos/ as *m/f, adj.* 4
fifth quinto/a 14
film, movie película *f* 7
finally por fin 9
finances finanzas *f/pl.* 2
fine, well bien 3
fine, ticket multa *f* 14
finger dedo *m* 9
fingernail uña *f* 9
fire fuego *m* 12
fireplace, chimney chimenea *f* 10
first primer 14
first primero/a 6
first class de primera clase 13
first floor primer piso *m* 10
first/second class ticket boleto de primera/ segunda clase round trip ticket 13
fish pescado *m* 4
fish pez *m* (los peces) 12
flat tire llanta desinflada 14
flat, deflated (tire) desinflado/a 14
flight vuelo *m* 13
flight attendant asistente de vuelo 13
floor suelo *m* 10
floor (of a building) piso *m* 10
flowers flores *f, pl.* 5
flu gripe *f* 9
fly mosca *f* 12
food, main meal comida *f* 3
foot pie *m* 9
football fútbol americano *m* 5
for, down, by, along, through por 7
for, in order to, toward, by para 14
forest bosque *m* 12
forest fires incendios *m, pl.* forestales 12
fork tenedor *m* 10
fourth cuarto/a 14
free of charge gratis 14
freedom libertad *f* 15
French (language) francés *m* 2
french fries papas fritas 4
frequently frecuentemente 6
frequently con frecuencia 2
Friday viernes 1
fried frito/a 4
friend amigo/a *m/f* 3
friendly, kind amable 3
friendship amistad *f* 11
from where? ¿de dónde...? 4
fruit fruta *f* 3
full-time job trabajo *m* a tiempo completo 5
furniture muebles *m, pl.* 10

G

game, match partido *m* 5
garage garaje *m* 10
garbage basura *f* 12
garbage can bote de basura *m* 10
garden jardín *m* 10

garlic ajo *m* 4
gas gasolina *f* 14
gas station gasolinera *f* 14
gate puerta de salida 13
gel gel *m* 6
generally generalmente 6
German (language) alemán *m* 2
gift regalo *m* 8
girl chica *f* 3
girl muchacha *f* 3
girlfriend novia *f* 3
glass (drinking) vaso *m* 10
global warming calentamento global *m* 12
gloves guantes *m, pl.* 8
go to the pharmacy Vaya a la farmacia 9
goblet copa *f* 10
gold oro *m* 8
golf golf *m* 5
good bueno/a 3
good afternoon buenas tardes 1
good evening/night buenas noches 1
good morning buenos días 1
good-bye adiós 1
good-looking, pretty bonito/a 3
good-looking, pretty/handsome guapo/a 3
good-looking, pretty/handsome hermoso/a 3
government gobierno *m* 15
GPS sistema GPS *m* 14
grade, score nota *f* 2
granddaughter nieta *f* 3
grandfather abuelo *m* 3
grandmother abuela *f* 3
grandparents abuelos *m, pl.* 3
grandson nieto *m* 3
grape uva *f* 4
grass hierba *f* 12
gray gris 5
great-grandfather bisabuelo *m* 3
great-grandmother bisabuela *f* 3
green verde 5
green bean judía *f* verde 4
grilled a la parrilla 4
Guatemalan guatemalteco/a *m/f, n., adj.* 1
guest huésped/a *m/f* 13
guitar guitarra *f* 4
gurney camilla *f* 9
gym, gymnasium gimnasio *m* 2

H

hair pelo *m* 9
hair dryer secador *m* de pelo 6
hair dryer secador *m* de pelo 6
half media *f* 1
half-brother medio hermano *m* 3
half-sister media hermana 3
ham jamón *m* 4
hamburger hamburguesa *f* 4

hand mano *f* 9
handsfree manos libres *m* 6
happy contento/a 3
hardworking trabajador/a 3
hat sombrero *m* 8
he; obj. prep. pron. him él *m, subj.* 6
head cabeza *f* 9
headache dolor *m* de cabeza 9
headache dolor *m* de cabeza *f* 9
headphones audífonos *m, pl.* 2
health salud *f* 8
heart corazón *m* 9
heating calefacción *f* 13
hello/hi hola 1
help! ¡Auxilio! 14
help! ¡Socorro! 14
here aquí 3
high school colegio *m* 3
highway autopista *f* 14
hill colina *f* 12
him, you, it lo *dir. obj. m* 5
his, her, its, your (formal), their su/sus 2
(of) his, (of) hers, (of) theirs, (of) yours (formal) suyo/a/os/as 8
history historia *f* 2
home, house casa 2
homeless people desamparados *m, pl.* 15
homemaker amo/a *m/f* de casa 6
homework, assignment, task tarea *f* 2
Honduran hondureño/a *m/f, n., adj.* 1
honest, sincere sincero/a 11
honeymoon luna de miel 11
horse caballo *m* 12
hospital hospital *m* 9
hostel hostal *m* 13
hot (temperature, not spiciness) caliente 5
hotel hotel *m* 13
house keeper amo/a *m/f* de casa 2
how are you? (formal) ¿cómo está usted?
how are you? (informal) ¿cómo estás? 1
how are you? (informal) ¿qué pasa? 1
how awful! ¡qué barbaridad! 14
how many? ¿cuántos/as? 3
how much? ¿cuánto/a? 4
how? ¿cómo? 1
human rights derechos *m, pl.* humanos 15
hunger hambre *f (but el* hambre) 15
husband esposo *m* 3
husband marido *m* 3
hybrid híbrido *m* 14

I

I yo *subj. pron.* 1
I am sorry Disculpe 1
I hope ojalá que... 11
I want to introduce . . . to you (informal); reflex. pron. yourself

(informal) te presento 1
I would like quisiera 4
I'm (so) sorry lo siento (mucho) 1
ice hielo *m* 4
ice cream helado *m* 4
immediately inmediatamente 6
in case en caso de que 14
in front of delante de 7
in front of, opposite enfrente de 7
in front of, opposite, facing frente a 7
in order to (do something) para que 12
in style a la moda 8
in the afternoon por la tarde 2
in the afternoon; P.M. (in the afternoon) de la tarde; por/en la tarde 2
in the evening, at night por la noche 2
in the evening, at night; P.M. (in the evening, at night) por/en la noche 1
in the morning por/en la mañana 2
in the morning por la mañana 2
in, at; on en 2; 7
inexpensive barato/a 8
infancy infancia *f* 11
infection infección *f* 9
injection inyección *f* 9
insects insectos *m, pl.* 12
inside dentro de 7
instead of en vez de 7
insurance seguro *m* 14
intelligent inteligente 3
interview entrevista *f* 15
island isla *f* 12
it rains llueve 5
it seems that . . . parece que 13
it's (very) cloudy nublado 5
it's (very) cold hace (mucho) frío 5
it's (very) hot/cool/cold/sunny/ windy hace (mucho) calor/fresco/ frío/sol/ viento 5
it's a pity ura lástima: es... 13
it's a shame lástima: es una... 13
it's better es mejor 13
it's good es bueno 13
it's horrible horrible: es... 13
it's important importante: es... 13
it's impossible imposible: es... 13
it's improbable improbable: es... 13
it's interesting interesante: es... 13
it's necessary necesario: es... 13
it's necessary preciso: es... 13
it's obvious obvio: es... 13
it's possible posible: es... 13
it's probable probable: es... 13
it's raining está lloviendo 5
it's ridiculous ridículo: es... 13
it's snowing está nevando 5
it's snowing nieva 5
it's strange extraño: es... 13
it's sunny hace sol 5
it's true verdad: es... 13

it's true, correct cierto: es... 13
it's unfair no es... 13
it's urgent urgente: es... 13
it's wonderful es fenomenal 13
Italian (language) italiano *m* 5

J

jacket chaqueta *f* 8
jam mermelada *f* 4
January enero 1
Japanese (language) japonés *m* 5
jealous celoso/a 11
jeans jeans *m, pl.* 8
jeans vaqueros *m, pl.* 8
jewelry joyas *f, pl.* 8
jewelry shop joyería *f* 7
job empleo 15
journalist periodista *m/f* 6
juice jugo *m* 4
juice zumo *m* 4
July julio 1
June junio 1
jungle selva *f* 12
justice justicia *f* 15

K

kayak kayak *m* 12
key llave *f* 13
keyboard teclado *m* 2
kilometer kilómetro *m* 14
kitchen cocina *f* 10
knife cuchillo *m* 10

L

laboratory laboratorio *m* 2
lake lago *m* 5
lamp lámpara *f* 10
laptop computadora portátil *f* 14
laptop/notebook (computer) computadora portátil *f* 13
last night anoche 6
last week semana *f* pasada 6
last weekend fin de semana pasado 6
last year/month/summer pasado: el año/ mes/ verano 6
later más tarde 2
law ley *f* 15
Lawyer abogado/a *m/f* 6
lazy perezoso/a 3
leader líder *m/f* 15
leather cuero *m* 8
leave, depart, to go away irse 11
leaves hojas *f, pl.* 5
leg pierna *f* 9
lemon limón *m* 4
less menos 4
lesson lección *f* 2
letter carta *f* 7
lettuce lechuga *f* 4

library biblioteca *f* 2
life vida *f* 11
light luz *f* 10
lightning relámpago *m* 12
line (of people or things) cola *f* 7
line (of people or things) fila *f* 7
link enlace *f* 14
lip labio *m* 9
literature literatura *f* 2
little (quantity) poco/a *m/f, adj.* 4
little poco *adv.* 4
living room sala *f* 10
lobster langosta *f* 4
long largo/a 8
long distance call llamada de larga distancia 11
long-/short-sleeved de manga larga/corta 8
long-sleeved de manga larga 8
love amor *m* 11
love at first sight amor a primera vista 11
luggage equipaje *m* 13
lunch almuerzo *m* 4
lung pulmón *m* 9

M

magazine revista *f* 7
maid (hotel) camarera *f* 13
mailbox buzón *m* 7
main floor planta baja 13
makeup maquillaje *m* 6
mall, shopping center centro comercial 7
man hombre *m* 3
manager gerente *m/f* 15
map mapa *m* 2
March marzo 1
market mercado *m* 3
married casado/a 11
mathematics matemáticas *f, pl.* 2
May mayo 1
me mí *obj. prep. pron.* 6
me; *ind.* **obj. me (to/for me);** *refl. pron.* **myself** me *dir. obj.* 5
meat, beef carne *f* 4
medicine medicina *f* 15
metro, subway metro *m* 7
Mexican mexicano/a *m/f, n., adj.* 1
microwave microondas *m* 10
midnight medianoche *f* 1
milk leche *f* 4
mirror espejo *m* 10
misdemeanor, crime delito *m* 15
Monday lunes *m* 1
money dinero *m* 6
monitor monitor 14
month mes *m* 1
moon luna *f* 12
more más 4
mosquito mosquito *m* 12

mother madre *f* 3
mother-in-law suegra *f* 3
motor motor *m* 14
motorcycle motocicleta *f* 14
mountain biking ciclismo *m* de montaña 12
mountain climbing alpinismo/el andinismo *m* 12
mountain climbing andinismo *m,* alpinismo *m* 11
mountains montañas *f, pl.* 3
mouse ratón *m* 2
mouth boca *f* 9
movie theater, cinema cine *m* 7
much, a lot; mucho/a/os/as *m/f* mucho *adv. adj.*
much, a lot, many times, often muchas veces *f* 8
museum museo *m* 7
music música *f* 2
my mi/mis 2
my name is . . . me llamo... 1
my soul mate, other half mi media naranja 11

N

napkin servilleta *f* 10
nasal congestion congestión *f* nasal 9
natural resources recursos *m, pl.* naturales 12
nature naturaleza *f* 12
nausea náuseas *f, pl.* 8
near cerca de 7
neck cuello *m* 9
necklace collar *m* 8
neighbor vecino/a *m/f* 10
neither . . . nor ni... ni 8
neither, not either tampoco 8
nephew sobrino *m* 3
nervous nervioso/a 3
never nunca 2
new nuevo/a 3
newlyweds recién casados *m, pl.* 11
news noticias *f, pl.* 7
newscast noticiero *m* 15
newspaper periódico *m* 7
newsstand quiosco *m* 7
next próximo/a 5
next month/year/summer el próximo mes/ año / verano 5
Nicaraguan nicaragüense *m/f, n., adj.* 1
nice meeting you too igualmente 1
nice, likeable simpático/a 3
niece sobrina *f* 3
night noche *f* 1
nightstand mesita *f* de noche 10
ninth noveno/a 14
no one, nobody nadie 8
no, none, no one ningún (ninguno/a) 8
noise ruido *m* 10

noon mediodía *m* 1
normally normalmente 6
nose nariz *f* 9
nor, not even ni 8
not much *(informal)* pues nada 1
notebook cuaderno *m* 2
notes apuntes *m, pl.* 2
nothing nada 8
November noviembre 1
now ahora 2
nurse enfermero/a *m/f* 6

O

ocean océano *m* 12
October octubre 1
Of course! ¡Claro! 14
Of course! ¡Por supuesto! 14
of mine mío/a/os/as 7
of yours *(informal)* tuyo/a/os/as 7
of, from de *prep* 1
office oficina *f* 2
Oh my gosh! ¡Caramba! 14
oil aceite *m* 4
OK, so-so regular 1
old viejo/a 3
old (elderly); older mayor 3
old age vejez 11
olive aceituna *f* 4
on sobre 7
on time a tiempo 2
on top of, above encima de 7
once, one time una vez 9
one-way ticket billete/boleto de ida/ sencillo *m* 13
onion cebolla *f* 4
open abierto/a 3
open your mouth abra la boca 9
or o 8
or . . . either o... o 8
orange (color) anaranjado/a 5
orange (fruit) naranja *f* 4
other otros/as 4
ought to, should (do something) deber + *infinitive* 5
our; (of) ours nuestro/a/os/as 8
outdoors aire libre *m* 12
outer space exploration exploración *f* del espacio 15
outside fuera de 7
oven horno *m* 10
overpopulation sobrepoblación *f* 15
ozone layer capa *f* de ozono 12

P

package paquete *m* 7
page página *f* 2
pants pantalones *m, pl.* 8
paper papel *m* 2
paper (academic) trabajo *m* escrito 15

paramedics paramédicos *m, pl.* 9
pardon me, excuse me con permiso 1
pardon me, excuse me perdón 1
parents padres *m, pl.* 3
park parque *m* 7
parking estacionamiento, aparcamiento *m* 14
partner, significant other, couple pareja *f* 11
part-time job trabajo a tiempo parcial 5
party fiesta *f* 2
passenger pasajero/a *m/f* 13
passport pasaporte *m* 13
pastry shop, bakery pastelería *f* 7
patient paciente *m/f* 9
pea guisante *m* 4
peace paz *f* 15
peace agreement acuerdo *m* de paz *f* 15
peach durazno *m* 4
peach melocotón *m* 4
pear pera *f* 4
pen bolígrafo *m* 2
pen pluma *f* 2
pencil lápiz *m* 2
people gente *f* 7
pepper pimienta *f* 4
personally personalmente 6
pharmacy farmacia *f* 9
philosophy filosofía *f* 2
phone book guía *f* telefónica 11
physics física *f* 2
picture, painting cuadro *m* 4
pie, pastry pastel *m* 4
pig cerdo *m* 12
pillow almohada *f* 13
pilot piloto/a *m/f* 13
pineapple piña *f* 4
pink rosado/a 5
pizzeria pizzería *f* 7
place lugar *m* 7
planet planeta *m* 12
plant planta *f* 12
platform andén *m* 13
play obra *f* de teatro 7
plaza, town square plaza *f* 7
please por favor 1
pleased to meet you mucho gusto 1
poisonous pesticide tóxico/pesticida *f* 12
policeman policía *m* 14
policewoman mujer policía 14
political science ciencias *f, pl.* políticas 2
pollution contaminación *f* 12
poor pobre 3
Poor me! (What am I going to do?) ¡Ay de mí! 14
pork carne de cerdo/puerco *f* 4
pork chop chuleta *f* de cerdo/puerco 4
possibly posiblemente 6
post card tarjeta postal 7

post office oficina de correos 8
poster póster, afiche *m* 10
potato patata, papa *f* 4
poverty pobreza *f* 15
pregnant embarazada 9
prejudice prejuicio *m* 15
prescription receta *f* 9
price precio *m* 8
printer impresora *f* 2
private bath baño privado 13
probably probablemente 6
problem problema *m* 12
professor profesor/a *m/f* 2
psychology psicología *f* 2
Puerto Rican puertorriqueño/a *m/f, n., adj.* 1
purple morado/a 5
purse, bag bolso/a *m* 8

Q

question pregunta *f* 2
quiz prueba *f* 2

R

raft balsa *f* 12
rafting balsismo *m* 12
railroad station estación de ferrocarril 14
rain lluvia *f* 5
raincoat impermeable *m* 8
rapidly rápidamente 6
rarely casi nunca 2
razor rasuradora *f* 6
recently recientemente 6
reception, front desk recepción *f* 9
receptionist recepcionista *m/f* 13
red rojo/a 5
refrigerator refrigerador *m* 10
relative pariente *m* 3
religion religión *f* 2
remote control control remoto *m* 14
reporter reportero/a 15
research investigación *f* 15
reservation reservación *f* 13
responsible responsable 3
rest descanse 9
restaurant restaurante *m* 2
restroom aseos *m, pl.* 13
restroom baño *m* 14
rice arroz *m* 4
rich rico/a 3
ring anillo *m* 8
ring sortija *f* 8
river río *m* 15
road camino *m*, carretera *f* 14
roof techo *m* 10
room cuarto *m* 2
room habitación *f* 10
room service servicio de habitación 13

roommate compañero/a *m/f* de cuarto 6
round trip ticket billete/boleto de ida y vuelta *m* 13
routine rutina *f* 6
rug, carpet alfombra *f* 10
Russian (language) ruso *m* 5

S

sad triste 3
safe seguro/a 14
salad ensalada *f* 4
sales rebajas *f* 8
salt sal *f* 4
sand arena *f* 12
sand castle castillo de arena *m* 12
sandals sandalias *f, pl.* 8
sandwich bocadillo *m* 4
sandwich sándwich *m* 4
satellite satélite *m* 14
Saturday sábado *m* 1
sausage chorizo *m* 4
sausage salchicha *f* 4
Say ah! Diga iah! 9
scarf bufanda *f* 8
schedule horario *m* 13
scissors tijeras *f, pl.* 6
screen pantalla *f* 2
sea mar *m* 12
seafood marisco *m* 3
search engine buscador *m* 14
season estación *f* 4
seat asiento *m* 13
second segundo/a 14
second class de segunda clase 14
second floor segundo piso 10
secretary secretario/a *m/f* 6
see you soon hasta pronto 1
see you tomorrow hasta mañana 1
sign señal *f* 14
September septiembre 1
serious wound herida *f* grave 9
serious, dependable serio/a 3
service/gas station estación de servicio/la gasolinera 14
seventh séptimo/a 14
shampoo champú *m* 6
shaving cream crema de afeitar *f* 6
she obj. of prep. her ella *f, subj.* 1
sheet sábana *f* 13
sheet of paper hoja *f* de papel 2
shirt camisa *f* 8
shoe store zapatería *f* 7
shoes zapatos *m, pl.* 8
shop taller *m* mecánico 14
short bajo/a 3
short corto/a 8
short- sleeved de manga corta 8
shorts pantalones cortos 8
shoulder hombro *m* 9
shower ducha *f* 10

shrimp gamba *f*; camarón *m* 4
sick enfermo/a 3
silk seda *f* 8
silver plata *f* 8
single soltero/a 11
single bed cama sencilla 6
single room habitación sencilla 13
sink (bathroom) lavabo, lavamanos *m* 10
sink (kitchen) fregadero *m* 10
sister hermana *f* 3
sister-in-law cuñada *f* 3
sixth sexto/a 14
size (clothing) talla *f* 8
skinny flaco/a 3
skirt falda *f* 8
sky cielo *m* 12
skyscraper rascacielos *m* 7
sleeping bag saco *m* de dormir 12
sleeve manga *f* 8
slow lento 14
slowly lentamente 6
small, little pequeño/a 3
snack merienda *f* 3
snake serpiente *f* 12
snow nieve *f* 5
so that, in order that para + *infinitivo* 7
soap jabón *m* 6
soccer fútbol *m* 5
social network red social *f* 14
society sociedad *f* 15
sociology sociología *f* 2
socks calcetines *m, pl.* 8
sofa sofá *m* 10
soft drink refresco *m* 4
software programa (de computadora) *m* 14
some unos/unas 2
someone, somebody alguien 8
something algo 8
sometimes a veces 2
son hijo *m* 3
sore throat dolor de garganta *f* 9
sore throat dolor *m* de garganta 9
soup sopa *f* 4
space ship nave *f* espacial 15
Spanish español/española *m/f, n., adj.* 1
Spanish (language) español *m* 2
speed velocidad *f* 14
speed limit límite de velocidad *m* 14
spider araña *f* 12
spoon cuchara *f* 10
sport deporte *m* 5
spring primavera *f* 5
stages of life etapas *f, pl.* de la vida 11
stairs escalera *f* 10
stamp estampilla *f* 7
stamp sello *m* 7
star estrella *f* 12
statue estatua *f* 7
steak bistec *m* 4
steering wheel volante *m* 14

stepbrother hermanastro *m* 3
stepfather padrastro *m* 3
stepmother madrastra *f* 3
stepsister hermanastra *f* 3
stereo estéreo *m* 10
Stick out your tongue. Saque la lengua. 9
still, yet todavía 4
stockings, hose, socks medias *f, pl.* 8
stomach estómago *m* 9
stomach ache dolor de estómago *m* 9
stomachache dolor *m* de estómago 9
store clerk dependiente/a *m/f* 6
store, shop tienda *f* 6
storm tormenta *f* 12
stove estufa *f* 10
straight, straight ahead derecho 14
strawberry fresa *f* 4
street calle *f* 7
street corner esquina *f* 14
stressed estresado/a 3
strong fuerte 3
student alumno/a *m/f* 2
student estudiante *m/f* 2
student center centro estudiantil 2
student desk pupitre *m* 2
student dorm residencia *f* estudiantil 2
suddenly de repente 9
sugar azúcar *m* 4
suit traje *m* 8
suitcase maleta *f* 13
summer verano *m* 5
sun sol *m* 12
Sunday domingo *m* 1
sunglasses gafas de sol 8
supper, dinner cena *f* 3
sweater suéter *m* 8
swimming pool piscina *f* 13

T

table mesa *f* 2
Take a deep breath. Respire profundamente. 7
Take aspirin/the pills/the capsules. Tome aspirinas/las pastillas/las cápsulas. 9
Take liquids. Tome líquidos. 9
take out, to withdraw retirar 7
Take the prescription to the pharmacy. Lleve la receta a la farmacia. 9
tall alto/a 3
tank tanque *m* 14
taxi taxi *m* 7
tea té *m* 4
teacher maestro/a *m/f* 2
teacher's desk escritorio *m* 2
team equipo *m* 5
teaspoon cucharita *f* 10
telephone call llamada *f* telefónica 11
television set televisor *m* 2
tennis tenis *m* 5

tennis shoes zapatos de tenis 8
tent tienda de campaña 12
tenth décimo/a 14
terrific fenomenal 1
terrorism terrorismo *m* 15
text message mensaje de texto *m* 14
thank you (very much) (muchas) gracias 1
thank you/thanks gracias 1
that aquel/aquella *adj.* 6
that ese/a *adj.* 6
that que 4
that on aquél/aquélla *pron.* 6
that one ése/a *pron.* 6
that which lo que 14
the el *m, definite article* 2
the las *f, pl. definite article* 2
the line is busy línea está ocupada 11
the pleasure is mine el gusto es mío 1
the weather is nice/bad hace buen/ mal tiempo 5
the; *dir. obj.* **her, you (f), it (f)** la *f, definite article* 5
theater teatro *m* 7
them (f), you (f, pl.) las *dir. obj.* 5
them, you; *m, pl., definite article* **the** los *m, dir. obj.* 6; 2
then entonces 6
then luego 6
there allí 3
there is/are hay 2
thermometer termómetro *m* 9
these estos/as *adj.* 6
these estos/as *pron.* 6
they obj. of prep. them ellas *f, subj* 1
they obj. of prep. them ellos *m, subj* 1
thin delgado/a 3
thing cosa *f* 8
third tercero/a 14
this este/a *adj.* 6
this afternoon esta tarde 3
this morning esta mañana 2
this one éste/a *pron.* 6
this, that esta 6
those aquéllos/as *pron.*; aquellos/as *adj.* 6
those esos/as *adj.* 6
those ésos/as *pron.* 6
throat garganta *f* 9
Thursday jueves *m* 1
ticket billete, boleto *m* 13
ticket window taquilla *f* 13
tie corbata *f* 8
time hora *f* 1
tip propina *f* 13
tire llanta *f* 14
tired cansado/a 3
to advise aconsejar 11
to answer contestar 7
to apply for (job) solicitar 15
to arrive llegar 2

to ask preguntar 8
to ask for, request, order pedir (i, i) 4
to attend asistir (a) 2
to avoid evitar 12
to be estar 3
to be ser 2
to be able, can poder (ue) 4
to be afraid tener miedo 12
to be against estar en contra de 15
to be annoying to, to bother molestar 11
to be born nacer 11
to be careful tener cuidado 14
to be engaged estar comprometido/a 11
to be engaged estar prometido/a 11
to be fascinating to, to fascinate fascinar 11
to be glad (about) alegrarse (de) 11
to be hot/cold tener calor/frío 5
to be hungry/thirsty tener hambre/ sed 4
to be important to, to matter importar 12
to be in a hurry tener prisa 13
to be in favor of estar a favor de 15
to be in love (with) estar enamorado/a de 11
to be interesting to, to interest interesar 12
to be jealous tener celos 11
to be married (to) estar casado/a (con) 11
to be on vacation estar de vacaciones f, pl. 12
to be pregnant estar embarazada 11
to be ready estar listo 12
to be ready listo/a: estar... 11
to be seated estar sentado/a 9
to be sleepy, tired tener sueño 6
to be sorry, regret sentir (ie, i) 11
to be standing estar de pie 8
to be standing estar de pie 9
to be successful tener éxito 15
to be sure of estar seguro/a (de) 12
to be together estar juntos/as 11
to be together juntos/as: estar... 11
to begin empezar (ie) (a) 7
to believe creer 11
to break romper 10, romperse 14
to break one's (arm/leg) fracturar(se) (el brazo/ la pierna) 9
to break up (with) romper (con) 11
to bring traer 5
to brush one's hair cepillarse el pelo 6
to brush one's teeth cepillarse los dientes 6
to buy comprar 14
to call llamar 3
to camp acampar 12
to cash, to charge cobrar 7
to change, exchange cambiar 7

to check over revisar 14
to check (baggage) facturar 13
to choose escoger 15
to clean limpiar 5
to clear the table quitar:... la mesa 10
to climb (the mountain) escalar (la montaña) 12
to close cerrar (ie) 7
to comb one's hair peinarse 6
to come venir (ie) 5
to communicate comunicarse 11
to complain about quejarse de 11
to continue continuar 14
to continue, follow seguir (i, i) 14
to contribute contribuir (y) 12
to cook cocinar 4
to cost costar (ue) 4
to cough toser 9
to count, tell, narrate (a story or incident) contar (ue) 7, 8
to crash, collide chocar 14
to cross cruzar 14
to cry llorar 11
to cut one's hair/nails/a finger cortarse el pelo/ las uñas/ el dedo 6
to cut oneself cortarse 5
to cut the lawn cortar:... el césped 10
to dance bailar 5
to delight encantar 11
to deposit depositar 7
to die morir (ue, u) 7
to do, make hacer 2
to doubt dudar 12
to draw blood sacar sangre 9
to drink beber 2
to drive conducir 14
to drive manejar 5
to dry (oneself) secarse 6
to dry the dishes secar:... los pl.atos 9
to eat comer 2
to eliminate eliminar 15
to enchant encantar 11
to enjoy (something) disfrutar de 13
to enter, go into entrar (en/a) 7
to examine examinar 9
to exercise, to do exercises hacer ejercicio 5
to exercise, work out, do exercises hacer ejercicio 5
to explain explicar 8
to fall in love (with) enamorarse (de) 11
to fasten one's seat belt abrocharse el cinturón 13
to fear, be afraid of temer 11
to feed dar de comer 15
to feel sentirse (ie, i) 9
to feel like (doing something) tener ganas de + infinitivo 5
to fight (for) luchar (por) 15
to fill (the tank) llenar (el tanque) 14
to find encontrar (ue) 7

to find out, inquire averiguar 6
to finish terminar 7
to fish pescar 12
to fly volar (ue) 13
to forget olvidar/ olvidarse de 11
to get (stand) in line hacer cola 7
to get (stand) in line hacer fila 6
to get a grade sacar una nota 2
to get along well/badly llevarse bien/ mal 11
to get angry enojarse 11
to get broken romperse 14
to get divorced divorciarse 11
to get dressed vestirse (i) 6
to get engaged (to) comprometerse (con) 11
to get married (to) casarse (con) 11
to get off, to get out of . . . bajarse de 13
to get on, board subirse a 13
to get passports sacar los pasaportes 13
to get tired cansarse 9
to get up levantarse 6
to get/become sick enfermarse 9
to give dar 5
to give (as a gift) regalar 8
to give a shot/vaccination poner una inyección/ una vacuna 9
to give birth dar a lu 11
to go ir 2
to go down bajar 10
to go on a cruise, take a trip on a ship/ boat/cruise ship hacer un viaje en crucero/ en barco 12
to go on vacation ir(se) de vacaciones 12
to go out (with), date salir (con) 11
to go parachute jumping saltar en paracaídas 12
to go parasailing practicar el parasail 12
to go shopping ir de compras 5
to go snorkeling hacer esnórquel 12
to go to bed acostarse (ue) 6
to go to sleep, to fall asleep dormir (ue) 6
to go up subir 10
to go white-water rafting rafting: practicar el... 12
to go white-water rafting practicar el descenso de ríos 12
to have a good time divertirse (ie) 6
to have a layover hacer escala 13
to have breakfast desayunar 2
to have dinner cenar 2
to have lunch almorzar (ue) 4
to have to . . . (do something) tener que + infinitivo 5
to hear oír 5
to help ayudar (a) 10
to hug abrazar 3
to hurt oneself lastimarse 9
to inform informar/ reportar 15
to insist (on) insistir (en) 11

to intend/plan (to do something) pensar (ie) + *infinitivo* 5
to invest invertir (ie, i) 7
to invite invitar (a) 7
to keep guardar 10
to kill matar 11
to kiss besar 3
to know (facts, information); to know how to (skills) saber 5
to land aterrizar 13
to laugh at reírse (de) 11
to learn aprender 2
to leave dejar 13
to leave a message dejar un mensaje 11
to leave behind dejarse 13
to leave, go out salir 2
to legalize legalizar 15
to lend prestar 8
to lie mentir 11
to lift weights levantar pesas 5
to like gustar 4
to listen to escuchar 2
to live vivir 2
to look at mirar 8
to look for buscar 2
to lose perder (ie) 7
to love amar 3
to make an appointment hacer una cita 9
to make reservations hacer reservaciones/ reservas 14
to make the bed hacer la cama 10
to meet up (with) (by chance) encontrarse (ue) (con) 11
to meet, get together reunirse (con) 11
to meet, know, be acquainted with conocer 5
to miss extrañar 11
to miss the train perder el tren 13
to move (from house to house) mudarse 10
to move (oneself) mover(se) (ue) 10
to need necesitar 4
to open abrir 7
to pack empacar 13
to pack hacer las maletas 13
to paint pintar 5
to park estacionar 14
to pay (for) pagar 7
to pick up, gather recoger 12
to play (instruments) tocar 5
to play/to play (sport) jugar (ue)/ jugar al (deporte) 5
to practice practicar 2
to prefer preferir (ie, i) 4
to prepare preparar 2
to prevent prevenir 12
to print imprimir 2
to prohibit prohibir 15
to protect proteger 12
to put gas (in the tank) echar gasolina 14

to put on (shoes, clothes, etc.) ponerse (los zapatos, la ropa, etc.) 6
to put on makeup maquillarse 6
to put, place poner 5
to rain llover (ue) 5
to read leer 2
to really like, love; to delight, to enchant encantar 12
to receive recibir 7
to recommend recomendar (ie) 11
to recycle reciclar 12
to reduce reducir 12
to register registrarse 13
to remember acordarse (ue) de 11
to remember recordar (ue) 11
to rent alquilar 10
to repair reparar 14
to repeat repetir (i, i) 7
to report reportar 15
to rest descansar 5
to return regresar 2
to return (something) devolver (ue) 8
to return, to go back volver (ue) 4
to ride horseback montar a caballo 12
to ring, to sound sonar (ue) 6
to rob robar 15
to row remar 12
to run correr 5
to run, work, function (machine) funcionar 14
to save guardar 14
to save (money) ahorrar 7
to save, conserve conservar 12
to say good-bye despedirse (i, i) 13
to say, tell decir (i) 5
to scuba dive, skin dive bucear 12
to see ver 5
to sell vender 4
to send enviar 2
to send mandar 2
to separate separarse (de) 11
to serve servir (i, i) 4
to set the table poner la mesa 10
to shave afeitarse 6
to show mostrar (ue) 8
to sign firmar 7
to sing cantar 5
to sit down sentarse (ie, i) 9
to ski esquiar 5
to sleep dormirse (ue) 4
to smoke fumar 5
to sneeze estornudar 9
to snow nevar (ie) 5
to solve/resolve resolver (ue) 10
to speak hablar 2
to spend gastar 7
to spend (time), to happen, pass pasar 7
to sprain (one's ankle) torcer(se) (ue) 9
to stay quedarse 9
to stop (movement) parar 14
to study estudiar 2

to suffer sufrir 15
to suggest sugerir (ie, i) 11
to sunbathe tomar el sol 5
to support (a candidate/cause) apoyar 15
to surf hacer surf 12
to surf the Web navegar por la red 2
to swim nadar 12
to take a bath, bathe bañarse 6
to take a hike dar una caminata 12
to take a shower ducharse 6
to take a walk/stroll dar un paseo 5
to take care of cuidar 2
to take notes tomar apuntes *m, pl.* 2
to take off despegar 13
to take off (clothes, etc.) quitarse la ropa 6
to take one's blood pressure tomar la presión arterial 9
to take one's pulse tomar el pulso 9
to take one's temperature tomar la temperatura 9
to take out the garbage sacar la basura 10
to take photos sacar fotos *f, pl.* 11
to take photos tomar fotos *f, pl.* 12
to take, drink tomar 4
to the left izquierda *f:* a la... 14
to the right derecha: a la ... 14
to think pensar (ie) 4
to think about (someone or something) pensar (ie) en 11
to tidy (the room) ordenar (el cuarto) 10
to travel viajar 5
to try intentar 14
to try to (do something) tratar de + *infinitivo* 14
to tune the motor afinar el motor 14
to turn doblar 14
to turn off apagar 10
to turn on prender 10
to understand comprender 2
to understand entender (ie) 4
to use usar 2
to vacuum pasar la aspiradora 10
to visit visitar 3
to vomit vomitar 9
to vote (for) votar (por) 15
to wait (for); to hope, expect esperar 7; 11
to wake up despertarse (ie) 6
to walk caminar 5
to want, love querer (ie) 4
to wash one's hands/face lavarse las manos/ la cara 6
to wash oneself lavarse 5
to wash the dishes lavar:... los platos 10
to waste desperdiciar 12
to watch TV ver la tele(visión) 5
to wear llevar 8
to win, to earn, make money ganar 5; 6

to work; trabajar para... to work for trabajar 6
to worry (about) preocuparse (por) 9
to write escribir 2
to x-ray sacar una radiografía 9
today hoy 1
toilet inodoro m 10
toilet paper papel higiénico 6
tomato tomate m 4
tomorrow, morning mañana f 1
tongue lengua f 9
tonight esta noche 2
too, too much demasiado adv. 14
tooth diente m 9
toothbrush cepillo de dientes 6
toothpaste pasta f de dientes 6
towel toalla f 6
traffic tráfico m 14
traffic tránsito m 14
traffic light semáforo m 14
train tren m 14
trash can cubo m de la basura 10
traveler's check cheque de viajero 7
tree árbol m 5
truck camión m 14
trunk maletero m 14
T-shirt, undershirt camiseta f 8
Tuesday martes m 1
tune the motor afinar el motor 14
tutor tutor/a 15

U

ugly feo/a 3
umbrella paraguas m 8
umbrella sombrilla f 8
uncle tío m 3
understanding comprensivo/a 11
underwear ropa f interior 8
unemployment desempleo m 15
unfortunately desafortunadamente 6
unless a menos (de) que 14
until hasta que 15
upon (doing something) al + infinitivo 7
Uruguayan uruguayo/a m/f, n., adj. 1
(USB) port puerto (USB) m 14
us; ind. obj. us (to/for us); refl. pron. ourselves nos dir. obj. 5

V

vacation vacaciones f, pl. 12
vaccination vacuna f 9
valley valle m 12
VCR, video VCR m 2
vegetable legumbre f 3
vegetable verdura f 3
very muy 3
very well muy bien 1
victim víctima f 15
(video) camera cámara (de video) f 14

video game videojuego m 14
video game playing device videoconsola f 14
vinegar vinagre m 4
violence violencia f 15
volleyball voleibol m 5
volunteer voluntario/a m/f 15
volunteer work trabajo voluntario m 15
vomit vómito m 9

W

waiter/waitress mesero/a m/f 6
waiting room sala de espera 9
wall pared f 10
wallet billetera/la cartera f 8
wallet cartera f 8
want, wish desear 4
war guerra f 15
washer lavadora f 10
wastebasket papelera 2
water agua f (but el agua) 4
waterfall cascada f 12
waterfall catarata f 12
watermelon sandía f 4
wave ola f 12
we; obj. prep. us nosotros/as m/f, subj. pron. 1
weak débil 3
weapon arma f 15
weather clima m 5
weather tiempo m 5
Web page página web 2
Web site sitio web m 2
wedding boda f 11
Wednesday miércoles m 1
week semana f 1
weekend fin m de semana 2
welcome bienvenido/a 13
well pues 1
what ¿qué? 4
What a mess! ¡Qué lío! 14
What a shame! ¡Qué lástima! 14
What luck!/ How lucky! ¡Qué suerte! 14
what, that which lo que 4
what's happening? (informal) ¿qué tal? 1
what's new? (informal) ¿qué hay de nuevo? 1
What's your name (formal)? ¿Cómo se llama usted? 1
What's your name? (informal) ¿Cómo te llamas? 1
wheel chair silla de ruedas 9
when cuando 4
when? ¿cuándo? 2
where ¿dónde? 3
(to) where? ¿adónde? 2
(to) where? ¿adónde? 2
which (one)? ¿cuál? 4
which (ones)? ¿cuáles? 4

while mientras 9
white blanco/a 5
who? ¿quién/quiénes? 3
whose? ¿de quién? 4
why? ¿por qué? 4
widower/widow viudo/a m/f 11
wife esposa f 3
window ventana f 2
window (airplane, train, car) ventanilla f 13
windshield parabrisas m 14
wine vino m 4
winter invierno m 5
with con 4;
without sin 4
woman, wife mujer f 3
wool lana f 8
work trabajo m 6
world mundo m 12
world politics política f mundial 15
worried preocupado/a 3
worse Peor 10

Y

year año m 4
years old tener... años 3
yellow amarillo/a 5
yesterday ayer 6
you (formal); obj. prep. you (formal) usted subj. pron. 1; 6
you (informal) ti obj. prep. 6
you (informal) tú subj. pron. 1
you (informal); ind. obj. you (to/for you) (informal) te dir. obj. 5
you (informal, pl., Sp.); obj. prep. you (informal, pl., Sp.) vosotros/as m/f, subj 6
you (pl.); ind. obj. you (to/for you); refl. pron. yourselves os dir. obj. 5
you (pl.); obj. prep. you (pl.) ustedes subj. pron. 1; 6
you, him, her (to/for . . .) le ind. obj. 8
you, them (to/for you, them) les ind. obj. 8
you're welcome de nada 1
young joven 3
young people, adolescents jóvenes m, pl. /los adolescentes 11
younger menor 3
your (informal) tu/tus 2
your (informal); (of) yours (informal) vuestro/a/os/as 7
yourself, himself, herself, themselves se reflex. pron. 5
youth juventud f 11

Índice

Frontispiece. Lancelot Brown, 1716–1783. A portrait attributed to Richard Cosway.

CAPABILITY
BROWN

Dorothy Stroud

WITH AN
INTRODUCTION BY
CHRISTOPHER HUSSEY

faber and faber
LONDON · BOSTON

First published in this new edition in 1975
by Faber and Faber Limited
3 Queen Square London WC1N 3AU
First published in Faber Paperbacks in 1984

Printed in Great Britain by
BAS Printers Ltd. Over Wallop Hampshire
All rights reserved

Publisher's Note

*We are grateful for the
generous financial contribution
the COUNTRYSIDE COMMISSION
have made towards the cost of publishing
this Faber Paperback edition*

Library of Congress Cataloging in Publication Data

Stroud, Dorothy.
  Capability Brown.
  Bibliography: p.
  Includes index.
    1. Brown, Lancelot, 1716–1783.   2. Landscape
architects—England—Biography.   I. Title.
[SB470.B7S7 1984]   712′.092′4 [B]   84-13541

ISBN 0-571-13405-X (pbk.)

British Library Cataloguing in Publication Data

Stroud, Dorothy
Capability Brown.—[New ed.]
  1. Brown, Capability
    I. Title
712′.092′4   SB470.B7
  ISBN 0-571-13405-X

FOREWORD

IT IS NOW more than thirty-five years since I first began to collect material for a life of Lancelot Brown, a man whose name was frequently turning up in writings on houses and gardens, but only in the vaguest way. Who was this familiar but insubstantial character, alleged to have altered the appearance of much of the English countryside, but about whom so few facts seemed to be recorded? I determined to find out, but no sooner had I begun than the Second World War put a stop to research until 1945, and for a considerable time after it ended the shadow remained, with many houses continuing to be occupied by official departments, while family papers were stored away and their owners were engaged on more urgent matters. It was certainly not the most favourable time in which to conduct research, but with many of Brown's landscapes threatened by the difficulties of maintenance, and the selling up of estates through taxation, it seemed desirable to proceed with such material as could be found, and a book eventually emerged in 1950.

In the years since the first editions were published, there has been an increasing interest in, and concern for, historic houses and gardens. Old letters and accounts have been sorted by their owners or handed over to County Record Offices, drawings have come to light in cupboards and attics, and the pursuit of architectural history is now encouraged as never before. Brown has received his share of the resulting discoveries, and enough new material has now been found about him to justify a complete re-writing of the earlier book. In the main I have kept to the chronological pattern used previously with the exception of two chapters where the works seem to justify treatment as a group, that is, the West Country commissions which began with Longleat (Chapter IV), and those in the Staffordshire area (Chapter IX). Although it has not been possible to mention all Brown's known or attributed works in the body of the text, these have been listed at the end, and numbered to facilitate location on the accompanying map (see pages 212–13).

7

As many of Brown's plans as could be photographed have been included, but some were found to be too fragile or too large to give satisfactory results. Inevitably, a reduction in scale has lessened the effect of the delicate details in the originals.

Her Majesty the Queen has graciously given permission for the inclusion among the illustrations of a plan by Brown for Richmond Old Park (now Kew Gardens) from a portfolio at Windsor Castle. I would express my gratitude to all the owners who have answered my enquiries. Their help and interest has been much appreciated. In particular I am grateful to the following: Mrs. Mavis Batey, Mr. Geoffrey Beard, The Duke of Buccleuch, Mr. Marcus Binney, Mrs. F. J. Charlton, Mr. George Clarke, Lady Mary Clive, Mr. Howard Colvin, Mr. John Cornforth, Miss J. R. Cripps, Dr. J. Mordaunt Crook, Mrs. J. G. Dower, Pamela, Lady Egremont, Lady Fairfax-Lucy, Mr. Cecil Farthing, Sir Keith Fraser, Mr. Michael Gibbon, Mr. Christopher Gilbert, Mr. M. G. Glover (Brocklesby Estate Office), Mr. David Green, Mr. P. B. Grimes (Grimsthorpe Estate Office) Dr. Ivan Hall, Mr. John Harris, Mr. J. B. Henderson (Croome Estate Office), Mr. David Hicks, Sir Joslan Ingilby, Sir Giles Isham, Mr. Gervase Jackson-Stops, Miss Alison Kelly, Mr. John Kerslake, Mr. J. M. Lees-Milne, Captain H. Love-grove, Col. A. A. McBean, the Duke of Marlborough, Miss Mary Mauchline, the Lord Methuen, Mr. Anthony Mitchell, Mr. Thomas Newman, Mr. A. S. Oswald, Miss Anne Parry, Mrs. G. F. Pettit, Professor Sir Nikolaus Pevsner, Colonel Sir Charles Ponsonby, Mr. Hugh Prince, Mr. Roger Rawcliffe, Mr. Alistair Rowan, Mr. Lawrence W. Robson, Mr. Oliver Stirling-Lee, the Earl Spencer, the Lord Stafford, Mr. Tatton Sykes, Dr. Eric Till, Mr. G. B. Williams, Captain T. C. Turner, Mr. David Udy, the Rev. A. H. Walker (Vicar of Kirkharle and Cambo), Dr. Peter Willis, and Mr. Anthony Wood. I am no less grateful to the staff of the various County Record Offices and City Libraries who have produced relevant material in their care, notably those at Carlisle, Cumberland and Westmorland, Essex, Gloucester, Hertfordshire, Leeds, Lincolnshire, Northamptonshire, Stafford, East Sussex, Warwickshire; the University Library, Cambridge, the Bodleian Library, Oxford, the Department of History of Art, Oxford, the Library of the Royal Botanic Gardens at Kew, the Public Libraries of Lambeth and Richmond, the Scottish Record Office and the National Library of Wales. I have also received help from the National Monuments Record, the National Register of Archives, the Royal Institute of British Architects (Drawings Collection), the Society of Antiquaries, and the National Trust.

To my very great regret several of those whose help was of value in the preparation of the original editions are no longer alive to receive my renewed thanks, notably Mr. Christopher Hussey, whose knowledge of eighteenth-century landscape gardening has not been surpassed, and whose introduction to my earlier book is here reprinted. The late Mr. G. R. M. Pakenham was a descendant of Brown by whose kindness I was

FOREWORD

allowed the use of a folder of the latter's correspondence; and the late Mrs. F. M. Morrice lent me Brown's surviving account book which had descended in her husband's family. This has now been placed on permanent loan to the Royal Horticultural Society by her daughter-in-law, Mrs. Humphrey Morrice.

DOROTHY STROUD

1974

CONTENTS

CONTENTS

CONTENTS

ILLUSTRATIONS

ABBREVIATIONS

C.R.O.	County Record Office (e.g. Essex, Hertfordshire, etc.)
G.L.C.	Greater London Council
H.M.C.	Historical Manuscripts Commission
P.C.C.	Prerogative Court of Canterbury (wills at Public Record Office)
P.R.O.	Public Record Office
V.C.H.	Victoria County History

INTRODUCTION

Written by the late Christopher Hussey for the original edition

THIS DOCUMENTED ACCOUNT of the life and work of the most celebrated English landscape architect of the eighteenth century fills a gap in the history of national art that has been as regrettable as it can now be perceived to be large. The designing of 'natural' landscapes, contrasted with the baroque geometry of the French school of Le Notre, is a unique English contribution to the arts, and, typically English in its union of beauty with use, an art of which our countryside itself constitutes the principal display.

Miss Dorothy Stroud's study of Capability Brown can be welcomed on that account alone. But it proves, in addition, to have the engaging human qualities of a 'success story' and to contain the fruits of much historical research. Not only does it reveal the remarkable and likeable personality of the man so long masked by his apt if slightly ridiculous nickname; it establishes many illuminating connections in the social and artistic life of the eighteenth century that were unsuspected or conjectural.

Whether the shade of Capability was employed to landscape the Elysian fields, as one contemporary, hoping to predecease Brown on that account, feared might be the case, his terrestrial reputation has had to wait 150 years for a biographer. Some examination of the causes for the delay is worth while, since it will show the timeliness of the present work and set the subject in focus with the general aesthetic trend of his and our own times.

One obvious reason has, of course, been lack of material. Brown, unlike his successor Repton, did not write a book on his *Theory and Practice*, did not supply his clients with prettily got-up picture books of his proposals, and it happens that very few of his working plans have survived. The bringing to light of Brown's account book in the possession of a descendant now enables a number of unsuspected works to be identified

and a chronological sequence to be assigned to a large proportion of them – though the notes cover only twenty-three of the forty-four years of his activity. This is valuable enough. And it has established the fact, denied hitherto by some authorities in such emphatic terms that they can scarcely be defended from a charge of bias, that Brown had an extensive architectural practice. It was this practice that was inherited by his son-in-law Henry Holland, who transmitted it to his pupil John Soane. So the importance of this MS material is evident. I understand, however, that this book was already in preparation prior to its discovery, which did not, therefore, provide the initial stimulus.

Its main impulse has undoubtedly been the growing concern with problems of country planning, preservation of scenery, and relation of buildings to their setting. These problems have renewed in the present generation an aesthetic and technical interest in landscape almost as widespread as that traditional to Englishmen before the Industrial Revolution. In proportion as the man-made origin of English rural scenery has been recognised, together with the debt owed to the landscape architects of the eighteenth century, the reputation of Brown has been re-established. This recognition has not been confined to England. In Europe the *jardin anglais*, grotesque as often were its parodies, has been influencing contemporary planning and leading to the desire to study its origins in Kent's and Brown's landscape system. In the United States, Frederick Law Olmsted was largely responsible during the latter half of the nineteenth century for establishing a vigorous tradition and profession of landscape architecture on lines which were freely admitted to owe much to English eighteenth-century precedent, at a time when Brown, its outstanding exponent, was remembered only in this country for what he had destroyed.

The recollection of his destructions of earlier formal gardens was all too well founded, and has been one of the deterrents to his appreciation. In this respect the prejudice, which still exists, originated in the romantic reaction in taste which took place soon after his death and began effectively to distract attention from his positive achievements. As these had gradually matured, their artificial origin tended to be forgotten and to be mistaken for natural effects. This is the inevitable fate of successful landscape architecture in the naturalistic manner and one foretold in an apt obituary appreciation of Brown: 'Where he was the happiest man he will be least remembered; so closely did he copy nature that his works will be mistaken' for nature.

The campaign of ridicule and denigration directed in the 1790s at Brown's system of improvement was less concerned, however, with his naturalism, or lack of it, than with the difference of his conception of design from that advocated by the impresarios of the Picturesque. The visual and architectonic values stressed by Uvedale Price and Payne Knight, and the importance attached by them to a building's pictorial unity with its setting, led them to recognise the necessity of some architectural setting for country

houses, which Brown's aesthetic had as strenuously denied. The distinctions between the later, visual, approach to landscape design and the ideological nature of Brown's will be touched on in a moment. Here the relevant point is that the pictorial approach to landscape design led to a revival of some degree of formality in the immediate neighbourhood of the house, whether of that unfortunate kind that J. C. Loudon in the next generation was to term 'the gardenesque', or the Italianate architectural layouts associated with Charles Barry and Nesfield. The former led directly to the Victorian concentration on horticulture, and both trends narrowed the attention of designers and their clients to the garden itself at the expense of the wider vision of the Georgian land-owning class. Whilst the decline in power and wealth, after 1832, of the landed interest was partly responsible for this contraction of outlook, the prevailing sentimentalism, which preferred to see in landscape the hand of nature guided only by history and time, also played its part. In the later years of the nineteenth century the revolt from garden-esque horticulture conducted by William Robinson and Gertrude Jekyll applied the greatly enriched botanical resources of the age to realising the intensified natural effects and 'wild gardens' which had been visualised by the Picturesque school a century before. At the same time the amateurs of formality achieved a notable revival of the seventeenth-century types of geometrical gardening. But both schools confined their attention to the garden. Landscape, in the old sense, was beyond their scope.

This sequence of trends had the effect of relegating the larger considerations of land-scape, where these existed, to the forester, the huntsman, and the gamekeeper, though there has survived even to the present time, among the larger landowners of Great Britain a remarkable if instinctive tradition of personal interest in the landscape scenery of their estates. In general, however, the result has been that, until the recent perception of the social bearing of landscape, the range and ideals of Brown's scenic architecture, and still more so the details of his life, lay beyond the field of vision whether of gar-deners, architects, or intelligent critics.

The range of Brown's scenic architecture, the enormous areas of park and woodland that he handled, are evident from some of the photographs and plans reproduced here. But what was he aiming at? What really were the effects he wished to produce, and to achieve which people were prepared to give him such large sums of money? Merely to say that the fashion, forsaking the formality of the seventeenth century, demanded the reverse, is to note the effect but ignore the causes of a great extension of aesthetic sensibility. It is no coincidence that Brown began his astonishingly successful career as a landscape designer (1751) in the same decade that Hogarth published *The Analysis of Beauty* (1753) and Burke his *Inquiry into the Origin of Our Ideas of the Sublime and Beautiful* (1756). The influence of these books on Brown may have been no more than indirect and contributory; but his conception of landscape represents so exactly Burke's

of 'Beauty', and made such notorious use of Hogarth's serpentine 'line of beauty', that we must regard all three as complementary exponents of the *Zeitgeist*.

Brown's work has closer affinity to Burke's aesthetic of sentiment than to William Kent's visual approach to landscape. In the introduction to *The Work of William Kent*, by Miss Margaret Jourdain, I suggested how the theory of aesthetic morality propounded by Shaftesbury, identifying beauty of life and beauty of form as complementary aspects of the humanist ideal, underlay Palladian taste and Kent's high-priesthood of the visual arts. The Christian humanist conception of Nature, derived from Aristotle, of an immanent force always striving to produce perfection of form, but always deflected from perfection by evil 'accidents', until enabled to do so by Man's divinely rational faculties, was the conception generally held by the earlier eighteenth-century thinkers and artists. The perfectly humanised forms of classic architecture should therefore, it was felt, have a setting of perfectly humanised Nature. Hence Kent the architect's conversion to Kent the landscape gardener. But Kent was also a painter, and approached landscape design with a painter's eye to some extent trained in the appreciation of Claude and Poussin's pictorial compositions.

Brown was never a painter. Indeed I do not think he was particularly sensitive to visual impressions. Miss Stroud quotes an illuminating passage in which he actually told Hannah More that 'he compared his art to literary composition', setting a comma here, a full-stop there. Those are not the symbols that a visual artist would use; rather those of a literary mind. Miss Stroud makes a convincing case for Brown's having worked with and under Kent personally at Stowe. There is, indeed, a section of the grounds at Stowe, the Grecian Valley, which it is probable that Brown was responsible for forming under Kent's direction. In the *Guide* of 1769 it is described as 'a large and beautiful vale adorned with Statues of various kinds intermixed with Clumps of Trees beautifully disposed'. If its present appearance corresponds at all to the original description (with the significant use of the term 'clumps') the Grecian Valley must be recognised as an important scene in the history of landscape architecture: the actual point of junction between Kent's and Brown's styles. But much as the young gardener may have learnt from the old Palladian about his general conception of landscape design, Brown did not acquire the painter's method of pictorial approach, except in a very generalised way. Yet at Stowe, Brown could have absorbed, and almost certainly did absorb, the essentially poetic conception of scenery that he translated into his landscapes and that Burke analysed in the *Inquiry*. Stowe, under Lord Cobham, had become the capital seat of what has been called the Grand Whiggery, the geographical and artistic centre of the cult of humane and political liberty subscribed to by the supporters of the elder Pitt. The political bias underlying the scenery of Stowe is traceable in many of the dedications of its monuments. The same spirit undoubtedly influenced Cobham's and Pitt's pro-

gressive loosening, with Kent's help, of Bridgeman's landscape design into harmony with the age's humanism, its faith in disciplined freedom, its respect for natural qualities, its belief in the individual whether man or tree, and its hatred of tyranny whether in politics or plantations.

At Stowe was worked out, as in some grand didactic poem, a vision of landscape wherein Nature was perfected, 'raised to the human mind' as James Thomson phrased it, and by the same process the human mind was 'raised' by exhibiting Nature's 'purest truth': Nature as a manlike Deity intended her to be before man's Fall dragged her down with him. A noble if, to our science-conditioned minds, presumptuous undertaking, but one which was felt by contemporaries to have been realised at Stowe, and which Brown, whatever his actual share in the later landscapes at Stowe, used as the foundation of his system for developing the capabilities of scores of Whig noblemen's parks.

Thus the foundation of his landscape conception was intellectual in so far as he aimed to create, or recreate, an ideal state of nature by selecting representative forms and eliminating 'false accidents'. Yet the basis of selection and the medium of composition had necessarily to be physical. The Georgian aesthete, however idealistic in theory, was not satisfied by abstractions but required imaginative conceptions to be interpreted into sensuous shape. The landscape architect must evolve, from remembered pictures, from literary descriptions, from the actual terrain, scenic shapes that suggested the ideal by physical means.

It is in Brown's selected range of natural forms that lies the close analogy of his landscapes to the conception of beauty as defined in *The Analysis*. Burke's thesis was that all emotion is sensation with a physical basis, and that all physical phenomena were divisible into the Sublime and the Beautiful according as they aroused sensations of danger or appealed ultimately to the sexual emotions. The phenomena producing the sensation of Beauty, and identified by him as its attributes, were Smallness, Smoothness, Gradual Variation, and Delicacy of form. In describing the sensation produced by Beauty, Burke indicates the physical basis of the 'waving' and 'serpentine' forms felt by Hogarth to constitute the 'line of beauty' and predominant in the lines of Chippendale's furniture no less than in the serpentine paths and lakes of Brown's landscapes. Indeed his description of the sensation aroused by Beauty expresses exactly the *feeling* which Brown evidently aimed to produce in his landscapes and which served contemporaries as the physical counterpart of their idealism. 'Most people,' Burke explained, 'must have observed the sort of sense they have had of being swiftly drawn in an easy coach on a smooth turf, with gradual ascents and declivities. This will give a better idea of the Beautiful than almost anything else.'

Brownian landscape was, therefore, fundamentally physical and intellectual in its appeal. He aimed to create the gentle serenity that Richard Wilson infused into his

contemporary landscape painting. The visual qualities – of texture, colour, contrast – scarcely entered into it. It was this lack of visual excitement which provided the chief ground of attack for the Picturesque critics.

> *Oft when I've seen some lonely mansion stand*
> *Fresh from th' improvers desolating hand,*
> *'Midst shaven lawns that far around it creep*
> *In one eternal undulating sweep*

– exclaimed Payne Knight in *The Landscape* (1794). He felt, he continued, impelled to cry:

> *Hence, hence! thou haggard fiend, however called,*
> *This meagre genius of the bare and bald.*
> *Thy spade and mattock here at length lay down,*
> *And follow to the tomb thy fav'rite Brown:*
> *Thy fav'rite Brown whose desolating hand*
> *First dealt thy curses o'er the fertile land.*

Less passionate and more judicial, Uvedale Price admitted that Brown's 'really commendable forte was in the middle distance garden' where, he pointed out, he greatly developed and improved upon the handling initiated by Kent. By the 'middle distance garden' Price meant what we would call park landscape: those familiar, yet uniquely English, scenes of sweeping turf accented by groups of noble trees casting long shadows, the contours sloping to glimpses of a broad winding river and rising beyond to melt into the skyline of encircling woodlands.

When analysed, Brown's typical park landscape resolves itself into a few quite obvious elements. The park is bounded by an encircling belt of woodland, excluding the agricultural hinterland but interrupted to admit any distant prospect or object of pictorial interest. The inner edge of the belt is irregular, receding or projecting according to the contours, and softened by outlying clumps or individual trees which hide by their lower branches the line of the belt's containing fence. Similarly the clumps, where Brown's intention was followed, have become free-standing groups of stately trees. But for the first fifty years of their lives they no doubt looked tight and stiff, fenced as they had to be against cattle. The strictures of Payne Knight against clumps must have been largely due to the intention of opening them out as the trees grew having been forgotten. In the same way the belts must have presented a hard outline until the front trees were sufficiently grown for the fence to be set back and leave the outliers to form an open fringe, when the undergrowth would disappear and yield to grass and bracken. Price was right in attributing the origin of the clump to Kent;

a sketch by him for a group of clumps is preserved at Holkham and is reproduced by Mr. H. F. Clark in *The English Landscape Garden*. Belts had been largely used at Stowe, but their development into something more than a boundary is attributed to the amateur Philip Southcote, whose *ferme ornée* at Woburn Farm, near Chertsey, was regarded by contemporaries as having first demonstrated the value of the belt for providing a woodland walk around and overlooking the park. The poet Shenstone at the Leasowes made the successive cross-views from the belt-walk, with incidental seats and objects, the principal feature of his small but famous *ferme ornée*; and its possibilities were early exploited at Wotton, whether by Brown or the Grenville family. The value of the circuit, as the belt-walk was called, lay in providing a whole sequence of points of view from which the composition must be adjusted, in addition to the prospects from and towards the mansion.

Wherever possible the middle distance was enlivened by water, in the form of an artificial river where none existed and there was a valley and stream of some kind to be dammed; or of a lake where there was not. The notion of an artificial river goes back to Wise at Blenheim and Bridgeman at Chiswick; and Kent was probably responsible for serpentining the originally geometrical waters at Stowe. One of Brown's dogmas was that the ends of an artificial river must be concealed, whether by contours or planting, or be otherwise masked. He seems in his later works to have dropped Kent's naïve use for this purpose of a grotto, as at the head of the 'Worthies River' at Stowe and the grotto-cascades at Chiswick and Wanstead. Masking was most effectively done by means of a real or dummy bridge – a well-known example is the wooden silhouette of a bridge at the end of the lake at Kenwood, though Brown is not known to have been employed there. One of the dams in the Wotton river is combined with a bridge that entirely conceals the subterfuge until the spectator notices that the water level differs on each side. The most spectacular of Brown's handlings of water by this device was his enhancement of the Glyme at Blenheim into a river worthy of Vanbrugh's majestic bridge. That it pleased him is to be presumed from his reputed apostrophe: 'Thames, Thames, you will never forgive me!'

Brown was subsequently criticised for the nakedness of his river banks. There is some justice in Knight's and Price's strictures on this score, but it should be remembered that they both were accustomed to the abruptly contoured Welsh borderland where raised viewpoints are normal, enabling water to be seen above riparian vegetation. In the usually flatter scenes of Brown's activity there was the danger that waterside planting might entirely conceal the water, as has in fact occurred in many of them. Moreover, there is no doubt that the pre-Picturesque eye relished the sinuous margin of a limpid stream laving emerald turf – as numerous contemporary poets more or less said.

The concealed dam in an artificial river was an application of the concealed fence or

ha-ha, the introduction of which by Switzer and Bridgeman early in the century made possible Kent's development of the landscape garden idea. In this enumeration of the component parts of a Brown landscape scheme, the ha-ha has been mentioned last, although, in point of location, it naturally was the nearest to the mansion. In effect, however, it was invisible from that direction, its purpose being that, if there were cattle,

> *the dubious eye*
> *Decides not if they crop the mead or lawn.*

Brown's existing plans do not indicate, as many of Repton's do, the previous use of the terrain. But when he formed a park landscape where none existed before, the grubbing and levelling of hedgerows, with the concomitant burying of land-drains to take the place of field ditches, was one of the biggest operations. Repton, and no doubt Brown, was careful to retain selected hedgerow timber, where suitably placed, to furnish the new landscape, though any obvious alignment was 'broken' as sedulously as the majority of avenues. William Mason succinctly versified the process and the emotions involved in this stage of realising an estate's capabilities:

> *Pity, sure,*
> *Will spare the long cathedral aisle of shade …*
> *The axe must do its office. Cruel task,*
> *Yet needful. Trust me, though I bid thee strike,*
> *Reluctantly I bid thee, for my soul*
> *Holds dear an antient oak, nothing more dear;*
> *It is an antient friend. Stay then thy hand;*
> *And try by saplings tall, discreetly placed,*
> *Before, behind, between, in scattered groups,*
> *To break th' obdurate line. So mayest thou save*
> *A chosen few … Parted now*
> *Each tree becomes the father of a tribe.*

By such means the new parks were to some extent provided with mature trees. Nevertheless the amount of planting for which Brown was responsible must have been very large, and not the least of the accounts in which posterity is indebted to him. The timber in a Brown landscape is predominantly hardwoods – elms, oak, or beeches, according to locality, and many ashes and limes – with a mixture of Scots firs and larches, and usually a few cedars sited to give special emphasis.

Brown had no particular purveyor of trees. In some cases no doubt his clients possessed or proceeded to establish their own tree-nurseries. Unlike London and Wise in Queen Anne's reign, with their own famous nurseries at Brompton, Brown had

34

recourse to commerical tree-raisers, of whom his favourites seem to have been in the London region. At Ashridge trees were supplied by a Mr. Scott, who also supplied 100 larches and 40 planes to Lord Shelburne for Wycombe Abbey and Bowood at a cost of £9 10s 0d. The latter accounts also refer to a Mr. Ash, 'Nurseryman at Twickenham', who supplied 100 elms at 9d per tree and quicksetts at 6d per hundred. For Corsham a number of trees were purchased from Kennedy and Lee of Hammersmith.

In all Brown's landscapes these trees are now at or past their prime, so that it requires an imaginative effort to remind ourselves that these established and venerable scenes, so much part of the England that we accept as continuous and unchanging, were in fact consciously projected by men who could not hope to see the finished picture yet were animated by the faith and foresight to visualise that which we now too readily accept as the gift of Providence or Nature.

The habitual foresight of our ancestral planters of trees, among whom Lancelot Brown must be acknowledged the Director-General, should put us to shame who, men of little faith, seek an immediate return for such niggardly sums as are expended in public plantations by resorting to flowering crabs and shrubberies. When the last private landowners, whose families and tenants set the trees we fell, have been 'liqui-dated', it is an unanswered question who will renew the English landscape. The Forestry Commission is restricted to purely commercial timber production; such government departments and local authorities as are implicated in tree-planting are not sufficiently animated by nepotism and primogeniture to plant forest trees in quantities along the new arterial roads or around housing estates; and, if they were, the depredations of undisciplined urchins would soon bring their intentions to nought. We may look to the National Trust and some corporate landowners to ensure a succession of young trees in the estates they administer. At least the profession established by Capability Brown in his own person is now incorporated in the Institute of Landscape Architects. Among its growing membership is an increasing body of 'improvers', qualified to apply his traditions to the practical and social problems that have taken the place of the aesthetic ideals ministered to by him. But the practitioner is dependent upon patrons with ideas as large and sight as long as is necessitated by this four-dimensional art.

In no way, perhaps, can this requisite largeness and length of vision, this responsi-bility of ours to posterity, be better cultivated than by appreciating the extent of what we owe in this respect to Capability Brown – the last of the great English eighteenth-century artists to be accorded his due because only now, when they face extinction, are his works esteemed at their true worth.

I

NORTHUMBRIAN BACKGROUND
AND EARLY DAYS

O, ye Northumbrian shades, which overlook
The rocky pavement and the mossy falls,
Of solitary Wansbeck, limpid stream;
How gladly I recall your well-known seats,
Beloved of old, and that delightful time
When all alone, for many a summer's day
I wandered through your calm recesses.

Mark Akenside, *Pleasures of Imagination,*
Book IV, 1.40 (1770)

IT WAS IN this Wansbeck region of Northumberland, an area of great natural beauty where the hills dip to fertile valleys, and where Roman sites and medieval remains are witness to its eventful history, that Lancelot Brown was born in 1716. The story of how, in later life, he acquired his nickname of Capability, from a habit of referring to the capabilities of the places on which he was consulted, has often been recounted. Less familiar, however, are the details of his life. A few authors, notably Horace Walpole and Humphry Repton, paid tribute to Brown's works, but neither in his own century, nor in that which followed, was any serious biographical account of him undertaken, and such brief outlines as were printed by the editors of the *Beauties of England and Wales*, the *Encyclopaedia of Gardening*, or even the *Dictionary of National Biography* are vague and in many respects inaccurate.

Brown's birthplace was the small village of Kirkharle in which his family, of yeoman farming stock, had come to live from Ravenscleugh in the nearby valley of Redesdale where they had long been established.[1] The Ravenscleugh farm-house was rebuilt shortly before 1800, when it was described as standing 'snugly under the hill'. His father, William Browne (the name originally ended with an 'e'), was the son of Dorothy

and Lancelot Browne who died in 1699 and 1700 respectively. Henry Browne of Myre-law (now Mirelaw) House who married Jane Jobson in St. Wilfrid's Church,[2] Kirkharle, in 1707, and George Browne of Shelhoe-hill (now Shielhill) whose twin daughters were baptised here in 1716, were probably his brothers. The name of William's wife is not recorded, but they were married some time before 1704 when a daughter Dorothy was born on 18 May and baptised on 8 June. Another daughter, Mary, was born on 22 August, 1706. John arrived early in 1708 and was baptised on 3 February, followed five years later by George whose baptism was recorded in the parish register on 29 October, 1713. Lancelot came in 1716 and was baptised on 30 August, while Margaret was the last child, being baptised on 1 November, 1719. Her father did not, however, live long enough to see his younger children grow up for he died in 1720, and was buried in the church-yard at Kirkharle on 5 April.[3] The house in which they first lived was pulled down some years later when the village was rebuilt on a new site. The vicar at the time of Lancelot's birth and childhood was Richard Ward who was at Kirkharle from 1672 until 1725.

No doubt the children in their early years went to the village school at Kirkharle, but, as he advanced, Lancelot is known to have attended that at Cambo, two miles away. This was an establishment of some repute which occupied a stone building partly incorporated in the present village hall (Plate 1c). The road which now runs on the east side of Wallington Hall had not then been formed, and his way to school would have been by a track through Little Harle leading to a ford over the Wansbeck, close to a now vanished mill. From here the path climbs steeply to Cambo, skirting Wallington on the west. The school master at this time appears to have been Thomas Gastle, under whose supervision it was later said that 'the fertile and ingenious mind of Capability Brown underwent the first processes of cultivation, and had those seeds of useful learning sown upon it which enabled him to rise to the head of a new and elegant profession.'[4] It was, therefore, a lad of reasonable education and undoubted intelligence who, having come to the end of his school days in 1732, had to decide on his future. In this comparatively remote and sparsely populated area, the prospects were limited. He might have followed a farming life, as did his elder brother George, but instead he took employment with the principle land-owner of Kirkharle, Sir William Loraine.

Up to the early years of that century, Northumberland remained little touched by the tastes and fashions of the south. Constant warfare in the middle ages and subsequent sporadic invasions made keeps and pele towers a necessity long after they were disused elsewhere. A few castles such as Chipchase and Belsay received Jacobean additions, Chillingham was remodelled in the second quarter of the seventeenth century, and there followed some essays by a remarkable Newcastle architect, Robert Trollope, whose particular brand of baroque may still be seen at Capheaton. In general, however, house-

building was a matter of exigency rather than aggrandisement, while gardens remained small, formal, and within hedge or wall – until the wind of change began to blow over the county boundaries in the second decade of the following century, bringing with it that new concept in which landscaping and improvement went hand-in-hand.

As the late Christopher Hussey pointed out in his introduction, written for the first edition of this book and now re-printed, the movement which began soon after 1700 as a revolt from strict formality, and which in due course developed into the fully-fledged landscape garden, was not only a manifestation of changing taste in design, but reflected developments in other directions at the same period. Of these the Palladian revival, which emerged with Leoni's translation of *I Quattro Libri* in 1715, was to be supremely important, but there were other factors which, although of a more practical nature, helped to provide the right conditions. They included the passing of Acts for the enclosure of large areas of hitherto common land, new methods of reclamation and husbandry, the making of better roads, and the importation of new species of trees and shrubs, all of which came under the general heading of 'improvement'. While improvement did not necessarily imply landscaping, no landscape could hope to flourish unless due attention had been paid to the ground on which it was to be formed, and the proper cultivation of the trees with which it was to be planted. On the grand scale such undertakings called for wealth, and enthusiasm tempered by patience from those who participated, but in return they offered enjoyment and relaxation, and not infrequently consolation, in retirement. 'This place affords no News', Lord Orford wrote from Houghton to Colonel Charles Churchill in June, 1743, after he had withdrawn from office as Prime Minister, 'no subjects of Amusement, or Entertainment, to fine men. Men of Wit and Pleasure about town understand not the language, nor taste the pleasures, of the inanimate World. My Flatterers here are all Mutes. The Oaks, the Beeches, the Chestnuts seem to contend, which shall best please the Lord of the Manour. They cannot deceive; they will not lye. I, in sincerity, admire them; and have as many beauties about me as fill up all my hours of dangling, and no disgrace attends me from 67 years of age.'[5] Similarly John Aislabie, retreating from the débâcle of the South Sea Bubble, immersed himself in the transformation of Studley Royal. Before long, however, the pleasures of embellishment and improvement had penetrated to another strata of society, and by 1739 a writer in *The World* commented that 'Every man now, be his fortune what it will, is to be doing something at his Place, as the fashionable phrase is, and you hardly meet with anybody who, after the first compliments, does not inform you that he is in Mortar and moving of Earth, the modest terms for Building and Gardening. One large Room, a Serpentine River and a Wood are become the absolute Necessities of Life, without which a gentleman of the smallest fortune thinks he makes no Figure in the country.'

The counties in which these activities first became apparent on an extensive scale were Surrey and Yorkshire, and it is significant that in both the majority of pioneers in the creation of early 'natural', or transitional, gardens were members of the Kit-Cat Club. That select coterie which met regularly at Jacob Tonson's Thames-side house, Barn Elms, to wine, dine and exchange ideas included the Dukes of Newcastle and Grafton, the former's cousin, Henry Pelham, the Earls of Carlisle and Scarbrough, Sir Richard Temple (later Lord Cobham), Sir John Vanbrugh[6] and the poet Alexander Pope, who was soon to create his own miniature landscape across the water at Twickenham. Other literary members included Joseph Addison and Sir Richard Steele, both of whose pleas for a return to natural gardening had been voiced in the *Guardian* and the *Spectator*.[7]

The creation of Castle Howard by Vanbrugh for Lord Carlisle undoubtedly set an example which was quickly to be followed, if less extensively, by other landowners in the region. Designs for the house were drawn out in 1699 and work began two years later, the carcase being more or less complete by 1707, although it was not occupied for some years. The creation of its setting was a more gradual process during which it it is evident that Lord Carlisle and his architect became increasingly partial to the charms of landscaping, and to the potentialities of reclamation. Although Vanbrugh's parterre to the south of the house was to remain essentially formal, the great Grass Walk extending south-east to the Temple of the Winds, and the creation of a sequence of winding paths, open glades and a cascade descending to a serpentine stream within Wray Wood to the north-east, revealed that growing appreciation of picturesque scenes which led Vanbrugh to plead with the Duchess of Marlborough for the preservation of Woodstock Manor in the Blenheim landscape. This, he urged, with judicious planting, would make 'one of the Most Agreeable Objects that the best of Landskip Painters can invent.'[8]

Although alterations continued to be made to both the building and the grounds at Castle Howard during the next two decades, Vanbrugh was able to describe them in 1721 as 'The Top Seat and Garden of England', adding modestly, 'Of the house I say nothing; The other [the grounds] I may commend because Nature made them; I pretend to no more Merrit in them than a Midwife, who helps to bring a fine child into the World, out of Bushes, Boggs and Bryars.'[9]

Three weeks later he noted in another letter that 'Several Gentlemen in the[se] Parts ... are possess'd w[ith] the Spirit of Building'.[10] and he could have added 'of gardening', for many other landowners had been emulating Lord Carlisle in tackling the bushes, bogs and briars to produce remarkable results. Of these the most spectacular were the semi-natural grounds of Studley Royal, Bramham, Ebberston and Duncombe, the latter with its terrace embanked by a ha-ha, and overlooking the ruins of Rievaulx

Abbey. All had been initiated in the second decade of the century and played an important part in spreading the new principles in garden design, and an interest in 'improvement', not only in Yorkshire but in the more northerly counties of Durham and Northumberland, where Vanbrugh's personal influence was making itself felt from 1719 through his work at Lumley Castle and Seaton Delaval.

It was in the same year in which these two latter works were conceived that William Loraine succeeded, on the death of his father, to the title of second baronet and the family estate at KIRKHARLE (Map 111) (Plates 1A, B and 2A) which he was to transform in the course of the next twenty years. Already sixty at the time of his inheritance, Sir William was a man of wide interests and considerable ability, having practised for several years as a barrister, and being 'skilled in architecture and physic.'[11] His maternal uncle, Sir John Fenwick of Wallington, had married Lady Mary Howard, daughter of the Earl of Carlisle, and he must therefore have followed the activities at Castle Howard with particular interest. Whether he had even a nodding acquaintance with Vanbrugh can only be a matter of speculation, but it is possible that they may have met at some point during the many years spent by Loraine in London, where he had studied law at Lincoln's Inn, and married his first wife, Elizabeth Lawrence, daughter of a City Lord Mayor. After her death he married in 1695 Anne, daughter of Richard Smith of Preston Bissett, a village some three miles from the town of Buckingham. In 1701–2 he represented Northumberland in Parliament and subsequently, as a magistrate and deputy-lieutenant of that county, took a prominent part in public work, in the course of which he would have been well aware of such activities in the neighbourhood as the building of Morpeth Town Hall, the design of which was ascribed to Vanbrugh in 1714. Moreover, Great Bavington, a property which was close to his own at Kirkharle, belonged at this time to Admiral Delaval, the owner of Seaton, whom he must therefore have known well, and whose rebuilding of the latter house would again have been a reason for interest in Vanbrugh's work. The latter's local activities may therefore have been, consciously or unconsciously, an influence when Sir William, acting as his own architect, began the improvement of his comparatively modest domain.

The Kirkharle programme included the remodelling of Sir William's house to form a square stone block with wings at the rear, and new domestic quarters. To the Church of St. Wilfrid he added a west gable, porch and bell turret, this probably following an unfavourable report by the Archdeacon on the condition of the building after a visit on 11 September, 1723.[12] The old village was removed from a site in the shadow of the mansion and rebuilt on higher ground some distance away, and the formal parterre laid out by Sir William's grandfather was also removed to make way for extensive lawns, although a good many mature trees were retained to form groups in the new scene. Further afield Sir William is said to have planted some 24,000 forest trees, nearly

500,000 quick-growing varieties, and 580 fruit trees in the course of improving his estate 'by his industry and his wives' portions'.[13]

How much of this ambitious programme had been accomplished by the time that Lancelot Brown was taken on in 1732 it is not possible to define, but there would have been plenty still in hand to give the young man a thorough knowledge of reclamation, husbandry and horticulture, as well as some familiarity with building construction. That his ability in the former soon became apparent can be judged from the fact that Sir William was within a few years entrusting him with transforming a hitherto rough and boggy tract of land to the north of his house. Over this Brown, in the words of John Hodgson, 'contrived to throw the sweetest charms . . . and to convert the landscape . . . into a "woody theatre of stateliest view".' This tribute was confirmed by Sir William Loraine's great-great-grandson almost a century later when he wrote that this achievement at Kirkharle was 'the first landscape work ever entrusted to his [Sir William's] gardener, afterwards known throughout England as *Capability* Brown.'[14] The Loraines ceased to live at Kirkharle after 1832 when the property was sold to Thomas Anderson of Little Harle who, having another residence, pulled down the mansion but left enough of the domestic quarters to form the present farm house. In the surrounding meadows are groups of venerable trees and, here and there, remains of old foundations visible among the grass. To the north a drive leads to the crest of a hill where stands St. Wilfrid's Church, and it is only from this ridge that the full beauty of the more distant landscape is revealed, the ground dipping sharply to the Parson's Burn, and then rising again across the valley, the whole set with fine plantations of beech, oak and chestnut. If, as now appears certain, this landscape survives from Brown's first creation, it confirms his inherent genius and that remarkable self-confidence which enabled him to tackle large-scale works from the outset of his career. From the experience gained in the employment of Sir William Loraine he had no hesitation in altering land contours, forming lakes or transplanting mature trees. The scale on which his designs were conceived must also, however, have owed much to the natural grandeur of those Northumbrian hills and valleys in which he had been reared, and this characteristic of his work was to distinguish it from the restricted essays of his predecessor, William Kent.[15]

The creation of the landscape at Kirkharle was complete by 1738, and Sir William Loraine, on the threshhold of eighty, was able to sit back and enjoy this achievement for the years that were left to him, which in fact proved to be seven. For Brown the work had earned a reputation further afield, and a commission from Robert Shafto of BENWELL TOWER[16] (Map 22), on the outskirts of Newcastle, to landscape his grounds which lay along the north bank of the Tyne. The only traces of this today are a few fine trees immediately around the house which, remodelled in 1831, stands amid a suburban development.[17]

42

Whether Brown at this time played some part in the various changes then taking place in the grounds of Wallington Hall, which lay across the Wansbeck from Kirkharle, is doubtful. Certainly he had been familiar since childhood with the estate which, originally the home of Sir William Loraine's mother, née Grace Fenwick, had passed to the Blacketts *circa* 1690. On inheriting the property from an uncle in 1728, Sir Walter Calverley Blackett, who would have been well aware of the improvements which had for several years been proceeding at Kirkharle, decided to emulate his neighbour and kinsman. For the improvements to the house he employed Daniel Garrett, who had been one of Lord Burlington's draughtsmen. But the early garden designs which survive, and which, from their semi-natural character with meandering walks threading through tight plantations of trees and a circular pool, appear to be of the mid-1730s, were probably by a 'Mr Joyce' who gave Sir Walter an estimate of £2,155 9s 2d for 'the terrace on the south front' in 1737. If Brown was consulted by Sir Walter at any point in this decade, the proposals seem not to have been committed to paper, but several years later he made changes in that part of the Wallington garden which lies to the east of the Cambo–Kirkharle road (formed about 1755, and carried over the bridge designed by James Paine in that year).[18] At this later date Brown also gave Sir Walter designs for the lakes at Rothley, to the north of the Wallington estate (see page 137).

The wave of landscaping and improvement which passed over this region in the middle of the eighteenth century suggests a strong Brownian influence, but whether he was personally involved in more than two or three cases before 1760 is difficult to establish. The Rev. John Wallis, who was rector of Simonburn, and numbered Brown's brother John among the subscribers to his *History of Northumberland*,[19] describes some of the places which had recently been landscaped, including Gawen Aynsley's 'ancient Tower' overlooking the Wansbeck at Little Harle, with the 'great improvements about it by gardening, plantations and enclosures'; and Hartburn Vicarage, where a 'bank of wood . . . cut into many agreeable walks' had been formed by Archdeacon Sharp, who also added a grotto and a falling stream, as well as making prospects to Thurston Wells and the neighbouring seat of Long Witton. At Capheaton Wallis mentions the 'south lawn' and large park-like enclosure with its small clumps of forest trees through which the 'spire of the tempieto of Belsay', and the 'precipice and villa of Harnham' could be seen.

It is doubtful, however, whether any of these were as early as Mr. Shafto's enterprise at Benwell, and while health may have had a part in Brown's decision to make for a milder climate in the south, ambition is more likely to have been the spur to his seeking wider opportunities than a few local commissions could provide. In the course of his work for Sir William Loraine he would have become familiar with the names of those

men of an older generation who had attained eminence as garden designers, but who were relatively few in number. Vanbrugh had died in 1726 leaving only three practitioners of note – Henry Wise (1655–1738), Charles Bridgeman (?1680–1738) and Stephen Switzer (1682–1745).

Wise had collaborated with Vanbrugh at Blenheim and Hampton Court, while Bridgeman worked with him at Eastbury, Claremont and Stowe. Switzer's principal claim to fame rested on his books of which *The Nobleman's, Gentleman's and Gardeners' Recreation*, first published in 1715 and enlarged to two volumes under the title of *Iconographia Rustica* in 1718, had become a popular manual for those who wished to devise their own improvements. In 1728 Bridgeman was appointed Royal Gardener, a post which he held until his death, although ill-health made him increasingly inactive in the 1730s. It was at the beginning of the latter decade that another figure was coming to the fore in the realm of garden design. This was William Kent, Yorkshire-born but Italian-trained as a painter. Largely through the encouragement of Lord Burlington, Kent turned from painting, in which his reputation was indifferent, to architecture and then to landscape gardening.[20] It was Kent who freed the eighteenth century from the last traces of formality and, in Horace Walpole's words, 'struck out a system from the twilight of imperfect essays', thereby formulating the principles of pure landscape which Brown was in due course to carry to perfection.

For all his genius, William Kent suffered from poor health, a tendency to indolence, and a strong dislike of travelling. As a result his practice was restricted to commissions from the relatively few patient patrons who were prepared to wait for his spasmodic visits and to sort out the muddles which frequently ensued through his inexplicit directions.[21] At Stowe, Bridgeman and Kent were for some years in the 1730s both working for Lord Cobham, the former no doubt finishing schemes which he had initiated, while the latter was designing new buildings and perhaps proposing changes in the garden layout. Joseph Spence, referring to Kent as 'the sole beginner of the present National Taste in Gardening', says that he 'had shown his skill at Lord Cobham's' before 1733,[22] but of this garden work no firm evidence has yet come to light.

In 1738 Wise and Bridgeman died within a few months of each other. News of their demise may therefore have strengthened Brown's resolve to try his luck in the south, where the only figure then left in the front rank of professional garden designers was Kent, to whose brilliance was attached the shadow of reluctant mobility and scant practical knowledge of horticulture. Whatever the incentive, Brown left Kirkharle in 1739.

Whether he had at this time any inkling of a romance which was, some four years later, to link his family with that of his previous employer is not revealed but in 1743 his brother John married Jane, the youngest of Sir William Loraine's four daughters. Jane was then forty, and the only one of the sisters still unmarried. If her parents enter-

tained any reservations about the match, they hid them with good grace, and the marriage took place at Hartburn Church in the parish adjoining Kirkharle on 23 April of that year. It proved entirely happy, and produced three sons, George, William and Richard.[23] According to Sir Lambton Loraine, John Brown subsequently acted as steward for the Kirkharle estate, and Hodgson records that he was the Duke of Portland's agent for the management of the latter's property at Ogle, near Belsay. He appears to have died *circa* 1770. Jane was to survive both her husband and her celebrated brother-in-law by several years, dying in April, 1788.[24]

Five days after John Brown's wedding, another of Lancelot's brothers, George, was married to Catherine, daughter of Thomas Fenwick of Hartburn. He and his family continued to reside at Cambo, from where his one surviving letter of 1773 is addressed to Lancelot (see page 162).[25]

1 The Rev. John Hodgson, *A History of Northumberland*, 1827, Part II, Vol. I, p. 243. This author also mentions, p. 106, that one William Browne of Redesdale was concerned with the conveyancing of land here in 1438.

2 A fourteenth-century church, restored in the seventeenth and eighteenth centuries, and again in 1884.

3 For help over these entries I am greatly indebted to the Rev. A. H. Walker, Vicar of Cambo, which parish is now combined with that of Kirkharle.

4 John Hodgson, *op. cit.* Hodgson's position as one of the foremost historians of Northumberland gives his remarks authority. Much of his life had been spent in this part of the county where he was incumbent successively of the villages of Kirk Whelpington and Hartburn, adjoining Cambo. He must have met many people acquainted with Brown and his relations.

5 Quoted in Rev. Joseph Spence, *Anecdotes of Books and Men*, 1820, p. 407.

6 Knighted in 1714, and given the newly-created post of Surveyor of the Gardens and Waters of the Palaces of England in the following year.

7 Notably Addison in the *Spectator*, 1 March, 1711, 25 June, 1712, and 6 December, 1712; and Steele in the *Guardian*, 29 September, 1713.

8 *The Complete Works of Sir John Vanbrugh*, Vol. IV (*The Letters*), ed. Geoffrey Webb, 1928, p. 30. Letter dated 11 June, 1709.

9 *Op. cit.* To the Duke of Newcastle, 8 August, 1721, p. 136.

10 *Op. cit.* To Brigadier Watkins, 26 August, 1721, p. 138.

11 Quoted in Hodgson, *op. cit.*

12 A summary of the report is noted in the Kirkharle Parish register.

13 Hodgson, *op. cit.*

14 Sir Lambton Loraine, 11th Baronet, *Pedigree and Memoirs of the Family of Loraine of Kirkharle*, printed for private circulation, 1902. A later plan by Brown for further alterations to the Kirkharle grounds was not adopted. Dr. Peter Willis, 'Capability Brown in Northumberland', *Garden History*, Vol. IX, No. 2, 1981.

15 Even Horace Walpole had to admit that Kent's 'ideas were rarely great owing to the novelty of his art. The features in his landscapes were seldom majestic; he aimed at immediate effect. His clumps were puny.' *Essay in Modern Gardening*, 1770.

16 John Hodgson, *op. cit.*

17 The 'Mr. Shafto' mentioned several years later in a letter from Lord Cadogan to Brown, and who

is said to be represented in the drawing in Plate 53 was probably his nephew and heir of the same name.

18 Sir Charles Trevelyan, *Wallington, its History and Treasures*, 1950, p. 18.

19 Rev. John Wallis, *Natural History and Antiquities of Northumberland*, Vol. II, 1769.

20 Margaret Jourdain, *The Work of William Kent*, 1948.

21 Sir Thomas Robinson, *H.M.C. Carlisle*, Part VI. 'The Signior [Kent] ... often gave his orders when he was full of claret and as he did not perhaps see the works for several months after, he had indeed a pretty concise, though arbitrary, manner to set all right, for he would order, without consulting his employer, three or four hundred pounds worth of work to be directly pulled down, and then correct the plan to what it ought to have been at first.'

22 Rev. Joseph Spence, *Anecdotes of Books and Men*, 1820, p. xxxi.

23 This Richard received a legacy under the will of his maternal grandmother, Lady Loraine, in 1756, and another, some thirty years later, from his Uncle Lancelot.

24 That the ties between the two families were maintained by the next generation is confirmed by the presence on 23 November, 1780, of Lancelot Brown's son of the same name, by then a barrister of Lincoln's Inn, as a godfather at the Kirkharle christening of the baby William Loraine, later 9th Baronet.

25 28 April, 1743. *History of Northumberland*, Vol. XII, p. 368.

II

STOWE:
A STEPPING STONE TO SUCCESS

WHEN BROWN left Northumberland in 1739, he headed in the direction of the Oxfordshire–Buckinghamshire border, and there is little doubt that the reason lay in an introduction to Lady Loraine's father, Richard Smith, then close on ninety years old and still living at Preston Bissett, the estate which he had inherited together with land at Padbury from his father, Harris Smith.[1] In 1724 Richard Smith had served as High Sheriff of Buckinghamshire, and he was well known over a wide area. He was therefore in a position to help in a quest for employment, and is likely to have been responsible for recommending Brown to the owner of KIDDINGTON HALL (Map 108) (Plate 2B) near Woodstock, a little way over the Oxfordshire border.

This owner was Sir Charles Browne, second Baronet, with whose antecedents Lancelot could not, however, claim a connection. The former's great-grandfather had purchased the property *circa* 1613, but the house had been largely rebuilt over old foundations by the first Baronet in 1673. Sir Charles's wife, Mary, was a daughter of George Pitt of Stratfieldsaye and was thus a distant cousin of William Pitt, whose friendship with Lord Cobham of Stowe was long-standing. The Brownes were probably well acquainted with Stowe and the garden activities proceeding there, which possibly inspired Sir Charles's decision to landscape his own comparatively modest grounds at Kiddington *circa* 1740.

The authority for attributing the lake there to Lancelot Brown rests on John Penn, the Buckinghamshire landowner and man of letters who, in his *History and Descriptive Account of Stoke Park*, published in 1813, stated that 'the first piece of water which he formed was at Lady Mostyn's in Oxfordshire.' Lady Mostyn of Kiddington was in fact the only grandchild of Sir Charles Browne who, dying in 1751, was succeeded by his son George.[2] The latter survived him by only three years, Kiddington then passing to his daughter Barbara who had by this time married Sir Edward Mostyn of Talacre, Flintshire. After her husband's death in 1775, she returned to live at her childhood

home. Although she later re-married, she seems to have been known mostly as Lady, or Dame Barbara, Mostyn, which would account for John Penn's remembering her by this name.

It is not difficult to accept the lake at Kiddington as an early Brown work. From the house[3] and nearby medieval church the ground slopes steeply southward to the water where the little river Glyme assumes, by damming, a lake-like proportion and boasts a small tree-covered island at its widest point. On the far side the ground rises again, and is planted with groups of trees, many of which are of considerable age. Upstream, where it narrows, the river is crossed by a bridge, now rebuilt, originally carrying a road to the house and church before the making of the present drive. Assuming that the lake was formed in 1740, Barbara Browne would have been ten years old, and certainly old enough to recollect the undertaking which she may herself have recounted in later life to John Penn.

In giving a brief outline of Brown's early career in his *History*, Penn stated that he had found 'uncommonly few notices concerning him in books of reference [which] furnish materials to the biographer'. He therefore proceeded to give his own account of how Brown, shortly after the Kiddington commission, came to the notice of Lord Cobham who asked a local nurseryman 'whether he knew of anyone who could continue with him at Stow, able to converse instructively on his favourite pursuit, but free from the vanity and conceit which had rendered his former assistants disinclined to alterations upon which he had determined'. The nurseryman, according to Penn, thereupon recommended Brown who, 'already a landscape gardener, became an inmate of that princely mansion'. Penn added, however, that 'though Lord Cobham zealously patronised him, he there allowed him no opportunity for substituting any designs of his own.'

There are several facts which give credence to Penn's account. Born in 1760, he spent most of his life at STOKE HOUSE (Map 175), having succeeded in 1775 to the property which his father, Thomas Penn, had acquired from the executors of Lady Cobham. It was to Stoke, which came to her from her father, that she had retired after the death of Lord Cobham in 1749.[4] Her resuming residence here no doubt prompted the 'plan for modernising Stoke' which Penn says was drawn out in 1750 'by another genius, the celebrated Brown, who had long lived with Lord Cobham assisting him in the improvements at Stow[e]. This plan, having remained at the old house when purchased [by Thomas Penn] is in the possession of the present owner, and had in common with that afterwards adopted the object of producing the appearance of a natural river, by linking five quandrangular pieces of water more suited to the taste of former times.' This proposal, however, was apparently shelved, though it formed the basis for the alterations carried out by Richmond some years later.[5]

To Stoke House John Penn added, at the turn of the century, the adjoining estate of Stoke Park, previously owned by Field Marshall Sir George Howard for whom it had been landscaped by Brown in 1765–7, when, in Penn's words, the latter's reputation 'having made him known to the new possessor, he was invited back to the county in which he had so long resided,' a fact later confirmed by Brown's account book where he noted the receipt of £800 for this work.

As well as having lived for most of his life in what had been Lady Cobham's home, Penn was a close friend of the younger generation of her husband's relations, and particularly the Hon. Thomas Grenville of Wotton to whom he sent a copy of his *History* on its publication in 1813. With this went a letter bearing his 'compliments to Lords and Ladies Grenville and Nugent'.[6] He would therefore have taken care to make any references to Lord Cobham as accurate as possible. As he was twenty-three at the time of Brown's death, he could well have met him, and certainly was acquainted with a number of those who had been his friends or clients. It is equally certain that a stroke can now be put through the tradition which has hitherto persisted that Brown was, on coming south, first given work as a garden labourer at Wotton by Richard Grenville, and from there worked his way to Stowe. It is just possible that Grenville may have employed him as early as 1740, but not in a menial capacity, and it is far more likely that the designs which Brown gave for Wotton were made, with Cobham's agreement, after he had settled at Stowe in or after 1742, when Grenville was able by Act of Parliament to enclose more land.[7]

That Lord Cobham did on occasion 'lend' his head gardener is now confirmed, as will be seen later in this chapter.

*   *   *   *   *

When Lancelot Brown took up his duties at STOWE (Map 180) (Plates 3A and B) he was twenty-four, and his total years did not equal those which Lord Cobham had already devoted to the embellishment of his house and gardens. Inheriting the estate as Sir Richard Temple, second Baronet, in 1697, he had been too deeply engaged in Marlborough's campaigns to pay much attention to his estate until temporary retirement in 1710. Resuming military and political activities in 1713, he gained a barony in 1714, and four years later was created Viscount Cobham. His own financial resources were augmented at this time by a share of the booty from the successful attack on Vigo, in Spain, in which Cobham took command. He was thus able to carry out further work at Stowe until 1733 when political disagreement with Sir Robert Walpole brought about his final retirement, although he continued to take a keen interest in politics. From then he was free to devote himself whole-heartedly to his passion for building and garden-

49

ing, a passion in which he was supported by a close circle of friends and relations which included the 'mob of nephews' from Wotton, the Lytteltons of Hagley, and the poets Alexander Pope, Gilbert West (another nephew), and James Thomson. There was also that brilliant but then impecunious young cornet from his own regiment, William Pitt, who had now turned to politics and was later to marry Cobham's niece, Hester Grenville. Later, Pitt was himself to emerge as an amateur landscape designer of considerable ability.

According to Joseph Spence,[8] it was just prior to Cobham's retirement in 1733 that William Kent made his first contribution to the Stowe scene, and by 1734 Sir Thomas Robinson described the grounds here, with those of Claremont and Chiswick, as being 'now full of labourers to lay them out without level or line after Mr. Kent's notion.'[9] Charles Bridgeman, whose professional advice had hitherto contributed extensively to what was accomplished at Stowe, was now bowing himself out, probably due to increasing ill-health,[10] leaving Kent to carry on with the Temples of Venus, Contemplation, Ancient Virtue and British Worthies, and the gradual naturalising of the hitherto semi-formal groves and plantations. Kent's actual visits are, however, a matter of speculation, but his aversion to travel was probably tempered in this case by the degree of comfort prevailing in Lord Cobham's hospitable household. For the first years of the 1740s he probably continued to come at intervals, and to give Lord Cobham drawings for his proposals which would then be handed on to Brown for execution, and thereby exert their influence on the latter. It is, however, likely that as Lord and Lady Cobham usually spent the winter months in London, the house in Hanover Square may have provided a rendezvous for Kent to discuss his schemes. It is to be hoped that more details will one day emerge to provide fuller details of Kent's participation at Stowe. Meanwhile the vast corpus of Temple–Grenville–Buckingham material deposited in the Huntington Library[11] has already yielded a number of facts relating to Lancelot Brown's ten years here.[12] They confirm John Penn's assertion that Brown was in fact recognised as an able undertaker of garden projects by the time he entered Lord Cobham's service.

Up to the beginning of 1741 there had been no appropriate opening at Stowe, but in February of that year one offered itself through the departure of William Love, who had held the post of head gardener here for fifteen years, and who is named as a subscriber to Stephen Switzer's *Practical Husbandman and Planter* of 1733–4. Love had supervised the making of the Eleven-Acre Lake under Bridgeman's direction, and the creation of the Elysian Fields. In succeeding him Brown therefore found himself in a responsible position, acting as paymaster and taking charge of some forty men working in the grounds.

The accounting procedure at this time required that the head gardener's bills should

be rendered regularly to the steward at Stowe, by whom they were forwarded to a London steward, Mr. Smith. This routine Brown followed from the second week of March, 1741. The Stowe steward at the time of his arrival was William Roberts but within six months the latter had committed suicide, apparently for the reasons given in a letter from Ralph Verney of Claydon to his father on 23 August, 1741: 'Lord Cobham's steward hang'd himself soon after the Assizes, he has left 4 or 5 children behind him. He was reputed an Atheist and was a great favourite of Lord C. He was uneasy at Mr. D—'s conviction of the Deer Stealer and used Mr. D— at the Assize not so civily as he should upon which he complained to Lord C. who reprimanded him for it, which vex'd him so much that he made away with himself.'[13] Lord Cobham undertook the expense of educating three of Roberts's children, while the place of steward was filled by Thomas Potts, although Leonard Lloyd of Buckingham was brought in to check the latter's accounts before sending them on to Smith in London. This soon led to quarrels between the two men, but was justified in the following year when suspicion grew as to Potts's honesty, and culminated in his disappearance with a considerable sum of money. Lloyd was thereupon appointed steward as from October, 1742.

Meanwhile Lancelot Brown, having settled down at Stowe in spite of these dramas, earned for himself general esteem and a reputation for integrity which led to his being entrusted with the disbursement of money not only to the under-gardeners, but to the carpenters, carters, sawyers, plasterers and masons: in fact, it is clear that he was virtually acting as Clerk of the Works for the many alterations in hand at this period to buildings as well as in the grounds. With a non-resident steward (Lloyd lived 'near the Church in Buckingham'), his duties were exacting and reveal the remarkable degree of competence which he possessed in spite of comparative youth, as well as a good measure of tact which was essential in a situation where the owner considered himself the presiding genius.

Within two or three years Brown was increasing his knowledge of architecture and familiarising himself with technical terms by copying out a fifteen page glossary. The explanations are in many cases identical with, or a paraphrasing of, those in the *Builder's Dictionary or Gentleman's and Architect's Companion* of 1734,[14] and leave no doubt that it was on this useful manual that he based the exercise. By 1747 he had become competent in drawing out building plans, and a garden account for April in that year is endorsed with a note that he would be sending – presumably to Lord Cobham in London – a 'plan of the Long Room' which he had been unable to finish in time for that day's post. It is evident that in the presentation of his landscape designs Brown was strongly influenced by William Kent's style of delineation, as well as by the latter's theories. No example of his drawing prior to his arrival at Stowe has been found, but there has now come to light an outline drawing on which the endorsement 'Upright

of Gibbs' Building' is written in Brown's hand. Although this is not conclusive evidence that the elevation itself was drawn by him, the latter is probably a copy made by him, perhaps at the time of some proposed alteration previous to those for which Giambattista Borra scribbled notes in French on the drawing, *circa* 1753. In Brown's first surviving landscape drawing (a rough sketch for the park at Packington *circa* 1749), the general outlines, the rocky cascade, and the effective representation of both hardwoods and softwoods owes much to Kent, many of whose drawings he must have seen at Stowe, although only one – a sketch for the shrine of British Worthies – remains in the house today.

While there is no single feature in the grounds which can be ascribed with certainty to Brown alone, the creation of the Grecian Valley must by date and deduction be largely his work. The replacing of Bridgeman's parterre by a lawn to the south of the house in 1743, the cutting of cross views through the avenues, and some alteration of the lakes were all carried out under his supervision, as was the planting of thousands of trees, mainly beech, elm and Scots fir. Many of these trees were already of considerable size at the time of transplanting, and it may have been for their removal that Brown invented a machine to lever them out and carry them to a new site.[15] In 1742–3 he was organising the supplies of stone from three different quarries, and the work of four masons then employed on work in the house (the library and chapel), the Palladian Bridge, the Gothic and Lady's Temples, and a grotto in the grounds; as well as new stables and coach-houses. He would also have been concerned with the building in 1747 of the octagonal column, 115 feet in height, and intended by Lord Cobham as a prospect tower from which to survey the landscape achievements of a lifetime. Probably the latter had in mind the column erected by Sarah, Duchess of Marlborough, to the memory of the 1st Duke, and the similarity was heightened when, after his death two years later, Cobham's widow turned the tower into a memorial to her husband.[16] Appropriate tributes inscribed on the base while over the lantern Cobham's statue presided until struck by lightning in 1957. The column stands as a focal point at the end of the 'Grecian diagonal', that is, the oblique south-easterly view which is obtained from the steps of the Temple of Concord, and which is at an angle to the Grecian Valley. The Valley itself was the last great work to be carried out in Cobham's life, and involved the removal of some 23,500 cubic yards of earth[17] to form an extensive glade of dog-leg outline with thickly planted slopes.

It is possible that the first idea of the Grecian Valley may have stemmed from William Kent in the course of one of his spasmodic visits or discussions in London earlier in the decade, but he certainly would not have seen the inception of the work over which 'Mr. Brown', as he is styled in the accounts from 1747 onwards, presided. By now he was no longer afraid to put forward a little reasoning of his own to Lord

Cobham, and in a letter of 24 February, 1746 to the latter, then in London, he excuses himself for some apparent misunderstanding as to 'finishing the Head of the Oval' (that is, the Valley), and continues: 'I had never formed any other idea on it than what your Lordship gave me which was to Forme the Laurell Plantation with the sweep under it and Concave to the Ovall that the Slope of the Head your Lordship thought might some time or other have statues put upon it, but gave me no absolute Orders to finish it and indeed I think it would be better not finished this season, I thinking that a sumer's talk and tryels about it may make it a very fine thing.' A very fine thing it did indeed become, and it now seems clear that its ultimate beauty was not the outcome of Kent's genius but of constant 'talk and tyrels' on the part of Lord Cobham and his right-hand man.

Lord Cobham's willingness to lend his head gardener suggests that it may have been Brown who was involved in the strange incident described in a letter of 31 December, 1741, from Ralph Verney to his father. This concerned a neighbour, Mr. Souldern, who was tricked by an imposter over the sale of his house, near Aynho. Several local tradesmen were similarly deceived by the man who subsequently disappeared after arranging for a builder to re-front the house, and for 'Lord Cobham's gardener to lay out the garden.'[18] In the following year, Richard Grenville (later Earl Temple) was extending his estate at WOTTON (Map 206) (Plate 4A), and although regrettably few details have so far come to light, it is certain that Brown was playing some part in the changes made to his grounds early in the 1740s. Fragmentary evidence comes in entries made in Grenville's 'personal account'[19] for small payments to 'Browne, ye Stowe Gardener' in 1742, 1744 and 1746, these probably representing gratuities. Richard was the elder son of Richard Grenville who had married Lord Cobham's sister. As heir to the childless owner of Stowe, he spent almost as much time there as at his own home, and shared his uncle's passion for landscaping. The loan of Brown for the designing of his own grounds is therefore not surprising, and resulted in a splendid scene with the house[20] standing on a ridge from which the garden front overlooks gentle slopes to the lake. The appearance of the grounds in their prime is described by Thomas Whately, who mentions the various adornments including the octagon near the water, and a Chinese tea-house which survived until the 1930s. Another feature, which later disappeared, was the 'elegant bridge, with a colonnade upon it', which sounds like a version of the Palladian bridge at Stowe.[21] This was seen by Thomas Jefferson in the course of his brief visit to Wotton on 5 April, 1786, when he noted that Whately had not referred to it in his book.[22]

Brown also undertook for Richard Grenville the improvement of the grounds of FINMERE RECTORY (Map 75), a modest stone house in this North Oxfordshire village. The property had been acquired by the latter from the executors of Nathaniel Bacon

in 1748. The house was pulled down and the gardens largely destroyed when a new Rectory was built in the 1830s; the appearance of the eighteenth-century miniature landscape is now known only from Lord Selborne's description of it as 'A slope of green turf ... [with] cedars, spruce firs, groups of other well chosen trees and shrubs and pretty flower beds; all so disposed as to produce the effect of a long perspective and considerable space where there was really little.'[23]

In the autumn of 1745 Brown was to be borrowed again, this time for altering the grounds of NEWNHAM PADDOX (Map 138) (Plate 4B), the home of the Cobham's close friends, Lord and Lady Denbigh. Returning to England in 1741 after a lengthy stay abroad, the 5th Earl and Isabella his Countess embarked on the improvement of both their country and London houses, the latter being in Hanover Square where they were neighbours of the Cobhams during the winter months which both couples usually spent in town. A Building Book[24] covering the 1740s shows that some minor garden work was in hand at Newnham in 1742–3, before Brown was consulted. In the summer of the latter year Hester Grenville went to stay there and returned with an injunction to find out what would be the best trees to form a hedge. 'I have enquired of all the learned,' she wrote to the Countess on 15 September, 'and they all agree that Dutch Elm is the properest, but my Lord [Cobham] say's they will form a quicker and better hedge still if mixed with English Elm.'[25] Not only was Lord Cobham's advice forthcoming, but also the loan of £500 and, later on, of his garden assistant.

The first written reference to Brown's plan for Newnham Paddox comes in the Building Book, where it was noted under 28 April, 1746, that work had begun on 'the alteration of ye great canal, and carrying it on to ye head of ye Pond in the Park by a plan and the direction of Mr. Brown, Gardener to Lord Cobham, with other work done in consequence of this.' The plan, by which the old formal ponds and canals were turned into a serpentine lake, is likely to have been drawn out some months before, and was probably discussed during Lady Denbigh's visit to Stowe in the preceding August.[26] Alterations continued during 1747–8 when Brown appears to have spent several days at Newnham towards the end of July, probably planning the levelling of the 'End of the Serpentine Water', and laying out the surroundings of the 'First pond in the Park ... with hanging slopes.' A gap in the Building Book between August 1749 and 1753 suggests that the Denbigh's finances were again at a low ebb. By the time garden work was resumed under Brown's direction, the latter had left Stowe and had set up his own practice on the outskirts of London. Later still he was to draw up plans for the remodelling of the house (see page 71).

The completion of the house and grounds at WAKEFIELD (Map 194), five miles north-east of Stowe, is said to have been undertaken by Brown in, or possibly before, 1748. It had been designed by Kent as a hunting lodge (although an unusually grand

one) for his 'true friend', the Duke of Grafton, but the work had dragged on and was still not finished at the time of Kent's death, so that consultation with Brown would have been a likely course.[27] Horace Walpole, who saw the place in the course of his tour in 1751, considered it 'too heavy',[28] and there is a massive grandeur about the exterior which is Vanbrugian rather than Palladian. This is largely due to the Tuscan portico, and the lunette windows, like half-closed eyes, above the *piano nobile*. The entrance hall, however, is a reflection of Inigo Jones's Queen's House at Greenwich, running the full height of the main storeys with a gallery at first-floor level supported on consoles. The house stands on a slight hill, the grounds sloping to a lake on the far side of which stretches what was once 'a noble lawn, nearly a mile in extent; the smooth features and soft tints of which are finely contrasted by the bold and abrupt aspect of a dense woodland scene terminating the view.'[29] Most of this is now farmland.

* * * * *

Lord Cobham's death on 13 September, 1749, marked the end of an era at Stowe. Having no son, his estates passed to his sister, the widow of Richard Grenville, who had died in 1727. Hester was created Countess Temple in 1750, but survived for only two years, being succeeded by her elder son Richard. Meanwhile Cobham's widow had moved to Stoke House, the property left to her by her father, Edmund Halsey.

For Brown these changes indicated that the time had come to establish an independent practice. Most of the features with which he had been concerned in the Stowe gardens were completed or nearing completion at the time of Lord Cobham's death, and the first phase of activity at Newnham Paddox was also half-finished. By now he was a family man, having married on 22 November, 1744, Bridget Wayet, one of the daughters of a 'very respectable county family of Boston and Tumby-in-Bain, Lincolnshire'.[30] The wedding took place in St. Mary's Church, Stowe, the small medieval building which stands within a few hundred yards of the house although screened from it by trees. Here in due course their first child, a daughter, was christened Bridget (Plate 64A) in 1746 and two years later the christening of a son, Lancelot, was recorded on 13 January, 1748. William's name followed on 17 April, 1750, but he survived less than a month, and the last Brown child to be christened at Stowe was named John on 23 April, 1751.

Brown did not move from Stowe until the late autumn of 1751,[31] when his place was filled by one Woodward, 'who lived to a great age in Buckingham.'[32] During the preceding two years, however, he had been building up the foundation for his future practice by undertaking a group of commissions within a fifty-mile radius. While that for Packington concerned the grounds and garden buildings only, structural work was involved at Warwick Castle, and at Croome he was to design a new house as well as the carcase of the church in a landscape setting.

PACKINGTON HALL (Map 144) (Plates 5A, B, and 6A, B) had been built by Sir Clement Fisher early in the eighteenth century. Although it was described in 1732 as 'new and very beautiful . . . in the Middle of a Spacious Park,'[33] no illustration of it is known, and the structure was later incorporated in the present Hall, built in 1766–72 by the elder Matthew Brettingham for the 3rd Earl of Aylesford. It was this Earl who, as Lord Guernsey (the 2nd Earl being still alive but then living at Albury) had some sixteen years earlier obtained Brown's designs for the grounds which are preserved in the house. The first drawing is a rough survey, unsigned and undated, but clearly in his hand and of about 1750. Over the existing layout he has superimposed his ideas for 'improvement', sketching in the course of a serpentine lake, a new curving drive to replace a straight avenue, and new plantations, writing over one of the original thickets 'Take this away'.

In the following year Brown's ideas were drawn out neatly on the 'Plan for the disposition of the ground at Packington, the Seat of the Rt. Hon. The Lord Guernsey', with marginal details for three proposed features, 'My Lady's Lodge', new entrance gates and a grotto, the trees growing above the latter shown in a curiously stylised manner which he does not seem to have used again, and which was probably an experiment in draughtsmanship. Neither the gates nor the lodge were executed, but traces of the grotto in a simplified form are still visible at the east end of the lake, while some of the plantations can also be identified although many more were added by the 4th Earl in the nineteenth century. It was, however, in Brown's landscape that Brettingham subsequently carried out the remodelling of the old house, and Joseph Bonomi built in 1789 a remarkable neo-classical church.[34]

On the reverse of Brown's first rough sketch of the layout at Packington is scribbled an outline drawing which has recently been identified as showing the house and garden at CHARLECOTE (Map 40), some twenty miles to the south-west.[35] This suggests that Brown visited the latter on the same expedition in 1750, but some time elapsed before any results materialised. George Lucy had inherited Charlecote from an elder brother in 1744, and spent a quiet bachelor life in this Elizabethan house,[36] the domestic arrangements of which were in the care of Mrs. Hayes, a widowed lady who kept a *Memorandum Book* which is useful in providing dates for various events. Brown may have been recommended by Anne, Countess of Coventry, a distant cousin of the 6th Earl and a close friend of George Lucy. On 29 September, 1757, Mrs. Hayes noted in her book that 'Mr. Brown began to make alterations upon Wellsborn Brook', these being in the charge of Horsbrough, a man who had previously worked for David Hiorne on the construction of a bridge over the same brook.

In May, 1760, Mr. Lucy signed an agreement with Brown by which the latter undertook to widen the river Avon, and lay its banks so as to give them a 'natural and easy level'. He was also to make the fosse, or sunk fence, surrounding the meadow; to fill

up the old ponds by the north front of the house; and to lay the lawns. The Welles-bourne was dammed to form a cascade at the point where it joins the Avon, Scotch firs were planted in the 'wilderness', and by Hiorne's bridge, while cedars of Lebanon and other trees were introduced on the lawns around the house. By this time Horsbrough seems to have left and John Midgely, later to become Brown's foreman at Castle Ashby, was put in charge.

George Lucy went off to Bath for a change in April, 1761, only to find Brown staying there, probably *en route* for Corsham or Longleat. Brown had called on him, as he wrote to a friend, 'not on business, as he said, but to enquire after my health, and told me he should not be at Charlecote till May, which I suppose will be June at soonest. I did not well know how to construe this visit; I told him the time was elapsed for a second payment which he said was no matter as he did not want money, but upon my offering him a £100 note he pulled out his pocket book and carried it off with him'[37] Brown had by then no doubt learnt the truth of the adage that a bird in the hand was worth two in the bush. Whether he reached Charlecote in May or June is not recorded, but the work was duly completed, and much of it remains today.

The transformation of CROOME (Map 55) (Plates 7A, B and 8A, B), in Worcestershire, was to be one of the largest undertakings of Brown's early practice, and a considerable amount of reclamation had to be tackled before any building work could be put in hand. His practical experience no doubt weighed in the decision of Lord Deerhurst (who succeeded as 6th Earl of Coventry in March, 1751) to place the commission in his hands in or possibly just before 1750. The estate lies in a low plain between the rivers Avon and Severn, and at this time was still virtually the marshland which had created constant problems for the owners of earlier houses on the site. The first house of which there is a record was Jacobean, but this had been replaced at the end of the seventeenth century by a three-storey double pile house of eleven bays, flanked by lower wings, each divided into five bays by Ionic pilasters, with oval windows in an attic storey.[38] There was a small formal parterre with two gazebos in front of the house, and a number of half-timbered farm buildings and sheds in the flat rough ground immediately adjacent.

A suggestion for the thorough reclamation of the environs seems first to have come from Lord Coventry's friend Sanderson Miller, himself an able amateur architect, for, when the project was nearing completion, the Earl wrote to him 'Whatever merit Croomb may in future time boast, it will be ungrateful not to acknowledge you the primary Author ... It was to your assurance that Nature had been more liberal to me than I apprehended.'[39] In fact it is more than likely that Miller may have been responsible for introducing Brown for he certainly knew him and had recorded that in the course of a short visit to Stowe on 7 November, 1749, he had walked 'in the Garden with the Comp. [company] and Mr. Brown and Dorrel: 5 h[ours].' In the following summer he

recorded that Brown had visited him at Radway Grange, his home near Edgehill in Warwickshire, on 10 August. 'W[alked] with him to the Castle etc., he dined here – rode with him across ye Valley etc.' The 'castle', an octagonal gothic tower set among 'ruins' on the slopes of Edgehill had recently been completed by Miller and provided a favourite object for exercise. On the 26th of the same month he noted that he had written 'to Lord Cobham and Mr. Brown.'[40] Unfortunately there is no clue as to the contents of the letter to Brown, but Croome is likely to have come into this, and certainly into their conversations.

Brown tackled the drainage problems at Croome by laying extensive culverts from the old house to the artificial 'river' which was to form part of the landscape, thereby rendering the old foundations sufficiently dry to serve as a substructure for the new building. The house itself was to be a Palladian essay of stone with corner turrets rising above the main block. There are eleven bays to the principal facades, as in the earlier house, and it is evident that a good deal of the old masonry was retained, which accounts for the transverse corridor following the 'spine' of the original double pile building. The north front has a pediment over the three centre bays, while on the south a tetrastyle portico projects from the *piano nobile*. The design is similar to that for Newnham Paddox which Brown drew out shortly afterwards.[41] The new stable block to the east of the house was built in brick with stone dressings, although it may originally have been intended to face the whole range with ashlar.

Work on the house proceeded swiftly and to the Earl's satisfaction for on 14 November, 1752 he wrote to Miller: 'Mr. Brown has done very well by me, and indeed I think has studied both my Place and my Pocket, which are not always conjunctively the Objects of Prospectors'.[42] Two weeks later Sir Edward Turner wrote: 'Lord Coventry is furnishing his house with elegance.'[43] At this stage, however, the 'furnishing' would have related to those entertaining rooms for the decoration of which Brown had been responsible, that is, the entrance hall, with its screen of fluted doric columns, the dining room, billiard room and the saloon, in the centre of the south range, which has an enriched cornice and massive central doorcase flanked by Corinthian columns supporting a broken pediment. The long gallery, occupying the full extent of the west side of the house, and the tapestry (originally breakfast) room[44] on the south-east were to await decoration by Robert Adam who gave his first design for a ceiling (unexecuted) in September, 1760.[45] On the 30th of that month, however, a shadow was cast over Croome by the death of Lady Coventry. Work was eventually resumed, and the Adam rooms were completed in time for the Earl's second marriage in 1764.

Meanwhile Brown's work in the grounds had continued during the 1750s when the sinuous outline of the 'river' was formed, beginning with a wide pool, fed from a spring, then narrowing to wind past the west front of the house where it was crossed by a

timber (now iron) bridge. Widening again in an eastward turn, it was then brought into view of the garden front before another turn southward carried it to the extremity of the park. Although Adam was later to design the greenhouse and more distant panorama tower, Brown appears to have been responsible for the rotunda on the knoll to the south. He also devised the grotto at the head of the water, and the arched tunnel which runs under the road to Upton, and links the grounds with a further area to the north.[46] On the island in the wider part of the lake he built a small summerhouse with a Corinthian order. In this were set, some years later, three Coade stone plaques, Mrs. Eleanor Coade's receipt noting that she was paid £26 13s od for these and other items on 12 July, 1778 by a 'draft drawn on Messrs. Drummond sent to me by Lancelot Brown Esqr.'[47]

Brown's surviving account book begins too late to include details of his first contract with Lord Coventry, but it does give a few details of payments made after June, 1760. From this it appears that Benjamin Read was the foreman left in charge. Small sums for unspecified work are also noted as paid to William and David Hiorne, the brothers who carried out a considerable amount of building in the Warwickshire area at this time.

Brown's next important task at Croome was the rebuilding on a new site of the CHURCH OF ST. JAMES THE APOSTLE (Map 55), which stands in the park, to the east of the house. The faculty for taking down the earlier church is dated 16 March, 1758, and the deed of conveyance drawn up on 4 July, the attached plan proposing a classical structure with a tetrastyle portico.[48] As carried out, however, the design was gothic, with an almost square aisled nave and a chancel in which were re-erected the early Coventry monuments from the old church. The tower is in three stages with a pierced parapet and pinnacles. The decoration of the interior was again left to Robert Adam, whose executed work follows fairly closely his original drawings[49] which are dated 1761. His bills submitted to Lord Coventry include an item of £7 7s od for 'sections of the inside . . . finishings' of the church, and designs for a gothic chair and a painted window in the chancel, priced at £2 2s od and £10 10s od.[50]

In 1758 Lord Coventry, anxious to have a worthy record of the transformation which had taken place, commissioned Richard Wilson to paint the house and its surroundings, and in November paid him twenty-one guineas on account. The new church, which was to feature in the background, can barely have been begun, but it kept pace with the painting which must have been more or less finished in May of the following year when Wilson was paid another thirty guineas 'in full of all demands by me'. In its representation of the house bathed in sunlight, the rotunda on its hill and the bridge over the water, the painting portrays the ideal landscape scene.[51]

Such perfection, however, required continual care and maintenance, and in 1772 the lake began to give trouble. 'The head is faulty,' Lord Coventry wrote to Brown on

21 November, 'my conjurers have tried to rectify it, but find the work beyond their skill. I must therefore desire that you will send me a man of practice and sound direction for that important work. I call it so, because all the enjoyment of Croome next summer will depend upon it . . . Cou'd Mr. Read be spar'd? As he first made the Head he wou'd be the fittest person to restore it.[52] I believe the roots of the Trees have been a chief cause of the fissures in the bank. I must also beg that you will send the plan of the Farm House etc. that we may lay our foundations early in the spring. I mean to stay here till the new year and heartily invite you to a Christmas gambol.'[53]

The farmhouse plan was for one on the Croome estate, but at about this time Brown was also to design a modest house for Lord Coventry at Spring Hill, some three miles south-east of Broadway, and about fifteen from Croome. This was apparently intended as a retreat from the social involvements of the latter where, as the Earl had complained to Sanderson Miller some years before, 'The Hospitality my ancestors exercised for some generations at Croome makes it impossible for me to effect any privacy or retirement there. It has always been an Inn and always must remain so.'[54] The house which was duly built still stands but has been altered out of recognition by Victorian additions to its original five bays. The surrounding heights were planted with shelter belts, but further planting was carried out after the property had been sold in 1830 to General Lygon, a veteran of Waterloo, who is said to have set his beech clumps to represent the positions of British divisions during the battle.

Lord Coventry was among the most long-lived of all Brown's clients, dying at the age of eighty-seven in 1809, and remembering his friend long after the latter's death in 1783, for in 1797 he had erected by the lake-side path a memorial in the form of a casket[55] on a pedestal bearing the inscription:

To the Memory of
Lancelot Brown
who by the powers of
his inimitable
and creative genius
formed this garden scene
out of a morass.

The work which Brown was to carry out at WARWICK CASTLE (Map 196) (Plate 10A) for Francis Lord Brooke, later 1st Earl of Warwick, ran almost parallel with that for Lord Coventry and was probably already in hand by the beginning of 1750. Lord Brooke had for some years been engaged on a sequence of improvements which was to continue for the rest of his life, and in 1744 took a preparatory step toward garden schemes by obtaining powers to close a footway which had previously passed close to

the west side of the Castle and led to two riverside watering places. The land thus gained was then taken into the Castle grounds where the garden still consisted of four parterres and an ancient mound on the west.[56] It was this area which first received Brown's attention, together with the stoney river bank immediately below the Castle walls, for although no drawings or accounts have so far come to light for this early phase, sufficient had been accomplished to earn Horace Walpole's commendation during a brief visit in the summer of 1751. Writing to George Montague on 22 July he described the Castle as enchanting, and continued:

> The view pleased me more than I can express; the river Avon tumbles down a cascade at the foot of it. It is well laid out by one Brown who has set up on a few ideas of Kent and Mr. Southcote. One sees what the prevalence of taste does; little Brooke who would have chuckled to have been born in an age of clipt hedges and cockle-shell avenues, has submitted to let his garden and park be natural.[57]

In the transformation the mount and parterres had disappeared, their place being taken by a grassy slope to the river, planted with groups of trees. At that time the main Warwick road was carried over the Avon by the old town bridge which stood nearer to the Castle, giving a closer view of its massive walls, with Castle Meadow and the cascade below. This bridge later collapsed and was rebuilt by Robert Mylne further to the east in 1765.

The terms on which the first work was carried out are not known, but in 1753 Brown entered into a new agreement with Lord Brooke whereby he undertook alterations in the Castle itself. This included the rebuilding of the porch and stairs to the Great Hall, removing garden steps by the Watergate Tower, making a way to Caesar's Tower from the domestic offices, levelling the courtyard and making a drive into it, as well as other minor items.[58] The Castle Vouchers for 1755 show that most of this work had been completed by this date but in Castle Park, which lay on the south side of the river, Brown was supervising considerable landscape undertakings for the rest of the decade. In 1758 a wooden bridge was built to his orders over the Avon near Spiers' Lodge, and in 1761 he planned the construction of a dam in the Ram Brook.

In addition to the miscellaneous items already mentioned, Brown also appears to have been responsible for enlarging a suite of rooms in the Castle for the family's use, these being contrived by cutting into the thickness of the walls in the range to the east of the Great Hall. These must have been completed by September, 1754 when they invoked Thomas Gray's unflattering comment that Lord Brooke now had 'a little burrough in the massy walls of the place for his little self and his children, which is hung with paper and printed linnen, and carved chimneypieces in the exact manner of Berkeley Square or Argyle-Buildings.'[59] A somewhat later visitor was more kind, and thought

that 'By diminishing the walls [the Earl] has made many that were before small closets, comfortable rooms.'[60]

Although the Earl was to employ other architects at the Castle from time to time, he and Brown continued on friendly terms over the ensuing years. In 1758, when still Lord Brooke, he had added his signature to the petition for Brown to be given a royal appointment (see page 121), and they were still corresponding in 1772 when the Earl sought help over a new gardener to take charge at Warwick Castle.

> Lord Warwick's compliments of the season attend his Old Friend Mr. Brown [he wrote on 4 January], who he desires to send him a character of John Beecroft, gardener. One is wanted for W[arwick] Castle, to take care of the Garden, Hothouse etc. but particularly an extream sober man.

Brown had apparently found one for him on a previous occasion, but although the latter had 'seemed very understanding in busynes [he] had in a few weeks gott Drunk

Fig. 1. Stowe, from a drawing by F. M. Piper

often and at last fell down stairs, broke his scull and dyed shockingly. Our town', the Earl added, 'is enough to debauch anybody that is not steady and sober by nature.'[61] As a successor to this unfortunate character, Brown thought of a man then out of work but previously employed by the Duke of Northumberland, to whom he at once dispatched a note. 'I received your letter,' the Duke replied on 6 January, 1773, 'and immediately wrote to Lord Warwick concerning him [Beecroft] in such a way as I hope will induce his Lordship to take him as his gardener: for tho' I do not think him a Master of his business yet his Situation makes it a consideration of compassion not to hinder him from getting his bread.'[62] Whether Beecroft proved better equipped to withstand the temptations of Warwick, history does not, however, relate.

1 *Victoria County History, Buckinghamshire*, Vol. IV, p. 214. Harris Smith (d. 1690) and his wife Francisca (d. 1705) are buried in Padbury Church, where is also a floor slab to Richard Smith (d. 1742).

2 Alexander Pope's character of Sir Plume in *The Rape of the Lock* was said to be based on Sir George, who was thereby much offended. A footnote quoted in the Rev. A. W. Eaton's edition of 1901 refers to 'the amiable Miss Barbara, only daughter and sole heir of Sir George Browne of Kiddington', who married Sir Edward Mostyn in 1748.

3 Rebuilt by Sir Charles Barry *circa* 1850 after a fire.

4 The manor house was demolished in 1789 except for the west wing which still stands. John Penn's new mansion was designed by Robert Nasmith in that year, and completed by James Wyatt in 1801.

5 The story of Stoke Manor formed the basis of *The Long Story*, dedicated by Thomas Gray to Lady Cobham who befriended him and his mother when they resided at nearby West End Cottage.

6 This copy, with Thomas Grenville's bookplate and the letter, is now in the British Museum, G.16211.

7 Private Act 15, Geo. II, cap 39, for the enclosure of 1,668 acres by Richard Grenville and other local land-owners.

8 *Anecdotes of Books and Men*, 1820.

9 *H.M.C. Carlisle*, 15th Report.

10 The engravings of his celebrated *Plan* were published by his widow in 1739, the year after his death.

11 At San Marino, California. See Jean Preston, 'Collections of English Historical Manuscripts in the Huntington Library', *Archives*, Vol. VI, No. 30, 1962.

12 These have been assembled by the patient researches of Mr. George Clarke who has generously made the results available for the writing of this chapter. His own accounts of the gradual development of the gardens at Stowe have appeared in *The Stoic* for December 1969, July 1971 and December 1971. This will eventually form part of the *History of Stowe* which Mr. Clarke is writing in collaboration with Mr. M. J. Gibbon.

13 Margaret Lady Verney, *Verney Letters of the Eighteenth Century*, 1930, Vol. ii, p. 189.

14 This work, in two octavo volumes, is prefaced by a note: 'We have perused these two volumes of the *Builder's Dictionary* and do think they contain a great deal of useful Knowledge in the Building Business,

Nicholas Hawksmoor
John James
James Gibbs.'

The MS of The Glossary is in the Huntington Library, San Marino.

15 The invention came into general use later on, and a representation of it is given by Sir George Steuart in *The Planter's Guide* of 1828.
16 The column, attributed to James Gibbs, was subsequently altered by Vincenzo Valdré. Payments in connection with its construction were made through Brown to Richard Batchelor, statuary mason of Buckingham, during 1746. (See Dr. Michael McCarthy, 'The Rebuilding of Stowe House 1770–77', *Huntington Library Quarterly*, May, 1973.)
17 Estimated from the accounts.
18 Margaret Lady Verney, *op. cit.*, p. 190.
19 Huntington Library. Richard Earl Temple's Personal Account, 1732–79. Temple-Grenville Muniments.
20 Burnt in 1820 and rebuilt by Sir John Soane who kept to the original design except for lowering the roof.
21 Thomas Whately, *Observations on Modern Gardening*, 1771, p. 87.
22 E. M. Betts, *Thomas Jefferson's Garden Book*, 1944.
23 Roundell Palmer, Earl of Selborne, *Memorials, Family and Personal*, 1896.
24 Warwickshire C.R.O., Box 4/14.
25 *H.M.C. Denbigh*, Part V.
26 Margaret, Lady Verney, *op. cit.*, p. 235.
27 This attribution is given by The Hon. Alicia Amherst, *A History of Gardening in England*, 1895, but the 10th Duke of Grafton, in a letter to the present writer in 1944, confirmed a family tradition to this effect.
28 'Visits to Country Seats', *Walpole Society*, Vol. XVI, p. 45.
29 J. Evans and J. Britton, *The Beauties of . . . Northamptonshire*, 1810.
30 Parish Register, now in Bucks. C.R.O., '1774, Launcelot Brown and Bridget Wayet, both of this Parish, were married . . .'. For a note on the Wayet family see Sir George Gilbert Scott, *Recollections*, 1879, p. 2.
31 A letter from Brown in the Petworth archives was written from Stowe in October, 1751.
32 Duke of Buckingham, 'The History of Stowe', *Transactions of Bucks. Architectural and Archaeological Society*, Vol. V, 1878, p. 349.
33 John Macky, *Journal Through England*, 1732.
34 Marcus Binney, 'Packington Hall, Warwicks.', *Country Life*, 9 and 16 July, 1970.
35 The identification was made by the staff of the Warwickshire C.R.O. to whom I am grateful for bringing it to my notice.
36 Extensively remodelled in the nineteenth century.
37 Alice Buchan (Lady Lucy), *Charlecote and the Lucys*, 1958, pp. 225ff.
38 A drawing by Henry Beighton made in 1714 is in the Prattington Collection of Worcestershire History Box I, Society of Antiquaries.
39 14 November, 1752. L. Dickens and M. Stanton, *An Eighteenth Century Correspondence*, 1910.
40 Sanderson Miller's *Diary*, 1 October, 1749–28 September, 1750. For these extracts I am indebted to Mr. Anthony Wood who is now working on the *Diary*.
41 Bodleian Library, Oxford. Gough Maps, 32ff. 28v.
42 Unpublished correspondence, Warwickshire C.R.O., CR 125 (153).
43 L. Dickens and M. Stanton, *op. cit.*
44 Removed in 1957 and re-erected in the Metropolitan Museum, New York.
45 Adam Drawings, Sir John Soane's Museum.
46 H. Repton, *Theory and Practise of Landscape Gardening*, 1803, p. 201, says: 'It often happens that a walk .. ᵥis crossed by a road or driftway; this has been ingeniously obviated (I believe originally by Mr. Brown) by making the one pass over the other.' In fact Alexander Pope had employed a

1a.
KIRKHARLE, NORTHUMBERLAND. Looking north from the Church. *see page 41*

1b.
ST. WILFRID'S CHURCH, KIRKHARLE. *see page 41*

1c.
CAMBO, NORTHUMBERLAND. The Village Hall, incorporating part of the old school house. *see page 38*

2a. KIRKHARLE TOWER, NORTHUMBERLAND. An early nineteenth century water-colour, from *Memoirs of the Family of Loraine.* see page 41

2b. KIDDINGTON HALL, OXFORDSHIRE. An air view showing Brown's lake formed out of the river Glyme. see page 47

3a. STOWE, BUCKINGHAMSHIRE. The south front at the time of Brown's arrival in 1741. From an engraving by Jacques Rigaud and Bernard Baron. *see page 49*

3b. STOWE. The Grecian Valley as laid out during Brown's years here. From an engraving published by George Bickham, 1753. *see page 52*

4a. WOTTON, BUCKINGHAMSHIRE. The lake and temple. *see page 53*

4b. NEWNHAM PADDOX, WARWICKSHIRE. An elevation probably drawn by Brown. *see page 54*

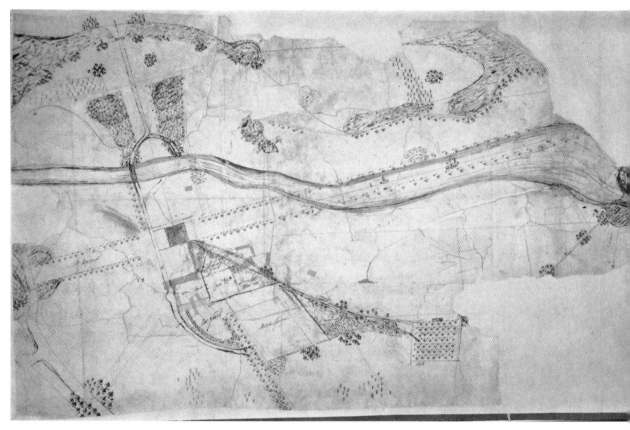

5a. PACKINGTON, WARWICKSHIRE. Brown's first sketch plan proposing the lay-out for the grounds.
see page 56

5b. PACKINGTON. Looking west from the house.

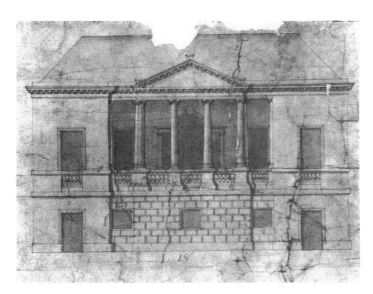

6a. PACKINGTON. 'My Lady's Lodge'. A detail from Brown's finished plan of 1751. *see page 56*

6b. PACKINGTON. The entrance gates proposed on Brown's plan. Neither these nor the 'Lady's Lodge' were carried out.

6c. KIRTLINGTON PARK, OXFORDSHIRE. Brown's plan for the grounds, initialled and dated 1752. *see page 69*

7a. CROOME COURT, WORCESTERSHIRE. The house and stable court from the north-west. *see page 57*

7b. CROOME COURT. The north and west fronts.

8a.

Croome, Worcestershire. The Church of St. James the Apostle, built by Brown in 1759. Robert Adam's designs for decorating the interior were prepared in 1761. *see page 59*

8b.

Croome Court. The summerhouse on the island, with wall plaques by Mrs. Coade. *see page 59*

8c.   Petworth, Sussex. Looking south-east over the park to the lake. *see page 68*

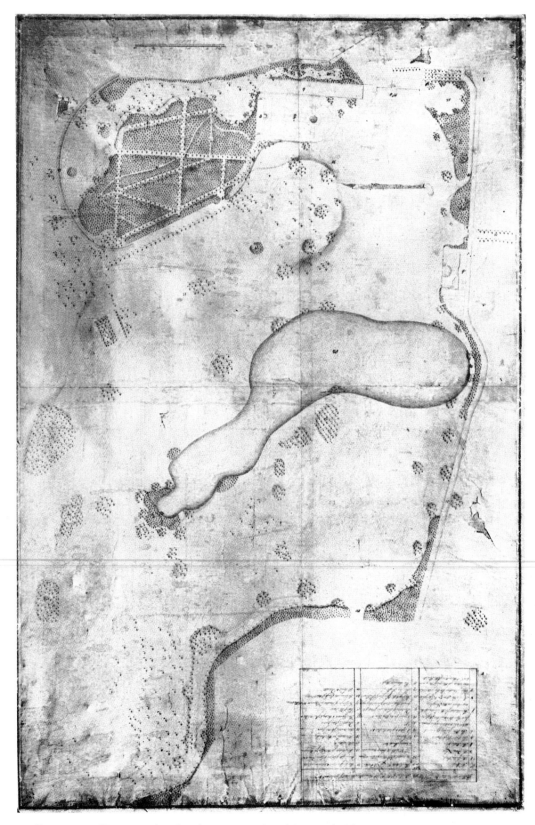

9. PETWORTH. Brown's plan for the park, undated but probably 1753. *see page 68*

10a. WARWICK CASTLE with the Avon in the foreground.
see page 60

10b. MOOR PARK, HERTFORDSHIRE. From an old photograph showing statuary beneath a cedar tree near the Temple, now destroyed. *see page 69*

11a.   MOOR PARK. A painting by Richard Wilson showing the house before the wings were removed. *see page 70*

11b.   LONGLEAT, WILTSHIRE. Looking over the park from the parapet of the house. *see page 85*

12a. BURGHLEY, NORTHANTS. The south and west fronts seen from across the lake. *see page 75*

12b. BURGHLEY. Looking over the lake to the bridge. The bridge is almost identical with one in Brown's landscape at Shortgrove.

13a. BURGHLEY. The greenhouse designed by Brown. *see page 77*

13b. BURGHLEY. The stable block for which Brown's design survives.

14a.
BURGHLEY. The garden house by the lake. *see page 77*

14b.
BURGHLEY. The Grand Staircase for which Brown supplied designs 1780–81. *see page 78*

14c. CORSHAM COURT, WILTSHIRE. The south front, enlarged by Brown 1760–64. *see page 86*

15a. CORSHAM COURT. The Picture Gallery. *see page 88*

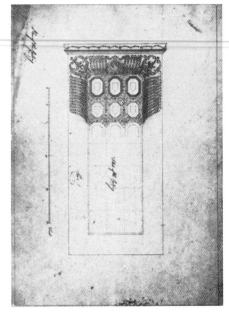

15b. BURTON CONSTABLE, YORKSHIRE. Brown's design for a ceiling originally prepared for Burton Constable but subsequently adopted at Corsham.

16a.
CORSHAM COURT. The Breakfast Room, originally the Library, in Brown's extended west wing. *see page 89*

16c.
CORSHAM COURT. The gothic Bath House in the North Walk. *see page 88*

16b.
CORSHAM COURT. Detail of the plaster frieze in the Breakfast Room.

more elaborate form of 'grotto chamber' to connect the two parts of his Twickenham gardens. Repton himself made use of the idea in the grounds of Gayhurst, Bucks.

47 Miss Alison Kelly's work on the Coade Manufactory, now in preparation.

48 Registers, Diocese of Worcestershire.

49 Adam Drawings, Sir John Soane's Museum.

50 Adam's accounts for his work in the house, his garden buildings, and the decoration of the interior of the church are preserved in the Estate Office at High Green, near Croome.

51 The painting is the property of the Trustees, Croome Settled Estates.

52 Probably the same Read who was subsequently working at Blenheim.

53 Pakenham Correspondence.

54 L. Dickens and M. Stanton, *op. cit.*

55 The casket was in Coade stone. The memorial has recently been restored.

56 As shown on a Warwick Street plan *circa* 1711, Warwickshire C.R.O.

57 R. Toynbee, *Letters of Horace Walpole*. Mr. Southcote was Philip Southcote of Wooburn Farm in Surrey, an amateur gardening enthusiast.

58 M. W. Farr, *Victoria County History, Warwickshire*, Vol. VIII, pp. 461ff.

59 P. Toynbee and L. Whibley, *Correspondence of Thomas Gray, Letter 192.*

60 Viscount Grimston, *Tour*, 1769. *H.M.C., Verulam*, Vol. 1, pp. 275-7.

61 Pakenham Correspondence.

62 *Ibid.*

III

PROSPECTS AND CAPABILITIES

O<small>N LEAVING STOWE</small> in the late autumn of 1751, Brown settled in Hammersmith, then a riverside hamlet in the parish of Fulham, an area where several celebrated horticulturists and nurserymen were already established.[1] He took a house on the Mall where his letters were to be addressed for the next fourteen years.[2] He was now thirty-five, with a reputation which had been enhanced by the building of Croome.

That Brown should have extended his practice to architecture as well as landscape gardening was in part due to the lack of practitioners at this juncture, for many of the older generation of Palladians were dead or in retirement. William Chambers and the Adam brothers had not yet arrived on the scene. He also felt, as did William Mason, that the two arts of architecture and landscape were inseparable. 'I am uniformly of opinion,' the latter wrote, 'that where a place is to be formed, he who disposes the ground and arranges the plantations ought to fix the situation at least, if not to determine the shape and size of the ornamental buildings. Brown, I know, was ridiculed for turning architect, but I always thought he did it from a kind of necessity having found the great difficulty which must frequently have occurred to him in forming a picturesque whole, where the previous building had been ill-placeed, or of improper dimentions.'[3]

Humphry Repton, who was to become the leading garden designer after Brown's death, was the first to publish a list of the latter's architectural works for which purpose he borrowed the relevant papers from Brown's son-in-law, Henry Holland. The list can therefore be taken as having a fair degree of accuracy, and although the Holland papers were later destroyed by a nephew, documents from other sources confirm the majority of attributions. Repton also gave his own assessment of Brown's building achievements: 'Mr. Brown's fame as an architect seems to have been eclipsed by his celebrity as a landscape gardener, he being the only professor of the one art, while he had many jealous competitors in the other. But when I consider the number of excellent works in architecture designed and executed by him, it becomes an act of justice to his memory to record that, if he was superior to all in what related to his own particular profession, he was inferior to none in what related to the comfort, convenience, taste,

and propriety of design in the several mansions and other buildings which he planned.' Repton was aware that Brown had lacked any formal training, but considered that, through 'intercourse with men of genius and science, natural quickness of perception [and] his habitual correctness of observation, he became acquainted with . . . the higher requisites of the art relating to *form*, to *proportion*, to *character*, and above all, to *arrangement*.'[4]

Brown was, in fact, increasingly to be involved with architecture of one kind or another during the ensuing decades. It was for this reason that he ultimately, at the end of the 1760s, decided to take a partner to help with this side of his practice; but during the 1750s he carried on by himself, and even for garden work had no regular assistants until 1764, when John Spyers was engaged to help over land surveys. Although there are from time to time hints of impatience in letters from some of those who sought his advice and found themselves kept waiting, the amount of travelling in which he was involved, the quantity of plans to be drawn out, or letters written and accounts kept, added up to a volume of work by which he must often have felt weighed down.

The presentation of his schemes was to vary from large plans, occasionally on vellum but more usually on thick paper, to sheets some twelve to fifteen inches across which were generally used for details such as bridges, heads of water or garden buildings such as those for Blenheim or Rothley. The unexecuted designs for Belvoir are described in his account book as 'all the drawing made very descriptive, fair, and neat, with trees etc. etc., bound into a book', and a similar set for Stanstead showed alterations for the house, offices, and grounds with 'very fair descriptive drawings'. The proposals would be submitted either for the owner to put them into execution himself, or for Brown to undertake the work over a given period, for which a contract was usually made, setting out terms and details as to who should provide the men, horses and materials. These contracts might come to £3,000 or more, made up by quarterly or half-yearly payments spread over an agreed time. At Harewood the total came to over £6,000, and at Blenheim to over £21,500, and there were others equally large. The cost of preparatory surveys varied, that for Wilton being reckoned at 8d per acre including expenses, but at Byram the charge was a shilling per acre, probably because it was for only 373 as compared with 1,300 acres, and the travelling expenses were greater.

Where Brown was responsible for the execution of the work, there could be no argument as to the results being of his devising, but in cases where he only supplied the owner with drawings, the latter was sometimes tempted to take credit for the conception as at King's Weston, and probably at Tong Castle. Few were as generous in their acknowledgements to him as Lord Coventry, who erected a lake-side memorial to his skill at Croome, or Jemima, Marchioness de Grey, who included Brown's name with that of her husband in a commemorative column at Wrest Park.

Although Brown must have kept several account books, only one has survived, and that does not begin until 1759, but other sources show that from the time of his arrival in Hammersmith new commissions poured in, while earlier undertakings were still to be completed. The principal new works begun at this time were Petworth, Kirtlington, Moor Park, Beechwood, Belhus and Burghley, as well as the resumed phase of activity at Newnham Paddox, and schemes for Ragley. At the end of the decade, Brown also made his first designs for Burton Constable.

The project for PETWORTH (Map 148) (Plate 8c and Plate 9) must have been put to him while he was still at Stowe: from there he made his first visit, but the scheme only took shape in 1752 with further journeys from Hammersmith, resulting in the 'several plans' for the Petworth grounds which are mentioned in an early account with Lord Egremont.[5] His recommendation to the latter had come from George Grenville of Wotton, whose wife Elizabeth was the Earl's sister. On 1 May, 1753, a contract was signed by which Brown undertook to carry out an agreed scheme for £1,175. This was followed by a second contract in 1754, for a lake to be made near the Half Moon Wood, and two more dated 1 June, 1755, and 4 May, 1756.

The surviving plan by Brown, recently discovered at Petworth, is undated but must be one of those prepared in 1752. It relates to the ground lying to the west of the house, and shows the great lake proposed for the middle distance, very much as it was carried out, and the way in which Brown retained a considerable amount of mature timber to form groups in the new scene. Some of the adornments listed were either not carried out, or disappeared later, such as the 'sham bridge' and the grotto at the head of the water. Several other items can however be traced, notably 'The Terrass reduced to a Fine Undulated hill adorned with groups of Cedars, Pines etc.' to the north-west of the house; the distant 'Clumps of Beeches and Chestnuts etc. on the hill'; the 'Foss to keep out the Deer', which still performs this function; and the south-west 'plantations of shrubbs and plants of low growth that will not prevent the prospects', although the trees have now outlived the shrubs.

Brown's reference to 'a gravel path through the mena[gerie] etc. with its borders adorned with Flowering Shrubbs,' gardens for aloes and bay trees, plantations of evergreens and a cypress walk shows his care for these details in a garden scheme, and a bill from the nurseryman John Williamson in 1753 is of interest as showing the variety of material in use at the time, and the part it played in Brown's layout:

80 Sweet Briony	5 Oriental Collutea	8 Candleberry Trees
30 Honeysuckle	6 Cockgyreas [sic]	6 Butchers' Broom
10 Altheas	6 Bird Cherry	10 Ilex
6 Spirea	6 Double Cherry	60 Sweet Briars

10 Double Thorn	7 American Maples	5 Rosa Mundi
8 Persian Jasmin	4 Sea Buckthorns	5 Maiden's Blush
10 Virginia Schumachs	4 Trumpet Flowers	4 York and Lancaster
10 Virginia Raspberry	80 Roses	20 Laburnhams
4 Tamarisks	6 Portugal Laurels	50 Lilacs
		20 Acacias

While the more ephemeral material inevitably perished after a few decades, much of the hardwood of Brown's planting still plays its part with later additions in making Petworth an outstanding example of an eighteenth-century landscape.

Simultaneously with his Petworth work, Brown was carrying out alterations to the grounds of KIRTLINGTON PARK (Map 112) (Plate 6c) in Oxfordshire. The owner, Sir James Dashwood, had in 1741 obtained designs for a palatial mansion, with flanking pavilions joined to it by low walls, to be set in a clearing made in what had previously been known as the Great Wood on his estate. His architect for the house was John Sanderson who collaborated over the building with William Smith of Warwick.[6] The house was ready for occupation in August, 1746. Sir James had already turned his attention to the grounds and had been supplied with a plan by the then Royal Gardener, Thomas Greening,[7] some part of which was certainly carried out; but by the end of 1751, Greening's layout no longer pleased, and Sir James signed a contract for the grounds to be landscaped by Brown, who had probably been recommended by their mutual friend Sanderson Miller. On 17 January, 1752, Sir James entered in his notebook that he had paid Brown £100 'for work he is doing.'

Of three garden drawings which survive, one is endorsed 'Greening's plan totally changed by Brown', and shows the former's semi-natural scheme of wiggley paths and small clearings to the west of the house, with very little done to the existing woodland on the east. The other two drawings are in Brown's hand, one being for the area around the house, almost entirely encircled by a ha-ha, or 'fosse' as he calls it, and, instead of Greening's wildernesses, compact plantations flanking the house and stables. Before the two main fronts are open sweeps of lawn lightly sprinkled with small groups of individual trees. The second Brown drawing shows the more distant grounds to the north, and includes a particularly large clump of trees which has been scored through in pen as though Sir James had not approved of it. The work took some four years to complete, Sir James's notebook showing that payments varying between £100 and £500 were made to him intermittently until 1757.

Brown's recommendation to Admiral Lord Anson of MOOR PARK (Map 136) (Plate 10B) in 1753 appears to have come through his client at Petworth, Lord Egremont. 'I am sorry to hear of your indisposition by Lord Egremont', Lord Anson wrote on

26 September. 'I am going to Moor Park to-day and shall be there till Sunday. The next week I shall go down on Thursday and shall not return till Monday by which time I hope and wish you may think yourself well enough to let me see you ... Put me in mind of a message Mrs. Yorke left with me for you.'[8] The house at Moor Park, built in 1720 for Benjamin Styles by Giacomo Leoni, replaced the earlier home of Lucy, Countess of Bedford whose celebrated garden had been praised by Sir William Temple as the 'perfectest figure of a garden' he had ever seen.[9] Much of this had gone when the wealthy Mr. Styles had, in 1725, removed a sizeable hill which obscured the south view from the house at a cost of £5,000.[10]

Brown considered that the surroundings of the house were not sufficiently varied, and endeavoured to remedy this by scooping out more earth in front of it, and by building up some hillocks at either side. A painting by Richard Wilson[11] shows the results soon after completion (Plate 11A). On the margin of a lake formed in what had been the 'old pleasure ground', an Ionic temple was erected and dedicated to the Winds. It was this feature which later inspired Dr. Johnson, in the course of a visit, to compose the couplet which was duly inscribed on its walls:

A grateful mind I praise! All to the winds he owed
And so upon the Winds a Temple he bestowed.

Lord Anson did not enjoy his new park for long as he died in 1762, after which it was sold to Sir Lawrence Dundas. There are no surviving accounts for Brown's work for the Admiral, but Horace Walpole, who saw Moor Park in July, 1760, remarked that it had cost Lord Anson £86,000, and that he had laid out a further £6,000 in 'improving the grounds under Brown's direction.' Of the results he was critical: 'I was not much struck with it after all the miracles I had heard that Brown had performed there. He has undulated the horizon in so many artificial mole-hills that it is full as unnatural as if it was drawn with a rule and compasses.'[12] It was, in fact, far too soon to judge the full effect, and Thomas Whately, who described the grounds in detail in 1770, when the trees were reaching a reasonable size, was much impressed by these hillocks, which he pointed out were not diminutive in size, and were enhanced by the 'fine clumps which distinguish them. They recede one beyond another, and the outline waves agreeably amongst them. They do more than conceal the sharpness of the edge; they convert a deformity into a beauty, and greatly contribute to the embellishment of this most lovely scene.'[13] Building development has bitten deeply into the estate, but a considerable area has been retained as a golf course and gives some idea of its former character. The temple was recently demolished after being damaged by a falling tree.

Another Hertfordshire property for which Brown was asked to give designs at about the same time as Moor Park was BEECHWOOD (Map 17), some ten miles to the north-

east. His client here was Sir John Sebright who, at the age of thirteen, had succeeded his elder brother as 5th Baronet in 1736. The house hides its irregular and partly Elizabethan structure behind a fine entrance facade of about 1702, in red brick with stone quoins (although the window frames which appear contemporary were in fact a later addition). Originally called St. Giles in the Wood, both this and its present name imply the thick natural woods by which it was surrounded so that Brown's task here was to thin out rather than to plant on any extensive scale. This is confirmed by comparison of his plan, dated 1754, with a survey prepared in the preceding year. His drawing, which bears his initials and the date in a rococo cartouche, sweeps away the original small garden – shown on the survey as rectangular, with rounded 'bastions' at the angles – and introduces a tree-studded lawn to the south west, surrounded by a sweeping belt formed largely of existing trees. A number of other drawings unsigned but almost certainly by Brown, show that he made some alterations to the house at this time, mainly in the first-floor rooms. A plan for an ice-house is also attributable to him, and one for a small bath-house which is endorsed 'to stand obliquely in order to show its side in perspective to ye windows of ye house', but the latter, if it was built, has not survived.[14]

The year 1753 was also to see a renewal of activity at Newnham Paddox. Nothing of importance had been done here since 1749, probably because Lord Denbigh's finances were temporarily at a low ebb. Now Brown was to begin work on the house itself, altering the bedchamber floor and the nursery wing. On 2 April, 1754, the workmen 'Began to pull down part of the old house' in preparation for the building of Brown's new facade.[15] An unsigned elevation in the Bodleian Library can almost certainly be identified as one of his drawings for this.[16] In its eleven-window, two-storey composition, with angle turrets and a central pediment, it follows closely the design for Croome, although the resemblance was to be blurred in the second half of the nineteenth century by the addition of an attic storey, a balustraded parapet and an elaboration of decorative detail. The work at Newnham suffered a set-back through the death of Lord Denbigh in 1755, but his successor, Basil, the 6th Earl, continued the various activities no doubt with his impending marriage in mind, although at first finance was again a problem.[17] This, however, was soon to be solved for 'when he was about to finish Newnham he said . . . an old rich Aunt had very kindly given him £2,000 to be laid out in the house or gardens. He preferred the latter; for though the great room, with his fine Vandyke portraits, was built with spaces between the windows to receive the largest glass mirrors from Paris, yet he would prefer completing his large piece of water and bridge, which were absolutely necessary for the whole place.'[18] In fact the mirrors were eventually hung as intended.

On 18 May 'Mr. Lancelot Brown' was paid £200 for measuring, surveying, planning,

and all other demands in connection with 'his building of the house at Newnham', and a loose sheet in the Building Book dated 31 December of that year notes payments to 'Mr. Brown the architect', and several of the craftsmen employed, including John Hobcroft for woodwork, John Lovell for chimneypieces, John Cobb for furniture, and Joseph Duffour of Paris for glasses which would have been those which were placed between the windows of the 'great room'. The John Smallbones who paid the masons in 1768 can probably be identified with Mr. Smalebones, the carpenter who was working at Stowe early in the 1740s, and perhaps with the man of the same name who later occupied a lodge in Blenheim Park.[19]

Long before the work was completed Lord and Lady Denbigh were receiving visits from friends and neighbours anxious to see how things were progressing, and among them was Lord Warwick whose curiosity led him to make what he called 'a great excursion' from Warwick to Newnham for the purpose of seeing the alterations in general, and the Vandyke paintings in particular. The house he subsequently described in a letter to Lord Dacre as 'very convenient', although he added that he never approved of 'an Apartment above and one below to serve the same purposes, particularly in respect to a Dining Room above stairs which here is. They are finishing a large saloon for six of his best Vandykes to hang in [but] I don't love a deep cove.'[20] Lord Warwick's visit was followed by one from Horace Walpole in September when the latter noted a 'new garden making and serpentine water. Two exceedingly large ash trees. Plain good brick front built by this Earl before the old house designed by Brown the gardener.'[21] At the time of T. H. Wyatt's drastic alterations to the house in the late 1870s, the southern extremity of Brown's sinuous lake was filled in to make room for a formal garden to the east end of the house. The house itself was demolished in 1952, but a gothic entrance arch to the surviving stable range may belong to Brown's period of activity here.

Although Brown's first visit did not materialise until the autumn of 1753, the possibility of his landscaping the grounds at BELHUS (Map 18), in Essex, had been under discussion for some time. The property to which Lord Dacre had succeeded in 1745 had been neglected by his grandfather for many years, and gave the new owner an opportunity of exercising his keen antiquarian and architectural interests on the restoration of the delapidated Tudor house in what he considered to be a 'true gothic' manner. This programme, begun with such enthusiasm, was brought to a sudden halt by the death of Lord and Lady Dacre's only child, Barbara, in 1749, and to alleviate their unhappiness they subsequently travelled abroad, returning to Belhus in 1751. Their close friendship with Sanderson Miller was a likely source of Brown's introduction as garden adviser in the following year but on account of the latter's ill-health several dates were postponed. Eventually in October, 1753, Lord Dacre was

able to inform Miller that 'Brown has been here, and by what I find has really been very ill; he made me a great many very serious professions how ready he was to serve me and while he stayed here slaved at setting out the road and rest of the Shrubbery all day and drew Plans all evening, and was in the best humour imaginable; and of his own accord promised to come again next month. Upon the whole I begin now to think that he has not grown too great to Despise my little Business. He attributed to many different hindrances his being so long absent, and says I ought to remember that for two months in summer I myself was not here . . .'[22]

Brown's proposals, whatever they were, appear to have been put in hand without any complications. By 1756 Lord Dacre was toying with the idea of further work in his park, and another letter to Miller, written from Bruton Street, told the latter that 'Brown went with me about a month agoe to Belhouse in order to give me his opinion about some plantations, etc., I had a mind to make there.' There is no clue as to whether these were carried out, but it seems probable. Lord Dacre's appetite for 'improvement', however, was apt to be checked by indifferent health or lack of funds, and there was a lull until 1759 when his health and his finances were both strong enough for him to consider further schemes. On 26 January he wrote to Miller:

> In the state I am in you will perhaps think me a Bold man to begin such a great work as I am going to mention to you: and yet should I not Live to enjoy it perfected, it will so far as I go on with it be an amusement to my mind and a Temptation to me to use Exercise. In a word then, I have had Brown down with me at Belhouse and am going to make a Pool where now the run of water is, in the lower part of my Park: its size will be about ten acres: its Form very irregular and 'twill be a quarter of a mile long. Brown and indeed my own little Judgment tells me that it will be a very great ornament to that side of the Park and quite change the Face of it. By what I have said you will immediately conceive that all the rushy part of Bumstead Mead will be converted into water, and that the Black moory soil will be taken away till we come to the parts of the meadow that rise and where the soil is gravel . . .[23]

As it transpired the lake had to be shelved for the time being, but work on the lawns and plantations continued until they had absorbed all the money he could spare for the next two years. By the beginning of 1761 he and Brown were again deep in plans for the lake, and in February Lord Dacre wrote off to tell Miller:

> I am much pleased that you think of paying us a visit at Belhouse this spring . . . You will find the Place, if not much altered since you was there, yet a good deal improved by the Turff being got older and consequently smoother and greener, and by the Shrubberys being now in good measure come to perfection. My Breakfast Room

too has been entirely new fitted up and somewhat enlarged in a manner I flatter
myself you will not disapprove of. I have a number of Expences on me this year
and yet I doubt whether I shall have prudence enough to abstain from meddling
with my water in the lower part of the Park; the truth is that I never ride that way
without longing to do something there; as I know that that coarse meadow and moory
sided canal might be converted into a very pleasing scene: and Brown is of the same
opinion: we now have another Scheme for it of much less (tho' still a good deal) of
Expence; it is to make it in the River stile instead of the Lake.

Although this scheme seems to have hung fire for several years, some attempt at improving the 'coarse meadow and moory sided canal' seems to have been initiated in 1770 with the help of a local man, Richard Woods, who was later to set up as a professional landscape gardener (see page 207). At that time Woods was a tenant of nearby North Ockendon Hall, and by January, 1771, Lord Dacre had paid him £175.[24] Another payment of £42 to a carpenter for 'painting and building the Bridge in the Park'[25] in the following July strengthens the likelihood that Woods supervised work on the Long Pond at this time, but in general Lord Dacre continued to rely on Brown for ideas, and in the autumn of 1773 could not conceal his disappointment that the latter's ill-health had prevented him from visiting Belhus in the previous month. Writing on 7 November he was now fussing about his own ailments, and the 'damp cold as one is to expect' which would keep him, in his invalid state, from going out of doors with Brown during the ensuing weeks. He was, however, determined not to 'move a step without your advice, and I fear the operations here must now be postponed till we come hither next spring when I shall hope nothing will hinder me the pleasure of a visit from you ... As soon as the Trees have got their leaves next spring I shall flatter myself you will hold yourself engaged to me. In the meantime I most sincerely wish you a speedy recovery from your disorder and hope that ... when your affairs call you to London, you will do me the pleasure of calling on me.'[26]

Brown was certainly at Belhus again in 1774, when Lord Dacre paid him £10 for his journey, and their friendship ended only with Capability's death. Belhus remained in the hands of Lord Dacre's descendants until the late 1930s when the property was acquired by the London County (now Greater London) Council, although the house stood in a ruined condition until the late 1950s when it was demolished. Since then the grounds have been extensively developed, and nothing remains of the delectable scenes which had once been the apple of Lord Dacre's eye.

At the end of 1754 Brown was consulted by Brownlow, 9th Earl of Exeter, who put into his hands the alteration of the house, and the landscaping of the grounds at BURGHLEY (Map 31) (Plates 12A, B, 13A, B, and 14A, B), a commission which proved to

be one of the most important of his career and which lasted for over a quarter of a century. The Earl had succeeded in November of that year and at once set about putting his somewhat neglected estate into order. Begun in 1552 for Elizabeth I's Lord High Treasurer, William Cecil, Burghley stands on the site of Burghe Minster, fragments of which were incorporated in the hall, chapel and kitchen. Ranged on the four sides of an inner court, the house crowns a slight hill in what is otherwise a flat area, and still presents that remarkable sky-line which Daniel Defoe described as 'more like a town than a house at which avenue soever you come to it; the towers and pinnacles so high, and placed at such a distance from one another ... Like so many distant parish churches.'[27] It is more or less contemporary with that other prodigy house, Longleat, where Brown carried out landscaping work from 1758.

Although Brown's own record of payments from Lord Exeter was to be continued in the surviving account book after 1769, his book containing the earlier entries is lost. There are, however, enough fragments from other sources to confirm his activities which began with alterations to the grounds in 1755 while his various proposals for the house were still under discussion. By the spring of 1756 the latter materialised, and some of his signed drawings have now come to light at Burghley. These include a plan of the whole house and elevations for the north and south fronts showing the proposed alterations. The south front today follows closely his design for raising the facade by several feet, and introducing 'gothic' sashes to the widows[28]. Another far-reaching proposal to which Lord Exeter agreed was the removal by Brown of the western of the two wings which had previously projected northward from the house. By this demolition, an extensive view was opened out across the park and lake from the north forecourt. In May, 1756, Lord Dacre was writing to Sanderson Miller:

> *Brown tells me that he has the alteration of Burleigh, and that not only of the Park but of the House which wherever it is Gothick he intends to preserve in that stile: and whatever new ornaments he adds are to be so. For example in the old Hall whose sides he says is now quite naked. I advised him however not to lace it too much: he says he would give the world you should see his designs: having the highest opinion of your skill in this way; I asked him why he did not send them to you; that I knew your good nature: but his answer was that the Drawings were so large it was impossible. He wanted much to know whether there was any chance of seeing you soon in this part of the world ...*[29]

Brown apparently followed Lord Dacre's advice and kept adornment in the hall to a minimum, although Victorian alterations make it impossible to be precise over the nature of his design for it. Certainly the upper part of the walls, above the nineteenth-

75

century panelling and bookcases, was left plain as a foil for the splendid mid-sixteenth-century double hammer-beam roof. The chapel on the upper floor of the north-east angle of the house, has some details attributable to Brown, and he was no doubt responsible for the introduction, slightly later, of the lamp-holders in the form of ten Coade stone *Virgins* set round the walls, and probably obtained at about the same time as the four lions for the bridge which came from the Coade manufactory in 1777. Other rooms in the north range altered under Brown's supervision include the Billiard Room, which has a 'gothic' ceiling, and the Green Library with its pedimented book-cases.

By the time Horace Walpole visited Burghley in July, 1763, much had been completed, and he was able to comment: 'A noble Pile! Brown is ornamenting the Park and has built a gothic greenhouse and stables which are not bad, except that they do not accord with the house, which is not Gothic.'[30]

Before this Brown had been making himself useful to Lord Exeter in another direction, the latter at the end of 1757 having had the idea of parting with the lease of his London house. Brown, with a wide circle of wealthy clients, was in a position to know of a possible purchaser, and three letters in the British Museum[31] show that he was soon successful in interesting Philip, 1st Earl of Hardwicke,[32] then Lord Chief Justice, to whom he wrote on 3 January, 1758:

> *Mr Lord,*
>
> *By information I find there is sixty years unexpired in the Lease: the Ground Rent is eighteen Pounds: the expence to the Square has been usually two Pounds per annum. All the Fixtures which Lord Brooke left, to go with the House. The price, six thousand, two hundred pounds.*
>
> *I have had another application about the House, but I will give no answer 'till I am honoured with your Lordship's Determination . . .*

Before Lord Hardwicke had time to reply, Lord Exeter changed his mind about parting with the house. Brown hastened to pass on the news:

> *I wrote to Lord Exeter to let his Lordship know what I had said relative to his Lordship's House in Grosvenor Square, and to my Astonishment rec'd a Letter from His Lordship in answer to it this Day; to inform me that he had determined to keep the House and live in it himself. I thought it my Duty to give your Lordship the earliest Notice that your Lordship might not have any unnecessary Trouble or Disappointment about it . . .*

That, however, was not to be the end of the matter for within six months Lord Exeter

was changing his mind yet again. Brown found that Lord Hardwicke was still interested and wrote off on 15 July:

> *I have this morning called at Lord Exeter's House and find that his Lordship has made no Additions to the Fixtures. I therefore conclude when your Lordship reads over my Commission from his Lordship which is underwritten I apprehend there needs no Delay.*

Having quoted Lord Exeter's instructions as to price – 'it ought not to go under Six thousand four hundred Pounds but [I] leave fifty Pounds in your Power' – Brown added that the house was in extremely good order and that two marble tables in the dining room were to go with it. This time the transaction went through satisfactorily and Lord Hardwicke took up residence in Grosvenor Square from 1758 until his death.

Meanwhile work had been proceeding at Burghley, particularly on the greenhouse and stables on which Walpole had commented after his visit. The greenhouse extends at an angle to the north-east range of the house and screens domestic offices in this area. Eleven bays across, it has slender turrets at the extremities and flanking the central door-way. These turrets terminate in lanterns with ogee caps echoing those on the house. Each of the greenhouse windows is set beneath a pointed arch, while the upper part of the ashlar facing, between the windows and the crenellated parapet, is worked with slender vertical panels, a feature which Brown was to use elsewhere, and which is pro-bably a recollection on his part of the similar treatment in Gibbs's Gothic Temple at Stowe. Adjoining the greenhouse on the east is the stable block, ranged on three sides of a courtyard entered from the north. Its treatment is simple, the two-storey walls being faced with stone and rising to a crenellated parapet, while the mullion windows are set under flat dripstones.

By 1767 Lord Exeter was giving some attention to the south range of the house, although the major work of inserting a new staircase was not to come for another thirteen years. At the earlier date, he was making minor re-arrangements, one of which involved displaying a celebrated antique Bacchus in the Marble Hall. For this purpose Brown was requested to design a pedestal, the Earl writing to him on 1 December with the dimensions of the figure which measured four feet ten inches from the 'top of the head to the sole of the foot.'[33] In the grounds, where the course of the river had been widened and a new four-acre kitchen garden laid out, several small buildings were to go up in the seventeen sixties, including a game keeper's lodge and a dairy with an elaborate plaster ceiling. To this period, too, belongs the little summerhouse, set back from the lake against a group of cedars against whose dark foliage its 'Jacobean' pin-nacles and lacey parapet show up to perfection. Its design is clearly inspired by one of the small banqueting houses at Chipping Campden which are almost the only surviving

fragments of the great house built early in the seventeenth century by Sir Baptist Hicks.

To cross the western extremity of the lake, after it had wound its way past the south front of the house, Brown designed a handsome stone bridge, sending the drawings to Burghley at the end of 1772 to await Lord Exeter's return. Acknowledging them on 4 January, 1773, the latter wrote:

> *On my return home last night, I was treated with the sight of the plans . . . Both [are] elegant but at present I prefer that with three arches [but] shall not finally determine till we meet. May happy new years ever attend the family at Hampton is the sincere wish of yrs. Exeter.*[34]

His preference for the three-arched version remained, and later in the year the mason, Thomas Manton, began to assemble stone for the work which began in 1774. It was completed in the spring of 1777 when 'four Lyons' supplied by Mrs. Eleanor Coade at £115 12s 0d were placed on the balustraded parapet.[35] Harrod, writing of the grounds at Burghley in 1785, described them as 'laid out of a rude mass by the late ingenious Launcelot Brown', who had formed 'an agreeable serpentine river, a mile long, and over this a bridge, [which] sweetly enlivens the landscape to the admiration of those who were acquainted with the spot of 20 years ago.'[36]

The sums which Brown noted as received from Lord Exeter in respect of work done after 1770 are confirmed in a day book at Burghley kept from this time by the Earl's accountant, John Clarke.[37] From this source come the details of the last important phase of work within the house, for which Brown supplied plans in 1781–2. These were for a new staircase and hall giving direct access to the suite of state rooms on the principal floor of the south range, and known as the George Rooms. These contain a wealth of late seventeenth-century carving and plasterwork, but their chief glory lies in the wall paintings by Antonio Verrio. With the 5th Earl's death in 1700 work came to an end in these rooms and for close on a century they were not used. The 9th Earl's decision to open up the suite led to plans for replacing an existing and perhaps inadequate staircase which rose from the ground floor to the upper room containing Verrio's unfinished paintings of the *Horrors of War* (generally known as the *Hell* room, in contrast to the adjoining *Heaven* room). It appears that Robert Adam heard rumours of this intention, and in 1779 drew out a scheme which he submitted to Lord Exeter, one copy surviving at Burghley, and one in the Adam collection in the Soane Museum. His attempt to attract Lord Exeter's patronage with this colourful essay, in which blue scagliola columns with gilded capitals are set against pale green walls, did not prove successful, and Brown's account book records that he delivered plans for the staircase as built in 1781 and 1782. This rises in two stages beginning with a single flight which then divides and turns to rise in two flights against the walls to the level of the *Hell*

room, the floor of which received support from a screen of four doric columns or Ketton stone set *in antis* on the floor below. The unfinished paintings by Verrio in the upper room were later completed by Thomas Stothard. Although Brown's final designs were not delivered until 1781 and 1782, they must have been under discussion, and preparations made, in the preceding year for by December, 1780 several loads of Ketton stone for this had already been assembled in anticipation of the final drawings and by the following March Thomas Manton was at work on it. In August the doric columns were rising, but Brown did not live to see the completion, and the elegant balustrade of diagonal ironwork, made by N. Beetham[38] in London, was not ready until 1783, when a waggon and team of horses left Burghley in July to collect it.

Burghley was to prove not only the longest but one of the happiest of Brown's commissions, and it was one in which he took immense pride. As he wrote to Lord Harcourt while staying there in 1778, 'This is a great place, where I have had twenty-five years pleasure in restoring the monument of a great minister to a great Queen.'[39] His death in 1783 brought the total years to thirty, and few things would have pleased him more than to find that Lord Exeter had paid him the compliment of placing his portrait by Nathaniel Dance in the Pagoda Room at Burghley, where it still hangs. His regular visits to inspect the various works here would have made it easy for Brown to take in two more commissions which materialised in the later 1750's: Madingley, on the outskirts of Cambridge; and Wrest Park in Bedfordshire.

Brown must have called at MADINGLEY HALL (Map 130), which then belonged to Sir John Hynde Cotton, during the summer or early autumn of 1756 for a draft contract was prepared and dated 16 November of that year. This set out four *Articles* or clauses outlining the work which he was to undertake. In fact, the contract was never signed, and it is evident from a surviving copy that mutual trust was sufficient, for Sir John endorsed it 'Never executed nor any other but all was done upon honour on both sides and never repented by either.'[40] The articles are, however, useful in defining the scope of the work. The first provided for the making of a lawn before the north front, clearing certain trees and planting others, and filling up the old canal to 'give the whole a natural and corresponding Level with the Park House and Grove'. The second article related mainly to making a gravel walk some eight feet wide round the new lawn, and for the sowing or turfing of the lawn itself. The last two clauses provided for making a coach road, and a fosse from the house to the wood and the north-east grove: also the filling up of the 'bason' and all other pieces of water except the 'lowermost of the square Pieces' which was to become part of the lake. The draft concluded with the undertaking by Brown to complete the work 'in the best manner' by August, 1757, for £500, this to include the cost of his journeys and survey, but Sir John was to provide horses, carts and wheelbarrows as well as trees and shrubs.

Although the house at Madingley is now occupied by a department of Cambridge University, and a good deal of new building has been carried out on the site of its stables and elsewhere, there are traces of Brown's lawn and lake on the perimeter of the well-kept formal garden which was re-introduced at the end of the nineteenth century.

His commission for WREST PARK (Map 207) (Plate 62B) came from Philip Yorke and his wife. The former was the eldest son of Lord Chief Justice Hardwicke to whom Brown in this year successfully negotiated the sale of Lord Exeter's town house. Mr. Yorke had married in 1740 Lady Jemima Campbell, daughter of the 3rd Earl of Breadalbane, and grand-daughter of the Duke of Kent from whom she inherited the estate at Wrest, and the titles of Marchioness de Grey and Baroness Lucas of Crudwell, the first of which she continued to use after her marriage.

At first sight there is little at Wrest to bring Brown to mind. Its present external appearance of a *chateau* set down in some flat acres of Bedfordshire provide no clue, nor does that part of the ground immediately around it. Until its rebuilding by James Clephane, for Earl de Grey in 1834, the house was, however, largely Jacobean although the entrance front had been re-faced towards the end of the seventeenth century. Before its south front stretches a formal parterre, and beyond that lies a canal at the far end of which is a domed brick pavilion, built to a design by Thomas Archer *circa* 1710. The retention of these early features in a garden on which Brown was consulted was unusual, but no doubt he had to adapt his ideas to suit those of the Marchioness de Grey, a dominant character by whom the memory and achievements of her grandfather were revered. Although she was anxious to keep much of what he had created in the gardens, she was equally anxious to make improvements of her own, and for this reason in the years following their marriage she and her husband made a number of expeditions to see what had recently been carried out elsewhere, notably at Holkham, and at Warwick Castle.[41] In 1748 they visited Stowe when Brown may first have come to their notice.

Documentation for Brown's contribution to Wrest is scanty, and there have been many innovations since his time, but on the evidence of Horace Walpole he was responsible for the Bath House – a curious domed, pseudo-ruin of rough-hewn stone standing by a pond. He also raised the ground level round Archer's pavilion (now lowered again) and carried out a considerable amount of planting, his contributions to the scene being acknowledged when, in due course, the Marchioness erected a memorial column, topped by an acorn-shaped urn, and banded with square blocks of rustication. It bears an inscription recording that the gardens 'were begun in the year 1706 by the Duke of Kent, who continued to beautify them until the year 1740; the work was again carried on by Philip Earl of Hardwicke, and Jemima, Marchioness de Grey, with the professional assistance of Lancelot Brown, Esq., 1758–60.'

Some part of the latter's work was, however, still in hand in 1769 when the Marchioness wrote to a friend: 'Mr. Brown has been leading me such a fairy circle and his magic wand has raised such landscapes to the eye, not visionary, for they were all there, but his touch has brought them out with the same effect as a painter's pencil upon canvas, that after having hobbled over rough ground to points that I had never seen before for two hours, I return half tired and half foot-sore and must really break off.'[42] The retention of the formal features was not calculated to meet with the approval of Horace Walpole who, in one of his sourer moods when he visited Wrest some four years later, described it as a 'wretched low bad house'. The gardens he found 'very ugly in the old fashioned manner with high hedges and canals, at the end of the principal one of which is a frightful Temple designed by Mr. Archer', but he conceded that 'Mr. Brown has much corrected this garden and built a hermitage and cold bath in a bold good taste.'[43]

A small, but unusual and noteworthy, work which Brown was to carry out in about 1756 or 1757 was that undertaken for David Garrick in the gardens of his house beside the Thames at Hampton, now known as GARRICK'S VILLA (Map 89). Garrick had purchased this small estate, some way to the west of Hampton Court Palace, in 1754. Although the house itself was to be altered by his friend Robert Adam in 1772, the latter was abroad when Garrick moved in, and when the actor conceived the idea of building a Temple on the river bank. 'Garrick is building a graceful temple to Shakespeare,' Walpole wrote to Richard Bentley in August, 1755, and soon after the octagonal walls were ready to take their leaden dome. The drawback to this riverside portion of his estate lay in its separation from the rest by the road to Hampton village, and it was to overcome this problem that he consulted Brown. The latter's advice was that a tunnel should be made beneath the road in preference to spanning it by a bridge; a solution which he had already employed at Croome. Mrs. Garrick liked to recall that when this recommendation had been reported to Dr. Johnson, he gave his approval, adding 'David, David, what can't be over-done, may be under-done.'[44] The work must have been completed well before February, 1759 when Robert Adam, newly returned from Italy, and his brother James, accompanied by Alexander Carlyle and John Home, spent a day at Hampton with their golf clubs. Home, seeing the tunnel, offered to drive his ball through it in three strokes, a feat which he accomplished. The ball, however, came to rest in the shallows of the river from where it was retrieved by Garrick and kept as a memento.

This brief essay in landscaping appears to have provided Garrick with an idea for a new passage in his play *Lethe, or Æsop in the Shades*, first produced in 1740. In the fifth edition of 1757 he was to introduce the character of Lord Chalkstone, a gouty peer who, waiting to be rowed across the Styx, turns his spy glass on the Elysian Fields, and comments to Mr. Æsop that they are:

laid out most detestably – no taste! No fancy in the whole world! Your river there,
what d'ye call it? *Aye, Styx – Why 'tis as straight as Fleet-ditch. You should have
given it a serpentine sweep, and sloped the banks of it. The place indeed has fine*
capabilities; *but you should clear the wood to the left and clump the trees on the
right. In short the whole wants variety, extent, contrast, inequality* [going towards
the orchestra stops suddenly, and looks into the Pit] *Upon my word, here's a
fine hah-hah! And a most curious collection of evergreens and flowering shrubs!*

The part of Chalkstone was played by Garrick himself, and became one of his
favourites.

The existence of a ceiling design prepared by Brown and submitted to William
Constable of Burton Constable (Map 32) (Plate 15B) before 1760 indicates that he must
have visited that house towards the end of the previous decade. No details of this early
project have, however, come to light so far, and his other schemes for Mr. Constable
are later in date. That the early ceiling design was submitted, rejected, and then accepted
by another client will be seen in the following chapter.

Fig. 2. Garrick's Garden

1 Miles Hadfield, *A History of Gardening*, 1960, mentions Henry Marsh, James Lee, Lewis Kennedy
  and Christopher Grey as living in the locality.
2 It has not been identified but was probably one of those demolished and rebuilt in the early nineteenth century.
3 Letter to H. Repton, 24 April, 1792, quoted in *Sketches and Hints*, 1795, p. 53.
4 H. Repton, *The Theory and Practice of Landscape Gardening*, 1803, p. 266.
5 Petworth archives.
6 Plans and elevations in *Vitruvius Britannicus*, Vol. IV, 1767, plates 32–6.

7 Warrants for Greening's royal appointment are in P.R.O. Works 1/2, folios 18–20. He made a design for Corsham (see page 87). Robert Greening who was employed at Wimpole in 1753 may have been a brother or son. The *Gentleman's Magazine* for 1757 notes the death on 4 February of 'Thomas Greening Esq. late Gardener to His Majesty', and in 1781 on 11 June at Turnham Green, the death of 'Mrs. Greening, widow of Thos. Greening Esq. head gardener to his late Majesty King George II.' Repton, who made a slip in calling him Greenway, refers to his having preceded Brown in the grounds at Longleat (*Fragments*, 1816).

8 Pakenham Correspondence. Mrs. Yorke would have been his wife's sister-in-law as he had married Elizabeth Yorke, eldest daughter of Lord Hardwicke.

9 Sir William Temple, *Works*, 1720.

10 A scathing allusion to this was made by Alexander Pope in his *Moral Essays*, 1731.

11 In the possession of the Marquess of Zetland. It includes the wings added to the house by Robert Adam *circa* 1763, and pulled down in the 1780s.

12 'Visits to Country Seats', *Walpole Society*, Vol. XVI.

13 *Observations on Modern Gardening*, 1770, pp. 4–5.

14 Drawings preserved in the house, now Beechwood Preparatory School. Permission for their reproduction in this book has unfortunately not been granted.

15 Denbigh Papers, Building Book (Box 4/14).

16 Bodleian Library, Oxford, Gough Maps, 32f., 28 v.

17 He married in 1757 Mary, third daughter and co-heir of Sir John Bruce Cotton of Connington.

18 Joseph Cradock, *Literary and Miscellaneous Memoirs*, 1828, Vol. 4, p. 187.

19 T. Wharton, *History of Oxfordshire*, 1783, p. 60.

20 Dated 27 July, 1768. Dacre Correspondence, Essex C.R.O., D/DL C43/3/237.

21 'Visits To Country Seats', *Walpole Society*, Vol. XVI.

22 L. Dickens and M. Stanton, *An Eighteenth Century Correspondence*, 1910.

23 L. Dickens and M. Stanton, *op. cit.*

24 Essex C.R.O., D/DL F13312.

25 Essex C.R.O., D/DL E72.

26 Pakenham Correspondence.

27 *Tour Through England and Wales*, 1724–7.

28 A detailed account of Brown's work at Burghley is in preparation by Dr. Eric Till and will in due course be published in *Country Life*. His continuing researches may produce still more drawings, and I am grateful to him for allowing me to see those which have so far come to light, and for giving me the benefit of his knowledge of the house and its history.

29 L. Dickens and M. Stanton, *An Eighteenth Century Correspondence*, 1910.

30 'Visits to Country Seats', *Walpole Society*, Vol. XVI.

31 British Museum, Add. MSS 35595, F. 1–3.

32 Father of the Hon. Philip Yorke, then of Wrest Park.

33 Pakenham Correspondence. This Bacchus was described by Dallaway (*Anecdotes*, 1800, p. 390) as one 'which would grace any collection even in Italy'. Dr. Till has found that this pedestal was duly supplied to Brown's design by Ince and Mayhew. For many years, however, the Bacchus has stood out of doors in the North Court, the original pedestal being replaced with one of stone.

34 Pakenham Correspondence.

35 Day Book, Burghley Archives.

36 William Harrod, *Antiquities of Stamford*, 1785.

37 Information kindly supplied by Dr. E. C. Till.

38 Beetham worked for Brown at Benham and Claremont, and for Holland at Carlton House.

39 E. W. Harcourt, *Harcourt Papers*, Vol. 8, p. 266.

40 Antrobus Papers, Box 2, at Wootton Rivers, Wilts.
41 Joyce Godber, *History of Bedfordshire*, 1969, pp. 301–2.
42 19 September, 1769. Lucas Papers, Beds. C.R.O. I am indebted to Mr. John Kerslake for bringing this letter to my attention.
43 June, 1771. 'Visits to Country Seats', *Walpole Society*, Vol. XVI, p. 71.
44 Percy FitzGerald, *The Life of David Garrick*, 1866.

IV

WEST COUNTRY COMMISSIONS

By 1757 Brown's practice was extending into the west country with enquiries arriving from Lord Weymouth, Mr. Methuen, Lord Shelburne and Lord Bruce in that and the following two or three years.

Thomas Thynne, 3rd Viscount Weymouth and later 1st Marquess of Bath, succeeded his father in 1751 when he was seventeen, and some years were to pass before he embarked on alterations to the park at Longleat (Map 127) (Plate 11B), the great Renaissance house begun by Sir John Thynne in 1554. Johannes Kip's engraving of *circa* 1700 shows the house as surrounded by a formal layout, the most extensive area being to the east where, beyond a parterre and a canal formed out of monastic stew-ponds, several straight alleys radiated from an axial walk. Much of this formality was still in existence when, in October, 1757, Lord Weymouth signed the first contract with Brown in the sum of £1,450. This contract set out the alterations which were to be made to the garden, park, terrace and water, and work began at once. Away went the parterres, to be replaced with lawn, while the canal was re-cast into a chain of lakes and the rigid alleys were broken into groups of trees. On the south, a curving drive wound its way to the house in place of the previous straight approach. Brown did, however, retain the fine avenue of elms on the east, which survived until recent years. In the more distant park-land, where the ground begins to climb upward from the plain in which the house lies, he planned the plantations of beech, oak and chestnut with which they are still clothed.

The second year's work, as set out in the contract, provided for the making of walks from 'the Hall door to High Wood', and from High Wood to the kitchen garden, the verges of the latter being adorned 'with shrubs, trees of curious sorts, and turfe'. There were also to be stews formed in the kitchen garden, followed in 1759 by a new drive from Horningham, and the draining, levelling and sowing of the surrounding meadows, Brown undertaking that 'should any part of it fail', he would 'sow it over again till it does answer'. Altogether something over £3,300 was spent by 1760, after which a

further £1,200 was involved in the construction of more sunk fences and another drive 'from the stables past Rottenbury Hill to the Frome road,' with additional draining and planting. To supervise this extensive programme in his absence Brown employed one Sanderson as foreman.

Mrs. Delany visited Longleat in November, 1760, and found that 'there is not much alteration in the house, but *the gardens are no more*. They are succeeded by a fine lawn, a serpentine river, wooded hills, gravel paths meandering round a shrubbery, all modernised by the ingenious and much sought-after Mr. Brown. There are schemes for further improvements. Lord Weymouth is so fond of the place that he leaves it with reluctance.'[1] Walpole, who was there two years later, was more critical and thought that 'the water is not well contrived, the ponds do not unite well, and the Cascades have not water enough. There is a new [flower] garden making, and a gate built, designed by Brown, too small, and in a false taste.'[2] Humphry Repton was to carry out a number of alterations in the grounds near the house, including a form of 'Palladian' bridge built over the dam formed between two lakes by Brown. Repton also deepened and broadened the water, and introduced a tree-covered island, but in the main, and particularly in its further reaches, the park at Longleat is of Brown's creation.

In 1760 Brown was commissioned to enlarge CORSHAM COURT (Map 54) (Plates 14C, 15A, B, and 16A, B, C) and to alter the grounds. The property had been purchased some fifteen years earlier by Paul Methuen, a young cousin and god-son of the ambassador Sir Paul Methuen who, with his father, had been responsible for negotiating Britain's port wine treaty with Portugal. Sir Paul had intimated an intention of leaving his famous collection of pictures and other works of art to his cousin on the understanding that it should be suitably housed, and it was with this in mind that Mr. Methuen in due course set about the enlargement and re-decoration of what was still largely a gabled Elizabethan house, although the north front had been refaced in a classical manner in about 1749.

While the main objective was the provision of a suite of state rooms in which the pictures could be hung, more living accommodation was also required, and to provide both Brown doubled the wings of the house, repeating the existing gables on the south front. For the new east front, behind which were to be the state rooms, and the north returns, he designed classical facades. The former was of seven bays, those at either end breaking forward slightly, and the whole being surmounted by a balustraded parapet set at intervals with stone vases. The return walls of these additions were brought into line with the existing classical north facade which carried a pediment over the three centre windows. The windows of the extensions were 'venetian'. Within the new east wing the state rooms were to consist of a picture gallery, 72 feet long and 24 feet across, and leading into a cabinet room, state bedroom and octagon room at its south end.

In the corresponding wing on the west, Brown built a new library, now the breakfast room, with bedrooms above.

The site of the house and garden did not present ideal landscaping material, lying immediately to the south of Corsham village, with its forecourt guarded by massive gate piers and gabled Jacobean stable blocks, that on the east adjoining the church and church-yard. To the north lay a small formal garden with a rectangular pool for which a design signed by Thomas Greening survives in the Corsham archives. Beyond this garden, a seventeenth century avenue of limes stretching away from the north front was brought to a sudden halt by the Bath–Chippenham road, while the ground immediately to the west of the house was occupied by domestic offices with kitchen gardens beyond. That left only the east in which to project any extensive landscape, and here Brown proposed a lake, to be constructed at the foot of the ground which slopes gently away from the house. This was not to be one of his favourite serpentines, but an irregular oval backed by woods. In the foreground a sunk fence was constructed, and continued as a boundary to the north lawn from which stretched the lime avenue which he retained, although removing, as can be seen from his surviving plan,[3] certain trees so as to give cross views. From the northern extremity of the avenue a belt of trees, known as the Mynte Wood, was planted eastward to screen the rest of the park from the main road. On the north lawn Greening's pool was to be given an irregular outline, but the lake proposed on Brown's plan was not executed at the time. It was later adopted as part of Repton's work here in the 1790s.

Brown's estimate for the garden work is dated 6 December, 1760, and provides for:

> *Making the great Walks and sunke Fence between the House and the Chippenham Road. The Draining the ground between the Sunke Fence and the line of the garden. To making the Water in the Parks, as also the leveling round it. The leveling round the House, as also on Front the New Building. The Sunke Fence on the Front of the Church-yard. All the Planting included Mr. Methuen to find trees and [sic] alterations which have been made in the Garden. The Above Articles come to one Thousand and twenty Pounds.*[4]

The trees planted in this decade probably included the oriental plane near the north-east angle of the house, now one of the most majestic in the country.

On 6 September, 1761, Brown wrote to Mr. Methuen from Hammersmith to acknowledge a payment of £200 for work already in hand, and continued:

> *I hope you have rec'd the plan [for the grounds] and that it has your approbation. I have desired Sanderson, my foreman at Longleat, to come over and give a few directions. He will want the plan. My health which has been extremely bad is now on the mend . . .*

Work on the enlarging of the house must have been begun in this year, and the new wings are outlined on the plan of the park, although detailed drawings for the exterior have not survived. Nor, with one exception, have those for the interiors, the one survivor being a detail for the library. There is, however, a list of some of the drawings which Brown supplied, which confirms the extent of the alterations:

No.
1. Elevation of Anti Room
2. Cieling [*sic*] of Anti Room & Dressing Room
3. Cieling of Bedchamber
4. Mouldings & margins for Anti & Dressing Room
5. Cornice to Dressing Room, firplace & Plint[h] base to Dito, & Entablature for Doors in Bedroom & Dressing Room
6. Elevation of Alcove Bedchamber
7. Elevation of the Dressing Room
8. Elevation of the Gallery
9. Sketch of Cieling for Dito
10. Principal Story for Corsham
11. Plan of the North Front
12. Dito of the East or Gallery Front
13. Chimney Piece Dressing Room
14. Chimney Piece Bedchamber
15. Cold Bath, Room over & Drawings of Dito

Against most of the entries is written either 'Brown' or 'Boucher', apparently an indication as to who held the drawings at the time when the list was prepared. Boucher was Mr. Methuen's steward whose name occurs over a long period in the Corsham day-books. The last item on the list, the Cold Bath, refers to the elegant little gothic building which stands to the west of the north walk, the bath itself being sunk in the floor behind the open triple arches of the ground floor. Above the arches a two-light window, flanked by pinnacled niches lights a dressing room, while a crenellated parapet with more pinnacles encircles the stone-tiled roof. Behind the bath house a short passage, its walls originally set with a decorative pattern of fir cones, which survived until recent years, leads to a walled garden on the north-west.

One of the outstanding features of the decoration in the new rooms was the plaster-work. To carry this out Brown employed Thomas Stocking of Bristol, a skilful crafts-man about whom little is known save that he died 'esteemed and respected' in 1806. Brown's design for the Picture Gallery ceiling appears not to have been made for Mr. Methuen in the first place: it was, in fact, the graceful rococo design (mentioned at the end of the preceding chapter) which he had previously submitted to Mr. Constable

for the hall at Burton Constable, but which that gentleman had turned down in favour of a scheme for his Great Hall by Thomas Lightoler, carried out *circa* 1760.[5] When Brown first envisaged this elaborate piece of plasterwork with its S-scrolls, baskets of flowers and highly modelled *putti*, he probably had in mind the skilled band of York plasterers for its execution. Now the able Mr. Stocking was at hand and Brown saw an opportunity of taking his rejected masterpiece down from the shelf for submission to Mr. Methuen. It duly found favour, and by 1763 Stocking was at work on the Gallery and other state room ceilings. There were a few hitches as Brown was frequently elsewhere, and failed to deliver some of the required drawings at the appointed time. Stocking, growing desperate, wrote to him from Bristol on 27 December, 1763:

> *Sr*
>
> *I make bold to trouble you with this to beg the favour of sending me down the Drawings for the Drawing room Vestiable & Cove bedchamber, the Cornice of the Two later are finish'd.*
>
> *I have been obliged to keep my Ornament Stands on Mouldings for sum time past which is hurtfull to mee, and at this time wee have nothing to do, and the Cieling of the Cove bedchamber will be to dry for to recive the Ornaments, if wee don't recive them soon. I shall be exstreemly glad if you'll send them to Corsham as soon as you are at leasure . . .*

The designs apparently arrived without further delay and on 16 March, 1764, Brown, who had been ill, wrote to Mr. Methuen:

> *I have enclosed to you a Plan for the turning the Bow Window in the Dressing Room into a sort of Alcove, but you will be so obliging as to keep this till I have the honour of waiting on you which shall be as soon as possible. I have enclosed a letter from Stocking and beg you will be so good as to send the Plan he mentions. As to what he writes about the green House I must first talk with you & be on the spot likewise before that can be settled. I will answer Mr. Boucher's letter directly. I cough night & day. I mean to take a little journey by way of changing the air and when I return you may depend on seeing me.*[6]

The doors and window cases in the state rooms were executed by John Hobcroft,[7] and by 1769 the walls of the Gallery were ready to receive their covering of crimson silk damask, supplied by Morris and Young at 14s the half-yard (i.e. a yard of 18 in. width).[8]

Thomas Stocking was also responsible for the plasterwork in what was then the library in the west wing of the house. Here the ceiling carries numerous roundels, each containing a coat-of-arms for some branch of the Methuen family tree, and linked to

each other by entwined plaster 'ribbons'. The ceiling rests on an arcaded cornice with dozens of tiny modelled heads. Each head differs from its neighbours, one being said to represent George III, while Shakespearean characters have been suggested for several of the others. The similarity with plasterwork formerly in the Bath House at Arnos Castle, Brislington, establishes Stocking's connection with the latter building.[9]

Brown's connection with Corsham continued for many years. By 1767 Mr. Methuen noted in his day-book payments amounting to £1,050 for designs and superintending the work. In 1780 Brown received £10 for a set of hot-house plans. When John Nash and Humphry Repton came to carry out their alterations to Corsham in 1795 they fortunately left the state rooms undisturbed, although the gothic bookcases in the library were removed, and a new library formed in the adjoining room. Externally their work was a good deal more drastic, involving the application of 'Jacobean' detailing to the east front, and the replacement of the north facade with a semi-octagonal feature modelled on Henry VII's Chapel at Westminster. Shoddy workmanship in the latter, however, doomed it to a short life, and Thomas Bellamy's present facade eventually succeeded it.[10]

It had probably been in the course of his autumn journey to Longleat in 1757 that Brown first visited BOWOOD (Map 26) (Plates 17A and B) at the request of John, 1st Earl of Shelburne, although it produced little result at the time and the Earl wrote ruefully to his son:

> *What wou'd you give to know the consequences of the visit of the famous Mr. Brown and the fruit of the 30 guineas which I gave him? He passed two days with me . . . and twenty times assured me that he does not know a finer place in England than Bowood Park, and that he is sure no Prince in Europe has so fine a fruit garden.*

This, as the Earl observed, seemed little return for his 'three-times-ten guineas', but he concluded philosophically, 'I am persuaded that the man means to present me at some future time with a well-digested plan for this place, and perhaps to come to me to explain it.'[11] While he was disappointed in the hope of seeing Brown's final design, which is dated 1763, it appears from the payment to the latter of £500 in April,[12] 1761, that a rough scheme had in fact already been agreed, and preliminary work begun, before the Earl's death on 10 May that year.

In August, 1762, a contract was signed by the 2nd Earl and Brown, setting out the course of the work for the next four years.

The landscaping of the grounds was envisaged as complementary to the considerable alterations to the house which Robert Adam was designing at the same time, and which were to be supervised by Henry Holland, the builder,[13] who had previously worked at Bowood for the 1st Earl in 1754. Now he was to act as paymaster, and to deal with a

variety of issues which included fetching the painter, Cipriani, from London to work on the panels which formed part of Adam's decorative schemes. For some time before the 1st Earl's death the Bowood estate, originally of modest extent, had been enlarged by the gradual purchase of adjoining land. This gave scope for Brown's extensive scheme in which the main feature was to be a large sheet of water of sinuous outline, this to be made in two converging valleys by damming the Washway stream to the south and the Whetham brook to the east, the latter also involving the removal of a cluster of cottages. Another important feature was to be the mausoleum which the 1st Earl's widow erected to his memory, and for which she commissioned a design from Robert Adam. The site selected was against a background of trees on the crest of a knoll to the south-west, overlooking the extremity of Brown's lake after it had swept in a curve below the house. Adam could hardly have hoped for a more advantageous setting for his fine classical essay, with its doric portico guarding the entrance to a domed, top-lit cella containing Carlini's monument to the Earl, a simple sarcophagus resting on a high plinth with an inscribed tablet.[14]

In his contract with Lord Shelburne, Brown undertook responsibility for the general planting and sowing of the grounds, and for making the lake, the sham bridge, sunk fences, and drives to the house from the Calne and Derryhill entrances. He was also to 'Make the Great Plantations . . . each side of the Mausoleum and all those plantations proposed to Verge the Park', which included the magnificent beech woods by which the estate is still encircled. He was to find the stones for the 'dry wall . . . and head of the water as also for the sham bridge', and to supply all forest trees and underwood. Lord Shelburne agreed to produce 'the curious trees and tree seeds' for Brown to plant, and to provide six able horses with carts for use in the course of the work. The agreed payments, amounting to £4,300 in all, were to be made half-yearly from 1763 to 1766.

Early in 1765 Lord Shelburne married Lady Sophia Carteret who was to share his enthusiasm for the alterations at Bowood, and whose diary contains a number of references to the making of the landscape. On 30 May that year she noted that Brown's plantations 'are very young but promising', while on 5 August, 'Mr. Brown the gardener came to dinner and spent the evening giving directions to his men.' By the following June considerable progress had been made. 'As soon as breakfast was over', Lady Shelburne noted on the 16th, 'we took a walk and were vastly pleased with the effect of the water which flows into a magnificent river and only wants now to rise to its proper height, which it comes nearer to every day'.[15] The work continued for two years after the agreed time, and Brown wrote to Lord Shelburne at the end of 1768 to explain that £130 additional expenditure had been incurred in 'forming the Island, and in lowering the hill between the wood and the house'. The matter of reimbursement, however, he was content to leave 'entirely to your Lordship's pleasure'. He must have been well

aware of the Earl's renewed interest in politics at this time, for he closed his letter with the information that he had just returned from a visit to Lord Chatham at Hayes, 'where I found things as I dare say your Lordship wishes, (viz.) well.'[16]

Although on Brown's plan of 1763 there is a reference to 'rock-work' at the extremity of the lake, and his contract refers to 'stones for the head of the water', it appears that the latter was subsequently elaborated, *circa* 1785, into a cascade of considerable size by the Hon. Charles Hamilton of Painshill, who 'took a picture of N. Poussin's for his model. Mr. Josiah Lane assisted in the function of this stupendous work, but it was *finished* under the direction of the present Marquis.'[17] Lane's was not the only name to appear in connection with the grounds in that decade for in 1781, two years before Brown's death, 'Mr. Eames' is mentioned in the Bowood accounts as directing improvements in the park. His payment of £21 does not, however, suggest anything extensive, and the park as it survives today is essentially a Brownian conception, grand in scale, tranquil in atmosphere, and providing constant variety by the texture and colour of its trees, and the reflections in its lake.

Over the same period as his work for Lord Shelburne at Bowood, Brown was also carrying out changes in the grounds of what is now WYCOMBE ABBEY (Map 209) in Buckinghamshire, a property which had come to the Earl from a maternal uncle in 1751. Originally called Loakes, it was a fairly small estate entered by a handsome pair of gates erected in 1762, but now moved to the approach to St. Mary's Parish Church. Brown was then on the point of making his first visit, for the Earl's agent, Samuel Auld, wrote to him on 8 October: 'The Iron Gates is up and much esteem'd by our neighbours as being a great ornament to the Town. I wish your Lordship wd. make them a visit. I have regulated the Ground near the Gates. The rest I leave to Mr. Brown. When he come's I shall accommodate him according to your Lordship's direction to me to Day.'[18]

Brown's account shows that he was responsible for a considerable amount of planting, which was carried out by the foreman John Simpson. It also records that for this purpose 100 elm trees at 9d each were purchased from Ash's nursery at Twickenham, as well as 12,000 quick-sets at 6d per 100, while 100 larches and 40 planes were bought from another nurseryman, Scott.[19]

Although his appointment as royal gardener in 1764 was to bring Brown into contact with several members of the King's household, he was by this time already acquainted with Lord Bruce, then Lord of the Bedchamber. The date of his first visit to Lord Bruce's home, TOTTENHAM PARK (Map 191), is unrecorded, but it was probably towards the end of 1763 for in the following year the latter noted that the 'Piers and Court wall' in front of the house had been taken down, which suggests that landscaping had begun. Baron Bruce, later 1st Earl of Ailesbury, had married in 1761 Susanna, daughter of

Henry Hoare of Stourhead, and widow of Viscount Dungarvan. His house, in the heart of Savernake Forest, had been designed by Lord Burlington, whose sister married Charles, third holder of the earlier Ailesbury title. A painting of *circa* 1740[20] shows the house as of red brick with stone dressings and angle turrets, an appearance which it retained until 1825 when Samuel Cundy encased it in stucco. The same painting also shows the semi-circular forecourt and stone piers to which Lord Bruce alluded in his note.

The first document in the Ailesbury archives which refers to Brown's activities is a sketch in red chalk showing the house flanked by trees, but with the southern approach opened up with lawns. On the reverse is pencilled another very rough sketch plan, while folded with it is a strip of paper bearing the words 'Sketch by Mr. Hoare of what he understands to be Mr. Brown's idea for improvements in the forest so as to make it one Great Whole.' Although it is undated, it must belong to the time of preliminary discussions, when Mr. Hoare, Lord Bruce's father-in-law and the creator of that outstanding example of amateur landscaping, Stourhead, was obviously consulted over Brown's proposals.

It was agreed that in the vicinity of the house the alterations should include removing the rectangular pools which had previously flanked the forecourt, as well as the forecourt itself; creating a new walled kitchen and flower garden, screened by trees, to the north of the house; and opening up the ground before the north-west and south-east fronts. The great rides through the surrounding forest were left more or less undisturbed, but the thickets near the house were substantially thinned, while two garden buildings, designed by Lord Burlington and standing at some distance on either side of the house, were retained.

In the spring of 1764 Lord Bruce noted that 'Mr. Spires [Spyers], Mr. Brown's surveyor, came here Tuesday April ye 10th and went from hence Friday May the 4th ... 3 weeks and 3 days', and the resulting measurements would have formed the basis of Brown's finished design, although this appears not to have survived.

Since Lord Bruce's official duties kept him away from home a good deal, reports were sent to him periodically by his agent, Charles Bill, who on 18 March, 1765, wrote:

Mr. Brown came here on Sunday to dinner. In the afternoon he took a view of the gardens in a storm of snow. Early this morning, which proved tolerably favourable, he allowed lining out and finally settled the serpentine walk all round the garden, marked such trees as were proposed to be taken away and gave general directions to Winckles [Lord Bruce's house steward] upon everything that occurr'd. He thinks it best to keep Howse a fortnight or three weeks longer to get the levelling Business forward. In general he approves of what has been done except the taking away [of]

a few large trees in one or two places. If the high bank and trees had been taken down,
great would have been the fall indeed, Brown would have excommunicated us all . . .

If Mr. Bill was troubled by Capability's autocratic manner, Lord Bruce was equally
exercised by his failure on this occasion to fix his charges. A request in September for
details of the yearly account brought a somewhat aggrieved reply on the 21st:

My Lord,

I am now in Staffordshire [i.e. Trentham] where I was honoured with your
Lordship's letter I believe ten days ago or more, but I have been so much out of
order that I have not been able to write nor do anything else. I sent up to my Clerk
to know what the demand was upon your Lordship which I did not know exactly
by the Book. He writes me word that the surveying and maping Bill with the man's
expense at 6d per acre comes to near twenty-five pounds and as to my Journeys and
Plans I have no fixed rule about it nor is it possible to do it but to charge less or
more according to the size and trouble. All I can say upon it is that I should be very
sorry to diminish my friends, and very sorry to increase my business, for I have so
much to do that it neither answers for profit nor pleasure, for when I am galloping
in one part of the world my men are making blunders and neglects which [make] it
very unpleas't.

Of one thing I can assure your Lordship that if I can be of use to your Lordship
I shall be very happy and as to money matters your Lordship will satisfy me when
your Lordship is pleas'd . . .

Lord Bruce apparently was satisfied with this arrangement, and everything proceeded
smoothly. In the following December, Brown was again at Tottenham when on the
12th, the agent noted the points which had been raised, including 'Lady Bruce's peep
from the large study window', of which 'Mr. Brown complained of its being a straight
line thro' a perfect avenue – he directed the cure of it by rounding off the plantation of
laurels at the entrance of it on the left hand. There is a fine Beech there, and he directed
the scrub trees to be cleared away a little from behind it which would also enlarge the
entrance to the narrow avenue.' Charles Bill concluded 'Mr. Brown thinks there is great
Capability about the Loggia and Octagon Buildings.'

In the autumn of the following year the kitchen garden was laid out after Brown,
who seems to have been singularly unfortunate in the weather for his visits to Tottenham, had spent a wet and windy September day examining the proposed site. The
capabilities of the garden buildings, however, remained in abeyance for another year
until, on 1 October, 1768, Winckles noted that the Octagon was to be re-faced with
stucco, and 'the Great building stucco'd and mended . . . the stucco to be jointed in
imitation of stone work'. At the same time, rose trees removed from the old kitchen

garden were planted out in the pleasure gardens, and 'the alteration of the West Corner of the House . . . done according to Mr. Brown's directions,' while laurels were planted behind the 'Umbrella Seat' – a feature which has not survived, but was probably modelled on one known from drawings to have stood in the gardens at Stourhead. Brown was again at Tottenham in the following March, spending the night of the 20th at Mr. Bill's house and proceeding next day to see Lord Suffolk at Charlton. By 1770 the work was more or less complete, although some minor changes were still in hand in 1772 when Lord Bruce wrote to Brown from Tottenham on 7 June:

> Upon our arrival here last night, we found what has been done towards the opening the Ladylawn Way much to our satisfaction, but we shall scarce venture to go a step farther to compleat it without your advice upon the spot, which we wish to have as soon as conveniently can be to yourself . . . I hope your family are well as mine is, Thank God, in general, excepting Lady Bruce who continues an invalid.[21]

To this Brown replied on 17 June:

> I am honoured with your Lordship's letter and I was very glad to find that the opening answers so well. I am going this week into Sussex and Hampshire. Does your Lordship wish to see me soon or more properly are your wants pressing? I know that opening requires some nice touches but I should think this is a bad time to execute that sort of work. Are not the men going to Hay making and after that the Harvest will follow. Your Lordship will be so obliging as to honour me with a line by the Cross Post, Lord Palmerston's near Romsey, Hants. immediately on the receipt of this, which will determine me to come from that place if I can possibly contrive it to your Lordship.
>
> I am sorry Lady Bruce is not as well as your Lordship would wish her but very glad that all the rest of the Family are well. Thank God mine are better than they have been this great while. I have got a very bad cold but I hope the journey I am about to take will carry it off . . .
>
> I shall get to Lord Palmerstons about Tuesday. Would not later in the summer be better for my coming? Come I will if I live because I wish the place and c. well.[22]

Tottenham has for many years been occupied by a school, but its magnificent setting, with the great Ionic column erected on the axis of the house by Lord Bruce after he had been created Earl of Ailesbury in 1776, is a remarkable survivor among eighteenth-century landscapes.

CHARLTON (Map 41), the house in the northern extremity of Wiltshire to which Brown had proceeded from Tottenham on 21 March, 1768, belongs to the group erected during James I's reign and including Hatfield, Blickling and Audley End. It was built for Catherine, Countess of Suffolk, whose descendant, the 12th Earl, succeeded to

the property in 1757 and some ten years later turned his attention to the remodelling of the house. With this in view he approached Brown and wrote to him on 5 July, 1767:

> *When you see the place I am inviting you to, you will wonder at my anxiety for your assistance – but a seat is like a Mistress where Beauty does not always charm. You gave me hopes of seeing you here this month I shall be here 'till the twenty seventh and made extremely happy by your immediate opinion on one or two favourite points, as well as by your general idea of the whole . . .*[23]

Brown's first visit was in that year, the one from Tottenham in 1768 being the second of the 'journeys twice there' noted in his account book, following which he submitted 'Plans and Elevations for the alterations of the House' as well as 'some sketches for water to be made near the house', and schemes for the kitchen garden. While the designs for the house failed to meet with Lord Suffolk's approval,[24] the design for the kitchen garden was adopted, the Earl writing to him on 19 November for the details 'that we may calculate and provide what quantity of bricks may still be wanting [for the walls]. My present stock is about 560,000.'[25] Two cottages which survive in the walled garden were almost certainly part of Brown's design. They were originally linked by a greenhouse which was later replaced by a curved colonnade which masks a potting shed.

The two attributed landscapes at SHARPHAM (Map 167), overlooking the river Dart, and WIDDICOMBE (Map 200), near Kingsbridge (see appendix, page 244), mark the western limit of Brown's practice in England, but not far from them in South Devon come the two schemes which he carried out at Mamhead and Ugbrooke. The sequence of events at UGBROOKE (Map 193) is not well documented since it must have come in an early and now non-existent ledger of Brown's, and the one design of his which survived until 1939 appears subsequently to have been mislaid. Fortunately the owner at that time recorded its inscription which ran: 'A Plan for the intended Alterations at Ugbrooke in Devonshire, the Seat of the Rt. Hon. Lord Clifford in 1761 by L. Brown.' He also observed in a letter that 'the design of the Park follows this plan fairly closely, except for the fact that there are now two lakes and a waterfall between them, instead of one lake, and a few extra clumps of trees have been planted at subsequent dates.'[26]

While there is no doubt that Brown laid out the grounds for the 4th Baron Clifford, the rebuilding of the old house presents a puzzle. Humphry Repton refers to it in his list of attributions to Brown as 'a new house' of his building. Robert Adam was redecorating the principal rooms here from 1766 until 1771, these dates being on his surviving drawings,[27] but none of the latter covers any structural work, and the carcase of the house must already have been built by then. This suggests that it had been begun somewhere about 1761, which is the year in which Brown's garden design was also prepared. A similar Brown–Adam arrangement had prevailed at Croome, where the latter decorated

rooms within a Brown carcase, and there is no reason to doubt that the same course was followed here, the straightforward design of the two-storey main elevation, with its end bays carried up to form angle turrets, being one of Brown's favourite themes at this period, although here given a gothic flavour by the addition of a crenellated parapet.

Lord Clifford had succeeded his father in 1732, but it was several years before he began the 'numerous improvements' which John Britton and Edward Brayley described as 'of late years effected in the house and scenery',[28] that is, before his death in 1783. Following the completion of the house, he obtained from the younger James Paine an elaborate neo-classical design for new stables in 1779[29] but this was not executed, and the simple block which eventually materialised in 1793 was by a local man, Joseph Rowe. To this later period also belong several rustic cottages which are an attractive feature of the estate, but thirty years earlier there appears to have been little in the way of architectural adornment in the park, and Brown's landscape relied for its effect on the water and plantations by which he emphasised the natural contours. From the house the ground slopes in a north-westerly direction to a wide valley and the stream which he dammed to form the two lakes which replace the single pool proposed on his plan of 1761. To the north the more distant ground rises sharply to an earthwork known as the Danish Encampment from where there are extensive views over the park.

In 1774 the beauties of the new landscape at Ugbrooke were to inspire two water-colours by Francis Towne showing views from the Encampment, and across the lower lake from a point known as Dryden's Seat, the poet having been a close friend of the 2nd Lord Clifford. Two years later appeared a lengthy and somewhat turgid poem by a Jesuit priest who had come to Lord Clifford's family as chaplain,[30] but while he extolls in detail the charms of the grounds, and the taste of his patron, his verses throw no light on the development of the house under Brown and Adam, and further evidence now seems unlikely to be forthcoming. It was, however, undoubtedly as a result of the former's work here that he was recommended in 1773 to Lord Clifford's brother, the Hon. Thomas Clifford of Tixall.

The building history of MAMHEAD (Map 132), four miles north-east of Ugbrooke, is even more confused than that of the latter house. The original structure was begun in 1681 by Sir Peter Ball, attorney to Queen Henrietta Maria, and was completed by his son Thomas, who died in 1749 and bequeathed the property to Thomas Hussey Aprice. He in turn sold it to Joseph Gascoigne Nightingale, whose daughter married the 3rd Viscount Lisburne (later 1st Earl). In 1769 Lord Lisburne asked Robert Adam to make designs for the ceilings of the principal rooms and these were presumably carried out. Three years later he wrote to Brown, whom he had met some months before. The letter, written from Mamhead on 17 August, 1772, explained that he intended 'to make some alterations at this place to render it more commodious and aggreeable, and continued:

I should esteem myself much obliged to you if I might hope for the favour of see-
ing you here any time during the autumn when it may best suit your other engage-
ments . . . I am encouraged to hope from you what you said [to] me when we met
accidentally last winter, that notwithstanding the distance, you may find an
opportunity to come here, as I should be glad to make what improvements the
scene is capable of under the Direction of a Genius whose Taste is so superior and
unrivalled. . .

It was apparently the following summer before the visit materialised, but in due course
Brown, after a two-day visit, submitted a structural survey of the house and tentative
suggestions for the grounds. After studying these, Lord Lisburne pointed out a few
inaccuracies in the former which, in a letter of 7 November, he asked Brown to correct
lest it 'should occasion you more Trouble and difficulty . . . in forming your Ideas of
what it is capable.' As to the proposals for the grounds, he continued that as these were
not intended as any 'capital feature, but merely as a private scene', Brown could deal
with them as he thought best. There had been difficulty in acquiring adjoining land
from a neighbour, and Lord Lisburne had therefore decided to incorporate more of his
own on the far side of the road. Meanwhile, he was 'inclosing the ground with railing
that you staked out, near the Great Wood, for planting and shall get as forward as I can
in these matters till the plan of the grounds is ready with your further directions how
to proceed.' There is no mention at this stage of any building work, and in the following year Robert Adam produced a design for an entirely new house, an elaborate
composition with a centre block and pavilions linked by low corridors. This proposal
was, however, rejected, and in the absence of other evidence, it may be assumed that
Lord Lisburne contented himself with having Brown's less ambitious suggestions for
improvements carried out by local builders. In 1828 the house was severely damaged by
fire, following which it was rebuilt to designs by Anthony Salvin.

In 1773 Henry, 8th Baron Arundell, was seeking Brown's help over the grounds of
WARDOUR CASTLE (Map 195), on the northern edge of Cranborne Chase, where the
fine classical house designed by James Paine in 1770 – the largest house in the county –
was nearing completion. Half a mile away on rising ground to the north-east the no less
striking ruins of the original fourteenth-century Castle stand in what is now a mar-
vellously mature scene, although beyond it recent soft-wood afforestation has nibbled
alarmingly close to the old oaks and beeches. Lord Arundell's first letter was written
to Brown on 16 August, and in it he explained that:

as I am making improvements here, I have long thought of desiring you to come here,
and having seen several specimens of yr. fine taste, I am come to a resolution of
having a General Plan from you for ye grounds, water etc., and as I am inform'd

98

you are to be some time this summer in my neighbourhood, I shou'd be glad [if] you wou'd fix a time please and let me know beforehand that I may not be from home . . . I hope it may be convenient for you to spend some days with me to take a full view of this place wh. I flatter myself will be worthy yr. attention . . .

Other commitments, followed by a bout of illness, made the visit impossible during the autumn, but on 13 December Lord Arundell was writing again:

I found ye favor of yours. I am very sorry to hear of yr. indisposition and that it prevented me ye pleasure of seeing you here, which I have long wished for, being convinc'd it is needless to go on with anything in ye grounds till you have taken a view of it, and I flatter myself you will find room to show your fine taste. I intend going to town for ye winter about ye latter end of January, and shou'd be very happy if it wou'd suit you to make me a visit here about ye 20th or before . . .[31]

Whether Brown did get there early in the new year is not recorded, but it is likely that he worked Wardour in with one or other of his visits to Milton Abbey in 1774. Entries in his account book show that in March 1780 he was paid £84, presumably for his plan or plans, although he noted that journeys since that date still had not been paid for.

Particularly splendid are the great lake – formed out of a stream in the valley to the east of the house – and the plantations on its further bank. Whether Brown was responsible for the design of the two-storey Gothic banqueting house, which abuts the bailey of the old Castle, it is not possible to say with certainty, but it is very much in his manner.

1 *The Autobiography and Correspondence of Mary Delany*, 1862.
2 July, 1762. 'Visits to Country Seats', *Walpole Society*, Vol. XVI, p. 45.
3 Corsham Archives.
4 Corsham Archives.
5 This design, with Brown's name on it, is preserved at Burton Constable.
6 This and the two foregoing letters are from the Corsham Archives.
7 Hobcroft, whom Brown had first met at Stowe, was engaged in many important country house works of the period and in later years turned architect himself, designing Wasing House, Berkshire, and Padworth House in the same county. He was probably related to Simon Hobcroft, 'ye carpenter', who worked in this area and is referred to in the *Purefoy Letters*.
8 In 1772 the four gilt mirrors and console tables for which Robert Adam had supplied designs were placed between the windows of this room.
9 Demolished in 1958 and re-erected at Portmeirion, Merionethshire.
10 It is said that the rubble from this unsatisfactory feature was used to fill up the pool laid out by Greening and retained by Brown, to the north of the house.
11 Quoted in 'Bowood Park' by the Earl of Kerry, *Wilts. Archaeological and Nat. History Magazine*, Vol. 42, December, 1924.
12 Brown's Account Book.
13 Henry Holland the elder, father of the architect.

14 See John Cornforth, 'The Making of the Bowood Landscape', *Country Life*, 7 September, 1972.
15 Lady Shelburne's Diary, preserved MSS at Bowood.
16 Dated 13 December, 1768, Bowood Archives.
17 J. Britton, *Beauties of Wiltshire*, Vol. II, p. 221.
18 E. Lionel Reynolds, 'Correspondence Relating to High Wycombe', *Records of Bucks.*, Vol. X, No. 5, 1914.
19 A drawing of Ash's nursery is in the British Museum, Kings Maps. Scott may have been Henry Scott, at one time Lord Burlington's gardener, who later set up on his own at Weybridge.
20 At Sturmy House, Savernake, where are also preserved the papers from which the quotations in these paragraphs are made unless marked otherwise.
21 Pakenham Correspondence.
22 Archives at Sturmy House.
23 Pakenham Correspondence.
24 An inscription on a rebuilt portion of the roof records that 'This edifice was rendered such as it is under the skilful direction of Matthew Brettingham, Architect. Begun 1772, finished 1776.'
25 Pakenham Correspondence.
26 Communicated to the author, 29 July, 1939.
27 Sir John Soane's Museum, Adam Drawings, Vols. 50, 11, and 22.
28 *Beauties of . . . Devonshire*, 1809.
29 British Museum, Add. MSS 31323, A³ L, M, N.
30 The Rev. Joseph Reeve, *Ugbrooke Park*, 1776.
31 This and the foregoing quotation are from the Pakenham Correspondence.

Fig. 3. Ugbrooke Park, from an engraving

V

GROWING PRACTICE

WHILE THE REFERENCES to the elder Holland in the accounts at Bowood, mentioned in the preceding chapter, and those under Ashridge in Brown's account book, confirm transactions between them early in the 1760s, their acquaintance had begun a good while before this and probably soon after Brown went to live at Hammersmith, in the same parish of Fulham and a short walk from Church Row, where the Holland family resided. Here this Henry had established a flourishing building firm and a reputation which led to his employment in many important country houses. Three years older than Brown, he had married in 1739 and had already produced several children of which the first boy, also named Henry, was born in 1745.[1] Holland *père* took an active part in parochial affairs, helped to hang a new peal of bells in the church tower, and served as church warden in 1756. He designed several substantial houses in the neighbourhood, where he also owned brick-fields, and in the 1760s began to participate in land speculation in the west end of London. Between Brown and himself work was to form an obvious common interest, while the latter's children, Margaret, Ann, Henry, Mary and Catherine, found kindred spirits in young Bridget, Lancelot and John. During the 1750s two more little Hollands and two more little Browns were to arrive, and from this time the families were increasingly to be drawn together.

On 7 September, 1761, Lancelot junior, usually called Lance by the family to avoid confusion with his father, was dispatched to Eton where his schoolfellows lost no time in dubbing him 'Capey', which confirms that Capability's nickname had already percolated to the ears of the junior members of society.[2]

Brown's first journeys to ASHRIDGE (Map 8), where in due course he was to pay the elder Holland for building work, were made in 1759. The Duke of Bridgewater, probably in anticipation of his marriage to the Duke of Hamilton's widow,[3] wished to improve both the house and the grounds, and Brown's drawings submitted in 1760, included four plans and two elevations for the former. A grangerised volume of Chauncey's *Hertfordshire* in the British Museum[4] contains three pen and wash drawings of 1796 showing the old Ashridge as a rambling house of which the great hall, with its

oriel window and lantern astride its roof, formed the nucleus. To this two and three storey blocks were added at different times, and finally an attempt had been made to give coherence to these by decking them out with crow-stepped gables, which were also added to the lodge. Whether these embellishments were in fact the result of Brown's proposals cannot now be established with any certainty, but it seems probable in view of a note at the end of his account with the Duke, which refers to a 'Balance paid to Holland and to James Symes of quite two thousand pounds', this being additional to £100 already paid to the former for the garden wall, and other incidental sums including an unspecified amount 'to Mr. Scott for Trees'.

The Park at Ashridge had by this time been extended to embrace rising ground on the west of the road to Dagnall from which a magnificent avenue leads to a crest from which there are extensive views to Ivinghoe Beacon.[5]

Soon after the programme of work had been put into operation, the Duke's matrimonial hopes were dashed. Disapproving of some antics of his fiancée's sister, Lady Coventry, he stipulated that the former should have no further contact with her, a command which she not unnaturally refused to observe. Embittered by this, he withdrew from social life and retired to his Lancashire estate at Worsley, there to immerse himself in developing its mineral resources and subsequently to embark with James Brindley on the construction of the canal which bears his name. The contract with Brown, however, could not very well be cancelled, so the improvements went on at Ashridge until 1768, when the latter delivered his final account including a note of £13 7s 7d extra for his attendance about 'the work not contracted for'. The old house was pulled down in 1800 to make way for the present Gothic mansion designed by James Wyatt, after which Humphry Repton introduced some changes in the proximity of the latter, but the park, and particularly that area of it which is known as the Golden Valley, remains much as Brown left it with fine plantations and open glades. Part is now used as a golf club, the remainder being National Trust property, while the house is occupied by a business management concern.

More ducal commissions arrived in or around 1760, for Henry, 1st Duke of Northumberland, consulted Brown on plans for two of his estates, Syon and Alnwick and at about the same time Brown was summoned to Chatsworth by the Duke of Devonshire. In 1758 the Duke of Northumberland had put his name to the petition for Brown to be given a post in one of the royal gardens, and it is therefore possible that the plans for Syon may have been discussed at that time, but there are no relevant archives in the house. His Duchess, whom he had married in 1739, was Elizabeth, daughter of the 7th Duke of Somerset, through whom there were Grenville, Egremont and Hertford connections which would doubtless have made Brown's name familiar, and led to his employment.

SYON

By 1761 enough changes were evident in the gardens at SYON (Map 183) (Plate 19A) for R. and J. Dodsley to give several lines to describing the removal of the old walls so as to form 'a fine lawn extending from Isleworth to Brentford', the making of a ha-ha and gravel walks, and the sloping of the ground towards the river so that the surface of the water might be seen, with a prospect over it to 'the King's gardens at Richmond [now Kew Gardens] as well as up and down the Thames.'[6] They also describe the making of a 'new serpentine river', the eastern end of which forms a sizeable lake. Even in its early stages the new landscape must have presented a striking picture across the Thames, and its progress must have interested the King on his regular visits to his favourite palace. Thus it may well have played a part in securing Royal approval for Brown's appointment as Royal Gardener at Richmond and Hampton Court in 1764. In 1767 his own account book takes over from a lost ledger, with notes of payments from the Duke for 'work at Sion', beginning with £200 and continuing with substantial amounts until 1773. Brown's frequent presence, after 1764, in the gardens across the river, and his accessibility to George III's ear, were to make him a useful medium in the political manoeuverings of both the Duke of Northumberland and Lord Chatham with the monarch, and, indeed, in the somewhat guarded relations existing between the two noblemen.

Alnwick is not mentioned in Brown's account book and must again have been in a missing ledger, but it can be regarded as following closely on the initiation of work at Syon. As early as 1752 Walpole had remarked that the Duke and Duchess were 'building at Northumberland House, at Sion, at Stanstead, at Alnwick and Wentworth Castles! They live by the etiquette of the old peerage, have Swiss porters, the Countess has her pipers – in short they will soon have no estate.'[7] The ducal coffers, however, proved to be deeper than he knew, and the improvements continued through this and the following decades. At ALNWICK (Map 3) (Plate 19B) Brown was once again to find himself working concurrently with James Paine and Robert Adam. The former was certainly making alterations to the Castle by 1760, and was probably responsible for some earlier changes noted by Adam's elder brother John in the course of a brief 'Jaint into England' in the spring of 1759.[8] The purpose of this was to see the 'Reparations & additions making by the Earl of Northumberland upon that Princely Pile. The dining-room and drawingroom that he has fitted up are all extremely noble and elegant in the Gothick taste, but the drawingroom pleased me most.'

The Castle crowns a ridge of high ground, the slopes of which are shown as unkempt and full of boulders in Canaletto's painting of circa 1750.[9] These Brown had cleared and turfed, and where the little Bow Burn had cut its way through a shallow valley, the ground was filled in to form a terrace walk below the Castle walls. Only a few groups of trees were planted here, but on the further slopes thick plantations were made,

through which the river Aln still winds its way, reflecting sky and trees in its calm waters, and crossed by Adam's handsome bridge which carries the park approach to the Castle.

Adam's many designs for the Duke were later to include two decorative details supplied in 1778 for what he called 'Haln Abbey', that is, the rehabilitated portion of Hulne Priory. For some years after its purchase by the Duke (then Earl) in 1755, this ruin of a Carmelite foundation had stood as a picturesque eye-catcher in the park, some two miles distant from Alnwick Castle. At some point in the late 1760s it was decided to build on the site of the Prior's tower, what was later described as a 'summer house', with gothic windows and a crenellated parapet. While there is no evidence as to its architect, Brown may well have been responsible, as it is in the manner of his remodelling of High Lodge at Blenheim. Adam's charge of £17 17s od for his design for '4 sides of a Room in the Gothic stile' and 'a design of a ceiling for said Room'[10] suggests that he was consulted later as to the decoration of the large first-floor room, although the work as carried out differs from a design for this which is among his drawings in the Soane Museum.

In July, 1774, Walter Stanhope, the young Yorkshire landowner who a few weeks later was unexpectedly to find himself competing with Brown's eldest son as a possible candidate for Cockermouth (see page 174) visited the Northumberlands at Alnwick. Although he wrote enthusiastically to his mother about the improvements, his comments on Hulne Priory were limited to the observation that it was 'the first convent of Carmelite Friars established in Europe . . . and it now forms a curious ruin and a menagerie.' Possibly he did not get close enough to see the 'summer house' in detail, though he mentions that Hulne Park alone was seventeen miles in circumference, and that the Duke was re-planting here. 'If he continues his operations a few years longer upon as large a scale, it will be the noblest as well as the most extensive place in the Kingdom' he wrote of Alnwick in general. 'I never saw plantations so large, better disposed, or that flourished more, notwithstanding they are exposed to an eastern Wind from the main Ocean at a distance of two or three Miles. We traversed Rides of ten miles of his Grace's own planting within these twelve years.'[11] Brown was still visiting Alnwick in 1778.

His CHATSWORTH (Map 42) (Plate 20B) commission does not come into his surviving account book, but he was certainly at work here well before August, 1761, when Horace Walpole wrote that the 4th Duke of Devonshire was 'making vast plantations . . . and levelling a great deal of ground to show the river under the direction of Brown.'[12] Jan Sieberechts's painting of 1707, which hangs in the house, shows that although the old formal gardens immediately around it had been luxuriant and varied, what lay outside the encircling stone wall was extremely rough and bare, while the charms of the

river Derwent were hidden from view by the steepness of its banks. It was to provide a prospect over the water that Brown sloped the ground away from the house on the west, and raised the river level by constructing a dam.

Once again his work was to proceed side by side with buildings designed by James Paine, which included a new wing with domestic offices to the north of the house, stables to the north-east, and an imposing bridge over the Derwent, its piers embellished with sculpture by Colley Cibber. This bridge was to carry Brown's new drive where it crossed the water on its way through the park, in and around which he made extensive plantations, particularly along the ridge of high ground to the east, where these now form a splendid mass. A second visit by Walpole in September, 1768, confirmed his impression that Chatsworth had been 'much improved', especially in the gardens where 'many foolish waterworks' had been taken away,[13] although in fact Brown had retained the celebrated cascade, constructed in 1694 and elaborated with a domed feature, probably designed by Thomas Archer, in 1702. From this lofty source the water has descended over a series of steps for close on three hundred years, a unique and lovely feature to which even Walpole could scarcely have objected. Although some formality was re-introduced to the south and west of the house by the 7th Duke in the mid-nineteenth century – an era when Chatsworth was to produce that Victorian genius, Sir Joseph Paxton – much of Brown's landscape survives in the park, creating a splendid foil to the grandeur of the house.

Other commissions which materialised in the first half of the 1760s included Harewood, Aynho and Castle Ashby. Brown was also working at this time on the first of a group of Midland gardens, but these will be mentioned in Chapter IX.

At HAREWOOD (Map 91) (Plate 20A), Brown was to find himself in company with John Carr and Robert Adam, both of whom were employed by Edwin Lascelles in the building of a new house on his Yorkshire estate. This was to replace a seventeenth-century manor house called Gawthorpe, a name which lingered for some time and was still used by Brown when he carried his account with Mr. Lascelles forward from a missing ledger to his surviving account book.

John Carr gave his designs for the new house in 1758, work beginning early in the following year. Although Adam's designs for gothicising the nearby church are dated 1759, none of his drawings for adding external details to the house, or for decorating the principal rooms, is earlier than 1765. Brown evidently paid his first visit to Harewood, or Gawthorpe, as he called it, at the beginning of 1758, but it may be that his reference to giving Mr. Lascelles 'Two General Plans for the House' was concerned with some proposal at the time to keep the old manor house on its low-lying site. The item listed as a 'general plan for the Ground' appears to belong to this early date, although the charges for three drawings were carried forward to the new account book

to join the much later entries for three journeys, and a 'Plan for the intended water etc.' which was supplied in 1772.

One of his earliest visits is confirmed by a letter from Robert Teesdale, Lord Carlisle's head gardener at Castle Howard, to Samuel Popplewell, the steward at Harewood. Written on 12 March, 1758, it is revealing not only in its reference to Brown, but in showing the interest which the gardeners of the great estates took in each other's work, and the interchange of ideas and produce. After acknowledging a letter from Popplewell, Teesdale wrote that he had already written to the Harewood gardener, John Turnbull, and 'signified my distress for want of a few Franks [probably the shrub Franklina Altamaha]', of which he had been promised a dozen. He continued that he had 'Likewise desired of him [i.e. Turnbull] a few random Pencil Strokes of Mr. Brown's Designs for your Place, but he told me he had left none. Parson Hodgson tells me he did, and as I am acquainted with your situation it would give me some satisfaction to see any thoughts that has [sic] drop'd from that Great Man. I hope it is determin'd to carry the fire walls the whole length of the garden.'[14]

A first contract made between Mr. Lascelles and Brown, and amounting to £5,500, was seen at Harewood circa 1913 but has not so far reappeared.[15] The latter's surviving account book, however, only takes up payments made after 1774, which leaves a considerable period undocumented. He received £400 in September, 1774, subsequent amounts varying from £200 to £700 until £6,203 had been settled by March, 1781. The course of the work had not run entirely without trouble, and in 1778 Mr. Lascelles had complained in strong terms to Popplewell. 'I hope to be down the beginning of the week before Easter Sunday,' he wrote from Portman Street, London, on 28 March, 'and expect to find the whole job that Dickenson has the direction of, quite completed. Mr. Brown was with me the other day to desire I wou'd give him a Draft for the remaining £400, part of the £900 which he was not to desire until the whole was certified and allowed to be done according to contract. I have always said and did insist upon it that the ground was Scandalous Lay'd, and beggarly sown, and that several other parts were slovenly run over and badly finish'd, particularly by the Island. Mr. Brown assures me that he will be at Harewood House, on purpose to meet me and to give me satisfaction the week before Easter.'[16]

From the account book it appears that Mr. Lascelles gave Brown the £400 for which he asked on 27 March, and a further £400 was made over on 21 September, so it may be assumed that the defects were remedied to the owner's satisfaction. Certainly, when they had time to mature, the grounds took their place among the great landscapes of Yorkshire, to be praised by poets and painted by Turner and Girtin.

Aynho (Map 12), for which Brown was to make a plan in 1760, lies about ten miles west of Stowe, and would have been a familiar landmark on his journeys to Banbury.

Bought by Richard Cartwright at the end of the seventeenth century, the house had been rebuilt soon after the Restoration under the direction of Edward Marshall, and was altered by Thomas Archer between 1707 and 1711. By the mid-eighteenth century it had come to William Cartwright, M.P. for Northampton, who commissioned Brown's survey and plan in 1760. The incentive to landscape his grounds may have been due in part to his wife's interest for, as a daughter of Sir Charles Cottrell Dormer, she had grown up at Rousham, and would have seen the later stages of Kent's work being carried out there.

Although the approach to the north (entrance) front of Aynho from the village is still formal, with its courtyard flanked by stable blocks, the long garden front overlooks a gently sloping lawn and plantations laid out by Brown. A ledger for expenditure at Aynho[17] refers to a payment of £263 1s 3d to him for his plan, and there are later entries amounting to £1,080 for carrying out the work between 1761 and 1763. Another and more consequential work in the same county materialised when, on 14 October, 1761, Charles, 7th Earl of Northampton, signed a contract with Brown for the land-scaping of the grounds at CASTLE ASHBY (Map 38) (Plate 18B). A parish survey made in the previous year shows the formal gardens as still surviving to the east of the house at that time, while four long avenues radiated to the points of the compass, presenting much the same appearance as when John Evelyn had visited the place a hundred years earlier and noted in his diary on 18 August, 1688, that the gardens were 'nothing extraordinary except the iron gate opening into the park which indeede was very good work.'

The alterations were initiated at once, but the Earl was not to see the results for he set out for a tour abroad shortly afterwards, and died at Naples in 1763. Brown noted that the 'work ordered by the late Earl . . . which was done during his absence from England' included 'pulling down the old ice house and Building a new one in a very Expensive manner and place', making a sunk fence and wall between the Red Deer paddock and kitchen garden, and preparing new ground. He had also prepared 'a great General Plan for Castle Ashby' costing £50 which brought the total sum to £1,816 10s 7d in 1763.

A younger brother, Spencer, succeeded as 8th Earl, and for him Brown continued the carrying out of his 'General Plan'. The north, east and west avenues were removed, but that on the south, leading to Yardley Chase, was retained. At the foot of the hill on which the house stands, he converted a string of small pools into the Park Pond and the Menagerie Pond, replacing the old boundary wall of the gardens with a sunk fence so that there appeared to be an uninterrupted sweep of lawn down to the water's edge. Extensive plantations were set around both ponds, and against the trees which framed the Menagerie Pond he set the Temple which was to present to the water a

stone-faced classical facade while screening a menagerie at the rear. The domed central space of this little building curves forward to provide shelter under a roof supported on Ionic columns. On either side are bays with semi-circular headed windows. Another garden building to Brown's design was the dairy which gave its name to the Dairy Walk, and in connection with the construction of which John Hobcroft, the carpenter, was paid for two visits. Here again an ashlar facade screened the functional purposes of the rooms behind, the centrepiece being an archway under a pediment, the opening being crossed by a pair of doric columns supporting an architrave.

Near the south end of the Menagerie Pond the water was crossed by a small bridge with a delicate ironwork balustrade, the original drawing for which exists[18] although the structure itself was replaced *circa* 1865 by the 'Terracotta Bridge'. In his planting Brown made use of a good deal of the existing timber, particularly the old oaks, filling in with beech and chestnut for the new groves and rides, with occasional cedars to give contrasting shape and colour. One of the latter, now of immense size and standing near the Temple, is said to be that over which the 8th Earl's son Charles, born in 1760, was forbidden to jump when he was a child.[19]

The foreman in charge of the Castle Ashby work was John Midgely, one of whose letters (undated) to Brown survives. It refers to alterations on the east side of the park where, as he explained:

> *I have taken down both the Elms as I cou'd not bring the Ground very well together with-out; and I have shorten'd the Spinny and taken down some of the Lims and trim'd some up so as to let your Eye thro' without making a Avenue which when the wall is taken away will make a fine Opening. I do intend not to take one of the walls down only Fence high till I see his Lordship or you as you did not fix where the sunk-fence was to go.*
>
> *You'l let me have Twenty Pounds against next Satterday night to Pay the Men.*[20]

A number of letters between Lord Northampton and Brown are also preserved among the Castle Ashby papers. One from the latter, dated 8 December, 1764, and written from Testwood in Hampshire while 'on my western expedition', proposed a visit in the course of his next trip to Northamptonshire, and took the opportunity of asking where he might be able to obtain more of the cough lozenges which Lady Northampton had given him when he was last there. Two years later Brown was writing from Trentham, on 30 July, 1766, ostensibly about the work at Castle Ashby, but ending with a reference to something else which was on his mind at this time, namely the possibility of acquiring a small estate of his own. With his royal appointment in 1764 had come the use of an official residence at Hampton Court, but although he became much attached

to this, it was Crown property which he would have to relinquish in the event of retirement. It appears that Lord Northampton, faced with increasing financial worries, was then contemplating the sale of one of his properties, the Manor of Fenstanton (Plate 18A) in Huntingdonshire,[21] and that he had already offered it to a Mr. Drummond.[22] A rumour of this had reached Brown's ears, for he raised the matter in this letter and asked for a first refusal should negotiations with Mr. Drummond fall through. The latter did not, in fact, proceed in the matter, but at this point the Earl wavered in his decision to part with Fenstanton, and would give Brown no definite answer. On the following 25 May Brown wrote again, reminding him that he was still interested in purchasing the property. However reluctant the Earl may have been to part with the Manor, the Northampton election of 1767 was to involve him in further financial difficulty so that there was little alternative but to use it in settlement of the debts incurred by work at Castle Ashby. Early in June, Brown heard that he could inspect the estate and make his offer. 'As soon as I possibly can see it, I will,' he wrote off to the Earl on the 8th, 'and your Lordship may depend on an immediate answer.' He would visit Castle Ashby on his return from a planned journey to Blenheim and houses in Worcestershire and Staffordshire. 'I shall be very unhappy if your Lordship should be from home as there are many things that should be settled . . . My man is going on with the map of Compton etc. but there is a monsterous quantity of it and of course cannot be done in a little time.'[23]

By 7 September, 1767, Brown was writing that 'my intention is to have the Estate at the price your Lordship had agreed with Mr. Drummond which was I think thirteen thousand pounds. It will not be very convenient for me to pay the whole of the money before Lady Day next. I could at Christmas pay six or seven thousand pounds. Your Lordship will be so good as to signify your pleasure in regard to the times of payment.' The deed of transfer was duly drawn up, and on his copy the Earl added in his own hand, 'I take the Manor of Fen Standon to belong to Lawrence [sic] Brown Taste, Esq., who gave Lord Northampton Taste in exchange for it.'

So Brown became the Lord of the Manor of Fenstanton, with paramount authority over Elsworth. The deed also conveyed to him certain tolls from navigation on the Ouse,[24] including the Manor Farm and its mid-eighteenth century brick house with stone dressings and a slate roof. The unusually high quality of its detailing, inside and out, suggests that it had been intended for private occupation, but although Brown paid insurance premiums on it, there seems to be no record of any of his family residing there, and it probably continued to be let to tenant-farmers.[25] The Manor House itself was a small, old-fashioned, gabled building standing virtually at the road-side, and it was presumably here that Brown stayed on his comparatively rare visits to his estate.[26]

Fig. 4. Chatsworth

1 D. Stroud, *Henry Holland*, 1966.
2 *Eton College Registers*, 1761–65.
3 One of the celebrated Gunning sisters, noted for their beauty. Another was the first wife of Brown's client, the Earl of Coventry.
4 British Museum, Add. MSS 9063 f. 304.
5 The 3rd Duke's statue, on a lofty column, was raised at this point in 1832.
6 R. and J. Dodsley, *London and its Environs*, Vol. VI, 1761.
7 P. Toynbee, *Letters of Horace Walpole*.
8 John Fleming, 'Adam Gothic', in the *Connoisseur*, October, 1958, p. 75.
9 At Alnwick.
10 Accounts at Alnwick Castle.
11 A. M. W. Pickering, *Annals of a Yorkshire House*, 1911, Vol. 1, p. 281.
12 'Visits to Country Seats', *Walpole Society*, Vol. XVI, p. 28.
13 *Walpole Society, op. cit.*
14 Harewood Archives, Bundle 2, Archives Department, Leeds Public Library. The fire walls were those with fireplaces and flues to warm them as a protection for fruit trees against frost. I am indebted to Miss Mary Mauchline, author of *Harewood House*, 1974, for drawing my attention to this letter.
15 John Swarbrick, *Robert Adam and His Brothers*, 1915, p. 210.
16 Harewood Archives, Bundle 4.
17 Now in Northants. C.R.O.
18 Castle Ashby Archives, F.D.1349, iii.
19 6th Marquess of Northampton, *The History of the Comptons*.
20 Castle Ashby Archives.
21 The Manor was originally granted by William the Conqueror to Gilbert de Gaunt but was subse-

quently escheated to the Crown. It came into the possession of Lord Northampton's ancestor, Sir John Spencer, in 1600.

22 Probably Mr. Drummond the Banker whose name appears frequently in Brown's accounts.

23 Castle Ashby Archives. The 'map' of Compton Wynyates, another of Lord Northampton's estates, is almost certainly that found by the present Marquess in recent years. It is signed by John Spyers and endorsed 'begun in 1765 and ended in 1771.'

24 *Victoria County History, Huntingdonshire*, Vol. II. In these rights Brown was succeeded by his son, Lancelot, of Stirtloe House, Buckden, who was followed by Admiral John Brown and the Rev. Thomas Brown at whose death in 1815 they passed to the latter's son, the Rev. Robert Brown. On his death they were held in Trust for two daughters, but between 1871 and 1885 the manor was sold in lots and the rights ceased.

25 I am indebted to Mr. Roger Rawcliffe for kindly lending me a copy of the relevant policy which is in his possession.

26 This was certainly the conviction of the late Miss G. M. Peet who resided in the Manor House for many years, and bequeathed to Cambridge University Library the survey which Brown had prepared of his estate (C.U.L. MS Plans 635).

VI

MAINLY EAST ANGLIA

Brown's first commission in Norfolk came in 1762 and took him to Holkham (Map 103), to continue the landscaping of the grounds laid out by William Kent for Thomas Coke, Earl of Leicester, some thirty years earlier. The house and its park lay in the extreme north of the county, an area then remarkable for its absence of trees except where, as Mrs. Delany observed after a visit, they had been planted by Cokes or Walpoles.[1] Kent's designs for the grounds, preserved at Holkham, show that his proposals were limited in extent, and his planting sparse, much of the luxuriant timber which is now a feature of the park evidently being due to Brown's appearance on the scene. The still later contribution by Humphry Repton was mainly concerned with lakeside alterations, but their combined achievements have now merged into a park of great splendour and diversity.

Brown's designs for Kimberley (Map 109) (Plate 21A) and Melton Constable (Map 133) were given in 1763 and 1764, the former being on a considerable scale and continuing over five years, during which nearly £3,000 passed through his hands for work carried out which included the enlarging of the lake to some twenty-eight acres. He also noted that he had given designs for 'alterations near the house', and for a new drying yard and greenhouse. A large plan for the alterations has recently been discovered among papers which had been removed from the house many years ago, and this is now back again. Initialled 'L.B.', it is dated 1763. For Melton Constable he provided Sir Edward Astley with schemes which again took five years to complete, and for which he provided drawings for a temple, aviary and a gothic summerhouse, his total bill coming to just under £2,500. At both places a good deal of the landscaping remains, although at Melton it is in a somewhat forlorn condition, and in the vicinity of the house formal bedding was introduced in the nineteenth century.

A visit to Redgrave (Map 155) (Plates 22 A, B and C), near Diss, in the course of one of his tours in 1763 led to a contract being signed in that year with the owner, Rowland Holt. Although this first agreement was probably for the grounds only, it is clear from Brown's account book that during the next five years the decision was made to remodel

the house, and that he had provided before 1768 designs for encasing the Tudor and Jacobean core within a shell of Suffolk white brick with stone dressings. This sounds as though Brown had successfully brought his powers of persuasion to bear on Mr. Holt as he is known not to have liked red brick in general, and Repton attributes to him the pronouncement that 'a red house puts the whole valley in a fever'.[2] The existing fabric no doubt dictated the somewhat monotonous nine-window facades that were then built, the only relief to which was the tetrastyle Ionic order which was applied to the centre of the south front, and supported a pediment in which were set the family arms. Much care and money was, however, lavished on the building work in which Henry Holland senior participated for bricklaying and masonry, while John Hobcroft was responsible for carpentry and joinery.[3] At the same time the landscaping was in progress, and Brown noted in his account that the making of the lake had involved additional expenditure in 1766, while in the following years alterations were in hand 'on the London side of the water', and the building of a boat house. By the autumn of 1771 William Hervey was able to note that 'at Redgrave Park the water very fine ... the house well situated, nine windows in front and nine in flank, a hall and a good room on each side.'[4] The seven-bay orangery probably went up at about the same time, but the various changes were not completed until September 1773, by which time Brown had received £10,000 of which £9,440 was passed on to Holland and Hobcroft. The orangery and a white brick lodge at the south-west entrance to the grounds survive, as does the fine lake, but the house itself was demolished in the 1950s.

Considering the size of his practice, the amounts of money which passed through his hands and the trust which he had to place in the foreman on the site, Brown ran into remarkably little trouble with his clients. On occasion they grew impatient at delays in his visits, but his reputation for integrity was never in doubt, and only rarely was there any serious disagreement over the carrying out of work or the amount of a bill. That two such occurrences should have happened in 1765, and in respect of places fairly close to each other, suggests that the two disgruntled owners may have put their heads together and resolved to dig their toes in when the bills came along. One of these was Sir John Griffin Griffin of Audley End, and the other Ambrose Dickens of Branches, a small estate on the Essex–Suffolk borders.

Sir John had inherited AUDLEY END (Map 11) in 1760, the house by then being the only remaining side of what had been a quandrangular Jacobean mansion. Within a year he had summoned Robert Adam to prepare schemes for re-decorating the principal rooms. Three years later Brown was given a contract for the landscaping of the grounds. His own account book references give the bare facts – a contract of £650 begun on 22 April, 1763, for which payments of £200 were to be made in June and September, with £250 on finishing the work. The owner's side of the story is made clear from relevant

bills and correspondence in the Braybrooke archives,[5] Sir John becoming dissatisfied not only on account of the delay, but because, in carrying out the plan, a wrong turn had been made in widening the river Cam to form a lake before the house. He claimed that the work should have been finished in 1764, although Brown noted in his book that on completion of the first contract, a second one was agreed. Sir John had paid a further £200 in May, 1766, but to his annoyance Brown pointed out that a sum was still outstanding in 1767. This, the latter maintained in a letter from Hampton Court on 9 October, had been due for a year, and that it should therefore carry interest. Sir John's tart reply that his opinion on the matter remained unchanged drew another from Brown, who considered himself 'not honourably treated', but said that he would not 'labour more to convince Sir John as he knows there is none so blind as him that will not see.' On that sour note the correspondence closed.

Seven years after Brown had withdrawn, one Joseph Hicks was employed by Sir John to carry out further work in the grounds at Audley End, including the 'correcting' of the river's course to the owner's original intention. The conception of the overall landscape, and much of its execution, is however basically due to Brown, and the calm scene in which the house stands to-day gives no hint of the recriminations which attended its creation.

The contract which had been made with Ambrose Dickens for work at BRANCHES (Map 27) proceeded over the two years from July, 1763 to September, 1765, by which time Brown had received £1,500. The alleged cause of trouble here was the sum of £58 1s 8d for 'Extra Work' carried out by the man in charge, Alexander Knox, during November and December, 1764, apparently at Mr. Dickens's orders, and added to Brown's bill. The matter was raised in a personal confrontation during Brown's final visit, when Mr. Dickens refused to pay, and the former subsequently noted in his account book, 'Mr. Brown could not get the money for the Extra Work and tore the account before Mr. Dickens face and said his say upon that Business to him.'

It was probably as a continuation of one of his northern journeys to see the progress of work at Chatsworth or Harewood that Brown travelled on to LOWTHER HALL (Map 128) (Plate 24), near Penrith, where Sir James Lowther[6] required advice on his gardens early in 1763. The house at this time was a Palladian essay of considerable size for which plans and elevations were included by Colin Campbell in *Vitruvius Britannicus*.[7] These show that on the north the main block was flanked by single storey wings coming forward on either side of a forecourt, while the south front overlooked a small formal layout, its parterre divided into four rectangular beds. This arrangement is confirmed by a survey made by F. Richardson in 1754 which also shows that the approach to the entrance front on the north had been by a long avenue on the axis of the forecourt. The surroundings of the south parterre are shown, and include a short canal to

the south-east, and orchards on the south-west, both encompassed by thick coppices.

Brown's plan, dated 1763,[8] proposed a wide expanse of lawn to the north, and the replacement of the avenue by a curving drive. On the south the parterre was to give way to another lawn, the canal being re-cast as a long pool of irregular outline in a glade, while the orchards to the west were replaced by shrubberies. In contrast to most of his schemes for places near a river, no opportunity was taken here to bring the river Lowther into view of the house except for one oblique and distant glimpse to the north-west.

Brown's account book refers to a second, undated, visit made to Lowther 'since 1763'. This was probably in 1771, which is the date of a further plan which he made to cover an area some way to the south of what had by then been accomplished. Altogether his charges for his journeys and the plans amounted to £200, which he noted as having been received from Sir James on 7 November, 1780. It is evident from comparison of his plans with one made by a later landscaper, John Webb, in 1807, that much of what he had proposed was not only still in existence, but was retained as a background for the 'Castle' designed by Robert Smirke in 1806 and subsequently built. Webb's proposals, superimposed on Brown's layout, consisted of a fussy infilling with thickets of trees on the south lawn, which would totally have destroyed any vistas, and an extraordinary network of rectangular and meaningless paths cut through the shrubbery on the west.

The landscaping of TEMPLE NEWSAM (Map 185) (Plate 23), on the outskirts of Leeds, was begun by Brown early in the 1760s, and continued for the rest of the decade. Although the house is maintained in excellent order as one of the Leeds City Museums, the further parts of the grounds are now in a sad state of neglect, largely as a result of their requisition during the last war for open-cast mining. Subsequent replacement of the top soil has been a totally inadequate compensation for the loss of scenes which had matured during two centuries.

In its heyday Temple Newsam was considered to be one of the great English land-scapes, having been evolved from what was originally a small seventeenth-century garden surrounded by a sporting estate. In 1710, ornamental pools, a bridge, and several plantations were introduced under the supervision of William Etty of York, who also worked for Vanbrugh at Castle Howard. Temple Newsam at this time belonged to Richard 5th Viscount Irwin, and an even stronger link with Castle Howard was provided by his marriage to the Earl of Carlisle's daughter Anne. Several of the features introduced by Etty were to be retained when Brown's plan materialised.

The first approach to Brown was made by Charles Ingram, later 9th Viscount Irwin, in the autumn of 1758, Temple Newsam having by then been given to him by his uncle, the 7th Viscount, who had retired to his Sussex estate at Hills, near Horsham.

Brown replied that although he would take the first opportunity of waiting on Mr. Ingram in Whitehall to discuss the project, he would not be able to make a Yorkshire journey before the following summer.[9] The date of his first visit is in fact unknown, but it may not have been until 1761, and it was certainly 1762 before he prepared the plan which is inscribed as for 'the Intended Alterations at Temple Newsham, Yorkshire, the Seat of Charles Ingram Esqr.' Even then he did not send it off, and Mr. Ingram had succeeded yet another uncle in the Irwin title by the time he penned a letter to Brown on 30 January, 1763, with a hint of impatience:

> *I am glad to find by your letter that the plans are ready and I must beg the favor of you to send them to the Temple as soon as possible and the most expeditious way will be by the Leeds Machine which sets out from the Swan and Two Necks, Lad-Lane. I am greatly surprised at your mentioning Frost. We are all here as Warm as a Toast . . .*[10]

The plans – in the plural, which indicates that there must have been more than the one which survives – duly arrived to reveal Brown's schemes for sloping the grounds away from the house with tree-planted lawns towards two large lakes. There was to be the usual sunk fence, and an extensive screen of beech woods to the north and west. The references on the surviving plan include sham bridges, a rotunda, a menagerie, a cottage and a dairy. All, including a grotto not mentioned but built, have since disappeared.[11] Brown not only retained traces of Etty's layout to the north-east of the house, but also an extensive coppice to the south in which eight alleys converged at a rond-point. The two large lakes proposed were not, however, made, and for water the so-called Menagerie Pond to the east, and the slender course of the river Aire to the south had to suffice.

Brown's account book notes the sums received for the work beginning with £200 in September, 1765, and continuing until 1770, but probably the first entries were in an earlier and now missing book. The total payments from 1765–70 amounted to £2,800, but at some time around the latter date the Temple Newsam archives show that he had given Lord Irwin further designs, including one for the Sphinx Gates which were to terminate a new drive. In this Brown obviously took as his model the gates for Chiswick House, Lord Burlington's drawing for which had been published by Isaac Ware in his *Designs of Inigo Jones and Others* (1735). Brown, however, set the ironwork on a curve between the rusticated stone piers which are topped by sphinxes. The ironwork was made by Robert Johnson 'according to Mr. Brown's design' for £47 5s 0d.[12] The gates are now in a state of neglect, this drive having fallen into disuse early in the present century when, with the advent of the motor-car, a new approach to the house was made.

It appears that there was a proposal at one stage during the landscaping that Brown should alter the south wing of the house, but although an outline plan, initialled and dated 1767, has survived, it was not adopted.

The year 1767 was also to see the appearance of a long and anonymous poem entitled *The Rise and Progress of the Present Taste in Planting Parks, Pleasure Grounds, Gardens, etc. from Henry the Eighth to King George III*, dedicated to Charles 9th Viscount Irwin. Although the work at Temple Newsam was by this time well advanced, it is nevertheless puzzling that Lord Irwin, who was not an outstanding public figure, should have been the object of this tribute. The poem itself is not without merit, but its particular interest in the present context lies in its references both to the changes at Temple Newsam and to three of Brown's other recent works. Of the former it says:

> *. . . you, my Lord, at Temple Newsham find,*
> *The charms of Nature gracefully combin'd,*
> *Sweet waving hills, with wood and verdure crown'd,*
> *And winding vales, where murmuring streams resound:*
> *Slopes fring'd with Oaks which gradual die away,*
> *And all around romantic scenes display.*
> *Delighted still along the Park we rove,*
> *Vary'd with Hill and Dale, with Wood and Grove:*
> *O'er velvet Lawns what noble prospect rise,*
> *Fair as the scenes, that Ruben's hand supplies.*
> *But when the Lake shall these sweet Groves adorn*
> *And light expanding like the eye of Morn*
> *Reflect whate'er above its surface rise,*
> *The Hills, the Rocks, the Woods, and varying Skies.*
> *Then will the wild and beautiful combine*
> *And Taste and Beauty grace your whole Design.*

The line 'When the Lake shall these sweet Groves adorn' implies that the writer had heard of the proposal for a great expanse of water which in fact did not materialise. Of Brown's work in general he was equally effusive, likening him to a painter of living scenes, comparable to the great masters:

> *At Blenheim, Croome and Caversham we trace*
> *Salvator's wildness, Claude's enlivening grace,*
> *Cascades and Lakes as fine as Risdale drew*
> *While Nature's vary'd in each charming view.*
> *To paint his works wou'd Poussin's Powers require,*
> *Milton's sublimity and Dryden's fire.*

Born to Grace Nature, and her works complete
With all that's beautiful, sublime and great!
For him each Muse enwreathes the Laurel Crown,
And consecrates to Fame immortal Brown.

Temple Newsam was not to be Brown's only work for Lord Irwin who, on the death of his uncle, had also inherited HILLS (Map 100), a fine Jacobean house with extensive grounds in Sussex. No drawings have come to light, and it is not mentioned in Brown's account book, but in October, 1769, he combined a visit there with one to Ashburnham (Plates 40 B and 41 A, B), and subsequently wrote to tell Lord Irwin that he had given the necessary directions for some work to be carried out at once, and with all possible care. At the same time he added, 'If anything is wanted at the Temple, my man that is at Lord Scarborough's shall come over about the gravel or any other thing that your Lordship may want to have done.'[13] The work was still in hand two years later, when Brown wrote from Hampton Court on 5 March, 1771, proposing another visit: 'As to Hills, the weather has been very unfavourable for outdoors work ... I propose going there tomorrow and intend setting out the gravel walk from the Dairy Place to the river and to make the necessary plantations.' All trace of this was, however, to vanish when the house was demolished *circa* 1820, and the estate divided up.[14]

The gentlemen of Dorset, perhaps because they were mainly housed in snug little manor houses, were less responsive to the wave of mid-eighteenth century improvement than their neighbours in Wiltshire and Hampshire, and the county yielded Brown only two landscape commissions, Milton Abbey in 1763, and a later one for Sherborne Castle in 1775.

MILTON (Map 134) (Plates 55A and B) was soon to be rebuilt by Sir William Chambers, but when Brown made his first visit, probably in early May[15] the house still formed part of the Abbey buildings which had been reduced, enlarged, or patched up at various times during the preceding centuries. A few yards away was the Abbey Church, in the shadow of which Market Street and High Street, with an inn, school house and a few cottages formed the remains of what had once been a flourishing medieval township. The Milton estate had been acquired by Joseph Damer, who had married a daughter of the Duke of Dorset and been created 1st Baron Milton in 1753. Brown's account with him opened with the receipt of £200 in August, 1763, for work in hand, although the contract was not signed until November, 1764. Payments continued regularly until October, 1770, by which time Brown had received £2,052 8s od. The first area of operations was no doubt to the north and east of the house, where the ground slopes to a valley in which it was hoped to create an extensive lake. It would have been for the lawns on these slopes that Brown recorded the purchase from Mr. Freeman

of Fawley Court of 1,120 lb. of Dutch clover seed. Across the valley and on the rising ground to the east of the house Brown made extensive plantations which, now grown into thick masses, clothe the hillsides.

From 1770 there was a lull so far as Brown was concerned while Lord Milton pondered about the future of the old house, deciding in the end to demolish it and rebuild to a design by Chambers which, in spite of its crenellated parapets, quatrefoils and dripstones, refused to look gothic.[16] The new walls were going up by the time Brown reappeared, no doubt taking care that his two visits in 1773 did not coincide with those of Chambers, whose *Dissertation*, with its unflattering innuendos about Capability, had been published in the previous year. By now, however, Chambers's relations with his client were beginning to wear thin, and on the 29th of the following March he was writing to Lord Milton,

> *Whether we part or not, the laying the new foundations must necessarily be done by me, else I should leave you in a labyrinth which probably neither your Lordship, nor your Lordship's new architect, would know how to get out of in building as in economy . . . I have now completed three-fourths of your great work, and tho' you have used me hardly I will certainly go through with the rest; at least as far as relates to the carcass . . . You would be very much Distressed were I to obey the dictates of my own resentment and leave you now.*

The carcase would, Chambers added, be finished by the following Christmas when 'any other man may do the remainder without difficulty.'[17] A few days earlier, he had indiscreetly written to the Earl of Pembroke, 'Unfortunately for me, I have three or four years past been building a cursed Gothick House for this unmannerly imperious Lord, who has treated me as he does everybody, ill . . .'[18] and the Earl, who had already made some trouble by talking to Lord Milton of his architect's derelictions, may have passed the contents of the letter on to the same quarter. If not for that, then for some other reason, Lord Milton ceased to consult Chambers, and James Wyatt was called in for the later stages of work on the house.

Meanwhile steps had been taken towards the building of a new village, and in April, 1773, Chambers sent Lord Milton 'a plan and elevation of a part of the intended village'. These appear to have been set aside, and in November, 1774 Brown noted that he had been at Milton again, and had given plans for the village for which he was paid £105. It seems certain, therefore, that he was the architect of this layout in which rows of semi-detached cottages with thatched roofs and trim gardens were built on either side of the road climbing a steep hill. Moving the inhabitants, however, was not accomplished without opposition, and some of those in an outlying area of the valley, where Lord Milton proposed to have his new lake, refused to go. All other inducements having

failed, he thereupon ordered the dammed-up waters of a stream to be released, which effectively put an end to the argument. To the disgruntled and dislodged cottagers it no doubt seemed like retribution from their autocratic landlord that the combined efforts of Lord Milton and his adviser were to prove unsuccessful in creating the desired expanse of water in the valley although, as a later writer observed,[19] vast sums of money had been spent on the project.

Elsewhere on the estate, all went well, and in December, 1781, Brown noted that Lord Milton paid him another £210 to cover various items up to that date, but he must have given more designs, or carried out further work in 1782, for his final entry is for the receipt of a further one hundred guineas in December of that year, only two months before his death closed the account.

1 Lady Llanover, *The Autobiography and Correspondence of Mary Delany*, 1862.
2 H. Repton, *Theory and Practice of Landscape Gardening*, 1803.
3 There are references to this work in a MS Price Book, Soane Museum, Architectural Library, Soane Case.
4 25 October, 1771. *Journals of Hon. William Hervey, 1755–1814.*
5 A detailed account of this work and the subsequent correspondence is given in J. D. William, *Audley End, The Restoration of 1762–1797*, Essex C.R.O. Publication 45, 1966.
6 In 1774 Sir James, by then a powerful but notorious figure in north country politics, was to treat young Lance Brown in shabby fashion over the Cockermouth contests. (See page 174.)
7 Vol. II, 1717, Plates 78–80. A plan of the gardens is in Vol. III, 1725, Plate 76.
8 Cumberland and Westmorland C.R.O., D/Lons./L Plans of Lowther Park.
9 25 November, 1758, Leeds Archives Department, T.N.Corr. 23a/27.
10 Pakenham Correspondence.
11 For a detailed account see Christopher Gilbert, 'The Park and Gardens at Temple Newsam', *Leeds Arts Calendar*, No. 53, 1963.
12 Leeds Archives Department, T.N. Estate Accounts, 12/10.
13 6 October, 1769, Leeds Archives Department, T.N. Corr.
14 The house is illustrated in T. W. Horsfield, *Topography of . . . Sussex*, Vol. 2, 1835, p. 264.
15 A letter of 24 May, 1763, to Mr. Methuen at Corsham acknowledges one to him received by Brown 'at Lord Milton's'.
16 John Harris, *Sir William Chambers*, 1969.
17 British Museum, Add. MSS 41, 136 f. 14.
18 Mavis Batey, 'Nuneham Courtenay', *Oxoniensia*, Vol. XXXIII, 1968.
19 *The Beauties of . . . Wiltshire*, 1809.

VII

THE ROYAL APPOINTMENT:
RICHMOND AND HAMPTON COURT

I N 1758, when he was forty-seven, there had been a move by Brown's friends to obtain for him an official post in the Royal Gardens. The nature of these posts had changed since the time when Charles Bridgeman had been appointed gardener to George II, a position which entailed responsibility for all the Royal gardens. After his death in 1738, the grounds at Windsor, Hampton Court (with Richmond) and Kensington (with St. James's) were each allotted to a different man. The petition putting forward Brown's name for a post at Kensington was dated March, 1758, and was submitted by several influential men who, 'being well-wishers of Mr. Browne, whose Abilities and Merit we are fully acquainted with, do most earnestly request the Duke of Newcastle to promote his speedy appointment to the care of Kensington Garden agreeable to his Grace's very obliging promises in that respect, the delay having already occasion'd great loss to Mr. Browne in his Business and great inconvenience to many Persons for whom he is Employ'd.' There followed the signatures of two dukes, eleven other peers, and one commoner:[1]

Anson	(Moor Park)
Temple	(Wotton and Stowe)
Ashburnham	(Ashburnham)
Egremont	(Petworth)
Holdernesse	(Syon Hill)
Midleton	(Peper Harow)
Stamford	(Enville)
Ancaster	(Grimsthorpe)
Exeter	(Burghley)
Coventry	(Croome)

Brooke	(Warwick Castle)
George Grenville	(Wotton)
Hertford	(Ragley)
Northumberland	(Syon and Alnwick)

The original source of this petition, of which a copy was given to the author in 1939, has not been traced. It does not appear among the four volumes of petitions to the Duke of Newcastle which are in the Manuscript Room of the British Museum.

This imposing list might have been expected to spur the Patronage Secretary into action, but the Duke of Newcastle was notoriously dilatory in such business and the petition for Brown was buried alongside dozens of others. When, three years later, the Duke was jogged into considering the matter of the Kensington vacancy, he gave it to a Dr. John Hill, much to the annoyance of Horace Walpole, who considered him to have 'little claim to favour'.[2]

A further move by Brown's supporters in 1764 was successful, and the *Gentleman's Magazine* announced in its July issue that Brown had been made 'Surveyor to His Majesty's Gardens and Waters at Hampton Court.' This was not entirely correct, for the Surveyorship was a sinecure held by the Hon. Charles Sloane Cadogan. Brown's post was that of Master Gardener, in which he succeeded James Greening.[3] In the same year, he was also appointed Gardener at St. James's, although this post seems to have taken second place, and made little demand on his time.[4] It does not come within his surviving account book as does Hampton Court. It does, however, explain the existence of a plan by Brown for a small portion of the garden at Buckingham House (now Palace) and his plan for St. James's Park (see Plate 54A and List of Works, page 232, under 'London').

Although his remuneration for Hampton Court and Richmond is set out in the warrant as £1,107 6s, plus £100 for 'raising pineapples', and £100 for 'parcel fruits', his own account book shows that from 1765 he received a salary of £2,000 a year. It came in quarterly payments of £500, handed to him by Sir William Bretton, George Mathias, or some other member of the King's household.[5] Out of this sum he had to pay the under-gardeners, and to meet the cost of replacing trees, plants and gravel. It would, however, have left a fair margin of profit, and the post brought the additional advantage of a residence at Hampton Court. This was Wilderness House (Plate 26B), a comfortable red brick building dating from the late seventeenth century. It stands within the Palace grounds a few hundred yards west of Lion Gate, and is little changed. Within, there are four panelled rooms on the ground floor (the large room on the east is a later addition), and a wide flight of shallow stairs leads to the upper rooms, Brown

lost no time in moving his family into their new home to which he became much attached, and even after he had purchased his own property at Fenstanton, he was never away from Wilderness House for longer than he could help.

When Brown took up his post he found installed as joint Clerks of the Works at Kew and Richmond Palaces Joshua Kirby, and the latter's son William, both of whom lived at Kew. Others who were currently holding official posts in his territory were James Paine, as Clerk of the Works at Richmond New Park Lodge, who had succeeded William Kent's assistant, Stephen Wright, in 1758; and William Rice, an obscure character who held office as Clerk of the Works at Hampton Court from 1758 until 1789. The two latter posts, however, were largely sinecures, and probably Brown saw little of either Paine or Rice in the royal gardens.

At HAMPTON COURT (Map 88) he made few perceptible changes although it is said that George III suggested that he should 'improve' the formal layout. Brown, however, 'had the good sense and honesty to decline "out of respect to himself and his profession" '[6] and confined his additions to replacing with grass and gravel slopes some terrace steps in the Privy Garden,[7] and planting the Great Vine. This remarkable specimen, said to have been grown from a cutting taken from a Black Hamburg vine at Valentines in Essex, still bears a considerable crop of grapes each year.[8] In the routine work Brown was assisted by young George Lowe, a nephew of his predecessor in office. The family had long been connected with Hampton Court, and young George, describing himself as 'used to fruit work', had petitioned unsuccessfully to be given the place of his uncle who had 'bred him up and was a father to him.'[9] For his failure in the petition he seems to have borne no grudge, and Brown obviously relied on him to carry on during his frequent absence.

The RICHMOND (Map 156) (Plate 26A) gardens were to take up far more of Brown's time and Joshua Kirby, in a report on 11 October, 1765, noted that 'great alteration and improvements are making . . . by Mr. Launcelot Browne'.[10] His activity was in what was then the Old Park, now the western portion of Kew Gardens. This long stretch of ground extended south from near to Kew Green, between the river and the parallel garden then belonging to the Dowager Princess of Wales, for whom William Chambers had been designing garden adornments since 1757. In view of Chambers's growing hostility to Brown, it was somewhat ironic that the pathway by which the two royal gardens were separated was called Love Lane.

Brown lost no time in preparing his plan for landscaping the King's gardens, an undertaking which involved not only the destruction of Bridgeman's layout, with its terraced walks and wildernesses, but that celebrated gothic extravaganza created by William Kent for Queen Caroline's amusement, 'Merlin's Cave'. The disappearance of this feature (the lead from its roof was sold to Devall for £31 14s 9¼d in 1765) was to

provide one of the derisory darts which William Mason later hurled at Sir William Chambers:

> *To Richmond come, for see, untutor'd Brown*
> *Destroys those wonders which were once thy own.*
> *Lo, from his melon-ground the peasant slave*
> *Has rudely rush'd, and levell'd Merlin's Cave* . . .[11]

Of Brown's one surviving plan there are three versions, one large and unsigned drawing having recently been identified in the Royal Botanical Library at Kew. A smaller drawing is in the Royal Library at Windsor Castle, the latter being endorsed L.B., although it lacks the boats on the Thames shown in the larger plan. The third version is in the Public Record Office.[12] In this scheme, the outlines of what was to become the Rhododendron Walk can be traced, and certain other features, but a good deal was changed in execution, and for a record of what was actually carried out the best evidence is to be found in the splendid Survey of the Royal Gardens of Richmond and Kew made by Thomas Richardson in 1771 *'Under the Direction of Peter Burrell Esqr. His Majesty's Surveyor General'*.[13] Here again there are three versions, the largest being in the Public Library at Richmond, while a smaller version is in the Royal Library at Windsor Castle. Even smaller is the third, mounted on a roller and preserved in a tooled leather case among the King's Maps in the British Museum.

For George III, his palace at Kew was a favourite retreat, and he followed each stage of the alterations in the grounds with interest, expecting Brown to be frequently at hand to discuss details. The latter must therefore have spent many hours driving or cantering to and from Hampton when the royal family were in residence at Richmond or drove down for the day. Sometimes there was little notice, and, on one occasion a hasty note, written by Brown's foreman informed him of the unexpected appearance of the King and Queen:

> *Their Majesty's came into the works on Saturday after you was gone. I told the King you stayed till two o'clock and that I had said to you that their Majestys seldom ever came after that time. He said He had been detained But should see you next Saturday. The King did not bid me inform you so. But I do it in case you should be engadged [so that] you can possibly put if of for that Day as I think he rather wishes to see you. He was much pleased with the Levels and asked if you ws. not so too. I told him you found no faults.*[14]

This Richmond priority may have led to some slackening of attention in the maintenance at Hampton Court for which the King had less regard, and in 1770 Brown was not a little annoyed to receive a letter from the Clerk Itinerant to the Board of Works,

William Robinson,[15] taking him to task for some apparent neglect. They were not, Robinson pointed out, 'in so good a condition as they ought to be ... none of the Walkes being fit for use, and most of the other parts of the Gardens much neglected.'

Brown, whose easy relations with the King at Richmond had rendered him unprepared for high-handed admonishments of this kind from petty officials, lost no time in replying with acerbity:

> *Sir,*
>
> *I recd. your Letter. I must acknowledge that I have lived long enough not to wonder at anything, therefore it did not surprize me, I believe I am the first King's Gardiner that the Board of Works ever interfered with, & they have taken times that seem odd. The first was when I recd. a very extraordinary Letter from a Gentleman of the Board of Works under the Colour of Friendship, at a time when I found it necessary to discharge three men. I seldom use Epithets otherwise I would translate that Letter as it deserves, because I know both the Author's meaning, & his Conduct on that Subject. I believe if any Body had a right to have censured my Conduct it was the Surveyor of the Gardens, which would have been very agreable to me, because I know the Gardens are in exceeding good order, & I can assure you that I lay out an hundred Pounds a Year more than my Predecessor did, my wish & my intention is to keep them better & to put them in better order than ever I saw them in, & have stopped at no Expence in procuring Trees & Plants, nor grudged any number of Hands that were necessary. I this Day went through the Gardens, & my Foreman told me they had more hands than they knew how to employ. But you Sir have only done your duty. You will be so good as to inform the Gentlemen of the Board of Works that Pique I pity, that Ideal Power I laugh at, that the Insolence of Office I despise, & that real Power I will ever disarm by doing my Duty.*

To this he added a postscript: 'The Gravel at H: Court is totaly worn out; I have been obliged in the course of this Year to break it up three times, otherwise it would have been as Green as Grass.'[16]

This exchange no doubt made him careful not to run the risk of further complaint, but when it was his turn to complain of repeated flooding in the kitchen of Wilderness House, Brown wasted no time in dealing with the Clerk Itinerant but went straight to John Robinson of the Treasury, who at once took the matter up with 'the Lords', and obtained their authority for a new kitchen to be built without delay.[17]

While George Lowe could be left in charge at Hampton Court, Brown found at the outset of his appointment that he would need reliable assistance not only at Richmond, but also in his private practice, for which two men were taken on in 1765. One was Samuel Lapidge who lived at Hampton and later married a daughter of the elder George

Lowe;[18] the other was John Spyers, who also lived at Hampton. Their work consisted mainly of preparing the initial surveys at the places on which Brown was consulted, Lapidge being mentioned as at Wrotham for this purpose in 1765, and Spyers being sent to Compton Wynyates in the same year. Both were to remain with Brown until his death.

Before he had engaged these draughtsmen, Brown had found a young Scottish gardener called Michael Milliken to work at Richmond. The latter had previously been employed at Chatsworth where Brown had first seen him, and learnt that Milliken wished to move south. After some preliminary soundings, he was able to write on 2 January, 1765:

> *I intend employing you in his Majesty's work at Richmond. I have spoken to the Lords of my intention and they aprove as it will be doing you a service: I would therefor have you aprize Mr. Barker of my intention with my compliments to him and I would have you give every enformation you can to Mr. Trevis and [tell] him about the finishing of the work that is to be done this season viz the finishing near the porters Lodge and Stables etc. etc. – I presume there can be but little carting done this winter time, but in everything consider the good of the work and the most prudent way of putting it in execution. Bring with you an exact acct. of the money you have recd. of Mr. Barker from the beginning to the time you leave the work. I again repeat, do all the good you can whilst you remain at Chatsworth, because for the sake of the great good man that is you and on all other accts. I wish it as well my own self. My best compliments to the Family. If you are up in a fortnight from this time it will do very well, but if it will be of any use to the work stay longer. Let me hear from you and believe me your Friend.*

Milliken, who had married only a few weeks earlier, lost no time in carrying out his instructions, and by the end of the month he was temporarily installed in the Coach and Horses inn, which still stands on the south-east side of Kew Green. The foregoing and several letters which passed between him and his wife Polly before she could join him are in the possession of a descendant, and passages from them throw an interesting light on his first weeks at Kew from where, on 27 January, he was able to write:

> *I am now settled as Foreman in his Majestys works at Richmond where the worke will last for many years if I have the Good Forton to give satisfaction as I have done hitherto. It will be much to my advantage. The way that Mr. Brown expressed himself to me was Friendly, let the event be what it will ... 'Milliken I sent for you here as I saide before to do you a service. This will be a great and lasting worke and where you will be known to his Majesty and other Great Men.' He have advanced my wages more than I expected But that must be intirley a secret between you and*

me as he never give so much to any man before. Nor am I to charge it in my accts. but receive it from his own hand that his Clark may not know of it as it would raise a murmoring amongst his other men. But my Dear Creature dont think I am puffed up with what apears for as I often told you before we was one that one Hours Displeasur may disapoint me of all I have agread. Many men at work and am much confined. The King and Quen come 2 or 3 days a week here and [he] talkes as free and I think is as Bent on the work as ever the Duke of Devonshire was. The Princ of Walls was all over the Garden esterday in a chise drawn by a mare and the other princ in the nurses armes for two hours notwithstanding the cooldness of the day indeed they are fine Lusty Boys and do not fear the coold.

What I am doing here is to begg my dear and loving wife that you will be with me asoon as possible you can. I have taken a house which I hope you will like very well. There is a good parlour below and kitchin fire places in both, a copper in the kitchin, places for coals and other conveniences, two chambers above, a fire place in one of them. Its a pleasan plac on Kew Green where houses are dearer than in the Citty there being few but Gentlemens houses in the place. I give 7 pounds a year for it . . . The man I take the house of favors me as I pay my men at his house [i.e. public house] which bring a dale of costom. . . . I can give you no other instruction of coming than . . . to send your things by the waggon and come yourself in the muskain [? machine]. I will meet you at the Inn. I beg my dr. Soull you will leet me hear from you asoon as you receive this. I intend going to London today to see about my chest but must go to Hampton Court this afternoon to Mr. Brown.

Polly's arrival was delayed owing to the sudden death of her father, but early in February there were fresh plans for her journey. Michael added in a postscript to a long letter,

My dear, I would have you see for a girl that you think will suit you and order her up in the waggon. We must have a maid. Good ones are hard to be got here. One cannot trust them. I intended [mentioning it] to you before but forgot. Plas yourself in wages. A pound is not throwed away on a good one and one that is honest.

Only one more letter was to be written before Polly set out: her husband bade her,

Take speciall care of yourself on the road, Want nothing that will do you good . . . You'll think of what I said about the girl. Mr. Brown asked on Monday how you did, when you could come . . . O How I long to embrace all that is dear to me now. I have an old srt. [servant] of Mr. Browns takes good care of my shoes boots &c. makes my fire and go[es] erands.

Polly arrived safely and set up house with her husband. Later they moved to a house of their own on the Green where they were to remain for the rest of their lives. Michael

Milliken was to outlive Brown by seventeen years, dying in 1800 after thirty-five years in the King's service.[19] An entry in his daughter's diary records his passing:

Thursday Jan. 16, 1800. The King called on Horseback a little after eleven oclock when William told him my beloved Father was dieing. He turned from the door and said 'Oh God! I am very sorry for it. He was as Honest a man as ever lived'.

Two hours later Milliken was dead. The King sent a message to say that his widow was to remain in the same house for as long as she pleased, and there she continued to live until her death in 1813. The surviving Milliken papers include a number of accounts passed and signed by the King for the years 1793–5, both in respect of Michael's salary of £150 a year, and of payments to tradesmen. His sword, a silver teapot, and Polly's green silk needlecase are other treasures which have also been handed down in the family.

1 The names of their country seats, although not on the original document, have been added here in brackets.
2 To Rev. Henry Zouch, 3 January, 1761. *Letters of Horace Walpole.*
3 P.R.O. Royal Warrant, Works 6/8, 228, of 16 July, 1764; and Works 4/13, of 1 March, 1765.
4 P.R.O. Works 6/13, 233, 1764.
5 Sir William Breton was knighted after he had represented the Duke of Aquitaine at the Coronation of George III in 1761. He is described as 'of the King's Chamber' in an obituary notice, 1773. George Mathias was one of a large family attached to the court, and mentioned in the diaries of Charlotte and Frances Burney.
6 E. Law, *The History of Hampton Court Palace,* 1885–91.
7 *V.C.H., Middlesex,* Vol. II, p. 385.
8 It is the subject of a detailed description in a contribution to *Notes and Queries,* Vol. XII, p. 404.
9 British Museum, Add. MSS 33055, f. 270.
10 P.R.O. Works, 4/13.
11 *Heroic Epistle to Sir William Chambers,* 1774.
12 P.R.O. Works, 32/96.
13 Peter Burrell, Surveyor of H.M. Crown Lands until his death in 1775, when he was succeeded by his son. Thomas Richardson was later appointed Gardener at Kensington and St. James's. He also prepared a survey of Wimbledon Park (see page 135).
14 Chatham Correspondence, P.R.O.
15 Previously Clerk of Works for Whitehall and Westminster. He is not to be confused with John Robinson of the Treasury, with whom Brown was on friendly terms.
16 P.R.O. Works 1/4, pp. 86–7. Letters dated 29 October and 5 November, 1770.
17 Pakenham Correspondence, 29 January, 1773.
18 Samuel Lapidge and Sarah Lowe were married on 9 July, 1778, at St. George's Church, Hanover Square. Their first son, Edward, was baptised at Hampton Court on 21 June, 1779, Lancelot Brown and Robert Lowe being godfathers. Edward Lapidge became a well-known Victorian architect.
19 William Mason quotes the story that soon after hearing of Brown's death, George III went to Richmond and, on seeing the under gardener, said: 'Brown is dead. Now Mellicant [*sic*] you and I can do here what we please.' Rev. J. Mitford, *Correspondence of H. Walpole and W. Mason,* 1851.

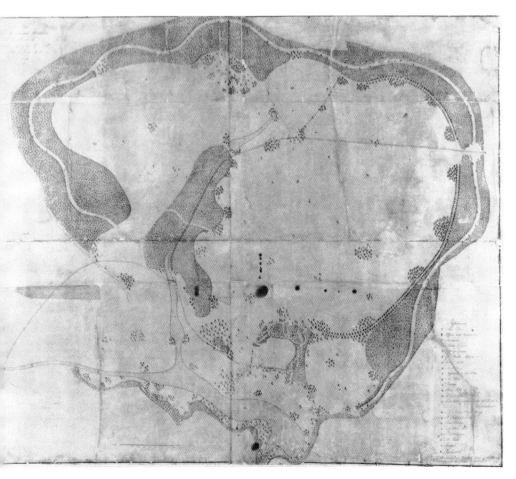

17a.
Bowood,
Wiltshire. Brown's
plan for the park,
dated 1763. *see
page 90*

17b.
Bowood. Looking
over the lake to the
temple.

18a. FENSTANTON, HUNTINGDONSHIRE. Decorative detail from the survey of the manor prepared for Brown by his draughtsman John Spyers in 1777. *see page 109*

18b. CASTLE ASHBY, NORTHAMPTONSHIRE. The lakeside menagerie. *see page 107*

19a. Syon House, Middlesex. From an engraving *circa* 1783. *see page 103*

19b. Alnwick Castle, Northumberland. Looking over the park from the ramparts. *see page 103*

20a.　HAREWOOD, YORKSHIRE. Looking south over the park from the terrace. *see page 105*

20b.　CHATSWORTH, DERBYSHIRE. Looking south over the park with James Paine's bridge in the foreground.
see page 104

21a. KIMBERLEY PARK, NORFOLK. An engraving from Morris's *Country Seats of Great Britain. see page 112*

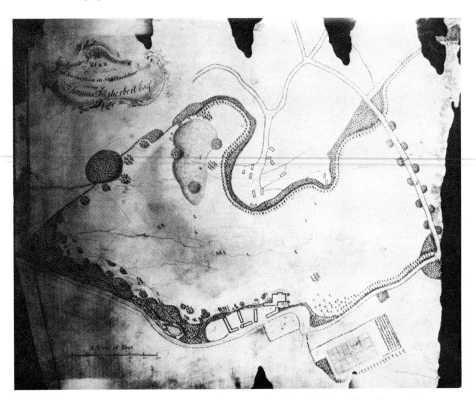

21b. SWINNERTON, STAFFORDSHIRE. Brown's undated plan for the park. *see page 147*

22a.
REDGRAVE HALL,
NORFOLK. The
house designed by
Brown. Now
demolished. *see
page 112*

22b.
REDGRAVE
HALL. The
orangery.

22c.
REDGRAVE HALL.
Detail of pediment
shortly before
demolition.

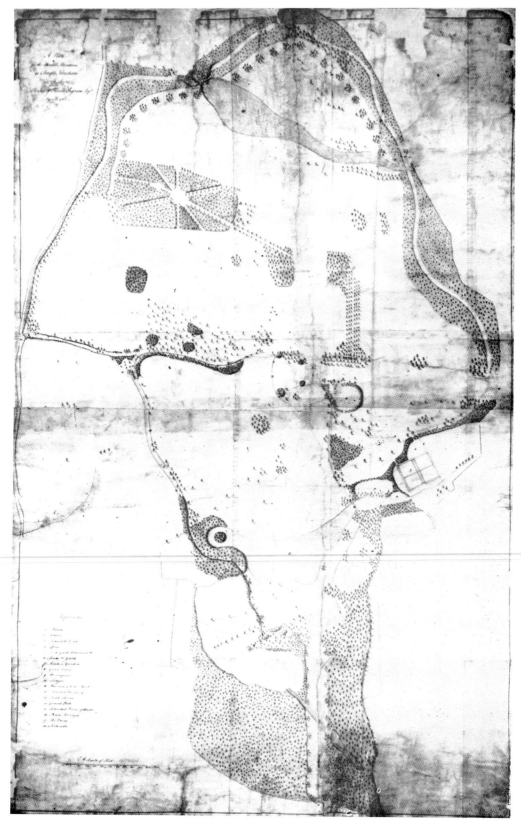

23. TEMPLE NEWSAM, YORKSHIRE. Brown's plan for the park dated 1762. *see page 116*

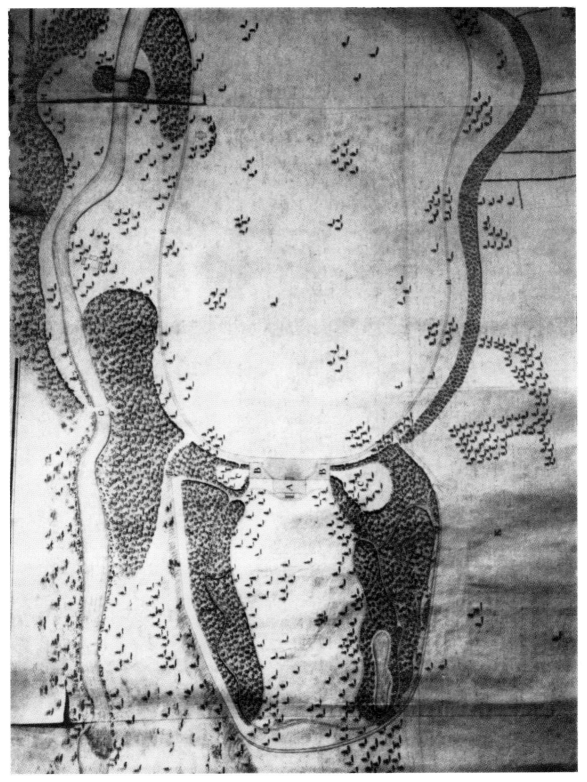

24. LOWTHER, WESTMORLAND. Brown's plan for the park, dated 1763. *see page 115*

25a. BROADLANDS, HAMPSHIRE. The west front and portico from across the river Test. *see page 137*

South Front for Broadlands

25b. BROADLANDS. Brown's design for remodelling the south front.

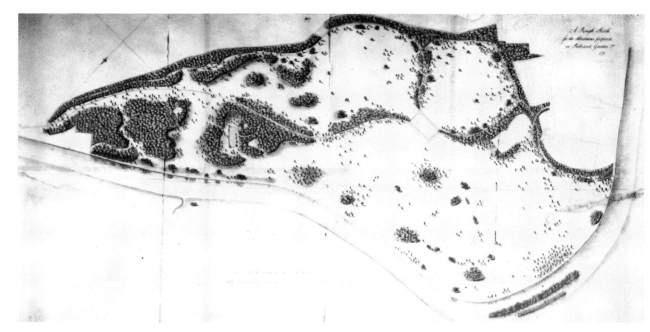

26a. Brown's first design for the ROYAL GARDENS AT RICHMOND, SURREY, now part of the Royal Botanical Gardens, Kew. *see page 123*

26b. WILDERNESS HOUSE, HAMPTON COURT, MIDDLESEX. Brown's official residence. *see page 122*

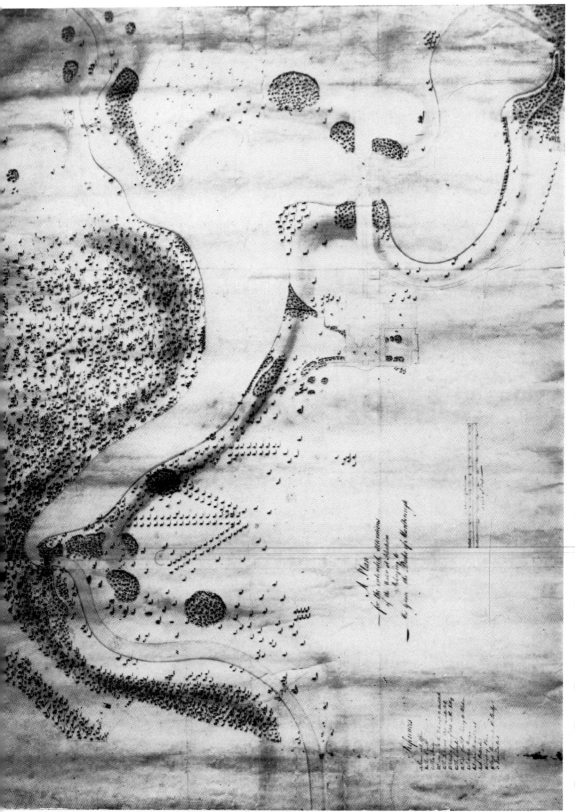

A Plan
for the intended alterations
of the water at Blenheim
as given the Duke of Marlborough

References

27. BLENHEIM PARK, OXFORDSHIRE. Brown's plan of 1764. *see page 129*

28a. BLENHEIM PARK. An air view looking north. *see page 129*

28b. BLENHEIM PARK. Looking west over the lake.

29a. BLENHEIM PARK. Looking towards the house and bridge from near the Woodstock entrance. *see page 129*

29b. BLENHEIM PARK. High Lodge. Remodelled and embattled in the early 1760s.

30a.
BLENHEIM PARK. Brown's design for the cascade. *see page 130*

30b.
BLENHEIM PARK. Brown's design for the Park Farm Granary, 1765. Partly carried out. *see page 131*

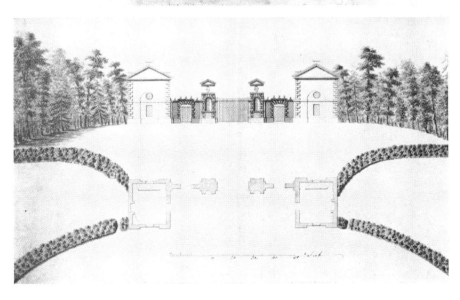

30c.
BLENHEIM PARK. Brown's unexecuted design for a gateway. *see page 130*

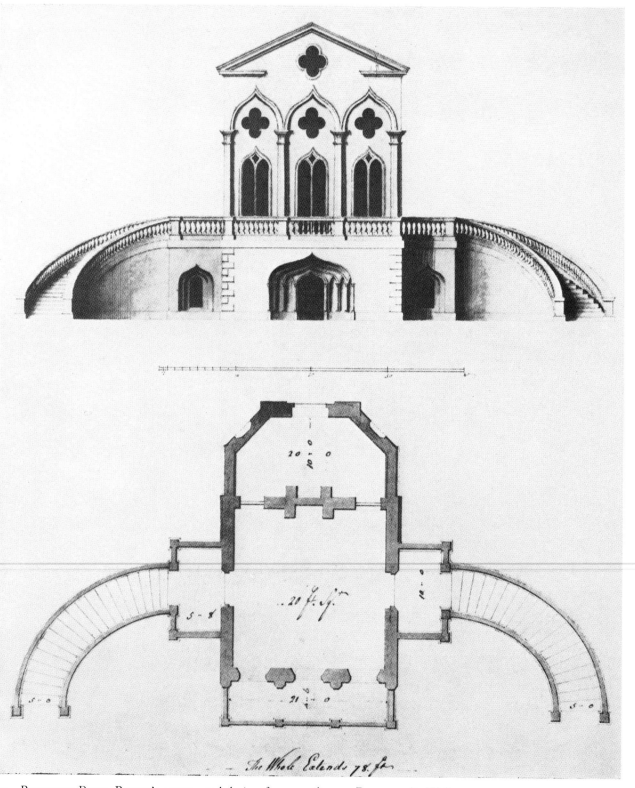

31. BLENHEIM PARK. Brown's unexecuted design for a pavilion at Rosamund's Well. *see page 130*

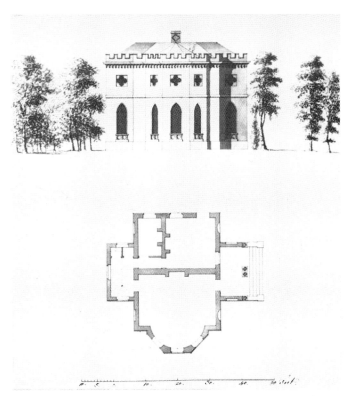

32a. ROTHLEY, NORTHUMBERLAND. Brown's design for a
lakeside lodge, unexecuted. *see page 137*

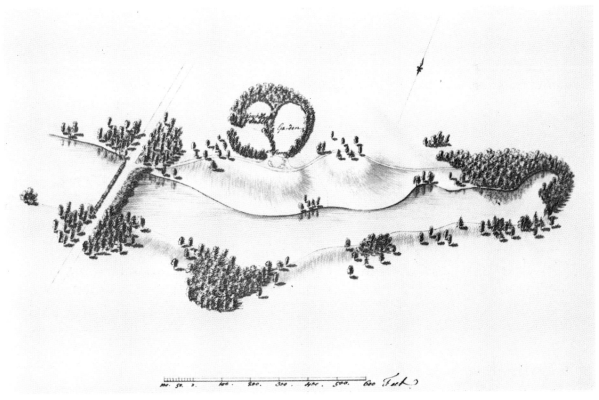

32b. ROTHLEY. Brown's design for the lake which he formed out of the Ewesley Burn, showing the site
proposed for the (unexecuted) Lodge and its garden.

VIII

THE CREST OF THE WAVE

THE YEAR 1764 which saw Brown installed as Royal Gardener at Hampton Court and Richmond, and as Lord of the Manor of Fenstanton, was also to see the first stages of work at BLENHEIM (Map 24) (Plates 27, 28A, 28B, 29A, 29B, 30A, 30B, 30C and 31) which, if it was not to be so lengthy as his undertaking at Burghley, was by its scale and virtuosity to attract wider notice, and which today is associated with Capability in the minds of those who would be at a loss to name any other of his works.

Sarah, Duchess of Marlborough, had died in 1744, having outlived the 1st Duke by twenty-two years, and their daughter, Henrietta Godolphin, who had succeeded her father as Duchess in her own right, by eleven years. The title of 3rd Duke had then gone to a grandson, Charles, who enjoyed an uneventful reign and died in 1758 when he was succeeded by his son George, aged nineteen. The 4th Duke was soon to show a keen interest in matters of taste and fashion, and was still only twenty-four when he turned his attention to the grounds of both Blenheim and Langley Park, on which he consulted Brown. The latter's plan for LANGLEY (Map 115) was produced early in the summer of 1763 and sent off to the Duke who acknowledged it in a letter from Blenheim on 29 June. 'I like [it] very well,' he wrote, but added 'As I cannot begin to make alterations (at least *expensive* ones) at this place and at the same time, I have a notion I shall begin here immediately so that the sooner you come the better.'[1]

Brown went, and although his 'Plan for the Intended Alterations'[2] is undated, it must have been prepared in that autumn for work was in hand at the beginning of 1764, the first two payments to him of £500 and £600 being made in February, followed by £800 in October. For the next ten years sums varying from £500 to £1,200 were noted as received for work in hand until they finally amounted to over £21,500.

The park at Blenheim has always been regarded as the epitome of Brown's achievement, and there is no doubt that the honey-coloured mass of Vanbrugh's palace, set on the crest of high ground, proved a spur to his genius. The course of the river Glyme, from the modest lake at Kiddington which he had constructed in 1740, to the shimmering magnificence of the water at Blenheim, is in fact a reflection of his own progress during twenty-four years. While it might appear that, by removing Henry Wise's

parterres and Bartholomew Peisley's canal, he ruthlessly destroyed what had been carried out under Vanbrugh's direction in the vicinity of the house, Brown's attention to the picturesque potentialities of the park in fact came surprisingly close to views expressed by Vanbrugh in his plea for preserving old Woodstock Manor. There Vanbrugh had observed: 'That Part of the Park which is Seen from the North front of the New Building, has Little Variety of Objects, Nor dos the Country beyond it Afford any of Vallue. It therefore Stands in Need of all the help that can be given which are only Two: Buildings and plantations. These rightly dispos'd will indeed Supply all the Wants of Nature in the Place.'[3] Brown's recognition of these 'wants' was to result both in his plantations, ranging from the smaller lake-side groups with their contrasting shapes and foliage to the more distant clumps; and in the designing of several gothic buildings, although not all of the latter materialised.

A comparison of Brown's plan for the grounds with one published in Volume II of *Vitruvius Britannicus* in 1725 shows the extent of his proposals whereby the geometrical precision both of the parterres and of the alleys radiating through tightly packed coppices gave way to lawns and scattered groups of trees. Although to the south-west he proposed the retention of three short radiating alleys and one straight tree-lined walk from the old layout these, too, disappeared in the execution, leaving only the great avenue on the axis of the house and Vanbrugh's walled kitchen garden as visible survivors. Not shown on his plan, and therefore probably an afterthought, was the forming of a tree-covered island from part of the old causeway through which the Glyme had previously flowed. Where the river narrows after taking a southerly turn from the great lake, Brown formed the Grand Cascade where the surrounding trees and shrubs form a green background for the white foam of the water as it surges over the mossy rocks. Half a mile further south again comes another cascade at the point where this river joins the Evenlode on its way to the Thames.

Brown's ambitious but unexecuted project for gothicising those walls of Woodstock which were visible from the park, and another unexecuted design for an elaborate gateway survive as well as four drawings for a 'Bathing House' intended to be built at Rosamund's Well. But no drawings have been found for the remodelling of High Lodge, a notable feature which stands on an eminence in the north-west area of the Great Park. This must have been in hand at a early stage as it was sufficiently complete for wallpaper to be supplied in the late spring of 1764.[4] The oldest of the park lodges, this was the house in which the profligate Earl of Rochester had come to the end of his short life. Boydell's engraving of 1752 shows it as a plain two-storey building with dormers in a steeply pitched roof. Brown's gothicising took the form of two-light pointed windows introduced on both storeys of the principal front, and the addition of a canted bay rising to a higher level, while the roof of the old house was largely

concealed by a crenellated parapet. Another of Brown's gothic buildings was the facade with a central gateway masking a granary and other outbuildings at Park Farm, for which his drawing survives. This design bears a close resemblance to the courtyard facade which he was to build at Burton Constable a few years later. The Park Farm screen survives, and although it has lost much of its original character, it ties up with a letter written from Brown to the Duke on 26 August, 1765:

> I have enclosed to your Grace the Sketch for the Front of the cart House, Granery etc. I mean the Granery to have two Floors besides Stages for Corn between them for the easy turning of the Grain, and letting it fall from one floor to the other which is the best way of keeping it sweet; there may be very good convenience for Grain over the Cart Hovel if wanted, and upon a level with the Floor in the Square Granery. If a Barn is wanted, the middle part may be very eas[il]y made into one by taking a piece of the Cart House on one side, and piece of the supposed Stable on the other, and the arch will make a good Entrance or barn door. I have supposed a Habitation for a Family on the Corner next to the Column; some of the stone which has been pull'd down in the sunk fence, may if your Grace pleases be made use of for the front: and I flatter myself that the Effect of the Building would be very proper for the situation.'[5]

Brown was no doubt also responsible for the menagerie which was built adjacent to Park Farm, and was apparently to number among its occupants the tiger which Lord Clive sent to the Duke of Marlborough in 1771.[6]

The man whom Brown entrusted with supervising the various works in his absence was 'Mr. Read' who had worked for him at Croome. On 6 August, 1767, Lord Cadogan, who in his youth had served as one of the 1st Duke of Marlborough's officers, and would therefore have had a particular interest in Blenheim, wrote to thank 'Dear Brother Brown' for having arranged his entry to Blenheim with a party of guests. He mentioned Brown's 'letter of recommendation' to Mr. Read 'by whose attention and civility we saw it to the greatest perfection, and indeed it *beggars* all description, as it would the owner of it had he not £40 or £50,000 a year to be doing with. The water is, by much, the finest artificial thing I ever saw; when I say that I include the banks and the advantageous manner in which you have set it off . . . .'.[7]

By 1768 much of the work had been completed, although final touches continued to be made. A visitor in September of that year wrote that although the cascade was already 'pleasing and magnificent, just now they are continuing it further,' and he added that 'The Provost of Eton, who converses with Brown, told us that he himself cries it up as the master-piece of his genius.'[8] Some years later Samuel Johnson and James Boswell visited Blenheim, and when they had walked round the grounds, the latter exclaimed to

the doctor, 'You and I, Sir, have, I think, seen together the extremes of what can be seen in Britain: the wild rough island of Mull, and Blenheim Park.'[9] The doctor's reply is unfortunately not recorded. Other distinguished visitors included Thomas Jefferson, who was impressed. In the course of his short tour of the more celebrated English gardens in April, 1786, his comments in general were not particularly flattering, although the principles of landscape layout were absorbed by him and later implemented in his Virginian creations. Blenheim received praise, however, particularly the cascade, though he found almost equally noteworthy the facts that the park contained 2,500 acres, that two hundred people were employed in its upkeep, and that the garden turf required to be mown every ten days.[10]

The second Baron Cadogan, whose remarks about Blenheim were quoted earlier, lived at CAVERSHAM PARK (Map 39) (Plate 35 A), some thirty miles south-east of Blenheim, and then on the outskirts of Reading by which it has now been swamped.[11] His letter, written from Caversham, had ended with the sentence 'I had the mortification to find on my return that I had miss'd you here. I flatter myself you found Justice done to your works in the manner of keeping them.' From this, and from the reference to the gardens of Caversham in the anonymous poem dedicated to Charles 9th Viscount Irwin (see page 117) it is evident that the landscaping had been put into Brown's hands at least three years earlier, and perhaps in 1764. No drawings, however, survive and the accounts must have been entered in one of Brown's lost ledgers.

The house, on the crest of a steep slope above the north bank of the Thames, had been rebuilt soon after 1660, probably by William Winde. Before Brown's arrival the gardens would still have been very much as depicted in *Vitruvius Britannicus*, Vol. III, where the formal terraces and parterres to the south of the house, with their vases, fountains and statues, including one to the 1st Duke of Marlborough, were said to have been laid out in 1723 by an appropriately named Mr. Acres. Brown in fact retained the long terrace with its two canals, but removed the parterres beyond and included the long sweep of previously rough ground to form the expanse of lawn dipping to the Thames. A good deal of clearing was carried out in the thickets which had previously hemmed in the old gardens and which had given rise to the remark, later attributed by Mrs. Lybbe Powys to Brown, that 'it was impossible to see the trees for the wood'. As she observed, he had 'By taking down some and leaving conspicuous the most noble [trees], made it one of the finest parks imaginable, and at the time of the whitethorns being in blow, which at Caversham are by far the oldest and most beautiful I ever saw, 'tis hardly possible to describe the scene it offers.'[12] Additions to the house at various dates in the nineteenth century transformed it into a characterless barrack, but it still sits forlornly on its hill amid the development which, since 1960, has flooded the estate with some fifteen hundred houses.

Before 1764 was out, Brown had given designs for the landscaping of Luton Hoo, Dodington in Gloucestershire and Wimbledon, although the contract for the latter was not signed until January, 1765.

However staunch his Whig proclivities outside his practice, Brown did not allow party politics to come between him and a good client, and his various works for the 3rd Earl of Bute reveal his respect for this distinguished scholar and patron of the arts to whom the founding of the Royal Botanical Gardens at Kew was largely due. The LUTON HOO (Map 129) (Plate 34A) estate had been purchased by the Earl in 1762, when he was Prime Minister, but he resigned in 1763, and in the following year began to consider schemes for the remodelling of the house by Robert Adam, and for the landscaping of the grounds by Brown. Little was in fact done to the old house for some years, but Brown's work went ahead without delay. Only one small fragment of his original plan is, however, known to survive, and that is now in the Metropolitan Museum, New York, having passed through a London sale-room in 1950. The position of the house, on the crest of a hill sloping to the river Lea on the east, provided possibilities of which Brown was quick to take advantage, making his lawns not in a single, flat expanse, but in a series of gentle undulations. The river was dammed to form a lake nearly a quarter of a mile wide, set with small wooded islands, while on the further side of the water, the ground was thickly planted. In view of his designing of a column at Burton Pynsent in the following year, it is possible that Brown may have had a hand in that erected at Luton to a former owner of the house, Francis Napier, which provides a feature in a prospect across the valley.

In 1767 there was a misunderstanding about some of the groups of trees which had been put in, and Brown, writing to Lord Bute on 11 March, hastened to inform him that:

> *I just got to Kew as your lordship left it, much mortified at not having the honour of paying my respects to your Lordship. I am very sorry that Blair has planted the Trees in a manner which is not agreeable to your Lordship. I am sure if your Lordship wished me there, I am certain nothing will give me more pleasure than to obey your Lordship's commands, be what and where they will.*
>
> *I am very glad your Lordship has taken William Ireland.[13] My order to him was to submit himself to your Lordship's terms. Your Lordship, I do believe, will find him sober, industrious and honest. We have got as many trees as we wanted this season from the Princess of Wales's garden, on which acct. I desired Mr. Haverfield to forward the trees for your Lordship as fast as possible. I have sent by the bearer another plan for the walls of the kitchen garden without a green house. The walls are the aspect that I think the best.*

In the same letter Brown was giving the Earl information about stone, probably in connection with the rebuilding of the house:

> *I have seen the Duke of Bridgwater, his Grace is for going on with Digging of stone, and I find the Duke of Bedford is working in the same Pitt. His Grace informs me that the pitt that Mr. Hill offered to your Lordship the Duke of Bedford had examined and was thought to be very bad on which acct. his Grace declined having it. I am sorry to give your Lordship so unsatisfactory an acct. of the stone pitt, but I hope soon to be in all the pitts that is at Tattenho when I shall be happy to be of use.*[14]

The final effect of the landscaping at Luton was only to be seen after several years, but Arthur Young was enthusiastic over what had already been accomplished by 1770, and devotes many lines to the 'finest water I have ever seen', the 'very fine beeches', and other trees through the openings among which 'the opposite hills are viewed in a pleasing stile'. He was also much taken with a sloop with ornamental sails and flying colours which, with two other boats, lay at anchor in the lake; and with the wooden bridge which concealed a twelve-foot dam. Beyond was the cascade which he described as then 'but a *capability*; when a little improved, and catched from a proper point of view, it will add to the variety of the scene.'[15]

By this time an additional 900 acres of farm and woodland had been taken into the new park, while two miles of highway had also been altered.[16] Brown's payments for the various works at Luton had amounted to £10,420 2s 9d by 1774, although he noted that this included an overpayment of £148 15s at one point, and made the appropriate credit to the Earl's account. His work for Lord Bute at Highcliffe will be mentioned later in this chapter.

DODINGTON (Map 64), in Gloucestershire, was the home of Sir William Codrington, and the house, later to be rebuilt by James Wyatt, was then a Tudor mansion of about 1560 with gardens which had been described by Alexander Pope as having 'a valley betwixt them with some mounts and waterfalls'. Brown's account book shows that between August, 1764 and December, 1767, he received £1,368 covering the two contracts made with Sir William, but although many estate plans for Dodington are now in the County Record Office at Gloucester, nothing relating to Brown has so far come to light. In front of the house a number of oaks which even then were of considerable age, were retained. For the water two lakes were made at different levels, there being a rocky cascade between them. The gothic bridge built over this fall is now attributed to James Wyatt, but the weir itself is almost certainly part of Brown's scheme.

Some time towards the end of 1764 Brown must have prepared a design for WIMBLEDON PARK (Map 202), for he noted in January, 1765, that a contract had been made with

Viscount [later 1st Earl] Spencer, to whom the estate had come from his great-grand-mother, Sarah, Duchess of Marlborough. It then covered some 1,200 acres which, from the ridge of high ground near the parish church, dropped sharply as they fanned out to the north. The house – the second of two built by the Duchess, and the fourth to be built here since Sir Thomas Cecil had acquired the estate in 1576 – stood close to what is now the upper end of Home Park Road, from where there is still a fine view towards inner London. The formal gardens of the earlier houses had already been much altered at the time of the Duchess's building activities, but two avenues remained to the north-east. Brown's proposals included the formation of the spectacular lake in the valley, cutting views through the avenues, and a considerable amount of new planting, as can be seen from a survey of the park prepared by Thomas Richardson in 1768.[17] The contract was for £1,760, to be paid quarterly over two years, and was more or less complete by the end of 1766. Twelve years later he was here again, supervising minor alterations for which he noted that he had been paid £200 in March, and £200 in May, 1779, out of which he made payments to Thomas Squires for a rail fence, and to John Watridge for painting it, while George Bowstreed was paid for work in the wood and 'various parts of the Park'. Brown was still receiving sums totalling £740 from Lord Spencer in 1781, though no further details are given.

During the 1870s much of the Park was sold for development. First to go were 500 acres on the Putney side, followed by further lots which provided sites for residences in Arthur, Home Park and Wimbledon Park Roads. A considerable portion, however, survives as the Wimbledon Park Golf Course, while a further area, north of the lake, is now a public recreation ground.

From 1765 Brown's activities were covering an incredibly wide area, ranging from Burton Pynsent in Somerset to Wallington in Northumberland in that year, Broadlands in Hampshire and Sandbeck in Yorkshire in 1766, and equally far-flung commissions during the years which followed, as well as several in the home counties. His work at BURTON PYNSENT (Map 33) (Plate 36A) followed the bequest of this property, over-looking the Vale of Sedgemoor, to William Pitt by Sir William Pynsent, a somewhat eccentric character whose interest in politics developed late in life, and was thus likened by Horace Walpole to 'the blooming of an aloe'. Dying at the age of ninety, his will infuriated his relations, but although their disputes were not settled until 1771, Pitt at once embarked on schemes for improving the Elizabethan house and its grounds, and the erecting of a column to his benefactor. Although Pitt was himself an accomplished landscape designer, the distance of Burton Pynsent from London made it difficult for him to give it his full attention, and for the column and its setting he sought the help of Brown, whom he had known since the latter's days at Stowe. On 10 September, 1765, Brown wrote to him:

135

I called at your Builder's in Bath but found he was set out for your house the same day I arrived at that Place. I shall have some other opportunity of talking to and giving him the best advice in my power concerning the construction of Pillars, the scaffolding and ca. agreeable to my promise.

I have sent you by your Steward a design for the Pillar which I hope will merit your approbation; if there are any parts you disaprove of, we can very easily correct them when I shall have the honor of seeing you. The figure I have put on the pedistal is that of Gratitude, conveying to Posterity the name of Pinsant; which indeed he himself has distinguished and without flattery done in the most effectual manner by making you His Heir. On this topic I could say more, but may my silence convey my respect. And that your King and your Country may be long, very long, very long blessed with your unparalleled abilities will be the constant wish of Sir, your most obliged and most obedient, humble servant.[18]

From his reference to advice 'concerning the construction of Pillars,' it is probable that Brown had in mind the column constructed at Stowe at the time of Lord Cobham's death, and with which he would have been closely concerned. This pillar, 150 feet high, carried an arcaded lantern surmounted by a statue. In its base (subsequently altered by Valdré) a small door leads to a stair which corkscrews its way to the summit. Brown's Tuscan essay for Burton Pynsent originally carried a figure symbolising Gratitude but this was replaced in the late nineteenth century by a classical urn.

In 1766 Pitt was raised to the peerage as 1st Earl of Chatham, but political preoccupations alternating with bouts of illness kept him from Burton Pynsent until the late summer of 1767. On 10 September Brown wrote to Lady Chatham:

I was most heartily rejoiced to find that Lord Chatham was well enough to move from North End, and that his Lordship and family were set out for Pynsent. I hope in God that his Lordship mended every Day, and that you have all had a good journey.

Pardon my Zeal! Pardon my Vanity, but I wish above all things to know [how] my Lord does, and how the Pillar pleases his Lordship.[19]

While there is no record of her reply to the latter question, there is little doubt that his Lordship was pleased, and the column still rises from its lofty site on the spur of high ground across a valley from the house.

Brown's several journeys to Northumberland in the 1760s in connection with work at Alnwick provided opportunities, rare in the early days of his practice, for visiting his brothers George and John, and their families at Cambo. It would have been in the course of one of these detours, probably in the summer of 1765, that he was consulted by Sir Walter Calverley Blackett about alterations to the east garden at WALLINGTON

(Map 197), and on the formation of the lakes on the latter's nearby estate at ROTHLEY (Map 162) (Plates 32 A, B and 33 A, B). The separation of the eastern part of the Wallington grounds had resulted from the building of a new road from Kirkharle to Cambo, which was carried over the Wansbeck by a bridge for which James Paine had given designs in 1755, and then climbed the hill to pass close to the east front of the house. Brown's remodelling of the earlier layout removed the rectangular plots of what had been the kitchen garden, and replaced them with grass and trees, now grown to enormous size, on the north side of the Garden Pond.[20] The outline of the China Pond, further west, was also altered to its present form. Wallis, writing in 1769 soon after the alterations had been carried out, says that the east garden by then contained 'a pinery, shrubberies, plantations and other ornaments.'[21]

The lakes at Rothley were formed by damming the Ewesley burn, the road from Cambo to Rothbury being carried across them on a bridge which is also a dam. For this project five unsigned and undated drawings in the Wallington portfolios have now been identified as in Brown's hand, two being plans for the lakes and surrounding plantations, more or less as carried out, one showing the rock-work adornment proposed for the arches of the bridge-dam but in fact omitted, and two being designs for a lakeside banqueting house, closely resembling the gothic bath house drawn by Brown for Rosamund's Well in Blenheim Park, but not built. Some six years later the new work had settled down sufficiently to meet with praise from Arthur Young, who described the young plantations round the 'fine new-made lake of Sir Walter Blackett's . . . which is a noble water; the bends and curves of the bank are bold and natural, and when the trees get up, the whole spot will be remarkably beautiful.'[22] Two hundred years later, the scene is still one of great beauty.

Humphry Repton's list of Brown's works, as given in the *Theory and Practice* of 1803, includes 'considerable additions' to BROADLANDS (Map 29) (Plates 25 A and B) for the 2nd Viscount Palmerston, and this is confirmed by references in Capability's account book. The property had been purchased in 1736 by the 1st Viscount who, before his death in 1757, began the deformalising of the gardens, 'giving away all the fine pyramid greens to those that will fetch them, of which many cartloads are gone already,'[23] but it was his successor who summoned Brown to carry out the landscaping and building work. This involved forming a new suite of reception rooms and a portico on the garden (west) side of the existing house, which Celia Fiennes had described some fifty years before as 'halfe a Roman H', that is, with wings coming forward from a narrow main block.

There may have been entries relating to the first stages of the work in one of Brown's earlier and lost account books, but the surviving ledger shows that in 1765 he was arranging with John Devall, the mason, and John Hobcroft, the carpenter, to carry out

work on the house. No plans of the date have so far come to light, but an unsigned drawing, almost certainly in Brown's hand, survives and shows the nine-window south front with its three centre bays breaking forward slightly and surmounted by a pediment.[24] Two unsigned elevational drawings at Broadlands relate to the decoration of the saloon behind the west portico, and the enrichment of one of the mahogany doors in the new suite.

The remodelled house was encased in white brick, no doubt from the kilns then in production in the Exbury neighbourhood some fifteen miles away.[25] The portico, quoins and window frames were of stone. In the grounds, water was provided in this rather flat terrain by the river Test, which flows in a wide sweep before the garden front. In addition to new lawns and plantations, Brown must have been responsible for alterations at this time to an earlier orangery which was given a five-bay extension at the rear, the entrance to this being set between two long windows adorned with a Coade stone urn set over an enriched frieze.

By June, 1766, Brown noted that he had been paid £500 'on account of the building' of the house, with a further £600 which he passed on to Devall. From then onwards large sums continued to be paid to him until 1778, by which time the total amounted to £20,750 out of which regular disbursements were made to Hobcroft, Devall, Payne, and the elder Holland. The entries closed with a note on 8 December, 1779, that Brown had 'Rec'd of Lord Palmerston the Balance of his Accounts on the Building and out of doors work, and in full of all demands'.

Although he does not record his journeys to Broadlands to supervise the course of the work during these years, his correspondence with his daughter Peggy includes an undated letter, written from there, and probably of about 1770, in which he describes how he had travelled down from London in ten hours, 'We came all the way as hard as four horses could lay feet to the ground', a servant having been sent on before to order fresh horses at the various posting stations. Five years after his death, more alterations were to be carried out in the house by his son-in-law, the younger Henry Holland, who remodelled the entrance front and dining room.

From 1763 James Paine was engaged on the building of a new house at SANDBECK (Map 164) for the 4th Earl of Scarbrough; three years after its inception, Brown was asked to prepare a scheme for landscaping the grounds. Although the house was regarded as secondary to the family seat at Lumley Castle, the site of Sandbeck had considerable potentialities, with the ruins of Roche Abbey (Plate 51B) standing beside a tributary of the river Ryton about a mile away, a scene which at once caught Brown's imagination. Following his visit in September, 1766 a plan was made, although no drawing has survived; in 1767 Brown's foreman, Andrew Gardiner, was sent to supervise some preliminary work, the nature of which is not specified in the account book,

and during the next year was again present. But it was not until 1774 that the Earl and Brown made a formal contract 'for the underwritten Articles of Work to be performed at Sandbeck'. The first four of the five clauses which followed were concerned with the usual provisions for making sunk fences, draining, and sowing with grass or Dutch clover seed. A good pond was also to be made near, and for the use of, the stables. Article 5 is that in which Brown sets out his proposals for Roche, where he undertook

to finish all the Valley of Roach Abbey in all its parts, according to the Ideas fixed on with Lord Scarbrough (With Poet's feeling and with Painter's Eye) beginning at the Head of the Hammer Pond, and continuing up the Valley towards Loton [Laughton] in the Morn as far as Lord Scarbrough's Ground goes, and to continue the Water and Dress the Valley up by the Present Farm House, until it comes to the separation fixed for the Boundary of the New Farm. N.B. The Paths in the Wood are included in this Discription and every thing but the Buildings.

For this work it was agreed that he should receive £3,000, but his account book records only £1,076 5s for the work, and for his own journeys over seven years.

From his reference to 'with Poet's feeling and with Painter's Eye', it can be taken that Brown had by now read the first three volumes of William Mason's *The English Garden*, which had been published in 1772,[26] and in line 20 of which he invokes 'Those magic seeds of Fancy, which produce A Poet's feeling, and a Painter's eye.' Brown's seeds of Fancy led him to grass over the horizontal outlines of the Abbey ruins, leaving only the upright fragments to rise from a green carpet of lawn. The course of the stream which flowed past the cloisters was altered, and dammed to form shallow cascades.

While his client must have wholly concurred with these changes which were certainly to produce a superbly serene scene, the treatment of the ruins occasioned a good deal of criticism from the antiquarian pundits, although William Gilpin, who visited the place in 1776, conceded that they, and the ground around them, had been 'in the roughest state when Mr. Brown was employed to adorn them'. He continued:

He is now at work and has nearly half completed his intention. This is the first subject of the kind he has attempted. Many a modern Palace he has adorned and beautified: but a ruin presented a new idea: which I doubt whether he has sufficiently considered. He has finished one of the valleys which looks towards Laughton spire, he has floated it with a lake and formed a very beautiful scene. But I fear it is too magificent and too artificial an appendage to be in unison with the ruins of an abbey. An abbey it is true, may stand by the side of a lake; and it is possible that this lake may, in some future time, become its situation; when the marks of the spade and the pick-axe are removed, – when its osiers flourish, and its naked banks become fringed and covered with wood . . . The ruin stands now on a neat bowling green.[27]

The 'bowling green' was in fact to be removed towards the end of the nineteenth century when antiquarian enthusiasm demanded that the bases of the piers and other foundations should be revealed once more, but in general this is still a Brownian scene of great beauty.

The year after his first visit to Sandbeck and Roche, Brown had to switch his attention to a 'ruin' of a very different kind, having been designed, but as yet not executed, by his old friend Sanderson Miller for WIMPOLE (Map 204) (Plates 39 A, B and 40 A) in Cambridgeshire. This estate had by then been inherited by Philip Yorke, by now 2nd Earl of Hardwicke, for whose wife Brown had worked at Wrest Park in the 1750s. Built for Thomas Chicheley in 1632, the house had been partly refaced. Some attempt had been made in the time of the 1st Earl to de-formalise the great parterres which had surrounded it, although the spectacular avenue to the south, and a shorter one to the north remained. It was to make a feature at the end of the latter, where the ground rises sharply to 'Johnson's Hill', that Miller had designed a castellated tower, similar to that at Hagley for which he was also responsible, and which had earned Horace Walpole's encomium for having 'the true rust of the Baron's Wars'. Although the design was prepared in 1752, there was considerable delay in putting it into execution. It was not until three years after the 2nd Earl had succeeded his father, and had commissioned Brown to plan the alteration of the grounds at Wimpole, that the project for the Castle was brought off the shelf again. On his plan, undated but *circa* 1767,[28] Brown noted the intended site on 'Johnson's Hill', while Lord Harwicke re-opened the matter with Miller. This is confirmed by two letters from the Earl's steward, Richard Barton, to Miller, the first of which, dated 6 April, 1768, urges him to press ahead with arrangements:

> *I was some time ago acquainted from my Lord that you had promised his Lordship that the Tower should be begun upon again the beginning of this month and he now expects the workmen are about it and is desirous to know what progress is made. Pray let no time be lost in carrying this Business on with all good speed . . .*

The second letter of 22 April was to let Miller know that Brown was expected at Wimpole on the following day, 'I presume before dinner, of which this is the earliest notice that cou'd possibly be given.'[29] A reference in Brown's account book to payment for 'what is doing at the tower', suggests, however, that in the end it was left to him rather than to Miller to carry out the building of the ruin.

Writing to Brown on Christmas Eve, 1767, Lord Hardwicke had expressed the hope that:

> *You will have leisure in the Holy-days to make out the minute for our proceedings at Wimple; specifying more particularly the plan of operating for next year with ye*

expence thereof; and making out dans le gros *the works for the 2 succeeding years, when* [viz. in 1770] *the Whole Plan is to be completed. Perhaps it is absurd to look so far forward but however the sketch of the whole may be of use in every event.*

He added a Christmas postscript with 'If it were not too old-fashioned I wd. make you the Complimts. of the season.'[30]

In his plan Brown retained the south avenue, but thinned that on the north so as to allow cross views while still giving the impression of a double line of trees when looking from the house to Miller's castle. The lake, formed out of a string of pools in the lower ground between the house and Johnson's Hill, is shown as crossed by a seven-arched bridge, the whole northern area being backed by a thick belt of trees through which a broad ride winds its way. His contract with Lord Hardwicke was in the sum of £2,400, which was settled in 1770, although additional sums amounting to £980 accrued in that and the two following years.

A letter addressed to Philip Yorke of Erddig – a cousin of Lord Hardwicke – by John Lawry in 1767 shows that Brown was at this time advising on the grounds of Lee, a long-vanished house which belonged to Sir Samuel Fludyer and stood on the road from Lewisham to Blackheath. Sir Samuel, who had amassed a fortune as a clothier, served as Lord Mayor of London in 1761, and as M.P. for Chippenham from 1754–68. 'Since I wrote last to you' Mr. Lawry informed his correspondent on 10 November, 'the great Brown hath appeared among us to correct and amend & inlarge the gardens of our worshipful Bart Sir Sam Fludyer. Sir Gregory Page who delighteth as our Friend Mr. Lloyd to see works going forward hath been called into the Council; and they have at last by lengthening their Fosses much beyond the first plan been able to inclose one fine spreading oak which is unique, and the glory & pride of the whole neighbourhood . . . it will turn out I believe notwithstanding all their skill, but a *soupe maigre* in comparison with those works where the liberal hand of nature hath afforded great materials in a large compass to work upon.'[31]

The Kentish Traveller's Companion of 1779 describes the 'elegant gardens and pleasure grounds belonging to Miss Fludyer, daughter and heiress of the late Sir Thomas Fludyer [a son of Sir Samuel]. The house is not large but hath a very handsome apartment upon the first floor towards the gardens and pleasure grounds and the prospects . . . onto Sir Gregory Page's grounds and park . . . are most picturesque and beautiful.' The house was demolished and the grounds extensively developed in the mid-nineteenth century.

The first reference to COMPTON VERNEY (Map 50) (Plates 38 A and B) comes in Brown's account book with the receipt of £120 as a first payment from Lord Willoughby de Broke on 19 November, 1768, by which time he had visited the place

and given plans. Earlier in the decade there had been extensive building activity here, with the addition of wings and a portico to the designs of Robert Adam, who also remodelled the interior of the house to form a great hall. The three-arched bridge with its pierced balustrade has been attributed to Adam but is more likely to have been from Brown's hand, as part of his scheme for uniting the five existing pools into a wide, serpentine river.[32] Elsewhere in the grounds Brown removed the parterres which had lain on three sides of the house, replacing them with lawns and trees, and carrying out a considerable amount of planting further afield. By May, 1770, the total of £1,000 on his first contract had been settled, and a new contract begun which by 1774 was to total another £2,830.

In the latter year Brown noted in his account book that he had supplied 'Drawings for the Chapel'. The old chapel at Compton Verney had stood close to the windows on the south side of the house, and its removal was therefore necessary if the rooms here were to have any view over the new landscape. It was demolished during or just before 1772, when an inscribed stone was laid to mark its site. There is little doubt that Brown's design was used for the new chapel, built to the north-east of the house. Externally it is a simple Palladian essay with a pedimented facade, and rusticated stonework to the ground floor. Internally, its decoration is confined to the ceiling, with square coffers containing rosettes, and the similar treatment of the window soffits. The altar tomb of Sir Richard Verney designed by Nicholas Stone in 1630, and a marble monument to Sir Greville Verney who died in 1668, were re-erected at the east end. At the west end a gallery is supported on coupled doric columns. It is likely that Brown was also responsible for the orangery, with its doric order and pediment, which was built in the grounds during the years of his activity here.

The decade of the 1760s culminated in the commission received from the 1st Lord Clive for the rebuilding of CLAREMONT (Map 47) (Plates 42 A, B, 43 A, B, 44 A, B and 45 A, B) in 1769. Lord Clive had purchased this Surrey property from the Duke of Newcastle's widow in 1768, a year after his second return from India. In contrast to the austerity which he had exercised during his Indian campaigns, Clive's homecoming was marked by a dazzling display of wealth. He established himself in a handsome house in Berkeley Square, and soon after bought two more estates at Walcot and Oakley in Shropshire, where he had already inherited the family home at Styche and entrusted its rebuilding to Sir William Chambers. Finally came the purchase of Claremont.

The existing house had originally been built by Vanbrugh as a residence for himself, but he subsequently sold it to the Duke of Newcastle for whom he made considerable additions, while Bridgeman, and later William Kent, gave designs for the gardens. Its situation in the grounds was low, and its rambling plan and castellated brick facades

made little appeal to the Prince of Nabobs. It was therefore demolished, and a site for a new house selected on high ground further north, although the lofty belvedere which Vanbrugh had set on a nearby mound, and his walled kitchen garden, were to be retained.

For the new house Lord Clive invited designs from both Chambers and Brown. Of the former's essay nothing is known, but whatever its merit, the client's choice lay with Brown's proposal, several of the drawings for which have survived.[33] These include seven contract drawings, each signed by Lord Clive and the architect, and endorsed 'referred to by us in our agreement'. A memorandum confirms that by their contract Brown was entrusted with the preparation of the designs, and with responsibility for their execution, although it transpired that from time to time his client changed his mind over details, as in the case of the hall floor. This was to have been plain but was later elaborated with black marble inlay 'at the request of Lord Clive at the time his Lordship went to see the pavement in the Hall at Sion House'.[34] The carcase of the house was to be built of white brick, although a quantity of old bricks from the Vanbrugh building were used for the inner walling and fillings. The lofty Corinthian portico to the south (entrance) front is of Portland stone, as are the window dressings and balustrade to the roof. The north front has four fluted pilasters supporting a pediment, a central doorway on the *piano nobile* being approached by a double flight of steps. Although the final drawings are dated 28 February, 1771, the first plans must have been drawn up towards the end of 1769, when preliminary work began. By January, 1771, Brown noted that he had received £4,000 for what had already been carried out on the foundations and carcase, and later in this year Henry Wood, the carver, was paid for the columns and other details for the portico.[35]

From the design of the new Claremont it is evident that Brown had by now shed his early and heavy Palladianism in favour of neo-classical precepts. Gone are the projecting tower blocks at the angles, with 'Venetian' windows and long transverse corridors. The plan is notable for its compact form in which the principal rooms on the *piano nobile* are ranged round an inner, top-lit, staircase hall. The service quarters in the basement are light and airy, with a wide surrounding area. Direct external access to the latter is by way of a short tunnel from one of the drives. Claremont was also given an elegant stone plunge bath in its basement.

On the north and south of the house Brown laid out sloping lawns flanked by trees but with uninterrupted views over what was then countryside. To the west much of the earlier planting was retained, as was the island in the lake on which stands William Kent's classical temple. This area of the grounds, including the hill dominated by Vanbrugh's belvedere, now belongs to the National Trust through whom commendable restoration is gradually taking place. A major change carried out by Brown was the re-aligning

of the Portsmouth road, which previously ran along the high ground beyond the belvedere, involving a steep climb and descent for travellers. This was replaced by a new road cut through lower ground further north, after which the old way was merged into the Claremont woodland.

It was the prospect of this considerable undertaking, on top of the mass of work already in hand, which made Brown realise that he must take a partner. His own sons showed not the slightest interest in architecture, Lance by this time being busy with his law studies at Lincoln's Inn, while John was already in the Navy, and Thomas still at school. His thoughts therefore centred on the son of his old friend Henry Holland the builder. Young Henry had for some years been working in his father's firm, and had thereby gained a considerable knowledge of architecture for which he had already shown a marked talent. He was now twenty-five and no doubt felt that the time had come to move outside the limits of the family business. Probably Brown, whose shrewd eye was not confined to landscapes, had foreseen that this might happen, and on discussion the advantages to both seemed obvious. In 1770 he took young Henry under his wing, introduced him to a large circle of influential clients, and encouraged him in the building up of his own practice. In return he was from this time to be relieved of a great deal of the detailing in Claremont and the later houses by an able collaborator who was eventually to become one of the country's most distinguished architects. The first product of this successful partnership, the internal finishing of Claremont, will be mentioned again in Chapter XI.

1 Pakenham Correspondence.
2 Mislaid for many years but found by Mr. David Green in a chest at Blenheim and now in the muniment room there with other Brown drawings except that for Woodstock which was presented by the late Duke to that Borough.
3 D. Green, *Blenheim Palace*, 1951, p. 303.
4 D. Green, *op. cit.*
5 Blenheim Archives.
6 *Oxford Journal* quoted in Mary Gretton, *Three Centuries in North Oxfordshire*, 1902.
7 Pakenham Correspondence.
8 J. Nichols, *Literary Illustrations*, Vol. 1, p. 134, 1817. The Provost was Dr. Edward Barrard.
9 G. B. Hill and L. F. Powell, *Boswell's Life of Johnson*, 1964, Vol. II, p. 451.
10 E. M. Betts, *Thomas Jefferson's Garden Book, 1766–1824*, 1944.
11 Lord Cadogan's marriage to Elizabeth, daughter and co-heiress of Sir Hans Sloane, had brought him a large area of land in Chelsea which was later to be developed as Hans Town by Brown's son-in-law. See D. Stroud, *Henry Holland*, 1966.
12 E. J. Climenson, *Diaries of Mrs. Lybbe Powys*, 1899.
13 Previously in charge at Burghley. Blair was not, however, dismissed and his name turns up in Brown's account book as having received £600 for disbursements at Luton in 1776.
14 British Museum, Add. MSS 5726. c.f. 72.
15 A. Young, *Six Months' Tour through the North of England*, Vol. II, 1770.
16 Hugh C. Prince, 'Parkland in the Chilterns', *American Geographical Review*, Vol. XLIX, 1959.

17 Minet Library, Wandsworth. He can be identified with the Thomas Richardson who prepared the survey of the gardens at Richmond (see page 124). On the Wimbledon drawing he describes himself as 'Surveyor of York Street'.

18 P.R.O. Chatham, MSS Bundle 24.

19 P.R.O. Chatham, MSS, Bundle 24.

20 Sir Charles Trevelyan, *Wallington, its History and Treasures*, 1950.

21 Rev. John Wallis, *History of Northumberland*, Vol. II, 1769.

22 A. Young, *Six Months Tour through the North of England*, Vol. III, 1771.

23 Letter to his son, archives at Broadlands. The 1st Viscount planted the maidenhair tree (Ginkgo biloba) on the west lawn which is labelled 1754, and which was retained in Brown's scheme. (Information from the late Lady Mount Templar to the author, 1943.)

24 Drawing now at Brightwell House, Brightwell Salome, Oxfordshire.

25 Dr. John Latham, notes for a projected History, British Museum, Add. MSS 26,774 and 26,780.

26 In his published notes on the poem, Mason says that it was begun in 1767.

27 W. Gilpin, *Observations relating chiefly to Picturesque Beauty*, 1776.

28 Preserved in the house, where are also some notes on 'Mr. Brown's Plan', dated 1768.

29 Both letters in British Museum, Add. MSS 6771, fs. 99 and 179.

30 Pakenham Correspondence.

31 From the Yorke Family Papers at Erddig, Denbighs., now a property of the National Trust. Mr. Gervase Jackson-Stops was kind enough to draw my attention to this letter.

32 Robin Chaplin, *The Landscape Lakes at Compton Verney, Warwickshire History*, Vol. 1, 1969.

33 In the possession of Lady Mary Clive.

34 T. E. C. Walker, 'The Clive's at Claremont', *Surrey Archaeological Collections*, Vol. LXV, 1968, p. 91.

35 Copies of tradesmen's accounts in Soane Museum Correspondence. There are also 'Accounts, estimates and memoranda relating to Claremont' in the Clive MSS, National Library of Wales, Aberystwyth.

Fig. 5. 'Moving a Tree' from *The Planter's Guide* by Sir Henry Steuart, 1828

IX

MIDLAND COMMISSIONS

WHILE THE FOREGOING works were in hand Brown had for some years been dealing with a group of commissions in the midlands which, although of varying size, importance and date, can most conveniently be grouped in one chapter. At Trentham and Fisherwick he was to rebuild older houses. At Tixall he proposed alterations which were carried out in part; at Himley some structural changes were made, all being in addition to garden work. At Ingestre, Chillington, Swinnerton and Weston he was to be concerned with the landscape only.

Fate has dealt harshly with the houses. Trentham, extensively remodelled by Sir Charles Barry in the following century, has since been reduced to a fraction of its original size. Fisherwick, into which a wealth of material and fine craftsmanship was poured, was razed to the ground within fifty years, and its gardens returned to arable. The Clifford house at Tixall disappeared many years ago, Tong suffered the same fate more recently, and Himley Hall was severely damaged by fire.

Brown's commissions for all but one of these places belong to the 1760s and 1770s, the exception being INGESTRE (Map 106) (Plate 46) to which he must first have been summoned in 1756. The house was still mainly Jacobean, although two plans among the Wren drawings at All Souls College, Oxford, show that there had been a project to rebuild the north (garden) front with a classical facade and giant order, presumably at the time when Wren was designing the nearby church.[1] Although this particular scheme did not materialise, some changes to the north front were in hand in 1698 when Celia Fiennes noted that it was 'new building of the fashion with sash windows.'[2] It was for the grounds stretching northward from this front that Brown submitted to Lord Chetwyn his plan 'for the Intended Lawn', which is initialled L.B. and dated 1756.[3] By 'lawns', however, he meant a fairly extensive area reaching well beyond the sunk fence which was proposed for the middle distance, and within which were to be retained a number of features from the earlier garden. This had been heavily wooded, with rides radiating from an axial point where Brown was to form his large area of sward. From its extremities three of the original rides were retained, shown on the plan as extending

into the distance, two of them being marked as 'The road to Weston Hall', and 'The road to Hopton'. No water of any size is mentioned, but a small lake is shown, and in the 'references' at the foot of the drawing is marked as to be 'inlarged with Sham Bridge at the Upper End'. There is also a 'reservoir inlarged and made Oval', while the 'Dutch barns in the Trent Walk' indicate the proximity of the garden to this river. Other early features to be retained were an obelisk in an octagonal pool, and a 'bastion' on which was set a doric rotunda. The feature of an obelisk in an octagon is similar, although smaller in scale, to one at Stowe shown in Charles Bridgeman's perspective drawing of *circa* 1720,[4] and subsequently described in a letter from Lord Perceval as 'a Gulio or pyramid at least 50 feet high, from the top of which it is designed that water shall fall.'[5] The 'Tower' and the 'Menagerie with ye Back Side ornamented' noted on Brown's plan were to be his additions, as were the belts of trees to screen existing farm buildings. In his new plantations he was to make use of trees already standing in the 'Iron Pitt Copy', 'Watering Copy' and 'Fiddler's Copy', i.e. coppices. Although the menagerie has gone and only the foundations of his tower are now visible, a good deal of Brown's planting has survived, and makes comparison with his plan all the more interesting.

The undated scheme which he drew out for SWINNERTON (Map 181) (Plate 21 b),[6] to the north of Stafford, is likely also to be of an early period since its description as 'A plan for the alteration of Swinerton . . . the Seat of Thomas Fitzherbert Esqr.' is in a rococo cartouche somewhat similar to the Packington and Beechwood drawings. Though the right-hand side, which presumably carried the references to the explanatory letters on the plan, is missing it is clear that he proposed the removal of a number of small buildings in the foreground of the house so as to obtain a wide sweep of lawn dipping on the south east to a lake. A thick belt of trees was intended to hide other buildings, probably farms, which had to be retained. The house had been built by Francis Smith of Warwick in 1738, and its position on the crest of a hill gives it fine views over its own park in which some part of Brown's scheme is discernible, and over the surrounding countryside.

The evidence for Brown's commission from Thomas Giffard of CHILLINGTON (Map 44) rests on James Paine's comment in his *Plans of Noblemen's and Gentlemen's Houses* of 1767 where he describes the park as 'confessedly one of the finest pieces of water, within an inclosure, that this Kingdom produces; the verges of which are bounded by fine plantations, intermixed with groves of venerable stately oaks . . .'. Paine had by then built a second bridge over the river feeding the lake, but of the earlier bridge he adds: 'At another neck of this beautiful water is erected another bridge, concealing the other extreme of the water, built by Lancelot Brown, Esq., who designed and conducted the execution of the improvements of this justly admired park.'

Brown's landscaping must have been carried out before 1761, the year in which a survey of the park was made by Thomas White,[7] showing the former's five-arched bridge as built, and the long lakeside walk which follows the eastern bank between groves of trees.

Chillington is barely three miles from two other estates with which Brown was shortly to be concerned, Tong, which lies due west and Weston, which is to the north-west.

The estate at TONG (Map 190) had been purchased early in the 1760s by George Durant, who decided to settle here after acquiring a considerable fortune in Havana. He then proceeded to demolish the greater part of a sixteenth-century house which had belonged to the Vernons whose tombs are still a feature of the nearby church. Possibly on the recommendation of his neighbour at Chillington, he approached Brown for schemes which were duly submitted, the latter noting in his account book that he had made 'several journeys there' and had in 1765 supplied Mr. Durant with 'various plans and elevations made for Tong Castle'. This puts in question the statement of George Griffiths who some fifty years later compiled a history of the parish in which he wrote that Mr. Durant had demolished the wings of the old Castle and

> encased the remaining portion in stone according to a fanciful design of his own, a mixture of Gothic and Moorish architecture. Surmounted by its lofty domes and pinnacles, the structure is noticeable principally for its massive and stately appearance, enhanced by its position at the edge of a broad rich greensward extending uninterruptedly to its very foot and the pretty low-lying sheet of water winding along the valley.

Further confusion comes with the claim of Theophilus Shelton,[8] an obscure eighteenth-century character who is said to have designed a house in a Gothic style near Shiffnal for 'General Durant who was his own architect'. If the owner was in fact his own architect, then Shelton could only have been the builder and not the designer, but it is even more likely that Mr. Durant made use of Brown's plans and passed them off as his own.

WESTON PARK (Map 198), near Shiffnal, was the home of Sir Henry Bridgeman, later 1st Earl of Bradford who, while Brown was working for him, commissioned James Paine to design a Temple of Diana and a Roman bridge as features in the grounds. Both of Brown's contracts with Sir Henry are preserved at Weston,[9] the first being dated September, 1765. This included the making of a sunk fence to sweep round the south side of the house, and to be of a sufficient depth to 'keep out the deer'; the preparation for planting 'all the trees and shrubs that may be deemed necessary for ornament or use'; the old Square Pond was to be filled up, and the surrounding ground levelled and sown with grass or Dutch clover. This contract was for £765, the work to be done in the two

following years, and Brown's record of payments over this period agreed with the figure.

The second contract was signed in July, 1766, before the first had been completed, and was for £960. This covered the continuation of the sunk fence 'to the Triangular Elm Grove where the Dairy and Greenhouse were Proposed to be', also finishing the slopes and levelling the ground between the east avenue and the sunk fence, 'lowering the Hill in the manner agreed to by Sr. Henry', and continuing the drive from the hall door of the house to the offices, all of which was duly carried out, and much of which survives in fine order today.

Brown's contribution to this corner of the west midlands was completed with Weston, but in the east of Staffordshire he was to be kept busy for a long time to come. At TRENTHAM (Map 192) (Plates 48 A and B), near Stoke-on-Trent, he had been at work for some time, for although his surviving account book only takes up the details from 1762, it records that he had begun 'a fresh account at the Earl Gower's' in that year, the first having clearly been made soon after the submission of his 'Plan for the Intended Alterations'[10] in 1759. James Leveson, the ancestor of Brown's client, had acquired the Trentham property in 1540, when fragments of an Augustinian priory were incorporated in a house of which there is no pictorial record. This in turn was replaced *circa* 1630 by a mansion built for Sir Richard Leveson which was to be altered by succeeding generations until, by the second decade of the eighteenth century, it had become a rambling pile set in a formal layout of parterres and long straight walks stretching southward, one of which was carried on an embankment over an extensive lake formed out of the river Trent, before disappearing into woodland. This raised walk had gone before Brown came on the scene, but the angular lake was to form the basis for the irregular expanse of water, with a tree-covered island in its midst, which he was now to create. Few commissions provided at the outset a sizeable river – usually he had to contend with the difficulty of producing from some insignificant stream a sufficient flow to make a worth-while lake – but here he was able to take advantage of an abundant natural supply, and constructed a weir at the southern point where the river rounded a slight bend between wooded banks.

At its northern end, under the 'Intended Stone Bridge' marked on Brown's plan, the lake narrowed to flow past the house after which it divided, one arm turning westward and passing under two bridges before entering a straight canal. The other arm flowed under the 'Town Bridge' and northward across the rest of the estate.

In the Trentham Estate accounts are a few references to disbursements for the gardens and plantations from 1759.[11] Brown's own record begins in 1762 with his 'Fresh Account', when he noted that 'His Lordship [was] so good as to say he will allow the Expense of Repairing the water'. Following this there are payments of £200 in 1764,

when he was making a new drive to the house, £300 in 1765, £200 in 1766, and £300 in December, 1767, when Brown noted that after another visit to Trentham he had given plans for 'the Lodges etc.'

In 1768 Lord Gower married for the third time, and having already four children, produced four more, which may have contributed to his decision to remodel his house although Lord Verulam, who visited the existing one in 1769, described it as 'very extensive and well adapted to receive a large family.'[12] Brown had by now taken young Henry Holland into partnership, and together they planned the alterations of which the foremost was the re-facing of the south front where the long range of fifteen windows was divided into groups of three by giant Corinthian pilasters set on pedestals. The end bays were given pediments, between which a balustraded parapet extended across the facade. A new wing was added to the east, and the whole exterior was to be encased in white Egyptian cement.[13]

Work began in 1775 and proceeded slowly, Brown noting that he had received £100 for his journeys in 1777, and that in the following year he had paid over to Holland £3,000 for disbursements on the building work. Another £2,800 was similarly disbursed in 1779 and £600 in 1780, by which time the house was more or less complete.

As Trentham was barely four miles away from Josiah Wedgwood's potteries at Etruria, it is hardly surprising that he should have hoped to enlist Lord Gower as a customer for some of the jasper-ware tablets, intended for chimneypieces, which he had perfected in 1776. The Earl responded by acquiring a tablet and two friezes for the library at Trentham, and by interesting Brown in this new ware. As Wedgwood later reported to his partner, Thomas Bentley,

He [Brown] express'd his strongest approbation and even admiration of what he had seen. He preferred them greatly to sculpture in marble, and would make use of them himself as an architect when he had an opportunity and recommend them everywhere. He assur'd me of his real attachment to our interest from the merit of our productions, and desir'd we would call upon him in town at any time when we thought he could be of any use to us with his advice or anything else in his power. We had nothing to fear he said from the opposition of the architects, for such things as those must come into use when seen.

Mr. B. and Ld. Gower objected to the blue ground unless it could be made in Lapis Lazuli. I showed them a sea green and some other colours to which Mr. Brown said they were pretty colours and he should not object to those for the ground of a room, but they did not come up to his idea of the ground of a tablet, nor would any other colour, unless it was a copy of some natural and valuable stone. All other color'd grounds give ideas of color'd paper, painting, compositions, casting, mould-

ing and c. and if we could not make our color'd grounds imitate marble or natural stones, he advises us to make the whole white, as like to statuary marble as we could. This is certainly orthodox doctrine and we must endeavour to profit by it. This gentleman, if there is any confidence to be placed in the greatest apparent sincerity and earnestness, means really to serve us, and he gives for his reason – because we deserve it.[14]

The last entry to be noted by Brown in his own hand for Trentham was for £600 received in June, 1780, but after his death Holland, as an executor, noted that a further sum of £380 had been settled by Lord Gower in 1781. A decade later John Byng described the house as 'wonderfully altered from the grand to the modern,' while in the grounds he found 'my old friend L. Brown is to be traced at every turn: he certainly was a grand planner and leveller of ground – and a judicious former of water; the lake, here, is very fine, but above the house.' He added, however, that in general he thought Brown 'too severe upon avenues [which] if narrow, are charming, shady walks, and if wide, grand things.'[15] In 1838 Trentham was again to be extensively remodelled when Lord Gower's grandson, the 2nd Duke of Sutherland, commissioned Charles Barry to enlarge the house, and Eden Nesfield to re-introduce formal terraces and parterres. By the end of the century, however, the smell of the polluted river Trent drove the 4th Duke to the extreme of pulling down most of the house and removing himself elsewhere. The grounds, still containing much of Brown's work in the further parts, were subsequently acquired by the municipality of Stoke as a public park.

Early documentation for the re-building of FISHERWICK (Map 76) (Plates 47 A and B) by Brown for the 5th Earl (later 1st Marquess) of Donegall, is scanty apart from the former's account book which shows that he received on 10 March, 1769, £300 for work already in hand, after which large sums continued to be paid at regular intervals, reaching a total of £7,225 by June 1776. On the 26th of that month, however, another agreement was drawn up and of this the Earl's copy does survive to provide more details.[16]

The Fisherwick estate lay in the south-east corner of the county where the rivers Tame and Trent converge. It had been acquired by the Earl in 1758, three years before his marriage. The old house, of which there is an engraving in Plot's *History of the Antiquities of Staffordshire* (1686) was mainly Elizabethan, with gabled roofs and a courtyard between two wings at the rear.

At the time of preparing his first plans, Brown had not yet taken Holland into partnership, and the external alteration of the house was therefore his own conception. As at Croome, he made use of the existing foundations for what was to rise as a large Palladian mansion, extended by new ranges on the north and west to form a quadrangle

round a central court. The main approach to the house was from the Whittington–Elford road, the drive passing a lodge and gateway before winding its way first between plantations, then through open ground, giving views across the park and countryside to Lichfield Cathedral and the fir-tipped slopes of Gentleshaw. The main front of the new house was to present a striking giant portico, hexastyle and of the Corinthian order.[17] The end windows of its eleven-bay facade were Venetian, the remainder of those on the ground floor having alternate elliptical and angular pediments.

It is evident from the wording of the contract that Brown's first designs for Fisherwick had included 'Elevations, sections and designs as well as for the fitting up and elegantly finishing the Great Hall, Eating Room and Hunting Parlour', the latter probably being a large room in the north range which had two chimneypieces, and a door leading directly to the north entrance to the house. Other items mentioned as among the early drawings are the stables, brewhouse, granary and lodgings for outdoor servants, as well as paving for the courtyard, and the building of a barn in the park. This work Brown undertook to carry out 'With all possible expedition . . . in the most substantial and workmanlike manner and . . . with the best materials' for the sum of £9,406. There seems, however, to have been considerable delay in the early stages and much remained to be done at the time of signing the agreement of 1776, when Holland's arrival in the office provided help over the decoration of the various rooms. In the description of the hall there are echoes of that at Claremont, the former having marble pilasters and, between them, 'niches neatly stuccoed and painted . . . [with] Trophies in circular pannels over the doors', while the floor was paved with Roche Abbey stone inset with black Warwickshire marble, a description which is confirmed in the sale catalogue.

The principal rooms were set on either side of this hall, and of these the sale catalogue is valuable in giving details of their decoration. The first drawing room, to the east of the hall, had blue silk damask walls, painted ceiling panels, and superports, which were to become a favourite feature in Holland's later work. The second drawing, or music, room was also hung with silk, while in the east range was yet a third drawing room hung with 'rarest India Japan panels'. Elsewhere there were two dining rooms, two libraries and a succession of smaller rooms and offices.

The work in the grounds which the contract mentions as still to be done included the sunk fence and various walks. The Hademore and Tamworth drives were still to be finished, as well as some laying-out, levelling and ornamenting in parts of the park, and the construction of an arched underground passage eight feet wide and eight feet high from the house to the pleasure garden. As was usual in such contracts, the Earl had again undertaken to find the cut timber necessary for garden buildings and fences, and to provide Brown's men with wheelbarrows, carts and 'four able horses'

although Brown was responsible for the carriage of building materials used on the house.

The ample waters of the Trent were again to be used in the landscaping at Fisherwick where a lake was created before the north front of the house. Where it narrowed to fall in a cascade, a stone bridge was constructed, while further downstream was another bridge of timber. Across the water, on a high bank, stood a small Chinese pavilion. Beyond, in the park proper, a prodigious amount of trees, mostly oak with conifers interplanted as 'nurses' formed the plantations which were soon to become celebrated. Brown assured Lord Donegall that altogether one hundred thousand trees had been put in, which he estimated might in due course fetch £100,000, and in 1779 these earned for their owner a medal for planting.

In the spring of 1773 Brown was helping to find Lord Donegall a suitable gardener to take charge at Fisherwick; one called Turner, who had worked previously for Lord Bristol, was eventually taken on. Writing to Brown on behalf of her husband, Lady Donegall thought that the new man 'promis's to do very well by the character . . . from Lord Bristol who says you know him and recommended him.' She concluded 'My young family, I have the pleasure to tell you, are all well. [I] hope you and Mrs. Brown are the same, and beg my compts. to her.'[18]

So substantial a house and such magnificent plantations might have been expected to weather the storms of at least one century, yet within forty years both were sold up, following Lord Donegall's death in 1799. The costly fittings, described in detail in a sale catalogue of 1808[19] were stripped from the house and auctioned, after which the shell was demolished. The Chinese pavilion and the greenhouse disappeared, lawns returned to arable, timber was cut down, and only a set of pen-and-wash drawings made by John Spyers in 1786 survives with a few engravings to show how the place appeared in its heyday.[20]

TIXALL (Map 189), the property of the Hon. Thomas Clifford, lay a short distance to the south of Ingestre, and within view of the northern slopes of Cannock Chase, that long ridge of high ground which extends across this part of the county. Mr. Clifford, a younger brother of the 4th Baron Clifford, and a cousin of William Constable of Burton Constable – both clients of Brown – had come into the Tixall estate by his marriage to Barbara, heiress daughter of Lord Aston. It included a sixteenth-century manor house, altered by Richard Trubshaw in 1729, and the fine gate-house which still stands. Brown's advice was sought circa 1773, when he visited the place (although the exact date is not given) and prepared plans and elevations for the alteration of the house. The charge, he noted in his account book, would be twenty or twenty-five guineas, about which he wrote to Mr. Clifford on 8 May, 1774. As the house was pulled down in 1925, evidence as to what was actually accomplished in the 1770s rests largely

on the *Description of the Parish of Tixall*, published in 1827 by Thomas and Arthur Clifford. In this they record that the Hon. Thomas (they do not state their relationship) had determined to add a new house to the unfinished quandrangle begun by Lord Aston *circa* 1748. This new mansion duly emerged in Tixall stone, 'ornamented with a portico of four columns of the doric order'. The principal front was extended on either side by a screen wall, on each extremity of which was set 'a lion . . . from Coade's Manufactory at Lambeth.'[21] Although the carcase was complete by 1782, there was delay in finishing the interior which a few years later was 'fitted up under the direction of Mr. Samuel Wyatt of the Albion Mills'. It was ready for habitation only by the time of Mr. Clifford's death in 1787, he having lived in the intervening years in a few rooms formed into a residence within the old quadrangle.

In the course of the first stages of the work on the new house, some stable blocks and cottages 'which obstructed the Prospect' had been removed. Two ponds were filled in, a new flower garden formed, and the churchyard screened by 'judicious plantations', while a 'handsome stone bridge' was built to carry a new drive over the river Sow. In conclusion the authors of the *Description* state that 'In the progress of these improvements, he [Mr. Clifford] was assisted by the taste and judgment of the celebrated Brown, and his pupil Eames', the latter having apparently completed the final touches in the grounds after Brown's death at the beginning of 1783.

The year 1774 also saw Brown's first proposals for HIMLEY (Map 102) on which he had been consulted by Viscount Dudley and Ward. No doubt Brown had fitted his visit in with one to Tixall, but Spyers was sent there on 22 September and spent 'about 14 days' making surveys on which Brown based his suggested alterations to the grounds. His plan, initialled 'L.B.' and dated 1774, has recently come to light and is now in the possession of the Metropolitan Borough of Dudley (West Midlands). The account book shows that on 31 January, 1780 he received £500 from Lord Dudley, with a further £700 on 25 October, 1781, and that on 14 May, 1782 he passed on to Henry Holland £20 'for his journeys to Himley relative to the intended Building Business'. The house was rebuilt by William Atkinson in 1824.

1 K. Downes, 'Three Drawings for Ingestre Hall', in *The Country Seat*, 1970.
2 C. Fiennes, *Journeys*, ed. Morris, 1947.
3 Staffs. C.R.O., D.240/U/3136.
4 Bodleian Library, Oxford, Gough Drawings, a. 4., fol. 46.
5 H.M.C., Egmont MSS, St. James's Palace.
6 Preserved in the house.
7 Staffs. C.R.O., 590/368. Thomas White later described as a pupil of Brown, may have been a younger relation of the master mason of the same name who had a wide practice in the west midlands in the first half of the eighteenth century.
8 *Architectural Publications Society's Dictionary.*
9 Muniment Room, Parcel 17.

10 Staffs. C.R.O., D.593/H/13/1.
11 Staffs. C.R.O., Trentham Estate Accounts and Vouchers 1691–1815, F/3/2/33.
12 *H.M.C. Verulam, Northern Tour*, 1769.
13 J. Cornforth, 'Trentham', *Country Life*, 25 January, 1968, p. 176.
14 20 June, 1776. E. Meteyard, *Life of Josiah Wedgwood*, 1866, Vol. II, pp. 458–9.
15 28 June, 1792. C. Bruyn Andrews (ed.), *The Torrington Diaries*, Vol. III, p. 128.
16 Staffs. C.R.O., M/761/8.
17 Generally described as Corinthian, although the engraving in the sale catalogue of 1808 shows it as Ionic.
18 Pakenham Correspondence.
19 Staffs. C.R.O., Bundle 6, 115/41.
20 Preserved in the Salt Library, Stafford.
21 Probably similar to those ordered by Brown at about the same time for the bridge at Burghley.

X

LITERARY UNDERCURRENTS

B Y 1770 two authors had set to paper their thoughts on garden design, and had – presumably by chance – chosen for these dissertations almost identical titles. Thomas Whately, M.P. and literary critic, published in this year the first edition of his *Observations on Modern Gardening*, containing not only a lengthy discussion of current theories, but detailed accounts of several important examples in which Brown's works were well represented. Walpole's shorter and more generalised essay, *On Modern Gardening*, followed a few months later and in fact made reference to Whately's book. In it Walpole paid generous tribute to Brown, that 'very able master' by whose hand the landscape garden had arrived at its happy state. 'How rich, how gay, how picturesque the face of the country!' he exclaimed, 'Every journey is made through a succession of pictures; and even where taste is wanting in the spot improved, the general view is embellished by variety. If no relapse to barbarism, formality and seclusion is made, what landscapes will dignify every quarter of our island when the daily plantations that are making have attained venerable maturity.'

Two years later came the publication of William Mason's long poem *The English Garden*, in the notes to which the poet explained that he had used 'the general term *Gardening* for that peculiar species of modern improvement which is the subject of the poem, as it is distinguished from common horticulture and planting. – The Garden in my sense, and in that of the Poet, bears the same relation to the Kitchen-Gardener as the Painter does to the House-Painter.'

While Brown himself never ventured into print, there survives a draft of one letter in which he summarises his principles for the creation of a good landscape. The occasion was provided by a request received in 1775 from the Rev. Thomas Dyer of Marylebone, writing on behalf of a French friend who wanted to lay out his garden in the English style. Brown replied:

I have made a Plan according to your desire, as well as I could, from the survey and description you sent me, which I wish may be of use to the owner. In France they

do not exactly comprehend our ideas on Gardening and Place-making which when rightly understood will supply all the elegance and all the comforts which Mankind wants in the Country and (I will add) if right, be exactly fit for the owner, the Poet and the Painter. To produce these effects there wants a good plan, good execution, a perfect knowledge of the country and the objects in it, whether natural or artificial, and infinite delicacy in the planting etc., so much Beauty depending on the size of the trees and the colour of their leaves to produce the effect of light and shade so very essential to the perfecting a good plan: as also the hideing what is disagreeable and shewing what is beautifull, getting shade from the large trees and sweets from the smaller sorts of shrubs etc. I hope they will in time find out in France that Place-making, and a good English Garden, depend intirely upon Principle and have very little to do with Fashion; for it is a word that in my opinion disgraces Science where-ever it is found.[1]

On the back of his draft Brown wrote: 'Copy of Letter sent to the Revd. Mr. Dyer, June 2, 1775, to go into Frame with a Plan,' and their delivery in due course prompted a grateful acknowledgement. Mr. Dyer wrote on 24 June,

I am extremely obliged to you for ye Plan you have so readily and happily executed. Am struck with it much, and doubt not but it will please and give ye French a better Notion of Gardening and Place-making yn. they have ever hitherto had. Yr. Ideas of this noble Art I am vain enough to imagine, or rather flatter myself have always corresponded with mine . . . Yr. Architecture pleases me mightily. The Bridge will have a fine effect from ye House.

But I am only concerned about ye amends this French gentleman is to make you, for you know they are not over rich, these Messieurs, tho' they are call'd Noblesse, and are quite ignorant of what a value we in England put upon ye Designs of a Mr. Brown . . .[2]

Capability is unlikely to have thought of any remuneration from his old friend. As to the precepts put forward in his letter, while it is easy to regard them as a reflection of those qualities advocated by Edmund Burke's *Inquiry into the Sublime and the Beautiful*, that is, variety in shape, colour and texture, they in fact go back to Alexander Pope's edict that 'all the rules of Gardening are reducible to three heads: – the contrasts, the management of surprises, and the concealment of bounds,'[3] which the poet summed up in the lines:

He gains all ends, who pleasingly confounds,
Surprises, varies, and conceals the bounds.

These fundamentals are the essence of every Brownian plan, whatever its scale or situation, although their validity was later to be misunderstood or questioned by protagonists of the *picturesque* school.

While Walpole and Whately were occupying themselves with garden theory in 1770, Brown was taking some time off from that subject for some local duties in Huntingdon. Since his acquisition of the Fenstanton estate, he had become increasingly drawn into the orbit of the Earl of Sandwich,[4] whose home at Hinchingbrooke was only five miles away. It was probably through Lord Sandwich that Brown's name was successfully put forward for the office of High Sheriff of Huntingdonshire in 1770. No doubt he found, as other peers before him had done, that Brown made a useful medium in certain quarters. Their friendship, however, was of mutual benefit, and for Capability it eventually led to the opening of channels that enabled his eldest son to enter Parliament. In the meantime Lord Sandwich was to use his position as first Lord of the Admiralty to further the second son's first steps in his naval career. The only one of Brown's children to show a roving spirit, John was self-reliant and not afraid to argue with his father, and there had been an occasion when, home on leave, he had insisted that the journey from London to Exeter could be made in an impossibly short time. Brown, who was on the point of setting out with Lord Palmerston for Broadlands with relays of post horses, put this to the test, and found that it took twice as long even to reach Romsey. In a letter to Peggy that night he asked her to 'tell Jack if he is with you . . . that I will concede the sea to him, but the land he had better leave to me.'[5] In the following summer 'Jack' was at sea again and Lord Sandwich, writing to Brown on 11 August, 1772, was able to tell him:

> *The enclosed (which you will be so good as to return) will show you that your son has long before this time got a firm commission, as the Savage has been sailed above these two months, and is of course long ago arrived at her destination. I am allways happy when it is in my power to prove the truth and regard with which I am your very sincere friend.*[6]

Four months later Lord Sandwich was writing to Brown about some political manoeuvres in the constituency which his son, Viscount Hinchingbrooke, had won in the election of 1768, and managed to hold for over twenty years in spite of strong opposition:

> *I have seen some of your Fenstanton Friends and have received from them a confirmation of the good effects of your application. No candidate is as yet declared against us, nor have our opponents acquired any additional strength.*

As yet Lance had not been involved in politics having only recently completed his legal

studies at Lincoln's Inn. Within a few years he was to taste the excitements of party contests and, after some disappointments was successful, proving a useful ally for both Lord Sandwich and his son.

In spite of his Sheriff's duties, Brown still found time for three commissions in 1770, although one of them was so small and conveniently placed, that he probably fitted it in with his frequent rides through RICHMOND (Map 158) to Hampton Court, and no charge appears to have been made. However, the owner, Frederick Nicolay whose house was situated in Hill Street, made his request in such graceful terms that it deserves to be recorded:

> Sir [he wrote on 20 October], If you have five minutes to spare when you come to Richmond, I should take it as a great favour if you would give yourself the trouble to call at my house. I am in very great Distress and Trouble, which one Coup d'Oeil of yours into a large piece of ground of mine (allmost half an Acre) would soon relieve me from. I hope it is no offence to wish for a Miniature Picture from a Raphael.[7]

Although he described the house as having 'white Rails before it', and being 'next door to where Prince Ernest lived', it has not been possible to locate it precisely, although Mr. Nicolay's name occurs in contemporary Richmond rate books.

The commissions for RYCOTE (Map 163) in Oxfordshire, and HIGHCLERE (Map 97) in Hampshire were both of considerable extent. During the summer, Brown visited the 4th Earl of Abingdon at Rycote where the house was an important Tudor building of *circa* 1520, with later seventeenth-century formal gardens.[8] Brown's plan for altering the latter went into execution without delay, and in October Brown noted that he had paid out £288 7s 1d to the man in charge, James Hope. During the next two years he recorded several more visits to Rycote and noted receipt from Lord Abingdon of £50 in July, 1772 and £600 in 1773.

The Earl, to whom racing was a paramount interest, appears to have been the most easily satisfied of clients, giving Brown a free hand in the transformation of his grounds. As he said in an undated letter written from Newmarket,

> I pay so great Deference to your Taste, Prudence, and Judgment, that I never make the least Inquiry concerning the Improvements at Rycot, but shall always be happy to meet you there, or in any other part of the Globe. Transit [a race-horse] behav'd most ignominiously and lost what might have contributed considerably towards the adornment of Oxfordshire.[9]

In spite of this set-back, there was no apparent delay in settling Brown's accounts which by 1776 had amounted to well over £2,400. Lord Abingdon died in 1799, and within

a few years his successor, preferring another of his seats at Wytham, near Burford, decided to pull down most of Rycote. J. N. Brewer, writing in 1813, described the place as 'an extensive domain, desirably adorned with an alternation of wood and water. The mansion has recently been pulled down by order of the present Earl; but the chapel remains ... nor are the grounds yet disparked.[10] Part of the building was in fact retained and adapted to form the present house and a good deal of old timber also survives.

Brown's first visit to Highclere, near Newbury, was followed by a long visit from John Spyers who between 7 and 25 November, 1770, made full surveys both of the grounds and of the house. On these Brown in due course based the drawings which he submitted to Henry Herbert, later Earl of Carnarvon. These are listed as a general plan for the alteration of the grounds (charged at £40), a separate plan for the intended water (£10), and 'many plans for the alteration of the house and offices – a great deal of trouble to me' (£25). Spyers expenses were put at £52 10s which included copying an old survey. Although in this instance Brown was not responsible for the execution of his designs for the grounds, there is little doubt that they were used by Mr. Herbert's estate men for the splendid park which survives today. As to his proposals for the house, it is not possible to say whether any part of these was incorporated, for it was almost entirely rebuilt in an Elizabethan style by Sir Charles Barry for the 3rd Earl in 1839.

In 1771, when his term of office had ended, Brown undertook two more extensive commissions, both of which were in Lincolnshire. The first was for BROCKLESBY (Map 30) (Plates 59 A and B), where Charles Anderson Pelham, later to become the 1st Baron Yarborough, had inherited the estate from a great-uncle in 1763. Although Jacobean in origin, the house had been remodelled *circa* 1730 to a design said to be based on Buckingham House in London. Following his marriage in 1770, Mr. Pelham embarked on the alteration of the grounds, and later of the house. Brown's plan for the former was submitted in 1771. During the next year he re-visited the place for three days, making a plan for the more distant parts of the estate, including the ground 'round about the old Abbey', that is, the ruins of Newsome, many of the stones from which had been used for the foundations of the Jacobean house. Another three days were spent here in September, 1773, preparing a plan 'for the Improvement of Brocklesby Agreeable to the Building of a New House—[11] A great deal of trouble was it to me,' he added under this item in his account book. The latter project did not, however, material-ise and Brown was instead to make alterations in the existing mansion, including the east hall which rises through two storeys, with a deep coved ceiling, and plaster enrich-ments between the windows of the upper walls. Although much of the house was destroyed by fire in 1898, this hall was carefully reconstructed, but it is not possible

to identify any other rooms of his remodelling, although the 'offices' referred to in his accounts were probably the servants' quarters built as a single-storey extension to the north wing of the house.

Brown was at Brocklesby again in April, 1778, stopping at Wisbech on his return from where he wrote to tell Peggy that he had sent her some plovers' eggs. 'They were Boyl'd at Mr. Pelham's and packed in Bran. There is but a few, but it was all I could get'.[12] By now the plantations on this undulating wold terrain were beginning to make a show, and in this year he received £2,800 for his work, a further unspecified sum being paid in April, 1780, to balance the account. Much of his planting remains in the grounds immediately around the house, although some formality was introduced in the late nineteenth century with terraces and a canal before the east front. Further afield, the outlines have become blurred amid the extensive afforestation schemes which have been carried out since the 1920s.

GRIMSTHORPE (Map 85) (Plate 51 A) is in the south of Lincolnshire. Although the Duke of Ancaster's name had appeared among Brown's supporters on the petition of 1758, there is no evidence of Brown having worked at Grimsthorpe before 1770. It is likely, however, that he made changes in the grounds of the Duke's villa at Richmond during the early period. His first visit to Grimsthorpe was in December, 1771, after which Samuel Lapidge was sent there for several days to make surveys. In 1772 Brown sent the Duke 'a clean Drawing of the survey of the ground about the house and the oaks as it was when taken; also a plan for the alteration of the ground round the house and the oaks etc. etc.', with another for the 'boundary of the park and the fields taken into it'. Lastly came plans for 'the Water in the Bottom' and for 'a Sham Bridge to be placed at the head of that water the road to Grimsthorpe goes over'. To all of these there are references in his account book, but only two drawings have so far come to light, the very large plan for 'the park and the fields', and the design for the sham bridge, which was to be of eleven graduated arches in all, spanning some 350 feet.[13] The causeway between the two lakes, carried over a dam with rockwork arcading, is remarkably like Brown's project for the dam at Rothley but in fact appears to have been the work of John Grundy, engineer and surveyor, who was employed at Grimsthorpe in the two previous decades.

Although Brown noted that his charge for preparing the various drawings in 1772 was £105, he did not specify any sums for his expenses on the journey, leaving this to 'what his Grace pleases'. Nor was he to be responsible for putting the ideas into execution, this being left to the Duke's own estate staff. In the following year, however, Brown was to supervise work (perhaps a second phase to some earlier undertaking) at ANCASTER HOUSE (Map 157), a brown brick residence at the top of Richmond Hill built for the Duke in 1772, near the present Star and Garter Hospital. The items were

fairly trivial, Brown entering that he had 'paid out of my pocket to the labourers' £69 os 5¾d.

There is no evidence that Brown's northern commissions took him beyond Yorkshire in 1772, and there would thus have been no chance of visiting Cambo, but he was corresponding with his brother George towards the end of the year in concern about one of their sisters, who had run into financial difficulties over her farm in that neighbourhood. In a letter to his 'Dear Brother' on 28 January, 1773, George says that 'she will not hear of parting with her farm, tho' I can see no prospect she has to keep it but a bad one, her effects will not pay half her debts'. He had acted as surety for her in a loan of £30 so that she might get her crops in during the preceding autumn, but now she was in more trouble with a neighbour to whom she owed money. There is no hint as to how the problem was to be solved, but George ended on a more cheerful note with the news that all was well with his family, who sent their love, while he would be posting off 'a piece of hung beef' to Lancelot as soon as the weather improved.[14]

Fig. 6. Town Hall, Huntingdon

1 Pakenham Correspondence.
2 *Ibid.*
3 Rev. J. Spence, *Anecdotes . . . of Books and Men*, 1820, p. 260.
4 John Montagu, 4th Earl of Sandwich, Ambassador, Privy Councillor and Master of Trinity House. Walpole wrote that 'his passion for maritime affairs, his activity, industry, and flowing complaisance endeared him to the profession . . . No man in the Administration was so much master of business, so quick or so shrewd' (*Memoirs of the Reign of George III*).
5 Undated letter, *circa* 1770, Pakenham Correspondence.
6 *Ibid.*
7 Pakenham Correspondence.
8 As shown in Knyffe and Kip's engraving in *Le Nouveau Théatre de la Grande Bretagne*, 1714.

9 Pakenham Correspondence.
10 *Beauties . . . of Oxfordshire*, 1813.
11 These plans are preserved at Brocklesby.
12 Pakenham Correspondence.
13 Lincolnshire Archives Committee, 5 Anc. 5A 10/10a, and 3 Anc. 5/85. The former, endorsed 'L.B. 1772', is nearly five feet across. Earlier work on the lakes carried out by John Grundy is referred to in one of his notebooks, now in the Library of the Institute of Civil Engineers.
14 Pakenham Correspondence.

XI

DETRACTORS AND CHAMPIONS

WHILE IT WAS said that Sir William Chambers's jealousy of Brown was kindled by Lord Clive's rejection of his design for Claremont in favour of one by Capability,[1] it had probably been smouldering for a long time, and there is no evidence of any cordiality when each was engaged on royal works on either side of Love Lane at Kew in the preceding years. Chambers should have remembered that in 1765 he had been the successful participant in designs for Peper Harow, and that Brown's plan for that house had been turned down by Lord Midleton. The Claremont incident, however, brought about a culmination of his resentment which was unleashed in several scarcely veiled and unflattering references in his *Dissertation on Oriental Gardening*, published in 1772.

The bewilderment which this publication caused is understandable. Here was the respected and talented leader of the architectural profession, H.M. Surveyor-General, and Treasurer of the Royal Academy, expounding some extraordinary theories under the name of oriental taste and wisdom. No one would have disagreed that the principle of adding liveliness to the landscape was admirable but Chambers was in error in attributing to the Chinese the planting of deciduous trees in order to obtain varied colouring. It had been advocated by Burke in his *Inquiry* of 1756, and practised by Brown for even longer, while the idea of 'placing amongst them decayed trees, pollards and dead stumps of picturesque form' had been attempted by William Kent in Kensington Gardens and ridiculed by his critics, in the 1730s. To recommend that picturesque scenes could be obtained by the introduction of 'ruins of castles and deserted religious houses' when professional and amateur architects from Vanbrugh to Sanderson Miller had been cherishing old, or building new, ruins for precisely this purpose was foolish enough; but to commend to a generation that had given particular care to the building of orangeries and greenhouses the oriental novelty of placing rare shrubs and flowers in 'frames of glass, disposed in the form of temples or other buildings' called conservatories, was inviting derision. Even Chambers's

friend Archdeacon Robert Clive, to whom he had sent a complimentary copy, had to admit that, although grateful for the present, 'I may not perhaps, even after the second reading of your *Dissertation*, have been able to comprehend so as to explain to another your precise idea of Oriental Gardening; and how far upon the whole it differs from, for in some respects it seems to coincide with, the European, or rather the modern English style of gardening . . .'[2]

As to the more fanciful notions – the pavilions and walks 'occupied by the fairest and most accomplished concubines', the introduction of 'vultures, wolves, tigers, jackalls and half-famished animals' among the woods in order to present a scene of terror, and a general mixing-up of the seasons so that primroses and lupins are blended in a 'rich harmonious mass', these were more than could be taken seriously. The average English landowner, stalwart, hard-riding and practical, was quite content with foxes to hunt, and perhaps a 'menagerie' for a few monkeys or bear cubs.

The tilts at Brown in the *Dissertation* stick out like quills on a porcupine in such phrases as 'this island is abandoned to kitchen gardeners well skilled in the culture of salads', and 'peasants emerge from the melon ground to take the periwig and turn professor.' After contradicting himself in the matter of 'gardens which differ little from common fields, so closely are they copied from vulgar nature', and 'those which owe most of their excellence to nature and so cannot be improved by art', Sir William bursts forth in a final crescendo of indignation: 'Whole woods have been swept away to make room for a little grass and a few American weeds. Our virtuosi have scarcely left an acre of shade, nor three trees growing in a line, from Land's End to the Tweed, and if their humour for devastation continues to rage much longer there will not be a forest-tree left standing in the whole Kingdom.'

This at least must have raised a smile on the part of Capability, remembering the thousands of oaks, beeches and chestnuts which he had planted up and down the country. For the rest, secure in his unrivalled practice, he could afford to ignore the affront. The incident was not, however, to pass unchallenged. Even before its publication, Horace Walpole had read of the imminence of the *Dissertation* and wrote to Mason:

> *The newspapers tell me that Mr. Chambers the Architect, who has Sir-Williami̯ea himself, by the desire as he says of the Knights of the Polar Star, his brethren, . . . is going to publish a treatise on ornamental gardening; that is, I suppose, considering a garden as a subject to be built upon . . .*[3]

Both men were therefore ready for the book when it arrived, and Mason, considering it quite outrageous, set to work and produced a masterpiece of sarcasm addressed to the Knight of the Polar Star,[4]

> *by Fortune Plac'd*
> *To shine the Cynosure of British Taste ...*
> *O, let the Muse attend thy march sublime*
> *And with thy prose, comparison her rhyme;*
> *Teach her, like thee, to gild her splendid song*
> *With scenes of Yven-Ming and sayings of Li-Tsong;*
> *Like thee to scorn Dame Nature's simple fence,*
> *Leap each Ha-Ha of truth and commonsense.*

This poem, entitled *An Heroic Epistle to Sir William Chambers*, was published anonymously in 1774, and its authorship was at first disputed. There is a story that Colonel Barré called on Capability one morning, and, noticing the book on a table, exclaimed, '*This is too much! – too much indeed!*' Whereupon Brown looked at him earnestly and said, 'Upon my honour, Sir, I did not write it.' Then the rumour went round that it had been written by Walpole and 'buckram'd by Mason',[5] and finally Reynolds confirmed that it was from Mason's pen. 'His being found out to be the Author of the Heroick Epistle', wrote Mrs. Thrale, 'shews he has under that appearance of Coldness – a large portion of Fire and Pungent Satire; and I shall for ever esteem Sir Joshua Reynolds for finding out that he *did* write the Poem to Chambers.'[6]

Sir Joshua was not above having a joke. Some time after the appearance of the *Epistle* he begged Mason to dine with him, his nieces and a brother artist. Mason in all innocence accepted, and the brother artist turned out to be Sir William Chambers. Mason took it well, and reported the incident amid much laughter to Lord Harcourt. 'Well, now you certainly told Sir Joshua my dislike of a *witty* Society, for sure enough he did treat me with the reverse t'other day, and who should he pitch upon to meet me of all people but *Sir Wm. Chambers*. Of all *men alive*: comical enough! To ask *me* to dine with Sir William *Chambers*.'[7]

Chambers was not the only architect to be jealous of Brown; and James Paine, although he made one or two complimentary references to his work in the first volume of his *Plans of Noblemen's and Gentlemen's Houses*, included less flattering allusions in the Introduction to the second edition of 1783, where he says:

> *The great Vitruvius has enumerated the qualifications of an architect, and the catalogue is formidable enough to deter a man of a moderate share of modesty and abilities, from attempting to pursue its study; what surprizing genius's then must those be who are* born *architects? how much above every other order of men? but, as nothing is impossible with the great Author of nature, so we have seen a genius of this kind, who, after having been from his youth confined against his nature, to the serpentine walks of horticulture, emerge, at once, a compleat architect, and*

produce such things, as none but those who were born *with such amazing* capability, *could possibly have done; nor is the foregoing a singular instance (except in that of* birth); *there are many of the same, and other professions, who have suddenly commenced architects, and their works seldom fail of discovering the schools in which they prosecuted their studies.*

No doubt Paine intended that Brown should see these remarks, but the latter's sudden death while the book was in preparation, saved him that annoyance, and the challenge was taken up by two later writers, the first of whom was Humphry Repton who, in his *Red Book* for Panshanger, says:

In the dispute betwixt him and Pain[e] the architect, the latter seemed to have the advantage because Brown has left nothing in writing, but if we compare the houses built by each, we shall discover that Brown has left many good specimens of his skill while Pain[e] never built a house that was comfortable without great alteration.[8]

Brown's second champion in this issue was *Roger Shanigan, Gent.* under which pseudonym the elder Robert Smirke published his comments entitled *The Exhibition . . . at the Royal Academy* (undated but 1780). In this he says of Paine's introduction:

At times he endeavours to be witty, and would ridicule the architectonic Abilities of Mr. Brown, because he has presumed to build without serving an Apprenticeship. But his arrows are unwieldy, and pointed with lead. If they chance to reach their mark, they only give a dub against the celestial corslet of his Antagonist, and fall blunted. It perhaps may be impossible to receive from our mothers the knowledge necessary for a practical Architect; but Mr. Paine himself is the best example that can be produced to prove that, without natural Abilities, architectonic Breeding is of little avail.

More support was coming from James Wyatt who told Joseph Farington that he 'did not think Brown can any more be represented as a mannerist than great masters in painting may be – He had a peculiar way of thinking on the subject of laying out the grounds, and it was scarcely possible that it should not produce a style of his own. Many of his imitators have merely copied his *manner* and most of them his defects only but their imperfections cannot with justice be attributed to him'.[9]

The posthumous abuse heaped on Brown in the 1790's by Richard Payne Knight and Uvedale Price was, of course, generated by their participation in the Picturesque movement, in which Repton was also involved, but the unattractive character of Mr. Layout, 'designer in taste and gardening', in Joseph Cradock's *Village Memoirs* appeared in Brown's lifetime. Cradock, however, had the grace subsequently to admit

that Mr. Layout was based entirely on hearsay. When eventually he met Brown at Hampton Court, he was delighted to find him a most agreeable and unassuming man. 'I cannot,' he exclaimed to his companion Joah Bates, 'recognise an atom of the Capability Brown I have heard so much talk of'. Mr. Bates agreed but was surprised that they had not met before since Brown often stayed with Lord Sandwich at Hinchingbrooke. Later on Brown and Cradock were to meet at the home of their friend Professor Mainwaring, at Church Stretton, where Cradock remarked confidentially to his host that he could detect nothing of the presumption of Brown's having exclaimed, on completing the lakes at Blenheim, 'Thames, you will never forgive me'; or of another story in circulation at the time which credited him with saying to the owner of a particularly dreary estate, 'My Lord, there is nothing to be done here unless you plant one half of your estate and lay the other under water.'[10]

Early in the 1770s, while Chambers and Mason were letting off their literary squibs, Brown was proceeding with the original cause of the trouble, Claremont. Holland had been able to relieve him of much of the internal detailing, and the responsibility for subcontracting with the various craftsmen. Several of the principal rooms still have their fine marble chimneypieces, finely carved door and window cases, and enriched plaster ceilings.[11] Particularly elegant is the entrance hall, with its oval ring of scagliola columns set within a rectangular space, and wall panels of martial trophies in plaster relief, a design in which the then youthful John Soane, who had been taken on as a draughtsman, later claimed to have had a hand.

The Brown–Holland partnership was now to be cemented by more personal ties for towards the end of 1772 Henry proposed to his childhood friend, Bridget Brown. The first hint of their engagement comes in a letter from Mrs. Jodrell of Manchester, thanking Brown for a gift of venison, which the latter was no doubt able to obtain from time to time from the Hampton Court herd.

> The Venison came perfectly sweet [she wrote], was extreamly good, and has feasted me and my Friends. We drank your health as the Founder of our Feast, nor did we forget the rest of your family who always shair in our best wishes. I shall be glad of any occation [sic] of Congratulation. You have indeed set my dear daughters and myself of longing to know who the fortunate Swain is who will soon be blessed with your daughter's fair hand at ye altar. May Heaven shower down its choisest Blessings on them, and grant her that felicity she merits.[12]

The wedding took place at St. George's, Hanover Square, on 11 February, 1773. Apart from a dowry settled on Bridget, Brown made over to Holland on 3 March £5,000 in 3 per cent consolidated stock, a transaction confirmed by Drummonds Bank two days later.[13] The young couple took a house in Half Moon Street where their first child,

a daughter, was born in the following year. Later they moved into a house built by Henry in Hertford Street.

The decoration and furnishing of Claremont was more or less complete in 1773, when on 4 November Sir John Lambert wrote from Paris to inform Brown that the 'glasses for Claremont which I ordered at ye manufactury' were ready, but that as the makers had 'lost ye drawing with the measure of the severall seizes', he would not take possession until he was sure that they were right. He therefore sought Brown's help in supplying fresh dimensions.[14] By June, 1774, Brown noted that he had received £27,612 on account of Lord Clive's house and grounds, but for the latter there was to be no joy in his magnificent new home. On 22 November, in a mood of acute depression, he committed suicide. Brown's account book records that Lord Clive's executors made two further payments of £3,000 each in 1776 and 1778, but not without a good deal of argument and criticism for deviations from the contract drawings which had been agreed verbally between client and architect.[15] A small sum still remained to be settled in 1780. From 1774 the house was occupied successively by Lord Galway, Lord Tyrconnell and Lord Seaford. In 1816 it was acquired by the Commissioners of Woods and Forests as a country residence for Princess Charlotte and her husband, Prince Leopold. Later it became the holiday retreat of Queen Victoria in her childhood and early married life, eventually passing to her daughter-in-law, the Duchess of Albany who resided here until her death in 1922, when the house was sold. After private occupation for several years, it was acquired by its present owners, the Claremont School Trust, while the further part of the grounds, extending over some fifty acres, belong to the National Trust.

MOUNT CLARE (Map 161), Roehampton, built in 1772–3 for George Clive, and so-named, it was said, 'in compliment to his relation', was almost certainly a product of the Brown–Holland collaboration, many of its details following closely those of Claremont. Only a trivial sum of £200 is mentioned in Brown's account book under 'George Clive Esqr. at Roehampton' in 1774, and the building work is likely to have been entered in one of Holland's now lost ledgers.[16] Their client had acquired the property when portions of Putney Park were sold off in 1770. Mount Clare was enlarged and given a portico in 1780 by a Milanese architect then resident in London, Signor Placidio Colombani, and continued as a unique example of a country mansion in a London postal district complete with landscaped grounds and cows in its farm buildings until the 1930s. Only the house now survives, a lonely relic in the Roehampton Housing Estate.

COMBE ABBEY, in Warwickshire, and BENHAM, in Berkshire (Maps 49 and 21) (Plate 52B), were two undertakings begun by Brown for the 6th Baron Craven (Plate 53) in the early 1770s. Lord Craven had married in 1769 Elizabeth, daughter of the Earl of Berkeley, who bore him two sons and two daughters in the next ten years, but whose

later antics gave rise to much comment, and ultimately to separation.[17] Her *Memoirs*, published in 1826, were not always accurate, and one instance comes in her reference to Brown, of whom she wrote:

> *The famous man called Capability Brown was desirous of being employed [at Benham] but as he had already laid out twelve thousand pounds for Lord Craven at Coombe Abbey, I thought it unnecessary to be more plundered, and trusted to myself for adding to Nature.*

An undated letter from Lord Craven to Brown, perhaps of late August, 1770,[18] and addressed to him care of Lord Willoughby de Broke at Compton Verney, urged him to proceed to Combe, although he himself was unable to leave London for a few days owing to Lady Craven's imminent confinement. Once that had taken place, he could probably join Brown there, but in the meantime 'I have wrote to Watts who will give you the meeting and show you everything. All that I have further to observe,' he added, 'is that I desire you to exert yr. utmost abilities to improve the place and shall leave everything else to you. I hope you will not leave Combe till you have made a plan and estimate and that you will get the man you mentioned to me, and begin directly.'[19]

Work was in hand by September, 1771, Brown noting between then and May, 1774, payments amounting to £7,150. It is possible that in addition to the landscaping, he was also responsible for some minor internal changes, including the insertion of new chimneypieces in several rooms, which were carried out at about this time, but these are not referred to in his account. The gardens were altered again in the nineteenth century when William Nesfield re-introduced a formal layout.

The building of Benham was under discussion in 1773. At this time, on his periodic visits, Lord Craven stayed at an old house on the estate and from there wrote to Brown on 3 June:

> *If you can possibly spare a day next week, I shall be very happy to see you here, as I much wish to know your sentiments respecting this place, particularly the turning of the Road. I am more desirous of seeing you soon as Lady Craven wishes much to make some alterations here and to begin immediately, as I shall stay here only a month longer ... You will be sure to find me at home every day next week.*

At this point in the letter the name of one of Brown's Northumbrian friends turns up for Lord Craven ends, 'Mr. Shafto is here and desires his comps. and will be glad to pledge you in the Wooden Vessel.'[20]

The outcome of Brown's visit was a decision to build a new house, for which an estimate was prepared in consultation with Henry Holland, and submitted in September,

1773. This was to be of two storeys, nine bays across, and faced with ashlar. On the south, overlooking the fine landscape is an Ionic portico of Portland stone which originally carried a pediment, now replaced by a pierced balustrade, which is repeated on the roof where another storey has been added. Work began on the carcase in the summer of 1774, when the old house was pulled down, and allowances made for material from its walls and chimneys.[21] Having left the accounting for the building side of the work to Holland, Brown's own record of payments is presumably for the landscaping, and in fact is so marked in January 1776 (although in this instance the £2,400 received included similar work done at Combe during 1775). Earlier payments amounting to £4,500 in 1774–5 are marked as for Benham alone.

The grounds slope from the house, which is backed by thick plantations, to the river Kennet and retain that character of 'simplicity and beauty' on which a writer remarked in 1801, although there is now no trace of the 'small wooden bridge of three arches, built after a Chinese design' which he noted.[22]

The fact that his second home at Fenstanton was only ten miles from Cambridge meant that Brown was to see a good deal more of his friends in the University after 1765. Among the latter, a notable figure was Professor John Mainwaring, a renowned theologian, a Fellow of St. John's College, and a close friend of William Mason and Thomas Gray. His interests extended to painting, sculpture and music, but above all to embellishing his miniature estate at the foot of Caer Caradoc, near Church Stretton, to which he retired whenever his academic duties permitted. Landscape gardening thus provided a bond between him and Brown. Unhappily for both, they also shared the affliction of asthma, although their reactions were different, Brown never sparing himself in his long and arduous journeys, while the Professor was a complete hypochondriac, apprehensively studying the thermometer every hour and donning wooden clogs if there was any likelihood of having to stand on a stone floor.

Various schemes for the improvement of the buildings and grounds at St. John's (Map 36) had been discussed since 1765, when Charles Miller, first Curator of the Cambridge Botanical Garden, and son of Phillip Miller, the compiler of *The Gardener's Dictionary*, was asked for his advice on the latter. For this the College Conclusion Book recommended that he be paid two guineas, from which it may be presumed that his suggestions were as negligible as his recompense. Early in the 1770s, when the college had launched out on an ambitious project for encasing the first court in stone, the authorities were anxious to secure a scheme of comparable scale for the grounds. The chief supporters for this proposal were Professor Mainwaring and the Master, Dr. Powell, who shared the professor's enthusiasm for gardening to the extent of eventually bequeathing him £200 for further work at Church Stretton. It is therefore not surprising to find them consulting Brown, whose name first occurs in the College records

for 10 July, 1772, when it was agreed that the bank of the river Cam should be repaired under his direction.[23]

His plan for the alteration of the grounds was submitted for consideration a few months later, and there is a story in Nichol's *Anecdotes*[24] which sheds light on the circumstances attending its acceptance. Dr. Powell, it appears, called a meeting of the Fellows in February, 1773, and explained that in addition to the structural work then in hand, it was estimated that the execution of Brown's proposals would amount to at least £800 – a heavy burden in view of their limited funds. He suggested that there were probably many past members of the College who would be willing to assist if approached, and that if the Fellows saw fit to open a subscription, he would himself set it going with a donation of £500. With the generous Doctor's assistance the scheme went through, and soon work on the Wilderness, or Fellows' Garden, commenced. It occupied the site of an old bowling green and two adjoining rectangular plots previously called The Walks which, buttoned down with stiff little bushes, are shown on Loggan's map of 1688. In their place a lawn was laid, fringed with trees. Various changes made elsewhere in the College grounds during the nineteenth century fortunately left the Wilderness undisturbed and it remains a delicious retreat, enhanced by the inspiration of establishing, in more recent years, a flourishing colony of Martagon lilies beneath its lofty trees. There was to be some embarrassment among the Fellows as to how Brown could be compensated for his trouble, and it was eventually decided to present him with a piece of plate to the value of £50.

Soon after Brown had delivered his plan for the Wilderness, he had set off on a west country and Herefordshire tour, while the Professor, taking advantage of the summer vacation, had gone to Caer Caradoc where he was looking forward to a visit from Capability. Brown, however, found that his schedule was upset by having to spend more time than anticipated at Lord Clive's Shropshire house, OAKLEY PARK (Map 143), and had to let the Professor know that he could not come. In his reply of 21 August, the latter expressed regret, but hoped for another opportunity:

> *Tho' Fortune has so order'd it now, that you could not cast a look at my little mansion, she may be less cruel another year, and your kindness, I know, will ever be ye same. I am happy in finding that you think so highly of Oakley Park, because I have no doubt of Lord Clive's concurring with your opinion, and of your making it, rude and savage as it now lies, the glory of this county, if not of England itself... Two of Lord Clive's sisters are now at my house and my Lord himself did me the honor to call on me two days ago, but I was so unlucky as to be from home.*[25]

Whether Brown managed a visit to Caer Caradoc in the next two years is not recorded, but he was certainly in Herefordshire in 1775, after a hazardous journey in which 'the

post Boys were so obliging as to take me through a River that filled my Chaise with water.'

Scarcely back from his west country tour of August, 1773, Brown was off again in September to Yorkshire, taking in Brocklesby, Burton Constable, Harewood, Scampston and probably Temple Newsam. The journey had been projected during the summer, and early in July William Constable, hearing a rumour of it, asked him to call at Burton Constable (Plates 50 A and B) where he was 'quite at a stand' with the work then being carried out to Brown's later designs, that is, the South Courtyard block, with its embattled wall and arched entrance, and an extensive garden layout, the drawings for all of which survive. Brown apparently replied that he would come if he could, which drew another letter from Mr. Constable on 22 July:

> *I am truly obliged to you Dr. Sir, for your kind favor. Permit me to hope that the If is merely possible. Was I young and provident I would not press, but feeble and keen in my wants a year seems to me an age. Mr. Lascelles flatters himself with seeing you in September. By Lincoln I lie in the Road and most sincerely hope and wish you may think so.*

Brown must have told him that his son Lance was now a fully-fledged barrister, for Mr. Constable added:

> *Whenever I deal in Law, which by the way, I have often been subject to, the young Chancellor shall be troubled with my Grievances. A Graft from Genius cannot fail where so many Blocks allmost flourish. Indeed I long to see you and that you should see my poor country in its best Feather. I beg leave most sincerely to assure you that none of your many and great friends will more gratefully acknowledge the favor of your company.*[26]

Brown was to be at Burton Constable again in September, 1774, when he gave further plans, including one for a bridge; and at the beginning of September, 1778, when he wrote to his wife that he had arrived at Mr. Constable's *en route* for Alnwick Castle, having had 'a most shocking passage over the Humber'.

Sir William St. Quintin of Scampton (Map 166) (Plates 44 A and B) was one of the owners who, having obtained a plan from Brown, set about having it executed by his own estate workmen. Brown had visited the place in the autumn of 1772 and subsequently sent his proposals for the grounds. In the following spring he sent a design for the 'Bridge Building' and the cascade. The bridge in fact screens the head of the water, being solid on one side, while on the other four pairs of Ionic columns support the roof and the small central pediment. This superstructure is built over a low, three-arch

bridge, and the whole is a modest version of the Palladian bridge at Stowe. On 2 March, 1773, Sir William had written to Brown:

> *I have rec'd the favor of your letter with the plan inclosed for the Cascade, which I like very much: I am obliged to you for your enquiry after Scampston. I have made the sunk fence on both sides of the gate-way, which has a most charming effect. I have also fill'd the angle of the water at the west end, and have also made an Island where the water was too broad, and have widen'd it to ye north of the Bridge according to your Plan, which answers prodigiously well, for which I return you many thanks. I shall be in London some time next month, and will certainly wait on you. I beg your acceptance of some Yorkshire Hams . . .*[27]

The house was altered by Thomas Leverton in 1803, but the grounds survive much as they were when Sir William put Brown's suggestions into effect.

When Brown had mentioned to Mr. Constable in the preceding summer that his eldest son was now set on a legal course, there was no hint that the young man would later turn his attention to politics. By 1774, however, the idea had taken root – perhaps at the instigation of Lord Sandwich, although both the seats over which he exerted an influence, that is, for the town and the county of Huntingdon, were at this time filled. Brown junior had therefore to look elsewhere for a nomination, and for some undisclosed reasons chose to seek the patronage of Sir James Lowther for whom his father had landscaped the grounds of Lowther Hall in the early 1760s. Sir James's influence was by now enormous, and the notoriety attached to his electioneering methods in proportion, Alexander Carlyle describing him as a 'madman too influential to be locked up' and one who 'used every species of threat, fear, menace, and all the engines of distress and persecution' to gain his ends.

Whether Lance knew of his devious reputation before he sought the Baronet's help is doubtful. When Parliament was unexpectedly dissolved in the autumn of 1774, he was hopeful of being nominated for Cockermouth, unaware that he had a rival in the person of Walter Spencer Stanhope, a kinsman of Sir James, and equally keen to enter Parliament. Stanhope had been on his way to visit Lowther when news of the dissolution reached him, and he arrived to find that his host had only just returned from London. 'You are come in right time,' said Sir James in greeting. 'We have plenty on our hands, and *we want young men!*' Stanhope's thoughts flew to the vacancy at Cockermouth, and his hopes soared; then he found that he had a competitor in young Brown. Their mutual discomfort was no doubt a source of considerable entertainment to Sir James, who was in no hurry to choose his candidate, and let both his victims linger in an agony of uncertainty.

After weeks of suspense, Stanhope wrote to his uncle, James Spencer Stanhope of

Cannon Hall, in Yorkshire, 'The case stands thus. The Baronet has not said one word to me directly upon the subject. He has given me several Hints which may be all equivocal ... Everybody about him takes it for granted that I shall be one, and Brown, ye Son of Capability, the other; and I know he has said no more, if so much, to him as he has to me.' At the end of December the luckless couple were still on tenterhooks. Stanhope wrote to his uncle again:

> *Tomorrow morning is the day fixed for our setting out for Lowther. What to do, upon my word, I know not! Mr. Brown is equally uninformed who is the other ostensible man, and goes down along with us. One thing I know – that the Seat shall not be vacated till the next meeting of Parliament, a month hence; another whole Month of damnable doubt and uncertainty.*
>
> *I lose all patience and begin to wish it was all over and were lost, rather than in this state of tantalization. They say it is good to know all things. How well do I know the value of independence, and what a cursed thing it must be to wear one's life out in the Manner I have fretted away these last two months!*[28]

A fortnight later, Brown heard that he was out of the running. Sir James, Walter Stanhope wrote, had 'explained himself to Mr. Brown, who is now here, and has excused himself from bringing him in ... I may be chosen rather than him; but it is full as possible that I may be disappointed in the same manner.' In spite of his disappointment, Brown did not give up hope, but he had to wait for six years before taking his place in the House as Member for Totnes. His father's patience was to be taxed even further, for it was ten years before Sir James remembered to settle Capability's final account of 1771.

1 H. Walpole, *Anecdotes of Painting*, Vol. V.
2 28 March, 1774. British Museum, Add. MSS 41, 136, f. 14 v.
3 9 May, 1772. J. Mitford, *Correspondence of Horace Walpole and William Mason*, 1851.
4 The order bestowed on Chambers by the King of Sweden, on account of which George III allowed him to assume the title of knighthood.
5 Hill-Powell (ed.), *Boswell's Johnson*, Vol. IV, p. 315: 'One day at Mr. Courtenay's, when a gentleman expressed his opinion that there was more energy [in the *Heroic Epistle*] than could be expected from Mr. Walpole, Mr. Warton, the late Laureate, observed, "It may have been written by Walpole, and buckram'd by Mason".'
6 K. C. Balderston, *Thraliana: The Diary of Mrs. Hester Lynch Thrale*, 1942.
7 Lesser poets also had their fun at Chambers's expense, e.g. in *The Estate Orators* (1774) where there are the lines:
>   'Brown in quaint art whom Chambers may excel,
>   But ne'er could *capabilitate* so well'.
8 J. C. Loudon, *Collected Edition of the Works of Humphry Repton*, 1840.
9 J. Farington, *Diary*, 23 December, 1798.

10 Joseph Cradock, *Literary and Miscellaneous Memoirs*, 1828. Joah Bates, musician and sometime private secretary to Lord Sandwich, was also a Commissioner at the Victualling Office.
11 D. Stroud, *Henry Holland*, 1966.
12 Pakenham Correspondence.
13 *Ibid.* He also settled on them a house in Great Carrington Street. G.L.C. Records, Q/E, V. 51.
14 Pakenham Correspondence.
15 Clive MSS, National Library of Wales, Aberystwyth.
16 Destroyed with all his office papers after his death by his nephew, Henry Rowles.
17 After Lord Craven's death she married the Margrave of Anspach.
18 Lord Craven's heir was born on 1 September, 1770.
19 Pakenham Correspondence.
20 Pakenham Correspondence. Mr. Shafto was perhaps the nephew of Brown's early client, and by now his successor, at Benwell.
21 Soane Museum, copies of accounts relating to Benham, etc. in Soane Correspondence.
22 E. W. Brayley and J. Britton, *The Beauties of ... Berkshire.*
23 Possibly Brown had read Lord Kames's essay, *Gardening and Architecture* (1762) in which the latter observed that 'It is a sad truth that the young student, familiarized to the dirtiness and disorder of many colleges pent within narrow bounds in populous cities, is rendered in a measure insensible to the elegant beauties of art and nature. Good professors are not more essential to a college than a spacious garden sweetly ornamented, but without anything staring or fantastic, so as upon the whole to inspire our youth with a taste no less for simplicity than for elegance.'
24 John Nichol, *Literary Anecdotes of the Eighteenth Century*, 1812–15.
25 Pakenham Correspondence.
26 Pakenham Correspondence.
27 Pakenham Correspondence.
28 A. M. W. Stirling, *Annals of a Yorkshire House*, 1911.

A Sketch for the Head of the intended Piece of Water.
N.B. The Earth to be taken away from the Banks to give it this form and the Head to be made 25 feet wide at the top.

33a. ROTHLEY. Brown's alternative plan for the head of the water. *see page 137*
33b. ROTHLEY. Design for the 'grotto' bridge. Although the bridge carrying the road across the lake was built, no trace of the rock-work has been found.

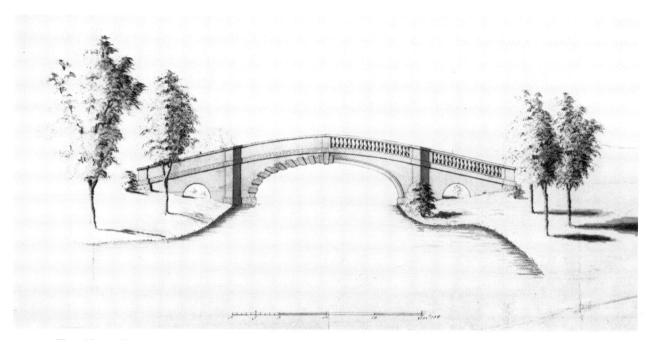

34a. THE HOO, HERTFORDSHIRE. Brown's unexecuted design for a bridge prepared for Thomas Brand *circa* 1762. *see page 229*

34b. PRIOR PARK, SOMERSET. Looking to the house with the Palladian Bridge in the distance *see page 236*

35a. CAVERSHAM PARK, BERKSHIRE. From an engraving. *see page 132*

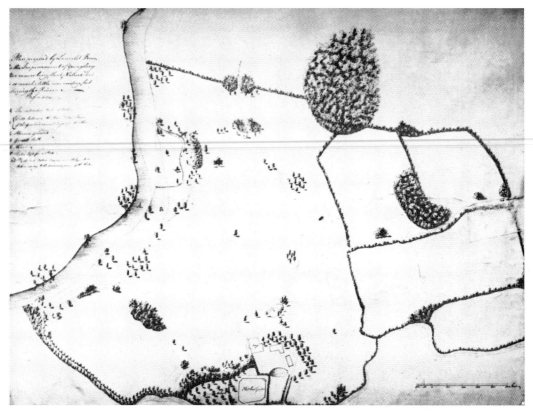

35b. YOUNGSBURY, HERTFORDSHIRE. Brown's plan for the 'Improvement' of the park.
see page 245

36a.
BURTON
PYNSENT,
SOMERSET.
Looking
towards the
Pynsent
column
designed
by Brown.
see page 135

36b. PAULTONS, HAMPSHIRE. A watercolour attributed to Brown. *see page 236*

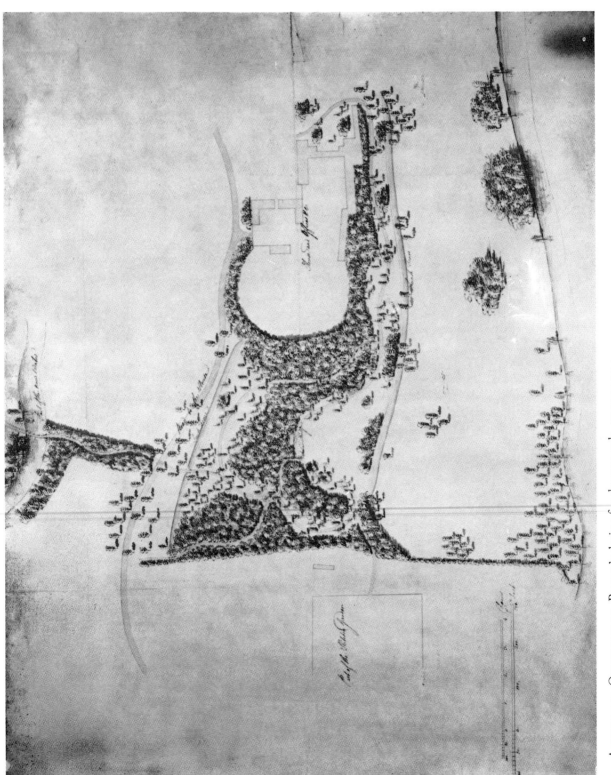

37. ADDERBURY, OXFORDSHIRE. Brown's design for the grounds. *see page 214*

38a.
COMPTON VERNEY,
WARWICKSHIRE. The lake
formed out of the earlier
mill pools. *see page 142*

38b.
COMPTON VERNEY. The
Chapel rebuilt by Brown.

39a.
WIMPOLE, CAMBRIDGESHIRE.
Looking north over the park
to the 'ruin'. *see page 140*

39b.
WIMPOLE. The 'ruin'
designed by Sanderson Miller
and erected under Brown's
direction. *see page 140*

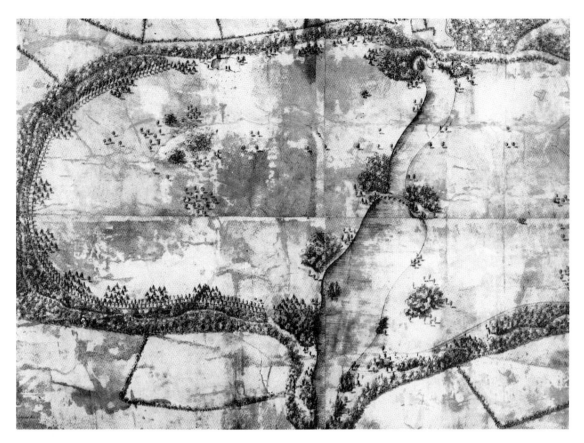

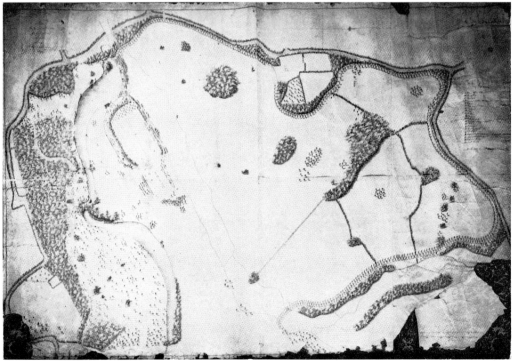

40a. WIMPOLE. Part of Brown's design for the park. *see page 140*

40b. ASHBURNHAM, SUSSEX. Brown's plan, dated 1767. *see page 118*

41a. ASHBURNHAM. Looking south-east across the lake. *see page 118*

41b. ASHBURNHAM. The Cascade.

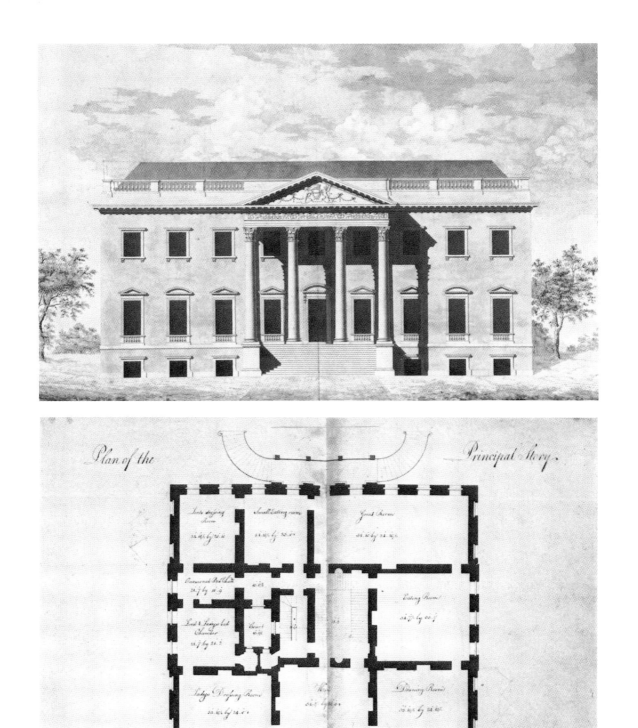

42a. CLAREMONT, SURREY. Brown's final contract elevation dated 1771. *see page 143*

42b. CLAREMONT. Brown's plan of the house, principal floor.

43a. CLAREMONT. The south portico with the Clive arms and supporters. *see page 143*

43b. CLAREMONT. The north front.

44a.
CLAREMONT. The
entrance hall. *see
page 143*

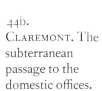

44b.
CLAREMONT. The
subterranean
passage to the
domestic offices.

45a.
CLAREMONT. The south portico with one of the giant cedars by which it is flanked.

see page 143

45b.
CLAREMONT. The lake enlarged by Brown.

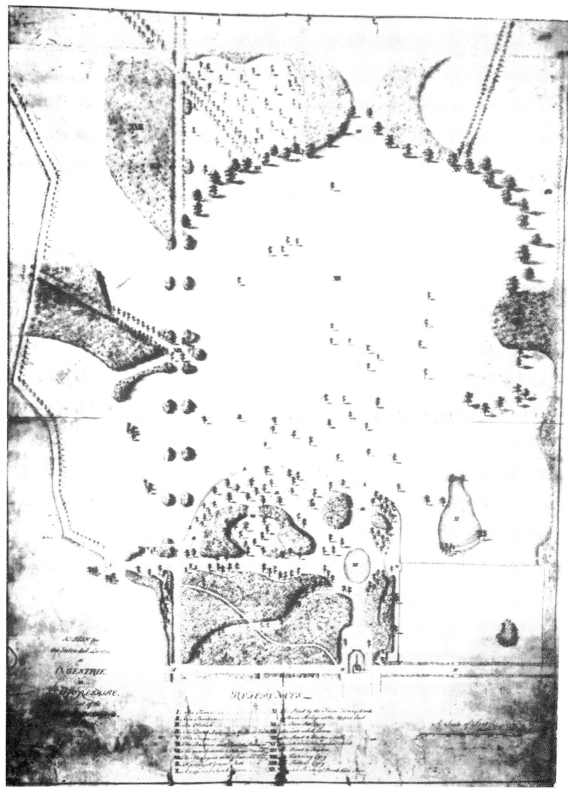

46. INGESTRE, STAFFORDSHIRE. Brown's plan, initialled and dated 1756. *see page 146*

47a. FISHERWICK, STAFFORDSHIRE. The principal elevation, from the Sale Catalogue of 1808. *see page 151*

47b. FISHERWICK. View from across the park, painted by John Spyers in 1786. *see page 153*

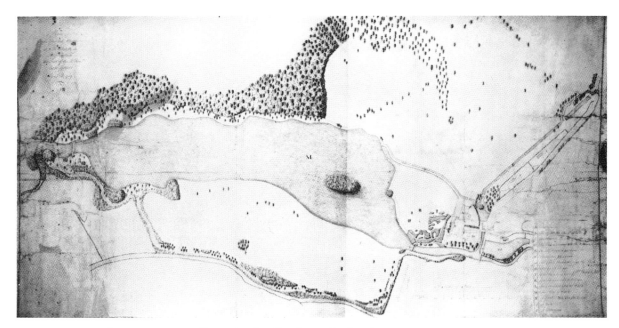

48a. Trentham, Staffordshire. Brown's plan for the park, dated 1759. *see page 149*

48b. Trentham. The house and Brown's landscape *circa* 1790. From a drawing reproduced in Stebbing Shaw's *History and Antiquities of Staffordshire.*

XII

SEASIDE VILLAS AND WELSH CASTLES

'I STAY'D WITH Lord Bute two nights and each Day we drank a bottle of Toka[y] wine which was rather too much for me as my cough has been very troublesome,' Brown wrote to his wife on 11 December, 1775 (Plate 63), and it was no doubt in this convivial atmosphere that the Earl told Brown of the various ideas which were then in his mind for a new seaside retreat. By the time the latter penned his letter to Biddy, however, he had left Luton, spent a night at FAWSLEY (Map 74) *en route*, and arrived at Combe Abbey, only to find that Lord Craven was away. During the day there was 'out of doors work' to be inspected, and in the evening he found himself sleeping in a guest room where hung 'pictures of King Charles, Bishop Laud, the unfortunate Lord Strafford, and some other man that they do not know. He looks as dismal as the others, on which account I conclude he was as unfortunate.' Being alone, Brown told her, he had been 'very much upon the Phylosophick strain', but 'a Day so spent is not one of the worst we spend and just to conclude it, I have entered into a conversation with you which has every charm except your company which will ever be the sincere and the principal delight, my dear Biddy, of your affectionate h[husband].'[1]

A month or two earlier he had seen the initiation of an important undertaking for the Hon. Robert Drummond, who had acquired an estate near Fawley, in Hampshire, and wished to build a house of moderate size on high ground overlooking the Solent. For this Brown and Holland collaborated on the design, and CADLAND (Map 35) (Plate 52A), as it was to be called, emerged as an elegant marine villa, compact in plan and simple in elevation, its two-storey facades devoid of elaboration other than a slight breaking forward of the three centre bays under a pediment. It was built of local white brick with stone dressings, the estimate for the carcase amounting to £3,050, while that for the 'Finishings' came to £2,574 9s 11d.[2] There appears to have been a quantity of woodland already on the estate which was to be useful as a basis for Brown's plantations in the grounds which sloped away to the sea on the east.

By 1778 Brown had noted the receipt of payments totalling £12,500 'on account of the building', with an unspecified balance still to be settled in January, 1779. Against

177

an entry for £100 received for 'Out of Doors work' in July of that year, Brown wrote 'see the letter about it', and this ties up with one in the Drummond archives in which he informed Mr. Drummond that:

> On looking over the Accts. I find you added for my trouble on the Out of Doors work, two hundred pounds, which is more than I can possibly accept of from you, by one hundred pounds, I having a reasonable profit in the Building on which Acct. I have annexed a Rect: to you for one hundred pounds on that of what is now doing at Cadlands . . .[3]

House and grounds were more or less complete by 1780, and by the end of that decade presented a scene over which William Gilpin was to write enthusiastically:

> Tho' quite plain, it is one of the most elegant and seems to me one of the most comfortable houses in the country . . . [the] abundance of old timber gives the house, tho' lately built, so much the air and dignity of an ancient mansion that Mr. Brown, the ingenious improver of it, used to say 'It was the oldest new place he knew in England'. The clumps he has managed with great judgment.[4]

Gilpin added that although many of the trees had been blown down in a great storm of 1781, those left 'adorned the natural scene and were just such as the picturesque eye would wish to introduce in an artificial landscape'. The original Cadland House was demolished for the building of the Fawley Refinery when the name was given to a modern house further south on the estate. This incorporated a fishing lodge by Brown and Holland.[5]

The second vanished house in this part of Hampshire probably emerged soon after Brown's talks with Lord Bute in the late autumn of 1775. Some eighteen miles south-west of Cadland, it stood on the cliffs above Christchurch bay, from which derived its name of HIGHCLIFFE (Map 98). It was said that Lord Bute had lost his heart to the site when after relinquishing office as Prime Minister in 1762 he then devoted a good deal of time to a favourite pursuit of searching for rare plants, which brought him to this part of Hampshire. Repton's list of Brown's works includes a 'bathing Place' for the Earl, but documentary evidence as to its building is scanty, and it has sometimes been attributed to Robert Adam although there is no mention of it among the Adam drawings in the Soane Museum or elsewhere. An engraving of 1784 in Watts's *Views of Seats* is accompanied by a caption describing it as 'a little Box', but in fact shows a house of considerable size, with two bays breaking forward in its long facade overlooking the sea.

Brown must have kept the full accounts for the building work in some lost ledger, but two brief items relating to it found their way into the surviving account book, under other work which he was carrying out for Lord Bute at Luton Hoo and South Audley Street, London. They record the receipt in February, 1777 of £140 in respect

of Highcliffe, and again, in July, 1778, of £184 to settle a balance due on this house. Into its gardens Lord Bute introduced many of the rare plants which he had found in the neighbourhood, while in the library specimens were mounted and classified to provide the basis for his nine-volume work on the different species of British flora.

William Gilpin was to be less flattering about Highcliffe than he had been about Cadland,[6] calling it a 'pompous pile' containing much 'curiosity', though he conceded that the situation was good. 'Lord Bute has made an attempt to adorn the cliff around him with a plantation', he added, but doubted whether it would flourish owing to the exposed position, but time was to prove his doubts groundless. After the Earl's death in 1792, the property was acquired by a Mr. Penleaze who rebuilt the house, but the new one was equally short-lived, and in 1830 the present Highcliffe Castle was built on the site by W. J. Donthorne for Lord Stuart de Rothesay, using a large amount of material brought to England from the demolished Hotel des Andelys in Normandy. Only a pair of lodges survive from Lord Bute's time.

The 'London House' referred to in Brown's later accounts with Lord Bute would have been No. 73 SOUTH AUDLEY STREET (Map 125), which the latter had purchased after selling his Berkeley Square mansion, to be re-named Lansdowne House, to the Earl of Shelburne in 1768. There are references to the extensive alterations which were carried out in one of Soane's early notebooks labelled *Copies of Bills*,[7] including external masonry and brickwork, as well as internal details, to the extent of £1,319 9s 9d. Brown's account book shows that he and Holland eventually received £3,700 for the undertaking. The house has been refaced and considerably altered. The fact that Soane noted these details suggests that he was probably put to work here while employed by Brown and Holland early in the 1770's.

While Brown and Holland were carrying out these works for the Earl, the latter's son John was created Baron Cardiff of CARDIFF CASTLE (Map 37) in May, 1776. As he is referred to in the account book as 'the Lord Mount Stuart' it would seem that Brown had been consulted before that event. He probably made his first visit in the summer of 1775 when he was *en route* for Dynevor, near Llandilo. Lord Mount Stuart asked for designs for the rehabilitation of a largely ruined agglomeration of medieval and later periods. As a preliminary, an extensive range of old buildings to the South of the Keep was cleared in this year. Early in 1777 Spyers spent some time at Cardiff measuring up the site and existing elevations, and in May Brown joined him. The resulting proposals were ready soon after. In the meantime Robert Adam (whether by invitation or on his own initiative) had drawn out a project for the Castle,[8] but one which could hardly have been seriously considered on account of its vast extent: the original buildings being duplicated and linked by a block of strange quasi-gothic form. Even to have seen it must have strengthened Lord Mount

Stuart's resolve to adopt Brown and Holland's design whereby the existing block on the west of the inner precincts was restored. This block abutted a long stretch of immensely thick Norman walling, from the west side of which rises the Octagon Tower built by Richard Earl of Warwick early in the fifteenth century. Four smaller towers project from the east facade, all of which were incorporated in the remodelling. A new entrance was formed on this side, leading directly into the old hall, a drawing room being built to the north of the latter and domestic offices to the south, with bedrooms on the floors above. Of two storeys and three bays each, externally these north and south additions carried battlements, but the windows were sashed, which later caused criticism from antiquarian enthusiasts. Within the Castle walls Brown laid out a sweeping drive, and turfed the ground, planting some small groups of trees on and around the mount of the Keep, and on the outer ramparts. The work went ahead without delay, and on 7 July, 1778 Brown noted that he had passed on £500 to Holland, with a further £3,000 on 11 October. There was another entry in 1782 for the receipt of £4,000 from Lord Mount Stuart, of which £1,000 was passed to Holland, but Brown's death early in 1783 ended these records, and any outstanding amounts probably went direct to his son-in-law. William Burges's drastic remodelling of the domestic range of the Castle in 1875 has left scarcely a trace of the eighteenth-century work.

Brown entered his account with the Rt. Hon. George Rice, P.C., M.P.,[9] under the name of NEWTON CASTLE (Map 139), although the mansion was subsequently renamed after the medieval castle of Dynevor which is a prominent feature in the grounds. Brown visited Newton in August, 1775, following which he gave plans, including one for the kitchen garden and garden walls. In February, 1776, he submitted plans for an 'Entrance to Newton'. The amount of the charge is not specified but he noted that the bill was settled in February, 1778. The park plan included the five fine clumps of beech which still stand, and the walk to the old Castle which still bears the name of 'Brown's Walk'.

It was following his August visit that Capability's itinerary took him on to Eywood in Herefordshire, and then to Staffordshire, where at Fisherwick he received a letter from Mr. Rice. This he answered after moving on to Trentham:

> *I was honoured with your obliging letter at Lord Donegalls for which & the great kindness with which I was treated at Newton Castle I return my sincere thanks. I wish my journey may prove to be of use to the Place, which if it should, it will be very flattering to me. Nature has been truly bountiful and Art has done no harm. My health which is not of the best kind but I assure you [is] not the worse for my Welsh journey. The Day I left you I was very ill. I found the Judges were at Hereford which determined me to go to Lord Oxfords & the post Boys were so*

obliging as to take me through a River that filled my Chaise with water. However I am thank God much better than I was when I was in Heriffordshire.[10]

For some time before 1776 Brown, no doubt fired by his success with the gardens of St. John's College, had been toying with the idea of further CAMBRIDGE (Map 36) (Plates 56 and 57) embellishment, involving the ground on either side of the river Cam between Peterhouse and Magdalene. Over the years individual colleges had carried out occasional improvements from 1725, when Charles Bridgeman had devised some new walks and plantations for King's, to John Fortin's alterations in the grove of Queen's, *circa* 1750, and some garden activity at Trinity ten years later. To Brown, however, it must have been tempting to think of their combined acres as potential parkland, with King's representing the mansion, while Trinity and St. John's could stand for subsidiary buildings, and the Cam be broadened in his mind's eye into a splendid lake. He must have outlined his thoughts to one or two influential and landscape-minded friends, such as Dr. Powell and Professor Mainwaring, who in turn persuaded the Senate to give their sanction for a drawing to be made.

It obviously took a considerable time to prepare, but when the vision eventually materialised in pen and wash it measured 58 in. by 30 in. In the left-hand top corner, against a decorative background of trees and rock-work, the inscription reads: 'A Plan Presented to the University of Cambridge for some Alterations by Lancelot Brown, 1779.'[11] While the scheme would have delighted the landscape enthusiasts, there was probably a good deal of misgiving among the more conservative dons on seeing this rather alarming proposal which took no account of the privacy dear to academic souls, or the petty rivalries to which colleges are as prone as any other aggregation of bodies. From his usual dealings with clients who were paramount in their own domains, Brown failed to see that the nobility of his conception would inevitably tread on a number of sensitive toes whose owners were united in little except their apprehension at the prospect of a communal pleasaunce. Even the offer of a young Duke who was up at the time, to open a subscription with £1,000, failed to rouse any general enthusiasm, and the scheme passed into the limbo of forgotten things. By 1814 the drawing had found its way to the University Library where George Dyer noticed it hanging in the entrance hall. 'The eye,' he observed, 'would certainly have been pleased with walks more winding, with a greater variety of trees, with something more of a winter garden of evergreens, and of light underwood near the river, and that without affecting to bring the Wye or Usk to these haunts, or obstructing the navigation.'[12] Elsewhere, however, he expressed the view that a distinction should be drawn between gardens and public walks, between a nobleman's pleasure ground and a spot to be adopted for the health and exercise of students or academic retreats; and that no doubt had been precisely the

feeling of those who had composed the Senate when the plan had been submitted. At the same time they had not wanted to appear ungrateful for Brown's trouble and followed the example of the Fellows of St. John's in voting £50 to be presented to him for the purchase of a piece of silver.[13] This materialised as a silver tray (Plate 64B) which can almost certainly be identified with one which, after descending in Brown's family until the 1960s, passed through a London saleroom and is now in a private collection. Made by John Wakelin and William Taylor of London in 1780, it was of oval outline with a gadrooned border, and bears within a wreath the arms of the University and the inscription *Ex dono de Academiae* Cantabrigiensis A.D. MDCCLXXX.[14]

In the mid-1770s Brown carried out work for Morrough O'Bryen, later 5th Earl of Inchquin, to whom the TAPLOW and CLIVEDEN (Map 184) estates had come by his marriage to his cousin Mary, heiress daughter of the 4th Earl. Closely related to the Earl of Egremont, Mr. O'Bryen had probably been acquainted with Brown through the latter's Petworth and Shortgrove activities, but the date of his own consultations is uncertain as the work is poorly documented. Capability's account book only takes up the story with an undated entry for 'Mr. Spyers' time and Expences taking plans of Taplow etc.', and a reference to his own journeys. Payments are noted in 1778–9 but the work had been in hand for a good while before that, for Mr. O'Bryen had not yet succeeded to the title which came to him in 1777 when he wrote an undated letter to Brown, asking him to be

> *so good as to remember my Plantations, and as I am entirely unacquainted with the method of proceeding, when, and how to begin, what Seeds Shrubbs and Trees are proper, and wishing it to be well and successfully executed, [I] shall be obliged to you to let me have a person to set us well to work.*

He added, however, that he realised this might

> *affront my own manager [but] shall not much regard his first chagrin ... When convenient I shall hope for your answer and much more so the pleasure of seeing you. I have passed this summer in Ireland and not long returned.*[15]

Although Brown received £100 from him in February, 1778, on account of work carried out to that date, and a promissory note for a similar sum a year later, there are no further details, but the '&c.' after Taplow at the head of the account suggests that it included the Cliveden part of the estate, and that the grounds of the latter may owe much of their present splendour to Capability's hand.

The activities of Sir Watkin Williams-Wynne, 4th baronet, in improving his house at WYNNSTAY (Map 210), in Denbighshire, began very soon after his return from making the grand tour in 1769, when he was still in his early twenties. In this year he

married Lady Henrietta Somerset, a daughter of the 4th Duke of Beaufort, but she died in 1770, and in the following year he married again, his second wife being Charlotte, daughter of George Grenville of Wotton.

Full of ideas for his property, Sir Watkin had obtained while in Rome a design for a new house from James Byres, but this was set aside, and in 1770 he added a 'great room' to the existing house, probably from a design by Thomas Pritchard of Shrewsbury, although Robert Adam was to supply drawings for the decoration of several rooms later in the decade.

In the account of his *Tour* of 1769 Lord Verulam had noted that Wynnstay was 'situated in a well-wooded park which has all the advantages that the genius of Mr. Brown, who is coming down here to superintend his works, can call for.'[16] Brown's account book only takes up the story from 1777 when he enumerates plans, sent in that and the two following years, for the house and offices, the grounds near the house, the water, the further parts of the grounds, and finally a new dairy. While the designs for the house were not adopted – it was eventually altered by James Wyatt in 1785 – those for the grounds went into execution, and he noted that he had visited Wynnstay each year up to and including 1782, by which time he had been paid £300 for the designs and journeys, the actual work being carried out by Sir Watkin's own staff. A further unspecified but probably small amount was settled with Brown's executors after his death. There can be no doubt, therefore, concerning his part in the transformation of the park which had been brought about by this time. But some thirty years later the editor of the Welsh volumes of the *Beauties of England and Wales* gave the credit for the plantations and the fine sheet of water to John Evans, a cartographer of Oswestry, under whose direction 'the waters of several brooks and rills were made confluent, so as to form a torrent; which dashing over a lofty ledge of artificial rock-work, covered with mosses and lichens, assumes the appearance of a natural cascade; and very similar to the much admired one in the Marquis of Lansdown's park at Calne [Bowood].' The explanation may be that Evans completed the few remaining touches after Brown's death, and that he, an acquaintance of the editor of the *Beauties of England and Wales*, was given credit for the whole work where in fact only a small part was due.

1 Pakenham Correspondence.
2 D. Stroud, *Henry Holland*, 1966.
3 This bears out the correctness of Horace Walpole's remark that Brown had 'great integrity in his dealings with those for whom he laid out ground, and returned money he had received on account if more than the expense he had incurred.'
4 *Remarks on Forest Scenery*, 1791.
5 Two drawings for the grounds stretching southward from the original Cadland House towards the sea have recently come to light, one in Brown's hand and the other with the initials of his draughtsman, John Spyers. They indicate the position of the fishing lodge now incorporated in the modern house.

6 *Op. cit.*

7 Soane Museum.

8 Sir John Soane's Museum, Adam Collection.

9 Mr. Rice was Treasurer to the King's Chamber, Lord Lieutenant of Carmarthenshire, and Lord Commissioner of the Board of Trade. He was also one of the Duke of Newcastle's political managers in Wales.

10 Archives at Dynevor Castle.

11 The framed drawing now hangs in the University Library, Cambridge.

12 George Dyer, *A History of the University and Colleges of Cambridge*, 1814.

13 *Liber Gratiarum*, 1772–1809.

14 I am indebted to Mr. David Udy for pointing out that the decorative inner border is of a design which he has not met elsewhere in this type of silverware. Possibly the serpentine line of tiny seed-like beads, housing in its convolutions formalised motifs of flowers and leaves was devised by Brown himself as symbolic of his art.

15 Pakenham Correspondence.

16 *H.M.C., Verulam, Northern Tour.*

XIII

WHIGS AND TORIES

REFERENCE HAS ALREADY been made to the work undertaken by Brown for Lord Chatham at Burton Pynsent (see page 135), but the friendship which the Earl had extended to him from his early days at Stowe was to continue over the years. In addition to those quoted in the Chatham Correspondence, other letters which passed between them, or between Lady Chatham and Brown, are to be found in the latter's own correspondence, and in the Chatham MSS at the Public Record Office.[1] While not in themselves of any great importance, they show the extent to which Brown was drawn into back-stage politics by those who sought to gain the King's interest through the medium of his Gardener at Richmond. One of the earlier letters shows that Brown was house-hunting for the Countess in the summer of 1767, at a time when the Earl was suffering from an acute attack of depression, and a change of scene had been recommended. Hayes Place, his much-loved house in Kent, had recently been sold to Thomas Walpole, but after Brown had made several enquiries as to 'things about Town in the Villa way that would do', Mr. Walpole consented to hand back Hayes, and further searching became unnecessary.

Apart from the correspondence, the gossips of the day recount numerous anecdotes about the Earl and Brown. Mrs. Thrale recorded hearing from Sir William Weller Pepys of their chance meeting at Staines. When the two men had dined together and were about to resume their respective journeys, Lord Chatham concluded, 'Go you and adorn England', to which Brown was said to have replied, 'Go you and preserve it'.[2] John Taylor's version of the story places the scene on the stairs of St. James's Palace, down which the statesman, crippled with gout, was painfully making his way. Brown came forward and gave him an arm to his carriage. 'Now, sir,' said the Earl after thanking him, 'go and adorn your country', to which came the answer 'Go you, my Lord, and save it.'[3]

Whether or not Lord Chatham and Lancelot Brown did exchange these particular exhortations on the threshold of St. James's Palace or elsewhere is of no great consequence. The fact remains that Brown's profound admiration for the Earl was

reciprocated by the latter's appreciation of his character and abilities, even if he indulged in an occasional mild joke about his rapid rise to eminence. He assured Grizel, wife of the 2nd Earl Stanhope in a letter of 1777,[4]

> *I will not fail to obey your Ladyship's commands by writing to Brown. I do so with particular pleasure, persuaded that you cannot take any other advice so intelligent or more honest. The chapter of my friend's dignity must not be omitted. He writes Lancelot Brown, Esquire,* en titre d'office; *please to consider, he shares the private hours of the King, dines familiarly with his neighbour of Sion [the Duke of Northumberland] and sits down at the tables of all the House of Lords, and c. To be serious, Madam, he is deserving of the regard shown to him, for I know him, upon very long acquaintance, to be an honest man, and of sentiments much above his birth. As he lives at Hampton Court, and has many calls upon his time, he may not be at liberty.*[5]

The nature of Lady Stanhope's enquiry is not revealed, but may perhaps have concerned the landscaping of Chevening, in Kent, which is set in a splendid landscape.

While his own political sympathies were undoubtedly with the Whigs, Brown numbered several prominent Tories among his clients, which on occasion led to his being regarded as a potential negotiator with the other party. One such occasion had arisen in 1771 when Lord Bute endeavoured, unsuccessfully, to gain Chatham's ear through Brown and John Calcraft. In 1777 Brown was acting as intermediary between the Earl and George III. Writing from Hampton Court on 3 May he reported:

> *In a conversation I have lately had [with the King] I was heard with attention. I went as far as I durst, upon such tender ground. My reason for troubling your Lordship with this, is owing to a conversation I had with the Duke of Northumberland. I told his Grace the state of your Lordship's health; on which he told me he would immediately wait on your Lordship. When he comes. I hope your Lordship will be well enough to see his Grace – no man is more truly devoted to your Lordship's interest than he is. There was a meeting yesterday amongst the **Lords** Rockingham, Camden, Shelburne, Grafton, Abingdon, Craven, etc.*
>
> *I hope your Lordship will excuse my officiousness, and believe it arises from the purest motives of love to my country, and being with the most convinced mind of your Lordship's character.*

No doubt the first conversation referred to was intended to leave the King in no doubt as to Lord Chatham's anxiety that an end should be put to American hostilities, a matter on which he was to address the House of Lords later in that month. However attentively the King may have listened to Brown's carefully chosen words, he was incensed

by the Earl's subsequent speech. 'Like most of the other productions of that extraordinary brain,' he wrote to Lord North, 'it contains nothing but specious words and malevolence.' Clearly Brown's good offices had suffered a setback; but in the autumn Lord Chatham again became the subject of a conversation with the King, and Brown was writing to the Countess:

> *I have had no opportunity of returning my thanks to your Ladyship for the agreeable news of the restoration of Lord Chatham's health. I can assure your Ladyship that I did not fail in putting it to the use I wished and meant to have it for. One part of it did inexpressible good: which was that of informing me, that you had wrote to your brother, 'for fear a newspaper description might alarm his Lordship'.*
>
> *To-day, and indeed many opportunities have occurred of late, in which I have had very favourable conversations [with the King] – no acrimony, nor ill will appeared. I was told, that Lord Chatham was perfectly restored; much conversation arose on the word restored. I was then informed, that his Lordship was to come up to oppose the Address for the Speech; I said, that it was very unlike Lord Chatham to declare he would oppose before he knew the subject. I was told the intelligence was from an enemy's quarter; but that quarter had it from Lord Camden, or in his channel. I then ventured to repeat what he had seen in your Ladyship's letter, that Lord Chatham was not changed in sentiment; that I was very sure what his Lordship had advanced was meant for the dignity of the crown, the happiness of his Majesty and the royal family, and the lustre of the whole empire; that I had always considered his Lordship in the light of being a friend to the whole, not parts of the empire; that he was a friend to correction, where it was necessary, but that he had rather have the rod kissed than make use of it; that some people have very much injured Lord Chatham in calling him an American, abstracted from the duty of a good English subject; because I knew, after forty years' experience, that no man loved his country more; indeed, nothing could be so strong a proof of it, as his Lordship standing alone, unconnected with party or faction. His answer was, that Lord Chatham had too much good sense to wish harm to his country.*
>
> *My opinion is, that we are in great distress; the bad news well authenticated, the good has had no confirmation. The court sal-volatile is Lord Amherst; who comforts them with a total annihilation of Washington's army, etc. Your Ladyship will be so good as to excuse this long letter, and take the will for the deed. My motives and wish are the happiness of the King and the country.*

Writing from Hayes, Lady Chatham replied on 13 November:

> *Neither I nor my Lord have wanted any assurance that your conduct respecting him, at all times, is ever dictated by your kind friendship towards us. The letter*

I have just received from you is an additional proof of it, and claims our sincerest thanks. It is impossible not to feel sensibly the animation of your conversation, in support of the rectitude of my Lord's principles, and of his zeal for the prosperity of the whole empire, and the true solid glory of his Majesty.

You may be persuaded that your having been 'heard favourably', and 'without acrimony', affords real comfort and happiness to my Lord; who is most undoubtedly actuated in all he does, or means to do, by the purest motives of disinterested concern for the King, and for the country. You know that this is not words, but an existing truth, to which his conduct has been always consistent. His view of things now tells him, that ruin *is at our door, if not* immediately *prevented. From the stamp-act to this day, his judgments, he says, concerning America, have never varied. In the present terrifying crisis, to be silent on the first day of the session would be want of duty to the King, and utter insensibility to the public calamities. The ardent wish of my heart co-operates entirely with his, that the past may be redeemed by happier councils. You join, I am sure, in the same honest hope. The sentiments of esteem and friendship which my Lord and myself have for you are of the most unfeigned sort; which I beg you to believe . . .*

She concluded with a postscript: 'The sal-volatile mentioned in your letter is, indeed, a poor cordial; and, considering the quarter it comes from, *astonishing*.[6]

How very real was 'the great distress' and the 'terrifying crisis' became apparent to government and opposition alike during the winter. There were repeated rumours that Lord Chatham was to be recalled to office. Strenuous efforts were made to reconcile his views with those of Lord Rockingham's adherents, but the hopes of his supporters were to be cut short by the Earl's sudden seizure while speaking in the House of Lords, on 7 April, and his death at Hayes on 11 May.

To Brown, the passing of the great statesman was a cause for very real concern, severing as it did their long and cordial friendship. He felt, moreover, an intense aversion to the American hostilities, 'so unfortunate and disgracefull a war', as he termed it.[7] His feelings on events in America were intensified by the fact that his sailor son John had been serving there since early in 1773, and had been engaged in several dangerous skirmishes. Letters from him were few, but there had been news in the autumn of 1775 when he had arrived at Boston in the *Nautilus* and wrote to his father on 14 November with an account of the tense atmosphere then prevailing. An attack threatened from 'the people who surround us', the town of Falmouth in Cases Bay had already been destroyed, and it was 'beyond conception how well they [the rebels] are prepar'd all along the coast'. In one encounter his own ship had been fired on, two men wounded and the sails damaged.

Three years later there was renewed anxiety, particularly in the months following Lord Chatham's death, when rumours were constantly passed around. Writing to his wife from Burton Constable on 1 September, Brown expressed his fears but could only 'hope we shall have better news from New York and poor Jack. Those accounts that came from there last in my opinion are very disagreeable.'[8] In spite of his worries, the war in fact seems to have had little repercussion on Brown's practice, and the policy of putting money back into an estate was still regarded as a safe course to pursue by Whigs and Tories alike.

A commission from a prominent Tory materialised in the spring of 1778 when Brown and Holland were consulted over the building of a new house, and the landscaping of its surroundings, at BERRINGTON (Map 23) in Herefordshire. The Hon. Thomas Harley, after an eventful career in the City of London, had decided earlier in the decade to stand as parliamentary candidate for Herefordshire where a second cousin, the 3rd Earl of Oxford, was then in occupation of the family estates at Eywood and Brampton Bryan. Brown had already visited EYWOOD (Map 72) in 1775, and may have owed to the Earl his subsequent recommendation to Mr. Harley. The latter, after an unsuccessful election in 1774, was returned as Member for the county in 1776, after which he purchased the Berrington estate and sought the advice of Brown and Holland. Although Brown was to concern himself with the landscape, he appears to have left the designing of the house to his son-in-law and the only relevant document present there today is an estimate in the latter's hand for 'The Several Works proposed to be done in Building a new House for the Rt. Honble. Thomas Harley . . . from the designs made by Henry Holland jnr. Architect, 1778.' As in the case of Claremont and Benham, this estimate is in two parts: that for the 'Shell of the House' being followed by the 'Finishing of the House'. As executed, it in fact echoes Claremont in several respects, particularly in its compact plan, its top-lit central staircase, and the entrance hall with martial trophies in relief set in panels over the doorways.[9]

'Mr. Holland sets out for Herefordshire tomorrow and I for Yorkshire', Brown wrote from Trentham to his daughter Peggy on 15 April, 1778,[10] and this was no doubt the time at which Holland made his first notes, but the work of building was to continue over several years, and the landscaping of the park was still receiving Brown's attention in 1780 when, after two more journeys himself, he sent Spyers to make a survey. Further work was in hand between July, 1781 and September, 1782, his account book showing that this cost £1,600, but no accounts seem to have survived for earlier stages of progress either in the house or the grounds.

The letter in which Brown had expressed his feelings about the 'unfortunate and disgracefull' war in 1778 had been addressed in August of that year to the 2nd Earl Harcourt who had sought his advice on NUNEHAM COURTENAY (Map 142) (Plates 60 A

and B) in Oxfordshire. The estate of Newnham, as it was originally spelt, had been acquired in 1712 by Sir Simon Harcourt but the family continued to reside at the old home at Stanton Harcourt for many years. In 1755 the 1st Earl decided to build a new house on the crest of a hill at Nuneham where the slopes, overlooking the Thames, the existing timber and the distant views over Radley to Oxford, presented ideal land-' scaping potentialities. The fact that a medieval village immediately to the north of this site had to be removed in the process seems to have troubled him not at all,[11] while a few years later he embarked with equal gusto on replacing the ancient church of All Saints with one in classical form, drawing out the first plans himself, and then giving them to James Stuart to knock into shape.

For the building of the new house, the Earl asked Stiff Leadbetter for designs which were under discussion in 1756, when Lady Harcourt wrote in October to her son, then abroad, about a 'design we have of building a villa at Nuneham, and not a seat, as was talk'd of: for beside the immense sum such a thing would cost, there is absolutely not a spot upon the whole Estate, as my Ld., Mr. Fanquier, and several others think, so proper for a house, as near the clump of elms, which you are sensible cannot contain a large building. However, I think the situation will make amends for the smallness of the building.'[12] In the following July she sent him full details with dimensions and was only prevented from sending an elevation because Leadbetter was too busy to draw it out. By December the walls were several feet above the level of the first-floor windows, but Lady Harcourt was having misgivings about the location of the domestic quarters. As originally planned, the laundry, brewhouse, etc., were to be detached, 'there not being room sufficient for them to be joined to the house, the hill dropping too suddenly to admit of it', but now it was decided to place these in low wings coming forward on either side of the east (entrance) front. This left the garden front with the appearance of a simple villa, three storeys in height, and with an angular bay in the centre.

The first landscaping was carried out to Lord Harcourt's own designs, and consisted mainly of thinning existing trees to create 'prospects' from this lofty site; he also devised a long north terrace walk, providing a vista and direct approach to the new church, which was completed in 1764. By 1772 the Earl's elder son George, then in his mid-thirties and imbued with reactionary ideals largely derived from his 'divine philosopher', Jean Jacques Rousseau, began to show an interest in gardening. Having gained the friendship of the Rev. William Mason, he prevailed on the latter to design a 'Flower Garden' for Nuneham. Mason, who was in the same year to publish the first book of his long didactic poem, *The English Garden*, had already supplied other close friends with similar designs, and now obliged Lord Nuneham. Having 'begged an acre' from his father, he proceeded to put it into execution about a quarter of a mile to the south-east

of the house, where it attracted a good deal of attention and favourable comment during the ensuing years.[13]

Lord Nuneham's gardening proclivities elsewhere on the estate had to wait, however, until 1777 when the 1st Earl met a sudden and tragic death endeavouring to rescue his pet dog from a well in the grounds at Nuneham. Within a fortnight of his succession, the new Earl was consulting William Mason on changes in the grounds, which were to result in the breaking up of the formal avenue between the house and the church into picturesque groups and views.

Up to this time the pleasure grounds at Nuneham had been confined more or less to the east, west and north of the house, but in 1778 the Earl decided to include about a thousand acres of land to the south. At the same time he required improved service quarters for the house, and more rooms for entertaining, having by now shed his early reactionary principles, and been drawn into Court circles and the gay social life which his wife enjoyed. During the summer Brown was summoned, but his visit was slightly delayed, and in August he was writing from Burghley:

> *I fully intended to have had the honor of waiting on your Lordship before this time but I was prevented by two causes. One was that of illness, and being with that and business, and the addition of hot weather totally exhausted; the other was that I had not a man to spare at that time to have put into execution anything we might determine. I am now at Lord Exeter's, on my way to the North, from which journey I mean to make Nuneham my road home again.*[14]

The alterations to the grounds did not pose any major problems for, unlike Blenheim or Croome, no great upheaval of earth or draining of swamps was involved, and the Thames itself was already gliding through the meadows below the house. What was required was a grooming of the old deer park on the east of the house so as to make a tree-sprinkled lawn; and the laying out of the new ground to the south. Here he set thick plantations, threading through them an undulating walk with vistas over the river, and enlivened with a small Doric temple of timber before it eventually opened out on to a plateau, where it was intended to have a gothic feature. This William Mason offered to design, but it happened that in 1786 Lord Harcourt was presented with the Carfax Conduit from Oxford, and this proved a suitable eye-catcher. Brown's plan, which survives,[15] is endorsed as for the 'intended Alterations at Newnham in Oxfordshire the seat of the Earl of Harcourt, L.B. 1779'. On it Mason's flower garden is shown as a small enclosure to the north-east of the house and church.

The poet was in fact consulted on Brown's proposals, and suggested a few minor changes. From their subsequent correspondence it appears that the Earl, who enjoyed baiting Brown, asked Mason to be present at the time of Capability's next visit, in order

that they might enjoy any display of irritation on the latter's part. Mason, however, was too gentle a character to relish the game of twisting Brown's tail, and wrote to the Earl:

> *I see plainly from your Lordship's letter that you wish me to be at Nuneham when Brown is there, that relying on my conciliatory and soothing arts, you may have the pleasure of putting him out of humour every moment and of treating him en grand seigneur, and yet for all that get all the good you can out of him, thro' the medium of my politesse.*[16]

Also participating in this somewhat infantile game was Lord Harcourt's other poetical crony, William Whitehead, once his tutor, and a constant visitor to Nuneham after his appointment as Poet Laureate in 1757. The latter had thought to add to the fun by teasing Mason: 'I long to have Brown find fault with some trifle or other in Mason's alterations; your Lordship at least must tell him [Mason] when you write that he [Brown] has done so, and it would not be amiss to magnify it a little, or put it into Miss Fauquier's hands if she should happen to see him in the North. I will undertake Mason's defence afterwards for I will not suffer him to be run down.'[17] Whitehead was, in fact, to admire the results of Brown's proposals and later composed a light-hearted pastoral on *The Late Improvements at Nuneham* in which Brown and Dame Nature contend with each other as creators of the scene.[18] It ends with the Dame admitting his superiority, when she 'dropp'd him a curtsie, and blushing withdrew', but consoled herself with the thought that

> *I may have my revenge on this fellow at last*
> *For a lucky conjecture comes into my head,*
> *That, whate'er he has done, and whate'er he has said,*
> *The world's little malice will balk his design:*
> *Each fault they'll call his, and each excellence mine.*

Walpole, writing to Mason on 7 February, 1782, reproached him for forgetting to tell him of Whitehead's verses on Nuneham; 'I am charmed with them. They are the best he ever wrote except *Variety*.'[19] Walpole had by then entirely reversed his first opinion of Nuneham, which he had described in 1773 as 'rough as a bear', although on the second day he had conceded that it was 'capable of being made a most agreeable scene'. Now he found it 'one of the most beautiful landscapes in the world.' The owner, too, for all his baiting of Brown was pleased with the results and Repton recorded that 'Lord Harcourt gives the whole merit of this [the flower] garden to Mason the poet, as he does of his pleasure grounds to Brown.'[20]

Alongside the garden work, gradually schemes for the alteration of the house were taking shape. One of the *References* at the side of Brown's plan notes the 'Place for the

intended additional offices'. The drawings for these, which have not survived, were prepared in collaboration with Henry Holland and put into execution in 1781, when the servants' quarters were moved to a new block beyond the south wing of the house. Both of the original wings were raised to three storeys, that on the north now accommodating a library and private suite for Lord and Lady Harcourt. A new top-lit staircase was made in the centre of the house, and the rooms on the lower level of the west side were turned into living rooms, with direct access to the garden.[21] Only a fragmentary reference is included in Brown's surviving account book, having obviously been entered in some other ledger, but the figures noted as settled in 1782 come to £1,700 of which £700 was passed on to Holland. By the autumn of that year the work was virtually complete, both on the house and in the grounds, and so they were to remain for half a century until Robert Smirke began his extensive alterations for Archbishop Harcourt in 1832.[22]

Fig. 7. Southill *circa* 1780

1 Pakenham Correspondence, and P.R.O., Chatham MSS, Bundle 24.
2 K. C. Balderston, *Thraliana: The Diary of Mrs. Hester Lynch Thrale*, 1942.
3 John Taylor, *Record of my Life*, 1832.
4 A second cousin of Lord Chatham through his mother, née Lucy Pitt. Charles, elder son of Lord and Lady Stanhope married in 1774 Hester, daughter of Lord and Lady Chatham.
5 W. S. Taylor and J. H. Pringle, *Chatham Correspondence*, 1838–40, Vol. IV, p. 430. The letter is dated only 1777.
6 Pakenham Correspondence.
7 E. H. Harcourt, *The Harcourt Papers*, 1880–1905.

8 Pakenham Correspondence.

9 D. Stroud, *Henry Holland*, 1966, pp. 52–5.

10 Pakenham Correspondence.

11 The villagers were duly re-housed more than a mile away in two rows of neatly planned cottages on either side of the Oxford-Henley road, where was also built a new inn with the Earl's arms on its facade. Although this new accommodation was a good deal more convenient and healthy than that which it replaced, the removal caused considerable repining, and almost certainly was the subject of Oliver Goldsmith's poem *The Deserted Village*, of 1770.

12 E. W. Harcourt, *The Harcourt Papers*, Vol. III, 1889–1905.

13 Mavis Batey, *Garden History Society's Journal*, Vol. I, No. II, February 1973.

14 *Harcourt Papers, op. cit.*, Vol. VIII.

15 In the possession of Lord Harcourt.

16 *Harcourt Papers, op. cit.*

17 Mavis Batey, *op. cit.*

18 Printed in *The Annual Register*, 1787.

19 J. Mitford, *Correspondence of H. Walpole and W. Mason*, 1851, p. 219.

20 *Theory and Practice of Landscape Gardening*, 1803, p. 215.

21 Mavis Batey, *Nuneham Court, Oxon: A Short History and Description*, 1970.

22 The Nuneham Estate was purchased from the 2nd Viscount Harcourt in 1948. After extensive restoration, completed in 1968, the house was leased by the University of Oxford to Culham College of Education. The history and development of both the house and its grounds have been the subject of considerable research by Mrs. Mavis Batey.

XIV

THE GENIUS AND THE BLUE STOCKING

ELIZABETH MONTAGU, 'Queen of the Blue Stockings', was well past middle age when she embarked on building operations at SANDLEFORD PRIORY (Map 165) in Berkshire. Her husband, a wealthy colliery owner and fine mathematician whose talents were overshadowed by Mrs. Montagu's literary proclivities, died in 1775, and shortly after his widow commissioned 'Athenian' Stuart to design her new London house in Portman Square. She then turned her attention to Sandleford, with James Wyatt acting as architect. The Priory was a house of medieval origin which, after many vicissitudes, had been acquired by her husband in 1730. Apart from the enlargement of the monks' stews into a small pond, neither house nor grounds were altered during his lifetime, but Mrs. Montagu's insatiable fondness for entertaining, which increased rather than diminished in her widowhood, called for more accommodation. Wyatt's additions consisted of an elliptical, domed drawing room, the 'Chapel Bedroom', and the conversion of the chapel itself, then in ruins, into a dining room. Mrs. Montagu called it her *reformed chapel*, 'for I think what has been taken from the owls, the bats, the rats, and mice to be dedicated to the sober use of sober society, and a temperate dinner preceded and concluded by a grace, may be rather esteemed, reformed and purified than polluted and debased.'[1] In order to bring the gardens into line with this embellishment of the house, she then consulted Brown, and together they planned the 'arched roof of twilight groves' which was to be formed immediately outside the great three-light window which Wyatt had inserted in the east wall of the old chapel.

If Mrs. Montagu found Wyatt an exasperating and dilatory architect, she had nothing but praise for Brown, and her letters have frequent references to 'my good friend' and his work. He first visited Sandleford in July, 1781, taking Spyers with him to assist in making a survey. 'He is an agreeable, pleasant companion,' she wrote, 'as well as a great genius in his profession. I consider him a great poet.' For his part Brown made a felicitous remark to Mrs. Montagu's sister-in-law, which was duly passed on to the old lady who, for all her shrewdness, enjoyed a little flattery. 'I am very glad Mr. Brown likes me as a correspondent,' she confided to Mrs. Robinson, 'for I am obliged to make

a very paltry figure to him as an employer. He is narrowly circumscrib'd, both in space and expense; but he really gives the poor widow and her paltry plans as great attention as he could bestow on an unlimited commission and an unbounded space. He has made a plan to make my grounds, in prospect of the house and new rooms, very pleasing and will execute as much of it every year as I choose, the expense being agreed upon, which will keep pace with the improvements.'

In July, 1782, she gave a supper to all the labourers then working under Brown's direction, of whom there were twenty men engaged on the wood and grove. 'They are poor weavers,' she wrote to Mrs. Carter, 'who by the decay of our manufacture at Newbury are void of employment, and not having been trained to the business of agriculture are not dexterous at the rake and pitchfork, but the plain digging and driving wheel barrows they can perform and are very glad to get their daily subsistence.' Another letter, written in December of the same year, describes Brown's transformation of the gardens into 'a lovely pastoral – a sweet arcadian scene. In not attempting more, she continued, 'he adapts his scheme to the character of the place and my purse. We shall not erect temples to heathen gods, build proud bridges over humble rivulets, or do any of the marvellous things suggested by caprice, and indulged by the wantonness of wealth.'[2]

Two months before, on 15 October, Brown had written to Mrs. Montagu from York, where he had stopped after a visit to Byram:

> *On my return to this Place today I was honoured with your letter which is an exact Picture of your mind, full of Compassion and good will to all; the Season has been such as I never saw before, and I am doubtfull the consequence of it will be tolerable to the Poor in many places. I am glad my Foreman has behaved in such manner as to merit your approbation. You inform me you intend staying till the twenty-fifth of this month. I hope and mean to pay my respects to you at Sandford [sic] before you leave it. Your sister does me honour in mentioning me. I am sure I was the gainer by having that pleasure. It seems as if you had parted with your young companions at a time when they are most wanted, but you have every resource that mortals can wish for, and may you long possess them is the sincere wish of, madam, your most obliged and most devoted humble servant.*[3]

As it transpired, this small but agreeable commission was to be cut short by Brown's death, but the work continued although, as Mrs. Montagu wrote afterwards, 'My pleasure in those improvements was mixed with regret for his death. Happily for me, he made a plan for all that is intended to be done here. As I do not allow my yearly expenses to exceed my yearly income, I go on softly; so that the plan will hardly be completed by this time two years.'

It was, in fact, just as the final touches were being carried out in 1784, that the peaceful flow of daily life at Sandleford was upset by a commotion which Mrs. Montagu later described to the Duchess of Portland, and which was caused by Brown's foreman:

> *The pleasure grounds and woods have been much improved and beautified by the late Mr. Brown, but a distress has arisen today, even from what usually produces great pleasure. The person under whose directions Mr. Brown's plan is going forward, has for some time given indication of madness, and yesterday, while he was ordering the workmen how to apply their spades, he fell on his knees and muttered prayers; he is now so wild I know not what to do with him. I am going to write to Mr. Lapidge, who is to finish [what] Mr. Brown began, to come with all speed to take care of this poor creature; in the meantime I dare not walk about the grounds.*

The victim, it appeared, had started life as a boxer who took to drink, and went temporarily out of his mind. When he recovered, he made every effort not to sink into bad habits again, drank nothing stronger than small beer, and was given a helping hand by Brown, who set him to superintend the enlarging of the pond and other work at Sandleford. On receiving Mrs. Montagu's urgent summons, Lapidge, then engaged on work at Chiswick House, set off for Berkshire. In her next letter to the Duchess Mrs. Montagu continued the story.

'All matters were prepared to carry our lunatic away on Thursday morning', she wrote, and she had proposed to recommend him for St. Luke's or Bedlam, but he had knocked down the men looking after him, and made his escape. 'I am under great apprehensions that it will be difficult to find him, for in his religious enthusiasm he fancies he must atone for his past offences by living like Nebuchadnezzar and it has been difficult to persuade him to sleep in a house, and he has endeavoured to eat grass.'[4] Enquiries were made in every village for miles round, but no news had come to hand by the time Mrs. Montagu's letter was dispatched.

Elsewhere, during what were to be his last two years, Brown was giving thought to a small group of works in Suffolk, the most important of which was a scheme for Heveningham commissioned by Sir Gerard Vanneck in 1781. This was followed by a proposal for a new building at Ickworth, where he had already altered the grounds in 1769, and some plans for Mr. (later Sir Charles) Kent at Fornham St. Genevieve. Brown's drawing for ICKWORTH (Map 105) was ready to be shown to the Earl Bishop of Bristol early in 1782, and the latter's brother, William Hervey, noted on 1 February 'Mr. Brown came and brought with him a plan for a house.' On the following day Sir Gerard Vanneck, Sir John Rouse and Mr. Kent dined there, and two days later Brown went over to Mr. Kent's house at FORNHAM (Map 78), returning to Ickworth later in the week.[5] Although his design for Lord Bristol, like those prepared by several other

architects for this client during the next few years, failed to materialise, the Fornham project seemed at first more promising, and Spyers was sent there in March to make surveys. In September Brown arrived again with Lapidge, subsequently submitting plans for the alteration of the house and a design for rebuilding the church which had been burnt during the previous summer. In the end these proposals, too, were shelved.

Meanwhile the HEVENINGHAM (Map 96) (Plates 61A, B and 62A) commission was proving more satisfactory. There his first plan for altering the immediate surroundings of the house, recently completed from Sir Robert Taylor's design, was put into execution. On this surviving plan, dated 1781, most of the objects listed in one corner can be identified although the peach house has disappeared, and the stables as built were not oval as shown. The site of the 'garden building' corresponds with the position of the present orangery, but the structure which eventually went up probably belongs to the architectural works which James Wyatt was to carry out at Heveningham soon after 1788.

The second of Brown's plans, some ten feet across and dated 1782, relates to the more distant parts of the grounds, and the 'Alteration and Continuance of the Water.' It proposed that the stream should be widened into a sizeable river crossed by two bridges, and followed for much of its course by the drive to the house. The scale of the 'river' as proposed apparently evoked criticism from the neighbouring owners of riparian rights, and was replaced by a more modest lake of irregular outline, fed by springs in the park, and crossed by one of his bridge-dams.[6] Brown's account book refers to his journeys and the preparation of the plans, but no sum is mentioned as he had died before completing the entries. Lapidge, however, endorsed the page with a note that Sir Gerard had paid the executors whatever was owing.

Other visits made in 1781 included Berrington, where the final stages of landscaping the grounds round the new house were in hand. Spyers had already been there to make surveys, and in July Brown noted receipt of a payment of £400 towards a total figure of £1,600 for the garden work; earlier expenditure was probably noted in Henry Holland's papers and subsequently lost. Plans for NORTH CRAY (Map 141), ADDINGTON (Map 2), and STANSTEAD (Map 174) in Sussex were others delivered in this year (see Appendix), while WOODCHESTER (Map 205), LLEWANEY (Map 122) and BYRAM (Map 34) followed in 1782. His Yorkshire journey to see the latter house was combined with another commission which presents a so-far unresolved puzzle. The entry for this is given in his account book under the heading 'The Right Honourable the Lord Stourton for STOURTON HOUSE in Yorkshire' (Map 179).

The title to which Charles Philip, 17th Baron Stourton succeeded on 3 October 1781, came originally from a family estate at Stourton in Wiltshire, but this had been sold by the 13th Baron several years earlier, when the nearby manor of Bonham became his

residence. The words 'Stourton House, Yorkshire' in the account can hardly have been a slip of the pen: Brown was certainly in Yorkshire at the time noted, and had visited Byram on the same journey before proceeding to York whence, on 15 October, he wrote the letter to Mrs. Montagu quoted earlier in this chapter. He noted, moreover, that Spyers had been sent to 'Stourton' and had stayed on the spot from 31 October to 4 December, making surveys.

In 1805 Lord Stourton bought an estate of Allerton Mauleverer, some eleven miles north-west of York, and gave it the name of Stourton. It is possible that he had already been living in that neighbourhood for several years in a rented property – perhaps Allerton Park itself – which he may have wished to embellish with an eye to purchasing it in due course. That does not explain why Brown should have called it 'Stourton' in 1781 unless his client had mentioned an intention of giving the property his own name. Although it was largely rebuilt in a gothic style *circa* 1848, fragments remain of the eighteenth-century house, and there are both stables and a garden temple which belong to the latter part of that century. Whatever the explanation of the Stourton reference, Brown's account for £69 10s was settled with his executors after his death, and John Bigland, writing in the *Beauties of England* (1812) described the grounds as 'charmingly picturesque, presenting a great variety of hills, dales and groves, delightfully inter-spersed. A beautiful lake contributes to ornament the scenery'.

Meanwhile, towards the end of 1781 Brown was to be confronted by a family prob-lem which arose when his younger daughter, Margaret, began to have doubts about an attachment which had existed for some time between herself and a Mr. Gee, and which had received the blessing of her parents. From their few surviving letters it is clear that although Brown was a fond father to all his children, she was his favourite, the 'daughter that I love dearly', as he told her. Although her mother addressed her as 'Margaret' in her letters, to her father she was always 'Peggy', and it was she who cherished not only his letters to her, but such fragments of his general correspondence as came her way, thus forming the invaluable collection which has been quoted extensively in these pages. Brown had hoped to see her happily married and was therefore much concerned when she confided her misgivings to him in a letter written from Hertford Street, while staying with her sister Bridget early in January, 1782. To this Brown replied from Hampton Court on 19 January:

> *I need not tell my dear Peggy the anxiety of mind her unhappiness has given to her mother and myself which makes me send her this letter with my Blessing and advice but with no commands. I pitty the feelings and distress of your mind. I wish to God it was in my power to alleviate and give comfort to you. You know your situation with Mr. Gee to which situation I have only contributed my wish and good will for*

your happiness. He you have made miserable and if this thing goes off you will be much blamed . . . I on comparing all things together hope you will find that the best thing you can do is to marry Mr. Gee. Remember my Dear Child that I lay no commands, that my wish is your happiness which that you may be is the ardent prayer of, dear, dear Peggy, your afft. father.[7]

On reflection, however, Peggy made up her mind that she could not go on with the engagement, and a sad Mr. Gee was given his congé. She had made no new attachment by the time of her father's death, but in 1784 married the man of her choice, James Rust of Huntingdon, a match which proved entirely happy.

1 Reginald Blunt, *Mrs. Montagu: Her Letters and Friendships*, Vol. II, 1923.
2 Blunt, *op. cit.*
3 Letter in the possession of the late Sir Eardley Holland.
4 *H.M.C., Bath, Papers at Longleat.*
5 *Journals of the Hon. W. Hervey*, 1755–1814.
6 Both drawings survive in the Vanneck family papers.
7 Pakenham Correspondence.

XV

'DAME NATURE'S SECOND HUSBAND'

WHILE THE SUMMER of 1782 had been as busy as ever for Brown, the weather had also been extremely wet. Walpole complained that he had been almost drowned at Strawberry Hill, and that the Thames was giving itself Rhone airs – 'none of your home-brewed rivers that Mr. Brown makes with a spade and a watering-pot.'

In compensation, December was mild and sunny. Capability was at Wilderness House, making plans for another journey to Suffolk as his old friend and patron, the Duke of Grafton, had asked him to visit Euston again. Hannah More, staying at Hampton Court with Mrs. Garrick, met him strolling through the Palace grounds one day and took a lesson in the art of landscaping. Later she wrote to her sisters: 'Never was such delicious weather! I passed two hours in the garden the other day as if it had been April with my friend Mr. Brown. I took a very agreeable lecture from him in his art, and he promised to give me taste by inoculation. He illustrates everything he says about gardening by some literary or grammatical allusion. He told me he compared his art to literary composition. "Now *there*," said he, pointing his finger, "I make a comma, and there," pointing to another spot, "where a more decided turn is proper, I make a colon; at another part, where an interruption is desirable to break the view, a parenthesis; now a full stop, and then I begin another subject".'[1]

On 13 January, Brown noted that he had received his usual quarterly payment of £500 from the King, and it was probably just after this that he set off for Euston Hall. By the beginning of February he was back in London, staying with the Hollands in Hertford Street from where, on 6 February, he went to call on Lord Coventry at his house in Piccadilly. On returning, he suddenly collapsed and fell to the ground so heavily that he died almost at once.

Walpole wrote off to break the news to Lady Ossory. 'Your Dryads must go into black gloves, Madam. Their father-in-law, Lady Nature's second husband, is dead! Mr. Brown dropped down at his own door yesterday.' To William Mason, however, he dropped his flippancy: 'Are you not concerned for the death of Brown? I made a

bad epitaph for him, which, if you please, you may recolour with any tints that remain on your pallet with which you repainted Fresnoy: here it is:

> *With one Lost Paradise the name*
> *Of our first ancestor is stained;*
> *Brown shall enjoy unsullied fame*
> *For many a Paradise he regained.*[2]

Into his notebook Walpole pasted a printed obituary notice of the man whom he had known for more than thirty years.

> *February 6, 1783, about nine o'clock, died Lancelot Brown, Esq., of Hampton-court, aged 67. His death was probably occasioned by a violent blow he received falling in a fit in the street as he was returning from a visit at Lord Coventry's house in Piccadilly to the house of his son-in-law in Hertford Street. For above thirty years he had laboured under a very troublesome asthma, and though he bore it with an uncommon degree of fortitude and good spirits, yet at times it reduced his life to alarming situations, and had lately prevailed so as to make him consider himself as drawing near that period, which he believed (with great strength of mind and resignation) as the price of a future state of perfect happiness. His great and fine genius stood unrivalled, and it was the peculiar felicity of it that it was allowed by all ranks and degrees of society in this country, and by many noble and great personages in other countries. Those who knew him best, or practised near him, were not able to determine whether the quickness of his eye, or its correctness, were most to be admired. It was comprehensive and elegant, and perhaps it may be said never to have failed him. Such, however, was the effect of his genius that when he was the happiest man, he will be least remembered; so closely did he copy nature that his works will be mistaken.*
>
> *His truth, his integrity, and his good humour, were very effectual, and will hold a place in the memory of his friends, more likely to continue, though not less to be esteemed.*[3]

So died one of the most remarkable characters of the eighteenth century, a man of few enemies and many friends; whose list of employers reads like Debrett; whom Walpole described as having 'wit, learning and great integrity';[4] who after thirty years of work in this country could afford to refuse the Duke of Leinster's offer of £1,000 on landing if only he would go to Ireland, excusing himself on the grounds that 'he had not yet finished England.' It seems, however, that even if he did not himself set foot on Irish soil, he supplied Lord Conyngham with designs for alterations at Slane. (See List of Works under 'Ireland', page 246.)

'I certainly held him very high as an artist,' Lord Coventry wrote to Humphry Repton some years later, 'and esteemed him as a most sincere friend. In spite of detraction, his works will ever speak for him. I write from a house which he built for me which, without any pretension to architecture, is, perhaps, a model for every internal and domestic convenience. I may be partial to my place at Croome, which was entirely his creation, and, I believe, originally as hopeless a spot as any in the island.'[5]

The Earl was to be consulted by Brown's son Lancelot over the epitaph which it was proposed to inscribe on his monument in Fenstanton Church. 'The great friendship your Lordship honor'd my father with, when living, convinces me that every tribute paid to his memory will be acceptable to your Lordship,' he wrote on 27 November, adding 'The lines I send are the product of Mr. Mason's pen.' They were duly incorporated in the memorial panel set against the chancel wall where the inscription reads:

Lancelot Brown Esq. died Feb. 6, 1783, aged 67 years

Ye sons of elegance, who truly taste
The simple charms that genuine art supplies,
Come from the sylvan scene his genius grac'd
And offer here your tributary sighs
But know that more than genius slumbers here.
Virtues were his, which arts best powers transcend.
Come, ye superior train, who these revere
And weep the Christian, Husband, Father, Friend.

In the years to come, it was the writer of the obituary notice preserved by Walpole who proved correct in his prophecy. By the time Brown's gardens and parks had reached maturity, their creator was almost forgotten. Ungrateful posterity, taking so much of the English landscape for granted, has remembered him only for his curious nickname or as the *destroyer* of formal gardens.

With his death, Bridget Brown had to leave Wilderness House and went to live in Kensington where the four remaining years of her life were cheered by her children, grandchildren and many friends. She died on 24 June, 1786, and was buried at Fenstanton near her husband, where her three sons and Lance's wife Frances were eventually to be interred with them.

Brown had made his will on 26 March, 1779,[6] recommending his soul to his Creator, and desiring his body to be committed to the earth at the direction of his executors. Any uncompleted contracts were to be carried out by Samuel Lapidge 'who knows my accounts', and who for this work was to be given one hundred guineas over and above his wages. As well as an annuity of four hundred pounds a year, and an outright sum

of a thousand pounds, his wife was to receive all his household goods and furniture, books, plate, china, linen, jewels, rings, watches, snuff boxes, prints and pictures, as well as his chariot or coach, two coach horses, and a saddle horse. Lancelot was left four thousand pounds clear, three thousand to purchase a house for himself in London, and all Capability's instruments. Bridget, who had received her dowry on her marriage to Henry Holland, was left a thousand pounds and, 'as I wish her to believe I love her with unchangeable affection', a flat silver candlestick which she had been promised. His second son, John, 'in His Majesty's Navy whom God preserve in his hazardous employment,' received two thousand five hundred pounds, while Margaret and Thomas were to have six thousand pounds each. To his 'men and maid servants' Brown left a year's wages, with an extra £20 and £10 to the two men William and George Davis. There were several bequests to other friends and relatives, including £100 to his brother George Brown, £10 for a mourning ring to his wife's brother, John Wayet, and £100 to her niece Phillis Cooke. His sister Mary Hudson, his 'good friends' John Edison of Cooper's Hall, and the elder Henry Holland are also mentioned. After his death it was found that, either by chance or some presentiment, Brown had written a brief codicil to his will on the previous day. This codicil, the authenticity of which was later testified by his executors, made a few minor changes from which it is evident that the children of his brother George were by now all dead, but that George himself and their sister Mary were still alive. The residue of the estate was put into trust.

By 1783 John Brown, as well as Bridget, was married, his wife being Mary, ninth child of John Linton of Freiston Priory. He subsequently rose to the rank of Admiral of the Blue, and died at Bath on 3 May, 1808.

Lancelot junior, having represented Totnes in Parliament for four years, went abroad in the year following his father's death and made a longish stay in Lausanne. There he met and married Frances Fuller, sister of Rose Fuller of Rose Hall, Sussex. The Browns were still at Lausanne when Charles James Fox arrived on his way through Switzerland, and Lancelot wrote to Lord Sandwich that they had spent two very pleasant days together. On their return to England, Brown was nominated by the Earl as Tory Member for the Borough of Huntingdon,[7] but when the latter required this seat for another candidate to whom he was under an obligation, Brown applied for the Stewardship of the Chiltern Hundreds. Later he drew Lord Sandwich's attention to his promise to nominate him for the General Election of 1790, but it was not to be fulfilled until 1792, when the Earl's heir, Viscount Hinchingbrooke, was called to the House of Lords on the death of his father. The seat was hotly contested by Lord Carysfort, who was probably responsible for a scurrilous handbill printed over the pseudonym 'Verax', and circulated shortly before the election. In this voters were besought not to return 'a person who (from his youth up even until now) has been the tool of a neighbouring

Peer, and who can never have any *Capability* to render them even the slightest service, being literally a meer *mushroom* sprung from a Dung-hill in Stowe-gardens'. The mushroom, however, proved to be more popular than Verax anticipated, and for the next two years kept this seat warm, until 1794 when Lord Sandwich's heir came of age. Brown then applied again for the Stewardship of the Chiltern Hundreds. By a warrant issued on 28 January, 1795, Brown was sworn in as a Gentleman of the King's Privy Chamber,[8] an office which he held until his death in 1802.

Margaret Brown married James Rust of Huntingdon on 29 September, 1788, and produced a family of two sons and three daughters. Her youngest brother Thomas, who had entered the Church, married Susannah, daughter of the Rev. Samuel Dickens, and had two sons and one daughter. The elder of these sons, another Lancelot, also became a parson and was a great pluralist, being Rector of Kelsale, Carlton, Thornyton and Saxmundham at the same time. It is said that he was fond of driving a four-in-hand coach, and was a noted *bon viveur*, after whom a brand of sherry was named the 'L.R.B.'. A letter from the elder Thomas Brown, son of Capability, written from Conington on 5 September, 1810, to Sir Joseph Banks reminds him that they had met sometime before at Woburn and Holkham, and that his father was 'an old friend' of Banks.[9] Thomas's elder brother, Lance, was also a correspondent of Sir Joseph. Many years earlier (19 January, 1778) Lance wrote to him from Hampton Court enclosing an inscription to the memory of Sir Robert Worsley, Baronet (d. 1747) which he had copied from a monument at Appuldurcombe in the Isle of Wight. While there, Lancelot added, he had not succeeded in finding a rock ousel for Sir Joseph, but had asked Sir Richard Worsley's keeper to send the first one he shot. Capability himself was to give Sir Richard Worsley a design for Appuldurcombe in 1779. (See List of Works, page 215.)

1 R. B. Johnson, *Letters of Hannah More*, 1925.
2 J. Mitford, *Correspondence of H. Walpole and W. Mason*, 1851, p. 329, 10 February, 1783.
3 This 'quickness of his eye' was also commented on by the French writer, François de La Rochefoucauld. In his *Melanges sur Angleterre*, published after a visit to England in 1784, he observed that 'Le Brun' had so quick and sure an eye that on riding round a park for an hour he could conceive a design for the whole place, and that afterwards half a day sufficed for him to mark it out on the ground.
4 H. Walpole, *Anecdotes of Painting*, Vol. V.
5 The letter was written from Spring Hill and was quoted by Repton in the *Theory and Practice of Landscape Gardening*, 1803. The 'detraction' mentioned by Lord Coventry referred to the attacks on Brown's work by Richard Payne Knight and Uvedale Price.
6 P.R.O., P.C.C., Cornwallis, 108.
7 *V.C.H., Hunts.*, Vol. II, p. 46.
8 P.R.O., L.C.3. 68.
9 Warren R. Dawson, *The Banks Letters*, 1958.

XVI

CONCLUSION. BROWN'S PRINCIPLES: INFLUENCES AND INTERPRETATIONS

ALTHOUGH BROWN, realising the uncertain state of his health, had drawn up a will in 1778, and in this charged his assistant surveyor Samuel Lapidge to see that any unfinished work was completed, Capability's sudden death in 1783 left a gap which no one man was sufficiently gifted to fill until Humphry Repton turned to landscape gardening five years later. A man of culture and a talented artist, who had also gained experience in the practical side of planting and husbandry on his own modest estate in Norfolk, Repton proved to be the third and last outstanding figure in the landscape movement, the decline of which after about 1815 he recognized and deplored. Before his appearance in this field, however, the few men who, towards the end of Brown's life or immediately after it, had attempted to emulate his precepts, can be said to have met with only moderate success. One or two claimed to be 'pupils'; others called themselves, more correctly, followers, for Brown is not known to have taken any pupils as such. Henry Holland, as his architectural collaborator, made designs for laying out the immediate surroundings of Althorp and the Brighton Pavilion but took no further part in garden design. Lapidge, who challenged Holland's right to provide the Althorp plan, achieved little beyond completing Brown's schemes elsewhere, and carrying out work to the extent of £384 at the Brighton Pavilion in 1802, probably to Repton's design.[1] John Spyers, Brown's other surveyor and a competent draughtsman in watercolours, submitted a *Design of a grotto* to the Royal Academy in 1780, when his address was given as Hampton Court. He exhibited a *View in Richmond Park* in 1783, and a *View of Mrs. Garrick's at Hampton* in 1790. His *Drawing for Brickley Lodge*, dated 1786, is in the British Museum,[2] and one entitled *A Cascade in Bushy Park* is in a private collection.

Other men whose names appear in Brown's one surviving account book, or more rarely in his correspondence, were the working gardeners or foremen who did not aspire to the status of designers. They were Benjamin Read (Blenheim and Croome), Cornelius Dickinson (Harewood, Ditton and Sherborne), Alexander Knox (North

Stoneham and Branches, and Cornelius Griffin (Maiden Early, Copt Hall and Red-grave.) Andrew Gardiner is mentioned twice (Sandbeck and North Stoneham) as is George Bowstreed (Southill and Wimbledon). William Ireland worked for Brown at Burghley, Luton Hoo, Stapleford and Trentham. John Midgely's name occurs in correspondence relating to Charlecote and Castle Ashby, where he acted as foreman. Lowy, Avery and Bissell were garden labourers employed on Philip Stephens's grounds at Fulham.

Nowhere in Brown's account book is there any mention of Richmond or Eames (sometimes spelt Emes), both of whom set up as designers while he was still alive and outlived him by several years. Brown must, however, have been acquainted with Richard Woods, who lived close to Belhus and carried out some minor work for Lord Dacre, possibly suggested by Brown, in the 1770s (see page 74). Woods built up a practice as an improver in East Anglia but also claimed two commissions in York-shire.[3] All three of these men were obviously strongly influenced by Brown, and each made for himself a modest reputation, Richmond being described by Walpole in 1780 as a 'scholar of Brown', who was then working for Thomas Barrett at Lee Priory in Kent, while John Penn in 1812 mentions him as having carried out the landscaping of Stoke Park, on the lines of a design given by Brown some years before. William Eames, although described as 'of Derby', covered a fairly extensive field, being mentioned in Lord Verulam's *Tour* as working at Chirk and Crewe. He is also said to have had a hand in the grounds of Hawkstone, Belton, Tixall, Beaudesert, and Cuffnells. His not very imaginative designs for alterations to the garden at Statfold for Samuel Wolferstan (1777), and Oak Edge for Thomas Anson (1771), are in the Staffordshire County Record Office, as is a survey of Green Wood made for Thomas Clifford in 1767, the latter apparently being the earlier name of Oak Edge before it was sold to Mr. Anson.

John Stuart of Allanbank, near Berwick, writing to John Soane in 1782, says that it is no longer necessary to consult 'Mr. Yeames' [*sic*] as he has 'got a Mr. White . . . who is carrying on some great works in the beautifying way, to look at Allanbank.'[4] This mention of White must refer to the Thomas of whom Sir Henry Steuart, in *The Planter's Guide* (1828) says that he was a 'pupil' of Brown, and he was almost certainly the man of that name who made a survey of Chillington soon after Brown's work there had been carried out (see page 148). His name also turns up on a plan of the grounds at Burton Constable *circa* 1772. This Thomas's son continued in his father's profession and 'improved' Allanton, of which an illustration is included in *The Planter's Guide*. Sir Henry also mentions as a 'disciple and admirer' of Brown a 'Mr. Pontey' who was the author of *The Rural Improver* (1825).

Another so-called 'pupil of the celebrated Capability Brown' was Thomas Cook, who is thus described in a manuscript note added to Langley's *Hundred of Desborough*

(1797) in the Society of Antiquaries' Library. The note continues that he was an eminent land surveyor whose 'peculiar skill and taste is exemplified in the happy disposition of the pleasure grounds at West Wycombe, Bucks., where he was employed for ten or twelve years by Lord le Despencer who left him a handsome annuity.' As a maker of cascades and grottos, the name of 'Mr. Lane' appears at Bowood, Wycombe, Painshill, Wardour and Oatlands, Joseph Farington giving a fairly full description of the latter which survived until the 1950s when it was wantonly demolished.[5] John Webb probably came nearest to Eames for the extent of his practice, which included work at Shugborough, Tatton, Somerford, Crewe, Rode, Quernmore and Lamport, at some of which Repton was also working, which makes an assessment difficult. Some correspondence with him is preserved at the latter house, but the only plan which has so far come to light is that for Lowther, which scarcely impresses by its fussy planting, superimposed on Brown's earlier layout, and obscuring its outlines.

It was with the inept imitators that Humphry Repton laid the blame for bringing Brown's principles into disrepute for, as he wrote in *Sketches and Hints* (1795), the latter's critics attributed to him 'all the bad taste of the day-labourers who became his successors.' In his next book, *The Theory and Practice of Landscape Gardening* (1803), he again pointed out that few of Brown's followers possessed his 'force of genius'; they copied the means he used 'without considering the effect which he intended to produce. Thus Brown has been treated with ridicule by the contemptuous observation that all his improvements consisted in *belting*, *clumping* and *dotting*,' the critics not realising that the last two were temporary measures whereby he formed 'small clumps fenced together, containing a number of trees calculated to shelter each other and to promote the growth of those few which might be ultimately destined to remain.'

Repton's practical experience gave him the insight, and the foresight, to understand the intentions behind Brown's schemes which took years to mature, a fact which the literary pundits, notably Richard Payne Knight and Uvedale Price, failed to appreciate when they opened the wordy battle of the picturesque in 1794. In that year the former published his didactic poem, *The Landscape*, while the latter produced his *Essay*, both of which castigated the recent school of designers in general, and Brown in particular. As Repton's *Sketches and Hints* was then on the point of going to press, he was able to slip in a footnote defending Capability, and concluding with the view that, however great the appeal of mouldering abbeys and antiquated cottages covered with ivy might be to the painter, 'in whatever relates to man, propriety and convenience are not less objects of good taste than picturesque effect.' Much heat was to be generated in the next six years among the various protagonists, culminating in a quarrel between Knight and Price in 1801 over the very subject which had previously united them. Writing to Repton, Daniel Malthus made some sensible comments on the controversy, and con-

49a. SCAMPSTON, YORKSHIRE. The bridge-pavilion. *see page 173*

49b. The cascade at the back of the pavilion.

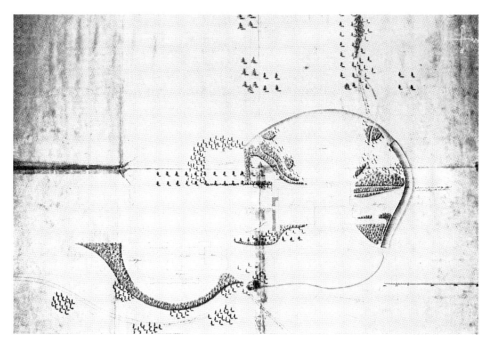

50a. BURTON CONSTABLE, YORKSHIRE. Brown's plan for the grounds. *see page 173*

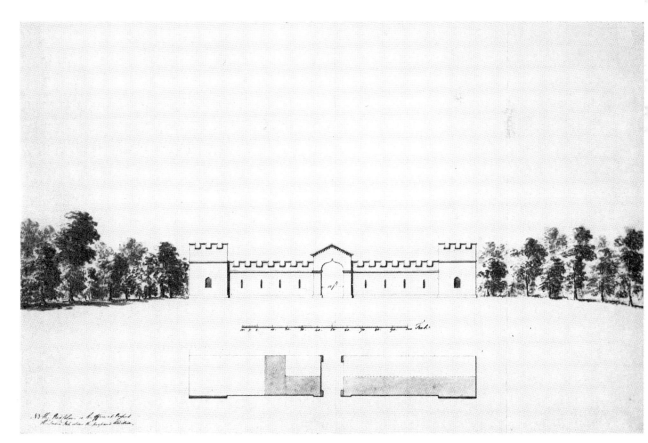

50b. BURTON CONSTABLE. 'A Plan & Elevation Mr. Brown recommends Mr. Constable to add to the offices at Burton Constable.'

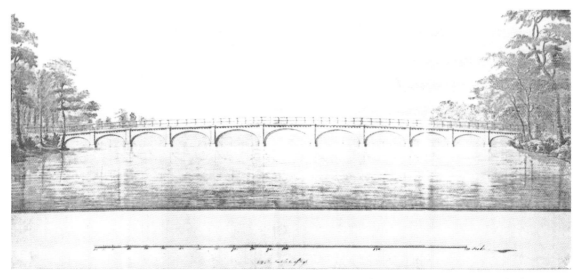

51a. GRIMSTHORPE, LINCOLNSHIRE. Brown's unexecuted project for a sham bridge over the lake, endorsed 'N.B. The rail to be 4ft. high'. *see page 161*

51b. ROCHE ABBEY (SANDBECK PARK), YORKSHIRE. The Abbey ruins in Brown's landscape. *see page 138*

52a. CADLAND PARK, HAMPSHIRE (demolished). An engraving of the house as built by Brown and Holland. *see page 177*

52b. BENHAM, BERKSHIRE. The south elevation. The original hipped roof of slate, and the pediment to the portico, were replaced with balustrading when another storey was added at the end of the nineteenth century. *see page 171*

53. A drawing believed to represent BROWN (right) with LORD CRAVEN (left, wearing a hat), MR. SHAFTO and, according to an inscription on the back of the frame, 'MR. COSWAY, who sketched this'. *see page 169*

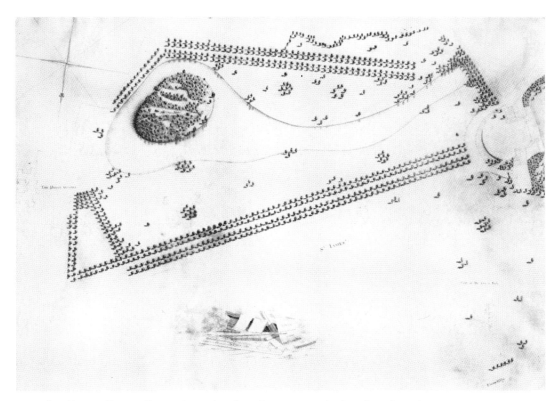

54a. ST. JAMES PARK. Brown's undated and unexecuted plan for alteration. *see page 122*

54b. SHEFFIELD PARK, SUSSEX. Brown's plan was supplied in 1776. Additional planting was carried out by Humphry Repton in 1789, and in the late nineteenth century. *see page 238*

55a. MILTON ABBEY, DORSET. An engraving from Morris's *Country Seats of Great Britain*. *see page 118*

55b. MILTON ABBAS VILLAGE, DORSET. Pairs of thatched cottages along the road. *see page 119*

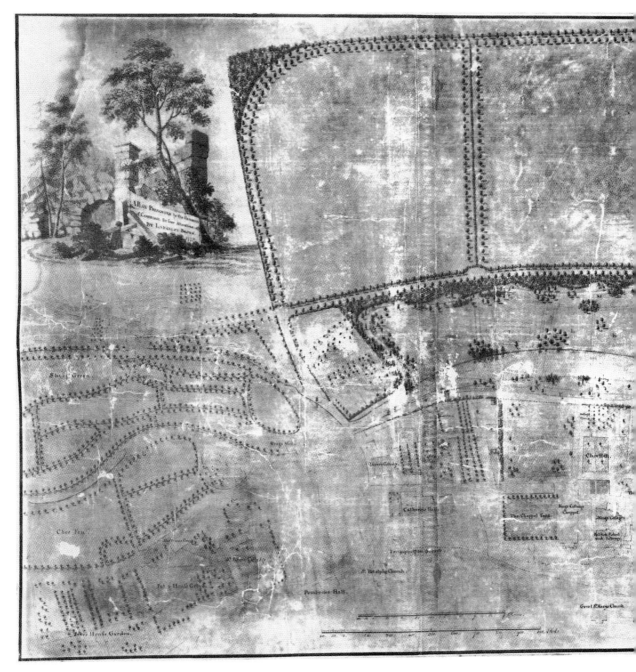

56–7. Brown's plan for landscaping 'THE BACKS', CAMBRIDGE. *see page 181*

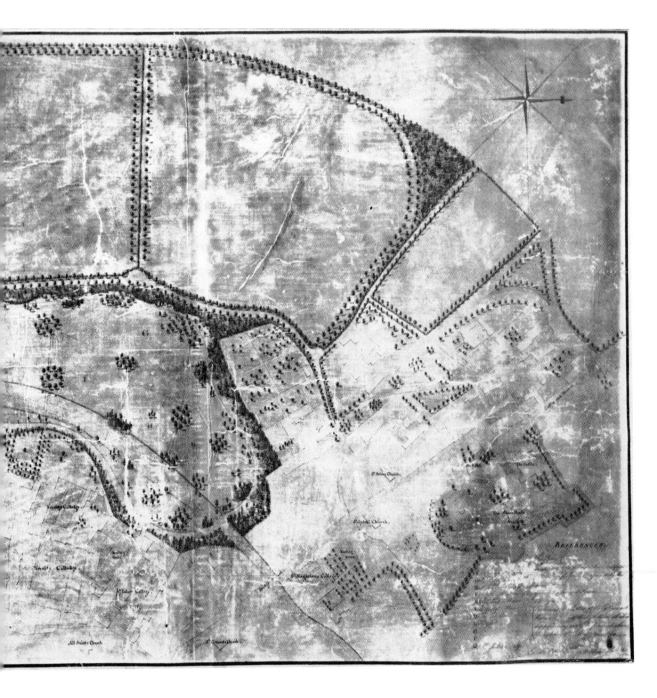

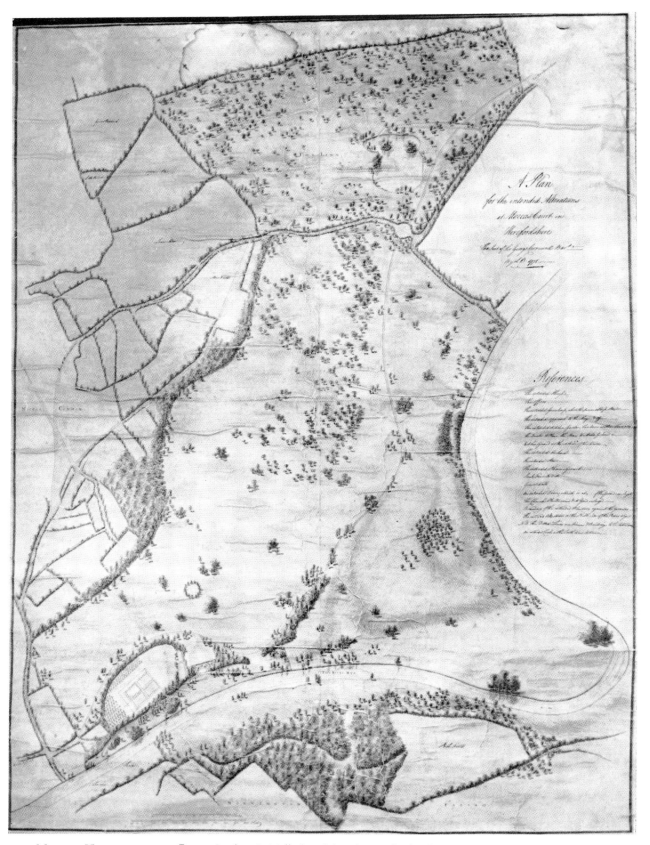

58. MOCCAS, HEREFORDSHIRE. Brown's plan, initialled and dated 1778 for landscaping the grounds overlooking the Wye. Partly executed. *see page 233*

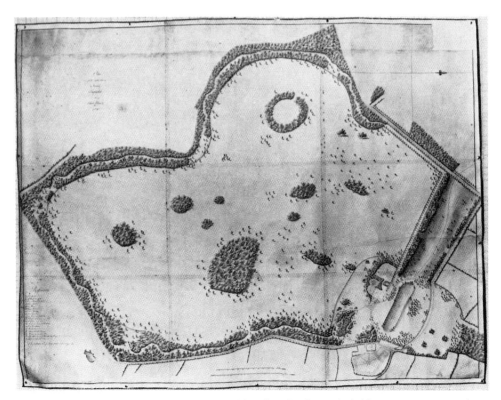

59a. BROCKLESBY, LINCOLNSHIRE. 'A Plan for the Intended Alteration, . . . 1771'.
see page 160

59b.
BROCKLESBY. Brown's 'Plan for the Improvement of Brocklesby agreeable to the design of a new house and situation.' The 'new house' was not built.

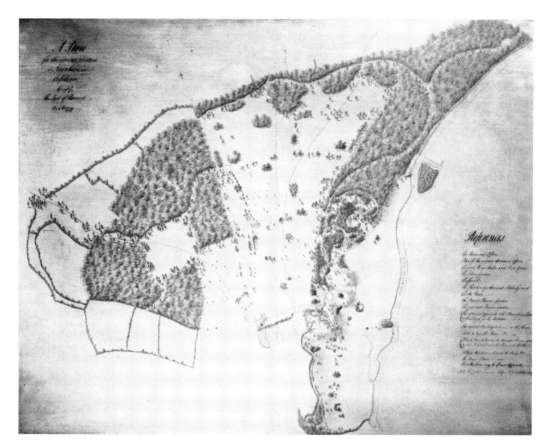

60a. NUNEHAM COURTENAY, OXFORDSHIRE. Brown's plan of 1779. *see page 191*

60b. NUNEHAM COURTENAY. An engraving showing the landscape from 'Brown's Hill' with the introduction of the Oxford Carfax, presented to Lord Harcourt in 1786. This was used as a feature where Brown had proposed to set a 'Gothic Tower' designed by William Mason.

61a. HEVENINGHAM, SUFFOLK. An engraving of 1782 by W. Watts after Thomas Hearne. *see page 198*

61b. HEVENINGHAM. The house from across the lake.

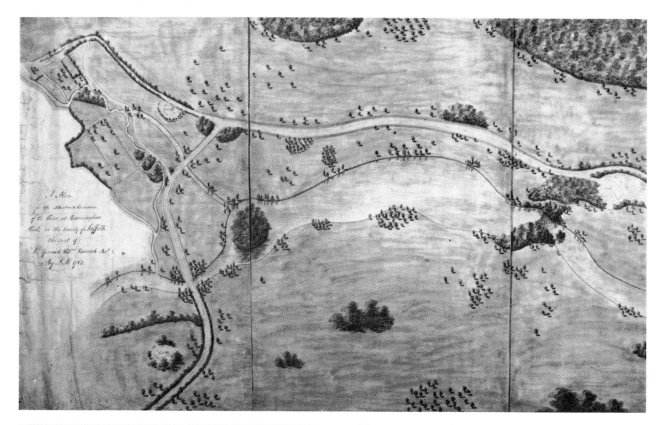

62a. HEVENINGHAM. One of Brown's plans for the further part of the park, dated 1782. *see page 198*

62b. WREST PARK, BEDFORDSHIRE. The column erected by Lady de Grey commemorating the work carried out by her father, her husband and herself, 'with the professional assistance of Lancelot Brown, Esq., 1758–60'. *see page 80*

I am quite allone at this Place, and as I
had no body to talk to I have been
very much upon the Phylosophick
strain, a Day so spent it is not one of
the worst we spend, and just to conclude
it, I have enterd into a conversation with you
which has every charm except your
Company which will ever be the sincere
and the principal delight of my
Dear Biddy   your Affectionate Hd Ye

Lancelot Brown

M: you will give my Love & Blessing
to those that are with you, you will
be so good as to write to me at Low Country,
by Thursdays Post or Friday at furthest you may
enclose to his Lordship —

63. Part of a LETTER written by Lancelot Brown to his wife, Biddy, 11 December, 1775. *see page 177*

64a.
BRIDGET BROWN, eldest child of
Lancelot Brown, and later wife of Henry
Holland the architect. From a miniature.
see page 168

64b.
The SILVER TRAY presented to Brown in
1780 by the University of Cambridge
as a mark of appreciation for his design
intended for 'the Backs' (unexecuted).
see page 182

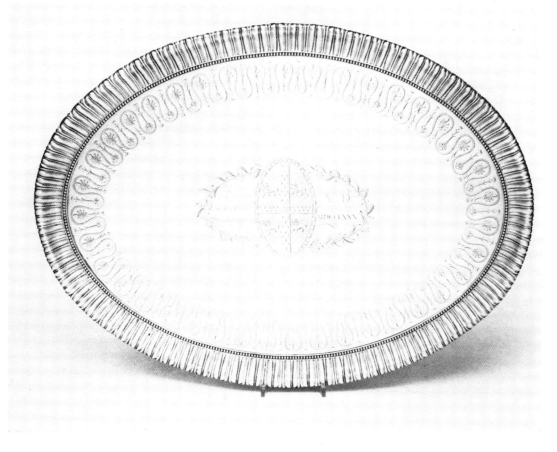

cluded: 'I know the abilities of the two gentlemen, and am sorry they have made themselves such pupils of the Warburtonian school as to appear more like Luther and Calvin than a couple of west country gentlemen, talking of gravel walks and syringas. To be sure, one would imagine they would have broiled poor Brown, but I hope not.'[6]

Repton was by no means alone in the line which he took, and from Strawberry Hill growls of protest were to issue when Walpole, then approaching eighty, read *The Landscape*. Pronouncing it an 'insolent and self-conceited poem . . . by a trumpery prosaic poetaster', he implored Mason to compose a poem in defence of Brown, but the muse which had produced the *Heroic Epistle* more than twenty years earlier, no longer felt equal to the effort. As it transpired, the squib of the Picturesque which had at first fizzled so brightly and fiercely, petered out with the first years of the new century, leaving Repton as the last upholder of the Georgian landscape garden.

The influence of the landscape movement abroad, although extensive, was not entirely happy. In addition to the designs which Brown himself supplied to the Duke of Brunswick in 1767, and to a French enthusiast through Thomas Dyer in 1775, there can be no doubt that his work had a considerable influence on such visitors to this country as F. L. Belanger, and F. M. Piper. The latter prepared a MSS treatise on the *Idea and General Plan for an English Pleasure Park*, and while here made many watercolour sketches now in the Art Academy at Stockholm, on the basis of which he subsequently laid out 'English Parks' at Drottningholm, Haga, Bergshamra, Valinge, Eodegard and Forsmark. Belanger, who had come to England in 1766 at the invitation of Lord Shelburne, returned to carry on his architectural practice in France in the course of which he also laid out many gardens, the more notable being Bagatelle, Sainte James at Neuilly, Maison des Champs at Pantin, and Santeny for Mme. Belanger, these being illustrated in Krafft's *Receuil*.[7] This book also includes several other examples of the *jardin anglais* but from these it is apparent that there was little real understanding of the principles either in France or elsewhere in Europe. The engravings assembled by Le Rouge under the title of *Cahiers des Nouveaux Jardins á la Mode* (1776–88) includes a number of English gardens, but those of continental imitations show that many were a travesty of English landscaping ideals with a frenzied winding of paths through half an acre of shrubbery, and a piling up of bridges, temples, grottos, hermitages and other features which would have appalled Brown and even his least perspicacious followers in England. The *Englische garten* frequently to be found in Germany, and examples in Italy and Russia, show the strength of the influence even where, as in the latter, climatic conditions were not ideal.

In America the eighteenth-century landscape garden found a sympathetic interpreter in the gifted personality of Thomas Jefferson. His knowledge and love of architecture was staunchly classical, deriving not only from the writings of Palladio and other early

authors, but from a first-hand study made during his European tour of 1785–6. Towards the end of these travels he came to England and spent most of April in the latter year visiting country houses and gardens, basing his intinerary mainly on those places mentioned in Thomas Whately's *Observations on Modern Gardening* of 1770. While the notes made in his Memorandum of these excursions are fairly brief and not always flattering, it is clear that what he saw at Claremont, Caversham, Wotton, Stowe, Blenheim and Moor Park, to name only a few on the list, collectively made a deep impression and left him in no doubt as to the ideal setting for the architectural concepts which he was to put in hand on his return to America.[8] At his own home, Monticello, Albemarle, he devised a landscape of great sensibility, and the same ideals were applied to the settings of the Virginia State Capitol, and the later University of Virginia.

Fig. 8. Rockwork underpass at Wardour Castle

1 Windsor Castle Archives, Brighton Accounts, 33524.
2 King's Maps, XXXVIII, 49a.
3 For a list of his works see Hugh Prince, *Parks in England*, 1967.
4 Soane Museum Correspondence.

5 *Diary*, Vol. 1, 30 October, 1793.
6 This letter was included by Repton in his *Theory and Practice*. It is also quoted in D. Stroud, *Humphry Repton*, 1962.
7 J. C. Krafft, *Receuil d'Architecture Civile*, 1811.
8 Edwin Morris Betts, *Thomas Jefferson's Garden Book, 1766–1824*, 1944.

(The map on the following pages was completed before the realignments of the county boundaries came into force.)

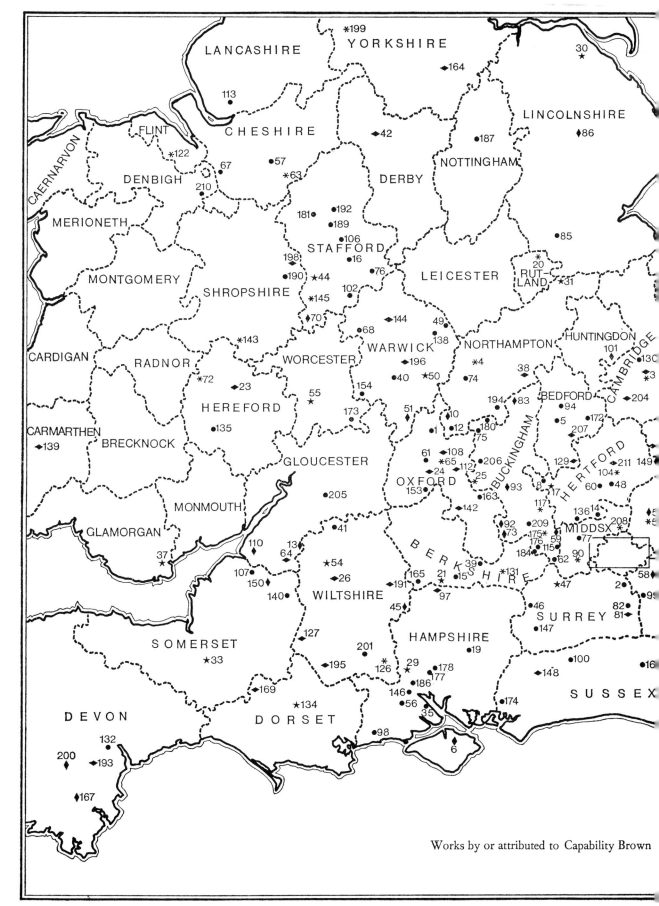

Works by or attributed to Capability Brown

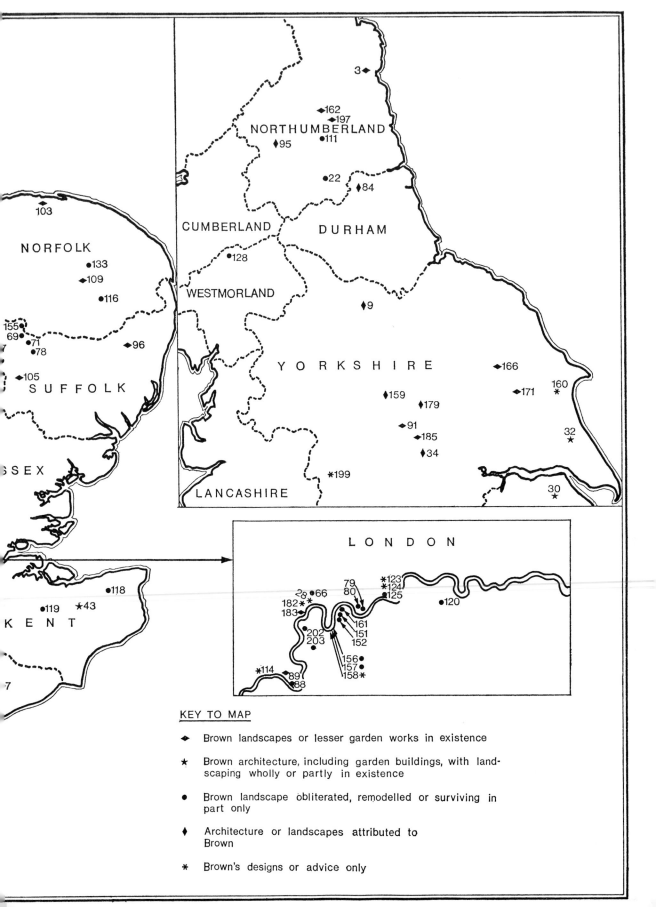

3◆

NORTHUMBERLAND
◆162
◆197
◆95 ●111

●22 ◆84

103◆

NORFOLK
●133
◆109
●116

CUMBERLAND   DURHAM

●128

WESTMORLAND

155●
69●
●71
●78
◆96

◆105   SUFFOLK

SSEX

♦9

Y O R K S H I R E   ◆166

◆159   ◆171   160
◆179   ✳

◆91   32
◆185   ★

◆34

✳199   30
★

L O N D O N

79   ✳123
80   ✳124
28 ●66   ●125   ●120
182✳✳
183●
161
202   151
203   152

156●
157●
114   158✳
89●
88●

●118
119● ★43

K E N T

7

KEY TO MAP

◆   Brown landscapes or lesser garden works in existence

★   Brown architecture, including garden buildings, with land-
     scaping wholly or partly in existence

●   Brown landscape obliterated, remodelled or surviving in
     part only

♦   Architecture or landscapes attributed to
     Brown

✳   Brown's designs or advice only

LIST OF WORKS KNOWN TO BE BY, OR ATTRIBUTED TO, CAPABILITY BROWN

Where given in quotation marks, the name of the owner is as written in Brown's account book. In such cases, the figures and dates quoted are from the same sources. Where a single date is given it is for the beginning of a commission which may have continued over several years.

House and Map Number		*Client*	*Notes*
ENGLAND AND WALES			
1 Adderbury, Oxon.	●	'His Grace the Duke of Buccleuch'	Brown made an undated note of a journey to Adderbury and preparation of a plan 'for alteration of the Park and Gardens'. Now property of Oxfordshire County Council. See Plate 37.
2 Addington Place, Surrey	●	'James Trecothick Esqr.'	Brown received £800 for work carried out in 1781–2. There are remains of a fine landscape on the periphery of the present golf course and notable cedar trees near the house.
3 Alnwick Castle, Northumberland	◆	1st Duke of Northumberland	*circa* 1760. See page 102 and Plate 19B.
4 Althorp, Northants.	✳	1st Earl Spencer	On 24 January, 1780, Georgiana, widow of the 1st Earl Spencer, wrote to Mrs. Howe: 'Mr. Brown has been giving some very excellent advice about this place. He is adverse from many things

House and Map Number	Client	Notes
		that I thought he had been for, and I think all his ideas are good. He is against removing your Barns [probably the Tuscan stable block]'. (Correspondence at Althorp.) The advice as to the landscape had not been carried out at the time of his death, but may have influenced Henry Holland's subsequent design.
5 Ampthill, Beds.	● 'The Earl of Upper Ossory'	Work carried out from February, 1771, to November, 1772, for which Brown received £2,396 9s 7d.
Ancaster House, *see* Richmond		
6 Appuldurcombe, Isle of Wight	◆ 'Sir Richard Worsley, Bt.'	Payment of £52 10s for a journey in 1779 and subsequent plan for 'alterations of the Place.' See page 205.
7 Ashburnham Place, Sussex	◆ 1st Earl of Ashburnham	Brown's plan of 1767 for this work is in the East Sussex C.R.O. The mansion is now greatly reduced in size, and a good deal of timber has been felled. See Plates 40B, 41 A and B.
8 Ashridge, Herts.	● 'His Grace the Duke of Bridgewater'	1759. See page 101.
9 Aske, Yorks.	◆ 'Sr Lawrence Dundass, Bt.'	Brown's undated account notes a journey and 'Plans for a bridge and the Head of the Water where the new road was to go over.' A bridge answering this

House and Map Number		Client	Notes
			description survives as does the drive, and a stream passing over a cascade in a wooded valley.
10 Astrop, Northants.	♦	Sir John Willes	A MS poem (undated) in the Methuen archives at Corsham begins: *At Astrop Brown his skill display'd In Woods and Lawns and clear Cascades, The first from fetter'd Rules set free, And made the Lawns with these agree....* The park shows signs of having been landscaped. Sir John Willes died in 1761.
11 Audley End, Essex	◆	'Sr. John Griffin Griffin'	1763. See page 113.
12 Aynho, Northants.	●	William Cartwright Esq.	1760. See page 106.
13 Badminton, Glos.	♦	4th or 5th Duke of Beaufort	Brown is traditionally said to have carried out further work here, following Kent's landscaping. An undated ground plan of the house by Brown, proposing slight internal changes, exists.
14 Barnet, East (Littlegrove) Herts.	●	'The Honble. Judge Willis'	Brown received £700 from Edward Willis for work carried out in 1768. The site has been built over.
15 Basildon Berks.	●	'Francis Sykes, Esqr.'	Journeys and plans for kitchen garden, etc., *circa* 1778.

House and Map Number		Client	Notes
16 Beaudesert, Staffs.	●		The Hon. Adelaide Drummond in her *Memoirs* (1915) states that when staying at Beaudesert as a child her host showed her a book containing a plan for developing the grounds by Brown, but he added that he thought this was only partly carried out.
17 Beechwood, Herts.	★	Sir John Sebright	1754. See page 31.
18 Belhus, Essex	●	17th Baron Dacre	1754. See page 72.
19 Belmont, later Warnford Park, Hants.	●	'The Earl of Clanricarde'	Undated journey and survey noted. A letter from the Earl to Brown of 13 April, 1773, asks if he can arrange for Lord and Lady Wandesford to have a 'view of Kew Gardens' (Pakenham Correspondence).
	●		
20 Belvoir Castle, Rutland	✱	'His Grace the Duke of Rutland	In 1779 Brown visited the Castle and sent Spyers to make surveys from which a detailed set of drawings was subsequently prepared for both the remodelling of the building and the grounds, 'all very descriptive, fair and neat with Trees etc. bound into a book'. Brown showed them to Walpole who thought they 'showed judgement and would be magnificent', but the project was abandoned. The account for £496 was settled with Brown's executors.

House and Map Number		Client	Notes
21 Benham, Berks.	★	'The Rt. Honble. Lord Craven'	See page 169 and Plate 52 B.
22 Benwell Tower, Northumberland	●	Robert Shafto Esq.	*Circa* 1738. See p. 42.
23 Berrington, Herefordshire	◆	'The Right Honorable Thomas Harley Esqr.'	1776 and 1781. See page 189.
24 Blenheim, Oxon.	◆	'His Grace the Duke of Marlborough'	1763. See page 111 and Plates 27, 28 A, B, 29 A, B, 30 A, B, C and 31.
25 Boarstall, Bucks.	✳	'John Aubery, Esqr.'	Two journeys noted by Brown, but without a date. The charge was £15 15s.
26 Bowood, Wilts.	◆	'The Earl of Shelburne'	1957. See page 90 and Plates 17 A and B.
27 Branches, Suffolk	●	'Ambrose Dickens Esqr.'	1763. See page 114.
28 Brentford, Middlesex	✳	'The Honble. Edward Stratford Esqr. now Earl of Aldborough'	Plans and elevations for a house intended to be built, charged at £46 in 1773.
29 Broadlands, Hants.	★	'The Rt. Honble. the Lord Palmerston'	1764. See page 137 and Plates 25 A and B.
30 Brocklesby, Lincs.	★	'Charles Pelham Esqr.'	1771. See page 160 and Plates 59 A and B
31 Burghley, Northants.	★	'The Earl of Exeter'	1754. See page 75 and Plates 12 A, B, 13 A, B and 14 A, B.
32 Burton Constable, Yorks.	★	'William Constable Esqr.'	*Circa* 1759 and 1770. See pages 82, 88, 173 and Plates 15 B, 50 A and B.

House and Map Number		*Client*	*Notes*
33 Burton Pynsent, Somerset	★	1st Earl of Chatham	1765. See page 135 and Plate 36 A.
34 Byram, Yorks.	♦	'Sir John Ramsden Bart.'	Visited by Brown and survey prepared by Spyers, 1782. Brown's 'General plan for the alteration of the place' sent in December of that year.
35 Cadland, Hants.	●	'Robt. Drummond Esqr.'	1775. See page 177 and Plate 52 A.
36 Cambridge St. John's College	◆	i The Masters and Fellows of St. John's College	1772. See page 171.
The Backs	✳	ii The Caput, or Synod, of the University	1776–8. See page 181 and Plates 56 and 57.
37 Cardiff Castle, Glam.	★	'The Right Honble the Lord Mount Stuart'	1771. See page 179.
38 Castle Ashby, Northants.	◆	'The Earl of Northampton'	1761. See page 107 and Plate 18 B.
39 Caversham, Berks.	●	2nd Baron Cadogan	*Circa* 1764. See page 132 and Plate 35 A.
40 Charlecote, Warwicks.	●	George Lucy Esq.	1757. See page 56.
41 Charlton Park, Wilts.	●	'The Earl of Suffolk'	1767. See page 95.
42 Chatsworth, Derbyshire	◆	4th Duke of Devonshire	1760. See page 104 and Plate 20 B.
43 Chilham Castle, Kent	★	' – Heron Esqr.'	Brown gave Thomas Heron a plan for 'alterations of the place' in 1777, followed by designs for

House and Map Number		Client	Notes
			a greenhouse, offices and stables in the next two years. In 1781 he supplied designs for the lodges and gates, which were almost certainly used for the gothic buildings which survived until 1862.
44 Chillington, Staffs.		Thomas Giffard Esq.	1760. See page 147.
45 Chute Lodge, Wilts.	♦		An advertisement in *The Salisbury and Winchester Journal* for 14 September, 1795, announced the sale of this house together with 900 acres of freehold land. The latter included 'extensive plantations and rides, in the best taste, by Brown & Emes.' There appear to be no other references to Brown's work here.
46 Clandon, Surrey	●	1st Earl of Onslow	Brown's plan, initialled L.B. and dated 1781, was seen at Clandon in 1927 but cannot now be found. In addition to landscaping the grounds, Brown built a new stable range some way to the west of the house, recently demolished.
47 Claremont, Surrey	★	'The Rt. Honble. the Lord Clive'	1769. See pages 142, 168 and Plates 42 A, B, 43 A, B, 44 A, B and 45 A, B.
Cliveden, *see* Taplow, Bucks.			
48 Cole Green, Herts.	●	2nd Earl Cowper	The Cowper MSS deposited in Herts. C.R.O. show that Brown

House and Map Number		Client	Notes
			was paid £154 7s 6d in 1756 'on account of works done in the Garden' at Cole Green. The house was demolished in 1801 to make way for Panshanger House, now also demolished and the grounds in a desolate condition.
49 Combe Abbey, Warwicks.	●	'The Rt. Honble. Lord Craven	1771. See page 169.
50 Compton Verney, Warwicks.	★	'The Rt. Honble. the Lord Willough-by de Broke'	1768. See page 142 and Plates 38 A and B.
51 Compton Wynyates, Warwicks.	◆	'The Earl of Northampton'	Brown sent John Spyers to prepare a survey, 'begun in 1765', which is probably that mentioned in his letter to the Earl of 8 June, 1767, and which has survived. See pages 109, 111.
52 Coopersale, Essex	◆	' – Archer Esqr.'	Brown's journeys and plans of 1774 were charged at £36 15s, but no other details are given.
53 Copt Hall, Essex	✳	'John Conyers Esqr.'	Brown noted a charge of £31 10s for 'My journeys and trouble and Mr. Griffin's Demeasurement of the ground round the House' but gave no date.
54 Corsham Court Wilts.	★	Paul Methuen Esq.	1760. See page 86 and Plates 14 C, 15 A, B, and 16 A, B, C,
55 Croome Court and Church, Worcs.	★	'Earl of Coventry'	House, 1750; Church, 1758. See page 57 and Plates 7 A, B and 8 A, B.
56 Cuffnells, Hants.	●	'Sir Thomas Tancred Bart.'	Brown received £165 for 'Work done at Cuffnells before it was

House and Map Number		Client	Notes
			sold to George Rose' who, according to the Rev. William Gilpin, continued the landscaping (*Forest Scenery*, 1791). House now demolished.
57 Crew Hall, Cheshire	●	John Crewe Esq.	In his *Tour* of 1768 Lord Verulam says 'the three fronts [of house] look into a park which has been admirably laid out by Mr. Brown.' (*H.M.C., Verulam*)
58 Danson Park, Kent	◆	Alderman John Boyd	An unsigned plan in the possession of the Borough of Bexley is attributed to Brown but the delineation is not characteristic. The management of the rather flat terrain and fine lake has, however, Brown-ish qualities.
59 Denham Place Bucks.	◆	Benjamin Way Esq. M.P.	*Buildings of England: Buckinghamshire* (1960) attributes the landscaping here to Brown.
60 Digswell, Herts.	●	' – Willes Esqr.'	The entry shows over £1,100 received by Brown for work carried out between June, 1771, and February, 1773, for Mr., later Sir John, Willes.
61 Ditchley Park, Oxon.	●	3rd Earl of Lichfield	Grounds landscaped by Brown shortly before the Earl's death in 1777. A lake in middle distance fed from a triple-arched dam. On a hillock nearby is a rotunda built by John Hopper from a design by Stiff Leadbetter.
62 Ditton Park, Bucks.	●	'Lord Vist. Montague'	Lying a short distance to the south of Langley (q.v.), Ditton

House and Map Number		Client	Notes
			was landscaped by Brown between 1768 and 1774 at a cost of some £3,450. Traces of the work remain.
63 Doddington, Cheshire	✱	'Sr. Thomas Broughton Bart.'	Brown's plan and elevations for a new house, prepared *circa* 1770, were rejected in favour of those by Samuel Wyatt but some part of his garden design may have been adopted.
64 Dodington, Glos.	◆	'Sir William Codrington Bart.'	1764. See page 134.
65 Dornford, Oxon.	✱	'John Weyland Esqr.'	A 'General plan for the alteration of his seat' was sent in November, 1775 and charged at £31. The house stood near the Dorn rivulet before it joined the Glyme, and belonged to the Crisps. It was burnt in 1770 when the land was bought by Thomas Southam and later acquired by the Duke of Marlborough. Possibly between these dates Mr. Weyland had taken it with an intention of rebuilding; alternatively Brown may have confused it with the Weyland seat at Woodeaton.
Dynevor Castle, Carn.			1775. See page 180.
66 Ealing Place, Middlesex	●	(?) Sir Francis Dashwood, Baronet	Humphry Repton, in his *Fragments* (1816), says that 'Brown, whose work this appears to have been, surrounded the whole place by a narrow belt of plantation

House and Map Number	Client	Notes
		...'. Lysons (*Environs*, 1795) mentions Ealing Place-house of which 'the grounds are agreeabl sprinkled with wood and are adorned by a spacious sheet of water'. Now built over.
67 Eaton Hall, Cheshire	● 1st Earl Grosvenor	Lord Verulam in his *Tour* (*H.M.C., Verulam*) refers to the house as standing in 'a good Park, which Mr. Brown has attempted to improve'. Extensive nineteenth-century rebuilding and the reintroduction of formal gardens by W. E. Nesfield have obscured the outlines.
68 Edgbaston, Warwicks. (now within the City of Birmingham)	● 'Sir Henry Gough Bart.'	'Plans for General Alterations' were sent in January, 1776 and probably adopted for the park and lake which in part survives as a golf course.
69 Eldon [Elvedon], Suffolk	● 'The Honble. General Keppell'	Between October, 1765 and January, 1769 Brown received £1,460 for work carried out in the grounds here for General Keppell.
70 Enville, Staffs.	♦ 4th Earl of Stamford	Lord Stamford gave his signature to Brown's petition of 1758 for a Royal appointment which suggests that he may have consulted the latter, although the landscaping of his grounds is usually attributed to William Shenstone.
71 Euston Hall, Suffolk	● 'His Grace the Duke of Grafton'	Between 1767 and 1769 Brown received £900 from the Duke of

House and Map Number		Client	Notes
			Grafton for work carried out in the gardens, first landscaped by Kent.
72 Eywood, Herefordshire	*	'The Earl of Oxford'	There is an entry for a journey to Eywood in August, 1775, but no further details are given. The landscape has now been destroyed.
73 Fawley Court, Bucks.	♦	S. Freeman Esq.	The grounds said by Mrs. Lybbe Powys (*Diary*, October, 1771) to be 'laid out by Mr. Brown with his usual taste'. They contained a menagerie and 'most elegant dairy'.
74 Fawsley, Northants.	●	'Lucy Knightley Esqr.'	Horace Walpole, *Visits to Country Seats*, says 'the ground Brown is laying out and making a large piece of water' (July, 1763). Brown's plans, believed to be extant in 1943, cannot now be traced.
75 Finmere Rectory, Bucks.	●	Richard Grenville, later Earl Temple	*Circa* 1748. See page 53.
76 Fisherwick, Staffs.	●	'The Earl of Donegal'	*Circa* 1768. See page 151 and Plates 47 A and B.
77 Flamberts, or Flambards, Middlesex	●	'Francis Herne Esqr.'	Alterations carried out to house and gardens in 1768. Brown notes that he received £600 in August of that year and £2,020 in 1770, with further large sums of which £5,300 was handed over to the elder Holland for building work. The house was rebuilt when part of the estate was

House and Map Number	Client	Notes
		developed by Harrow School but some trees and the lake must be remnants of the landscape.
78 Fornham Genevieve,● Suffolk	'Charles Kent Esqr.'	1782. See page 197.
79 Fulham, London ●	'Philip Stephens Esqr.'	Brown's work in the grounds of this house, later known as Ranelagh House, was carried out in 1774 and 1778, and amounted to £1,206 15s 11d. Part of the ground is now covered by Putney Bridge Station.
80 Fulham, London ●	'The Right Honble. the Earl of Peterborough'	A survey taken by Spyers in 1774 and in the following year work began on carrying out Brown's proposals, for which he received a total of £1,206 15s 11d in 1778.
81 Gatton Park, Surrey ◆	'Sr. George Colebook, Bart.'	An extensive commission involving 'several journeys' and the expenditure of £3,055 between 1762–8. Brown noted that he supplied a plan for the 'great water menagerie'. Part of the landscape remains, but the house is occupied by a school.
82 Gatton, Upper, Surrey ●	'The Late Revd. Mr. Tattersall'	Brown gave a 'general plan of the place' with some sketches for lodges, and noted visits made in 1765, 1766 and 1774. His bill for these was £52 10s.
Gawthorpe, *see* Harewood		

House and Map Number		Client	Notes
83 Gayhurst, Bucks.	♦	? George Wright, Esq.	Horace Walpole attributed the grounds to Brown (before 1763), but further work was carried out by Humphry Repton.
84 Gibside, Co. Durham	♦	George Bowes	By tradition the grounds of this now ruined house were laid out by Brown, but the only known relevant document is his reply to George Bowes' request for the dimensions of the column to Lord Cobham at Stowe. Brown's letter, dated 22 October, 1750, is in the Strathmore Collection, Durham County Record Office, D/St. 347/37.
85 Grimsthorpe, Lincs.	●	'His Grace the Duke of Ancaster'	1771. See page 161 and Plate 51 A.
86 Hainton, Lincs.	♦	George Heneage, Esq.	An unsigned pencil sketch for planting a belt of trees round the park, c. 1780, is at Hainton and may be from Brown's hand. Mr. Heneage was a brother-in-law of Brown's client, the 9th Lord Petre at Thorndon.
87 Hallingbury, Essex	✳	'Jacob Houblon, Esqr.'	Brown's 'General Plan' for the grounds and 'Plans for Lodges' were charged at £105, and paid for in July 1778.
88 Hampton Court, Middlesex	●	'The King's Most Excellent Majesty'	Royal appointment, 1764. See page 122.
89 Hampton, Garrick's Villa, Middlesex	◆	David Garrick Esq.	C. 1756. See page 81 and Fig. 2.
90 Hanwell, Middlesex	✳	' – Bayly, Esqr.'	An undated charge of £8 8s was made for Brown's 'trouble and journey', and a survey made by Samuel Lapidge.

House and Map Number		Client	Notes
91 Harewood, Yorks.	◆	'Edwin Lascelles, Esqr'.	1758 and 1772. See page 105 and Plate 20 A.
92 Harleyford, Bucks.	◆	Sir W. Clayton, Baronet	The grounds of this house, built by Sir Robert Taylor in 1755, are traditionally said to be by Brown but no documentary evidence has so far come to light.
93 Hartwell, Bucks.	◆	1st Baron Vernon	Capt. W. H. Smyth, in *Aedes Hartwellianae*, 1851, states that 'Brown was a great intermeddler at various seats in Buckinghamshire, but especially at Stowe and Hartwell'. The tradition is that Brown did away with the formal gardens as shown in a set of early eighteenth-century paintings which exist.
94 Hawnes, Beds.	●	Henry Frederick Carteret, Esq.	In a letter of 29 April, 1778, to his daughter Peggy, Brown says that he is proceeding from Wisbech to Hawnes, and that Henry Holland should let him know by post 'the state of matters' with Mr. Carteret. There is still a good park, but the house is now a school.
95 Hesleyside, Northumberland	◆?	Edward or William Charlton, Esq.	An unsigned survey of 1776 in the house is attributed to Brown but bears little resemblance to his usual designs and was probably prepared by a local man. Brown is traditionally credited with the landscape which still

House and Map Number		Client	Notes
			has fine timber and a small cascade on the Hesleyside Burn.
96 Heveningham Suffolk	◆	Sir Gerard William Vanneck, Baronet	1781. See page 198 and Plates 61 A, B and 62 A.
97 Highclere (High Clear) Hants.	◆	'Henry Herbert Esqr.'	1770. See page 159.
98 Highcliffe, Hants.	●	'The Earl of Bute'	*Circa* 1775. See page 178
99 Hill Park (later Valons or Valence), Kent	●	'The Earl of Hillsborough'	Brown was paid £1,200 for work carried out between December, 1772, and June, 1775.
100 Hills, Sussex	●	9th Viscount Irwin	1769. See page 118.
101 Hilton, Hunts.	◆	' – Pigot Esqr.'	Brown's account book refers to plan supplied to Mr. Pigot 'for the alterations of his Place over there'. No date is given but the charge was £42. Mr. (later General) Pigot succeeded to his brother's baronetcy in 1777. Hilton adjoins Fenstanton on the east, and there is a tradition that the Green here was laid out by Brown.
102 Himley, Staffs.	●	'The Right Honble. The Lord Visct. Dudley & Ward'	1774. See page 154.
103 Holkham, Norfolk	◆	Margaret, widow of the Earl of Leicester	1762. See page 112.
104 Hoo, The Herts.	✳	Thomas Brand Esq.	Brown is said to have laid out the grounds here *circa* 1760–2.

House and Map Number		Client	Notes
			A drawing by him for a bridge survives but was not executed. See Plate 34 A.
105 Ickworth, Suffolk	◆	'The Earl of Bristol'	Brown's garden designs were carried out between 1769 and 1776 when he received the final payment of £581 8s. In 1781 he supplied 'Plans and elevations for an 'Intire New House' for which, with two journeys, his charge was £105. These were not executed. See page 197.
106 Ingestre, Staffs.	●	The Hon. Thomas Clifford	1756. See page 146 and Plate 46.
107 Kelstone, Somerset	●	'Caesar Hawkins, Esqr.'	Brown was paid £500 for work executed for Mr., later Sir Caesar, Hawkins in 1767–8. The house, built by the younger John Wood, overlooks a wooded slope to the river Avon.
Kew, *See* Richmond			
108 Kiddington, Oxon.	◆	Sir Charles Browne	*Circa* 1740. See page 47 and Plate 2 B.
109 Kimberley, Norfolk	◆	'Sr. Armine Wodehouse'	1763. See page 112 and Plate 21 A.
110 King's Weston, Glos.	◆	'Edward Southwell Esqr.'	Brown's General Plan for the 'Alterations about the House and Terras' was charged at £84. The entry is undated.
111 Kirkharle, Northumberland	●	Sir William Loraine, Baronet	1732–9. See p. 41 and Plates 1 A, B and 2 A.
112 Kirtlington, Oxon.	◆	Sir James Dash- wood, Baronet	See page 69 and Plate 6 C.

House and Map Number		Client	Notes
113 Knowsley, Lancs.	●	'The Earl of Derby Order of Lord Strange'.	Plans given for 'alterations' and £100 received on account in 1775. Further plans supplied in 1776 for the kitchen garden and 'grounds round the house' now much changed.
114 Laleham, Middlesex	✻	'Sr. James Lowther, Bart.'	A survey and plans supplied. No date but after 1763.
115 Langley, Bucks.	●	'His Grace the Duke of Marlborough'	A plan was supplied and a contract made for £2,810. Although the Duke considered postponing the work (see under Blenheim) it was carried out in the 1760s. The Park retains much fine timber, and a sizeable lake to the south of the house.
116 Langley Park, Norfolk	●	Sir T. Proctor Beauchamp	The house, now a school, stands in a good park for which Brown's drawing was seen there in recent years, but cannot now be traced.
117 Latimers, or Islehampstead, Bucks.	✻	Lord Cavendish	George Johnson's *History of English Gardening* (1829) refers to 'the view which he [Brown] procured of Cheyney Church to Latimers, a seat of Lord Cavendish.'
118 Lee, Kent	●	Thomas Barrett, Esq., M.P.	Walpole says that the grounds were 'much improved under the direction of Richmond', scholar of Brown.
Lee, London, *see* Lewisham			
119 Leeds Abbey, Kent	●	'John Calcraft Esqr.'	£2,000 received by Brown, 1771–2, for work in hand. Now destroyed.

House and Map Number		Client	Notes
120 Lewisham, Lee, London	●	Sir Samuel Fludyer, Baronet	Sir Samuel Fludyer, 1767. See page 141.
121 Littlegrove, *see* Barnet, East			
122 Llewaney, Flints.	✱	'The Honourable Thomas Fitz-maurice, Esqr.'	Visited by Brown in September, 1781 when it was agreed that he should supply a plan for £100, an amount which was later settled with his executors.
LONDON *See also* under Ful-ham, Lewisham, Putney, Richmond, Roehampton, Syon, Wimbledon.			
123 St. James's Park, Buckingham House	✱	H.M. The King	Brown's undated plan for part of the garden is in the Royal Library at Windsor Castle (Royal Palace Portfolio). Prob-ably not executed. See Plate 54 A.
124 St. James's Park	✱	H.M. The King	A plan for the Park, initialled but undated, passed through a sale room in 1966. The plan shows that Brown proposed the turning of the straight canal into a ser-pentine, widening at its east end to encircle a tree-covered island. Its similarity to the present lake suggests that John Nash may have seen this drawing and re-membered it as a basis for his own creation here.
125 South Audley Street, No. 73	●	'The Earl of Bute'	*Circa* 1770. See page 179.

House and Map Number		Client	Notes
126 Longford Castle, Wilts.	✳	'Lord Folkestone' (later 'Lord Radnor')	Two visits noted by Brown before 1777, followed by surveys by Spyers in June 1778. Brown 'sent a letter to Lord Radnor naming 50 gns for my trouble.'
127 Longleat, Wilts.	◆	3rd Viscount Weymouth	1757. See page 85 and Plate 11 B.
128 Lowther Castle, Westmorland	●	'Sr. James Lowther, Bart.'	1763. See page 114 and Plate 24.
129 Luton Hoo, Beds.	◆	'Earl of Bute'	1764. See page 133.
130 Madingley, Cambs.	●	Sir John Hynde Cotton, Baronet	1756. See page 79.
131 Maiden Early, Berks.	✳	'William Mathew Burt, Esqr.'	Brown charged £31 10s for 'my trouble, journeys and plans', and £6 6s for the expenses of his man Griffin in making a preliminary survey. No date is given.
132 Mamhead, Devon	●	'The Right Honble. The Lord Visct. Lisburne.'	1772. See page 97.
133 Melton Constable Norfolk	●	'Sr. Edward Astley, Bart.'	1764. See page 112.
134 Milton Abbey and village of Milton Abbas, Dorset	★	'The Right Honble. Milton.'	1763. See page 118.
135 Moccas, Herefordshire	●	'Sir George Cornewall, Bart.'	Sir George paid Brown £100 for his journeys and plans. One of the latter survives, inscribed as for 'the Intended alterations at Moccas Court, L.B., 1778', and

House and Map Number		Client	Notes
			some part of his scheme appears to have been carried out. See Plate 58.
136 Moor Park, Herts.	●	Baron Anson	See page 69 and Plates 10 B and 11 A.
Mount Clare, *see* Roehampton			
137 Navestock, Essex	●	'The Earl Waldegrave'	From October, 1763 until 1773 Brown received half-yearly payments of between £200 and £300 for landscaping the grounds here, totalling £4,550. A further £250 was paid to him in 1782. The house was demolished in 1811, when the materials were sold and the grounds reverted to arable.
138 Newnham Paddox, Warwicks.	●	5th and 6th Earls of Denbigh	1745–8 and 1753. See pages 54, 71 and Plate 4 B.
139 Newton Castle (Dynevor), Carn.	◆	'George Rice Esq., M.P.'	1775. See page 180.
140 Newton Park, Somerset	●	William Gore Langton Esq.	In a letter of 29 March, 1761, George Lucy described the grounds as 'laid out by Mr. Brown' (archives at Charlecote). This is confirmed by Humphry Repton's *Red Book* for Newton where he speaks of Brown's treatment of the lay-out, particularly the water, and adds: 'I will do Mr. Brown the justice to observe that in no instance have I ever seen him inattentive to this consideration.'

House and Map Number		Client	Notes
141 North Cray Place, Kent	●	'Thomas Coventry Esqr.'	Brown carried out work in 1871 to the amount of £1,300 for Mr. Coventry, a Sub-Governor of the South Sea Company. The gardens lie behind a fine wrought iron gate.
North Stoneham, *see* Stoneham			
142 Nuneham Courtenay, Oxon.	◆	'Earl Harcourt'	1778. See page 189 and Plates 60 A and B.
143 Oakley Park, Salop.	✱	'The Right Honble. the Lord Clive'	Brown's account book records a visit to Oakley in August, 1772, and a letter to him from J. Mainwaring confirms this: 'I am happy in finding that you think so highly of Oakley Park' he writes, 'because I have no doubt of Lord Clive's concurring with your opinion . . .' Lord Clive's death in 1774, however, put an end to any proposals Brown may have made.
144 Packington, Warwicks.	◆	3rd Earl of Aylesford	*Circa* 1750. See page 56 and Plates 5 A, B and 6 A, B.
145 (?) Patshull, Staffs.	✱	'Lord Pigot'	There is an undated account book entry under Lord Pigot for a 'general plan for the Place and Journeys – £52 10s', but no location or date is given. Lord Pigot, a Governor of Madras, lived at Patshull when he was in England, but he returned to India in 1775 and died there. The *Beauties of . . . Staffordshire*

House and Map Number		Client	Notes
			(1813) describes the house as a 'very magnificent and spacious building adorned in front by a delightful serpentine expanse of water.'
146 Paultons, Hants.	●	'The Rt. Honble. Hans Stanley Esq.'	Work was carried out on the grounds here betweeen 1772 and 1774, amounting to £640. A drawing showing the house in its landscape and attributed to Brown, and was reproduced in *Country Life*, 17 September, 1938, page 276. See Plate 36 B.
147 Peper Harow, Surrey	●	3rd Lord Midleton	Brown was already landscaping the grounds when he was asked to give designs for a new house. The result, however, was rejected. An elevation of the south-west front is in a private collection. See page 164.
Peterborough House, *see* Fulham			
148 Petworth, Sussex	◆	2nd Earl of Egremont	1751. See page 68 and Plates 8 C and 9.
149 Pishiobury, Herts.	◆	? Mills, Esq.	The lake is attributed to Brown in *The Builings of England; Hertfordshire*, 1953.
150 Prior Park, Somerset	◆	Ralph Allen, Esq.	*Circa* 1764. Included in Repton's list of Brown's works. The Palladian bridge is similar to that at Stowe. See Plate 34 B.
151 Putney Heath, London	●	'Baron Tracey', (later 6th Viscount	Brown received £26 5s in 1774 for 'waiting on the Baron three

House and Map Number		*Client*	*Notes*
		Tracey of Tod- dington)	times and a plan for the altera- tions' but the house has not been identified.
152 Putney, West Hill, London	●	Daniel Rucker	William Angus's *Seats of the Nobility*, 1787. describes the grounds of Mr. Rucker's house as originally planned by Brown but somewhat altered by Rep- ton. The house disappeared in the nineteenth century but gave its name to the road leading to Putney Heath.
153 Radley, Oxon.	●	'Sr. William Stonhouse Bart.'	Brown received a total of £672 for work carried out here during 1770–71.
154 Ragley, Warwicks.	●	1st Marquess of Hertford	No accounts appear to have survived, but Walpole, writing to George Montague on 20 August, 1758, says 'Browne [*sic*] has improved both the grounds and the water though not quite to perfection.' Earlier wrought- iron gates were retained as an entrance to a new kitchen garden.
Ranelagh, London, *see* Fulham			
155 Redgrave, Suffolk	●	'Rowland Holt Esqr.'	1763. See page 112 and Plates 22 A, B and C.
156 Richmond and Kew, Surrey	●	H.M. The King	1764–1783. See page 123 and Plate 26 A.
157 Richmond Hill, Surrey	●	'His Grace the Duke of Ancaster'	1773. See page 161.

House and Map Number		Client	Notes
158 Richmond Hill, Surrey	✳	Frederick Nicolay Esq.	1770. See page 159.
159 Ripley Castle, Yorks.	♦	Joshua Ingilby	No documents have come to light but a family tradition ascribes the landscaping of the grounds to Brown.
160 Rise, Yorks. Roche Abbey, *see* Sandbeck, Yorks.	✳	'William Bethell Esqr.'	Brown supplied a 'General Plan of the Place' in 1775.
161 Roehampton, Mount Clare, London	●	'George Clive Esqr.'	1772. See page 169.
162 Rothley, Northumberland	◆	Sir Walter Calverley Blackett, Bart.	1765. See page 137 and Plates 32 A, B and 33 A, B.
163 Rycote, Oxon.	●	'The Earl of Abingdon'	1770. See page 159.
164 Sandbeck, Yorks.	◆	'The Earl of Scarborough'	1766. See page 138 and Plate 51 B.
165 Sandleford Priory, Berks.	●	'Mrs. E. Montague'.	1781. See page 195.
166 Scampston, Yorks.	◆	'Sr. William St. Quintin, Bart.'	1772. See page 173 and Plates 49 A and B.
167 Sharpham, S. Devon	♦	(?) John Bastard, Esq.	The fine landscape in a bend of the river Dart is traditionally attributed to Brown.
168 Sheffield Place, Sussex	●	'John Baker Holroyd Esqr.'	Brown made several journeys, and from 23 May to 1 June, 1776, Spyers was surveying the ground for Capability's subsequent plan 'for the alteration of the place particularly . . . the water and the ground about it.'

House and Map Number	Client	Notes
		Further work was carried out by H. Repton in 1789. See Plate 54 B.
169 Sherborne Castle, Dorset ◆	'The Right Honble. the Lord Digby'	Although Lord Ilchester had advised in 1756 that Brown should be consulted on some problems connected with forming a cascade, Lord Digby appears not to have done so until 1775 when Brown signed a contract for general landscaping which was carried out during the next four years at a cost of just over £1,250.
170 Shortgrove, Essex ◆	Percy [Wyndham] O'Brien, later Earl of Thomond	The presence of a receipt from Brown for £63 in respect of Shortgrove in the Petworth archives is explained by the inheritance of this Essex property by Lord Egremont's younger brother, Percy Wyndham. The receipt, dated 27 April, 1758, refers to making a pond for the newly created Earl of Thomond. Peter Muilman's *History of Essex* (1770) described the place as recently improved, and having a 'lawn . . . encompassed by fine plantations'. There was also an 'elegant stone bridge of three arches' over the river. This survives as does much of the planting. The bridge is almost identical with that at Burghley except that it

House and Map Number	*Client*	*Notes*
		does not have stone lions guarding the approaches.
171 Sledmere, Yorks.	◆ Christopher Sykes, Esq.	Brown's plan for the grounds survives in the house and is dated 1777. Most of the proposals were carried out for Mr. Sykes to whom the property had been made over in 1771. The village was moved to a higher site, and much planting introduced.
172 Southill, Beds.	● 'The Right Honble. the Lord Visct. Torrington'	Brown received £500 for his 'various plans' and the many journeys' made in 1777 to supervise their execution by George Bowstreed, his foreman. The property was sold in 1795 to Samuel Whitbread, for whose son Henry Holland was to remodel the house.
173 Spring Hill, Worcs.	● 6th Earl of Coventry	Built by Brown *circa* 1760 on a Cotswold hillside as a retreat from the demanding social life at Croome. Much altered. See page 60.
174 Stanstead Park, Sussex	● 'Richard Barwell Esqr.'	Brown made two journeys to Stanstead in 1781, taking Spyers on the second to make surveys. Brown subsequently submitted 'many plans' for remodelling both house and grounds, including the stables, kitchen gardens, greenhouses, farms, etc. Walpole says that he was employed here at the time of his

House and Map Number		Client	Notes
			death in 1783, but there is no further evidence, and later both James Wyatt and Joseph Bonomi were to work on the house.
175 Stoke House, Bucks.	✳	Lady Cobham	*Circa* 1750. See page 48.
176 Stoke Park, Bucks.	●	'General Howard'	1765–7. See page 49.
177 Stoneham, Hants.	●	'Hans Sloane Stanley Esqr.'	Brown's first payment for work here was in May, 1772, but payments continued intermittently until 1780 when they totalled £1,050. The estate is now largely built over.
178 Stoneham, North Hants.	●	'John Fleming Esqr.'	Plans for alterations were made by Brown in 1775 and carried out by his men Knox and Gardiner. The work was completed by 1778 when he was paid £1,400. The lake and some traces of the landscape remain.
179 Stourton House, Yorks.	♦	'The Right Honourable the Lord Stourton'	1782. See page 198.
180 Stowe, Bucks.	●	1st Viscount Cobham	Brown employed here 1741–51. See page 49, Plates 3 A and B and Fig. 1.
181 Swinnerton, Staffs.	●	Thomas Fitzherbert, Esq.	Undated plan. See page 147 and Plate 21 B.
182 Syon Hill, Middlesex	✳	4th Earl of Holdernesse	The Earl's name features in the petition of 1758 for Brown to be given a royal appointment. As

House and Map Number		Client	Notes
			most of the other signatories were clients, it is likely that Brown had given a design for the landscaping carried out here prior to this date.
183 Syon House, Middlesex	◆	'His Grace the Duke of Northumberland'	*Circa* 1760. See page 102 and Plate 19 A.
184 Taplow (perhaps with Cliveden) Bucks.	●	'M. O'Bryen Esqr.'	*Circa* 1776. See page 182.
185 Temple Newsam, Yorks.	◆	'The Rt. Honble. The Lord Visct. Irwin.'	1762. See page 115 and Plate 23.
186 Testwood, Hants.	●	– Serle, Esq.	An undated letter from Mr. Serle to Brown invites him to dine or stay the night when on his way to North Stonham. He adds 'Mrs. Serle flatters herself Mr. Brown will not for ever pass by Testwood without taking any notice of his friends there whose best comps. and good wishes always attend him.' Brown is likely to have given a design for the grounds here, but the house, although well maintained, is now on the edge of the heavily built-up area of Totton.
187 Thoresby, Notts.	●	The Duke of Kingston	Repton, in his *Theory and Practice* (1803) says 'I shall have occasion to propose a different idea to that suggested by Mr. Brown . . .'. No documents have

so far come to light to sub-
stantiate this reference, but the
fine park may well have owed
its outlines to Brown.

188	Thorndon Hall, Essex	● 9th Baron Petre	After a fire in 1878, only the shell remains of the house built by James Paine, and for the grounds of which Brown carried out landscaping between 1766 and 1772. The Petre Account Books (Essex C.R.O.) show that he was paid £5,059 2s for this work, but a good deal of planting had already been initiated by the 8th Baron. A survey by Spyers is dated 1778 (also in Essex C.R.O.). The lake and some vestiges of the plantations remain, but much of the ground is given over to a golf club.
189	Tixall, Staffs.	● 'The Honble. Clifford Esqr.'	1773. See page 153.
190	Tong Castle, Salop	● 'George Durant Esqr.'	1765. See page 148.
191	Tottenham Park, Wilts.	◆ 1st Baron Bruce	1763. See page 92.
192	Trentham, Staffs.	● 'The Earl Gower'	Circa 1759. See page 149 and Plates 48 A and B.
193	Ugbrooke, Devon	◆ 4th Baron Clifford	1761. See page 96 and Fig. 3.
194	Wakefield Lodge, Northants.	● 2nd Duke of Grafton	Circa 1748. See page 54.
195	Wardour Castle, Wilts.	◆ 'The Right Honble. Lord Arundel'	1773. See page 98 and Fig. 8.

House and Map Number		Client	Notes
Warnford, *see* Belmont			
196 Warwick Castle Warwicks.	◆	1st Earl of Warwick	1749–50. See page 60 and Plate 10 A.
197 Wallington, Northumberland	◆	Sir Walter Calverley Blackett, Baronet	1765. See pages 43, 137.
198 Weston Park, Salop	◆	'Sr. Henry Bridgman'	1765. See page 148.
199 Whitley Beaumont, Yorks.	✻	'R. H. Beaumont Esqr.'	Brown visited Whitley in 1779 after which a plan was sent for general alterations.
200 Widdicombe, Devon	◆	– Holdsworth, Esq.	Brown's account for £113 remained in the house until the 1920s, and presumably related to the lawns, plantations and pineapple house for which he is said to have given designs in the 1750s.
201 Wilton, Wilts.	●	'Earl of Pembroke'	Surveys prepared in 1779, followed by Brown's 'General plan for alterations', which probably included some of the surviving plantations.
202 Wimbledon Park, London	●	'The Right Honble. Lord Visct. Spencer'	1764. See page 135.
203 Wimbledon House, London	●	'Sr. Ellis Cunliffe'	This house was about half a mile from Wimbledon Park. Brown carried out work here in 1767 for which he was paid £450. The site (off Parkside Gardens) was developed at the end of the nineteenth century but there are traces of the lake.

House and Map Number		Client	Notes
204 Wimpole, Cambs.	◆	'The Earl of Hardwicke'	See page 140 and Plates 39 A, B and 40 A.
205 Woodchester Park, Glos.	●	'The Right Honble. the Lord Ducie Moreton'	In 1782 Brown visited the original Georgian house in its remote Cotswold valley and subsequently sent Spyers to make a survey. It was probably as a result of his proposals that the chain of lakes were formed into a continuous lake.
206 Wotton, Bucks.	●	The Hon. Richard Grenville, later Earl Temple	1742–6. See page 53 and Plate 4 A.
207 Wrest Park, Beds.	◆	Jemima, Marchioness de Grey	1758. See page 80 and Plate 62 B.
208 Wrotham Park, Herts.	✳	'George Byng, Esqr.'	A survey of the old park and gardens was prepared by Samuel Lapidge in 1765. Brown notes that he himself visited the place, but gives no further details. A later letter from Admiral Lord Howe, dated 18 December, 1773 invites him to Wrotham again as 'my ambition is to benefit by your lights.'
209 Wycombe Abbey, Bucks.	●	'The Earl of Shelburne'	*Circa* 1762. See page 92.
210 Wynnstay, Denbigh.	●	'Sr. Watkins Williams Wynne, Bart.'	1769. See page 182.
211 Youngsbury, Herts.	◆	Daniel Giles, Esq.	An undated 'Plan proposed by Lancelot Brown for the Improvement of Youngsbury after

House and Map Number	Client	Notes
		remarking that Nature had do[ne] so much that little was wanting, but enlarging the River', is now in Herts. C.R.O. The present course of the river corresponds roughly to that proposed on the plan. See Plate 35 B.
IRELAND		
Slane Castle, Co. Meath	1st Viscount Conyngham	A plan in the Murray Collection of architectural drawings in the National Library of Ireland, Dublin, shows suggestions for altering Slane Castle. A note written at the side reads: 'A specimen of Capability Brown's skill in architecture.' With this drawing is an elevation for the stable range with a gothic centrepiece. Although the design is unsigned it has every appearance of being by Brown, and corresponds to the existing facade. Slane is set in a fine landscape for which Brown may also have sent over a design.
FRANCE		
(?) location	'a French Gentleman'	Plan prepared in 1775. See page 156.
GERMANY		
(?) Herrenhausen	'His Serene Highness' (possibly the Duke of Brunswick Wolfenbuttel)	Major Emanuel Lutterton wrote to Brown on 28 October, 1767 about a plan for a park which his 'hereditary Prinz' wished to lay out' in the English way'.

House and Map Number	*Client*	*Notes*
		He asked to call on Brown in order to obtain his recommendations. The Duke of Brunswick had married, in 1764, Princess Augusta, daughter of the late Frederick Lewis, Prince of Wales.

BIBLIOGRAPHY

AMHERST, the Hon. Alicia, *A History of Gardening in England*, London, 1895

ANGUS, William, *The Seats of the Nobility and Gentry in Britain*, London, 1787

AUBIN, R. A., *Topographical Poetry in Eighteenth Century England*, New York, 1936

BEAN, W. J., *The Royal Botanic Gardens, Kew*, London, 1908

BETTS, Edwin Morris, *Thomas Jefferson's Garden Book*, American Philosophical Society, 1944

BOLTON, Arthur T., *The Architecture of Robert and James Adam*, London, 1922

BOSWELL, James, *Life of Johnson*, Oxford, 1940

BRAYLEY, Edward, BRITTON, John, and others, *The Beauties of England and Wales*, London, 1801–1815

BURKE, Edmund, *Enquiries into the Origin of our Ideas of the Sublime and Beautiful*, London, 1757

BYNG, John, Viscount Torrington, *The Torrington Diaries*, ed. C. Bruyn Andrews, London, 1934–8

CHAMBERS, Sir William, *Designs of Chinese Buildings*, London, 1757

CHAMBERS, Sir William, *A Dissertation on Oriental Gardening*, London, 1772

CLARKE, H. F., *The English Landscape Garden*, London, 1948

CLIMENSON, E. J., *Elizabeth Montagu: Her Correspondence*, London, 1906

COLVIN, H. M., *A Biographical Dictionary of English Architects, 1660–1840*, London, 1954

CRADOCK, Joseph, *Literary and Miscellaneous Memoirs*, London, 1828

DELANY, Mrs. Mary, *Autobiography and Correspondence*, ed. Lady Llanover, London, 1862

DE LA ROCHEFOUCAULD, François, *Mélanges sur l'Angleterre*, trans. S. C. Roberts, Cambridge, 1933

DICKENS, Lilian, and STANTON, M., *An Eighteenth Century Correspondence*, London, 1910

GILPIN, The Rev. William, *Remarks on Forest Scenery*, London, 1791

GILPIN, The Rev. William, *Three Essays: On Picturesque Beauty, On Picturesque Travel, On Sketching Landscape*, London, 1792

GREEN, David, *Blenheim Palace*, London, 1951

HADFIELD, Miles, *Gardening in Britain*, London, 1960

HANBURY, William, *Complete Body of Planting and Gardening*, London, 1770–1

HARRIS, John, *Sir William Chambers*, London, 1970

HODGSON, The Rev. John, *A History of Northumberland*, Newcastle-upon-Tyne, 1827

HOGARTH, William, *The Analysis of Beauty*, London, 1753

HUSSEY, Christopher, *The Picturesque*, London, 1927

HUSSEY, Christopher, *English Country Houses: Early Georgian*, 1955; *Mid Georgian*, 1956; and *Late Georgian*, 1958; London

HUSSEY, Christopher, *English Landscape Gardens*, London, 1967

JOURDAIN, Margaret, *The Works of William Kent*, London, 1948

KNIGHT, Richard Payne, *The Landscape*, London, 1794

LYSONS, Daniel, *The Environs of London*, London, 1792–6

MALINS, Edward, *English Landscaping and Literature, 1660–1840*, London, 1966

MANWARING, Elizabeth, *Italian Landscape in Eighteenth Century England*, London, 1925

MASON, The Rev. William, *The English Garden*, London, 1772–9

MASON, The Rev. William, *An Heroic Epistle to Sir William Chambers*, London, 1774

MITFORD, The Rev. John, *The Correspondence of Horace Walpole and William Mason*, London, 1851

NEALE, J. P., *Views of the Seats of Noblemen and Gentlemen*, London, 1824

PEVSNER, Nikolaus, and others, *The Buildings of England*, London, 1951–74

POWYS, Mrs. Philip Lybbe, *Passage from the Diaries*, ed. E. J. Climenson, London, 1899

PRICE, Sir Uvedale, *An Essay on the Picturesque*, London, 1794

REPTON, Humphry, *Sketches and Hints on Landscape Gardening*, London, 1794

REPTON, Humphry, *The Theory and Practice of Landscape Gardening*, London, 1803

REPTON, Humphry, *Fragments on the Theory and Practice of Landscape Gardening*, London, 1816

SIREN, Oswald, *China and the Gardens of Europe of the Eighteenth Century . . .*, London, 1950

SPENCE, Joseph, *Anecdotes, Observations and Characters of Books and Men*, London, 1820

STEUART, Sir George, *The Planter's Guide*, Edinburgh, 1828

STROUD, Dorothy, *Humphry Repton*, London, 1962

STROUD, Dorothy, *Henry Holland*, London, 1966

TAYLOR, W. S., and PRINGLE, J. H., *The Correspondence of William Pitt, Earl of Chatham*, London, 1838–40

WALLIS, The Rev. John, *Natural History and Antiquities of Northumberland*, London, 1769

WALPOLE, Horace, *Essay on Modern Gardening*, London, 1785

WALPOLE, Horace, *The Letters*, ed. Mrs. Paget Taynbee, Oxford, 1903–25

BIBLIOGRAPHY

WALPOLE, Horace, 'Journals of Visits to Country Seats', *Walpole Society*, Vol. 16, London, 1928

WATTS, William, *The Seats of the Nobility and Gentry*, London, 1779–86

WEBB, Geoffrey, *The Complete Works of Sir John Vanbrugh*, London, 1927

WHATELY, Thomas, *Observations on Modern Gardening*, London, 1770

YOUNG, Arthur, *Six Weeks' Tour through the Southern Counties*, London, 1768

YOUNG, Arthur, *Six Months' Tour through the North of England*, London, 1770

INDEX

Fig. 9. Lancelot Brown's book-plate

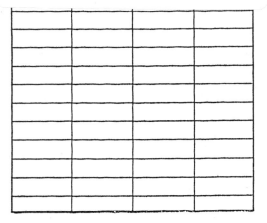

Credits

CAPABILITY BROWN

Born to grace Nature and her works complete,
With all that's beautiful, sublime and great!
For him each Muse enwreathes the Laurel Crown,
And consecrates to Fame immortal Brown.

The Rise and Progress of the
Present Taste in Planting
(Anon. 1767)

D1482154

How to use this guide

E-Z Legal's Made E-Z™ Guides can help you achieve an important legal objective conveniently, efficiently and economically. But it is important to properly use this guide if you are to avoid later difficulties.

◆ Carefully read all information, warnings and disclaimers concerning the legal forms in this guide. If after thorough examination you decide that you have circumstances that are not covered by the forms in this guide, or you do not feel confident about preparing your own documents, consult an attorney.

◆ Complete each blank on each legal form. Do not skip over inapplicable blanks or lines intended to be completed. If the blank is inapplicable, mark "N/A" or "None" or use a dash. This shows you have not overlooked the item.

◆ Always use pen or type on legal documents—never use pencil.

◆ Avoid erasures and "cross-outs" on final documents. Use photocopies of each document as worksheets, or as final copies. All documents submitted to the court must be printed on one side only.

◆ Correspondence forms may be reproduced on your own letterhead if you prefer.

◆ Whenever legal documents are to be executed by a partnership or corporation, the signatory should designate his or her title.

◆ It is important to remember that on legal contracts or agreements between parties all terms and conditions must be clearly stated. Provisions may not be enforceable unless in writing. All parties to the agreement should receive a copy.

◆ Instructions contained in this guide are for your benefit and protection, so follow them closely.

◆ You will find a glossary of useful terms at the end of this guide. Refer to this glossary if you encounter unfamiliar terms.

◆ Always keep legal documents in a safe place and in a location known to your spouse, family, personal representative or attorney.

Introduction to Last Wills Made E-Z™

In ancient Egypt, the pharaohs didn't need wills; they simply loaded up their tombs with all their worldly goods, to be taken with them into the afterlife.

Fortunately, we've wised up a bit since then.

You can't take it with you—but you can be sure about what happens to it after you pass from this life into the next by creating the single most important document you will ever make: your last will and testament.

Unfortunately, most people either think they don't need one or that there's plenty of time to make one. The truth is everybody needs one, and the sooner you make it the better.

Fortunately, it's not that complicated (unless you're someone like Bill Gates or Prince Charles, then you might have some work ahead of you). All you really need is this guide, and to decide two things: who you want to take care of distributing your worldly goods, and who you want to receive them. The rest will fall into place.

Of course, making a will involves a little more than signing your name at the bottom, and you may, in the end, decide you need to use an attorney to complete it. Either way, the information in this guide will help clear the cobwebs off this legal topic and leave you with a last will—made E-Z!

Everyone needs a will

1

Chapter 1

Everyone needs a will

What you'll find in this chapter:

⟹ What a last will & testament is

⟹ Why you need to make a will

⟹ Who can make a will

⟹ What an estate plan is

⟹ Other documents you need

What is a will?

DEFINITION

In its simplest terms, a will is a formal and legally enforceable statement of how you wish to dispose of your property upon your death. The person(s) who inherit your property are your *beneficiaries*.

A valid will allows your last wishes to be protected by state law. Because it can be changed at any time prior to your death, your will can be used to express a variety of emotions: kindness, anger, surprise, appreciation, etc.

> **E-Z TIP**
>
> Wills may be used to stimulate others to act, to express compassion, to provide the means to decide, to get revenge, to surprise beneficiaries, and to show appreciation for hard work and loyalty.

A will is the simplest form of an estate plan. It is also the most important document of any estate plan, since it is the one item that makes clear what you want done with the things you leave behind.

Why is a will important?

Without a will you cannot control who will inherit your property upon your death. Should you die without a will, your property will be distributed according to the laws of your state. This "state will" may be totally inconsistent with your personal wishes. The law may demand that your property be given to distant relatives whom you have little or no feeling for, instead of to a good friend and neighbor of 20 years whom you would choose to inherit your property.

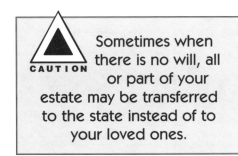

Sometimes when there is no will, all or part of your estate may be transferred to the state instead of to your loved ones.

Even if you believe that you have nothing of value, a will can cover an unexpected inheritance, an accident claim or even a wrongful death award. With a valid will, you decide who your beneficiaries will be. These are the people *you* want to inherit your property.

note

Your will may be used to forgive debts as well as to pay debts (including taxes) by designating what property is to be used to pay those debts.

A valid will enables you to name a guardian for your minor children. You can feel secure that you have guaranteed your children's education and upbringing. Your will also gives you the opportunity to select your *personal representative*. He or she is the person you choose to administer your estate.

DEFINITION

Who should make a will?

Every adult should have an up-to-date will. There are only two qualifications necessary to prepare a valid will:

1) **You must be of legal age.** The legal age in all states is 18, with these exceptions: in Alabama you must be 19 to bequeath real estate and 18 to bequeath personal property. In Georgia, you may be a minor older than 14 so long as you are also married and, therefore, considered emancipated. Iowa and New Hampshire also allow any married minor to make a will. Idaho allows any emancipated minor to make a will. Likewise, any member of the armed forces or maritime service is eligible in Indiana and Oregon.

DEFINITION

2) **You must be of sound mind** when you prepare and sign the will. "Sound mind" simply means that you must understand what you are giving away and to whom you are giving it. You must also prepare your will free from implied or actual threats, pressure or trickery. Even evidence of mental illness or ongoing psychiatric care does not automatically prevent you from preparing a valid will. Simple absent-mindedness or forgetfulness is not evidence of mental illness. Should you have a documented history of serious mental disorders, it may be wise to consult with a qualified medical practitioner just prior to preparing your will. This will help to establish your competency, which could be useful if the will should later be contested.

> *note*
> You must also prepare your will free of undue influence threats, pressure, trickery or other fraud. Most undue influence cases are filed against attorneys who are named as beneficiaries in a will they drafted for the suing client.

It is not necessary to be a citizen of the United States to make a will, but it is important to prepare your will in the state where you currently live. This makes the transfer of your personal property after your death much easier and smoother for your beneficiaries. If your will is valid in the state where it was drafted, it is valid in all other states.

In the course of making your will, and planning your estate, you must choose your domicile—your legal residence. If you live in more than two states, your legal residence is usually the state in which you pay taxes, register to vote, and have registered and titled your car.

Last will and estate planning

"Death and taxes are inevitable; at least death doesn't get worse every year..." The unknown author was right. Taxes and tax issues can become a serious concern for those who must settle an estate after a loved one passes. Without a will, you can't ensure that the property you leave behind goes to the people you want it to. In addition, without careful planning, your heirs may encounter some serious tax and property ownership issues. Therefore, it smart and considerate to have your estate in order today, before it is too late. A last will is the single most important thing you can do to prepare for this inevitable event. You may also take a few additional steps to help guarantee a more comfortable future for your loved ones, family and friends:

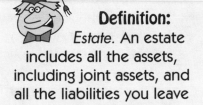

Definition:
Estate. An estate includes all the assets, including joint assets, and all the liabilities you leave at the time of your death.

• create a *Living Trust.* An excellent way to avoid the difficulties of probate, living trusts enable you to transfer your property directly to the trust of your beneficiaries during your life, without court involvement. After your death, the person you appoint to handle the trust may then simply transfer ownership to the beneficiaries you named in the trust.

• create a *Living Will & Power of Attorney for Healthcare*. These legal documents state your wishes about the type of medical treatment and life-prolonging procedures you would permit should disability leave you unable to speak on your own behalf. This helps ease the burden for your loved ones when striving to make important decisions on your behalf.

• organize and review your insurance and retirement benefits. Make certain your golden years are secure and your loved ones are cared for.

• seek tax advice to ensure your estate and loved ones are not overwhelmed with estate and death taxes (see appendix for financial resources).

When you begin planning for the future, even the simplest steps provide enormous peace-of-mind. E-Z Legal Forms, Inc. has the documents, the definitions, and the forms for your estate planning needs. The order form in the back of this guide provides more information to help you start today to plan for tomorrow.

Dying without a valid will

2

Chapter 2

Dying without a valid will

Unfortunately, people often delay preparing their wills. Some may dread the discussion of death. Some feel that their estates are not large enough to require a will. Some feel that they don't have the time to prepare a will.

Dying intestate

DEFINITION

When someone dies without having prepared a valid will, that person is said to have died "intestate."

> **note**
>
> Because he died without a will, the valuable estate of Pablo Picasso was one of the most complicated to settle of all time. It was finally settled at a cost of over 30 million. The estate of the 20th century's most famous artist included 1,885 paintings, 1,228 sculptures, 7,089 drawings, 30,000 prints, 150 sketchbooks, and 3,222 ceramic works as well as homes, gold, cash and bonds.

The laws that govern the distribution of property in such an estate are known as the Laws of Intestate Succession. These are state laws applied in exactly the same way to all estates that are not governed by wills. These laws determine who your beneficiaries, your administrator and the guardian of your children will be.

If you die intestate, your surviving spouse automatically inherits a certain percentage of your estate. That percentage differs from state to state, depending upon whom your other surviving relatives are. Any and all surviving parents, children, grandchildren or

> **Definition:** *Heir* vs. *beneficiary.*
> These words may be used interchangeably. To be technical, however, an heir is defined as a person legally due to inherit with or without a will (generally blood relations); but a beneficiary inherits through a will or other document, such as an insurance policy.

other descendants will affect how your estate's assets are divided. Again, you have absolutely no say in how your assets will be distributed if you leave no valid will.

For example, Bruce and Helen had a sizeable, jointly held estate, a home in Pennsylvania and no children together. Neither had found the time or realized the importance of preparing wills. Bruce died first, followed a few days later by Helen. The Pennsylvania laws of intestacy distributed all of the jointly held property to Helen's brother, whom Bruce hated. Unfortunately, Bruce's three children from a previous marriage received none of Bruce's jointly held assets.

> **Definition:** *Next of Kin* is not the same as the term *Heirs.* Next of kin refers exclusively to those who are related by blood while heirs usually refers to anyone who is entitled to inherit property from the deceased, under state law. Thus, a spouse is an heir but not next of kin.